You Can't Please All

By the Same Author

The Thoughts of Chairman Harold
(1966)

*The New Revolutionaries: A
Handbook of the International
Radical Left* (editor, 1969)

*Pakistan: Military Rule or People's
Power* (1970)

The Coming British Revolution
(1970)

1968 and After: Inside the Revolution
(1978)

*Chile, Lessons of the Coup: Which
Way to Workers' Power?* (1978)

*Can Pakistan Survive?: The Death of
a State* (1983)

*The Stalinist Legacy: Its Impact
on 20th-Century World Politics*
(editor, 1984)

*Who's Afraid of Margaret Thatcher?:
In Praise of Socialism* (1984)

*The Nehrus and the Gandhis: An
Indian Dynasty* (1985)

*Street Fighting Years: An
Autobiography of the Sixties*
(1987)

Iranian Nights (playscript, 1989)

Redemption (novel, 1990)

Moscow Gold (playscript, 1990)

Shadows of the Pomegranate Tree
(novel, 1992)

Necklaces (playscript, 1992)

*Revolution from Above: Where Is the
Soviet Union Going?* (1998)

1968: Marching in the Streets (1998)

Fear of Mirrors (novel, 1998)

Trotsky for Beginners (1998)

Ugly Rumours (playscript, 1998)

The Book of Saladin (novel, 1998)

Snogging Ken (playscript, 2000)

*Masters of the Universe: NATO's
Balkan Crusade* (editor, 2000)

The Stone Woman (novel, 2000)

The Clash of Fundamentalisms
(2002)

Bush in Babylon (2003)

Collateral Damage (playscript, 2003)

The Illustrious Corpse (playscript,
2003)

A Sultan in Palermo (novel, 2005)

Speaking of Empire and Resistance
(2005)

*Rough Music: Blair, Bombs, Baghdad,
London, Terror* (2005)

Conversations with Edward Said
(2006)

*Pirates of the Caribbean: Axis of
Hope* (2006)

The Leopard and the Fox (playscript,
2007)

*A Banker for all Seasons: Crooks and
Cheats Inc.* (playscript, 2007)

*The Duel: Pakistan on the Flight Path
of American Power* (2008)

*The Assassination: Who Killed Indira
G?* (playscript, 2008)

The Idea of Communism (2009)

The Protocols of the Elders of Sodom
(2009)

Night of the Golden Butterfly (novel,
2010)

The Obama Syndrome (2010)

*On History: Tariq Ali and Oliver
Stone in Conversation* (2011)

The Trials of Spinoza (playscript,
2011)

Kashmir: The Case for Freedom
(2011)

Desert Storm (playscript with
Thorvald Steen in Norwegian,
2013)

The New Adventures of Don Quixote
(playscript, 2015)

The Extreme Centre: A Warning
(2015)

*The Dilemmas of Lenin: Terrorism,
War, Empire, Love, Revolution*
(2017)

The Forty-Year War in Afghanistan
(2021)

*Winston Churchill: His Times, His
Crimes* (2022)

The Lenin Scenario (filmscript, 2024)

You Can't Please All

Memoirs 1980–2024

Tariq Ali

VERSO
London • New York

First published by Verso 2024
© Tariq Ali 2024
The author and publisher extend their gratitude to all those
publications in which earlier versions of these writings appeared.

1 3 5 7 9 10 8 6 4 2

Verso
UK: 6 Meard Street, London W1F 0EG
US: 388 Atlantic Avenue, Brooklyn, NY 11217
versobooks.com

Verso is the imprint of New Left Books

ISBN-13: 978-1-80429-090-3
ISBN-13: 978-1-80429-092-7 (US EBK)
ISBN-13: 978-1-80429-091-0 (UK EBK)

British Library Cataloguing in Publication Data
A catalogue record for this book is available from the British Library

Library of Congress Cataloging-in-Publication Data

Names: Ali, Tariq, author.
Title: You can't please all : memoirs 1980–2023 / Tariq Ali.
Description: London ; New York : Verso, 2024. | Includes index.
Identifiers: LCCN 2024023130 (print) | LCCN 2024023131 (ebook) | ISBN
   9781804290903 (hardback) | ISBN 9781804290927 (ebk)
Subjects: LCSH: Ali, Tariq. | Authors, English – Biography. | Political
   activists – Great Britain – Biography.
Classification: LCC PR6051.L44 Z46 2024 (print) | LCC PR6051.L44 (ebook)
   | DDC 823/.914 [B] – dc23/eng/20240523
LC record available at https://lccn.loc.gov/2024023130
LC ebook record available at https://lccn.loc.gov/2024023131

Typeset in Fermata by MJ & N Gavan, Truro, Cornwall
Printed and bound by CPI Group (UK) Ltd, Croydon, CR0 4YY

For Susan Watkins

Our life together is also the
time span of this book

Contents

Contents

Contents

Contents

Preface

Being in the World

The first public demonstration (and probably the last that year) protesting the CIA's assassination of the Congolese nationalist leader, Patrice Lumumba, took place in Lahore on the day his death was announced in the press: 17 February 1961. I remember this well because I organised it. Five hundred students from our college had assembled in the hall to hear a few of us explain what had happened. I said that though we were waiting for evidence there was little doubt in my mind that the United States was behind the killing and that its CIA executioners had done the deed. I suggested we march to the US consulate in the city. The vote was unanimous and marched we did, in open defiance of the martial law regulation banning all public demonstrations, imposed by the military dictatorship.

Today, of course, everybody interested in the early independence movements in Africa is aware of this fact. Good books have been written, moving poems have been sung, movies and documentaries have been made, and Lumumba lives. As do the slogans we chanted that day, in addition to others such as 'Down with the American dogs' and 'Down with US imperialism'. Alas, this last refuses to be buried.

A more detailed account of this event and its consequences appears in the first volume of my memoirs: *Street Fighting Years: An Autobiography of the Sixties.* To this day I still sometimes run into Pakistanis who ask: 'Remember our Lumumba demonstration?' Even those who weren't on it claim otherwise. That little march entered the collective imagination of the student population in 1960s Lahore. Everyone appears to have been on it.

It makes me very proud that a handful of us in Pakistan were politically ahead of the left in Western democracies and, for that matter, in India. I start with Lumumba to stress that I was interested in the world from a very young age. The anger I felt when they executed him was aroused again five years later in Bolivia when our team of observers realised that Che had been cornered. And then again when I witnessed children being maimed and killed by US bombs in North Vietnam. Soon after, a group of us were despatched to the Middle East by the Bertrand Russell Peace Foundation, after the Six-Day War and subsequent occupation in 1967. I visited the Palestinian refugee camps in Jordan, Syria, Egypt and, for the first time, properly understood what had happened from the first Nakba onwards. It was in Beirut that Walid Khalidi introduced me to the 1948 massacre at Deir Yassin.

The Palestinian refugees, intellectuals and politicians I met had no doubt at all. British imperialism had authorised the land grab, and the United States had taken charge after the Second World War, turning Israel into a crucial strategic asset. Both imperial states had failed to protect or save Jewish lives when the Third Reich was on the rampage, and were now using Jewish people to help fight the miserable and ugly Cold War and to crush the national sovereignty and independence won by the Arab peoples.

As we see every day on the television screens, this dirty business is far from being over. Completing this book against the backdrop of a genocidal war waged by Israel against a Gaza that symbolised the entire Palestinian nation was not an easy task. My life was taken up by the suffering of the Gazans, the expulsions from East Jerusalem, the regular assaults and hostage-taking on the West Bank. My own views on the situation are highlighted in the Epilogue.

A word about this book and its predecessor. *Street Fighting Years* was commissioned by Michael Fishwick at William Collins and published in 1987, one of the last to be taken on prior to the Murdoch takeover – a regression that damaged the book's distribution. But the book was widely reviewed and did well. Subsequently, two editions were published by Verso and a third to accompany this volume is currently under way. In the last published edition of *SFY*, I added a lengthy Introduction bringing some matters up to date and paying homage to Paul Foot and others who had passed away. To avoid confusion, I have not included that material in this volume even though the years fit better; with a rare exception: an enlarged essay on Edward Said, who is greatly missed (though it is worth mentioning that his three nephews – the Makdisi brothers, Saree, Ussama and Karim – are doing a very fine job in truth-promotion on US campuses).

I was in my forties when I wrote *Street Fighting Years*. I turned eighty while writing this volume. These last forty years have been so hectic what with writing books and essays and regular public talks on every continent that it has simply not been possible to cover everything in detail. Lack of space has been the only reason. I thought it best not to tempt fate by an extension that would have necessitated a third volume. As a result there is no account here of my trip to Tanzania where I was invited by Issa Shivji to give the annual Julius Nyerere Public Lecture, which compelled me to reread the Arusha Declaration, so much more radical than when it first appeared. Now it's a weapon against neoliberal capitalism. And there are too few descriptions of visits to the various cities and coasts of the United States. Much else besides has had to be left out. As it is, the book will be seen by some readers as too long already. My own generation I will forgive if they don't read it all. They have other promises to keep.

These memoirs are centred on politics of one sort or another. Are three separate chapters focusing on the *New Left Review* a bit excessive? Not for me. A large part of my intellectual life has been centred on the journal founded in 1960 and the publishing house it created in 1970.

I regret I have not been able to write a great deal on my plays and film scripts. Most of them have been published by Naveen Kishore of Seagull Books in Kolkata. Naveen is an old friend who has succeeded in creating one of the most internationalist English-language publishing houses in the world and who, along with his gifted design director Sunandini Banerjee, has created a new aesthetic. A Seagull book, regardless of its content or genre, is instantly recognisable by its colours and its collage style. A rare achievement.

In this volume I have included, as an intermission, an account I wrote of my family. Having avoided doing this for so long, I caved in to demands from family members, who insisted that 'nobody else will do it'. It may not be to everyone's taste, so my advice to the politicos is to bypass this section and move on to the next.

A final word on the book's structure and title. Because a chronological, narrative account was not possible for reasons of length, I kept to the pattern of *Street Fighting Years*. In that volume I wanted to avoid saying too much about myself or my internal journey to somewhere or other and instead sketch a constellation of encounters and engagements that have marked an active life. This explains the structures of the pieces themselves. Some are sourced from previous writings, some include unpublished extracts from diaries and fragments, others still (very few) come from talks or blogs; many of the pieces are new, others are borrowed from my own archives.

Many years ago a friend in Chicago had suggested a title for the memoir: 'Speaking Truth to Power'. I asked her to hand me a sick bag. I really hate that phrase on many levels. Above all, it's based on a falsehood. Power knows the truth. It knows what it's doing. It lies, it covers up, it pretends; but it knows everything. As for the actual title, I pinched it from a painting by my late friend, the Indian painter Bhupen Khakhar. In it an outsider enters a village where groups of people are busy getting on with their own lives and jobs. Ignored by them, the visitor mutters: 'You can't please all.' The fifteenth-century monk John Lydgate came up with the saying, later mimicked by Lincoln: 'You can please some people all of the time, all the people some of the time, but never all the people all of the time.' Almost a cliché. My meaning is somewhat different. For me, a correct reading of 'You can't please all' is 'In your political and intellectual functioning you don't have to please anyone at any time.'

Tariq Ali, 31 December 2023

Introduction

Spy Cops: On Being Spied on for Fifty Years

10 November 2021. It is lockdown year for most of Britain. I'm at the desk in my study, waiting for the Commission of Inquiry into the activities of spy cops to begin. A much-delayed official investigation into police spying on Marxist, anarchist, feminist activists and anti-war groups in general, from the sixties and seventies onward, is about to commence. It had originally been ordered in 2014 by the then Conservative home secretary, Theresa May, in response to the public anger that erupted when it was revealed that undercover cops had impregnated women activists they were spying on.

This traditional British exercise in neutering a crisis – the Official Inquiry – was presided over by a former senior judge, Sir John Mitting. Informally, he let the lawyers know that he had been busy reading Adam Zamoyski's *Phantom Terror* by way of preparation. The book is a readable history of the panic that gripped Europe after the French Revolution and the 'swarms of spies and agents provocateurs' that the governing classes mobilised to defeat and crush the radicals. As Zamoyski argues, however, what they unleashed 'only fed the fear, and led to the suppression of all dissent and the persecution of anyone whose attitude, or even manner of dress, aroused their wild suspicions'. A familiar ring, indeed.

As a 'core witness', I am watching a friendly engineer setting up a very large, brand-new government-supply iMac in my study. My one thought is whether there is any possible way this beautiful machine could be liberated for future use. After all, they did spy on me for decades and I would be prepared to accept this as tiny compensation for my shattered morale. I put this to the engineer. 'Afraid not!' comes the reply. I suggest a helpful possibility: 'What if between now and when you come back to collect, there's a burglary in the house?' He burst out laughing. 'Is that what you learn from all these books?'

As I waited for the Zoom proceedings to commence, related memories flitted by. Long after 1982, when I had left the International Marxist Group (IMG), I had sometimes wondered whether I was still under surveillance. I was.

Late summer, 1998. I was warming myself with a brisk jog on Hampstead Heath, prior to swimming in the men's pond, a long-established routine. Suddenly, I was waylaid by a stranger. I always groan inwardly when this happens on the Heath. It disrupts the rhythm; banalities are exchanged, often with someone who thinks they were with me at the LSE in 1968. I never was at the LSE, but as the years passed I stopped denying this imagined fact. It was harmless. It saved time. A smile and a nod and I could move on.

To avoid such disruptions, whenever I could see someone marching in my direction, I tended to look away and increase my jogging speed. This time, however, the man was determined. He blocked my path and stood resolutely in front of me.

'Are you Tariq Ali?'

I nodded.

'I can't believe it. I must tell you something important. You changed my wife's life.'

I was intrigued. We sat down on the nearest bench. His wife, he informed me, used to work at GCHQ in Cheltenham, the secret spy headquarters utilised by UK intelligence agencies. Her thankless task had been to listen in on my phone conversations.

'In 1981 or thereabouts were you breaking-up with your partner?'

I nodded. In fact, we had split up.

'My wife used to hear you talking or reading bedtime stories to your daughter on the phone. The evenings usually ended in tears.'

I had not thought about those days for a very long time. The fact that the secret state was spying on the private lives of its more critical citizens angered me. In Cold War folklore the Stasi (the former East German secret police) was the monster in the attic, spying on the daily lives of dissidents. That this was also happening as a matter of course in Britain did not surprise me as much as it should have. I asked whether his wife had worked shifts. Had it been a twenty-four-hour job? Were transcripts ever made? He smiled. I don't think he knew.

'She was so livid after she heard your seven-year-old daughter weeping that the very next day she went to her boss and handed in her resignation, pointing out that she had not joined GCHQ to eavesdrop on the private lives of others.'

I shook his hand warmly. 'Give her a big hug from me.'*

Another instance. Walking out of Brighton train station in autumn 2004, I was hailed by a relaxed-looking, jovial elderly man. He wanted to apologise: 'I was the postman delivering mail every day to your *Black Dwarf* offices in Soho. I worked in Rathbone Street. Did you know why your post was always late?'

---

* In October 1987, some years prior to this fortuitous encounter, Carol Sarler interviewed me for the *Sunday Times* series 'A Life in the Day Of'. In this I confessed that 'one conversation I have virtually every day is with my oldest friend Robin Blackburn ... our conversations encompass the state of the world, the state of British politics and culture, the latest storms in a coffee cup at the *New Left Review*, and character assessments of all and sundry, friends and foes.' And then I wondered aloud: 'I'm not sure if my phone is still tapped. It certainly was from the sixties until the early eighties and my post regularly opened. Anyway, I was wondering if they destroy the tapes or keep them. Because if they do keep them and one could have access to them, then – without wanting to sound immodest – I think my conversations with Robin would make a *fascinating* account of the last twenty years. If some stray MI5 officer is reading this, we would give him a good price for those tapes.' No such luck, and, as the Spy Cops Inquiry revealed, the surveillance was going on till the Iraq War in 2003. An edited version of the transcripts might have added another flavour to these reminiscences.

I did. In fact, everyone in the office had simply assumed the mail was being opened and read by the state. The ex-postman explained how the Special Branch would come early, go through the letters already steamed open by him and others, take copies of anything that seemed subversive as well as any letters written in foreign languages, and then depart.

'And', I added, 'often they put someone else's mail in our envelopes.'

He grinned. 'That was my way of warning you lot. I was too much of a coward to speak with you directly.'

Years later a retired engineer, once a regular in the Crouch End telephone exchange, sent me a Facebook message. He told me he had regularly switched off the apparatus tapping my home phone. I had tap-free days or hours. The workers certainly knew what was going on.

This is what the high command of secret state apparatuses never understands. Before recruiting employees, you can vet them as much as you like, but you can never predict individual human behaviour or what will cause someone to say 'Enough' and break with the system. Edward Snowden, working at the National Security Agency in the States, was shocked by the lies his boss was telling a Senate Committee. Chelsea (then Bradley) Manning, working for Signals, was horrified at witnessing the bloodlust of her fellow soldiers and pilots in Iraq. She became a whistleblower and sent all the material she'd gathered to the WikiLeaks team. Later, Julian Assange was framed and put in prison in 2019. The campaign against Assange, and his ongoing imprisonment, will go down as pure judicial thuggery on the part of the British state. The aim is to deter others, but it never works. The same technology used by the state to spy on groups and individuals is subverted by hackers and others who can uncover war crimes and make the evidence available.

Back to 2021. The scenario is surreal. The judge, the lawyers and the witnesses are all at home or in an office, visible only on the computer. A room for the press has been organised where the proceedings will be streamed. What was meant to be a public inquiry has seen the public removed. The lawyers' protests are to no avail. In the midst of the Covid-19 pandemic, the public cannot be allowed into any hall or room. Fine. But why then stop the inquiry being streamed live to everyone? No explanation was given, but the clear risk was that too many citizens might log in to watch and the event could find a global audience.

My own expectations were low. Nothing fateful was likely to be revealed. My instinct had been to steer clear of the whole business. There are too many commissions of one sort or another, usually set up to delay, obfuscate or cover up illegal activities and state lies or the orchestrated incompetence of the judiciary. Richard Parry, a radical lawyer from Saunders Solicitors, had persuaded me to take part, arguing that even though it might be a waste of time for me it would benefit others. And so I agreed. A meeting with the QC Rajiv Menon reinforced this decision. Answering questions from police lawyers at the inquiry was not a huge concern. It was the waste of time that bothered me.

Having flicked through the van-load of box files some days prior to the start, I noted that, apart from offering one or two critical analyses of speeches at International Marxist Group conferences, a spy cop reporting on a speech by IMG factional warlord, John Ross, found it somewhat schematic, heavy going and deadly dull. This was a rarity. Spy cop ideologues were generally short on programmatic reflections. Also, because the MI5 archives remained closed for this inquiry, much of the material I was given amounted to little more than a banal rendering of meetings attended, speeches made and articles written. An example:

> On Day X in Year Z at ... pm, TA chaired a meeting of the Red Circle, near Kings Cross. About 20 people were present. He seemed rather bored and brought the meeting to a rapid close.

Readers will forgive me for having nil recall of this key public event. This does not mean it did not take place or that the report was inaccurate.

There was one total fabrication. A police lawyer, after obtaining my permission to ask about a 'personal matter', referred to a spy report relating to a 1970s visit to give a talk at a Northern English college. Supposedly the spy had observed me 'in intimate contact with the president of the Students Union'. 'Was the Union president male or female?' I asked. (In those days, polite society in Britain – though not in South Asia – ignored the existence of non-binary gender variations.) 'Male,' came the reply.

It was a complete lie, as I informed the inquiry. Its only function could be to blackmail me if that became necessary. Homosexuality had been formally legalised a short while back, but the prejudice was still very strong and many took a long time coming out. Some preferred to keep it hidden. That would not have been my attitude had I been gay, but the spy cop in question had no way of knowing that.

I was aware that I had been placed under MI5 surveillance for demonstrating 'violently' with hundreds of others – including Labour MPs and many local councillors – against the South African ambassador in 1965 (he was pelted with rotten vegetables and eggs). And I had assumed that this ended in the '70s, or else when I left the IMG in 1982. In fact, it carried on at least until the Iraq War.

The most recent police report dated from 2003, when I was elected to the national committee of the Stop the War Coalition seeking to prevent the invasion of Iraq. Undercover officers were deployed to infiltrate this coalition, just as they had done during the campaign against the Vietnam War. Under the Tony Blair Labour government, Special Branch were still engaging in the same anti-democratic activity as they had been from the outset.

A year earlier, in March 2020, I had put together a sixty-six-page witness statement that set out my position clearly, going through events as well as raising a number of questions about the scope of the inquiry itself. My witness pack, to which I was being asked to respond, consisted of eighty Special Branch (SB) intelligence reports (and associated documents) dating between 17 March 1968 and 13 November 2003, plus eighteen press clippings and a transcript of part of the 'True Spies' Radio 4 documentary – my name had been mentioned in all these. The intelligence reports were largely based on the activities of officers from a Special Branch unit called the 'Special Demonstration Squad' (SDS), which had been set up in 1968 (albeit then called the 'Special Operation Squad'). The reports disclosed by this public inquiry were clearly only a fraction of the full 'registry file' held on me by MI5 and Special Branch, and even less of the files held on the organisations I joined, in particular the Vietnam Solidarity Campaign (VSC) and the International Marxist Group.

The names of the officers who had reported on our activities were conveniently obscured, but even then the catalogue was impressive:

i) DC HN299/342 'David Hughes' (deployed 1971–76 into the IMG, Troops Out and Anti-Internment League), (ii) DC HN68 'Sean Lynch' (deployed 1968–74 into the VSC, Sinn Fein and the Northern Ireland Civil Rights Campaign), (iii) DC HN301 'Bob Stubbs' (deployed 1971–76 into the International Socialists), (iv) DC HN321 'Paul Lewis' (deployed 1968–69 into the VSC), (v) DC HN326 'Douglas Edwards' (deployed 1968–71 into the Independent Labour Party, Tricontinental, et al), (vi) DC HN329 'John Graham' (deployed 1968–69 into the VSC and Revolutionary Socialist Students Federation), (vii) DS HN330 'Don De Freitas' (deployed 1968–69 into the VSC), (viii) DC HN336 'Dick Epps' (deployed 1969–72 into the VSC and IMG), (ix) DS HN340 'Alan Nixon' (deployed 1969–72 into the IMG and Irish Solidarity Campaign), (x) DC HN345 'Peter Fredericks' (deployed 1971 into 'Black Power' et al), (xi) DC HN331 (deployed 1968–69, probably into VSC, unknown cover name, now deceased)...

Quite a lot of what was reported was imaginary. For example, in October 1968, a spy cop called 'Colin Dixon' reported that fifty anarchists from Liverpool were planning to attack Scotland Yard. It never happened. Nor did the LSE students plan to attack the London Stock Exchange. Or the 400 Glaswegians with crash helmets, fireworks, ball-bearings and hat pins (!) for use as weapons – again, never happened. Dixon listed 'the political persuasion' of the VSC demonstrators as: 'Trotskyists, Communists, Anarchists, Maoists, Students, Foreign Elements'. I would be surprised if all of the 100,000 demonstrators characterised themselves in such terms. There were only 100 committed Maoists in Britain at the time.

More often, however, the witness pack was filled with tedious accounts of meetings. For example, one from June 1976 at Conway Hall, which focused on 'Building a Trotskyist International'. On that occasion, Sean Matgamna of the International Communist League (ICL) accused the IMG of 'chauvinism' for calling for a 'No' vote on the EU referendum. The IMG was condemned by the ICL for engaging in a 'broad front' politics (along with social democrats) that failed to offer a clear revolutionary programme, while the United Secretariat of the Fourth International (USFI) itself was characterised as a 'centrist' organisation. We were also charged with failing to elaborate a programme of political revolution for the states in the Soviet Union and the Eastern Bloc, and accused of effectively supporting their bureaucracies.

The police report deals with my role at this meeting: 'Tariq Ali, the last IMG speaker, attempted to change the atmosphere of recrimination which was developing by injecting some humour into the debate. His insistence, however, that the Russian and Chinese revolutions had made "some small advances for workers", which the ICL had failed to see, was not regarded as particularly amusing by the ICL members in the hall.' And the report concludes: 'The atmosphere of the meeting had, by its close, degenerated into a barely concealed mutual contempt. Future relations between IMG/ICL seem likely to be worse, as the ICL have now withdrawn even the critical support afforded to the IMG/USFI in the recent past.' This is hardly a description of an urgent threat to the nation's peace.

The reports told us little about what part, if any, SDS officers played in the sectarian rivalry between the groups they infiltrated. Was it actively encouraged? The evidence lays bare the degree of infiltration of the American Socialist Workers' Party (SWP), but this also seems to have been replicated in the UK, with Special Branch infiltration of the British SWP and other left-wing groups across the whole spectrum. As yet there has been no disclosure by the inquiry as to what the operational orders were for this SDS unit, but since they reported everything back to MI5, one wonders what use was then made of the information gathered.

One file contained the transcript of the Radio 4 'True Spies' documentary broadcast on 21 August 2002, in which I feature. This was made into a three-part TV series. I was told by the journalist Peter Taylor that an undercover officer ('Dan') in the IMG, someone I had known, had taken a copy of the keys to VSC and IMG premises; I was shocked at the time, as I thought that the Special Branch surveillance would not be quite so crude. MI5 then burgled the premises and stole information. 'Dan' apparently came under suspicion later, but I still don't know who he is.

In January 1980 there was another police file on an illustrated book project, *Trotsky for Beginners*, that I was putting together with the cartoonist Phil Evans. It shows how utterly out of control the British spying network was. Why should Phil's girlfriend be mentioned – not just her job as a teacher, but her address – as well as his friends and housemates? What use was made of all this prurient intelligence? Were any of the three women named in this report targeted by SDS or MI5? And if so, how? Mention is made of the photo of Phil being 'a very good likeness'. Where are the pictures of me from my file, and how often were they updated?

The verbatim extract below gives an idea of the day I spent in November 2021 testifying before the inquiry.

Lawyer I'd like to take you back, if I may, a little more than half a century to the days of the Vietnam Solidarity Campaign. You tell us in your witness statement that you were a member of the Ad Hoc Committee, which organised the March and October 1968 demonstrations. Did you also have a role organising the October 1967 demonstration?

T.A. Yes. And I was on the National Committee of the Vietnam Solidarity Campaign itself, which we created after Bertrand

Russell and Jean-Paul Sartre's tribunal trip to North Vietnam in '66. So, if my memory serves me right, VSC was set up in either '66 or '67.

Lawyer Thank you. You've helpfully in your witness statement directed us to your book, *Street Fighting Years*. I'm going to use your helpful book and read some passages from it. 'It was a nice Sunday. No rain and not too cold. We had expected a few thousand people at most, given that none of the established groups, such as CND or various front organisations of the Communist Party, had supported our call. When I arrived in Trafalgar Square for the rally, I saw a much larger crowd which had virtually filled the square. A number of us spoke and then, carrying NLF [National Liberation Front] flags and placards proclaiming 'Victory for Vietnam', 'Victory to the NLF', we began the march to Grosvenor Square. The plan had been to picket the American embassy, hand in a petition, chant slogans, sing pro-NLF songs and end the demonstration. The size of the crowd grew as we marched, and by the time we approached the embassy, there were about 10,000 people behind our banners, predominantly the young and largely students. The police, on their part, were equally surprised at our numbers. Their intelligence, which was usually based on ours, had let them down. We marched right up to the steps of the embassy before a thin blue line emerged to defend the citadel.' Do you stand by that account?

T.A. Yes.

Lawyer I'll continue: 'A few shoves and we were through. We actually reached the doors of the embassy before police rein-forcements dragged us back. There were hardly any arrests and very little violence. We were amazed that we had got so close to the enemy fortress. On the way back, we talked about what we would have done if we had managed to occupy the embassy. The most popular view was to open the files and embarrass the Labour government by publishing the list of MPs and journalists on the payroll or otherwise involved with the more sinister aspects of the embassy. This was a utopian hope but it was very strong at the time. We also dreamed of

10

using the embassy telex to cable the US embassy in Saigon and inform them that pro-Vietcong forces had seized the premises in Grosvenor Square.' Do you stand by that?

T.A. I do.

Lawyer Would it be a fair assessment to say that at least in your heart what you wanted to do was occupy the embassy and send that telex to Saigon?

T.A. Well, I suppose. I mean, it's difficult now, looking back nearly fifty years, but yes, our aim was to try and get into the embassy and occupy it. As a token gesture. You know, we were not intending to stay there, or anything like that. But yeah, we were thinking about that, yes.

Lawyer Thank you. I'll read on just a little bit further: 'The demonstration was judged to be a major success. Both its size and militancy were reward for all the hard work of VSC activists and a vindication of our political approach.' Might I ask you in what sense you were using the word 'militancy' there?

T.A. Well, mainly in the political sense, because within the broad left there was a disagreement. CND, for instance, or other anti–Vietnam War organisations were of the view that all they were demanding was peace in Vietnam. This was not our opinion at VSC. We said: yeah, we want peace, but not the peace of the graveyard, and the only way peace will come is if the occupying armies in Vietnam are defeated by the National Liberation Front. So 'militancy' referred to that. And that was quite well known at the time, because this debate was pretty much public, and we were denounced by quite a few people close to the Communist Party or their front peace organisations.

Lawyer And so just to explore that a bit further, having read that account to you, that was the sort of militancy that would involve shoving through a police line to get closer to the embassy?

T.A. Well, that's not how I meant it, really. I mean, what we meant by 'militancy' was giving support to the National Liberation Front. It was not particularly connected with entering the embassy. Because that was something that was an accident anyway that happened in October '67. We weren't prepared to do that; the police weren't prepared for it to happen. Some of us were hoping we could just take the embassy for ten minutes, as a token gesture. So it wasn't the central thing in our mind in October '67.

Lawyer If I'm understanding you correctly, you're saying that a central element of the militancy was essentially taking a partisan stance—

T.A. Yes.

Lawyer—and supporting the NLF?

T.A. Yeah, this was a big issue. And this was very new, actually to, you know, the press in the country at the moment, the radio, television, that there were a group of people saying that they actually wanted what was regarded by many in the British government as the enemy to win. And that is what created a stir, if one has got clippings from that period which demonstrate this. And that was, of course, you know, divisive on the left as well. But it was at the time a very sharp point of view to espouse. I mean, we were amazed that a Guardian opinion poll in that period showed that we were supported by 25 per cent ...

After nine hours of tedious questioning by police lawyers, the chairman of the inquiry, Sir John Mitting, asked a few questions of his own, relating specifically to Trotsky and Trotskyism. My answers were necessarily brief.

Chairman Can I turn now to an utterly different topic and seek your assistance. You have probably, amongst academic and semi-academic historians, the greatest knowledge of contemporary and recent Trotskyism of anyone in England. My own knowledge of Trotskyism is far and away – second, third, fourth or even further away – from yours, but correct me if I'm wrong, and I ask for your help on one or two questions.

First of all, my understanding is that the last time that Trotsky had any influence on a government was 1926, the year in which he was effectively removed from any exercise of power in the Soviet Union.

T.A. Yes, that is absolutely correct.

Chairman Secondly, before the Second World War, the only government anywhere in the world that had any Trotskyist influence upon it, as viewed by Stalin but not I think as viewed by Trotsky, was the Republican government in Spain where it was thought that Andreu Nin and the POUM had at least some influence. They may or may not have done, but there was disagreement about whether or not he and they were Trotskyists.

T.A. Yes, Trotsky denied that because they weren't pure enough for him. But they, on the other hand, were very keen that Trotsky come to Spain and help rebuild their armies so they could fight against Franco. And I mean, Trotsky obviously knew that the first minute he set foot in Spain, he would have been picked up either by the GPU, or by the Republicans or by the fascists, so he didn't go; it was not feasible. But the POUM, in my opinion, contained some of the best and most clearsighted people on the Republican side at the time.

Chairman But am I right in thinking that before the Second World War that was the only government that had any avowed Trotskyist influence?

T.A. Yes.

Chairman Since the Second World War, I think there is the Lanka Sama Samaja Party in Sri Lanka?

T.A. LSSP, yes.

Chairman Which has contested ordinary democratic elections for decades and occasionally supported governments...

T.A. And been government ministers.

Chairman Yes, but performing perfectly ordinary political tasks in a democracy.

T.A. Yes.

Chairman Now, you may know – I don't – about Bolivia. Could you put, in two/three sentences—

T.A. Well, the Trotskyist influence was largely organised through the miners' union, which they controlled. The party was called the POR, Partido Obrero Revolucionario, Revolutionary Workers' Party. They were very, very strong in the Bolivian tin miners' union, and the trade unions in general, and so whenever there was even a slightly radical government – I'm not sure whether they ever got a ministry – but they certainly collaborated with it.

Chairman Apart from those two instances, postwar, is there any other foreign government that has been influenced by avowed Trotskyists?

T.A. For a limited period, in Algeria, after independence, the Ben Bella government, which came to power after the French left, did have a very leading Greek Trotskyist, Michel Raptis – his underground name was Michel Pablo, so he was known as 'Pablo' – who was, if not in the government, very close to it, and advised the Algerian government on going down a non-bureaucratic path of state enterprises by having an element of democracy and workers' control right from the beginning, which would improve both productivity and class consciousness, was how he put it, and he remained close to Ben Bella until he was removed in a military coup.

Chairman You and others may wonder why I've been asking these questions. It's because of the definition of subversive activities given by Lord Harris in the House of Commons in 1975, which is a definition of subversion and subversive activities which has been carried through the decades in this country, and I simply wanted to see whether or not UK Trotskyists, even by reference to what was going on abroad, fell within it or not. I'm grateful for your answers and for your elucidation on a rather arcane topic. Thank you very much for your patience.

In February 2023, nine years after the home secretary first set up the inquiry, its leading counsel, Sir David Barr KC, made a preliminary report on the first tranche of documents (1968–82). He stressed the lack of accountability. Was the spying and the scale of intrusion justified? Was it legal? His conclusion was that the SDS had long been past its sell-by date and should have been disbanded. Why? Because, to quote him directly, 'these groups did not threaten the "safety or well-being of the state" … None was anywhere close to toppling multiparty democracy.'

This encounter with the inner workings of the British state was not exactly a Proustian madeleine. But it helped to catalyse the memories that follow, which concentrate on the aftermath of the sixties revolutions that I wrote about in *Street Fighting Years*. The struggle continued but in different forms. Rather than revolt, these were decades of resistance, where a few victories could still be won in skirmishes on the cultural front. They saw the onset of neoliberalism in the West, turmoil in Asia – Iranian revolution, Soviet invasion of Afghanistan, intensifying military dictatorship and hanging of Bhutto in Pakistan, assassination of Indira Gandhi in India, opening of China and its invasion of Vietnam – and the Gorbachev thaw in the USSR, before the Soviet system's final collapse and the onset of the new world order.

BOOK I

THE END OF
THE CENTURY

Part 1: Before the Fall

1

Police Riot in Southall, 23 April 1979

Ten days prior to the 1979 general election, I was campaigning in the west London suburb of Southall as the Socialist Unity (IMG, Big Flame and a few others) candidate. Tensions in the area were high. There was a total strike. All shops and banks had closed. The Socialist Unity 'shop' alone stayed open, busy manufacturing posters and placards – 'No Nazis in Southall' – and acting as a temporary HQ. When I arrived, I was besieged by angry young men asking what the plans for the day were.

Southall was regarded by the political parties and the state as a Punjabi encampment, largely proletarian and petty bourgeois in composition, but class boundaries remained fluid. A large section of workers, possibly over 50 per cent, belonged to the Indian Workers' Association (IWA – allied to the Communist Party of India back home) that served as both union and political organisation and was staunchly Labourist. They worked in local factories and many women were employed as cleaners at Heathrow airport.

The National Front (NF) often sent fascist vigilantes to create a ruckus, showering abuse, frightening women and children, and, when they could, physically assaulting migrant workers. The police were, to put it mildly, indifferent. Three years earlier, two fascists had walked up to a young engineering student, Gurdip Singh Chaggar, who was hanging out in the vicinity of the Dominion Cinema, stabbed him to death and disappeared. There was a huge protest the next day and after his funeral. The

Southall Youth Movement was formed that day to protect the community.

This latest protest had been organised by the Anti-Nazi League (ANL), who had called for a massive picket of the Town Hall, and it was intended to be a peaceful demonstration. The National Front had booked the Town Hall for an election meeting, no doubt encouraged by Thatcher's remark to the effect that she felt 'the country was getting a bit swamped' by migrants. The message had not reached a woman in her sixties who grabbed the loudhailer and addressed the youth in Punjabi, her intervention limited to a single sentence: 'Fight like lions today.'

The NF members had to be bussed to the meeting, since their local supporters were few in number and elderly. Southall Youth Movement activists stoned the bus and clashes with the police ensued. Along the route, tens of thousands of anti-fascists from all over London had assembled, including veterans from Cable Street. Also here were the police who, as we now know, were determined to crush the demonstration. As was later revealed at the Spy Cops inquiry, the police spies who were following me had been alerted to stay away in case they were beaten up as well.

The demonstrators were moving towards the Town Hall when mounted police with batons rode into the crowd. As an emergency measure, a medical centre had been set up in the People's Rights Centre, where the reggae band, Misty in Roots, myself and others were taken after they had played and I had addressed the demonstration.

At some point in the afternoon police broke into the People's Rights Centre and baton-charged doctors, nurses and solicitors. They hurled me down the stairs, grabbed the band by their dreadlocks, and made us walk a police gauntlet. Clarence Baker, the band's manager, was so badly injured that he was in a coma for six months. I lost consciousness. When I opened my eyes the police bus was transporting us to prison. Solicitors and others were told we were not in police custody. A lie. They let us out in the early morning, but not before I was handed a charge sheet, accused of 'threatening behaviour under the amended Public Order Act of 1977', an offence that threatened a trial without jury.

Only once I was out did I hear of the murder of Blair Peach the previous afternoon. A socialist teacher from New Zealand and an Anti-Nazi League member, Peach was on his way home from the demonstration when he was surrounded and clubbed to death by officers from the Met's Special Patrol Group (SPG).

I staggered back home, slept for a bit, biked over to the *Socialist Challenge* office on Upper Street in Islington, slept again, and then, my head still groggy from the unexpected encounter with police batons, sat down at the typewriter and wrote the front page for the next issue:

> They struck as he was trying to leave the demonstration. The police cornered him in a cul-de-sac and battered him to death with their truncheons. His horrified comrades saw him go down, little realizing they would never see him alive again. Blair Peach died later in the hospital, a victim of Labour's law protecting the fascist order.
>
> When everything else is forgotten about Southall, when the debate on tactics has died down, the memory of Blair Peach and how he was murdered will remain. He was a teacher in East London. Correction: he was a white teacher, a militant activist in the National Union of Teachers, a strong supporter of the Anti Nazi League. In the past he had been assaulted by fascists in London's East End, he had received threatening letters, local fascists had vowed to kill him. In the end the marauders in blue did the job for them.
>
> Southall resembled an armed encampment on Monday. Mounted police with long white truncheons paraded around the High Street like latter day Cossacks; riot shields were in evidence throughout. Groups of the hated Special Patrol Group moved around pouncing on Asians and West Indians, carting them off to police stations throughout London. While Southall was treated like an old imperialist colony, the leaders of the local Labour Party were nowhere to be seen.
>
> We were in the People's Rights Centre when the police charged the building, hitting everything and everybody in sight. With many others I was hurled and kicked down the stairs. Then the front door was opened and we were forced to crawl through a

gauntlet of baton-wielding police: 'Fucking bastards', 'niggers', 'let's kick their heads in' were amongst their more friendly war cries. At 2 a.m. they released us from Rochester Road [prison]. Only then did we learn that others had suffered more. Much more.

We remember Southall in June 1976 when Gurdip Singh Chaggar was murdered by white racists. Now it is Southall again, but this time the victim is Blair Peach, this time the killers wore blue uniforms. Blair was killed because he had wanted to march for the thousands of Chaggars who still live in Southall. And while Blair was dying 30 racist hoodlums, protected by 5000 police, were meeting in Southall Town Hall. What a strange public meeting that was!

Bernard Regan, a socialist teacher and friend of Blair Peach, was in the office helping with the issue. I asked him to cast an eye over the front page. 'It's fine, but you've misspelt the victim's name throughout.' In my groggy state I had typed Peachy.

Linton Kwesi Johnson's 'Reggae fi Peach', written in the wake of the murder, was an instant hit, including for many who had

Front page of *Socialist Challenge*.

little or no connection with the left but were shocked by the killing. The Bard of Brixton was attracting broader audiences, especially among the young, and this song was sung on most of the anti-racist marches of that time.

At the Royal Court Theatre, Max Stafford-Clark offered us the stage on a Sunday afternoon to raise funds for the legal and defence funds. Trevor Griffiths directed the show, a mélange of poetry, eye-witness accounts, speeches and songs that brought Southall to Sloane Square. I interviewed several women witnesses (many of them cleaners at Heathrow and none of them able to speak English) on the stage, simultaneously translating my questions and their answers from Punjabi into English. The women were all amazing, the audience was riveted by what was thirty minutes of oral history.

Paul Foot used satire as his weapon that evening to denounce the police, and at the end of the show both audience and the performers marched out onto Sloane Square and did a Chinese dragon dance. Was an effigy of a faceless SPG officer set on fire with a lit baton? Yes. It was a spirited evening, a show of defiance.

Linton sang his song:

Reggae fi Peach
Everywhere you go it's the talk of the day,
Everywhere you go you hear people say
That the Special Patrol them are murderers (murderers),
We cant make them get no furtherer,
The SPG them are murderers (murderers),
We cant make them get no furtherer,
Cos they killed Blair Peach the teacher,
Them killed Blair Peach, the dirty bleeders.
Blair Peach was an ordinary man,
Blair Peach he took a simple stand,
Against the fascists and their wicked plans,
So them beat him till him life was done.
...
Blair Peach was not an English man,
Him come from New Zealand,

25

Now they kill him and him dead and gone,
But his memory lingers on.
Oh ye people of England,
Great injustices are committed upon this land,
How long will you permit them, to carry on?
Is England becoming a fascist state
The answer lies at your own gate,
And in the answer lies your fate.

At the larger show taking place later that week, the Tory leader Margaret Thatcher gave full-throated support to the police. Law and order had to be preserved. And Blair Peach? Not a word from her or her deputy, Willie Whitelaw, nor from the right-wing Labour leaders then in office.

Blaming the victims is an old politico-judicial custom in England. The SPG was later disbanded, but there was never a full inquiry into the circumstances that led to the death in Southall. Lord Scarman's inquiry into the Red Lion Square anti-fascist clashes in 1976 that led to the death of Kevin Gately was not going to be repeated in this case.

Six months later there were rigged trials at Barnet Magistrates' Court. The stipendiary magistrate was a veteran of the Diplock Courts in Northern Ireland. The other three stars on the Bench were Canham, Cook and Badge. They shared many customs in common, but Canham excelled: he ordered the arrest of two witnesses on the grounds that they had been part of a 'hostile crowd'. Most reporters sitting in the public gallery failed to contextualise the trials. On 23 April, 5,000 cops and dozens of Alsatian dogs, with helicopters whirring above, had been sent to the area to make sure a colonial atmosphere prevailed. One protestor had been murdered, over a thousand Southall residents had been assaulted, and there were over 700 arrests.

In court along with 186 others – on a variety of charges, some serious, others less so – I was charged with 'threatening behaviour' and fined. The whole procedure was a farce. The cops lied. The magistrates found us guilty. All that was missing was a drum roll.

The only delight was listening to my defence lawyer, Len Woodley, later the first black QC in Britain, exposing all the inconsistencies in the police evidence. Given that they had burst into the People's Rights Centre to arrest me and others, where was the 'threatening behaviour'? One cop said I'd been waving my arms at the window from inside the house. There was some merriment in court. Another joker claimed that I had been escorted to the pavement and asked politely to leave. In his notebook there was no reference to the gauntlet or truncheons.

Why did they go through with all this? I think the original plan was to hand down serious punishments, but having killed Blair Peach they had to go easy. Len Woodley's performance in court that day was a masterclass for younger lawyers. It is a blatantly unjust system, he argued: policemen trained to tell lies and magistrates acting in concert. There may be a few good apples, but most are rotten. The legal system and much else needs urgent attention.

Observing the farce quietly but with a cold anger visible on his face was a young Suresh Grover, one of three brothers from Nelson, Lancashire, who were IMG/Fourth International activists. Anand Grover, the oldest, is now a leading civil rights lawyer in Mumbai. Satish remains a radical. His sleep in Dubai was joyfully disturbed when Jeremy Corbyn was elected Leader of the Labour Party. Suresh stayed on in Southall and became the founder and organiser of the Southall Monitoring Group that has compiled a record of racist killings in and out of custody. It is an archive that I hope will one day be published as a record of the Asian settlement in Britain. There is none other.

It would be terrible if the Asian presence in Britain was symbolised by the former Wall Street banker R. Sunak or the two far-right Tory activists Suella B and Pee-Pee (Priti Patel). Are they any worse than their Cabinet colleagues? No. Just the same. More provocative, certainly, since they imagine that their brown skin gives them leeway to promote ultra-right stupidities (of which Islamophobia and packing off refugees to Rwanda are only two among many). Sunak is more urbane, but all three are admirers of India's PM, Narendra Modi.

2

The Thatcher Consensus

Margaret Thatcher's electoral triumph in 1979 was a decisive turning point in postwar British politics.

There are, however, a few puzzling aspects regarding Thatcher's victory inside her party. It was generally assumed that Edward Heath would be re-elected as party leader in 1975. Derided and disliked though he was by many Tories, he had only narrowly lost the election the year before and had denied Labour an overall victory.

The only time I met Heath, in November 1963, I took an instant dislike to him. I had arrived in the UK just a few weeks previously. The Rector of my Oxford college (Exeter), Kenneth Wheare, was a genial Australian, an expert in constitutional law and very informal but, alas, a staunch believer in the British Commonwealth. He had persuaded a senior Tory Cabinet minister to come for a chat with a few PPE students and I was invited along for the talk and the dreaded sherry.

After his talk (not memorable) the minister, Heath, targeted me. 'What are your first impressions of this country?' I was tempted to say that the food was abysmal, the worst I'd ever had. What I said was that I was a bit surprised how similar both the political parties were. His fake laugh disappeared: 'You're probably too used to living under a dictatorship. You can't discern differences.' I couldn't believe my ears. The Rector, seeing the look on my face, moved Heath on to another victim. The next day he buttonholed me. 'What were you going to say to Mr Heath?'

I pointed out that Heath had got it a bit wrong. Living under a dictatorship usually led to appreciating even the slightest disagreement between politicians, the tiniest bit of democracy. Apart from that I wanted to remind him that our Sandhurst-trained dictator (General Ayub Khan) was loved by the British press and even the saintly Kingsley Martin had done a kind interview in the Staggers (*New Statesman*), not to mention the enticing invitation to lunch at Cliveden, where the general – captured on camera in ultra-tight swimming trunks, with rolls of stomach hanging over them like a decaying balcony – cavorted happily in David Astor's pool with Christine Keeler and some of her associates. The Profumo Affair was still fresh in our minds. Ken Wheare chuckled.

After Heath became party leader and then prime minister it soon became clear that he had a strategic project, the proto-neoliberal, pro-European programme crafted by the 'Selsdon Group', which my colleague Robin Blackburn described in a powerful essay in *Socialist Challenge* (later extended and reprinted in the *New Left Review*) as an attempt to chart a 'New Course for British Capitalism'.

Heath had distanced himself from Washington during the Yom Kippur war by refusing to allow British bases to be used. He fought hard to take the UK into the Common Market by convincing Pompidou that Britain was not a US Trojan donkey as De Gaulle had feared. He argued that a strong core Europe could chart a semi-independent course in relation to the US and adopt its own positions towards the Soviet Union and Eastern Europe. The French backed British entry. The House of Commons voted for entry in 1972, but with the narrowest of majorities: eight votes provided by the Labour right. It was Heath's initiatives and campaigning that laid the basis for the pro-Euro triumph in the 1975 referendum: 17.3 million for remaining in; 8.4 million against.

The Labour left was almost unanimously against, as was the far-left. I was still a member of the International Marxist Group. The IMG and the Fourth International to which it was affiliated were against, but with a sweet utopian palliative: 'For a Red Europe' were the headlines in all its European publications. We were against Europe as presently constituted by the capitalists, but for a socialist Europe. I voted for entry. Two reasons. If we wanted a socialist Europe, would it not make it easier if we were in the belly of the beast rather than outside? More truthfully, I had been completely won over by Tom Nairn's polemic 'The Left Against Europe?', which occupied a whole issue of the *New Left Review* and later became a Penguin title. In his inimitable fashion, combining erudition with forensic skills and humour, Tom wrote of 'the extraordinary dilemmas of a "national" left when confronted with a profound strategic threat, a threat to its traditional essence, rather than the more tactical challenges upon which it normally lives.'

It was one of Britain's convulsive economic crises that turned the tables on Heath. A huge tide of trade-union militancy – led by the miners and politically more conscious and effective than anything else (including the 1926 General Strike) in the twentieth century – shook the Heath government and appeared to contradict Robin's analysis. The miners came out on strike and were supported by the big battalions, the Engineers and the TGWU, led for the first time by the left: Scanlon, Cousins and Jones. The Labour leader was just as shaken by this development, but was mildly supportive of the workers in public. Silence was not an option.

The miners and other unions demanded a new election. Heath offered to negotiate with the National Union of Mineworkers (NUM) leadership. They agreed with my old friend from Scotland, Lawrence Daly, who was in an extremely recalcitrant mood and refused to show any respect at all. While waiting for Heath, he sat at the negotiating table, kept his hat on, leant back on the chair and put his feet on the table. When the prime minister entered, Lawrence remained seated. As Heath glowered, Lawrence touched his hat and said 'Hello, Sailor.' Some weeks later I asked him an obvious question: Too many wee drams? He swore he'd been stone-cold sober.

The negotiations came to naught. Effective picketing, with the Yorkshire NUM and their leader, Arthur Scargill, leading the flying pickets, saw clashes outside Saltley Gate storage depot in Birmingham and the inevitable tabloid headlines. No coal could enter the power stations. In January 1974 a desperate Heath ordered a three-day working week to save fuel.

In the *Private Eye* offices in Greek Street I walked into a heated debate. They were preparing the annual Christmas record, distributed with the mag every December and eagerly awaited by its readers. Peter Cook, vital to the process, was in charge and his spontaneous wit usually had everyone in stitches. Seeing me enter, Cook said, 'Ah. Here's the voice of reason. Our friend here (pointing at Richard Ingrams) is censoring my song on the Grocer.'

This was the nickname given Heath by the snootier Tories and taken up by *Private Eye* for slightly different reasons. Recently I asked Ingrams how the nickname 'Grocer' was chosen. He replied that 'curiously enough, a friend of Heath's close to the *Eye* once told us that he didn't mind the homophobic mockery, but hated being called the "Grocer". He thought of it as class snobbery, which it wasn't. Cook, Rushton and myself were talking about Heath's obsession with joining the EC. Cook said words to the effect that Heath was going on about the benefits of trade. "He's our PM, but goes on about profits and free trade like a grocer." Since then, the name stuck.'

Cook obligingly sang the offending opening line in a posh accent: 'Grocer Heath, Grocer Heath, put my prick between your teeth.' Little doubt that many miners would have appreciated it, but Ingrams remained firm. It stayed out. The song was funny enough without the addition.

Heath could have seen off the derision, but the confrontation with the miners ended in a political defeat for the Tory government. There were two options: send in troops to forcibly open the power stations and provide cover for an army of scabs (near impossible given the mood), or a general election to decide 'Who Rules?' Heath chose the drive to the palace and lost the election that followed. Tony Benn told me more than once of his conviction that the intelligence services, angered by Heath's anti-Americanism and his 'softness' on the unions, had played a part in toppling him.

In 1974 Labour was back in office. Prime Minister Harold Wilson left Downing Street early (incipient dementia) and

Jim Callaghan replaced him in 1976. The combination of an economic crisis with inflation led to more strikes in the public sector. Uncollected dustbins became an emblem for the vision-less government. A new opposition was beginning to gel, led by Tony Benn, a member of the Cabinet. Benn was opposed to the Common Market, but he understood that Britain as a state needed to be drastically reformed: abolition of the House of Lords; reduction of the monarchy to Scandinavian status, bicy-cling monarchs without any power whatsoever; a privilege-free education system, etc. These views matured over the decade.

This was the context in which Thatcher became leader of the Tory Party and, in 1979, prime minister. Her new course for British capitalism retained much of Heath's project, especially the concentration on finance capital, but toughened it up with the help of Keith Joseph and others. Unlike Heath she was a lukewarm European but a staunch defender of the 'special rela-tionship' with Washington.

Dozens of books on Thatcher's rise and fall, including her own memoirs, underplay the fact that she put into practice, in her own way, the plans that Heath had already outlined at Selsdon Park in 1970 – although, of course, she took the project much further. I never met her, had no desire to do so, and in both the wars she fought – in the Falklands and against the NUM – my sympathies were with the Argentinians and Arthur Scargill.

At least three of those who had served in her Cabinet shared my aversion. When I asked one of them (I think it was Norman Lamont, a university contemporary who was by then chief secretary to the Treasury) what it was like working with her, he was straightforward: 'Bloody awful.' Ian Gilmour was more sophisticated. He disliked the new dogmas and was critical in public and even more so in private. Likewise Michael Heseltine, my first employer. I received several jokey emails when he decided not so long ago (in 2022) to buy a large brutalist sculp-ture of Lenin and install it in the garden of his country house. A journo asked whether this was my influence. I replied that it was more likely a belated self-criticism for hanging out with Thatcher. Worth recalling that it was finally Heseltine and the

Tories who got rid of her in 1990. When needs be, I noted at the time, they are far more ruthless than their Labour equivalents.

Some on the broad left were mesmerised by Thatcher and admired her matronly domination of the public school levy in the Tory government. Christopher Hitchens, for one, already turned on by her prosecution of the Falklands/Malvinas war, was even more turned on when, as he bent to tie his shoelace in a House of Commons corridor, she affectionately spanked him with a rolled-up copy of the *Torygraph*. He told me so himself. A debate on Thatcherism, characterised by Stuart Hall as a form of 'authoritarian populism', had opened on the left. Hall and Eric Hobsbawm – principally in the pages of *Marxism Today*, the monthly journal of the Communist Party, but also in the *Guardian* – argued that something new was happening and that the left had to analyse the changes. They were ahead of us, even though Robin Blackburn's prescient *NLR* essay 'The Heath Government: A New Course for British Capitalism' had spelt out in brilliant detail what the Tories were planning as early as 1971.

That Hall and Hobsbawm were correct in alerting us to the changes should not obscure the fact that some of their more enthusiastic followers defended the measures being imposed: the ravaging of social provision, the deregulation of the utilities, the sale of council houses, the war fever, etc. It was all this that some of us opposed. Tony Benn and Ken Livingstone led the opposition from within the Labour Party; the miners and the poll tax dissenters from outside.

The 1970s and '80s in Britain, a period of intense class struggle, were dominated by a frontal assault on the postwar political consensus. Privatisation – the entry of private capital into what had hitherto been the hallowed domains of state social provision – and deindustrialisation required a pacified union movement.

Thatcher and her advisers actively wanted to provoke another miners strike so that 'the enemy within' could be decisively crushed. The plan was first to divide the NUM through an attritional campaign designed to force the miners to vote on the strike in the hope that a sizeable minority would vote against, then to use force to crush picketing and isolate the miners from other unions. A law against secondary picketing, which had been used to good effect during the previous strike waves, had already been considered by the Heath government.

Stuart Hall described this as a sign that marked an increase in the quotient of coercion relative to consent in British democracy. Later, Seumas Milne, a senior journalist at the *Guardian*, took this argument further in his trenchant analytical account of the miners' strike in *The Enemy Within*. It remains the best reference on the subject, never out of print.

3

Farewell to the Fourth

Thatcher's victory, followed by Reagan's in 1980, signalled the ebbing of a historical tide that had been under way for some time. The defeat of the Portuguese Revolution in November 1975 marked the end of the revolutionary period in Europe, just as the Warsaw Pact tanks that crushed the Prague Spring in the summer of 1968 had marked the beginning of the end for the USSR. Many far-left groups failed to grasp the depth of these political defeats. The Fourth International's 'turn to the working class' was a particularly crass attempt to deny reality.

What was to be done? We could pretend it was a temporary setback. And some did. We could engage in voluntarist fantasies and send our members into factories to toughen up the working class politically and become its leaders. This stupidity was sometimes referred to as 'colonising the working class'. It was pioneered by the US SWP and voted for by a huge majority of the Mandel wing of the FI. A handful of delegates, including myself, opposed the decision. It was a disaster.

To abandon a public sector in which we were relatively effective for an 'implantation' in industry where we barely existed was foolhardy. When the International Marxist Group became semi-paralysed by factional disputes – sociology versus politics – I left the organisation. I had not discussed this with anyone except Susan Watkins, both comrade and partner, Ralph Miliband and Peter Gowan – a long-time activist in the FI focused on political work in eastern Europe. It was Peter who suggested that, if I was leaving, I had better to do it with a bang, pre-empting any false accusations from whatever side.

By 1981, I concluded the only dynamic force on the left in Britain was that led by Tony Benn, Eric Heffer, Audrey Wise, Joan Lestor, Ken Livingstone and others in the Labour Party and the unions. The Labour-led Greater London Council was waging an opposition to the Tories more effective than the Labour front bench in Parliament.

That was my thinking when I decided to leave the IMG and apply for membership of my local Labour Party in Hornsey, North London. The only forward movement that existed, led by Benn, was left social-democratic in character. But it was inside the Labour Party. It would be foolish, I thought, for the left to isolate itself completely. Nor was I in favour of an 'entry-ist' project à la the Militant Tendency, i.e. pretending you were loyal Labour Party supporters, even functioning as such, while simultaneously having your own sect working as a separate entity inside the party. Everybody knew this was the case and that, sooner or later, if necessary, the Labour apparatus would pounce and remove the organisation as a 'party within a party'. This was what happened. And happened brutally, prefiguring in some ways the later purge of the Corbyn-led left, who were genuine Labour loyalists to their very core but who had scared the British state and its right-wing allies in Labour and the media.

But Benn was unlike Corbyn. He had been a Cabinet minister in the Wilson and Callaghan cabinets, understood pretty well how the state functioned, and had begun to move leftwards. The fact that he was not tied to the traditional Labour left gave him a certain freshness. His decision to fight for a modernised, democratic state and qualitatively increase democratic account-ability on the shop-floor and in local government generated a political excitement. His Achilles heel was his refusal to support proportional representation, defended by many of us on the left and argued for with great flair by Arthur Scargill in the pages of *New Left Review*.

In my view, time was now up for the IMG and the FI. My aim in joining the Labour Party was not only to strengthen (I hoped) the ranks of the Bennite left; the transition was also, as noted at the time by my opponents in Labour, the most useful tactical move for individuals politically fed-up with life in a sect.

There were changes afoot in the party. Some of the more intelligent members of the Labour right in Parliament – the former Cabinet ministers Roy Jenkins, Shirley Williams and David Owen – had decamped in January 1981 to form the Social Democratic Party because they were convinced our side was about to win and they wanted to inflict damage. But if the Labour right could split the party and create a brand-new outfit, why shouldn't the left strengthen itself and attempt to win the party leadership?

In contrast, both Denis Healey and Roy Hattersley believed that Labour would die if it became a left-wing rump. Along with many colleagues they chose to stay in and fight. Healey, while vicious in private, was convinced there was no room in Britain for a fourth hybrid party. The SDP would be a twelve-month wonder, destined either to collapse or to merge with the Liberals. The Healey–Hattersley faction may have been totally opposed to Tony Benn winning the leadership, but it was not in favour of suspending him from the Parliamentary Labour Party (PLP). In fact Healey had publicly campaigned for Benn (who had lost his Bristol seat) in the Chesterfield by-election, and both MPs had sung wartime left-wing songs in unison. But by now it was clear within the party that this was a civil war.

I decided to make my announcement, without malice or denunciation, in an article in the *Guardian* on 20 November 1981. The title was not mine. A well-meaning sub had imposed 'Bringing the Labour Party Back to Socialism' on the piece. Since I had never believed that Labour was a socialist party, the idea of bringing it back was inaccurate. Many of my friends in the IMG, the IS/SWP and the Communist Party were surprised; some were shocked and others were angry at being kept in the dark. But most remained either friends or friendly acquaintances.

A debate erupted, inaugurated by Neil Kinnock, who sent me a perfectly friendly letter asking me to withdraw and reapply in the new year. Since I was a Marxist, he saw my decision as being little more than a Jesuitical stratagem. His political argument was straightforward. My membership was to be 'resisted as resolutely as we resisted those who tried to pull the party away from its collectivism by weakening links with the trade unions and attempting to erase public ownership from our principles and programme'. (Confession: I'm giggling as I type out this quote.) More absurd was his argument that socialism was impossible in Britain, though he put it in his own way: I could not be a member unless I accepted 'that there is no plausible possibility of achieving socialism in this country by any means other than repeated parliamentary victory'.

The first phone call I received was from Paul Foot, who wanted a quick meeting. We both had childcare duties that day, so we took the kids to Golders Hill Park in North London. He was very surprised and pleaded with me to rethink. I explained why I thought that belonging to even the most tolerant sect was not getting anyone anywhere. One might as well work with the Bennites in the Labour Party. This made him nervous.

'Aren't you scared of moving to the right? Often when I'm sitting on the press benches at Labour Party conferences listening to the arguments, they're so dreadful, I feel like charging to the podium and joining the debate. Smashing the right.'

'Why don't you?'

'Inside the Labour Party, given my family links, I'd end up being an MP.'

'A left Foot in Parliament would not be such a bad thing. Bernadette [Devlin] showed what can be done.'

'Are you really going to apply?'

'Benn and Livingstone have suggested that I do so.'

Rose Foot's irritated voice interrupted us: 'Typical. Bloody typical. Men talking politics. I can't see the children anywhere. Have you lost them?'

We had done no such thing. In fact, the children were happily playing hide-and-seek and soon emerged demanding ice creams.

Our discussions continued over the phone in the weeks ahead. Despite political disagreements, we had been friends since 1966, meeting semi-regularly at *Private Eye* lunches and on numerous occasions at our homes or those of friends, always inspecting new additions to our libraries before supper was served. I can still recall Paul's childlike delight when he finally managed to obtain the last two books he needed to complete his set of Left Book Club volumes that Victor Gollancz had published in the 1930s and '40s.

Bibliophilia ran strong in the Foot bloodstream. His uncle Michael's library was the talk of Hampstead. Neither, however, could match the huge collection amassed by Raphael Samuel's uncle (and Jenny Abramsky's dad), Chimen Abramsky, in Highgate. Paul and I went to see it together and were staggered: A first edition of *Capital* that had once belonged to Engels and had his imprimatur on it. Many first editions of Engels's own works. A complete file of William Morris's weekly magazine *Commonweal*, in which his utopian novel *John Ball's Dream* was serialised. That was just the *hors d'oeuvres*. There were first editions of every Morris book, handwritten notes by Marx, Lenin's annotations on many volumes, Trotsky's and Luxemburg's documents and the latter's doctoral thesis.

Writing a proper history of the collection would have entailed commenting on what it contained and the evolution of the arguments. This was never done. The core of the library was sold by his family. There was no other option.

There had been a plan for Paul and me to discuss these books with Chimen on camera, directed by Christopher Hird. Paul's death put paid to that project, but on Chimen's insistence I did interview him, and Christopher did make a short film on the library that we first showed at Chimen's wake and, many years later, on Telesur. 'My Life, My Library and the Left' is still on YouTube.

The one occasion where I got very irritated with Paul was when he wrote a very silly and sectarian review of *Street Fighting Years* in the *Literary Review*. The high point was his attack on me as 'a rotten Marxist' for joining a tiny group (the IMG, with forty or so members) rather than the great and mighty SWP (which boasted 600 militants). Pathetic, I thought at the time, and still do.

It was obvious he hadn't read the book and in a few months my annoyance would have faded away, but as it happened, the very day the review appeared we were both dining with mutual friends, Christo Hird and Anna Howarth. Paul came forward offering his outstretched hand as if nothing had happened: 'Comrade, good to see you.' I stepped back, avoided him and returned the greeting: 'Hello, citizen.' Our charming and relaxed hosts were taken aback as the evening progressed, or rather didn't. It was tense, as Paul and I exchanged not a word.

He rang a few weeks later when I'd almost forgotten the episode, to apologise and admit he hadn't read the book. 'You should at least have read Hitchens's review in the *Observer*,' I told him. 'Warm and generous.' Normal relations were resumed.

After Paul, the next person to call me was Ernest Mandel, from the FI's HQ in Brussels. He was shocked that I had announced my departure in the *Guardian*, and very angry that I had not spoken to him before going public. He arrived in London the following week for lengthy discussions.

Of all the people I was close to, Ernest should not have been too surprised. He suggested that I remain a member-at-large and continue functioning on the 'leading bodies'. He understood that I was irritated with the IMG, but to end my membership of the FI after thirteen years without producing a balance sheet was 'irresponsible and light-minded'.

My problems were not simply with the IMG, however, but with the FI as a whole. Incapable of understanding the defeat or developing proper priorities, they had decided to dismantle their work in the public sector unions and 'colonise' industry. It was reminiscent of the Maoist line of 'serving the people' that was followed during the Cultural Revolution. That had made more sense than the FI policies, and allied to the latter was an anti-intellectualism that I found particularly distasteful. It was, by and large, a disaster. I had spoken and voted against it at the FI Congress and did not feel obliged to stay in any longer.

Perry Anderson, too, was annoyed. A stern, well-crafted, inimitable letter from him arrived in due course. His ostensible target was a text submitted to the *NLR* by Quintin Hoare and myself in which we argued strongly for an orientation to the Bennite current in the Labour Party as the only serious and defensible political project at the time. Quintin and I argued that the left outside Labour should strengthen Bennism. As Perry's response revealed, this was a debatable proposition, but what had really angered both Ernest and him was my very public decision to apply for Labour membership. Knowing this, my own response centred largely on that issue and the state of our wing of global Trotskyism.

I had totally forgotten this exchange, and that I had replied in writing, since I often did not keep carbon copies of my letters. Perry remembered and handed my letter over only recently. His own text had the collective thumbprint of the *NLR* editorial committee, but the individual authorship was obvious. Both letters are reproduced below, slightly edited.

Perry Anderson to Tariq Ali, 21 December 1981

The argument you develop in the second part of the article could be summarised thus: The Labour Party is at present the arena of 'an intensely antagonistic struggle between Labour and Capital', itself the exacerbation of the contradictions of the bourgeois order in the UK as a whole. The interests of labour within the Labour Party are represented essentially by the Bennite left. This is a 'novel phenomenon', not reducible to that of earlier revolts by the base of the party, such as those associated with names of Bevan or Cripps. It is new in two senses.

Firstly, it repudiates the right-wing record of the past Labour governments of the '60s and '70s, calling instead for policies representing a programme of 'radical reform'. Secondly, it challenges the traditional power structure of the party, and has already succeeded in imposing significant preliminary changes in it, of a more democratic cast. The result is that the tensions long endemic within the LP have polarised more sharply than ever before – precipitating the exit of the wing that now constitutes the SDP, weakening the position of the Right that has remained behind, and creating for the first time the possibility that a 'New Model Labour Party' might arise, of left-reformist or centrist complexion, battling for policies 'outrageous' to capital and mobilising the working class as a 'gigantic lever' of popular political impetus, to become 'a serious candidate for governmental power once again'.

This scenario is a possibility, but no certainty. It is all the more urgent therefore for socialists to put their shoulder to the wheel inside the LP. The argument that they would do better to remain organised in independent Marxist formations of an unambiguously socialist sort, outside the LP, has been invalidated by the failure of real mass parties – rather than small vanguard groups – to emerge anywhere in Western Europe, since the defeat of the Portuguese Revolution in 1975 and the period of (relative) reaction that has set in since then. Only work in the existing mass parties of the working class now affords any real hope of socialist advance.

We would like to put a number of questions in response to this perspective ...

1. How New is the Bennite Left?

The first premise of the case you develop is that there exists a qualitatively new kind of labour left today, which renders a participation in the Labour Party meaningful and hopeful in a way that it was not, or not so obviously, in the past. Now we are more in sympathy with the underlying judgement here than with the opposite conclusion that the current party struggle is simply a repetition of previous left–right fights with a similar conclusion more or less preordained.

But we still feel that the arguments advanced for it are too cursory and rapidly sketched for the weight they are made to bear in the text. What does it mean to say that the Bennite left is a new phenomenon? Two answers suggest themselves. Firstly, it is more radical or intransigent in policy terms than its predecessors. At times, your text represents it in these terms: e.g. 'the new Labour Left is different from its predecessors. Tens of thousands of constituency activists are interested in socialism and socialist measures.' But isn't it too summary a dismissal of the successive pre-Bennite lefts?

We do not pretend to have any definite answers here, but we would ask: is it really the case that tens of thousands of constituency activists were uninterested in socialism and socialist measures in the days of either Cripps or Bevan? Or was their interest less radical in its edge?

If we take the three major planks of Bennism today: (i) When did Tribune in the '50s ever argue for *less* than the AES [Bennite Alternative Economic Strategy]? Fewer nationalisations? (ii) Is unilateral nuclear disarmament for Britain intrinsically more radical a position than opposition to German conventional rearmament? Mightn't it be argued that the latter was actually more of a threat to vital US interests affecting the veritable keystone of NATO than the former? (iii) Does Benn or do his associates argue for any reform of the British state as radical as abolition of the first-past-the-post system, which was not only advocated but even implemented in the Commons by a Labour *government* in 1931 (rejected by the Lords)?

We're not saying that any of these three counter considerations are necessarily clinching. But we do think that the claim that Bennism represents a qualitatively new phenomenon in Labour left politics needs more careful evidence of a comparative sort and that such evidence would have to look at three critical axes: relation to British capital; relation to international alliances; relation to the UK state.

Nevertheless, even if little on paper separated Bennite from Bevanite or Crippsite (or Stracheyist) *policies*, it could still be argued that Bennism is a new phenomenon by reason of his greater *strength* within the Labour Party as a whole. This second case for the argument of novelty has two parts. Firstly, it would stress that Bennism comes after a long period of manifestly dismal and demoralising Labour governments, producing a more militant rejection of right-wing policies than in the past but above all on a much more widespread scale. Secondly, it would insist on a new drive for power within the party revealed by the Bennite left, crystallised in concrete reforms whose very implementation has weakened the right, produced an exodus of defections and thereby advantageously shifted the structural balance of forces in the Labour Party as a whole.

And there is much to be said for this view. However, some provisos may still be in order. Historically Bennism fits into the pattern of revulsion by the base against the experience of right-wing Labour governments, which produced the Lansbury regime in the '30s, and Bevanism in the '50s. But this time, of course the experience was far longer and in that respect was more traumatic. Above all, it antagonised not just the constituency activists, but many of the trade unions as well.

Hence the undoubtedly greater scale of the Bennite than the Bevanite revolt at the level of the conference mechanism, for it has up till now been able to canalise union as well as CLP votes whereby it has also been able to change the party rules in a somewhat more democratic direction. There is no doubt that it is important to make these crucial distinctions, but shouldn't we also be on our guard against any tendency to idealise them? There are two problems here. Firstly, is the intrinsic activist strength of Bennism really stronger than that of Bevanism before it?

...At the high tide of Bevanism, in 1954, Bevan seems to have enjoyed a degree of CLP support not very different from that of Benn in 1981. The caucus of Bevanite MPs was certainly no smaller, very probably larger than that of Bennite MPs today – and no doubt more gifted as well. (How many of the recent intake show the talents of, say, Mikardo?) What really differentiates Bevanism from Bennism in this respect is clearly the break-down of monolithic right-wing *unionism*. But this phenomenon has been an uneven, partial and *corporatist* dissociation from some of the specific anti-union measures of the Wilson–Callaghan governments ... the democratic reforms achieved by Bennism within the party *have been rendered possible only by the very union block-votes which put a rigid limit on the reforms*. Reselection and the electoral college are real gains: but they are marginal changes compared with the *central* obstacle of the 90% of conference votes controlled by the masters of Labour's 'dead souls', the union general secretaries who themselves for the most part enjoy life-tenures of a sort that no bourgeois politician would ever hope to enjoy, in a kind of bureaucratic monarchism ... Abolishing this House of Lords within Labour itself would be a far more radical measure than abolishing the House of Lords within the bourgeois state ...

In this formation as a whole, the recent exodus of the SDP seems to have led to a compensating shift inside the forces that remain, via the assimilation of the larger part of the former 'left' into the conventional Right – as Owen or Williams move outside, Kinnock or Lestor sidle in to take up their positions, so that everything happens as if a homeostatic mechanism ensured the same structured balance between Right and Left as before, in other words the basic mixture does not seem to have changed so far.

However, the evidence we have pointed to above is circumstantial, not necessarily dynamic. A new wave of turbulent industrial or social struggles, accidents of mortality in the PLP or TUC, an overdue turn by the Bennites towards hard inner party organisation, might – it could be argued – create a new balance of forces in the future; however, even were that so, surely one thing is absolutely certain: namely, that the right which created the Labour Party, has always dominated it, and regards it as its property, will never permit the left to actually take it over – that is to say, to occupy the same position within a unified organisation which it has always enjoyed.

Rather than see that happen, or even come near to happening, it will liquidate the party by organising a second and far larger split – this time taking the bulk of the PLP with it. The evidence for this is simply the history of the SDP itself, which walked out under very little provocation, and the declarations of many members or PLP leaders and troopers since. In other words, in addition to the *structural* barriers to any conquest of the Labour Party, there is the *political* fact that the right created the LP for its own purposes and will destroy the party as soon as it feels it no longer serves these purposes.

2. What Then Should Be the Attitude of Marxists towards the LP Today?

The remarks above have involved one major simplification. Clearly, the Labour Right is not – never was – a unified agent. The most dynamic and principled leaders of that Right, those with least liking for the mystifications of labourism itself, and so with the lowest threshold of tolerance for any advances whatsoever by the left within common party structures, have already organised their successful rival party, the SDP. It is this development which holds out the most immediate promise of a break in the logjam of British politics. For its conventional vacuities of social or economic policy are combined with a definite drive to abolish the first-past-the-post system and this could execute the long-delayed death sentence on labourism more speedily than any other prospect.

For once the electoral system is changed the Bennite left would be freed from the fate of sheer electoral extinction that has hitherto always chained the labour left to their bourgeois gaolers in the party. It is not certain but overwhelmingly probable that if an SDP electoral victory

45

was followed by electoral reform the LP itself would split again and disappear as an entity. The stage would then be cleared for a left Socialist Party with modest starting strength in regions like Scotland and a national poll of perhaps 7 to 8 per cent. The real dimensions of the struggle to overthrow British capitalism would become clear, and with them the conditions for actually advancing towards this overthrow by mass mobilisation against capital and all its minions (prominent among them the erstwhile parliamentary union representatives of labour).

Such a perspective does not depend on the conduct of the Marxist left today. It will be determined essentially by the ability of the SDP alliance to vanquish the two older parties at the next elections. But its likelihood must affect the choice of strategy of Marxists in the meanwhile. In your article you argue that all efforts should be thrown into the struggle within the Labour Party to create a new model Labour Party, in the wake of the failure of the revolutionary left to build mass parties outside it. It could be replied that if the Labour Party itself has no secure future, it certainly makes sense for socialists to work inside it in the perspective of an imminent split, to hasten the latter along – provoking further exits to the right, heightening political tension and turmoil, introducing new ideological and cultural emphases. Does it make sense, however, except as part of an organised and collective initiative? Individual additions or otherwise are a pragmatic matter. But can they affect the fate of the Labour Party? Certainly effective entry by Marxists of the sort that you advocate can only be based on disciplined common action ...

Tariq Ali to Perry Anderson, 15 January 1982

Dear Perry

Robin informs me that there was a feeling at your last meeting that Quintin and myself had not responded to all the queries raised in your comment on our text submitted for publication in the *NLR*. He also stated that the most burning question was one related to my plans and that regardless of what could or could not be stated in the text for tactical or other reasons it was my fraternal duty to explain what 'I was up to' to the *NLR* ...

Your comments, as always, are stimulating, invaluable and neither Quintin Hoare nor myself disregarded or ignored the substantive political points that you make. Where we agree (most notably on strengthening the comparative section on Bennism/Bevanism), we shall make suitable additions and deletions in the final draft. It is true that the organising cadres of Bevanism were more experienced, battle-hardened veterans, but this did not prevent most of them becoming the standard bearers of Wilson and Callaghan: Greenwood and Castle in 1964–74, and Foot and Driberg from 1974–79, symbolised the degeneration of this layer. Bevan himself ended up pathetically in both a political and a personal sense: politically, he decided to back the independent nuclear deterrent and privately he became a tame mascot to be produced for amusement at Lord Beaverbrook's lavish house parties. Beaverbrook paid him a retainer for the last ten years of his life and this insidious influence should not be underestimated either on Foot or Driberg. Ian Mikardo is a better figure, but was booted off the Labour NEC because he was initially engaged in a backroom manoeuvre to water down the reselection proposals!

The scale of Bennism's challenge is different and for a more fundamental reason: 1968 and three Labour governments. You will recall that Lenin in 'Left-wing Communism: An Infantile Disorder' stressed that the actual experience of Labour in office would be far more instructive for the masses than any variety of ultra-left syndicalism. This has proved correct except that for a variety of reasons (national and international) it was the SDP rather than a communist organisation, which threatened Labour ...

The central question preoccupying me is what revolutionary Marxists should be doing *today* to influence the process of re-composition currently underway in the arena of national politics. I am strongly of the view that we should be in the Labour Party ... to argue such a position is far removed from any 'conciliationist or liquidationist' temptations. It is, if anything, the opposite: a ruthless Leninist choice of where one intervenes and how one intervenes. In discussions with Octavio [Arraujo] and Norman [Geras], I was a bit shocked to realise that both comrades were simply unaware of the history of the Trotskyist movement in the '30s, '40s, '50s and early '60s. They seemed to regard it as ridiculous that Trotskyists should consider joining Labour!

As you are no doubt aware I had a lengthy discussion with Ernest Mandel in Brussels which lasted the best part of a day and with John Ross present in the afternoon. Ernest explained how the two people he had felt the closest to inside the FI in Britain had been Ken Coates and myself and how he was determined to prevent me from repeating the Coates 'experience'. I explained my views and ultimately we reached an agreement whereby I would remain in the FI, attend all meetings of its leading bodies, but in Britain the FI's discipline would be mediated via a regular meeting with an IMG leader (a similar arrangement exists with Adolfo Gilly in Mexico). We all agreed.

The leadership, however, prompted by Udry (EM's organisational eminence grise), rejected such a proposal. Ross then suggested to me that I should declare that there's been a split and constitute myself as 'a sympathising section' in Britain. This was a slightly unbalanced suggestion and it would have made a laughing stock of the FI. I told Ross that before he proceeded any further, he should get clearance from the Paris Bureau. Since that time not a single FI comrade from the Bureau has been in contact with me. I did catch a glimpse of Udry at the Liberty Sale, but I presumed he was exploring the possibilities of unionising the place and did not interrupt him.

My own differences with the IMG revolve around two interrelated questions: a section of the group is now besotted with a workerist, ultra-syndicalist vision of politics and this is a direct result of the FI's last World Congress decisions. More importantly there is little creative thought on how to develop a mode of functioning which is 'rigid' in defending the fundamentals of our programme, but is organisationally extremely flexible. I think what needs to be done is the creation of a large centrist united front inside the Labour Party in which a non-sectarian Marxist current is the far-left pole ... Clearly such an organisation would help develop international links and for me the FI offers the only viable programmatic alternative ...

You should, however, be aware of the state of the FI at the present time. The only country where we are doing well is Mexico, where the leadership has combined a creative electoral campaign with a benevolent attitude to two theoretical journals (not under the control of the PRT Central Committee) and a regular intervention in the daily *Uno mas Uno.* The heart of the FI, however, has been in Western Europe. Here the situation is bleak ...

The Spanish comrades have lost nearly half their members since 1976 and encouraged their intellectuals to depart. The consequences of this were that they were incapable of reacting to the development in the Communist Party in Catalonia or challenging it politically anywhere else. A number of Madrid cells of the PCE in 1977–78 were organising discussion circles around *Late Capitalism* and EM's other books but the local FI treated them with derision.

In France the gains of the post-1968 period were squandered, and the League lost a quarter of its membership to the whirling dervishes of Ayatollah Pierre Lambert. EM's naivete during this operation was staggering for someone who's been immersed in factional struggles since the age of sixteen. The German section has almost disappeared from view; the Italians have a small group of good friends; the IMG is now in a spin. The reasons for this are, in my opinion, a crisis of perspectives: the FI failed to see that November 1975 marked a turning point in European politics.

The Portuguese defeat coloured political developments throughout the continent. All attempts to make the leadership grasp this fact were answered by slanders and innuendos. I was labelled 'an agent of the NLR'; the French *Critique* was denounced by Udry as a 'plaything for intellectuals' and extinguished by the French CC; the early *Socialist Challenge* experiment was viewed as a threat by the FI centre since other sections want to emulate our progress, and Udry sent a powerful team to split the IMG leadership (then reunited after the crippling factional struggles of 1972–76) For those of us who have been struggling inside the FI since 1968, the last few years have been grim. This is not because of the objective situation. On that front having a Trotskyist formation is an incredibly powerful weapon. ('Indignation, anger, revulsion? Yes, even temporary weariness. All this is human, only too human. But I will not believe that you have succumbed to pessimism. This would be like passively and plaintively taking umbrage at history. How can one do that? History has to be taken as it is. And when she allows herself such extraordinary filthy outrages one must fight her back with one's fists' – Trotsky). An equally apt comment on Cambodia, Sino-Vietnamese war, Afghanistan, Poland, et cetera.

In other words, for me it was the deliberate shutting of eyes to history by the FI that was the biggest blow. The US SWP has played a major role in destabilising and weakening the political operation of the FI in Europe. We are now paying the price of their pernicious influence. And Udry's attempt to do a permanent deal with them on the basis of spheres of influence. The deal foundered because the Americans demanded Ernest's head on a platter. This Udry really couldn't do because the European sections were not structured like the US SWP and any attempt to displace Ernest would have encountered a stubborn resistance, but it was discussed in great detail. When Udry tried to mention his views on EM to me I denounced him in no uncertain terms and made the manoeuvre semi-public within the FI. In North America the best Marxists are outside the FI. Why did Mike Davis refuse to join the SWP? Or Charlie Post decline to re-enter it on the condition of recanting his former views? The question is, of course, rhetorical. You know the answers.

If you compare the theoretical-ideological-journalistic output of the FI today with what was being produced in the '50s and '60s by a tiny handful of comrades you cannot but fail to see that there has been a regression. Pablo, Frank, Maitan and Ernest (then deeply embedded inside Belgian social democracy) were producing monthly commentaries on all key world events. Ernest's analysis of successive CPSU conferences, Pablo's insightful texts on Stalinism, Frank's journalism on France and Algeria, Maitan's detailed studies of Latin America and Africa – where is all this today?

It's a sad fact that Ernest's powerful intellect is today the prisoner (albeit a willing one) of a tiny apparatus in Paris. His political instincts are suppressed in case they clash with purely internal priorities and battles. He has not produced a major text on Poland, Nicaragua, Iran, Afghanistan or France. What he has written is a barren polemic against [Pierre] Lambert, which was designed essentially to immunise the FI cadre by wrapping it in the cottonwool of *our* orthodoxy ...

Since I have been closely connected with *NLR*, in some way or other, for the last decade, I would like to give you my views on its evolution as well. The reason I was angry at the remarks about 'liquidationism' is the following: I am firmly of the opinion that if the *NLR* comrades (I mean the activists and not the House of Lords within the *NLR*) had joined the FI in 1969–70, the impact would have been very great. I have made this point to you and others on many occasions over the past ten years and you always had a ready excuse, till finally you ran out of excuses and I stopped asking the questions, though Ernest still entertains illusions on this score. I believed and still do that a synthesis of your and Ernest's strengths would have led to a powerful combination, helping both you and the FI.

The *Review*'s choice of articles in 1968–76 was, of course, not incidental, but it did not make up for your refusal to join the FI or for the staggered departure of RB [Robin Blackburn], QH [Quintin Hoare], BM and NG. FM [Francis Mulhern] promised to join for two years at a later stage but didn't. Mike Davis still states that he wants to join the FI, but doesn't. Of course it is not all one sided. AB [Anthony Barnett] was quite right to point out in a letter to me in 1977 that the *Black Dwarf* split had left many scars and that 'the political costs to all of us were very great'.

These missed opportunities could have been recuperated in a different way when you first completed *Considerations on Western Marxism*. I was of the view then that it should have been published in the *Review*, not to alter the broad-church character of the journal but in order to inaugurate a debate, which would have been of immense value for the entire left in the English-speaking world and elsewhere. You thought otherwise, added an afterword and published it as a book ...

Over the last few years the *Review* has been rudderless, floating from one show to another, without a clear project and extremely indulgent towards Brezhnevism. It is not sufficient to blame this exclusively on Ernest or other FI comrades not submitting material. I suggested that Robin and myself interview Tony Benn two years ago! I mention all these facts not to rake over old disputes but to explain why the accusation of 'liquidationism' hurled at me from 7 Carlisle St appeared somewhat bizarre ... I've been told that you have an article in the works by Ken Coates and are planning an interview with Tony Benn. This is excellent news and far more important than the article QH and I have submitted. What I would suggest however is that if our text cannot be published, you seriously consider commissioning Ted Grant and Peter Taaffe to spell out the *Militant* perspective ... Grant has done some extremely creative work on the dialectics of enabling acts which might be valuable ...

The Hornsey Labour Party led by Jeremy Corbyn took my shilling and handed me my first and only Labour Party card, signed by the wonderful Diana Minns. This led to fisticuffs in the local party, where my membership was strongly opposed by some leading right-wing intellectuals, including Max Morris. I was a bit shocked to hear that Peter Kellner, usually the gentlest of souls (and later a psephologist who failed to forecast the size of the Corbyn vote in 2015), had torn the necklace off Diana's neck.

To put it mildly, my decision had become a high-octane wrangle and within a matter of months the Labour NEC stepped in. I was expelled by 13 votes to 7. It created a hullabaloo at the time but is no more than a footnote now. On some key issues Perry has been proved right. On others my own political instincts regarding the far-left have been vindicated. Both of us were wrong on some points: the SDP could only survive by merging with the Liberal Party. A decade or so before she died, I encountered Shirley Williams at a dinner party in honour of Nadine Gordimer. We were seated next to each other. Conversation had to be made. I asked as neutrally as possible:

'Don't you regret leaving now? Surely Healey, Smith and Hattersley were right. We've got a Thatcherite Labour government.'

She smiled. 'Easy to say now. It is an odd feeling being in the Lib Dems and to the left of Blair.'

'But had you stayed your gang would have been in the Labour Cabinet. Now you'll be pushed into an alliance with the Tories.'

'We all make mistakes, don't we? Didn't you try and join the Labour Party after we left? That was a laugh and we all did.'

It was difficult to disagree.

4

Off to India

In 1982 I wrote my second book on the homeland, *Can Pakistan Survive?* The country was groaning under the military dictatorship of Zia al-Huq, who had overthrown the elected president, Zulfikar Ali Bhutto, in 1977 and then hanged him, with American collusion, in 1979.

I had last seen Bhutto in 1970, when the country was still exulting over the overthrow of the Ayub Khan dictatorship. Later that year would come the electoral victory of East Pakistan's Awami League, which the Pakistan Army tried to crush; then the Indian intervention and the birth of Bangladesh. Bhutto would become president in 1971 of a truncated country. I was there researching *Pakistan: Military Rule or People's Power?*, my first book on the troubled land. I interviewed Bhutto over dinner, and the conversation continued the following week. I had warned that if the Bengali people of East Pakistan were not given their rights, the province might find a way to 'detach itself'.

His response: 'What nonsense you talk. You're out of touch with politics here. You refused to join my party. So why aren't you off to Baluchistan with a gun, like Che Guevara?'

'I'm not ready yet to commit suicide.'

He glared at me.

We were interrupted by the entry of an ungainly figure and Bhutto hurriedly sent his deputy (Mustafa Khar) to whisper in my ear: 'He's General Yahya's son. So please keep silent.' Yahya Khan was the stopgap dictator who had promised general elections after his predecessor was toppled by the uprising; he kept his word. He was a colourful figure. His name in Punjabi meant

Fuck-Fuck and he was unstoppable in that regard – at the height of the civil war he had run out of his house in Peshawar inebriated and stark naked, followed by his mistress (nicknamed General Rani by local wags) who tried to drag him back and finally did so with the help of sentries. Word spread. How could it not?

Bhutto introduced Fuck-Fuck junior to me. We shook hands. He had a copy of *Private Eye* on him, half-buried inside a newspaper. I was slightly shaken. The two parts of my life had never collided like this before.

'Sir,' he asked Bhutto plaintively, 'have you seen "Letter from Pakistan"? What they have written about father and me? Do you know who writes these lies?'

'I have no idea,' came the reply, 'but ask Tariq. He lives there. Are you thinking of suing them?'

The portly figure looked at me. 'Mr Tariq, do you know the people of this magazine.'

'I do,' I said, trying to keep it as low-key as possible, 'and on my return I will make enquiries regarding this letter. I think it might be Sir William Rushton, who was at school with some Pakistani boy. But I'm not sure.'

Young Fuck-Fuck thanked me profusely before he left. Bhutto laughed. 'I saved you there. The whole world suspects you write that column about Pakistan. How could this oaf be so ignorant?'

I never saw Bhutto again. History kept us apart. But despite all our differences, I could never really dislike him. Once he came to power, I remained a critic. He was, without doubt, the most intelligent leader that Pakistan ever had, but his knowledge led to an over-bloated ego, a self-belief so strong that it bordered on madness.

As Bhutto became the leader of a rump Pakistan, he was faced with serious demands to 'hang the generals'. To teach them a lesson, in other words. Bhutto, only too aware that the new post-1971 state and its structures were weak, had many grandiose schemes but none that envisaged a serious reform of the army, uprooting it from its colonial roots and laying the foundations for a modern armed force with accountability built in. At the time there would have been huge popular support for any such move.

His response to these arguments was not stupid but did demonstrate some of his own weaknesses. He argued that the US military was deeply embedded in that country's own political structures, played an active part in decisions related to war and peace and could be overruled only by the president – though in extremis they could remove him to defend the national interest. As president, elected prime minister and chief martial law administrator, Bhutto would make sure that the Pakistan Army was kept under control. In other words, the only feasible form of governance he could envisage was a form of postcolonial Bonapartism that he must have known could not outlast him.

He supported the military assault on East Pakistan. As the supreme leader he tended to treat his own party colleagues as serfs. He rewarded sycophancy, punished dissent and boasted of how he occasionally utilised his hereditary landlord 'rights' to exercise the *droit du seigneur*: deflowering a woman on the eve of her marriage. Medieval European feudal practices of this nature never disappeared in Pakistan and were especially strong in Sindh, where Bhutto and other landlords dominated the landscape.

He was enraged when an old landlord friend, a fellow colleague in the government, addressed him at a Cabinet meeting as 'Zulfi'. The response was savage: 'Don't you Zulfi me just because I've fucked your wife.' This lofty exchange, too, mysteriously turned up in *Private Eye*. It didn't improve relations, annoying him greatly.

Can Pakistan Survive? was published in 1982, the title created a storm, and the book was banned in Pakistan. The question mark was important. The book was written ten years after the formation of Bangladesh at the conclusion of a brutal civil war. I had always warned that if the political and economic subjugation of Bengal by the predominantly Punjabi ruling class and army continued, the Bengali people would resist. Then, in 1979, the Pakistan Army, two years after they toppled Bhutto's government, decided to hang him.

It was these two events that compelled me to write *Can Pakistan Survive?* A warning to our rulers: if you carry on like before, what's left of Pakistan might collapse as well. The interior of Sindh had exploded in April, after Bhutto was hanged, and the repression by the police and paramilitary units was brutal. It was during one of these confrontations that a uniformed, indoctrinated policeman taunted a peasant woman he was assaulting: 'Your Bhutto. His mother was a Hindu.' The illiterate woman looked her oppressor in the eye and replied: 'Was our Prophet's mother a Muslim?' What a reply. Spontaneous. And unanswerable.

In Sindh people had chanted 'Indira Gandhi zindabad' (long live Indira Gandhi). After 1971 Punjab had become the dominant province in the new Pakistan. I did not think there was any possibility whatsoever of a united Punjab. It would be a challenge to two powerful state machines and would have ended Pakistan. That was not what I desired. I had speculated that Baluchistan and the Pakhtun nation could unite with their equivalents in Iran and Afghanistan, but this utopian thought was ended by the Soviet entry into Afghanistan in 1979 and the clerical revolution in Iran that same year. That ended all talk of unity in the region.

Even though the book was immediately banned in Pakistan, pirated editions (five in one month alone) circulated throughout the country. General Zia-ul-Haq, about to embark on a visit to India where the book was being widely read and reviewed, had been warned by his advisers not to mention it at all whatever the circumstances. Sage advice, but Zia could not resist. At his press conference two senior Indian journalists asked 'can Pakistan survive?' without mentioning the book. Zia denounced me and the book, insisting that Pakistan would exist forever and that the purpose of the book was to 'damage Indo-Pak relations'. Sales rocketed. For the US edition, Verso had the general's quote on the front jacket, along with a vicious response from Salman Rushdie.

It's not often that one of my books stirs a debate on the scale this one did. Many in Pakistan were shocked that the question in the title could even be posed. I was often buttonholed by senior civil servants and on one occasion by a serving general. My parents in Pakistan had a rougher time. Neil Middleton, my editor at Penguin, had commissioned two books from me. *The Stalinist Legacy: Its Impact on Twentieth-Century World Politics* was an anthology that he had thought would do better. He was thrilled they had to bring out a second edition of the Pakistan book within six months.

One outcome was a phone call from Carmen Callil at Chatto. 'Darling, can I give you lunch this week? I want to discuss an idea.' She had thought that a book on India might be an even bigger success. She said Sonny Mehta at Picador was also very keen and that they would do it together. I made it clear that my knowledge of India was nowhere as good as my knowledge of Pakistan. Nevertheless, agentless at the time, I suggested a book on the politics and culture of contemporary India. Contracts were exchanged, a modest advance offered and accepted.

I also applied for and obtained a grant from the Reemtsma Foundation in Hamburg, to cover travel, expenses and accommodation for two months. Jan Philipp Reemtsma was a leftist who had inherited a huge tobacco company, which he sold at just the right time and spread his investments. This was on the advice of Ernest Mandel, whom Reemtsma greatly admired and with whose books on capitalism he largely agreed. Many of us were surprised. Ernest's books had made a huge impact on us, but the notion that his analyses might guide dabbling in the stock market, leave alone scoring a big hit, had never entered my mind. 'It must be wonderful to observe the unity of theory and practice at such close quarters,' I teased him.

Thanks to the Foundation's grant, I was off to India in December 1983. I knew Northern India well, had lectured at Jawaharlal Nehru University and St Stephen's College in Delhi on a few occasions, and was a connoisseur of the street food and cafés in Chandni Chowk and South Mumbai. I had visited Kolkata in the East (my favourite Indian city) as well, but Southern India remained a mystery. Its culture, its languages, its histories had to be studied first-hand and I spent some very valuable time in Kerala, Hyderabad, Tamil Nadu, and Baroda in Gujarat.

The plan was to structure the book around individual characters in different domains, in order to build up a series of portraits that gave some idea of the country – a set of linked miniatures rather than a single, uninterrupted narrative. The project had already been inspected by two advisers: Ernest Mandel and Livio Maitan. Ernest questioned my proposal for a whole chapter on Indian cinema, suggesting that instead a few relevant footnotes where necessary would do the trick. Livio nodded sagely. I smiled politely but refused. And then a long-dead comrade came to the rescue: 'Well, of course,' Ernest now attempted a compromise, 'Lenin was very keen on cinema as a new mode of communication with the masses. Perhaps a chapter is not excessive.' Livio nodded sagely. I smiled again, but refrained from pointing out that Lenin's view on this matter was largely instrumentalist.

The project was approved. I typed and mailed off letters to the following:

Politicians: Indira Gandhi, Jyoti Basu, EMS Namboodiripad, George Fernandes, sundry trade union activists and Naxals
Journalists: Pritish Nandy, Khushwant Singh, Kuldip Nayyar, Sadanand Menon, Krishna Raj, Nikhil Chakravarty, Tavleen Singh
Intellectuals: Romila Thapar, Irfan Habib, Kosambi, Barun Dey, K. Damodoran, Utsa Patnaik, Jairus Banaji
Cinema: Satyajit Ray, Shyam Benegal, Mrinal Sen, Saeed Mirza, Adoor Gopalkrishnan, Aparna Sen, Shabana Azmi, Girish Karnad
Painters: Bhupen Khakhar, Gulam Sheikh, M.F. Husain, Vivan Sundaram, Geeta Kapur (art historian)
Dance: Chandralekha

Without exception, they all agreed. Mrs Gandhi's secretary rang the following week. They would confirm a time and date when I was in the country, and yes, I could attend the annual conference of the Congress Party in Kolkata.

Susan had given birth to our son, Chengiz, in February that year. We agreed that travelling all over India with a tiny baby was not a good idea. My parents insisted that mother and son hang out with them in Lahore. The winter weather there is usually beautiful. Warm, clear blue skies during the day, and chilly enough to have an open fire in the evening. At the time, I was banned from travelling to Pakistan by the Zia dictatorship, but we came up with a plan. They would join me in Delhi for a week or so at the end of my work tour and then we would fly back together. Ralph Miliband would be in Delhi, too, on his way back from a conference in Kolkata. I had promised to act as his tour guide.

Once the morning fog lifts, Delhi, too, is beautiful in December. I checked in at the India International Centre, neighbouring the Lodhi gardens and some tombs. Health-conscious lawyers, civil servants, etc., arrive punctually for their pre-breakfast power-walks around the gardens. There was very little chit-chat.

One of my first ports of call in this city is usually Maharani Bagh where Romila Thapar resides. On previous trips it was to exchange high-class political gossip from both our countries, catch up on intellectual debates in India and Europe, and much else besides.

Our conversations were always happily disordered. The interview for the book was very different in character. I wanted to discuss the iconology, philosophy and rituals of the Hindu sects in ancient times. In her writings, above all in the great *History of India: Volume One*, Romila had contextualised Hinduism in sociological and historical terms, attempting to break the textual domination and stress popular manifestations, including festivals and their links to polytheism. She had also compared ancient India to other ancient societies in the Mediterranean world and elsewhere. That would be the subject of our interview.

She agreed, but laughed disbelievingly, while immediately offering advice on other matters. 'If Mrs G[andhi] does see you, make sure you question her on the Emergency in some detail.'

The Thapars were Lahoris before Partition. Her brother, Romesh, was friends with my father and uncle. Their father, a surgeon-general and boss of the British Indian Army's medical services, often visited both my grandfathers when returning to Lahore after postings elsewhere. These family ties, especially after the bitter tears of 1947, meant that when Lahoris met up again there was an emotional charge.

The day after dining with Romila, I was dragged off to a lavish Sikh wedding at the Imperial Hotel, whose proprietors, too, were from Lahore and knew my family. Here I met many people who had attended my parents' wedding in December 1942. I had dinner with some of them the next day. After supper we retired to the living room. They all looked at me.

Had I done something terribly wrong? The most senior person present spoke: 'Just talk about Lahore.' He meant the Lahore 'after we were massacred or driven out'. I talked about what it was like growing up in a city of ghosts, of how many Lahoris mourned the deaths and the division of the Punjab, of how a sadness gripped my parents when we drove past houses or offices where their Sikh and Hindu friends had once lived and worked. The questions came thick and fast. What was life like in the post-Partition Government College? Was Professor X still alive? Were there mixed plays or had the participation of women been banned? Was a particular bookshop or café or street vendor still in existence? We spoke mainly in Punjabi. There were too many tearful eyes and I felt they needed cheering up a bit.

I recounted an incident concerning Bhutto at a massive public meeting in the city. Soon after West Pakistan became Pakistan and East Pakistan became Bangladesh, Zulfikar Ali Bhutto had a large majority in Parliament. As prime minister his main opposition came from the Jamaat-i-Islami (JI – the Party of Islam), led by the Saudi-favoured theologian Maulana Maududi and his cohort. A large public meeting had been planned to welcome Bhutto to Lahore, his first visit since becoming prime minister. Ambassadors and dignitaries were present, looking slightly nervous as they were told to note and report back on the new prime minister's popularity. The JI had decided to disrupt the gathering. A quarter of a million people had turned up. The changes Bhutto had promised – 'food, clothing and shelter for all' – had unsettled the various elites and delighted the poor.

Measures included opening up the public sector to employ women in large numbers, a ban on evictions of poor peasants and tenant farmers from the land, legalisation of trade unions and, in those early years, relatively few restrictions on thought or speech.

There were not enough JI activists to deal with the situation so they moved as close to the platform as they could. As was well-known, Bhutto, like Jinnah, enjoyed his whisky, and a minion carried a flask during campaigns for when he spoke at three or more meetings a day and needed a sip to clear his throat (as he once put it to me).

As he began to speak, he signalled his attendant, who poured the amber liquid, calmly adding ice and water. This was the cue for which the JI activists had been eagerly waiting. Some bearded men, young and old, stood up and started shouting: 'Look, look people, he is drinking sharab (alcohol).' Bhutto gestured they should calm down and let him quench his thirst. 'It's sherbet, it's sherbet' he told the crowd. The mullahs persisted: 'It is alcohol, it is alcohol.' Finally, the prime minister lost his cool and shouted through the microphone: 'Yes, it is alcohol, you sister-fuckers. Unlike you I don't drink the blood of our people.'

The crowd went delirious, a spontaneous chant arose and dominated the proceedings for the next few minutes. People roared with delight, stood up and danced: 'Jiye saadha Bhutto jiye, Piye saadha Bhutto piye' (Long may our Bhutto live, long may our Bhutto drink). My hosts in Delhi, too, applauded and laughed: 'Lahore is Lahore', 'only in Lahore', 'real spirit of the people', etc.

It was this that had created the new radical, post-Partition crowd in Lahore. Even at the time not all the 'people' were supporting Bhutto. A large majority of the 'crowd', however, was for him.

After Delhi I headed to Baroda to spend a week with my friend Bhupen Khakhar. He was working on a set of new 'coming out' paintings, mainly nudes of himself and his lover. The latter was in his sixties, older than Bhupen, and when he turned up one day he appealed to me: 'You're a friend of his. Don't you think

this painting is dirty?' I laughed. 'Look here V., nobody will recognise you without clothes. It's a very fine painting. Let him get
on with it.'

Bhupen must have known he was coming because he had
painted his lover's penis bright red. Naturally V. freaked out.
'Look at this, Tariq. Explain it to me.' I said it was an indication
of fire and passion. Then Bhupen took off the colour. I was dra-
gooned to accompany the couple to V.'s grandchild's birthday that
afternoon. Here petty-bourgeois 'normality' prevailed.

I moved on to Chennai and then to Kovalam beach in Kerala,
where I got the message that a date had been fixed for my meeting
with the prime minister. I flew back to Delhi the next day. After
the formal interview for the book, Mrs Gandhi turned to me:
'Now my turn to ask you some questions. I read your new book
[*Can Pakistan Survive?*]. You know these generals and how
they think and operate. I'm being told by my people here that
Pakistan is preparing a surprise attack on us in Kashmir. What
do you think?'

I was taken aback, and blunt in my response, pointing out that
with Pakistan heavily involved in running the Mujahideen on
behalf of the United States in Afghanistan, it was inconceivable
that they would want to open up a second front. It would be so
irrational that, even if some blowhards in the high command
wanted to, it would immediately be vetoed by Washington.

She persisted with her questioning, and I, in turn, refused to
accept that any such plan existed or was possible. I had used the
word irrational a great deal and she turned on me. 'I'm amazed
that someone like you thinks the generals are rational human
beings.' I burst out laughing. There was a certain irony. I, with a
near hydrophobic horror of military dictators, had been put in the
position of defending the Pakistan Army at a time when we had
the worst dictator of them all. 'But this would be so irrational that
it would be insane,' I replied. 'It would mean a state in which the
generals are deciding to commit suicide. They will not do that.
And I say this as someone who is completely opposed to them.
I'm still persona non grata in the country because of my views on
what they did in Bengal before your intervention.'

The discussion then took an amazing turn. 'Let me tell you something' she said. 'And this is about our generals. After Pakistan had surrendered, General Manekshaw walked into this very office where you're sitting and saluted me.' Mrs Gandhi, like Zulfikar Ali Bhutto, was a very good mimic, and her depiction was extremely diverting. What she went on to describe did surprise me a great deal. After the salute, General Manekshaw asked her whether the military high command had permission to 'finish the job'. This meant crossing the border into Lahore and taking West Pakistan as well. Given the demoralised state of the Pakistan Army, the outcome was preordained unless the Chinese and the United States entered the conflict.

'This being India,' Mrs Gandhi continued, 'I thanked the general and said the Cabinet would consider the suggestion.' She then summoned an emergency Cabinet meeting. 'When I reported the military request, the ministers were initially very excited. They were prepared to go along with it when the meeting began. I was alone. When it ended, we were unanimously in favour of a unilateral ceasefire. I tell you this to show you that even in India, generals can be very irrational. In Pakistan, as you know, they run the country.'

I repeated what I had said earlier and discussion on the subject finally came to an end. She then told me that the Israelis had offered to carry out a lightning strike against Pakistan's nuclear reactor, provided they could use an Indian Air Force base. 'I turned down this offer. I told them we can do it ourselves if we want to.'

The conversation concluded with her talking about Bhutto on his visit to Shimla to sign the peace treaty after the war in Bangladesh. Imagine how nervous he had been. She recalled my father being present on that occasion too, and said 'had it not been your father, who I've known since we were young, I would have been nervous myself. It was your father who convinced me that Bhutto was the only political leader in Pakistan to do business with. There was nobody else. And I did.'

She inquired after Bhutto's family, and asked me to convey her warm regards to Benazir when I next met her. 'You know, I was in prison myself when they hanged Bhutto. It upset me a great deal. Had I been prime minister, I would not have let it happen.' Mrs Gandhi seemed very sure on this front. I wondered what could she have done?

The next day, I was invited to an 'off the record' discussion at the India International Centre with twenty or so people, mainly senior civil servants, intelligence officials, and journalists representing the Soviet and American lobbies, respectively, etc. 'We hear you had a very interesting discussion with our prime minister yesterday,' said the chair. 'That's what we want to discuss.'

For two hours they tried to convince me that I was wrong, and that Pakistan was preparing a military strike in Kashmir. I remained patient, explaining at great length why this was impossible given the Afghan involvement and given that General Zia was extremely unpopular in his own country. Zia was hated in Sindh and in Baluchistan as well as in parts of the Frontier and even the Punjab. He could not afford any crazy war that he would lose. That is why he was desperate at that moment for some form of rapprochement, and kept turning up in India uninvited on the pretext of watching Indo-Pak cricket matches. What he really wanted was to speak with Mrs Gandhi. Most of the spooks present were not convinced. Finally, I lost my cool a bit and said: 'Look guys, if you want a pre-emptive strike against Pakistan, I can't stop you. But you should think up a better excuse since nobody in the world is going to believe that India was attacked first.'

This story has an amusing footnote. Back in London a few months later, I described the tone of this conversation to Benazir. She listened carefully, then asked: 'But why did you tell them that our generals weren't preparing an attack?' At that moment, she reminded me most of her father. She, too, thought that defeat in war would be the best way to break the military's grip on politics in Pakistan.

I recalled all these conversations vividly when I heard that Mrs Gandhi had been assassinated by her Sikh bodyguards in October 1984. It later emerged, according to both Indian and Pakistani intelligence sources, that one of the assassins (or a close relation of his) had visited Sikh training camps in Pakistan to meet some people. Even though no frontal assault was being prepared, the desire for revenge among sections of the military never evaporated.

Could it be that the CIA and the DIA had obtained information from their agents inside the Indian establishment suggesting that the Indians were seriously considering a 'pre-emptive strike' against Pakistan? This would certainly have destabilised the Afghan operation, not to mention the military dictatorship in Pakistan. Could a high-powered secret decision have been made in Washington to get rid of the Indian prime minister using Sikh hitmen? That was certainly the view of an Indian senior civil servant I met in New Delhi who told me that the internal report submitted to the new prime minister linked Pakistan to one of the assassins, and that the report had not been made public for fear of encouraging a new war fever.

'Could I read the report?' The request was denied.

The result of all this for me was a change of plan. Sonny Mehta insisted I write a book on the Nehru–Gandhi dynasty. 'Save the other idea for another occasion' said Carmen Callil. That's how I wrote *The Nehrus and the Gandhis: An Indian Dynasty* in six weeks flat for Chatto/Picador. It did extremely well and Sonny sold it all over the world, before advising me to get an agent and introducing me to Andrew Nurnberg.

The best review was whispered in my ear by Charles Wheeler, who had done a long, friendly interview for BBC Radio 4. As we were leaving he said: 'I enjoyed the book a lot, but you're a bit soft on the Indian bourgeoisie.' True, but my publishers had insisted they did not want a 'Marxist treatise'. Another BBC journalist who had overheard our exchange muttered: 'Have you decided to come out, Charlie?'

5

CLR

C.L.R. James was seventy-nine when I interviewed him for *Socialist Challenge*, by any standards an old man. He appeared somewhat frail, but this impression evaporated when he began to talk. It was almost as if one was being transported back to the polemical debates and arguments of the 1930s.

I had last heard him speak at the 'Dialectics of Liberation' conference in the Roundhouse in 1967. On that occasion he had clashed fiercely with the black American leader Stokely Carmichael. 'Race is decisive,' Carmichael had thundered. 'No,' James had replied with quiet dignity, 'it is class'. The same year James spoke at an International Marxist Group meeting in Birmingham, held to pay tribute to Malcolm X.

C.L.R. James was a Trotskyist and a member of the Fourth International (FI) for seventeen years. His conversations with Trotsky were published under a pseudonym. He left the FI because of differences on the class character of the Soviet Union.

When I met him in his hotel room, he stipulated one condition for the interview: It must end as the second Test match began. I did not want to miss a single minute of cricket.

T.A. What were the main literary influences on you in your youth? What were the first books you read and how much impact did they have on you?

C.L.R. The greatest literary influence on me before I left the Caribbean was William Makepeace Thackeray. I first read *Vanity Fair* when I was nine years old. Subsequently I read it on nine other occasions. I did not know it was a literary classic. My mother had Shakespeare, *Vanity Fair* and another book called *John Halifax, Gentleman*. These were on the shelf and I was living in the Caribbean countryside with nothing to do, so I read. Thackeray and his constant attacks on the aristocracy had more part in shaping my attitude towards the establishment than Marx.

T.A. Would you say your views have altered over the last decades at all, or are you still as intransigent as ever on the themes close to your heart?

C.L.R. My views haven't altered. I left the Trotskyist movement in 1951, but I have remained an independent Marxist ever since. I do not subordinate myself to any state. I have never been to Moscow, though I have much more sympathy with the Chinese developments. I am attached to no political organisation whatsoever.

T.A. But how would you view world politics today? The situation has altered in many ways since the thirties.

C.L.R. My view on world politics is based firmly on what Lenin said in 1919. He told us that this was going to be an epoch of wars: imperialist wars, nationalist wars, civil wars. And of course an epoch of revolution. I see the old societies falling apart, in severe crisis, and I don't think there is any way out except through building a new, socialist society. In that sense I have not changed since 1934, when I first joined the Fourth International. It was Marx who first stated that the choice confronting humanity was socialism or barbarism. I believe that. I believe that in the last half century we have seen many examples of barbarism.

T.A. On a related subject, could I ask you what is your attitude to Fidel and the Cuban Revolution. In the revised edition of *The Black Jacobins*, you make what I think is a rather attractive comparison between Fidel Castro and Toussaint L'Ouverture. Would you care to expand on that?

C.L.R. There was a great revolution in the Caribbean in the heat and excitement following the French Revolution, and in the wake of the crisis of the imperialist world today there emerged in the Caribbean another great revolution, the Cuban Revolution.

You ask me about Fidel. There are two things that come to mind. He made the revolution first and then the Russians helped him. They were not for the revolution before it was an accomplished fact. But secondly there are things about Fidel which I read which I am not too happy about. But I know another thing which for me is very important. If it were not for Fidel's army, Angola would now be under the control of the South African whites. The Cuban intervention in Angola was a tremendous event in the history of the world. I think Fidel is doing the best under the circumstances.

T.A. *The Black Jacobins* has been regarded by the revolutionary left as a classic for a long time, but it must have been galling for you that because of your politics it did not receive a wider recognition. Today it is being acclaimed in much wider circles. To me it has been obvious since I first read the book that it was tailor-made for an epic film. Not a Hollywood epic, but a people's epic. Why has that never happened?

C.L.R. Many people have talked about it, but where is the money to come from? A lot of people say that, and an American film-maker is studying the possibility today. I am prepared to write a film script provided we can find a capable filmmaker and the finance. But most of them are not too happy about the idea of making a revolutionary film.

T.A. What about the Cubans? They have a collection of very talented and very radical filmmakers. Don't you think they might be prepared to collaborate on a film?

C.L.R. There was talk at one stage of translating the book into Spanish by the Cubans. But the book has a few sharp attacks on the Russian regime and when they reached those pages they stopped the translation. They were saying before they reached those two pages that the book would be out in one or two months. But they stopped.

T.A. When I heard you talk many years ago in London, you polemicised sharply against Stokely Carmichael. Are your views on race and class the same or have you altered them in some way? At that time you were extremely emphatic that class was the ultimate arbiter.

C.L.R. I still believe that. I have not shifted, but it would be a great mistake to ignore the race question or the racial dimension. I am on the side of all those who are using their racial subordination as a means of getting together because in that way they can make as powerful an impact as possible. But for me the class question is still the dominant and crucial one.

T.A. These days there is a lot of talk about the 'crisis of Marxism'. Have you ever seriously questioned your Marxism or doubted its use as a method of investigation?

C.L.R. Never, never! In 1932 I came to this country for the first time. I looked around. I was very well read in history and literature. I had musical interests: Bach, Beethoven and Mozart were known to me. But my thought had no order about it. It was after reading Marx and Lenin and studying Trotsky's polemics against Stalin that I began to develop a coherent view of the world. In 1933 came Hitler and 'socialism or barbarism' appeared the only alternatives.

In the 1914–18 war capitalism killed eight million men, then it went to pieces in 1929 with the depression and as the economic recovery took place fascism was triumphant in Germany, Italy and, a few years on, in Spain, and then came the Second World War. Today they don't go to war because it would be suicide given the power of nuclear weapons. But I have no confidence in capitalism. None whatsoever. I have never entertained any serious doubts about Marxism over the last five decades of my life. Capitalism offers nothing that I want.

T.A. Leaving politics aside for the moment, could we discuss your other passion, cricket. Could I ask two initial questions: why is it that cricket in the Caribbean and India–Pakistan is a mass sport like football in Britain, and secondly, why did it not catch on in some of the other colonies such as Canada?

C.L.R. In Britain there is a very wide range of things that the people can be interested in, but the impact of cricket in India and the Caribbean was different. The overwhelming majority of the masses were illiterate. They saw cricket, which is a marvellous game altogether, as an art form. It was the easiest and most accessible part of Western civilisation that they could identify with, and it was also participatory.

In my book *Beyond a Boundary* I develop this theme in greater detail. Western literature, music, painting was only for the elite, but cricket the masses could adopt and take over. Instinctively they appreciated the artistic quality of the game. The great critics of the fine arts have yet to realise the fact that when 100,000 people go to see a football or a cricket match it is, even if they do not articulate it, an artistic event.

T.A. Could it not also be said that in some ways sport is the new opium of the masses?

C.L.R. Trotsky used to say that the working class was far too interested in sport. He said that far too much of their energy and interests was devoted to sport rather than the organisation of their own class. But I disagreed. I don't think so. I played cricket and football until I left the Caribbean and cricket has always meant a great deal to me. It has never interfered with my Marxist view. As to why it never caught on in Canada, I think the answer is simple: climate. You can't have a season in Canada. That's the chief reason.

T.A. Who would you regard as the most attractive cricketer today?

C.L.R. Viv Richards. The way he plays is something new. I used to think that George Headley was the greatest, better than Sobers or the three W's, but this boy Richards is a marvel. His batting is something we haven't known before. He is an extraordinary batsman altogether. The way they drop the ball on the off-stump or just outside and he keeps on hitting it through the on-side fieldsmen to the boundary. The precision of the shot is such that he could be playing billiards. I've never seen anything like it.

T.A. Do you regret any part of your life. Is there anything you would have done differently?

C.L.R. No. I have enjoyed reading books, which is what made me a Marxist.

As the Test match started the interview ended, with C.L.R. grumbling about the inclusion of Boycott in the English side. If he were an English selector: 'I would get rid of Boycott. He just demoralises the rest of the team. Pick two new openers and let them play in all five Tests. They'll ruin one or two, but they'll be good at the end.'

6

NLR: 'We Have an Editor!'

In 1983, *New Left Review* elected Robin Blackburn as its new editor, with Perry Anderson stepping down after twenty years at the helm. *NLR* was not immune to the changing currents of the early 1980s. The editorial committee, which I joined that year, would soon undergo a painful split.

The history of *NLR* dates back to the fusion in 1960 of two earlier journals, the *New Reasoner* and the *Universities and Left Review*. Both were created in the ferment resulting from two events in 1956. First, the Soviet suppression of the Hungarian revolt. Then, the Anglo-French-Israeli invasion of Egypt after Nasser nationalised the Suez Canal with the cry that galvanised the Arab and Third World: 'Let the imperialists choke in their rage.' The *New Reasoner* had been set up by dissident communists who had left the party; *Universities and Left Review* was created by students at Oxford University. By 1960, both were losing money.

In that year they decided to cut their financial losses and merge into one publication: the *New Left Review*. No extravagant manifestos were written to highlight the new arrival, and it was certainly not launched as a Marxist journal. It was much broader than that in bringing together the intellectual layer that had left the British Communist Party after Hungary and the anti-colonial, pro-CND Oxford students. The first layer included the party's most distinguished historians (minus Eric Hobsbawm, who had decided not to leave the party). The moving force was Edward Thompson, who had jointly edited the *New Reasoner* with John Saville.

Thompson was temperamentally impatient and determined to get the magazine off the ground as soon as possible. This seemed to flow into other parts of his life. Decades later, Christopher Hill confessed to me that the 'rudest and most obnoxious letter I have ever received in my life was from Edward'. Why? 'Because', he replied, 'I was taking too long to leave the CPGB.'

While the merger of the two journals produced the *NLR*, a ghost from the 1930s refused to disappear. During the Spanish Civil War, when Hitler and Mussolini helped Franco and his army to overthrow the elected Republican government, a strong anti-fascist magazine was born in Britain and named *Left Review*. In some ways it is more accurate to think of the *NLR* as the merger of three journals. Memories of the Spanish Civil War were still strong in the 1950s and only marginally less so in the 1960s.

The first *NLR* editor was Stuart Hall. In *Familiar Stranger*, Stuart describes the alienation he felt at not being 'formed' in the tradition of English socialist politics. It made him feel a neophyte. He was also in awe of E.P. Thompson and Raymond Williams: 'They were my fathers ... although I never felt their equal ... I found Raymond intellectually approachable and because of his intellectual interests, much closer to my own formation than Edward had ever been ... editorial boards were a nightmare for me'.

At a very early stage of the new publication, Thompson began to express dissatisfaction with Hall. As Stuart recalls in his memoirs, in editorial meetings he would 'indicate the possible contents of the next issue and then hold up my hands before the storm broke and the editors spoke'. John Saville 'protected me from the wrath that began to emanate from Halifax' (where Edward and Dorothy Thompson lived). Relations between the Thompsons and Stuart deteriorated. In the end, the 'immediate issue' that led to his walking out concerned 'the degree of editorial responsibility delegated to the New Left Clubs ... a delicate and complex issue' that culminated in a split at a meeting in Leeds. Stuart resigned.

There were interim solutions, till finally a desperate Board decided to interview a few candidates to settle on a permanent editor. One of these was Perry Anderson. In Oxford, Perry (who shared digs with Dennis Potter, an immensely charismatic figure) had helped set up the Sixty Group (in 1960), including Kenith Trodd, Robin Blackburn and Roger Smith and others, to discuss ideas for a new magazine. The editor of the *Daily Herald*, a respected Labour daily, met the group. Perry suggested a cultural supplement along the lines of what later became the *NYRB* and *LRB*. It turned out that the editor was only interested in securing the services of Dennis Potter, who he correctly saw as an up-and-coming media star. And he clearly liked a piece Potter had written on an obscure English football club in trouble.

Later, Potter's TV plays, including *Pennies from Heaven* and *The Singing Detective*, propelled him to a different level. He was happy to remain a left social democrat who loved England, minus the hullaballoo of royal parades and Union Jacks. Potter's England was peopled with miners, football crowds, and working-class children being sent free to university. This element of a socialist English nationalism had something in common with the Scottish civic nationalism that came later. As Dennis was dying of an incurable cancer in 1994, Melvyn Bragg conducted an interview with him on Channel 4. Dennis was in great form. He linked the 'pollution of the press' to the 'pollution of politics'. He startled his interviewer by calmly informing the huge audience that he had named his cancer 'Murdoch'. His loathing for Thatcher and her creation was written all over his face. But despite his strong links with the Oxford left in the early sixties, Dennis carved out his own path and remained aloof from all left magazines and organisations.

Back at the *NLR* in April 1962, Thompson was losing heart. Disappointed with Stuart, the Board accepted Edward's advice to interview selected candidates. The weekend interviews were successful, and Edward sent an excited handwritten postcard to an old friend: 'I think we have found our Lenin. More later.' The 'more later' came following the magazine's next Board meeting. It is the fullest account – perhaps because it was expressed in a private letter to a close friend – of Thompson's first thoughts on the person they had chosen to become the new editor of the *NLR*: Perry Anderson. It is an astonishing document on almost every level. Its prescience is remarkable: Perry's individual characteristics accurate to the last comma and still very present for those who have had regular dealings with him over the last half-century or more.

The letter also confirms Edward's position as the dominant political-organisational figure of the British New Left in the early sixties. It was he who effectively forced Stuart's resignation as editor (thought Stuart wasn't too disappointed) and he who recruited Perry as the replacement. He shouldn't have been too surprised when Perry slowly reorganised the *NLR* editorial committee, letting the 'old guard' leave (Tommy Wengraf and Mike Rustin hung on a bit longer) and putting his own very strong imprint on the journal. Edward had predicted the likelihood of this in his letter, which is reproduced below.

Halifax, Monday

Sorry to be so long with your letter which I put away last week for various reasons, partly the Board which came off this weekend. Now that is over, and by the skin of our teeth the New Left – at least, the review part of it is through all its bloody crises and steaming full ahead into optimistic seas. After all our run of bad luck – chiefly people with abundant qualities but some personal faults (Stuart's chameleon qualities, Raphael's delinquent monomanias) which upsets everything – we have lighted on a piece of good luck, better than we could have hoped for; perhaps better than we deserved, but then surely, we *did* deserve some good luck.

This curious bespectacled bat-like character, who came in as editor as an emergency, suddenly emerges as *the* missing link we have been looking for – politically, a mutation in which *NR* and *NLR* are fused, personally as tough as a Leninist, editorially tough, capable of taking criticism, capable of fighting the whole Board.

You would not believe it – in a month he has understood our problems, started at ground level, moved in, ordered a removal van, served notice on Stuart that every last thing of his would be sent to the tip if not removed from the office by the next morning, closed the office, repainted and reorganised it, dug out old MSS going back to '59, returned most of them, planned the next number, closed the old files, ordered a new file, sent a pair of Frances' shoes to the jumble (and bought her another when she threw a scene), instructed Frances on her office-hours, ordered a second telephone, examined the budget and the circulation figures, and so on.

Damn, he is an EDITOR. He can't speak and won't speak, has none of Stuart's sense of the movement, is a bit detached from practical politics; but he is the editor we need to build around. And though detached, he is political at the centre of his interests; that is, unlike Stuart – or myself – or, I suspect, Raphael – where our politics hits us first through values or obliquely, Perry really is a 'hard' political thinker; and he means to establish hard political criteria for the review – to reject on political grounds, and to use the review to clarify the whole theoretical position vis-à-vis communism and social democracy of the new left. In a sense he leans somewhat to the first, that is, he finds some of us ex-CPers affected by irrational attitudes to communism, regards it more objectively than we do, has not the least sympathy with orthodox CP organisation or theory but is *more* interested in the social and economic framework of the communist world than those of us who start with emotional blocks. And he is very tough indeed about the need for utter dissociation of the new left from anything tarred with Congress for Cultural Freedom, Encounterism, etc.

So. There we are. We have an editor – a tough one, perhaps tougher than we are, but the one who is needed – since surely a political review must essentially be edited by a political person. The review will establish a 'position' or '*tendence*': it will be somewhat detached from Clubs, CND, YS – though I can hope we can change this somewhat. But then what is required here is some new kind of weekly and new kind of organisation – the review never could serve all purposes.

But the greatest relief is that for the first time for *years* I feel that I can relax – I don't have to watch, nag, worry – *good* things will happen, initiatives will take place, without my nattering. I shan't agree with all of them. OK. But isn't it just bloody marvellous knowing we have someone there tough enough to send Frances' shoes to jumble, to throw Stuart's bag in the street, to reject in the same number pieces by EPT, Norman Birnbaum, Doris Lessing and John Hughes, to stand up to criticism, and who – I haven't mentioned this yet – refuses to get involved in amateur psycho-analysis, avoids factions, in every mess looks for the constructive way out, and so on?

Oh my god, what a stroke of luck. And I don't think I shall change my opinion in six months ... For the rest, Raphael's delinquencies – and they really were lousy, despite his admirable article in this number – I mean he went right through into that state he was in in the Partisan days when he was lying and playing politics with everyone until one felt he couldn't be trusted in any sense at all – were censured, but Raphael played truant from the Board so there was no great row. Raph will now go into a black mood in which he feels misunderstood and in which the new left etc. etc. is a gang of terrible people; I shall find it difficult to trust him again. Denis [Butt], however, behaved bloody well, came to the Board and took his censure, almost apologised, bears no malice, and we're still 'in friends' with him. Nick Faith is still resigned (in protest at Raph) but he may come back, and anyway with Perry there the business problems suddenly reduce themselves to a reasonable size.

So, so, so. After all, it was worth going back and fighting for it. We have saved, in all our curious collective ways (even Raph), an independent socialist review, perhaps even a revolutionary review which will live for many a year to fight. This probably seems very remote to you. It isn't really – it is important for the socialist movement, and so for all of us. But it is true that the rest of 'new leftism' has dwindled to very little, only a few Clubs and patchy, and the review won't have this activist bent. I think a new approach is needed to activist politics, but I am trying not to get too involved even in worrying about it ... And one of the things that has cheered me up a bit is that young Perry (24) really does seem to have been a little influenced by one or two of my written pieces – well, perhaps if I wrote a bit more carefully and better this would be as effective and useful as rushing round forming new societies ...

You say I must get out of it all, and yes, now perhaps I can. Can't you see it's much easier to get out when things are going well? It would have been awful to have got out and leave utter chaos – or a slick review run by Norm Fruchter – behind. That would have worked like poison – resentments – sense of failure – nagging responsibility – whatever else I tried to do. Sometimes one has to stay in one's corner, even if one loses a few good years. If we do pull it through, I can retire and become a minor

Olympian, a smug miniature Raymond. But lovely to look down from detached heights and see things moving *well* ...

Now here I am with a week in an empty house to finish the book [*The Making of the English Working Class*].

Apart from its other qualities, this letter will surprise those who assumed and still do (mainly lazy academics) that a permanent enmity coloured relations between the two men. It describes the real 'founding moment' of the *NLR* as it has existed from 1962 onwards. There have been political shifts, intellectual rows, resignations and returns. How could it be otherwise in a changing world that affects us all? But *NLR* has remained an indispensable journal of ideas for the international left.

When Robin was elected editor of *NLR* in 1983, he had already been holding the fort as managing editor for some years while Perry worked on his historical studies, *Passages from Antiquity to Feudalism* and *Lineages of the Absolutist State*, and launched New Left Books. There were several people on the *NLR* editorial committee (EC) who could have edited the magazine in different ways and with different political priorities, among them Anthony Barnett, Quintin Hoare, Francis Mulhern, Fred Halliday and Peter Wollen. Robin, apart from being a gifted writer, temperamentally non-dogmatic and capable of lateral thinking (a bit too lateral sometimes), represented a political and organisational continuity. Together with Perry, he had been amongst the first editors of the re-founded magazine.

Only in battle do some people find their allotted part. Robin, as a young lecturer, had supported the students occupying the LSE in 1969. When they were temporarily pushed out of the college, he had participated physically in helping them tear down the famous gates and re-enter the premises. For this, he and another lecturer, Nick Bateson, were sacked by the LSE. 'Revolting students', the 'end of civilisation', complained the Popperites. The far-left pleaded with other left-wing professors to come out in solidarity, but neither Ralph Miliband nor Bill Wedderburn had been in favour of the use of force. They agonised but stayed put.

Later, Ralph did resign and moved to Leeds, but not before Chris Harman (a leading light of the LSE International Socialists) had cruelly nicknamed him 'Professor Moribund'. I can't recall how many times Ralph expressed regret to me for not having left the LSE after Robin and Nick were fired. It haunted him. My own view was that these were tactical decisions. Others resigning immediately would not have led to the reinstatement of the LSE Two, but simply deprived the college of some very fine socialist academics. I don't think I ever convinced Ralph. He was a man of great integrity and felt he had made a mistake.

I remember at a *Red Mole* editorial board meeting in 1971, Robin gave a short talk critical of the inability of the far-left currents to provide a serious analysis of the ruling class and its politics. He pointed out that Marx and Engels, Lenin, Gramsci and Trotsky always put politics and not sociology in command. The left these days was too addicted to stale platitudes. He pointed to several examples, including from our own paper. Both at *Red Mole* and during his editorship of the *New Left Review*, Robin came up with ideas that challenged the verities of the left. It was this freshness of thought that made him indispensable to any left editorial board. At the *Red Mole* board meeting, for instance, he argued that Heath was exploiting the political weaknesses of the trade union movement to push through an aggressive set of policies intended to divide and defeat the workers' movement.

To demonstrate what he meant, Robin suggested that IMG members be encouraged to read in depth what the most intelligent and politically aware workers were saying. He held up that week's paper and read the following from an interview with Jack Gray, the convenor of shop-stewards at the occupied Plessey factory, that we had published (*Red Mole*, 20 October 1971). In answer to the first question, 'What political lessons have you learnt from the occupation?', Gray replied:

All the socialist press has been asking that question. The left-wing movement felt that we were politically motivated, but if they talk to the lads they find they are not. The only political motive is the feeling that this Government has to go whether it's over the Common Market or unemployment or the Industrial Relations Bill – it must be brought down. Its policies are totally against the working class. But the majority of the men don't like politics. Just look at that Union Jack out there. Someone brought in a Red Flag and about 50 said they would walk out if we put that up. It's their upbringing through the *Express* and the *Record* that men get frightened of Communism and nationalization and things like that – of the words I mean. They are doing what the socialists say, but they don't want to be politically involved.

With Robin as the new *NLR* editor, I was formally invited to join the editorial committee of the journal. As the left revolutionary tide of the '70s receded, however, rifts were starting to open up on the EC, leading to a split in the autumn of 1983. I was quite happy to carry on as before, but both Perry and Robin insisted otherwise. My own relations with a number of those who subsequently left for a variety of reasons – including feeling that Robin's appointment marked a new political phase (which it both did and didn't) – were friendly.

Tom Nairn had accepted my request to write an essay on the monarchy for *Socialist Challenge* in 1977. Later reprinted in the *NLR*, it was ultimately expanded into a book and became the most powerful account of the institution: *The Enchanted Glass*. Fred Halliday had been a fellow anti-imperialist since university. An unqualified supporter of Isaac Deutscher, he had edited a collection of his essays. He had also written in support of the Soviet intervention in Afghanistan in 1979 and, though I disagreed strongly with him, good relations were maintained. Peter Wollen and I had engaged in friendly debates on early Soviet literary and artistic movements. I was a huge fan of Peter's writings on the French *nouvelle vague* and culture in general, and we became good friends after he left the *NLR*.

Anthony Barnett wrote me a warm letter stressing that his departure had nothing to do with my formal induction to the EC and regretting that he had had to leave. There was a suggestion at the time that Robin and his new team should run the *Review*, while the exiters would remain on the Board if given charge of New Left Books/Verso, which had been launched in 1970. This proposal had no attractions for Perry, Robin or me. *NLR* had created the publishing house, and its programme of publishing modern European classics was closely linked to the intellectual priorities of the journal.

After this was made clear, two of the exiters – Jon Halliday and Peter Wollen – asked for a formal parley and I was assigned to meet with them. They had brought along a letter signed by others as well, explaining why they had left the EC. I pointed out that were we to publish this, Perry and Robin would certainly reply and challenge several points which even I could see were greatly exaggerated or misinterpreted. What good would that do anyone? It would not be a very edifying read. It would exaggerate differences, damage the journal and make conciliation at a later stage difficult if not impossible. My own time in a Trotskyist group, I pointed out, had made me allergic to this style of debate.

They were grumpy. They felt that Robin's appointment had been 'divisive' on a personal and political level, given that I was formally joining the EC, and a more neutral candidate could have been found. I rejected this view largely on the grounds of political continuity and urged them to stay on with the remainers and judge the *Review* under a new editor on its merits. The fact was that many exiters wanted to do their own things, writing for other magazines and publishing houses, etc. They felt that enough of their lives had been dominated by the *NLR*. After leaving, they did note that the *Review* maintained its high standards and many of them would return to its pages in more relaxed mode. Almost a decade later, Peter Wollen, now writing for the *NLR* again, expressed retrospective relief that we had stopped that 'barren debate' in its tracks. I couldn't resist: 'And the tracks weren't even in the direction of historical materialism.'

7

The Bandung File

In late 1984, in response to a *Time Out* column I had written on the new multicultural turn of Channel 4, I got a call from Farrukh Dhondy, the channel's commissioning editor, suggesting lunch. I had spoken a few times on anti-racist platforms with his wife, the writer Mala Sen, but had never really met him. He was part of the *Race Today* gang, itself inspired by C.L.R. James, whose nephew, Darcus Howe, edited the magazine.

What Farrukh suggested that afternoon surprised me. He wanted the daily lives and politico-cultural mores of Britain's ethnic minorities covered seriously on TV, going back to their roots and, whenever necessary, filming in South Asia and the Caribbean. The programme Dhondy envisaged, he told me, must be of a quality that appealed to and helped educate ignorant white citizens as well. According to his own account, when he first informed me that my co-editor would be Darcus Howe, my only response was, 'Oh God!'

Channel 4 was a publicly owned but commercially funded channel with a remit to deliver high-quality, alternative content that challenged the status quo. Conceived in the 1970s and launched in 1982 with the independently minded Jeremy Isaacs as CEO, it became a refuge for dissidents under the Thatcher ascendancy. Dhondy wanted to dump the existing programmes produced by LWT – *Eastern Eye* and *Black on Black* – that divided the non-white communities and were considered too mainstream for C4 in those early days. Samir Shah did South Asia, Trevor Phillips the Caribbean. They took it badly, but their careers prospered. Samir rose high (or slipped low, depending on one's opinion of Sir John Birt) at the BBC, and at the time of writing has been named as its next Chairman. Trevor migrated to the race relations industry and beyond, ending up a deeply conservative figure.

Darcus and I met up and shook hands. Both of us were aware that we had to work in unison. When Farrukh took the idea to Jeremy Isaacs, he was intrigued, but given the personnel involved had to clear it with the C4 chairman, Edmund Dell, a former Paymaster General in the Labour government and a hardened figure on the Labour Right. He said 'No' and asked Jeremy to think again. He did and, annoyed by Dell's prejudices, gave Farrukh the green light. Since neither Darcus nor I had any TV experience, it was suggested that we take on Greg Lanning of the TV History Workshop as a fellow producer. He had worked with Jeremy at Thames TV and would fit in well. Greg was a vital lynchpin in setting up the show and explaining the mechanisms to us in great detail. He managed to find some able directors (mainly women) as well. I found Asian researchers with an investigative background, Gita Sahgal, Vasudha Joshi, Seetha Kumar, Afshin Rattansi, Anjana Patel and others.

Jeremy Isaacs asked to see me. 'You've been on the screen for far too long,' were his first words. 'Time now to change gear and make programmes. It's a big opportunity to change minds.' And then he added, almost as an afterthought: 'Farrukh, others and myself are here to help. All I ask is if you want to do something naughty, warn us in advance so our lawyers can help from the start. Our lawyers are there to make sure you get the programme on air, not to stop you.' This turned out to be true. And the C4 lawyers, Don Christopher in particular, were always extremely helpful.

Meanwhile, I was working hard to finish my book on India for Sonny Mehta at Picador. Greg Lanning would ring regularly to tell me what was going but insisted that I decide on a name for the new company. The last time he rang I was writing about the Bandung Conference, the first meeting of newly independent heads of state from Africa and Asia: Nkrumah and Nehru, Chou En Lai, Sukarno and Nasser. I suggested Bandung Productions. Darcus and Greg were enthusiastic.

Asked to explain the title by a friendly journalist, I replied: 'People discover the name of a new town, the country where it is situated and the conference that took place there in the fifties. Symbolises the shows we will produce.' Debra Hauer, one of our first employees, who had set up the interview, informed her husband of this at their traditional family-and-friends Sunday supper in his restaurant, Le Caprice. Jeremy King suggested to me that 'You should add a sentence. Ban Dung. We're going to get rid of the shit on television.'

That's how it started. After I finished *The Nehrus and the Gandhis*, we moved from our tiny offices in Wardour Street in Soho to Carkers Lane in Kentish Town, where we constructed our four editing suites and reconstructed the offices into a giant open-plan space. This would be the Bandung base from 1984 till 1999.

It was painfully obvious that the number of black and Asian TV researchers, film editors and directors was extremely limited at the time. One of our tasks was to find and train new people, increasing diversity and quality simultaneously. I was strongly opposed to hiring replacements from mainstream companies. Greg's experience proved invaluable. He pointed out that as we built a new Bandung team we could also address the gender gap in television. We went headhunting and assembled a strong team of directors and editors, predominantly women, and on equal pay with their male colleagues. On my many trips to India I had met tough-minded investigative journalists and some of these were enticed to come and work for us in London. Darcus did the same in the Caribbean. We advertised as well and netted a few very fine people.

Farrukh commissioned some short documentaries in 1984–85, a rehearsal for what later became the regular *Bandung File*. There was some excitement in the air. Angela Carter, a dear friend since the late seventies who I first met through Liz Calder, and later, Susannah Clapp, wanted to know more about Bandung. We went for lunch. Angela asked if I'd ever read the novels of the Guyanese writer, Wilson Harris. I confessed I'd never heard of him.

'You must,' she said. 'He's like nobody else. He's not self-regarding. He doesn't promote his own work, he doesn't care too much if his books are reviewed, and yet his work is explosive. Why not a documentary on his life and work?'

'I better read his novels first. Which one?'

'Read them all. You could start with the Quartet.'

She told me that she had last run into Harris when they were both waiting to change trains at Crewe.

'He said something that day which made me think that he was a genius, not a word I throw around.'

'And from your tone it's obvious you're not going to tell me.'

'No.'

'Why?'

'I can't. It might not seem the same to you.'

I did as she asked, nevertheless, and read all his books. They were difficult till I began to read them aloud. As with Shakespeare, much of the meaning lay in the rhythm of the language and its mode of construction. Susan had a similar experience. It would be a huge challenge to make a documentary but stimulating as well. Could we do it? I rang Bill Webb at the *Guardian* for his opinion. He had read a few of Wilson's books and was very encouraging. Could he suggest a researcher? Bill was slightly embarrassed but only because his top recommendation was his daughter Kate, who had also read Harris. Kate Webb and I motored over to Chelmsford where Wilson and his wife lived. Bill had already told him. He was truly amazed that I wanted to make a documentary on his work.

'Why me, Tariq? I'm unknown.'

'That's why,' I said. 'There would be no point in making a documentary about [I mentioned a few names], but your work is so unusual that we must yank you out of the obscurity of the Guyanese forests and get people to read you.'

'A difficult task.'

'I agree. Hence a challenge.'

He had to be persuaded and Kate joined in. He was not being fussy, but genuinely saw no point in confusing the great British public further. We convinced him. I said that it was Angela Carter who had recommended him very strongly. 'Do you remember meeting her in the waiting room at Crewe station?'

He did.

'Was there anything special you said to her, to make her think you were a genius?'

'What are you talking about?'

'I don't know. I thought you might.'

He thought for a while but then shook his head. 'I can't think of anything unusual or striking that I said. She said I deserved the Nobel Prize. That made me laugh. I told her it was a politico-literary prize!'

'Well, she obviously meant it.'

I liked Wilson very much. Some critics regarded him as apolitical. Far from it. He was not above politics but repulsed by the form it had taken in his country, distanced himself from it and immersed his mind in literature. Guyanese ethnic unity between black and Asians was disrupted by the CIA, which engaged in a very sinister form of identity politics. They had bought off black leader Forbes Burnham and in 1953 toppled the radical Asian-origin prime minister Cheddi Jagan, whose white wife, Janet, had been a member of the US Communist Party. It was a joint US–UK operation, just like the overthrow of Mosaddegh in Iran in 1953, but less well known.

Wilson, too, knew the story well, but made it clear that the documentary should be about his work rather than history. In his own quiet way, he had admired Cheddi Jagan and had been pained by the coup and what followed. He didn't want to talk about it. It was one reason that he had decided to move to England. What left an indelible mark on him was his years of work as a land surveyor in the Guyanese rainforest. Nature was ever-present. The physical world 'behaving as quantum theory'.

Farrukh commissioned a sixty-minute documentary, and Greg agreed we needed an intelligent, aesthetically astute director. That's how I met Colin Nutley. He, too, found the books difficult. He, too, understood much more when he read them aloud and he, too, took a strong liking to the writer. We were in tandem. Colin got Wilson's approval to film the documentary using his novella *Da Silva, Da Silva* as a cinematic prop by filming scenes from it. It was our first ever documentary and, in my view, one of the best we ever made on every level. Wilson's participation lifted it further. Message from Jeremy Isaacs via Farrukh: 'Excellent. The channel was created to make documentaries like this ...'

Kate Webb wrote a very warm obituary when Wilson passed away in Chelmsford in 2018. The Guyanese embassy in London paid tribute to their greatest writer by showing our documentary. They had invited me to speak, but I was out of the country. Had I been present I would certainly have criticised him for accepting a knighthood from the British state. I did drop him a card at the time. No reply. The last time we met, Wilson had joked: 'Not even your wonderful documentary increased sales by too much. I did warn you!'

As for Colin Nutley, always unhappy with the mainstream TV companies in Britain, he emigrated to Sweden, and became one of their most popular film directors. He showed 'Da Silva, Da Silva' to a large, invited audience on one of my trips to Sweden, where I explained its genesis. The audience applauded enthusiastically, but thoughtfully. Decades later, flicking through the channels in a hotel in Rio, I bumped into a Swedish movie on Netflix. It was a well-directed, well-shot, high-class comedy. I had missed the opening credits. There were familiar touches that made me wonder. I checked it out immediately afterwards. It was indeed a Colin Nutley film.

Since its rightward, commercialising shift in the mid-1990s, Channel 4 has done all it can to eradicate memories of its radical early years. These days the work of *Bandung File* is hardly ever discussed. Yet during its years of existence, 1985–89, it was widely reviewed in the press and critically praised. Its viewing figures sometimes touched a million and more, especially after Michael Grade gave us a weekday prime-time slot. The average for the first year's broadcasting was 800,000. More interesting sociologically was that the non-white audience was 55 per cent. With white viewers accounting for the rest, this was exactly what Darcus, Greg and I were aiming for. We embarrassed many mainstream TV people not because what we did was 'radical' but because there was nothing (in most cases) to stop any other programme-maker in the country from doing the same inno-vative work. It was the decision to show parts of life here and abroad that could not be seen outside C4 that helped build our reputation.

Simultaneously, *Bandung File* could be and was very critical of 'problems' within the non-white community. We exposed fraud involving fake Asian votes in Sparkbrook, Roy Hattersley's par-liamentary constituency in Birmingham. This created a storm in the press. I was accused of harbouring grudges, which was absurd. On a personal level, I got on well enough with Hattersley, the deputy leader of the Labour Party. He was far more cultured and well read than most of the philistines serving under Keir Starmer today. The fact was that some Asian voters came and complained to one of our researchers. We investigated the story very carefully and there was no doubt that chicanery was taking place.

Hattersley was interviewed at length in the film, denying any corruption and saying that he and his constituency were tied together 'till death us do part'. We were lucky. During one interval in the filming, our cameraman allowed the tape to run till it finished so he could replace it. He informed me and I let him. A group of Asian voters arguing with each other in Punjabi spilt the beans by accident. They admitted that they had fibbed and that yes, they did engage in fraud but so did many others in other constituencies.

An Irish person present told me that this was small-scale compared to Northern Ireland, where the election day mobi-lising slogan in the Catholic community was 'Vote Early, Vote Often'. And nuns in particular had three shifts. (I asked if he was prepared to say this on screen. He refused.) The mistake I made was in not informing C4 lawyers that the decisive proof was uncovered by accident and that those who gave the game away were not aware they had been filmed. Edmund Dell, I was told, went berserk in private. I argued public interest, which Don Christopher said they could have defended in open court had I informed them. Knuckles were duly rapped, but I refused to apologise and defended the programme. We never made the same mistake again.

One day a young mixed-race woman walked into our offices and asked to see me. She was, I think, from Tower Hamlets, and had just got three A-levels and a place at Oxford. She had a story to tell and insisted it would help all young women. She informed me that her Bangladeshi father, bearded and pious (though he could just as well have been clean-shaven and agnostic, as some later instances described to us revealed), had sexually abused her since she was nine years old. She told her white mother, who initially refused to believe her and scared her into silence. The abuse continued. She pleaded with her mother again and again. Finally, the mother caught him in action, screamed abuse and rang the police. He was carted off, tried and received a prison sentence. The young woman allowed herself a few tears and pleaded: 'Please, please say you'll do the story. Even the *Guardian* refused.'

It was and remains an ultra-sensitive issue, usually hidden by layers of hypocrisy, misguided family loyalties and fear (of violence, death threats, disappearances). Nor was it confined to any one community. I was impressed by the woman's courage. She knew perfectly well that many other young women suffered the same fate and she wanted to encourage them to speak out. I agreed to do the programme and that we would film with her face hidden. Farrukh and Darcus agreed we should tell the story. Channel 4 legally cleared it and set up several helplines that were busy throughout the screening.

The young woman herself was calm, sober and very effective, arguing that silence in cases of this sort was a cop-out. She received hundreds of letters from her peers, most of them outlining their own experiences; social services throughout Britain used the documentary to help those in a similar situation. Another important result was that trust between us and the communities we served grew and grew.

With the exception of the apparatchiks from the mostly useless state-created anti-racist bodies, the show was widely respected. Confronted by a few of these jokers at a Bandung event, complaining that we never put them on screen, Darcus could be heard throughout the room as he shouted: 'I hate your self-promoting anti-racism. Just an excuse to cover up your corruption and your failure to do anything useful.' To help matters further, I added a few words: 'Payroll anti-racism. Why should we put you on screen? We talk to real people.' Linton Kwesi Johnson watched, listened, grimaced and grinned. He was a much-valued, unpaid member of our team. When we recorded and broadcast one of his concerts, our viewing figures doubled.

When Jeremy Isaacs left the channel to pursue his own interests, Michael Grade took over. We had all assumed that Issacs would become the Director-General of the BBC. So did he. Nobody doubted he was the best candidate. But the spook on the BBC Board of Governors vetoed him. Isaacs was punished for having shown a documentary on the Greek civil war, which I describe in my book on Winston Churchill.

There was much apprehension at the channel when Grade was appointed the new boss. Most independent producers were aware that access to Jeremy was usually possible as a last resort, and that as a high-quality programme-maker himself, he understood the problems we all faced. Grade was regarded as commercial and too aloof. The day before he formally took charge, he decided to watch every single programme going out on Channel 4. Useful homework as far as we were concerned. It was a weekend and *Bandung File* was in the Saturday 7 pm 'death-slot', called such since most young and not-so-young people were getting dressed or undressed for the evening.

Earlier that week we had been informed by campaigners that a senior police officer had agreed to attend the local council (Islington, North London) public inquiry on the latest death in custody (a young black man), to answer questions. They wanted us to film the meeting. I asked Vasudha Joshi, one of our toughest, no-nonsense researchers, to take command of the operation. She matched herself with one of our in-house directors and prepared the team. Bandung arrived at the Town Hall. The council official, delighted that TV cameras had arrived, asked eagerly, 'BBC?' Back came the Joshi reply: 'No, much better. *Bandung File*, Channel 4. It's open to all the press and media. Yes?'

The disappointed official nodded. The cameras were set up. Vasudha was banking on a quietish evening since no interviews were planned. The panel was ready, the local police boss, uniformed but nervous, was the last to join. Bandung started filming. Suddenly the cop stood up and turned to a council bigwig: 'I thought we had agreed that no TV cameras were allowed.' The packed hall hissed. The council person muttered words to the effect that not every network had been informed. Vasudha was on her feet, hands on hips, ready to have a go. The uniformed person asked her: 'Which programme?' '*Bandung File!*' replied Vasudha. The audience applauded. The cop walked out muttering, 'Fuck this for a laugh.' A Bandung technician on the stage insisted his words were less refined. What would the panel do?

Our intrepid researcher pre-empted the pandemonium about to break loose in the hall and mounted the stage: 'This is a public inquiry. Isn't it more democratic to screen it as well so more people are aware? Let's vote on this. If the public want us to leave we shall do so.' Hurried consultations on the panel. Another cop peeped through the side door. The panel agreed to the vote, which was unanimous. Not a single vote in favour of throwing us out. The Chair asked the police chief to rejoin them. Finally, he did so, to a mixture of cheers and boos, and the meeting restarted. We had a good film in the can and I insisted that Vasudha's democratic lesson to the assembled should be our starting point.

Michael Grade watched it and liked what he saw ('very good television'). At his meeting with C4's commissioning editors and programmers he asked them why *Bandung File* was being shown over the weekend. 'We had no choice,' replied Farrukh. He moved us to a prime-time weekday slot (Tuesdays at 8 p.m.) that compelled marketing and publicity – usually the most conservative section in most outfits – to take us seriously. Yvonne Taylor (a former IMG militant) at publicity was made responsible for our show and did a good job.

Given the obsession these days with identity politics, I've always been a bit surprised that no young academic has written a serious account of *Bandung File*. Riches await some enterprising scholar. To this day, whenever I'm asked to show and discuss a Bandung programme of my choice, whatever the continental location one question recurs: 'Was this actually shown on British television?' What they're really asking is whether it could ever be repeated.

We used to have a weekly staff meeting every Monday morning where Darcus, myself and Greg discussed our own ideas and those put forward by directors, researchers and others. By the end of the day we had decided the programme for the following week. Among the work we produced, two projects involved sending teams to India. One, led by Gita Sahgal, a senior researcher, went to investigate the horrifying story of 'Dowry Deaths', which were (and remain) prevalent. Young women were being enticed into marriage and then killed by their new husbands and mothers-in-law in tandem. 'Kill the bride, pocket the money' was the motto of these criminals. Our film was the first to expose this grisly ritual and created a tiny storm in the media and at festivals where it was shown. Whatever else, Bandung rarely indulged in feel-good docs.

At one of our editorial meetings, Vasudha Joshi asked how many of us had heard of the Vishwa Hindu Parishad (VHP). None of us had. The group was being funded as a Hindu cultural organisation by Ken Livingstone's Greater London Council (GLC). We smelt a scoop and Vasudha was authorised to investigate the issue. It emerged that they were an off-shoot of the far-right Hindu nationalist militia, the RSS, and essentially operated as a propaganda outfit. When Vasudha first approached them for an interview, they were delighted by her semi-sacred Hindu name and trusted her immediately. One of them disapproved of her chain-smoking. This was my only point of agreement with them.

In the interview, we left the difficult questions until the end. They denied they were an RSS front, but contradicted themselves by becoming very irate when we suggested that Gandhi's killer, Godse, had been a member of the RSS. Vasudha flew to India with a small crew to interview the distinguished historian Romila Thapar, who laughed and said on camera that everybody in India knew the VHP was an RSS outfit. We spoke to the brother of Gandhi's assassin, who showed zero remorse for the killing and calmly informed us on screen that both he and his brother had been with the RSS during their youth.

The VHP in India and its branch in London soon realised that the *Bandung File* investigation was not friendly. They refused to come on the programme to defend themselves. They began to complain to Channel 4 even before we had edited the piece. We assembled a rough cut that Farrukh and Don Christopher approved. Liz Forgan, the director of programmes, wanted us to double-check the facts. And we did. The documentary ended with our team confronting the GLC leader, Ken Livingstone. He accepted total blame for funding 'Indian fascists', took personal responsibility and apologised, stressing that the GLC should have checked more closely. 'We were taken for a ride.'

The VHP demanded a 'Right to Reply'. This was an innovative C4 programme designed to give aggrieved subjects of its factual documentaries a chance to respond. Gus Macdonald, later given a peerage and made Blair's Minister for the Cabinet Office, chaired the programme judiciously and, in this case, I was in the convict's seat. The VHP were extremely well prepared and went for me, demanding proof that the Godse brothers – one assassinated Gandhi, the other kept watch – had been RSS members. I repeated what Godse himself had said in the programme. Proof, they demanded. I pointed out that we had not been privileged enough to be shown their membership registers, if they even existed.

They were offended at the use of the term 'fascist' in describing the RSS. I replied that it was Jawaharlal Nehru, the country's first PM, who had pointed this out, specifically naming them and saying in public that 'Hindu communalism is a form of Indian fascism.' Bandung was often prescient in these matters, as revealed by the pogroms in Gujarat and the triumph of Narendra Modi, the BJP and the RSS combined, with the latter now exercising control over day-to-day policies. Modi was a long time RSS activist. One of his first tasks was to attend meetings of tiny far-left groups and report on their thinking to his bosses.

In 1991, our investigative work brought down a giant bank: the Bank of Credit and Commerce International (BCCI), also known to many of its own employees as the Bank of Crooks and Cheats

Incorporated. Founded by the Pakistani financier Agha Hasan Abedi, it was the seventh largest private bank in the world. It took a huge and complicated effort to get the information we needed to prove that it was a massive money-laundering operation, guilty of a number of other financial crimes. The investigation started in 1981, when an informant, a senior BCCI official who had seen the light, asked for a meeting. We first met late at night in his empty apartment in a London suburb. He did not permit me to use a tape-recorder so I took non-stop notes instead. If he was telling the truth, it was the endgame for the bank.

I rang Bruce Page, the editor of the *New Statesman*, and we met. I showed him my notes and he agreed we should publish a three-part piece anonymously revealing the hitherto secret names of the BCCI board of directors. It created an internal storm. I was the principal suspect, but they had no evidence whatsoever and the Staggers' lawyers had cleared the texts. My cousin Shahid Hyat (who worked at the bank and whose information had been very helpful) was summoned by Agha Hasan Abedi, the big boss, and questioned. He denied all knowledge.

A new editor at the magazine, Hugh Stephenson, despite strong advice to the contrary from his predecessor, caved in to the BCCI lawyers (in this case Geoffrey Bindman) and settled. I hope the mag demanded its money back when the BCCI finally went under. A Bank of England official announced in the wake of the closure of most of BCCI's operations that, at all costs, 'Western banking standards and values have to be preserved.' I think they were. It's certainly true that BCCI had had a louche career, beginning in the 1970s. Agha Hasan Abedi, the Pakistani son of a clerk employed by an aristocratic family in Lucknow, India, partly capitalised his bank in 1972 by issuing loans to the tune of $4 million from United Bank Ltd, where he oversaw foreign operations, to associates who lodged the money in the Cayman Islands. Abedi then wrote the loans off as bad debts and BCCI was on its way.

Abedi and his publicists claimed that BCCI was all for the little guy, or for little countries in the Third World in whose interests the bank would use its name to secure loans from the cruel First World. BCCI dealt with the little guys the way most big financial institutions do. It took the deposits of poor folk such as Asian shopkeepers in the north of England and then lent to rich folk who either spent the money on themselves or hired lackeys to do Washington's dirty work, and who rarely paid it back. Abedi's aim was to build the Third World's first multinational bank, large enough to dominate most of the rickety states with which it might do business. As Alexander Cockburn noted in the *Los Angeles Times* in 1991:

> It all worked out as planned. Starting with a close relationship with the late military dictator Zia-ul-Haq of Pakistan, BCCI became banker to Anastasio Somoza of Nicaragua. It had close dealings with the South Africans, with Gen. Manuel Noriega and the Medellin cartel. There were over a dozen BCCI branches in Medellin alone. Most important of all, BCCI enjoyed the backing of oil princes, notably the sheikh who ruled Abu Dhabi ... So, amid all the tut-tutting about BCCI, it's necessary to remember that Pakistanis have no monopoly on unsound banking practices; also that so long as there are illegal drugs there will be illegal drug profits, and so long as there are illegal drug profits there will be banks to wash them. The alternative is to keep the money under the bed, which is exactly what bankers were put on this Earth to prevent ...

Following the *New Statesman* story, the first of the two Bandung investigations of the BCCI was triggered by a phone call from John Moscow, a lead investigator in the New York District Attorney's office. He flew over from New York and spent half a day questioning me. He wanted to know how I got the story, and why it hadn't been taken up at the time. I told him. He smiled: 'Sorry we got to it late. I've checked it out carefully. You got everything right. And more information is now pouring in.'

At the next Bandung editorial meeting I suggested that we go for the BCCI. I rang C4 legal and told them that the NY District Attorney's office had more evidence and were conducting their own investigations. Anjana Patel's first task as researcher-director was to contact the Bank of England. She met a senior figure who posed a question in return: 'Why does Tariq want to bring down the only global Third World bank that tries to help the poor? I thought he would be sympathetic.' She smiled.

He did answer some of her questions. Within twenty-four hours I received a phone call from a very distinguished Pakistani surgeon who ran the Cromwell Hospital in London. During the Bhutto years the good doctor had a successful TV show in Pakistan explaining the necessity of hygiene to the poor. After the military coup he had moved to London. He said, 'I have an important message for you from Benazir (Bhutto) but we must meet today.' When we did meet there was no real message, but the following conversation took place:

Doctor Is it true you've decided to make a documentary on the BCCI for Channel 4?

T.A. Yes.

Doctor Your decision?

T.A. Yes.

Doctor So, if you wanted to cancel it, you could? Its entirely within your purview?

T.A. Yes.

Doctor I received a message from the Dubai people who are trying to clean up the bank and reform its management with the help of the Bank of England and who feel that your documentary could sabotage the process. It's a sensitive issue.

T.A. I know.

Doctor Look, I respect you a lot, but the BBC Drama people cancelled your three-part drama series on Bhutto and Zia.

T.A. It wasn't the Drama people. It was the editor-in-chief Alasdair Milne under pressure from the Foreign Office, who didn't want to destabilise General Zia.

Doctor Yes, yes, of course. How much would it cost if Bandung produced the series or made a film.

T.A. We could do it for £6 million.

Doctor (relieved and laughing) OK, OK. You have a terrible cough and cold. Let me give you some medicine. Where will you be tomorrow?

I was off to New York to meet John Moscow and others. I didn't give him my hotel details. He gave me a stiff brandy mixed with boiled water, lemon juice and honey. We parted. I rang a doctor friend later that evening to discuss the matter. 'Didn't you know?' he asked. 'The Cromwell is funded by the BCCI.' I should have guessed.

In New York I told John the story. He chuckled: 'They're desperate now. They're working closely with the Bank of England to save the bank via a drastic restructuring. Morgenthau (DA in NY) knows too much, including their links in this country and the politicians they've bribed in both parties. He won't accept a compromise.'

The next morning, I received a call at my hotel. It was the good doctor. He sounded cheerful. 'Salaam, salaam. Good news. Dubai has agreed to fund your Bhutto film. Where should they send the money?'

'To our account and tell them we will acknowledge it warmly on screen.'

'Very good. And you will cancel the documentary?'

'What?! I never agreed to that...'

The doc was in a state He couldn't believe it. He showered me with mild abuse.

'Tell your bosses', I said, 'that not everyone can be bought.'

The phone went dead.

I gave the story to the *Financial Times* who published it on their back page the next day. Another tiny nail in the coffin being prepared. Quite a few Pakistani friends felt the drama would have been more useful.

As John Moscow had indicated, the DA refused to do any deals with the Bank of England and his demeanour was threatening. We made our documentary. It was cleared by the C4 legal eagles. The day before it was due to go out, the BCCI served us with an injunction. We refused to accept. A judge at the Old Bailey summoned us for a hearing the next morning. Michael Grade and Liz Forgan were totally supportive. As part of their PR side, the bank had hired the distinguished QC Sydney Kentridge, Steve Biko's lawyer, to represent them.

I was confident for one simple reason. If they did stop us, we would demand to see all their files and produce witnesses from inside the bank. If the BCCI persisted it would be suicide. The injunction was just an attempt to delay; desperation had dictated the move. Just before the hearing began Kentridge informed our QC and the judge that the BCCI were withdrawing the injunction. Game and set.

We won the match a few years later in July 1991. I was commissioned to write a script but it was never made because US/CIA involvement in the whole business was highlighted. Naveen Kishore, wandering round my study, inquisitive as always, found this script and others, took them all back to Kolkata and his excellent Seagull Press published them under the title *A Banker for All Seasons*. The *New Statesman* articles were included as an appendix.

One of the senior BCCI managers who loathed his employers and had been very helpful with the research invited himself to a congratulatory lunch. 'I have one criticism. You should have ended the documentary by saying that the BCCI were what we always said they were, but there are other Western banks doing the same thing except more discreetly. Money laundering will remain, as long as crime syndicates exist. You really should have titled this one, "Our beautiful launderettes".'

We laughed as he recalled a last tit-bit of information: 'I know it was difficult to take on the Bank of England without tangible evidence, but they must have known everything. I was the BCCI executive who used to leave a locked Gladstone bag containing £250,000 in the cupboard of a cloakroom as an Xmas present at their seasonal party. No idea who picked it up and how it was divided, but it was always acknowledged via a phone call. Present much appreciated, my dear.'

Farrukh Dhondy interpreted his brief as C4 multicultural editor most creatively, commissioning cinema, plays and comedies. *Salaam Bombay* directed by Mira Nair (the film jump-started her career and remains the best she ever made) was shortlisted for the best foreign language film at the Oscars in 1989. Farrukh turned up to the ceremony sporting a black T-shirt with the logo 'Watch Bandung File' under his dinner jacket.

Most other commissioning editors during the first ten years took the Channel 4 remit more or less seriously. The late Alan Fountain, in particular, as commissioning editor for independent film and video, was a key figure who encouraged and disciplined (in the nicest possible way) indie filmmakers in Britain and South America. Jeremy Isaacs would later write:

> Season after season, *The Eleventh Hour* on Monday evenings at 11 o'clock presented an unpredictable melange: British independent film-makers Malcolm Le Grice or Margaret Tait, the new cinema of Latin America, film-making from Africa, Nicaragua, the emergent world, and long runs of Jean-Luc Godard. Ideas were traded and alliances formed, including one in Germany with Eckart Stein's 'Das Kleine Fernsehspiel', licensed to experiment by ZDF. Parochialism went out of the window; the world was our oyster.

To Dhondy and Fountain in those early years I would add Gwyn Pritchard, the commissioning editor for education for whom I prepared a series on philosophers. After Gwyn left, the number of thinkers we were allowed to cover was cut down from twenty-five to four. David Edgar wrote *Locke*, while Derek Jarman auteured *Wittgenstein* based on an original script by Terry Eagleton (both versions were published by the British Film Institute). April De Angelis turned in a fine script on *Aristophanes* and I wrote *Spinoza*, ably directed and edited by Christopher Spencer, a very gifted member of the Bandung team. I was really delighted to hear that his daughter, Harriet Spencer, a young extra in *Spinoza*, was an executive producer on the 2022 production *Sherwood*, one of the best BBC drama series for several decades.

In early 1989, after a four-year run, Darcus and I had to accept Channel 4's decision to bring the curtain down on *Bandung File*. Not so the TV critics (apart from Nancy Banks-Smith in the *Guardian*, who over the years never realised our show was even being aired). Richard Last in *The Times* and Peter Paterson in the *Mail on Sunday* published warm and appreciative obituaries, as did the *Independent* and others. After our last programme went out on 19 December 1989, Paterson wrote:

> British television will be the poorer for the passing of *Bandung File*. It may sometimes have been excessively strident ... but it brought our attention to issues like slavery, which still, amazingly, exists; to the exploitation by multi-national companies of the resources of poor countries; to the arms race which keeps the world's murderous brush fire wars going; to the crippling debt burden which crushes the hope out of many nations.
>
> Last night's final programme beautifully captured the Bandung spirit. Most of us think of the Nobel Prize for Literature as some kind of benefit for Western writers of whom we have all heard, but this dealt with the Egyptian novelist Naguib Mahfouz, who won the prize last year.
>
> OK, hardly anyone in Britain had even heard of Mahfouz, let alone read him. In terms of topicality, it was a year out of date. And the number of Egyptians settled in Britain cannot be large. Yet this was a timely reminder that the West does not have a cultural monopoly, and that important and interesting writers exist beyond the purview of the Booker jury.
>
> Channel Four, if Mr Grade needs reminding, was specifically set up to give television a multi-cultural dimension. If it can no longer be bothered to allow a showing to programmes like *Bandung File*, what on earth is it there for?

A question never answered. But another multicultural current affairs show was never to re-emerge on the channel. It would have been difficult for them to find something better than the *Bandung File*, so they gave up. What the channel seniors did discuss with me was an idea for a new series focused on ideas and culture. 'It must not be a repeat of the File,' Farrukh Dhondy opined, 'but infused with the same spirit.' A similar message emanated from Farrukh's bosses, Liz Forgan and Michael Grade. Our last show, on Naguib Mahfouz, shot in Cairo and extremely well directed and edited by Christopher Spencer, turned out to be the perfect bridge to something new.

That same week I wrote the proposal for *Rear Window* with 'modest' but coherent aims: 'To explore themes in the literature, art, music, cinema, architecture, and a history of ideas on all five continents, and make films that bring to light the earthy, sceptical, comic and life-affirming qualities present in most cultures, taking the broadest possible view of the word "multicultural".' The proposal was approved rapidly. Bandung Productions continued its life for another decade.

Darcus moved on to other fields, exploring new ideas for TV such as *The Devil's Advocate*, a role he had played in real life during the Mangrove trial in London's Notting Hill Gate (in its pre-boutique, pre-posh, pre-*Four Weddings and a Funeral* period), when he had defeated the corrupt and racist local police officers targeting him and the other West Indians who frequented the Mangrove Restaurant with constant arrests and cell-beatings. I had written about this in the *Black Dwarf* in the late sixties. Now, years later, we wished each other the best of luck and parted amicably, meeting up at odd events and occasions.

On one such where Farrukh was present, I asked: 'Why the hell didn't we film *The Black Jacobins*?' A silence fell. Farrukh said: 'Why didn't Bandung suggest it? We could have done it jointly with the education and drama departments, filmed in Cuba and made a few stars. £5 million would have been enough.' Darcus and I hung our heads in shame. Farrukh was correct. We could have made a stylish chamber epic strong on ideas, rather than a Hollywood extravaganza with long battle scenes.

Bandung File had interviewed C.L.R. James on two occasions. Once we took an awestruck Viv Richards to see him and film the two men talking. James was in his nineties and Viv was one of the very few cricketers who could score 90 between lunch and tea. The old man was excited at meeting the 'the world's greatest living batsman'. Darcus was hoping it would be a long conversation and C.L.R. did his best to help with questions like: 'Tell me Viv, why do you think our tiny islands in the Caribbean produce a rich crop of cricketers like ripened mangoes on trees? A wind blows and the mangoes drop to the ground. Batsmen, bowlers of every variety.' Viv's standard response to this and a few more C.L.R. questions was: 'Yes, I think you are right, C.L.R.' Darcus had to intervene to make sure we had a fifteen-minute insert for the next episode of the *Bandung File*.

We paid homage to *The Black Jacobins* in *Liberty's Scream*, a short play I wrote for *Bandung File* to mark the bicentenary of the French Revolution. But somehow filming the book had escaped our minds. Several years later, Danny Glover asked Hugo Chávez for help in putting C.L.R.'s classic on screen. I was in Caracas at the time and when asked for my opinion, I supported the project, even though, for some reason, Danny's scriptwriter, a very fine producer herself, was reluctant to let me read the script. I did not insist.

The big problem was funds. Over $100 million was being requested and many Venezuelan filmmakers protested, under-standably so. I suggested to Danny that he should abandon the idea of a lavish Hollywood-style movie. The model should not be *Lawrence of Arabia*, leave alone *Gandhi*, but the two rela-tively low-budget Pontecorvo masterpieces: *Battle of Algiers* and *Queimada (Burn!)*. He argued that they wouldn't get distribu-tion in the US unless they could compete with Hollywood. This argument always struck me as being based on a false premise and I told him so. It was a lesson of sorts. Even the most radical Hollywood productions get trapped by the system. I think the Venezuelan Film Institute offered $50 million or thereabouts. Nobody else wanted to lighten their purses, though the Mandela government in South Africa offered lots of freebies, including black soldiers as extras for the war scenes. Alas, the project col-lapsed. It need not have done so had a different vision been in play. A sad business.

8

Private Eye

I became a regular reader of *Private Eye* almost as soon as I arrived in Britain in September 1963, at the same time as I started to read the *New Left Review*. I was soon writing for both; to begin with more for the *Eye* than the *NLR*, at least till the seventies. The two magazines could have hardly been more different from each other, but they shared one quality in common: they had no wish to please and were not scared to offend. Perry Anderson was essentially a Sartrean Marxist and Robin Blackburn has written that while the *NLR* was not conceived of as a Marxist magazine, it developed in that direction later. At the *Eye*, Peter Cook and Richard Ingrams were unpredictable 'conservative anarchists'. Cook was more an anarchist than a conservative.

One anecdote illustrates what I mean. In the very first year of the magazine, Cook was blocked socially and permanently from one dining table in London NW1. Relations between Cook and Jonathan Miller (Miller, Cook, Alan Bennett and Dudley Moore had started their careers as Cambridge satirists in *Beyond the Fringe* and later graduated to the London stage) were abruptly truncated. Cook's view was that 'the Dr' had simply become 'a pompous bore'. This last word was one of the worst abuses in the *Eye* lexicon.

Miller told me decades later that Cook was impossible. He had written up dinner party conversations for the next fortnight's issue, naming and shaming Miller's guests. 'This was true,' said Ingrams, 'but so what? Lunches and dinners are always excellent locations for political gossip.' As if to institutionalise this assertion, the *Eye* started its own regular lunches above a Greek

Street pub, whose proprietor, Norman Balon, was as eccentric and rude (to guests) as the magazine for which he catered every week. Catered may be the wrong word. The food served at *Eye* lunches was utterly disgusting. Norman told me that this was on Ingrams's instructions. 'Let them eat public school lunches like we did.' Since Norman was very rarely rude to me I can only assume that his offensiveness, too, was an affectation. To a Tory MP who rightly complained that the coffee was lukewarm, Norman suggested: 'Why don't you fuck off then?' On almost every level there was a degree of contrariness that shocked some guests and attracted others. The lunches, at times, could be a display of S&M. Nonetheless, invitations were greedily accepted by politicians and others who the magazine later denounced and brought down. Paul Foot's relentless pursuit of the Tory grandee, Reginald Maudling, was a case in point.

I had first met Ingrams when I invited him to speak at the Oxford Union in the summer of 1965. He brought William Rushton along and we joked and laughed long after the event. Ingrams did not give up alcohol till a few years later. He asked me to drop by the *Eye* offices when I was next in London. It became a habit. I sat through many a lunch. The instruction was to listen to the guests and make discreet notes of what was being said by those who were there to provide information. These would later be analysed for credibility, which usually meant whether or not Ingrams found them convincing. Evidence of a serious nature was never required in those days, though it should be said that in 1966, when I went in fairly regularly, most of the stuff we were given turned out to be pretty accurate. I could have revealed more had I kept the notes, but most of the time we binned them.

My biggest treat at *Eye* lunchtimes was sitting next to Claud Cockburn. I met him before I knew his son Alexander or the younger siblings, or Sarah Caudwell, the elder step-sister who would later bring a very good play she had written to the Bandung offices. We spent a good few hours talking about her dad. He was quirky and eccentric and many other things, but she admired him nevertheless.

Everything written about Claud is true. He was a legendary figure for my generation. A witty and inspiring journalist with a sense of humour that varied from being highbrow to becoming vicious, scurrilous and rude. He once said to me: 'When you're in right-wing company always best to wear the mask. Never give anything away.' This was an art he had acquired as a *Times* correspondent in Europe in the 1930s. One story I heard him tell at the lunch table (I can still hear his voice) was an account of when he'd been sent to interview Al Capone in Chicago. The gangster wanted to make it clear where he stood. With his bodyguard 'Machine Gun' Jack McGurn watching Claud intensely, Capone informed him: 'Don't get the idea I'm a goddamned radical. Don't get the idea I'm knocking the American system. My rackets are run on strictly American lines. Capitalism, call it what you like, gives to each and every one of us a great opportunity if only we seize it with both hands and make the most of it.' Asked by his editor why he never sent in the article, Cockburn replied that Capone's remarks were almost identical to editorials in *The Times* itself, and he doubted whether the paper would be pleased to see itself in agreement with the most infamous racketeer in Chicago

On another occasion, when the perennial debate of those times as to how much information without a factual basis could be added to enhance the strength of an article was in progress, Claud was in full flow. When he finished, I stage whispered: 'Lenin forever stressed that facts are stubborn things.' Claud airily waved this aside: 'They're a bit more flexible than that.'

Apart from the flexibility or otherwise of facts, a parallel debate of sorts concerned Ingrams's and Cook's hostility to all sorts of 'bores'. Till Ingrams informed me, I had no idea that this, too, was partially inspired by Claud, who considered it a universal problem. Those of us who have had the misfortune to sit through innumerable public or interminable internal meetings (of which I have had more than my fair share) cannot but avoid sympathising with his words on the subject: 'One does right to treat bores as genuinely dangerous characters, not merely on account of the debilitating ennui with which they enervate one's faculties but because there is certainly something dangerously wrong with their mentality, character and general relationship to life.'

Ingrams later wrote that it was after the launch of *Private Eye* that he began to rely on Claud's instincts and humour a great deal: 'I came to know and love him. A brilliantly clever man, he could have been a professor, but being like his friend Graham Greene a lover of mischief, and because he had a genuine concern about all the bad things going on in this world, he chose the precarious life of a journalist.'

There is a footnote on boredom. In 2003, after the debacle of the US invasion and occupation of Iraq, and after a long absence, I went to an *Eye* lunch. The inducement was that Richard would be there as well. He came slightly late that Wednesday and while I was waiting, I watched Francis Wheen lecturing some young hangers-on. They were not smiling and one of them had glazed eyes. I got distracted by David Davis, a Tory MP very good on civil liberties, who was unburdening his soul to Paul Foot. By the time Ingrams arrived and sat opposite me, Francis was still hard at work. The following week Ingrams, Foot and I lunched at the Gay Hussar in Soho's Greek Street. We raged against Bush and Blair and their media minions. Foot remarked that Blair's vain and over-indulged PR person, Alastair Campbell, had served the late Robert Maxwell at the *Daily Mirror* with the same zeal. It was a character failing. Ingrams asked what my impression had been of the *Eye* lunch. I recalled the early years when our instructions re. information-gathering were clear: listen, take notes, question if necessary, do not speak too much yourself. I casually remarked that it had been fine and Ian Hislop had been a good choice in most ways, but Wheen appeared to be boring on too much. Had the rules been changed? A month or so later, a call from Ingrams: 'I've been noticing Francis. You were right. He does bore on.' Unbeknown to me Ingrams leaked his observation to the hacks and there were some mentions. And then, just as I was starting work on this book and as if to confirm his intense dislike of bores, he sent me his bubble captions for an old ragged and photocopied pic of Wheen and myself. Since he had never ever censored me, I had to return the compliment (see the first of this book's plate sections).

Ingrams, orphaned early, loved Claud like a father. At one point, not long after Claud died, Ingrams told me he might need my help to decipher some political codes were he ever to write a biography. Alexander had trusted me with what Claud's last words were as he lay dying. General Jaruzelski had that very day seized power in Poland with the aim of clamping down on the Solidarity movement. Alex passed on the news. Claud cheered up a bit: 'Am glad firm action is being taken at last.' Then he died.

Ingrams was thrilled. 'Completely in character,' he said as he laughed. He never wrote a biography because 'it would be too much hard work trying to understand Marxism and Communism. Why don't you?' I said the best person would be Alexander, who had adored his dad and in the years that followed once told me: 'Never a day goes by that I don't think of Claud.' He didn't write one either. Instead, Patrick, the youngest sibling, is hard at work on the book at the moment.

Ingrams and I rarely discussed his personal life, but one could tell that an inner sadness pervaded it. On one occasion we were sitting in his office in 34 Greek Street. He appeared depressed. But it turned out to be the opposite of what I thought. He wanted to nip over to Maison Bertaux for tea and cakes, but we couldn't because he'd agreed to be interviewed by the *Daily Mail* columnist Lynda Lee-Potter. I thought of a way of cutting the interview short, and as I heard her bouncing up the stairs I left the office.

From outside, I could hear Ingo bored out of his skull and monosyllabic. I went into the loo, stripped to my underpants, tied a tiny, filthy towel around my waist and with hands in Indian prayer mode re-entered the office, affecting the mannerism, pose and accent of a guru (these frauds were popular at the time). He managed, just about, to control himself. She nearly fainted. I said: 'Mr Ingrose, sir. Time for meditation. Please remove all clothes.' She apologised, hurriedly excused herself and almost ran out of the room. We laughed a lot at the ruse and then proceeded for tea and a killer marzipan pastry down the road. There have been other versions of this story. This is the only one that bears the seal of total accuracy.

One family matter that annoyed him greatly was his maternal uncles burning some important documents because Ingo's grandfather had so instructed in his will. 'Would you have ever done that?' he asked me. 'No,' I replied. 'Any idea what was in them?' He knew. His grandfather was Queen Victoria's private physician and accompanied her everywhere, including to Balmoral where her affair with her *ghillie*, John Brown, was no secret. Her physician kept notes on her health and on other matters, including John Brown's interventions. He was also her confidant and had kept diaries but, as Ingrams put it, 'my stupid uncles burnt them'. We looked at each other in horror. 'Off with their heads,' I said.

Despite his old and very close friendship with Trotskyist Paul Foot, Ingrams was cross with me when I joined the IMG in 1968. I was often attacked in the pages of the *Eye*, sometimes inaccurately but often wittily. Relations did not sour, however, though we met less, and in the late eighties friendly relations were restored. Ingrams has remained a good friend ever since, and we used to have a monthly lunch at the Gay Hussar during the *Oldie* days.

I missed the battle scenes during the struggle for succession in 1986, after Ingrams had decided to stop editing the *Eye* because he was tired and fed-up. The libel cases angered him. The choice of successor was either Ian Hislop, a twenty-something satirist from Oxford, or Auberon Waugh.

Bumping into Paul Foot at some meeting or another, I was apprised of what was going on. 'If he asks you, back Hislop.' We agreed that Bron was too right-wing. I had met Hislop a number of times. He seemed personable enough but might he be too safe a pair of hands, like much of his generation? Rather him than any of the others. Ingrams never asked me about any of this, but Cook did once, while sober. I said that Foot and Ingrams appeared to favour Ian and they were probably right. I didn't know him well enough to say more. Cook didn't say anything. And Hislop it was. Those who had assumed that Ingrams would remain the organ grinder were proved wrong. This was a good thing as new editors must be given their head. Otherwise, a magazine that just carries on as before when its new editor turns out to be a clone can suddenly go under.

With the national press largely polluted and the social networks flooded with fake news of one variety or another, the *Eye* is still an essential read. Its coverage of British politics and economy, exposing large-scale corruption in most of the institutions, has no competitor. Where it has changed noticeably is in its monotone foreign coverage. The tone is right-wing, sometimes reading like a handout from one of the UK/US intelligence agencies. Sad that this is hardly any different from most of the NATO-fawning European and US press. I think the turn began after 9/11. The *Eye* became a bit too 'civilisational'. My reading was that Christopher Hitchens's testicles – Francis Wheen and Nick Cohen – had captured the foreign desk. I just gave up reading this stuff.

When my papers arrived on the morning of 30 May 2023, in one of them, the *New York Times*, there was a whole-page investigation of how the other, the *Financial Times*, had aided and abetted a cover-up of a story exposing a senior British journalist as a serial groper. Several women were involved. Outed by the *NYT*, the *Observer* sacked him. None of this surprised me. Then I read: 'Even the investigative magazine *Private Eye* did not cover his departure.' When a reader emailed asking why, the editor replied: 'Coverage of Nick Cohen's departure from the *Observer* is obviously more problematic for the *Eye* than the others that you mention due to the fact that he used to write a freelance column for the magazine.'

I wondered which column that was. Purely by chance I was due to have lunch with Ingrams that week in Aldworth. He'd left London and moved to his old cottage in Berkshire a couple of years earlier. We spoke on the phone, but lunches in London were a thing of the past. He picked me up at the station and we caught up with news. I also met his wife, Sara Soudain, thirty years younger than him, and his god-daughter. In all these years I've never seen him so relaxed and happy, outwardly or inwardly. Sara is a medical researcher and whistleblower. She exposed a fraudulent neurologist, a research falsifier no less. Defended by his colleagues, he thought he'd got away with it, but she refused to give up. It went to the Appeal Court, which suspended him for twelve months.

We talked, as we always do, about Paul Foot. Richard wanted to know what the Foot boys were up to. I said no longer boys but footmen. After that it was the turn of the *Eye*. He complained about the lack of gossip. No criticisms of the BBC. Yes, we remembered how they had attacked John Birt non-stop and the Birstspeak leaks that used to pour in as a result. 'Some people say that Ian is too much in hock to the Beeb.'

And the foreign coverage? He was irritated that the IDF and settler attacks were no longer covered. 'Eye DF?' I suggested. Talking to him on the phone after 7 October he said, 'Ian is getting it in the neck for that cover suggesting that there had been enough killing.'

'That's pathetic,' was my response, 'but no reason to publish reports that are pure IDF propaganda, as they have done.'

9

Back in the USSR

It was pure luck that I observed the first inklings of reform in the Soviet Union. I was in Tashkent in April 1985, a few weeks after it was announced that the new leader of the country was Mikhail Gorbachev, the boy from Stavropol and protégé of the late Yuri Andropov. Three trips followed in 1988 to the Soviet capital, where I engaged with different wings of the intelligentsia. This resulted in a book, *Revolution from Above*, and a play cowritten with Howard Brenton, *Moscow Gold*, for the Royal Shakespeare Company. My last trip to the Soviet Union, in 1990, was with the RSC, who had been invited to stage several scenes from our play for a special performance in the massive children's theatre in Moscow. It was packed to capacity and from the laughter one could tell which audience members supported Gorbachev and which were attached to Boris Yeltsin. Impromptu debates on the pavement and in the bars followed the performance. That alone made the play worthwhile.

What follows are outtakes from a story of hope, disillusionment and finally defeat as the West outwitted Gorbachev, established firm control of Yeltsin and helped bring the Soviet Union to its knees. And all this without a shot being fired. Living conditions in Russia deteriorated and 'shock therapy' – as the Harvard economist Jeffrey Sachs later admitted – was a total disaster. It helped pave the way for Vladimir Putin, whose immense popularity was based on his capacity to revive the economy and restore a form of stability by preaching a new ultra-conservative nationalism. On these trips to Russia I kept more diary notes than usual, some confidential at the time. No longer. The history of this period is being erased, but it might return in a different way. Or perhaps not.

1985

My first-ever invite to speak at a conference in the Soviet Union. It was a joint invitation from the Soviet Academy of Sciences and the United Nations University in Tokyo. The venue was Tashkent. The conference might be dull, I thought, but it turned out to be serious, and in any case I wanted to see Soviet Central Asia for myself. Might we be taken to Samarkand and Bukhara, from where Mughal adventurers had started out on what became a one-way trip to India in the sixteenth century? It turned out that the cities were on our itinerary.

Moscow–Tashkent
24 April
I was being transported to Tashkent via Moscow. Arriving at the Heathrow departure lounge for the 11 a.m. Aeroflot flight I noted it was surrounded by tabloid photographers. A Soviet diplomat had been expelled. From inside the plane, I saw him arriving with his overdressed wife. They waved unashamedly to the vultures and boarded the flight.

At Moscow airport the customs search was thorough. A collection I had edited for Penguin Books, *The Stalinist Legacy: Its Impact on 20th-Century Politics*, was vetted by three men. They noticed I had a dozen copies in my suitcase. One of them looked nervous. They looked at the contents list: Trotsky, Rakovsky, Deutscher, Mandel, Khrushchev, Anderson, etc. I pointed to my name on the cover. 'Ah! It's by you.'

I smiled.

'You need it for the conference?'

I nod.

The books are let through. I'm met and transported to the Hotel of the Academy of Sciences.

25 April

At 1.30 p.m., Dima, a twenty-three-year-old student, picked me up to take me to the flat of Natalia P., a senior lecturer at the Oriental Institute then in her seventies. A portrait of her late father, a former Tsarist general, adorned the mantelpiece. Over lunch we discussed the whole world, but not the Soviet Union. The last of the gerontocrats, Konstantin Chernenko, has just died. I was curious to learn more about his much younger successor, Mikhail Gorbachev, but neither of them has anything to say about him.

Later, Dima insisted on practising his Urdu on me as he took me round the bookshops – where there was nothing on offer – but it soon became obvious that he was more interested in the Beatles than in Pakistan. This was a relief. When he discovered that I had known John Lennon, my stock rose phenomenally. 'When he died many of us went to the Lenin Hills and sang "Back in the USSR".'

Supper with Dev Murarka, an Indian friend who had been in Moscow for centuries as a correspondent for the *Economic and Political Weekly*, India's most respected magazine. We dined at an Azerbaijani restaurant. Drunken officials, loud music, vulgar dancing and mediocre food. We ignored the ambience. Dev talked endlessly about conditions in the Soviet Union. Awful. A secret report had confirmed that mass alcoholism had resulted in widespread sterility, with 25 per cent of Russian babies born with deformations. But he was strongly convinced that changes were on the way.

'The new man is an instinctive reformer.'

'Like Khrushchev?'

'Much more radical.'

I'm not sure I believe him.

26 April

To Moscow's domestic airport for the four-hour flight to Tashkent. There were some like-minded souls on the delegates-only plane. On arrival we were driven with a motorcycle police escort to a Communist Party guesthouse sixteen kilometres out of the city. The dinner was terrible, particularly depressing since real

Uzbek cuisine is usually very good. This was food for delegates attending conferences.

The conference organiser, Mushakoji, was a delightful person. I asked if he had been a member of the Kakumaru or Chukaku [two leading far-left currents in sixties Japan] in his student days. He laughed at the thought. 'No. I was in the JCP.'

Our two interpreters, Natasha and Oxanne, were funny, cynical in a good sense, relaxed. Good signs. The Soviet delegation was seated hierarchically at the dinner table, but lots of younger faces – people in their fifties, forties and even thirties. The delegation's leader, Yevgeni Primakov (candidate member of the Politburo), had absented himself; no doubt enjoying a meal with the local leadership and discussing the crisis. After dinner I convened a gathering of like-minded souls from New Zealand, Australia, Singapore, Malaysia, Fiji to discuss the conference. The Russian interpreters asked if they could attend. We agreed.

I warned our salon that the subject of the conference offered a few subversive possibilities: 'Peace and Security in Asia'. I did not intend to keep silent on Afghanistan. There was some nervousness.

I never submit papers in advance. It wrecks any possibility of spontaneity. I will not deny that advance conference papers have their uses. If one has read the paper before it is read to the conference in monotone, it gives one time to catch up on missed sleep from the previous night. An instinct matured over the years helps me to detect the more critical and questioning delegates present at these events regardless of locale or subject. We find a room (usually mine) where we assemble after official dinners and create a radical salon. Delegates introduce themselves, providing pen-portraits of the politicians who lead their countries. On this occasion, alcohol fuelled the conversation, and we sang radical songs, recited poetry, retold anti-authoritarian political jokes.

My opposition to the 1979 Soviet military intervention in Afghanistan had already isolated me on the international left. I was surprised that even Tony Cliff, the founder of the IS/SWP, was nervous on the subject. In those days, *Socialist Challenge*, the IMG newspaper I edited, was printed in the SWP print-shop, so they saw it before any IMG member. Paul Foot rang while they were typesetting the latest issue: 'Hi, Cliff asked me to ring. He said ask Tariq if he is 100 per cent sure that his position is correct.'

I'm never 100 per cent sure on anything, but in this case, I had very few doubts: 'I'm 90 per cent sure. Under no circumstances should this military intervention be supported by socialists. It will lead to a US response that will wreck the region for decades and God knows what else.'

I was later informed that my old sparring partner, Chris Harman, had wanted to support the Soviet line, no doubt with many caveats. Foot said that Cliff had overruled him. So at least one group from the Trotskyist tradition supported my views. The Fourth International backed the intervention. At their next Congress an over-excited Japanese comrade insisted that 'we fight alongside the Soviet Union'. I had to laugh out loud at this ridiculous notion, politically imbecilic and revealing a total ignorance of how the war was being fought, not to mention the region. I responded, suggesting that the comrade in question should learn to fly like Icarus or train to be a pilot, since the war was mainly being fought by bomber jets and helicopters.

E.P. Thompson and Ralph Miliband (and I think Stuart Hall) from the old New Left were also opposed to the entry of Soviet troops. In Thompson's case, when he rang some years into the war to ask whether he should accept an invitation to a conference sponsored by the Foreign Office and attended by all the anti-Soviet Afghan factions, I insisted very strongly that he should not. 'We should never support these right-wing forces come what may.' I'm glad he rejected the invitation. It's not an easy position to maintain but it's a necessary one for socialists and internationalists.

Doris Lessing, feminist novelist and Sufi saint, living locally and another opponent of the war, stopped me on Hampstead Heath one day: 'Tariq dear, is it the case that the Russians have now slaughtered twenty million people in Afghanistan?'

'No,' I replied. 'That is the entire population of the country. Are you sure you heard right? Twenty thousand is probably closer to the mark though even that seems high.'

It turned out that an Afghan woman speaker at the conference Thompson had turned down had mentioned the figure of 'tens of millions' to impress the British audience, which included Doris. It only succeeded in seriously upsetting her.

Tashkent
27 April
Woke up at 5 a.m. The light was stunning. The sky was a piercing blue. A gentle breeze was blowing as Kevin (New Zealand delegate) joined me for an hour-long jog through the Uzbek countryside and villages. The security guards at the guesthouse, astonished by our nerve (breaking rules, defying protocol), despatched a policeman on a motorbike to follow us at a discreet distance. The guesthouse itself, I'm sure, served as a trysting place for tired bureaucrats. It had that air about it.

Later that morning I gave my speech on Afghanistan, pointing out that it had been a huge mistake, explaining why, and calling for the withdrawal of all Soviet troops. My speech was well received with one exception: a CIA operative masquerading as a delegate from Thailand was angered by my references to the US role in Asia. I was eagerly awaiting the Soviet response after the lunch break. Lunch itself was interesting. I was surrounded by Soviet delegates who dragged me off to their table. One of them said: 'We never thought we would hear such a speech in our country in our lifetime.' Another asked: 'Are you aware that we have a new party leader?' I nodded. 'Well,' continued my interlocutor, 'some of us here, as Comrade Primakov will no doubt tell you in more detail, were at a top party cadre discussion on Afghanistan a few weeks ago, where Comrade Gorbachev made a speech that was more or less the same as your remarks this morning.'

I was astonished. They informed me that he was responding to growing unrest on this issue within the party and army. Soviet casualty figures were unacceptable. What Gorbachev had done was to bring the debate into the open. It would take them another four years to withdraw, but still. The frank exchange of views that followed convinced me that something new was in the air. Things were changing.

I went out in the evening to see Tashkent. A modern, if not a modernist, city. Earthquakes have destroyed a great deal of history. Lots of ugly buildings. Natasha jokes: 'We call this the Chernenko style in architecture. Dead! We called it that before he died.' Dinner at the Intourist Hotel in the city. Simply awful. Uzbek dance style: nice. Music: proto-rock. On the fringes of the hotel there are odd scenes taking place. A man is beating his wife as if it were an everyday occurrence. A black student is pleading, unsuccessfully, to be allowed to enter the hotel. The faces of Uzbek officialdom: overfed, corrupt, complacent, cynical, brutal. One of them who also hung out at the party guesthouse, and who I'd mentally categorised as a possible torturer, approached me – one Asian to another, in his words – to offer the services of a prostitute to complete the evening. I declined politely.

Rashidov, the Uzbek party leader, who personified corruption, had suddenly dropped dead just before the conference. That explains why he did not inaugurate the event. I ask the pimp-official how he died.

'A heart attack,' muttered a more senior guy.

'Are you sure it wasn't suicide?' I asked.

There was a tense silence. Our party broke up. On the coach back to the guesthouse, Natasha whispered in my ear: 'How did you know? It's meant to be a top secret.'

'I guessed.'

She doesn't believe me.

28 April

That afternoon at the conference the co-leader of the Soviet delegation confirmed in more diplomatic language (no mention of Gorbachev) what the younger 'top party cadres' had confided to me earlier. Academician Yevgeni Primakov stated very firmly that the USSR had no interest whatsoever in prolonging its military presence, and that a comprehensive agreement with Islamabad had been repeatedly sabotaged by the United States, mainly through the pouring in of money and weaponry to the military junta headed by General Zia-ul-Haq.

What was rejected as unrealistic, however, was my suggestion that a unilateral move by the USSR was necessary to regain the initiative on Afghanistan. Regarding Sino-Soviet relations, Primakov confirmed a general impression that both sides were moving towards some form of 'normalisation' – though without any reversion to the status quo ante.

Contrary to Cold War stereotypes and related prejudices, it was quite clear that the official intelligentsia of the USSR (members and aspirants of the Academy of Sciences) could not be dismissed wholesale as crude apparatchiks. It was undeniable that much published material on contemporary politics (as in the West) had an instrumental function largely serving diplomatic needs, but I found that knowledge and research on the West and the Third World – if not, ironically, on Eastern Europe – was often very impressive. The fact that much of this does not find its way into official publications was a grim reminder of the jealously guarded bureaucratic monopoly of information and knowledge, which irritated many established intellectuals and which they expected Gorbachev to modify or abolish altogether as part of the new reform programme. Private conversations with Academy members were often highly stimulating and instructive.

Primakov asked to see me later that evening. Very warm. 'We are on the same side now on Afghanistan.' He confirmed that Gorbachev had disliked the war from the very beginning. As had Andropov.

'Another imploded Brezhnevite fantasy.' I said. 'Trying to mimic the Americans is rarely a good idea.'

'On this question too, you will find our new leader in agreement. He is a genuine reformer. Have no doubt and I hope you will visit Moscow often to discuss with others. I know your past well. My younger colleagues got very excited by your speech and were asking me about your biography. To reassert party discipline in our ranks, I simply had to say that you were once a Trotskyist!'

'Was that sufficient?'

He laughed. 'Unfortunately not. The Gorbachev virus is spreading fast. I need your help on another matter. There was a serious incident last night. I hear you ran out of drink in your gossip parlour and needed another bottle. Last night someone walked into my empty hotel room and stole a bottle of the finest Soviet brandy. Preliminary investigations have revealed you were involved.'

I laughed. 'Guilty as charged except that I wouldn't use the word "stole". Why not "borrowed" or "liberated"?'

'OK, let's say "borrowed". When you next come to Moscow bring a replacement bottle. I don't mind if its French.'

29 April

The last day of conference, mostly taken over by a reception. A deadly event at Friendship House where the main speaker pays tribute to Harold Wilson as an architect of USSR–Great Britain friendship! An image of Auberon Waugh pontificating at a *Private Eye* lunch in Soho flashed by. Bron's friends in MI6, he tells us, were convinced Wilson was a Soviet agent and MI6 kept him under surveillance. Right-wing absurdism.

In the evening a farewell banquet with excellent local food that reminded me of the North Indian and Persian cuisines but sadly without chillies and more herbal than spicy. I am seated next to Dr Nodari Simonia, the Georgian deputy leader of the Soviet delegation. He was slight of build, bespectacled, with frizzled greying hair and smartly attired. He looked more like a connoisseur of Italian art than a senior figure in the state intelligentsia. After the meal he asks: 'Are you in the mood for drinking vodka and watching folk dances, or a serious conversation?' I opt for the latter. We move to a neighbouring café, virtually empty.

Simonia is ensconced in the Institute of Oriental Studies and reports directly to the Central Committee on Asia, Africa and South America.

'Let me start by telling you a story. I am of mixed Georgian-Ossetian ethnicity. In the late fifties I was on a summer vacation at home. It was a few years after Khrushchev electrified the 20th Party Congress with an account of Stalin's crimes. The atmosphere in the country was relaxed. The gulags were being emptied.

My grandfather sat me down in the kitchen and began to talk. He was in his nineties, had started adult life as a printer in Tbilisi and became a founding member of the Bolsheviks in that region. He joined the party in 1905. It was his clandestine print shop, constantly shifting locations, that printed fake passports and IDs, forged banknotes and all that was essential for moving comrades inside and outside the country. He also printed clandestine copies of *Iskra*. One of the local comrades who came to collect papers was Djugashvili, not yet Stalin. They were a nice bunch with their fair share of cynics and melancholics. There were also, grandfather told me, duds, windbags, boasters and braggarts. The majority were dedicated communists ready to sacrifice their lives for the revolution. He knew them all, but from the very beginning the only one he never trusted was Stalin.'

'But hang on, Nodari ...,' I protested.

He stopped me. 'Let me finish. So, we won the Revolution and the civil war. Then in 1927 messengers from the party centre arrived. They were compiling a list of all those who had been Bolsheviks prior to 1917. All the old comrades came to visit grandfather. They were happy: "Look we're going to get medals and a higher pension", etc. But my grandfather pleaded with them not to sign: "I smell Koba [Stalin's nickname] in all this. He wants our names so he can kill us all. Let that bastard think we're dead so we can stay alive." The others mocked him and filled in the forms. During the purges and trials of the thirties, all of them were imprisoned and killed. My grandfather, telling me the story with a sad smile on his face, died after reaching a hundred years old.'

When he asked the old man how he had been so sure, so early, he got the following reply: 'Its instinct but what made me suspicious was that when the others were laughing and joking and arguing, this Koba usually stayed quiet, nodding in all directions. He listened but did not take sides. Quiet but not out of shyness.' We agreed that this was not totally convincing. Instincts can be wrong. But in this case they had saved his grandfather's life. As for Nodari himself, he had joined the party as a teenager and had been a loyalist. He wept when Stalin died. However, the combination of his grandfather's stories (there were many) and Khrushchev's 1956 speech denouncing Stalin made him a critical member of the party. Nor was he alone. He described his own radicalisation:

'Something strange happened: I discovered Lenin. I had never read him before. His way of thinking was the exact opposite of how I had been taught at schools and universities and within the party. The only reason I read him was because I had ordered books from the proscribed section. There was a massive demand and you had to queue in a special, closed section of the library. These were books on the Soviet Union published in the West from differing viewpoints.

While waiting for my books I picked up a stray volume of Lenin. And then I read his collected works. The contrast between his conception of the Revolution and our realities shook me. That's the first time I told myself that the society in which we lived was not socialist and that Marx and Lenin would have denounced it as well. It was not that I was uncritical of either Marx or Lenin, but it was the sort of criticism they would have understood. My doctoral thesis of 1975 was a critical review of 'Marxism–Leninism' as ideology, of Russian history and the history of our party. I published it as a 300-page book in 1975. Of course, it was criticised, I was denounced, but nothing else happened.

Others were doing the same: the seeds of the current reforms were sown by people like me, state intellectuals who could still read critically. And let me also tell you that I agreed with almost everything you said and wrote on Afghanistan and Pakistan. Your books and essays on Pakistan are translated here in secret and available for scholars in our international relations institutes. Also books by Fred Halliday.'

'And Trotsky, Deutscher, Mandel?'

'Them too. Trotsky's writings were restricted but always available to the Central Committee and researchers linked to it like me, since they were already in Russian. The first copies of *Bulletin of the Opposition* smuggled into our country after Trotsky's exile reached the Soviet leadership before those for whom it was designed. Stalin, I was later told, often read articles with passages underlined for him by others! Deutscher's works were widely known. They circulated.

But it was not all one-sided. Robert Conquest, too, was widely read and Robert Service. And, by the way, Bukharin, Zinoviev, Kamenev will be officially rehabilitated later this year. Gorbachev liked Stephen Cohen's biography of Bukharin very much. A lot of us were told to read it. But not Trotsky. Nevertheless, I have here for you a quote from Trotsky. Whether they admit it or not, this is the heart of our reform programme; unless they panic. I've brought you a Russian facsimile and an English translation.'

He handed me the paragraphs he had typed in English. It was first published in the *Bulletin of the Opposition*, No. 31, 1932, p. 8. The first time I read it was in a Tashkent café:

> If there existed a universal brain, registering simultaneously all the processes of nature in society, measuring their dynamics, forecasting the results of their interactions, then such a brain would no doubt concoct a faultless and complete state plan. True, the bureaucracy sometimes considers that it has just such a brain. That is why it so easily frees itself from the supervision of the market and of Soviet democracy.
>
> The innumerable live participants in the economy, state collective and private, must make known their needs and their relative intensity not only through statistical compilations of planning commissions, but directly through the pressure of demand and supply. The plan is checked and to considerable extent realised through the market...

'What were your first impressions of Gorbachev?' I asked.

'For thirty years we have been suffocated. When Gorbachev became first secretary we heaved a collective sigh of relief. There will be big changes. We know him. We've talked to him. He's interested in new ideas, new thinking. Success is not guaranteed, of course, but it's a very serious attempt to transform Soviet society.'

On Afghanistan, Nodari says he was in complete agreement with me:

'They should never have gone in. I wrote a special paper for the Politburo before they went in, advising against the move.

Andropov was sympathetic, but Brezhnev wanted action. Then they got someone to denounce my paper.'

'Who?'

'One of their "prostitutes". I'm sure you can guess.'

I did. This is the first real conversation I have had with a Soviet communist intellectual. No banalities, no frills, to the point.

This and other conversations in Tashkent with Soviet delegates only a few weeks after Gorbachev's assumption of power made me think very seriously about the inner dynamics of Soviet society, and of Deutscher's last book, *The Unfinished Revolution*. As we were saying farewell, Yevgeni Primakov advised me not to underestimate the reform programme that was being prepared.

'It will surprise you. Our country will be transformed unless we lose our nerve. We will go way beyond Khrushchev.'

I got in a last question. 'And foreign policy?'

His face clouded but his frankness surprised me:

'Some are too keen to become like the US, to copy it in every way and to appease imperialism. That worries me. I am in favour of peaceful co-existence, but not capitulation. But everything is in flux. Everything is being discussed quite openly inside the top layers of the party. Come back soon. This is a serious invitation. I'm not being polite.'

Samarkand
30 April

We took a small plane to the magical city. Alexander had conquered it in the fourth century BC. Later the Caliphs of Baghdad had incorporated it into the growing Muslim Empire, and later still it saw the rise of Timur, who is buried here. The mosques, beautifully preserved, are a sensational example of Islamic architecture. The open market was a joy. Unlimited supplies of fruit, food, nuts, dried fruits, silks and satins. This was followed by a four-hour lunch at a model collective farm, then by a dance performance. We joined in the dancing.

The streets of old Samarkand have not changed for many centuries. Winding, long but narrow, with clay and brick constructions on either side. They were crowded as well, probably a bit less so than in the medieval period when this city was the centre of the world's silk trade, an essential stop for traders travelling from China to the Mediterranean, the capital city of Timur, the lame king who created the Timurid Empire. The clothes people wore had not changed. Exquisitely coloured tunics worn by both sexes. Skullcaps for men, light head-covers and shawls for women.

The main synagogue dates to the early twelfth century and was still in use. I was informed by a rabbi that there were a hundred thousand Jewish citizens here. The community had not been touched by the Second World War, except for sons who joined the Red Army to fight and defeat the Nazis. This theme was very common: 'We defeated the Germans. We destroyed their armies in Stalingrad and Kursk. We took Berlin.' Eric Hobsbawm always used to stress that Soviet Jews were not like their West European counterparts. They had fought and won. They never felt defeated. A rabbi confided that outside the worst phases of the Stalin period, there had been no trouble, no persecutions, and they were well integrated with all the different ethnic groups in the city.

'Had many departed for Israel?' I inquired.

'Not that many. Mainly young ones. Samarkand Jews', he told me, 'were well settled here for centuries. We have over a dozen kosher stores here. None in Moscow. Why move to someone else's country?'

I sat in the main square of the city for a while, admiring the domed mosques with turquoise tiles. Courting couples (some seated on the steps of the grand mosque) were dotted around the square. We were the only foreign tourists that day. I thought of Istanbul. Here was another centre of medieval Islam that, in this case, had merged well on some levels with the Soviet state. Women, if not architecture, had benefited a great deal. The new city was a Soviet city with similar buildings and huge posters lauding local party leaders who had no idea how close they were to becoming a new independent state: Uzbekistan.

Tashkent
1 May

The city was bedecked with red flags for the national celebration. We were taken to the reviewing stand and introduced as 'honoured guests'. My interpreter whispered, 'If only the people knew what mischief is discussed in your room, honoured guest,' and tried to contain her laughter. A march past of workers, students and party loyalists lasted for two hours. One point of interest for me: apart from portraits of the Politburo, Marx, Engels and Lenin, there was one of youthful Sergei Kirov as well! The man whose assassination in Leningrad was the pretext for the purge of the old Bolsheviks in the 1930s. I meant to ask the reason for this, but forgot.

In the evening our interpreter, Natasha, invited a few of us for a meal: 'My Igor is getting jealous seeing me work late and returning to him saying how much I'm enjoying this conference because of your bedroom salon. He'd better meet you.' We wandered over to the open-air market (less promising than Samarkand) to buy the raw materials for the meal, Uzbek wines, and a Moldavian red from a tiny stall that was unmarked. No label, no price. The seller insisted it was a remnant from the Tsar's cellar, which is why the price tag was on the high side ($30). Oxanne was unconvinced. It must be a fake, she warned, but I took the risk. Loaded with goodies we repaired to Igor's apartment. I cooked the meal: lamb in garlic and dried apricots, fresh coriander and thyme, soaked in a bottle of local red wine.

The dinner became an animated discussion on history and we talked till the early hours. The Moldavian red was without doubt from the Tsar's cellar. People spoke without fear on many subjects: Lenin, Trotsky, Kollontai, the old Bolsheviks murdered by Stalin, and Khrushchev's reforms. Natasha was surprised to hear us defending Khrushchev. She had accepted the Brezhnev line on him as a 'crude Ukrainian muzhik', etc. We argued back and forth as Igor grinned. *They've been having this debate since their university days and he's delighted by my support.*

Natasha turned to me: 'How do you know so much about our history?'

'It's our history as well.'

Natasha talked freely about the situation in Uzbekistan: massive corruption at the top, reinforced by violence and repression. As they spoke the picture became clearer. Rashidov, fearing an investigation, did commit suicide, but his men remained in place. In some of these Soviet Central Asian states the old pre-capitalist system had merged quite happily (for some) with the command-system created by Stalinism. The politics of the oriental bazaar.

Stories now came thick and fast. This one from Natasha:

'Rashidov was feeling like a fuck. A Russian woman, fresh from Moscow, who he had sighted and invited while in the capital, was staying at the party guesthouse. He sends for her. She is drunk and insists on riding to his place on the bonnet of his official convertible, breasts bare, her luscious, maroon-coloured hair flying in the wind with a vodka bottle in her hand. She soon shifts positions and transfers to the front seat so she can stand while the roof is down. In this fashion she is slowly driven the twenty kilometres to her port of call.

'This is not all. In the back seat of the car some live poultry are being transported for Comrade Rashidov's kitchen. In the centre of Tashkent later that evening, a bystander sees the half-naked woman. Then he sees a cock flying out of the back window and hears the woman laughing without restraint. A scene from Buñuel? Only too real. And to avoid misinterpretations, the male bureaucrat's version of *droit du seigneur* was not simply confined to Central Asia.'

Igor tries to compete on the anecdote front. 'There is an official reception for late gerontocrat Brezhnev. Locals bowing and scraping from the moment he arrives. One of Rashidov's acolytes presents Rashidov with a gold statuette of himself. The local boss smiles. Brezhnev grabs the statuette and feels it to ascertain that it really is gold. Rashidov asks with fake humility: "May we be so bold as to commission a larger one like this of you, comrade?" Brezhnev nods. The very next day he is presented with a solid gold replica of himself. It had been ready and waiting. Just local traditions of hospitality, you understand?'

Moscow

2 May

Back in Moscow, I lunched with a very old friend of my parents – a poet, regarded by critics as a bit of a hack. I gave him my impressions of the high expectations people had of Gorbachev. He laughed cynically. 'Look my young friend. There's always hope when a new Tsar is crowned.' This is a guy who has written poems extolling Stalin, Khrushchev and Brezhnev.

When I told him the Buñuelesque story about Rashidov, he laughed loudly. And then to annoy me: 'It started soon after the revolution. Anatoly Lunacharsky, our highly cultured Commissar for culture, one of our most talented orators and essayists, continued the Tsarist habit of picking a new ballerina from the Bolshoi for his personal use once a week. At least Rashidov's choice had a sense of humour and received payment.'

'How do you know about Lunacharsky?'

'The entire leadership knew. The person who told me was Svetlana Stalin. She was very reliable on such matters.'

More reliable it seems than the Australian academic Sheila Fitzpatrick, who forgot to mention it in her book on Lunacharsky.

1988

Moscow

20 April

Debates were raging on every level, including factory floors and classrooms. And, of course, in the party. The conservative faction felt that Gorbachev had gone too far, that Yeltsin's anti-corruption broadsides were destabilising the top layer of the party. Would all this come to naught? I thought not and this trip was a chance to see for myself. And so, almost exactly three years after my first trip, I returned to Moscow as a guest of the Writers' Union.

I was met at the airport by Maryam Salganik (Mira), a Union veteran and interpreter and an exceptionally gifted translator into Russian of Urdu, Persian and Turkish poetry. She loved Faiz and Nazim Hikmet's work, had visited Lahore a few times, and knew everyone on the left intellectual circuits. This was our first meeting. In the car to the hotel, she says: 'You will decide most of your own programme here. For this evening, a special treat. I've managed to get some tickets for the Bolshoi.'

I groaned inwardly. 'Is it the dreaded Swan Lake?'

'What? Why? Do you hate the ballet?'

'Not at all. I just prefer modern ballet. The Bolshoi should become more experimental. It's too outmoded. As an art form a show of technique, nothing more. You can tell. Even the dancers don't appear to enjoy it much. It could be easily re-enacted as a celebration of gay liberation with rainbow-coloured costumes.'

She informed me curtly that I was the first foreign guest who had turned down a visit to the Bolshoi Ballet.

'Ah,' I exclaimed, 'the joys of glasnost. You can't force me.'

The mood lightened. Slightly. 'Yes,' she said in a soft-spoken voice as we got into the car. 'It's glasnost time in our country. Do you think these new reforms will change the condition of women?'

'I was hoping to ask you that …'

She snorted, denouncing official Women's Day demonstrations and celebrations as pure ritual, an annual and strictly controlled mass outing for working-class Cinderellas. I scribbled down the figures she hurled at me: 'women: 53 per cent of the population, 60 per cent of whom are professionals; equal rights in most fields; 98 per cent of leadership in Russia and the republics are men … South Asia is better off, and you even have women prime ministers.'

Mira instructed the driver to drop me off at the Hotel Rossiya, the largest in the country, modelled on the latest US equivalents and, like them, totally characterless. In vain I pleaded to be transferred to an older, more historic place like the Metropol, but while sympathetic, she told me off. I was being honoured by being kept here. Best not to demand anything. Glasnost or no glasnost, she warned me, the bureaucracy functions as always. I capitulated. The location itself could not have been better: a five-minute walk from Red Square and the Kremlin, the river Moskva just across the road.

We dined at the Writers' Union Club. The tasteful dining room was once the ballroom of a grand mansion that Tolstoy had depicted as the Rostovs' residence in *War and Peace*. The Rostovs were themselves based on the writer's family, his sister-in-law to be precise. They had fled to the US after the Revolution but, Mira tells me: 'The old Countess returned last year, saw the building, and muttered to us, "Always knew the Bolsheviks wouldn't be able to maintain the place."' I thought they had maintained it rather well as I settled down to a second helping of the best pirozhki in town.

Could this be the same Writers' Union described by Bulgakov in *The Master and Margarita*? No, I was informed, that was a different building. And yet parts of the description appeared to fit. The Union, till very recently, acted as the ideological police of the Brezhnevites. There were still many careerists, writers high on their own mediocrity, drunks, but the atmosphere had changed. Everyone was talking politics. Everyone had a view. Mira herself, a hard-line Gorbachev supporter, was totally immersed in the factional struggle inside the party. It was bitterly divided, she confirmed. 'And Yeltsin?' I ask. Her face lights up with contempt: 'Very popular, but too much of a populist, a chameleon and not very bright. I doubt if he's ever read a whole book.'

A useful start to the trip, I thought, though the main reason I had wanted to get here was to study Constructivist Moscow in the 1920s in connection with a novel I was planning to write, *Fear of Mirrors*, about the early spies and the Fourth Department, aka Red Army Military Intelligence. I did manage some research, but the stormy present – lively and stimulating – disrupted the process. It was difficult to think of anything else. The Soviet Union was at the beginning of a major transformation that few in the West had predicted or foreseen.

It reminded me of Czechoslovakia in 1967: the reform programme that titled itself 'socialism with a human face'. Despite the regular reportage in the serious Western papers, it was only when I was in Moscow itself that I understood the scale of what was being attempted. The shared excitement of a new political movement is infectious.

21 April

I visited the offices of *Ogonyok*, the most innovative of the glasnost magazines. Korotich, the editor, was not present. 'Abroad as
usual,' his deputy said with a cynical laugh; his hostility to Yeltsin
smacked of careerism to me. When I pushed him, all he could say
was: 'Yeltsin is like Stalin! He's a workaholic. Works till late and
expects his staff to do the same.' I suggested strike action.

That afternoon I went to Boris Kagarlitsky's flat. In his early
thirties, Boris had been formed by Western Marxism and the
New Left Review and was probably the best-read intellectual
in Moscow. Talented, with more than a whiff of ultraleftism, he
was a leading light in the Moscow Federation of Socialist Clubs.
We shared similar aspirations and a common political language.
Boris's father Julius, a literary and theatre critic, remembered the
Revolution as a young boy and being taken by his father to hear
Trotsky and Lunacharsky speak. I had already read the proofs
of Kagarlitsky's book for Verso on the Soviet intelligentsia (*The
Thinking Reed*), an impressive study of its subject that I liked
very much.

After cake and tea, he dragged me willingly to a meeting of
the F-Soc Executive. I sat through this for five hours. It had a
familiar retro ring. It could have been a far-left gathering of
the seventies in any West European capital. The comrades in
Omsk were complaining that the paper was badly printed. The
comrades in Leningrad asked why all the key documents were
being written in Moscow. Socialists in the Urals demanded that
equipment be despatched to them so they could produce their
own material. An anarchist breakaway might be on the cards.
I met, amongst others, Victor Gershfeld, a German-Russian
former colonel in the Red Army, who had defended Moscow
as a fifteen-year-old citizen, rifle in hand, against the armies
of the Third Reich. He was both a party member and active in
the Socialist Clubs. We agree to meet up again for a lengthier
conversation.

22 April

I interviewed a guarded Otto Latsis, a dour Latvian and deputy editor of the party's theoretical journal, *Kommunist*. He defended the notion of a one-party state, but under firm questioning admitted that this notion did not flow from *any* stream or puddle of socialist theory. He did not reply when I gently inquired whether the time to dismantle the bureaucratic dictatorship had arrived.

Having finished the interview early I walked through the Arbat, lined with good second-hand bookshops. I bought a 1921 special edition of a magazine devoted entirely to Dostoevsky. I could find no first editions of Lenin or Bukharin, however. All Lenin's first editions were banned, and only doctored versions were available. The elderly woman who ran the shop knew of private libraries where they existed and promised that on my next trip she'd have them. And Trotsky? 'Perhaps in a few years, but very few people hid those. Discovery meant a prison sentence. It will be more difficult, but I will find some in provincial towns.'

The first person I should contact, Mira instructed, was the playwright Mikhail Shatrov. His trilogy – *Dictatorship of Conscience* (1985), *The Brest-Litovsk Peace* (1987) and *Onward! Onward! Onward!* (1988) – was having an impact throughout the country at the time. Where it was difficult to stage the plays, crowded public readings by actors served the same need to debate and to discuss. The plays were controversial and even those who claimed to support the reforms expressed hostility. The Brest-Litovsk play created a minor sensation. It marked the first appearance on the Soviet stage of Trotsky and Bukharin since the 1920s. Both men were depicted as being close to Lenin. The Shatrov project received official support when Gorbachev dragged almost the entire Politburo to the first night.

I asked to meet Shatrov. He agreed but insisted on taking me to a performance of *Dictatorship of Conscience* first. It was celebrating its third anniversary on the stage. I trooped along loyally to the Lencom (formerly the Moscow State Theatre). The building had been seized by the Moscow Federation of Anarchist Groups soon after the February Revolution and renamed the

House of Anarchy. It was packed, every seat taken. Apparently, it has been like this from the beginning. It was a mixed audience. Oldies mingled with school students; factory workers and Red Army soldiers seemed just as excited as segments of the Moscow intelligentsia.

The play itself was a frontal assault on Stalinism. 'The real strength of the state', a Shatrovian character declaimed, 'rests on the consciousness of the people'. The skeleton of the play is a mock trial of Lenin. The witnesses for the prosecution include Churchill, Hemingway and a Stalin substitute.

Why a substitute? 'When I prepared the script,' Shatrov tells me, 'it was still difficult to attack him directly in this fashion on the stage.' But the trial is constantly interrupted by everyday life. A young truck driver saunters on to the stage and is questioned by another actor. Why does he persist in displaying a picture of Stalin in his truck? 'Because Stalin was for law and order. People need to be disciplined!' Another actor responds: 'Ever heard of serfdom? Of slavery? That too was based on discipline ... Don't you know that Stalin's terror claimed millions of innocent lives?' Truck driver: 'We have never been taught this at school.' This remark is greeted with a massive round of applause from the audience.

In many ways, the dialogue between the actors and the audience generated even more electricity than the stage performances. The applause, the sighs, the questions, the silences as the watchers responded to the performers were an indication of Shatrov's popularity. A sense of the historical conjuncture united the audience with the playwright. Everything that was once taboo was now being discussed. At one point the actor playing Engels descended from the stage and, observing a row of Red Army officers, began a discussion on Afghanistan. Were they in favour of withdrawal? They certainly were, and the audience approved.

One of the high points is when a young woman, an idealist, attempts to join the Komsomol and discovers, to her amazement, that it is a nest of corruption and vice. When she expresses her horror to an apparatchik his only response is to rape her. Later in the play the same woman tells the audience: 'I told my great-grandmother all this; she told me that in the future there will be only one dictatorship. The dictatorship of conscience.' Loud and repeated applause greeted this remark. Shatrov's message is expressed through another voice on stage: 'We say we're living through a revolutionary process, but how can it be left in the hands of those who hate it?'

Shatrov has been writing plays since 1958. Like other artists, he attempted to circumvent censorship in the Brezhnev period by utilising the voice of Lenin. For over half a century Soviet history lay buried beneath a mountain of falsification. Historical truth, banished from the academy, sometimes found an outlet in the work of poets and playwrights, novelists and filmmakers. Shatrov's project was ambitious. He wanted to extend the limits of glasnost to their outermost boundaries so that no return was possible.

Onward! Onward! Onward! had been published in the Soviet press in January 1988, but the resulting debate meant a delay in its appearance on the stage. Shatrov was determined to fill in as many of the blank spaces in Soviet history as possible. As with all his work, the play functioned on several interrelated levels. The characters introduce themselves to the audience, but even this is not a linear process. The seventh character to introduce himself (Trotsky) accuses the eighth (Stalin) of having ordered his execution. Stalin does not deny this but explains why Trotsky has to be killed. This was not an issue that many people, especially academics, wanted to discuss. It was too sensitive and involved actions outside Soviet borders.

Stalin's attack on Lenin's widow; Rosa Luxemburg's strictures on democracy; Martov's criticisms of Trotsky … all this was there and a great deal else. The play was a another devastating indictment of Stalinism *as a system*, and it was this that created a panic atmosphere within the ranks of the reformers. Shatrov has stated openly that though his plays were historical they were always about the present. In *Onward! Onward! Onward!* Shatrov has Lenin saying:

A gigantic fossilised army of office-holders who will introduce reforms that undermine their domination? At whom are you laughing, gentlemen? To try to carry out a revolutionary transformation through such an apparatus is the greatest self-deception and deception of the people.

Unsurprisingly the editor of *Pravda*, Victor Afanasiev, was very upset. On 8 January 1988, at a meeting of media editors with Gorbachev, he launched a sharp attack on the playwright. Evidently Gorbachev remained silent as he listened to the arguments. This silence appears to have been interpreted as approval and a couple of days later *Pravda* carried a strong criticism of the play. Since the newspaper was correctly regarded as the voice of the Politburo, the conservatives could hardly believe their eyes. A group of status-quo historians followed up with a lengthy critique that was again published in *Pravda*. In response Shatrov was defended by *Moscow News* and *Sovetskaya Kultura*, and letters from readers poured in to these and provincial papers.

Shatrov had argued that Stalin's rise to power was not inevitable; it could have been avoided. 'There is no subjunctive mood in history,' stated an angry Stalinist in the pages of a Leningrad evening paper. Most of the letters, however, defended the playwright. His supporters also mounted a defence in the pages of *Pravda* in February 1988, and at a subsequent meeting with leading journalists some weeks later Gorbachev ended his remarks thus: 'We have to go ahead and look ahead. The purpose of these heart-to-heart talks is for things to sink in. So there must be no slipping back, no retreat, on the contrary. Onward and onward we go!'

This brought the anti-Shatrov campaign to a standstill. It is worth noting the remarkable fact that the Soviet Union was probably one of the few countries in the world, especially compared to the United States and Western Europe, where a play could polarise the political life of the country in such a sharp fashion. It could be argued that the major reason for this was the absence of any other structures through which dissent might be expressed. This was only partially true. The controversy over

Shatrov arose at a time when a great deal was being published in the Soviet media and there were wide-ranging debates within the academy. Moreover, the more the system was democratised the greater the impact of cultural events. The effect of the publication of Shatrov's play was a striking manifestation of mass involvement in affairs of this sort, not its opposite. The political culture of the Soviet Union was *potentially* vastly superior to that of the West.

23 April

An exhausting day. I met a handful of journalism professors at Moscow University. They appeared shell-shocked by glasnost. For years they had been teaching rubbish, defending the party's monopoly on information. I asked: 'Are you even mildly excited by the new trend of investigative journalism in the country?' There was no answer. The very question shocked them.

Dinner at the Writers' Club. Mira told me that Gorbachev's prepared speech for last November's seventieth anniversary of the Revolution was not delivered. The Politburo insisted on changes and he was forced to back down. I was taken aback. He still did not have a majority in the Politburo? The speech he did make was a weak and watery reflection of the original. While we ate, a musicologist acquaintance of Mira's walked over and sat at the table. He was the worse for wear and soon the vodka began to talk. He asked where I was from. Usually I say London. This time I said 'Pakistan'.

'Pakistan! You know my nephew was captured by the Afghan mujahideen. They castrated him. Stuffed his penis in his mouth, skinned him alive and sent his body back. What do you think of that?'

'Sounds straight out of Kipling.'

'What do YOU think of it?'

I express the expected shock and horror but can't resist pointing out that this wouldn't have happened had his nephew not been in Afghanistan.

'So, you don't defend them?'

'No.'

He appeared puzzled. He wanted Soviet troops out of that hell. We agreed. My criticism of the Afghan rebels bothered him. He drank some more. We discussed nationalism. I said it had its problems and, as for me, 'I am a rootless cosmopolitan.'

'Ah!' the vodka said, 'a Trotskyite.' The musicologist, if sober, might have had a more measured response, something like: 'But you're not a Jew.'

28 April

I spent half the day at Victor Alexandrovich Gershfeld's apartment. His bookshelves were lined with German editions of Goethe and Marx. 'I am equally fluent in both languages, but I prefer reading a book or an essay in the original language, if I can.'

He was born in Moscow in 1929. His paternal grandparents were doctors. His paternal grandfather was also in the army, an officer in 1905 and 1914. It was an old family tradition. 'If you go into Khiva,' he tells me, 'in the local history museum you can see a picture with the following inscription: "The generals Gershfeld and Garkhin are giving the command to attack".' Both his grandfathers and grandmothers were communists. His paternal grandfather joined the party during its first days and his father in 1918:

V.G. At the time he studied at Moscow University and it was from there that he joined the Red Guards first and then went into the Red Army and fought in the civil war. Later on, he directly reported to Lenin on the state of affairs at the front. In *Izvestia*, a map used to be published with the latest developments at the front, signed by my father. Till 1931, he held high posts. Being a general in the army then, he began to have some difficulties.

T.A. Do you remember your father ever talking about Trotsky?

V.G. Of course. The families of the old Bolsheviks knew each other very well, and they used to meet quite often. My father met Trotsky very often in the civil war period. Once they had a clash. In 1920 my father was in charge of troops on the Ural steppes. A revolt was shaping up and – just in case – my father put the Tsarist officers under house arrest, because the kulaks without military leaders were not a real force. Things were sorted out very rapidly, but afterwards he was summoned by Trotsky, removed from his command and sent to the Military Academy to study.

There is one fact that many of Trotsky's biographers overlook. They called him a leftist, holding very radical left views. What they forget is that it was he who recruited Tsarist officers and had some patronage over them. The famous General Brusilov rallied officers around himself in the Red Army. It just proved that Trotsky was a very sober-minded intellectual. His leftist views were not always manifested in his practical deeds.

After the war my father had some differences with Trotsky on the principles of building the Red Army. Trotsky was for a sort of police and militia system on the Swedish pattern. My father believed that we needed a permanent standing army. And I think my father was right. But once again, Trotsky was not the type to drive people by force into the army. On the contrary, he had quite liberal views even as far as the army was concerned. And this is what should be underlined and emphasised nowadays.

Having quarrelled with Brusilov and those who determined the political line of the army, my father took up a diplomatic post. He became first secretary of the Soviet embassy in Germany. At the time his brother Eugene was first secretary of the Soviet embassy in France. My father remained in this diplomatic post until 1937 and was quite familiar with Litvinov and others. In the thirties he used to report personally to Stalin. He would go personally from Germany, and then the usual happened. His brother was arrested and my father had to hand back his party card for not exposing the 'enemies of the people'. In 1938–39 Stalin demanded that he renounce his brother. He refused. Surprisingly, he got off quite lightly. He remained out of a job for a number of years and then started working for the Academy of Sciences.

T.A. But your uncle was killed?

V.G. He was killed in 1941 in the panic when the troops were retreating from Moscow, but without any trial. The Germans were already in the suburbs. My father and I joined the People's Militia, the volunteers recruited to defend Moscow.

T.A. But did you actually participate in the defence?

V.G. I did, and I returned to the army in 1944 as a sergeant. Towards the end of the war I was sent to military school, and afterwards, up to 1959, I served in the army. I left the army during Khrushchev's campaign to reduce the size of the armed forces, and joined Moscow University as a history student. After graduation I worked for some six months on the German-language newspaper and from then on until recently. It's only two years since I retired.

I was lucky to be in Moscow. It was the liveliest political capital in the world. Ideas of all sorts floating everywhere making one think that a political revolution was in the air. I felt at home and very happy.

At the *NLR*, my ex-IMG comrade and old friend Peter Gowan agreed with me; Robin was less convinced but hoped for the best. Quintin Hoare and Branka Magas were excited, speculating on the impact this could have in Eastern Europe and Yugoslavia. Perry too was excited to begin with, when Gorbachev came to power, but soon grew sceptical. Given the intellectual level of the leadership – he was disappointed by the level of the programmatic documents on offer – and no mass involvement, he was pretty much convinced that the process would lead to some form of messy restoration. I did ask myself 'Is this just me?' The overexcited impressionism of an outsider. But many others living in the country felt the same.

Victor Kuzin, for example, a non-party socialist. He told me how the first wind of pluralism had blown away the cobwebs. People could breathe again.

'Nowadays one can hardly be accused of over-exaggeration in asserting that our country is living through perhaps the most crucial and decisive moment in the whole seventy-year history of its existence since October 1917. The depth and acuity of the social contradictions which have now come to a head, as then, demand courage of thought and radical action in the choice of course and methods for overcoming the crisis.

April 1985, a definitive landmark on a distant and difficult road, has become the familiar line from which the democratic movement – previously nourished exclusively by the energy, persistence and heroism of isolated individuals, often resulting in self-sacrifice – began to assume the character of a developing process in improving the health of society. This process that was developing sluggishly and timidly is nevertheless gradually encroaching into more and more new areas. The democratic movement is striving to underpin socialism, its science, ideology, philosophy, economics, politics and legislation, with the only acceptable foundation: the extensive and free self-management of society.'

The problem for the conservative wing of the bureaucracy resisting change was that the central leaders of the party had given their support and strong approval to most of the measures under way. Popular consciousness was undergoing a daily transformation. When I had stopped over in Moscow in 1965 on my way to the last unified World Peace Congress in Helsinki, I'd been amazed at the number of people reading books on the Metro and the buses. This time it was newspapers and magazines, mostly free of censorship; the English-language daily *Moscow News* was astonishingly frank. The Western media today is by contrast conformist and loyalist to its respective governments.

Whether one spoke to ordinary members of the Communist Party, playwrights, musicians, artists or unofficial activists, the mood was one of hope. This was very refreshing, especially when compared to the gloom-laden voices of socialists in retreat in Western Europe and North America. By contrast, Moscow's streets and crowded benches in the city squares were filled with people talking to each other. Everyone discussing and debating politics, expressing their hopes and fears and speaking openly about the past. The press was filled with letters from ordinary readers from all over the country, especially workers. A woman worker in a ferro-concrete goods plant in Kurgan described in some detail the appalling conditions in which they worked.

She raged against corrupt managers and trade-union leaders, bad housing, inefficient public transport and the lack of safety measures and health provision. The sub-editor at *Izvestia*, which published the long letter, headed it 'We Want to Live Differently.' The letter concluded:

> Excuse me for writing what I think. I am not able to express all at once everything that is in my heart. We have been storing up insults for too long, while remaining silent. Now life has taken a new turn. We see changes for the better. We want to believe there will be more. Election of administrators, state product acceptance – all this is correct and necessary. But I am afraid that behind the restructuring of production, the restructuring of everyday life might be forgotten. To be honest, for me the main thing is my home and my family. I work for their sake. Believe me, most women here think the same. And if all around they are saying, 'We are restructuring,' and in the homes it remains as cold as before, and if you cannot squeeze into the public transport, and cannot buy anything in the stores, then for us it turns out there are no changes. That is what we think about. In a word, we want not only to work, but also to live differently than we have until now.

It was this change in the political atmosphere that made me want to write about the rebirth of hope in the Soviet Union; only a dead-end sectarian or a cynical hack could remain totally unaffected. That the process failed and ended with the imposition (backed by the US) of an authoritarian-oligarchic form of capitalism – first under a permanently inebriated, corrupt and unpopular Yeltsin, and after him with the Tsarist–White Russian nationalist Putin – was not the fault of those who wanted real change. It was what the US and its EU attachments wanted. It was only when Putin refused to do their bidding that they turned on him.

25 April
I had two final tasks to complete, leftovers from my trip to Tashkent three years before. To return Primakov's bottle of brandy

and to have lunch with Nodari Simonia. Both were fixed for the same day. Primakov was now the head of the KGB and suppressed a giggle when I entered his office. 'Yes, I've been promoted.'

I handed him the bottle of a very fine French brandy. He immediately hid it in the bottom drawer of his capacious desk.

'As you know my Boss has now banned alcohol. I don't want to arrest myself. So, I'll have to keep it safe till prohibition ends.'

'It never works with alcohol or literature. Just increases black-market prices as you know full well.'

As we sipped tea, I asked him for an off-the-record assessment of the situation. 'You are meeting Comrade Simonia for lunch today. He will explain the delicate situation to you. I read your book on the Nehru–Gandhi dynasty. Very informative and useful. I can say that in private but India is very important for us so I can't review it in *Izvestia*!'

'I know. And other states in other continents are important too. That's what Nodari is writing about these days. Close trade and diplomatic ties should not always supersede the necessary criticisms of these regimes.'

Primakov did not comment. As I was leaving, he walked me to the door and said *sotto voce*: 'My big worry is that the Boss is too prone to Western flattery. Naivete.'

In the car back to the hotel I wondered where Primakov might end up. He was very sharp, had nil illusions about Western democracies, was strongly in favour of glasnost and economic reforms, and was very well informed on the Middle East and Central and South Asia. He had seen the world. Why had Gorbachev not made him foreign minister? Compared to Primakov, the Georgian Eduard Shevardnadze was weakness personified. Worse even than Gorbachev in taking US promises and behind-the-scenes pledges seriously, and with not enough knowledge of the world outside the Soviet Union.

Was it already too late? Had the die been cast? A few hours later I discussed this with Nodari Simonia in a tiny Georgian café that he frequented. It was lovely seeing him again. He smiled, but his furrowed brow told a different story. He was worried. There was 'dual power in the party' and no Lenin in sight. Gorbachev was honest and well-meaning but not a strategist. I asked what his strength in the party was like.

'The ruling bureaucracy is badly divided. I would say 50–50. Amongst ordinary members and the intelligentsia, Gorbachev is much more popular, but for how long?'

'There is no such thing as permanent dual power,' I responded. 'The bubble must burst and better that Gorbachev unites all the hardcore reformists and takes on Ligachev and the conservatives, instead of playing the balancing act non-stop. We know what happens to those who only go half-way.'

'What would you do?'

'Mobilise the masses, storm the factories and the universities, listen to what people have to say, have free elections to a Constituent Assembly to prepare a new constitution. It may not have been possible in 1918, but it is now.'

'And multi-parties?'

'In principle, yes, but more important to revive the soviets. That was the most important institution created from below in European working-class history. A follow-on from the Paris Commune. Much more advanced. Then two, three, more parties make sense. The people elect representatives to the soviets and have the right to withdraw them. That would be more democratic than any democracy in the West. Given the total predominance of the working class it will not lead necessarily to a class divide but will certainly involve the people in politics: the corrupt versus the anti-corrupt, or less democracy versus more democracy, and – who knows – a women's soviet as well to discuss their needs and demands, etc., that were truncated in the 1930s.'

'Would it surprise you to learn that all this, excepting the reinstitution of real soviet power from below, is being discussed at virtually every level of the party?'

I was surprised and said so. There were two divides amongst the top layers: Yeltsin versus Gorbachev, and Ligachev versus Gorbachev and Yeltsin. I asked for his views on the latter. He raised both arms and shrugged his shoulders.

'To be honest, I don't know. If there was a vote in Moscow today, Yeltsin would defeat Ligachev's people and get a huge majority. His campaign against corruption and links between party bureaucrats and black-market gangsters is very popular. He is courageous. He names names and has been threatened by party hacks in return. It's good, but I don't trust Yeltsin. Too much demagogy, which can go either way.'

'Do you think it's a power struggle?'

'It could become one. Gorbachev has a bad habit of patronising those who disagree with him. I just don't know.'

I repeated Primakov's remarks. He already knew.

'Big problem and big danger. We are tired of telling Gorbachev and Shevardnadze that the Americans *only* act in their own interests. Neither their enemies nor their former enemies nor their allies matter where the US is involved. They've always been like that, whether it was grabbing huge chunks of Mexico or imposing the Monroe Doctrine. How can our leaders be taken in so easily? Sometimes I ask myself whether they are even materialists. Chinese, Cuban and Vietnamese leaders made revolutions. They learnt something from that process. Our leaders after Khrushchev were brought up inside and by the party-state bureaucracy. They had experienced war but not revolution.'

I turned the discussion towards Eastern European and the Baltics.

'This is regularly discussed. And the dreaded name of Beria crops up too.'

'Why him? He was such a swine.'

'True, but not unintelligent. Soon after Stalin's death and well before the 20th Party Congress, he came up with an interesting idea that he posed as a question to a Politburo that despised him. He said they had a choice. Discard Eastern Europe and keep the Soviet Union or possibly lose both. He proposed a treaty with the US. We will give Eastern Europe back to elected governments, permit a unified but neutral Germany and abolition of NATO and the Warsaw Pact.'

'The response?'

'He was executed for treason. I doubt this idea was the real reason. They wanted to destroy his apparatus and make an example of him.'

'He wasn't the first but let's hope he's the last. I can't help thinking if that had been done we would have avoided the Hungarian uprising and the Soviet invasion of Prague.'

'Perhaps. But would the Americans have accepted the Beria Plan? We don't want to fight a war with them, but they still want to destroy the product of 1917.'

'Public opinion in Europe would have been won over. But now? What's going on?'

Simonia laughed: 'We're broke. That's going on. We can't afford this level of military expenditure. Dismantling our bases in Eastern Europe would be a start. There is a Sino-Soviet summit in Beijing planned for next year. We are going to restore normal relations and withdraw the huge troop concentrations. Chinese party leaders have expressed a willingness to do the same.'

'But comrade, what will you get in return? Peace, I hope, and dismantling NATO and the Warsaw Pact. Is a peace treaty in preparation for both Moscow and Washington to sign?'

'Too early for that I think.'

Returning to the hotel, I saw my literary agent, Andrew Nurnberg, waiting in the reception. He was fluent in Russian and German, but was resisting Mandarin. He was in good spirits: 'Ready to write a book on these amazing goings-on?'

'I've been thinking about it.'

'I thought so. Dinner with Anthony Cheetham and Richard Cohen tonight? Can you manage a sheet outlining the project today?'

I could but was due to have dinner with Boris Kagarlitsky and his partner Irina that night. I agreed to join them at their restaurant later. Boris took me to an Indian joint called 'Delhi'. Awful, third-rate food. The cook told me they could not get the proper ingredients. I got away as soon as I could to meet Andrew and the publishers. Vodka had been flowing for some time. I ordered bread and borscht and handed over my single-page scribble on the book idea to Andrew. He read and nodded.

Anthony Cheetham asked me to summarise the situation and I gave them a fifteen-minute lecture. Then we headed off to the

Lenin Mausoleum to see the 'changing of the guard' at midnight. On the way back, Richard Cohen asked how long it would take me to write a book. 'I was impressed that you did *The Nehrus and the Gandhis* in six weeks.' I explained that I had made two longish trips to India for another book and conducted a very long interview with Mrs Gandhi; after she was assassinated, Sonny Mehta and Carmen Callil wanted to change the planned book into a biography of the Nehru family. It was not a cumbersome task. Cheetham interrupted: 'Write it soon. We'll get it out quickly.' And that was that. A book on the trajectory of the Soviet Union commissioned outside Lenin's Tomb.

II July

I returned to Moscow two months later for a conference on the cinema. Jonathan Steele, a friend, had recently arrived there as the new correspondent for the *Guardian*. This is very good news both for the paper and its readers. Jonathan is a meticulous and very inquisitive journalist. We meet up at his apartment at Gruzinsky Pereulok and chat. I give him my impressions and a list of people that he should meet sooner rather than later.

Then early lunch with the poet Robert Rozhdestvensky at the Writers' Club. A fascinating figure, part of the circle of poets who emerged after 1956, he angered Khrushchev some years later by writing a poem entitled 'The Yes-Men'. I ask what it was about. He looks around and replies: 'Use your imagination. The title is universal.'

He kept a low political profile, unlike his friend Yevtushenko, during the Brezhnev years, but argued for and got permission to rehabilitate poets and literary figures. Osip Mandelstam was the first on his list and he got himself appointed as the chairman of the Commission on the Literary Heritage of Osip Mandelstam.

'He was our finest poet after Pushkin. He died in the Gulag from ill-health. There were no orders to execute him, but the fact that he was in prison was a crime in itself. Pasternak used to tell a story: "One day in those terrible times I received a call from Stalin. He asked one question. 'How do you rate Mandelstam as a poet?' I knew that Stalin had read the orally transmitted poem on himself. And Stalin knew that I had done so as well. I paused but only for a moment and said: 'Comrade Stalin, he is our greatest living poet.' He thanked me. End of conversation."

'How do you explain this anomaly, Robert? According to the twisted logic of those times, Pasternak should have been taken to the Lubyanka and shot?'

His eyes expressed impatience. 'Years before the Revolution, Stalin dabbled in poetry. A collection of Georgian poetry was translated into Russian and published here. Pasternak reviewed it in a leading literary magazine and wrote that the poem by Djugashvili showed promise. Stalin never forgot that review and trusted Pasternak.'

'Would he have liked *Zhivago*?'

Robert laughed out aloud: 'It would never have been written in his lifetime. But none of us liked that novel. Akhmatova disliked it intensely and told him to stick to poetry. Of course, it should never have been banned even though the Cold War had given him the Nobel for writing it. Khrushchev could be very stupid on these matters. He remained a *muzhik*.'

'Did you ever meet Nadezhda Mandelstam? It was she who kept his work alive. I wish I'd met her.'

He had, and he described the May evening in 1965 when maths students at Moscow University had organised the first memorial meeting in Osip's honour on Russian soil. Many of his friends were present and Ilya Ehrenburg's memorial speech had people weeping. Ehrenburg had paid a warm tribute to Nadezhda: 'She lived through all the difficult years with Mandelstam, went into exile with him, saved all of his poems and I can't imagine his life without her.' Knowing it would annoy her, he could not resist informing the audience that the poet's widow was present in the hall. Thunderous applause and a standing ovation interrupted him and continued. Nadezhda was the only one left sitting. She finally stood up and said: 'Mandelstam once wrote, "I'm not yet accustomed to panegyrics..." Forget I'm here. Thank you.' But how could they forget? They simply carried on applauding.

It was getting late, and I had to rush to Progress publishing house for tea with the chief editor, who wanted to suggest a book on perestroika for Verso. The collection he proposed was predictable. I declined it on the spot but said we would be interested in other books. He was irritated. Tea was short.

Completely exhausted, I would have been happy to call it a day, but the Soviet Armenian composer, Mikael Tariverdiev, head of the Composers' Guild of the Soviet Cinematographers' Union, had invited me to supper at the Union restaurant. This was a problem. My knowledge of music in the Soviet Union was limited, making conversation a bit difficult. When he left the table to relieve himself, a couple in their late thirties walked up to me. My interpreter, Natasha Stepanova, explained who I was and why I was there. They nodded and the woman spoke: 'Don't waste time on him. He is a talentless, self-serving mediocrity. His music is awful. He prospered under Brezhnev, discouraged innovation, stopped us as students from organising a homage to Schoenberg. You seem to be alive. Why are you talking to a dead man?'

They saw him returning and scooted off. I soon discovered why he had wanted to meet up. Mira had told him that the RSC were thinking of a glasnost play. He wondered whether they might be interested in his music. He opened his briefcase and handed me some tapes. Natasha laughed as she gave me a lift back to the Rossiya. She too had enjoyed the couple's anger. 'What dead people am I seeing tomorrow?' I asked.

'Not one,' she said as I exited the car. My day was over.

12 July
On my single day off, I was asked what I wanted to do. I suggested Constructivist Moscow. Constructivism was the most exciting modernist movement of the twentieth century. Malevich, Rodchenko, Tatlin, Popova, Stepanova, Ginzburg and many others had laid the foundations of this universal form, proof of the early vitality of the Revolution, and, as such, they were household names for many in my generation.

I had dinner with Aidar Kurkchi, a Tatar architect working in Moscow. His father, he informed me, was in the Crimea where, fearful that their culture and language might disappear completely, he was working on a comprehensive dictionary of the

Tatar language. Aidar agreed to be my guide. There were scores of Constructivist buildings, he told me, many in a state of disrepair and it would need a week to see them all properly. I happily agreed to let him decide what we could see in a day.

On the tour most of the buildings, large and small, were still recognisable but sometimes hard to spot amidst the forest of other structures, many of them brutalist and others built for prestige during the stagnant years of Brezhnev, mimicking US skyscrapers. I spent a long time in each, with my knowledgeable guide pointing out all the special features. There was a workers' club with a cinema and library. The model for Tatlin's Tower was designed to celebrate the world revolution. Leonidov's design for the Lenin Institute of Librarianship was a display of total confidence in the new world of technology that was being born. Moise Ginzburg greeted it as the work of a true iconoclast, praising his pupil for having grasped the need for an architectural break with a 'system of methods, plans and elements that had become conformist and at best resulted in a uniformity of method, at worst in a threat of stylistic banality'. The special treat that awaited me was a low-rise apartment block for workers, a few miles from the Kremlin, in what had once been a new industrial zone built soon after the Revolution.

The Russian Revolution toppled much more than the decaying social and political pillars of the Romanov dynasty. During its first decade, it turned culture upside down. Discussions and debates on new forms dominated the literary and other cultural magazines and journals of the Soviet Union. New schools of literature, painting, cinema, sculpture and architecture became sites for important debates on the future shape of the revolutionary state. This explosion of ideas and theories resulted in new creative practices that were decades ahead of what was happening in the West.

Architecture as a form dominates all else. It changes cityscapes and is intimately connected with everyday life: where we live affects us all. The social priorities of architecture are determined by the social system in which it functions. Frank Lloyd Wright built amazing modernist homes for the rich out of

148

necessity rather than choice. Moise Ginzburg and his many colleagues were obsessed with communal housing, the construction of dwellings for workers and their families, factories, libraries, workers' clubs for leisure time, and office buildings: a practical utopianism. Ginzburg's classic work *Style and Epoch*, following *Rhythm in Architecture*, was first published in 1924, a year after Le Corbusier's *Vers une architecture*. Its first translation into English had to wait forty years. Ginzburg wrote:

> For nearly two centuries architectural creativity in Europe has lived parasitically off its past. At a time when the other arts somehow managed to move forward, systematically transforming their revolutionary innovators into 'classics,' architecture persisted, with unparalleled stubbornness, in refusing to tear its sights away from the ancient world or from the epoch of the Italian Renaissance ... Consequently, such 'academic' training yielded two results: the pupil lost touch with modernity and, at the same time, remained alienated from the true spirit of the great creations of the past. This also explains why artists seeking to express a purely modern understanding of form in their art often deliberately ignore all the aesthetic accomplishments of past epochs.

These views were not always reflected in the architecture of the Constructivists. Ginzburg's apartments expressed the new epoch. The apartment block to which Aidar took me marked a revolutionary shift. Communal laundries on each floor, dining rooms, a playground visible from every kitchen so that the children were in permanent sight when a parent could not be present. Spatial adjustments in every apartment allowing a room to be transformed into a different size using a strong wood partition on wheels. Ginzburg and his team had an intense dislike for corridors that connected rooms. Perhaps an aversion to dead space when everything should be alive and vibrant.

Many Constructivists loved nature and in later years designed deurbanised cities. Moving upwards was not a fad but necessary to preserve nature, and this, Ginzburg and Leonidov both insisted, could be done with four- or five-storey constructions flanked by commune houses, all linked to public spaces via enclosed highways. They hated repetitive rows of housing blocks. I was now in one of the Constructivist apartments.

'Who designed this one?' I asked my architect guide. 'My grandfather,' he whispered diffidently but with pride. It was a Ginzburg project, but the great theorist and practitioner worked best as part of a collective, uniting diverse individual talents to design the whole, a collaboration beneficial to all.

Ginzburg's colleague and student Ivan Leonidov produced some of the most imaginative designs and sketches that stunned not only Ginzburg and other colleagues, but also Le Corbusier and the Brazilian maestro of modernism Oscar Niemeyer. In his proposed 1927 design for the Lenin Institute he declared that his aim was to 'answer the needs of contemporary life through maximum use of the possibilities of technology envisaged'. The Dutch architect Rem Koolhaas remains a great admirer of Leonidov's style and method and is himself, in many ways, amongst the few truly gifted living successors of the Constructivists.

'In the mid-thirties,' Aidar tells me, 'the state began to close in, demanding blind obedience from its cultural workers, and it was then that priorities were changed.' A new instrumentalist architecture extolling the Stalinist regime was put in place: huge buildings with overly grand porticos, columns and sculptures that remind one of Mussolini's Milan in the same era. All this was followed in the postwar period by cheaply constructed brutalist building blocks.

Ginzburg, Leonidov, Tatlin, Rodchenko and Stepanova all died natural deaths. The Constructivist poet Mayakovsky committed suicide in 1930. His third eye could not bear the vision of what lay ahead in politics and culture. The Constructivist architecture that I saw in 1988 is still there but desperately needs a UNESCO preservation order to save it from oligarchic greed. Young architects from everywhere should see these constructions.

15–16 July

An informal dinner organised by Mira at the house of friends, with mainly intelligent Gorbachev supporters. Just before we sat at the table, a couple walked in. The man was a striking figure and I felt I had seen or met him before. After we were introduced I stared at him for a bit. He looked like a Tolstoyan character out of *War and Peace*. I got it. He was Prince Andrei. At this point and before I had said anything his wife whispered loudly in my ear: 'I'm not Natasha Rostov.' Everyone started laughing. Mira spoke: 'It's a mistake we Russians make, but you're the first foreigner to identify him as Prince Andrei!'

The dinner was lively. The future was the subject. We discussed the economy and most of them were in favour of a Scandinavian model. I disagreed. The country was huge. A market/state plan was needed or what they would get was not Sweden but Brazil. A thoughtless 'privatise everything' approach could wreck the country.

Prince Andrei: 'The existence of the Soviet Union was good for ending colonisation by the European powers and forcing them to introduce reforms at home. But here our people have suffered. You know that well. They need a chance.'

'They won't get a chance if you blindly mimic the US.'

The day ended as it had begun.

Earlier I had spent a few hours with a leading historian, Yuri Afanasiev, who was engaged in debating opponents on at least three fronts. A debate with the editors of *Pravda* on the limits of free speech and mass involvement in the reform process had been discussed by the Politburo. I managed to squeeze some time out of him over two days. For me his importance lay in the fact that he belonged to a milieu that was strongly opposed to a complete break with 1917. Things were going against them, but they carried on the debate. The interview I did with him summed up the strong feeling of hope that existed at the time. We focused in particular on the recent story that new history textbooks were being written.

T.A. Could you explain why the history exams have been can-celled throughout the Soviet Union?

Y.A. I think the answer is very simple, although the problem we confront is itself quite complex. The fact is that history textbooks in our country, especially those concerned with Soviet history, are completely falsified. These are not falsifications in some aspects or minor details of one sort of another, but total falsifications. And to make teenagers repeat all these lies during their exams is, quite frankly, immoral. We had no other option. Naturally this is only a temporary measure, but I think it was necessary.

T.A. And are new textbooks being written?

Y.A. Yes, some steps have been taken. Special teams of authors have been entrusted with this task. But you know here again there is something which I simply cannot accept, and I have expressed my disagreement on more than one occasion. I just think that it is unfair, incorrect and counter-productive if the whole country has to simply follow one textbook. This is a continuation of an authoritarian and monolithic approach in the field of pedagogy. It is based on the principle that you should know and learn only what you are given. Nothing more. Such an approach is totally negative and needs to be rejected. There must be a wide selection of texts available, a wide range of books, which may contradict each other. This is the only way to develop the critical faculties of our students. Both the teacher and the student must have a choice.

T.A. Of all the people involved in the debate on history you have been the most forthright in demanding justice for all the old Bolsheviks without exception. So far, the process of glasnost has rehabilitated almost everyone: Bukharin, Zinoviev, Kamenev, Rykov, Rakovsky, etc. Some have even been posthumously returned their party cards. The question of Trotsky, however, still remains unresolved. Why?

Y.A. First, none of the Bolshevik old guard around Lenin played such a major role as Trotsky in both the Revolution or the civil war that followed. Secondly, Trotsky is the only one of Lenin's old guard who for many years openly criticised Stalin and Stalinism. Thirdly, Trotsky is part and parcel of the history of the International, especially concerning a study and appraisal of Stalin's regime. That is why getting rid of the stereotypes of Trotsky in the Soviet Union is a measure of getting rid of the last vestiges of Stalinism in our society. This is why it is a special question.

I am not a Trotskyist sympathiser, but I am in favour of an objective assessment of his role in our history. We should report comprehensively on his work and activities and have an open mind on the question. It is impossible to get rid of the Stalinist legacy without getting rid of the Stalinist stereotype of Trotsky. That is why I insist on objectivity on the question of Trotsky and attach special importance to this issue. And that is why I call for Trotsky's rehabilitation.

T.A. Have you read Trotsky's *History of the Russian Revolution?*

Y.A. Yes, I have read it. Not in Russian, but in French. All his major works were available to me in French. I think the *History* is also available in Russian, but it was not published here.

T.A. As a historian, what is your estimate of it as a history?

Y.A. It is a noteworthy work and must be available along with other writings on the Revolution: Plekhanov, Sukhanov, Lenin, Martov, etc. All these writings need to be read and evaluated. There are histories by the proponents and architects of the Revolution and also others by its opponents. There are histories which defend the October Revolution and Trotsky's takes its place amongst them. Martov and Sukhanov are in a slightly different category. And then there are the outright opponents of October like Kerensky and Miliukov. There are different lines. All these books should be made available and judged on the basis of whether or not they correspond to logic and facts.

T.A. Before his death in 1967, Isaac Deutscher expressed the hope that his books would one day be published in the Soviet Union. With the advent of glasnost surely it is time?

Y.A. Personally, I think it is quite possible that Deutscher will be published one of these days. I know Deutscher's works and I must say that I think they are ideologically oriented. It is easier to publish non-Marxist historians because they aim at objectivity. Deutscher is ideological and party-oriented. I don't see anything unnatural in this and I think these books should be published. His Trotskyist sympathies are very clear, but this could be made clear in a publisher's statement.

T.A. Lastly, I would like to ask you about the debate on pluralism. It is a very interesting debate because those of us who are socialists in the West know that is quite possible to have three large parties who disagree about the pace of change, but never on the nature of change in capitalist society. So having more than one party doesn't *necessarily* mean a pluralism of ideas. I have followed very closely the debates inside the Soviet Union. The question is this: if you have a pluralism of ideas, you can't legislate that it should stop there. Suppose things reach a stage that people who believe in certain ideas wish to organise around these ideas with like-minded people. Ideas rarely exist in isolation for ever. In 1918–19, because of the civil war, all soviet parties were effectively banned, except for the ruling Bolshevik Party.

At the time of the 10th Party Conference in 1921 all the leaders of the Bolshevik Party stressed that the banning of tendencies and factions inside the party – in other words the outlawing of dissent within the ranks of Bolshevism – was a temporary measure. Stalin was to utilise this ban to institutionalise authoritarianism in the country. As I see it, it was the banning of other soviet parties such as the Left Mensheviks and the Left SRs that paved the way for barring pluralism inside the party itself.

Now we can see the film being reversed. If pluralism within the party leads to the emergence of other parties surely the heavens will not fall? Don't you think that it is possible to accommodate other parties within the soviet system? I would have thought that it was perfectly possible to move towards a form of soviet democracy which was much more real in terms of mass participation than any existing capitalist democracy.

Y.A. I have the same assessment as you of the 10th Party Conference. It was meant to be a temporary measure. This was indeed the spirit in which that resolution was passed. This 'temporary measure' has lasted from 1921 until 1988. It is impossible to regard this situation as normal. The party must not represent a monolith, because a monolith is like a boulder.

Of course, differences of opinion are perfectly normal in a

political party. I think that at the present stage there is very great scope for the development of a pluralism of ideas even within the framework of a one-party system. Of course, only if the party itself is radically transformed. What does this mean? It means the party must abandon the commandist and administrative methods of rule and instead offer guidance through persuasion and participation. In other words a party should lead not by the authority of its physical force, but rather through the force of its moral authority. This is what we are moving towards.

Secondly, I believe that tendencies and factions should exist inside the party that represent a community of independent ideas. We should have differing platforms articulating differing political positions, and that's what will happen soon. I think the existence of tendencies and factions is a positive phenomenon. It's healthy provided that the factions do not behave organisationally in a way that is contrary to the constitution. As for the presence of other organisations, it is already a fact. In Estonia there is the Popular Front for Perestroika which is legally registered. There are over 1,000 unofficial groups in our country. They are part of the new political reality.

The party should see this as part of the growing process of democratisation which needs to be taken into account. It must not be ignored and nor should the party treat these groups in a condescending fashion. I think our life is beginning to manifest what you said but perhaps not in such a clearcut and succinct fashion. There are still problems. There remains a hostile attitude to the mass movement and its leaders, but things are moving in the right direction.

T.A. There is a fear sometimes expressed both inside and outside the Soviet Union that in this critical time, given the balance of forces within the apparatus, they might remove Gorbachev and Yakovlev in much the same way as they dispensed with Khrushchev in 1964. Is this a possibility?

Y.A. The democratisation process in both the party and society has a long way to go. At the moment we have just drawn a sketch of the road that needs to be followed. Glasnost is a reality today and represents a tremendous gain for the whole country. But we still have to revive the soviets because till now they have been inanimate. Public and social organisations have to break from the old mould and begin to correspond to the needs of the democratic society.

We have a great deal to do in order to build up the institutions which can guarantee soviet democracy. We must not get hung up on the personal qualities of the leadership. Of course, we must rejoice that both Gorbachev and Yakovlev do possess such qualities, but these qualities alone are not enough to make the process of perestroika and democratisation irreversible.

T.A. Many of us who remain socialists in the West are beginning to regard the Soviet Union once again as a country of hope. Because if you succeed it could help in the rebirth of mass socialism elsewhere in the world.

Y.A. What will change things is not the quality of our publications and our debates. It is the change in life itself inside the USSR that will help socialism elsewhere in the world. Don't think we underestimate the difficulties confronted by socialist and workers' parties in the West having to fight for socialism when the model they had before them over the last two decades, for instance, was Brezhnev, Kunaev, etc. I am aware of how much we discredited socialism.

I completed my Russia book, *Revolution from Above: Where Is the Soviet Union Going?* There were two mistakes. At the time of writing, the most radical figure inside the party was Boris Yeltsin. This was acknowledged by Boris Kagarlitsky and others outside the party at the time. So, I dedicated the book to Boris Kagarlitsky and Boris Yeltsin. The latter name upset many comrades and friends. By the time the book was published the shifting trajectory of Yeltsin was beginning to come into view and this misjudgement on my part was later corrected in our play *Moscow Gold*.

A more serious mistake in the book was the absence of a response to the chess moves of the West, with Reagan and

Thatcher working in tandem. Apart from that I'm proud of the book as a reflection on an important moment in twentieth-century history: the collapse of the Soviet Union. I handed over the manuscript to Hutchinson in August 1988. It was published in December.

Over one lunch with Richard Cohen I reminded him that Hutchinson had published Mussolini's memoirs as well, and that had done very well, despite a fawning introduction by the former US ambassador to Italy. He replied in mock-serious mode:

'Our delayed punishment for that crime is that I'm now editing Jeffrey Archer's novels.'

'And your punishment for that is to publish me.'

1990

Moscow
11 October
Back in the USSR for a conference on the cinema. Ken McMullen's movie *Zina*, mostly filmed in the Deutscher home in North London, depicts Zina's nervous breakdown and her relationship with her father (Trotsky). It is Trotsky who insists that she sees an analyst. This was being shown at the conference together with *Partition*, a film on the last days of united India, which I scripted based on a short story by Saadat Hassan Manto.

The story, 'Toba Tek Singh', is set in the Lahore Mental Asylum. It is August 1947 and Sikh and Hindu inmates are being transferred to asylums in India, but they refuse, link arms with the Muslim inmates and must be forcibly parted. The writer is telling us that sanity in those crazed days could only be found in the asylum. The eighty-minute film was shot in two weeks in London, where we recreated the Lahore asylum in a warehouse in the deserted docks. The finished product divided opinion: Salman Rushdie and Hanif Kureshi hated it for aesthetic, not political, reasons. Arundhati Roy liked it very much.

In Moscow its style, pace and dialogue emptied the cinema within fifteen minutes. We had to laugh. *Zina*, however, was well received. It was the first time since the 1920s that Trotsky had been portrayed sympathetically on a Soviet screen. There were no simultaneous translators in the discussion that followed. Ken asked if I could translate the comments into English for him. I agreed. As the critics began to speak, I translated into Ken's ear as follows: 'Ken, don't panic but this guy is saying that the film is pure shit and that having a Welsh actor playing Trotsky is a Stalinist perversion.' Ken had his head in his hands.

The next critic loved the film and was smiling and nodding. My translation was a bit different: 'This guy appears well mannered but is saying that Zina in real life was very plain looking and you've cast an Italian beauty from a Tarkovsky film to play her. Oh my god Ken, he's asking whether you did so for non-cinematic reasons. I can't translate the next sentence. Its pornographic.' Ken was shattered.

I took pity on him and confessed that I wasn't a translator but an escaped inmate from the Lahore asylum who thinks he can speak Russian.

12 October

Documentary day at the conference. Fred Jameson and I sat through several films of varying quality including a well-meaning Soviet documentary on Afghanistan. We were hailed by S., a postgraduate student at Moscow University. 'Ah, Professor Jameson, I'm a huge admirer of your work. Hello, Tariq. Welcome. I am a regular reader of the *New Left Review*. What did you think of the documentaries?'

I pointed out that while we were in favour of Soviet troops coming out of Afghanistan, I didn't like the mystical, religious streak running through all the films. Why have three baptisms and two church weddings littering a doc on Afghanistan? I was slightly surprised when, in response, he began defending Dostoevsky's antisemitism and the Church: 'Our intelligentsia has always been heavily influenced by Christianity.' I reminded him of 1905 and 1917. 'Oh, that was the Jews.' So much for the Revolution. A canvas painted by the wicked Jews! Should we bother to engage? Fred and I exchanged looks and walked away. Later, I mention this to Boris Kagarlitsky. He laughs: 'This type of anti-semitism is ugly, but harmless.'

Dinner at the Writers' Club. I introduce Fred and Ken to Mira and the gang. Jonathan Steele and Ruth also present. A pleasant evening, but an exhausting day. As Ken and I return to the Rossiya we see a female Soviet official escorting several desolate sex workers, plastered with make-up and draped in imitation fur. She seems distracted but cheers up on sighting us. 'Are you two gentlemen part of the Turkish parliamentary delegation?' We shake our heads. She's upset. 'Where are they? They ordered these girls. Where are they?' We nod sympathetically and walk briskly to the lift. Too tired even to laugh.

13 October

The weather was changing on every front. I went to a children's store to look for Red Army Second World War models for my six-year-old son who was hooked on Jeremy Isaacs's TV series *The World at War* and Laurence Olivier's voiceover. He watched the Red Army episode at least once a week for months, and could recite the commentary with Olivier.

Lunch with Victor Gershfeld, who is getting nervous at 'Mishenka's [Gorbachev] increasing inability to take decisive action'. He describes a meeting with Politburo member and key reform intellectual Alexander Yakovlev. He is under daily attack by conservative opponents, is feeling isolated and is threatening to resign.

Supper with Aidar and his Georgian wife Irma at their apartment. A photograph of her parents prominently on display, both in Red Army uniform. Her father was arrested and killed by Stalin. We were joined by Mira and Kalpana Khosla, who I had last met in Delhi some years ago. Her husband, Romi Khosla, one of the top architects in the country and a radical to boot, had designed the new CPI(M) HQ in the capital. He told me that one of his funniest moments was being lobbied by every member of the Politburo individually. Each wanted a separate toilet!

Irma to me: 'If we fail, it will be a social and political Chernobyl.' What many people here want is democracy and a mixed economy.

16 October

A press conference called by the Popular Front socialists. A spokesperson describes how they met with the procurator's office to discuss implementation of the constitution. A productive conversation. The Front is strongly opposed to the victimisation of Yeltsin (his bureaucratic removal from the Moscow party leadership) and demands elections in Moscow. As a result, they inform us: 'Over the last ten days repression against us has increased. Some Brezhnevite measures are being used. More against us than the Democratic Union, which is a non-socialist liberal grouping.'

'How do you differ?' I ask.

'We are the most active, most rapidly developing social organisation. We believe in self-managed socialism, united workers, students and artistic groups who want to accelerate the process from below, fight against every violation of the law, or I don't know where it will go. Mishenka Gorbachev has broken from the past, but does he know where he's going?'

Another activist, Babushkin, takes the stand: 'I was arrested on the street last week while I was getting signatures demanding the rehabilitation of Boris Nikolaevich [Yeltsin], and released yesterday. I was sentenced on the spot to five days in prison for "disobeying police orders". I did get food, some of it was quite good like what we were given in Pioneer camps [laughter]. I talked to the police in the cell. They were friendly and all of them were very sympathetic to Yeltsin. He was the only politician who came out of the party conference with more prestige than when they went in. He reads now and learns.'

Misha Malyutin, another activist, and a party member, recounts a conversation with a party conservative, a Citizen Baranov.

Baranov: 'We don't allow perestroika from below.'

MM: 'Who is we?'

Baranov: 'The Party.'

MM: 'Which party? Mine, or yours.'

Baranov: 'You'll soon find out.'

MM: (sniffing) 'There is a whiff of Stalinism in the air. Did you leave the toilet door ajar?'

With a group of friends, I go to see a film made sixteen years ago but only just released: *Commissar*. Directed by Aleksandr Askoldov, it tells a civil war story, inspired by Babel. The action is set in a small town in Ukraine. Most of the characters, including the Red Army commissar, are Jews. That's why the film was shelved. The director was pressured to change the Jewish names but refused. The cinema was packed and the film was greeted with huge applause.

Over supper, one of the company informs us that Boris Zhutovsky, a gifted artist (and Khrushchev's son-in-law), was recently commissioned to illustrate a civil war story for *Yunost* magazine. Zhutovsky is left-handed so he had sketched guns in everyone's left hand. The *Yunost* editor only noticed that all the noses were Jewish.

17 October

Spent most of the day farewelling my new friends. Supper with V. Maximenko, one of the most gifted young academics in the party and a truth-teller. He had managed to secure a table at one of the few newly opened, privately owned restaurants in town. The 'Pirosmani', named after the great painter of the region, served only Georgian food and wine. The former very good, the latter very bad. Not permitting private restaurants or cafés for the last seven decades was an act of incomprehensible lunacy to me. For the Cubans to have mimicked this was even worse.

We had a wide-ranging discussion on the political crisis. Maximenko: 'The principal aim of the conservatives is to integrate Gorbachev into the apparatus so completely that he is suffocated by their collective hug and becomes one of them. This is a very real danger.' He felt that unless the system was opened up quickly the party reformers might lose all credibility. The apparatus that had outlasted the Tsar and Bolshevism must be dismantled.

He was passionate on the question: 'Gorbachev at the last conference stressed the importance of reviving the soviets, but quoting Lenin is not enough. Lenin's ideas varied. We must outflank Lenin from the left. The world has experienced bourgeois democracy, dictatorships of every sort, postcolonial disasters, and we can learn from all that. And the economy is crucial. Market, yes definitely. But accompanied by workers' self-management. The workers have more knowledge embedded in their experiences than bureaucrats and capitalists put together.'

The evening ended with a heated discussion on Turgenev. I was indifferent to his novels but Maximenko was a great admirer. He insisted that the novelist had some insights into the Russian character, such as mouthing effortless untruths, which he linked to centuries of serfdom. What about the Moscow Trials? He didn't reply.

I flew back to London the next day.

10

Moscow Gold

Amongst the first things I did on my return from Moscow in 1988 was fix lunch with Howard Brenton. I had worked with him before, and we had already got into some hot water.

Writing *Iranian Nights* together in a Royal Court dressing room over ten days had been a very enjoyable experience. We had laughed a lot and riffed off each other's jokes. The play had gone down very well except for a couple of lines that annoyed Salman Rushdie. The 'offending' lines were Brenton's brainchild, and the theatre resounded with laughter when they were spoken. It was an experience that many in the audience had shared. To contextualise: the first half of the play is a pastiche of *The Thousand and One Nights*, but also quotes bits of the actual stories to show that early Islam was far more tolerant on many levels than its modern, oil-fuelled heirs. This theme runs through my Islam Quintet novels as well. On the stage, Scheherazade reports a 'blasphemy' to the Caliph.

SCHEHEREZADE: From far away a messenger came with evil news. On a small island in Satan's thrall, where two queens sat on a single throne, a poet from an old family of believers in the East had written a poem. The blasphemous wretch.

CALIPH: Ah. Theology. Heads will roll. And what was the blasphemy?

SCHEHEREZADE: No one knows. It was a book that nobody could read ...

It was for this sense of mischief that I went to Howard with my idea for a play about what was going on in Russia. Before I left Moscow I had discussed the idea with Mira and suggested it would help if Howard were invited by the Writers' Union to Moscow so he could meet people and get a glimpse of the country in flux. She was delighted, and organised an invite. It was Howard's first trip, and he spent a couple of weeks in Moscow and Kiev. He had decided not to talk to any foreigners. He couldn't bear the thought of US tourists moaning that Red Square was 'too small' or asking the waiter at an Intourist restaurant whether they would be served meat or fish. A mean question, Howard thought, since nobody in the kitchen could answer it. They cooked what was provided.

I had strongly recommended he read Bulgakov to get into the mood, and especially *Black Snow*, a short satirical novel on the theatre backstage. That stood us in good stead. We met up the day after he returned from his trip. Even as I was wondering how we would write this play if he was up for it, he walked into the Soho restaurant grinning broadly.

'Spill the beans,' I said.

We exchanged accounts of what was going on in the Soviet Union. He was not sure of the outcome but was enthused by his trip.

'It would be great if we can get this on the stage. Should we go and see Max?'

Max Stafford-Clark had allowed us to stage *Iranian Nights* at the Royal Court at a time when others were fearful of 'Islamist reprisals'. And this in turn had led to Channel 4 agreeing to film the play and put it out the day after the run ended. Could we pull it off again?

'From what you've described,' said Howard, 'it's an epic. We need a big stage. The National or the RSC.'

'They'll never agree.'

'We have to find a director, someone who can't be easily turned down.'

'Peter Hall? Peter Brook?'

'Do you know John Dexter?'

I knew and liked his work, of course, but had never met him. And though writers and actors moaned at his exacting method he was undoubtedly one of the great English directors. He had done the Arnold Wesker plays at the Royal Court and *The Royal Hunt of the Sun* at the National, as well as Brenton's adaptation of Brecht's *Galileo* and much else.

Dexter and Laurence Olivier had set the tone for the new National Theatre. Olivier wrote to him: 'I think your work is glorious. And I'm giddily proud of it. It is with deliciously self-flattering pleasure that I like to think of you as my son.' But father and son, as often happens, had fallen out after a blazing row. Dexter's explanation for his many quarrels was subjective, but convincing: 'Fury for perfection makes me difficult to work with. The pressure that people feel is merely the afterburn of the blast off. They have no right to stand too close unless they are insured against fire.'

Dexter learnt how to read music after being offered the artistic leadership of the Metropolitan Opera House in New York. He stayed there for four years, his work a huge success. He was now back in London. His diaries testify that he had been to the Royal Court to see *Iranian Nights* and liked it. As had his partner Riggs O'Hara, a tough, no-nonsense American who complained, the first time I met him, that when they had gone to spend a weekend at Laurence Olivier's pad in the country, he had forbidden them to share the same bed. I asked: 'Morality or jealousy?' 'Probably both' came the reply.

Howard rang Dexter and he was very interested. We went over to Portland Road for lunch. I gave John my ideas for the play. Howard told him that we conceived it as a homage to Meyerhold and Brecht. He remained silent for too long, making us nervous. Then a burst of laughter. 'Great idea. Let's do it, boys. Go and write. Bring me the first draft as soon as you can and then we'll go in search of a theatre.' To his diary, he later confided: 'Howard and Tariq are the only authors I have ever worked with who are secure enough to set about writing a play with me in mind.' He was the only director I had ever worked with who was keen on ideas. His Brecht productions were astonishing, his description of the Brechtian *gest* original.

We met once a fortnight after that and it helped a great deal that Riggs was genuinely very keen on the play. I began to get an idea of the Dexter touch. He was a ruthless editor. While prepared to argue endlessly with the writer, he insisted on the final cut. That is what transformed so many of the new plays he directed. He could be very waspish. He hated writers walking into a rehearsal with friends simply to show off, and even more so if they whispered to each other. When Arnold Wesker did so on one occasion, Dexter raised his voice from the sixth row and rapped him hard on the knuckles: 'Daisy' – he had a female nickname for many writers and actors – 'if you don't shut up, I'll direct this play as you wrote it.'

We discussed casting with each other before we'd written a single line. Albert Finney or Anthony Hopkins as Gorbachev? Howard and I were very keen on David Calder, who was already part of the RSC ensemble and an excellent actor. He resembled Gorbachev too, and understood what we were up to in the play. He was also a relapsed member of the Workers Revolutionary Party, which in this case (if none other) was very useful.

Howard wrote in his diary about the week we spent before going to the state-subsidised theatres:

A West End producer whom Ali and I approached refused even to read our summary of the play and described us as 'a menace to the British theatre'. The agent of a 'star' actor was spotted by one of our spies on the Metropolitan line shouting and hitting the seat next to him with the outline of the script. These were encouraging signs that we were on the right track.

The National was not interested, so off we went to see Terry Hands, the artistic boss at the RSC, with a typed-up proposal. He was keen on the project and even more excited by the thought that Dexter might direct a big play at the Barbican. They had a phone conversation. JD confirmed that 'Grubby' Hands was enthusiastic. Within a week the RSC literary department had commissioned a first draft. It was now official. Everything – script discussions, casting, design, costumes – was now in earnest.

Dexter's reputation with writers preceded him. His monumental row with Peter Shaffer had lasted three years. Shaffer had come to prominence thanks to Dexter's direction of *The Royal Hunt of the Sun* at the National in 1964. The play centred on the battle, actual and ideological, between the last Inca emperor, Atahualpa Inca, and the Spanish conqueror, looter and despoiler, Francisco Pizarro. The staging was brilliant. The colours vibrant. It made the audience think. What more could one ask for? It became a huge commercial success, transferred to other theatres and was performed in New York and Sydney. It was this play especially that gave JD the reputation of being able to transform the roughest pigskin into a silk purse.

Shaffer knew this very well at the time and was thrilled. They began to discuss another 'two-hander'. This time the subject was music and egos and jealousy. The clash was based on the rivalry between Salieri and Mozart. The title was *Amadeus*. Work went on to create the best possible script over three years. Shaffer and Dexter fell out and the writer asked Peter Hall to direct the play. Shaffer declared he could not work with Dexter. The fall-out within theatrical circles was huge. Everyone took sides. JD's version is in his posthumous memoir, *The Honourable Beast*. After almost pledging never to work with living authors again, JD's entry for 21 June 1979 is acidic: 'And now that it's all over. *Never* again waste your time trying to turn the second rate into the first rate. You can't do it, because it should not be done at all, and because from the second rate there is nothing to be learned'

Howard and I had started work on the play in September 1989. We delivered the first draft in January. JD enjoyed the first read and started making notes on the script. Anthony Hopkins was too booked up. Dexter asked the RSC to check the availability of Klaus Maria Brandauer. He was booked up too. Howard and I pushed for David Calder, who I had already said would be better than Hopkins.

For *Iranian Nights*, Howard and I had taken turns on the typescript and it had worked. Here we divided up the scenes and each of us read the other's work critically and suggested additions, deletions, improvements. JD was in hospital having his heart looked at but insisted on a meeting at 6ish. He ordered a bottle of champagne and said we had to move forward on every front. Music: Shostakovich's Quartets were perfect for the script. For set design he wanted his regular, Josef Svoboda, to come up with something, but the Czech was in a grumpy mood and said he'd had enough of 'Vladimir Ilyiches' for one lifetime. After a week of tests, JD's surgeon advised surgery, promising a 90 per cent chance of success. John went home and slept well. In his diary of 12 March 1990 he writes: 'Tariq and Howard. V. good. Rewrites around Simple Soviet Woman and the people. *The Mother* as model.'

That afternoon what amazed me and boosted my confidence was JD's praise for a scene I had written, and that Howard also liked very much. A family in a state of disintegration just like the country. 'Pure Brecht,' were JD's words. Years later Howard told me that Richard Eyre had rejected the play for the NT from Scene 3 onwards. JD would have laughed a lot. In the meantime, he met Siobhan Brack (RSC casting director) and liked her. Next David Calder. Finally, we were all in agreement that he should play Gorbachev. JD was immersed in the play. We got the final green light from the RSC on 21 March 1990. I rang John at home and he was excited. One of his last ideas for the production was a choreographed opening five-minute dance sequence by Natalia Makarova, red flag and all. She had agreed and wanted to meet us all.

On 23 March, John went into the operating theatre for his heart operation. He died on the table. He was only sixty-four. We were devastated and did not much care whether the play happened or not. Our heads were full of JD. At his funeral, preceding a very jolly wake, one of his favourite actors, Frank Finlay, cheered us all up with an anecdote:

We were in the middle of rehearsals. John Gielgud and I were on stage. Suddenly John's inimitable voice interrupted us from the sixth row: 'Girls, I'm bored.' Slight pause, then we carried on as before. After a few minutes the same voice stopped us again: 'OK. Enough. A-team off the stage. B-team on the stage.' We walked

away. The understudies, feigning modesty, walked on. Their names
were Anthony Hopkins and Alan Bates.

To its credit, the RSC insisted on doing the play. Barry Kyle, an
in-house director, took charge and, though he must have been
irritated by JD's ghost whispering in Howard's and my ears, he
did a valiant job. His choice of designer, Stefanos Lazarides, was
brilliant, constructing the stage as a huge red Politburo table that
opened up to reveal the hidden truths. That Barry had mixed
feelings about the play is indicated by the fact that it's not in his
CV. Never mind. We respected him for doing it. Reviews were
mixed. The *FT* was totally positive. There were intelligent obser-
vations in the *TLS* and *The Sunday Times*. *Pravda* reported it on
its front page with a pic of Calder as Gorbachev.

Howard laughed: 'I wonder whether he [the editor of *Pravda*]
knew that Hare and I had done a play titled *Pravda*.' That play
was, in fact, a savage attack on Murdoch. The implication of the
title was that his newspapers were the Pravdas of Britain, supporting regime and state as uncritically as the Soviet paper of old.

'I did tell him, Howard, and he pointed out that his paper now
carried debates on a high level and there are more diverse voices
in the Soviet press than its British equivalents. You owe them a
retrospective apology.'

Many friends came to the opening. Angela Carter loved the
show. I received a very warm hug and kiss as she whispered:
'Amazing. How the hell did you manage to get it on?' Old enemies
were asking the same question but from the other side of the
divide and in public. A Murdoch columnist, Bryan Appleyard
(later awarded a CBE for his many services rendered), bristling
with anger and hostility, profiled me rudely in *The Sunday Times*.

Moscow, January 1990
We took three scenes from the play to perform at a large theatre
in Moscow. Many friends present. Mira says the situation is very
tense and the power struggle at a peak.

The massage scene [Act 2, Scene 3] that got a laugh every
day at the RSC makes the audience slightly nervous here. Raisa,

seeing how tired her husband is, insists on massaging him. He lies on his front. His back is knotted, a disintegrating Soviet Union. The Baltic states are his bum and bum-cheeks. Then, as he's totally relaxed, she speaks: 'Now turn over and I'll massage Yeltsin for you.'

The audience was taken by surprise. Many laugh, a few frown, others look nervous.

In August 1991, a foolish, desperate coup attempt by the anti-reform wing of the Communist Party of the Soviet Union was defeated. Jonathan Steele of the *Guardian* got himself a huge scoop by scrambling on to a plane and accompanying Gorbachev back safely to Moscow from the Crimea, where the Soviet president had been kept under house arrest.

What some of us had predicted, namely that the balancing act could not last, came to pass with dire results for the country and its people. Where I was wrong was imagining that the choice was either the status quo or a progressive social democracy. In the event we got neither. Just a huge mess that led to economic collapse and huge suffering for most citizens. A few days later Ukraine and Belarus declared independence, and Gorbachev resigned as general secretary. Boris Yeltsin took power in Russia and, as the Soviet Union collapsed, the US threw its political forces behind him. Yeltsin promptly dissolved the Central Committee and banned the party of which he had been a member for many decades. We watched the drama unfold as US secretary of state James Baker laid down conditions for extending help to the emergent republics. In December 1991, the Soviet Union ceased to exist and the Commonwealth of Independent States was recognised by the US and Russia.

My diary records that I rang B. in Moscow.

'So,' I asked. 'It's really over.'

'Yes,' he replied. 'And Gorbachev is finished too. Yeltsin won't last too long. It's a period of transition, but to where and what nobody knows. Any ideas?'

'The English Revolution lasted about twenty years, the French from 1789 to 1815, the Russian 1917 to 1991.'

'It's a defeat, Tariq. But sometimes new revolutions arise from past defeats. At least they can't revive the Tsar. No obvious candidate.'

'The US is now all-powerful. A huge triumph for their Empire. Gorbachev gave away everything without getting anything in return for his country and its people. Primakov, Simonia and others had warned him of the dangers in doing so. Western flattery went to his head. It's a defeat on every level. And that's how the world will see and feel it.'

'You're too pessimistic.'

I didn't think so. The tectonic plates on which the old global order had rested since 1917 had been badly dented.

11

Disrupting
Heavenly Peace

The events that led to the breakup of the Soviet Union were very different to those that preceded the challenge to the Communist Party in China in 1989. The debates over the state in the Soviet Union were largely confined to party bureaucrats and intellectuals, as I had witnessed during my three trips to that country. As a consequence, the reformers led by Gorbachev did not have the support of a mass movement as a backdrop.

In China in 1966, by contrast, a gigantic student movement – the Red Guards – was born which challenged the authority of the party. The Great Leap Forward had turned out to be a voluntarist disaster. The ensuing famine was a catastrophe with millions dying. Mao Zedong's position in the leadership was considerably weakened, politically and morally, as the leadership sought to reverse the policies he had imposed. Mao fought back by mobilising student youth with ideological slogans: 'To Rebel Is Justified', 'Bombard the party headquarters with pamphlets and leaflets', etc.

The Red Guards denounced Mao's opponents as bureaucrats and 'capitalist-roaders'. The Cultural Revolution, as it became known, plunged China into chaos for the best part of a decade. While a lot of score-settling took place, it was different from the Stalinist Terror. Where Stalin had used the repressive wings of the party and state apparatuses to exterminate his enemies, Mao and his allies utilised masses of youth and encouraged them to seize new liberties. As part of an anti-Confucius campaign, the young people challenged parental authority and confronted their teachers and professors. An uncontrollable movement from below gripped the country.

Despite the subsequent horrors, the movement's questioning of authority and challenging of established verities laid the foundations for a cohort of millions of citizens to eventually fight for political reforms in the spring of 1989.

In an interview conducted in Hong Kong in 1972, I discussed the early days of the Cultural Revolution with Yeung Cheng, a former leader of the Canton Red Guards, who had been forced to flee the army units sent in to restore order in 1968.

T.A. What were the exact circumstances that led to your becoming a Red Guard?

Y.C. 1966 was an important year in China. In the period preceding June 1966, the political atmosphere in the country was very tense. We felt that there would be an explosion fairly soon. In Peking High School, students had declared themselves Red Guards under the slogan: 'To Rebel Is Justified'. In our school in Canton in the same month there were only a few of us who were rebels, though we were very active. A few dozen in a school consisting of 1,400 students. We felt suppressed and uninvolved in the country's politics.

Our life was dull, routine and pedestrian. Before the Cultural Revolution I was very interested in reading political texts – Marx, Lenin, Mao – and was regarded as being weird since we were not supposed to show any independent interest in politics. In school, politics meant being taught what the party line was on this or that subject.

The June, Red Guards represented a trend to think independently. Our political level was very low and we put forward no demands as such. We merely made wall-posters condemning the section of the party in the school. I'd always hated the school headmaster, who was totally useless, a fact everyone in the school was aware of. He was there because he was a party member. He was a super-bureaucrat who ate separately not only from us students, but even from the rest of the teachers. While compelling us to take part in physical training, he used to stand at a distance under an umbrella. It made me want to get a stepladder and piss on his head. He was extremely authoritarian.

In June 1966 our wall-posters denounced him in rather emotional terms. We also snatched some of the rifles kept in the school and hid them. There were between twenty and thirty rifles in the school, but they were under the control of the children of PLA soldiers who also studied in the High School. We toppled the party organisation in the school and for a short period we elected a new administration. That was why Liu Shaoxi sent in work-teams to re-establish party control.

The work-teams claimed to support the Cultural Revolution, but in fact they suppressed us and warned us not to fight against the party section. Instead, they attempted to divert our wrath towards the non-party teachers, and it was on their instructions that many ordinary teachers were insulted and humiliated. Our spontaneity was crushed.

T.A. When did Mao intervene? And what was the impact?

Y.C. In August that year. Mao announced the sixteen points of the Cultural Revolution and the Red Guards were officially recognised. This action seemed to vindicate the June Red Guards as being genuine leftists and encouraged us to fight the 'capitalist-roaders'.

My isolation began to decrease and students began to speak to me again, but the school was still under the control of conservative elements (sons of Red Army soldiers). From August to October the minority Red Guards began to regroup. Our main difference with the conservatives was that they supported the work-teams, but even after the teams left our school in August, the conservatives did everything possible to steer the struggle well clear of the party bureaucracy. They did so by making scapegoats of the students who were of bourgeois origins and the latter were victimised rather brutally. Though I come from a working-class family myself, I nonetheless attacked the conservatives in very strong terms for their behaviour, which culminated in them actually killing a number of teachers and students of bourgeois origin. You must understand that this was a deliberate and conscious diversion. The period lasted from August to October 1966.

T.A. Did you go to Peking for the big event?

Y.C. In October, I left for Peking to observe the Cultural Revolution at its base and stayed there for three days. I saw the wall-posters, but not Mao. I met others like myself and then returned to Canton. I travelled with hundreds of others, free of charge, in trains, ferries, trucks. It was a fantastic experience seeing the country in this manner. We really did feel liberated travelling in this fashion without any restrictions and in the company of lots of other youths, discussing quite freely things we had not thought about in the past.

When I returned, I immediately set up a Red Guard HQ in our school, and we named our group 'The East Is Red Commune'. It consisted of about forty students at the start.

T.A. What did you discuss in 'The East Is Red Commune', and what actions did you initiate?

Y.C. The first action we took was to destroy the files of our school because they were used to keep the students under control. The party section, when it was dissatisfied with any student, opened a file on him which could be used against him in the future. For instance, such files could be utilised to prevent dissidents from reaching university and also to harm their job prospects. The files were an important weapon against us. After we had expropriated the files, I read the dossier on myself and could hardly recognise the picture it painted. We published the files, exposing them as a bunch of liars and lick-spittles ...

Yeung Cheng went on to describe the developing chaos, the entry of the PLA and Mao's approval of the order that they crush the movement and restore stability. Politically, the Chinese leader decided to hand over control to the 'capitalist-roaders'. Deng Xiaoping and his cohort took over the party and began to implement new economic policies: the Four Modernisations.

Although the Cultural Revolution was defeated, many good experiences stayed lodged in people's minds, not unlike memories of '68 in Europe. These stories were remembered, even idealised, and produced a striking literature. Two decades later the political leaders of the generation that followed unleashed what became the 1989 uprising. One of them, Wang Chaohua, had denounced school and parental authority as a fourteen-year-old back in 1967.

The idea that students and others could think critically for themselves had never disappeared from the historical consciousness during the intervening period. It was seen as one of the gains of the Cultural Revolution. With economic changes on the way, many intellectuals on campuses and in other professions had been circulating documents and open letters, polite in tone, demanding a Fifth Modernisation: democracy. Some form of accountability, a free press, open debates. And these ideas were also being discussed by the central leadership of the Chinese Communist Party as well as by provincial leaderships.

Confined at first to campuses, the student movement spread to the streets. In April 1989, the death of the popular party leader Hu Yaobang, who was considered supportive of the students, provided a cause to come out. They occupied the Square of Heavenly Peace (Tiananmen). The account of what happened given by Wang Chaohua, written eighteen years later, is still haunting:

> The government resolved the crisis by ordering regular troops, brought in from the provinces, to enforce martial law in Beijing, even at the cost of opening fire on the crowds and rolling tanks over peaceful protesters in order to seize control of Tiananmen Square, the most powerful symbolic space in modern China ... When the crackdown came on the night of 3–4 June, most of the victims were not students, but ordinary citizens. Strangers helped each other without asking questions, and some were killed as they tried to save the lives of others. The world remembers the image of a single man standing alone, in front of a column of advancing tanks. The city was full of such courageous people that night.

As the tanks entered the square in Beijing, I got a call from the current affairs editor at Channel 4. Given the emergency in China, he asked, could *Bandung File* join C4 News that evening, to take charge of the Chinese coverage and explain what was happening and why. We did exactly that. An archive was rapidly assembled. We sent a camera team to record vox pops in China-town in London's Soho. Many were weeping.

I contacted Gregor Benton and others in Leeds, which had the largest community of Chinese students in the country. They packed a large hall. When I got there to ask questions the students were in a state of shock. Some were in tears. 'Our army has fired on our people' was a popular refrain. 'We will never trust our leaders again' was another.

I interviewed Wang Fan-hsi in Professor Benton's house. Fan-Hsi had been an early member of the CPC; after being expelled in 1952 he had fled to Hong Kong and later Macau. He was in a wheelchair, which made it difficult to take him to the student assembly, but he gave his total support to the young people in the Square and, like the students, wondered whether this might be a huge turning point in Chinese politics.

'Restoration?' I asked.

His only response was a single salty tear.

Phone calls came from London. Could I ring the *Guardian* literary desk as soon as possible? Waldemar Januszczak, the literary editor, wondered whether I could write something, but a bit different from my op-eds for the paper. On the train back from Leeds I wrote a Brecht-style intervention that they published the following day and that was rapidly reprinted as a poster-poem by radical Hong Kong students:

> The frightened old man in his hospital bed,
> Haunted by the thought of his own demise
> Has ordered the murder of several thousand citizens.
> He imagines that this might prolong his own life;
> And in a country where there are a billion souls
> A million more or less will soon be forgotten;
> Or so he thinks,

The frightened old man in his hospital bed,
Trying desperately to banish his fear,
As he dreams of the successes of market Stalinism
And the glorious days when TIME magazine made him
Man Of The Year.
Outside the stench of death pervades the Square
As the corpses multiply;
He is still not satisfied.
More hides need to be flayed off
The tortured body of the Revolution.
More heads are needed
For his scrapheap of skulls.
He remembers with affection
The Khmer Rouge.
But still they are not frightened.
Still they keep pouring out.
And still they sing the 'Internationale',
He hears them now,
Their voices hoarse but clear:
'Frightened old man, in your hospital bed
Why are you still alive?
We wish you were dead!
Frightened of going on your own?
All alone?
Is that why we must die?
To accompany your cortege to Hell.
But old man, you are mistaken.
The people you have murdered
Will not go with you
They are travelling in the other direction.
And one of them has left you a message,
Scrawled in his own blood
And this is what it said:
'He won't go alone,
The Politburo of assassins will be at his side
And Li Peng will be at their head.'

Demonstration-sitting Paul and Monica Foot's son, John, in 1968, some years before he started writing books and became a professor. This photograph comes with a short story.

When I left for Britain in 1963 my father's wet nurse, Mrs Jaan Gheba, a firm Believer, who had also looked after me from birth onwards, weighed down my arms with a variety of amulets and whispered: 'Promise me that you will never marry a white woman.' I pointed out that both the amulets and marriage restrictions were, in fact, non-Islamic, but she insisted. Not having any intentions of marrying anyone, I promised.

My parents were visiting London in 1969. My mother liked this photograph very much and took it back with her to Lahore, where it was given pride of place on the mantelpiece in her bedroom. One day she observed Jaan Gheba clutching the photograph and kissing young John. On seeing my mother, she said: 'You can tell me. I don't mind. I know it's Tariq's son.' My mother denied it but to no avail. Jaan Gheba went to her grave convinced that John was my son.

With Mulk Raj Anand, Indian novelist and author of *Untouchable*, at the Helsinki peace conference in 1965 – the last peace conference to be attended by both China and the Soviet Union.

Red Mole cover after return from North Korea, July 1970.

Ho Chi Minh and Trotsky after a Comintern session, Moscow, 1920.

A polite rejection from Ho Chi Minh, 1966.

Richard Ingrams by Willie Rushton

Claud Cockburn (centre) surrounded by fans. Back row: Christopher Logue, Peter Cook, Christopher Booker. Middle Row: John Wells, Claud Cockburn, Richard Ingrams. Bottom row: Gerald Scarfe, Tony Rushton.

How *Private Eye* saw the Gott Affair, see Chapter 15.

Caption by Richard Ingrams. Bores were a much-mocked category in the *Eye* offices. Francis Wheen on the right.

With socialist dissident Boris Kagarlitsky, Moscow, 1988. Kagarlitsky is currently in Putin's prison for opposing the invasion of Ukraine.

Victor Gershfeld, who fought in the defence of Moscow at the age of sixteen, a leading international relations scholar and Gorbachev supporter.

Mikhail Shatrov – the bard of Glasnost.

Poster for *Moscow Gold*. After the RSC debut we took three key scenes to Moscow, where they were performed at the Children's Theatre.

With Howard Brenton in front of the Royal Court, defending Salman Rushdie against his would-be executioners.

Perry Anderson and Fidel Castro at an anti-imperialist conference in Havana, 2004.

Edward and Dorothy Thompson in Wick Episcopi during a shoot of the Bandung/*Rear Window* episode 'A Life of Dissent', 1993.

Part 2: Friends and Comrades

12

Derek Jarman

I first met Derek in 1992, on the edge of a radioactive sea. I was still producing films and documentaries for Bandung Productions, and Channel 4 was still interested in ideas. I suggested four films on philosophy, chamber epics constructed around the lives and ideas of Socrates, Spinoza, Locke and Wittgenstein.

They agreed to the four scripts on the spot, alerting me to the fact that budgets were small and that I could not exceed £200,000 per film. By the time the commissioning editor moved on, we had already filmed *Spinoza* (with Henry Goodman in the title role) and all the other scripts were written and approved. His successor was also enthusiastic but for some reason not keen on Socrates, and so the old Greek fell by the wayside. They asked who was going to direct *Wittgenstein*. I was still thinking. Spinoza had been beautifully filmed by Chris Spencer but the style was naturalistic. Wittgenstein needed to be different, slightly surreal.

On an impulse I rang Derek Jarman in Dungeness. I had never met him before, but had greatly admired two of his films, *Caravaggio* and *Edward II*. After speaking to him that morning I went out and bought a copy of *Modern Nature* from the Owl Bookshop on Kentish Town Road. I read it in the office for the rest of the day and finished it the next morning. To my great surprise I enjoyed it enormously. He was much more than a filmmaker or a gay saint.

I know the date I made the call because Jarman recorded it in his diary: 19 May 1992. His enthusiasm surprised me. He told me that he had always wanted to make a film on the philosopher but had never got beyond the title: 'Loony Ludwig'. I sent him Terry Eagleton's script, which was definitely not 'Loony Ludwig'.

He read it and rang me back the next day. He liked it and could transform it into a film. A week later I drove to Dungeness and found Prospect Cottage by the sea. The garden was, as had been claimed by every visitor, a work of art, but my enjoyment was slightly restrained by the fact that we were overlooked by a giant nuclear reactor.

It was at that first meeting that his illness really hit me. Nobody else I know would deliberately choose to live so close to a nuclear reactor. Derek no longer cared. AIDS would carry him off sooner rather than later and he enjoyed living on the edge. He grinned as he told me that it was so lovely to swim on a deserted beach. 'In the summer I often run out of the cottage naked and straight into the sea. It's radioactive all right. Friends have tested it with Geiger counters. Sometimes the reactor OD's and the whole place lights up. It's really sensational. You know what I mean?' I did.

We spent most of the day discussing Wittgenstein. He knew exactly what he wanted. No Merchant Ivory nonsense. No English Heritage atrocities. Apart from the aesthetics, we simply did not have the money to make that sort of a film. It must be austere, in keeping with the philosophy. Wittgenstein would record his life in front of black drapes straight into the camera. As Derek notes in his diaries, *Smiling in Slow Motion*: 'The visualisation must mirror the work – no competition from objects.' He was sure he could make it work. He asked which of his films I had seen and liked. I named them. He laughed.

After a pause I confessed that *Sebastiane* (the film based around Saint Sebastian that established Jarman as a gay director) had, alas, not succeeded in keeping me awake. It was sweet lemonade, whereas *Caravaggio* and *Edward II* were much stronger stuff.

'Why did you make *Sebastiane?*'

The reply was instant. 'There was only one real reason. To show a hard-on on the screen.'

We discussed production details and it was the only time on that occasion he mentioned his illness. 'You'd better put an extra director in the budget. The insurers will insist on it. His name is

Ken Butler and he shot the best two scenes in Edward II when I had to go into hospital.'

He looked so well that day that it was difficult to imagine him in hospital. As I was about to leave, I suggested to him that with *Wittgenstein* he should shock his fans.

'What do you mean? What do you mean?'

'Not a single bum or willy. Let the audience have withdrawal symptoms.'

He laughed. 'It's a deal. It'll make a change.'

And so it came about that the only sex in Wittgenstein is one fairly chaste kiss on the lips exchanged between Wittgenstein and Johnnie. Today the controllers of our TV channels would insist on maximum exposure.

We talked on the phone over the next few days and then I returned to Dungeness, this time by train. We went, as he records, to have lunch in the pub at Lydd and talked about everything. There was no God, there were no ghosts. He was prepared for blindness and death. It did not frighten him. He said something which has always stayed with me: 'If you want nothing, hope for nothing and fear nothing, you can never be an artist.'

He hated the monarchy and savaged the honours system. He was very angry with Ian McKellen for accepting a knighthood and entering 10 Downing Street. I was amused, but not in the least surprised, to note the following entry in his diary. This is the voice I remember so well:

Vivienne Westwood accepts an OBE, dipsy bitch. The silly season's with us: our punk friends accept their little medals of betrayal, sit in their vacuous salons and destroy the creative – like the wood-worm in my dresser, which I will paint with insecticide tomorrow. I would love to place a man-sized insectocutor, lit with royal-blue, to burn up this clothes-moth and her like.

I had seen a reference in *Modern Nature* (a book which contained Derek's reflections on natural history as well as his own and was so well constructed that a Belgian producer actually staged it in 1993) to a trip he made to Pakistan, and questioned him on it.

It emerged that his father had been a senior air force officer in India and had been seconded to help establish the Pakistan air force after independence in 1947. Throughout the fifties, Derek had spent part of the summer holidays in the Himalayan foothills in northern Pakistan. The air force had a special holiday resort in Kalabagh, two miles north of Nathiagali, where my family spent every summer to escape the heat of the plains.

The thought that a young Jarman had been only a few miles away from where I also spent the summer amused both of us. He had not discovered his sexuality at the time and roared when I told him that homosexuality in that part of Pakistan was very pronounced. The more snobby locals traced it back to the Greek generals and soldiers left behind after Alexander's conquests. 'If you had shown the slightest interest, Derek,' I told him, 'there would have been a queue outside your cottage.'

As we began preparations to film *Wittgenstein* he moved into the Bandung offices in Kentish Town, with Ken Butler at his side. We watched *Spinoza* together. He loved the puppet show I had inserted to explain the history of the period. Scripts were rewritten, actors auditioned. There was always a very special place in his heart for Tilda Swinton. 'If only she'd been a boy,' he would mutter.

Those were joyous days. We were short of money. Ben Gibson at the BFI helped out, but not enough. Derek was enraged. 'They've just given X a million and we can't even get a few hundred thousand.' He asked me to telephone a Japanese producer who was 'always good for £50,000 or so'. Takashi did not let us down. Still, there wasn't enough to make a film that could be shown on the big screen. In order to make it happen, people worked virtually for free.

During filming, we were all amazed. Derek's energy was staggering. He drew on all his reserves and worked twelve-hour days for two whole weeks. Ken Butler was not needed in the end, though his presence cheered us all. Throughout this period, Arif, Bandung's in-house cameraman, recorded Derek at work. There are fifteen hours of tape and I watched some for the first time before writing this to refresh my memory: the zest for life dominates.

After the film was finished, we stayed in touch. I went to the preview of *Blue*, Derek's film tribute to the painter Yves Klein, laughing to myself as sundry celebrities whispered to each other in bewilderment. They couldn't believe that all they would see was a blue screen with a voiceover. Paul Schofield tapped my shoulder from the row behind and whispered, 'Is this all we're going to see. A blue screen?'

The next day, over lunch at a greasy-spoon Chinese in Soho's Lisle Street, we discussed 'The Raft of the Medusa'. Derek wanted to make a film based on the Gericault painting. It would be a film about death. The people on the raft would all be AIDS victims. He wanted me to get a commission. I rang George Faber at the BBC who commissioned it without delay. A script was begun.

We used to meet and talk. A new biography of J. Edgar Hoover had just appeared, which revealed that he had always been a homosexual and a secret transvestite. We laughed and laughed. I suggested that *The Raft* might take a surreal turn. We should have a limo surrounded by G-men entering the studio and Hoover in a stunning red dress steps out and orders his cops to arrest the director. I suggested it might lighten the mood. Derek agreed.

Some months later I got a letter from the St Petersburg Film Festival. They wanted to show *Wittgenstein* and were inviting Derek and me to introduce the film. I informed them that he was dead and I did not wish to travel alone.

13

Ho Chi Minh

In the summer of 1992, when I was filming *Wittgenstein* with Derek Jarman, the Bandung hotline began ringing with urgent calls from US journalists. Both the major networks, CBS and NBC, wanted interviews for that day's news. It was Bill Clinton's first campaign for the presidency. A senior Republican figure had stated that Clinton was a 'traitor' and had been a leader of the anti–Vietnam War campaign in England. Evidently, he had attended a meeting where I spoke and played the role of *tertium gaudens* in the debate. It was with great pleasure that I denied all knowledge of Clinton's involvement. I informed them that there had been a sizeable group of anti-war Americans in Britain at the time. I knew their leaders well and Governor Clinton was not one of them. It was the truth and undoubtedly it was useful for the Democrats.

A fortnight after Clinton's victory in November 1992 I got a visit from a Washington journalist who 'was writing a book' on the period. After a few questions, he confessed that he was a friend of the Clintons, told me that what I had said had been very helpful and asked whether there was anything he could do in return.

In a more frivolous mood, I might have said that a dinner invitation to the White House for my friend Christopher Hitchens would be much appreciated by him. Feeling more practical, I told him about the long-standing restrictions on my entry to the US. Apparently I had been banned as a punishment for burning the US flag outside the London embassy in 1969. I could not remember the occasion, but a consular official had held up a copy of *The*

Times with a front-page photograph, commemorating the event. I responded that many leading US anti-war activists did the same. But from 1969 onwards, universities and others inviting me to the US had to apply for a State Department waiver on the ban.

Macalester College in Minneapolis was the first to do so; they were confident of getting the waiver since Hubert Humphrey, the US vice-president, was one of their alumni. They were right. Others were more hit-and-miss affairs. This time-consuming procedure could be a nuisance, though from the 1980s on, the waivers were usually granted.

Now I suggested to the *clintonista* journalist that this bureaucratic punishment could be called off. He was a bit shocked and promised it would be done. Within a fortnight I got a call from the US visa office asking me to come in and bring my passport along. Assuming this was about a waiver I had applied for a few months earlier, I traipsed over to Grosvenor Square.

A huddle of unfriendly British journos were waiting in line for their visas and made their irritation clear when I was whisked in ahead of them. The US embassy official shook my hand, took my passport and stamped in a ten-year visa, muttering that my name would be removed from the banned list very soon. Feeling slightly triumphant I brandished my new visa at the more unpleasant journos and said, 'If some of your tongues weren't permanently stuck cleaning the State Department's posterior, you might have more luck.' They spluttered as they tried to work out a response. I decided not to wait.

But the memory of those young Americans who had worked with us in the Vietnam Solidarity Campaign in the sixties brought back another, of an ambition still unfulfilled. A few weeks after leaving university, in June 1965, I was lunched by Anthony Blond, a leading London publisher. 'What book would you most like to write?' he asked.

The war in Indochina was beginning to escalate, with more and more US 'advisers' arriving after the defeat of their local stand-ins at the Battle of Ap Bac in January 1963. I had sabotaged my finals at Oxford by bringing Vietnam into every answer. I responded to one economics question that asked us to detail the cheapest form of subsidised transport in the world by noting that US helicopters carrying soldiers into the jungle did not charge at all. There was a slight drawback: they often returned without their passengers.

My answer to the publisher's question, therefore, maintained a certain continuity: 'A biography of Ho Chi Minh.' Did I read French? No. Vietnamese? No. 'Well,' Blond said thoughtfully, handing me the teach yourself French manual he also published, 'you better start a crash course in French straight away and now let's go back to my office and send Ho a telegram'. We did. A month later there was an excited call from Blond. 'Come to the office immediately. A fascinating telegram from Ho.' That he bothered to reply at all had created excitement in the office. The message was unequivocal: 'Thank you for your interest. The thought of you writing my biography never occurred to me. Ho Chi Minh.'

Just as well. It would have been impossible to discover anything new, though I would like to have known where Ho had lodged in Crouch End, a somewhat dilapidated London suburb, while working as a waiter in a local greasy spoon. Was it anywhere near my bedsit where I threw a bash to celebrate the NLF's tenth birthday in 1967? The two North Vietnamese diplomats who attended blew out the candles and we all sang the Internationale and danced the night away. Robin Blackburn was there, along with Richard Gott and Peter Jackson and his wife Christine. Peter was a Labour MP from High Peak. Over a hundred MPs supported the Vietnamese.

What the Vietnamese leader wanted the world to know about him was already in the public domain. Born in 1890 to a middle-ranking mandarin family, Nguyen Tat Thanh – the name he took at the age of ten – grew up in the village of Kim Lien in Nghe An province, a few hundred miles south of Hanoi. His father was a Confucian scholar who worked as an administrator till he lost his job for ordering the flogging of a landlord – the latter's misdemeanour has not been specified. His mother did the hard work in the fields and on the loom to help earn money to feed and educate the children. The Frenchman who taught Ho history, an ardent Jacobin, was pleased to observe his pupil's radicalisation. Ho became a nationalist who, like many of his generation, wanted to free his country from French domination, if necessary by the Robespierrean combination of virtue and terror.

I didn't give up on making notes for the biography. In 1911, Ho left for Marseille, leaving behind a landlord's daughter with whom he had fallen in love. His aim was to broaden his mind and, most importantly, to meet other Vietnamese nationalist students already in France. He did not linger in the south, moving rapidly to Paris and later London. 'It doesn't matter where you come from or where you are,' he told an American journalist in 1946, 'the important thing is to know where you're going.' He had no doubts: he was going to liberate his country by recruiting others to the noble cause. He got involved with the French Socialist Party, some of whose leaders were staunch opponents of French colonialism.

One of them, Marcel Cachin, advised him to go to Versailles, where the peace conference was taking place, and argue the case for Vietnamese self-rule. One of Woodrow Wilson's aides met him briefly, but self-determination was a privilege restricted to Europeans (though not Germans). He looks awkward in the photograph taken at Versailles: a sleek, well-dressed young man who found it difficult to manage the obligatory smile.

The rebuff radicalised him further. At the Socialist Party Congress in Tours in 1920, Ho backed the pro-Bolshevik faction that created the French Communist Party, thus becoming a founder member. Officially, he first visited Moscow in 1923, not long before Lenin died, but a photograph with Trotsky published in the 2003 biography by Pierre Brocheux suggests he was there in 1921.

I had always admired the poetry of Osip Mandelstam, but it was only when I was sent a copy of his collected prose that I discovered he had met Ho. In December 1923, young Mandelstam had been sent by the Soviet weekly *Ogonyok* (The Flame) to interview Nguyen Ai Quoc. In Moscow, the poet was impressed by the young revolutionary. And appalled to learn how the

French were exploiting the peasants and making alcohol obligatory in Cochin China:

> Nguyen Ai Quoc pronounces the word 'civilization' with disgust. He has travelled throughout most of the colonial world, he has been in northern and central Africa, and he has seen enough. He often uses the word 'brothers' in conversation. By 'brothers' he means Negroes, Chinese, Indians and Arabs … I could vividly picture in my mind how the gentle people with their love of tact and moderation and their hatred for excess had been forced to drink … European civilization operates with bayonets and liquor, concealing them beneath the Catholic missionary's *soutane*. Nguyen Ai Quoc breathes culture, not European culture, but perhaps the culture of the future.

On his part Ho Chi Minh informs the poet:

> Right now, in Paris there is a group of comrades from the French colonies – five or six men from Cochin China, Sudan, Madagascar, Haiti – publishing a little magazine, the *Pariah*, dedicated to the struggle against French colonial policy. It's a very small magazine. Instead of receiving honoraria, the staff members pay for the publication of each issue out of their own pockets. A bamboo cane with an appeal scratched on it was circulated surreptitiously among the villages. It was replanted in each village and a secret compact was made. It cost the Annamese dearly – there were executions, hundreds of heads fell.

In London, Ho learned English and worked as a waiter, first in the greasy spoon, then in a posh West End restaurant. A plaque in Piccadilly suggests that he was apprenticed as a sous-chef to Escoffier at the Carlton Hotel. In *State and Revolution*, Lenin had written that the final goal of communism was the 'withering away' of all oppressive structures – a time when, as an interpreter of the book suggested, a cook could run the state. Perhaps Ho had that in mind. At the end of his life Lenin said that Stalin should be removed as general secretary: 'This cook', he said, 'will prepare only peppery dishes.' (Of course, the more peppery a dish, the more popular it would be in Indochina and most of Asia. A young waitress at the Reunification Hotel in Hanoi giggled as I ate all the chillies from a decorative plant on the dining table in 1966. Despite this display of Punjabi manhood, I wasn't allowed to accompany her to the rooftop later to fire a few salvoes from the anti-aircraft guns at the long-distance bombers. The guests were firmly told to stay in the air-raid shelter.)

The young Ho Chi Minh soon gave up his culinary endeavours and became a full-time revolutionary working for the Communist International. He was despatched to China to link up with Vietnamese exiles there and organise the Indochinese Communist Party, a task he performed well. His travels through China in the late 1920s, as the civil war began, and the friendships he established with Chinese communist leaders, would have made fascinating memoir material. No such luck: only photographs survive. Hong Kong was a crucial base of operations for Vietnamese and Chinese revolutionaries, and here Ho fell in love again. In October 1926 he married Tang Tuyet Minh, a Chinese communist from a Catholic family.

Ho was condemned to death in absentia by a colonial Vietnamese court in 1930 and went underground. The following year he was arrested by the British in Hong Kong and deported two years later. He never saw Tang again: after the Vietnamese revolution in 1945 he was portrayed as the father of the nation who had given up all personal involvement for the sake of the revolution. All their attempts to contact each other were rebuffed by the Politburos of both countries. Tang died in 1991.

Most biographies of Ho mention his personal life only in passing. This might seem refreshing, but in Ho's case the personal is tied to the political. The Vietnamese novelist Duong Thu Huong spent fifteen years researching one story, and a gruesome tale it turns out to be. Her writing is banned in her native country because of her strong criticisms of the present regime. She told me she didn't care since millions read her books, interviews and essays online. We share a publisher in France, Sabine Wespieser, who introduced us a long time ago. Her novel *The Zenith* (2009), Duong told me, has no historical account that is not true. And yes, it is a *roman à clef*.

The Zenith interweaves four related stories, but the heart of the novel is a fictionalised account of Ho Chi Minh's tragic and hidden affair with a much younger woman in the 1950s. Duong portrays Ho as a good man surrounded by evil subordinates. There is a riveting account of a Politburo attempt to kill him when he is returning from a visit to China, but instead of crashing the plane into a lake the pilot lands it safely. Duong describes the leader looking sadly at the pilots and his guards, knowing full well that they won't have much longer to live.

Duong's own political credentials are impeccable: she fought in the war against the United States (her father was a veteran of the anti-French resistance), and chronicled Deng Xiaoping's 1979 war on her country (fought largely to demonstrate China's willingness to kowtow to Washington and to punish Hanoi for having removed Pol Pot from power). She was expelled from the Communist Party for writing a series of devastating novels depicting life from below during the war and giving a scornful account of postwar disillusion, and was later imprisoned before going into exile in Paris. She wrote about the struggles of ordinary people, and her work was hugely popular.

In *Beyond Illusions* (1987), we see how bureaucracy takes over everyday life. An intelligent and independent journalist is sucked into the machine. His wife leaves him in disgust. She has an affair with a composer, then realises that he, too, has been compromised by the system. Many communist veterans began to despise a life that had seemed necessary during the war but after the victory was more alienating than anything else. People couldn't decide anything for themselves. Petty bureaucrats made life difficult in the villages and murderous at a higher political level. Vietnam had won the war, but lost the peace.

Novel without a Name (1991), an account of the last phase of the war against the US, is rightly regarded as a masterpiece in Vietnam. In it, Duong, dispensing with official notions of heroism, writes instead of a generation that had no option but to

resist the occupation, young men and women physically toughened by the experience, who sacrificed a great deal and hoped
for a better life after the war. But their hopes were betrayed and
disillusion soon set in.

The affair described in *The Zenith* takes place just before
the 1954 Viet Minh victory over the French. In 1945 the Vietnamese resistance, led by the communists and with Ho at its
head, declared the country an independent republic. The French,
backed by the British and Americans, refused to surrender the
colony. The Viet Minh retreated to the countryside and waged
an effective guerrilla war culminating in the siege and defeat of
the French garrison at Dien Bien Phu in 1954. It was during this
period that Ho met Miss Xuan, a young woman from the Tay
ethnic minority in the mountains. He was in his early sixties;
she was nineteen. They quickly had two children, a boy and a
girl, and he promised to marry her, but his status meant that
Politburo permission had to be sought. The men who had fought
under him for years, many of them openly polygamous, told him
that the revolution came before all personal considerations. His
comrades ordered him not to marry:

> Immediately Sau [Le Duan] turned around and retorted strongly:
> 'We need not be shy; we don't need to weigh our words. We face the
> life and death of the revolution ... we must protect its interests at
> all costs ... The elderly father of the nation is the roof that shelters
> the people. For years now, people have absorbed this metaphor. The
> president needs to remind Miss Xuan about this point, if she contin-
> ues to demand to be officially recognised.' Thuan [Prime Minister
> Pham Van Dong] intervened, lifting his arm and continuing in a
> firm manner as if to have the last word: 'I believe that all of us are of
> one mind: the matter of recognising Miss Xuan cannot be done. We
> cannot even think about it. I hope that, in a spirit of high responsi-
> bility before the whole nation, the president accepts this decision.'

Ho accepted the unanimous decision. Isn't the Party always
right? In return, he was promised that Miss Xuan and the children would be 'treated properly, just as long as they willingly live

out of sight, behind the revolution'. Duong imagines her hero's response as he watches the Politburo, their 'plastic faces all puffed up, twisted', and 'a high wall just collapsed inside his heart. His soul emptied; his brain paralysed ... a sentence of death ... a realisation of his powerlessness.'

In the months that followed someone decided that separation was not enough. All traces must be removed. Miss Xuan and her two children were living in modest government quarters in Hanoi while Ho was recuperating from various ailments elsewhere. The thuggish minister of the interior, Tran Quoc Hoan – a rootless former criminal and protégé of Le Duan, whom he had first met in a Southern prison, and the most despised and feared member of the Politburo – decided (or was he instructed?) to kill Miss Xuan and her sister. Duong writes that Tran would regularly go to Miss Xuan's apartment and rape her, pressing her to marry him and leave the 'old man' alone. What is beyond dispute is that Tran murdered the two women. In the novel Xuan's brother-in-law receives the news of the murders while serving at the front. His friend writes:

Dear brother,

There is something you have surely guessed but didn't know for certain. Miss Xuan and Miss Dong were both killed in the year of the rooster (1957), their skulls smashed with a wooden mallet. The body of Miss Xuan was thrown on the side of a road outside Hanoi, making it appear that a car had hit her, pretending it was a traffic accident; and Miss Dong was thrown under the bridge across Khe Lan, on the road to That Khe.

Ho died in 1969, a broken-hearted old man. Duong portrays him grappling in his head with the contradictions of his life. (Some of her reconstructions work better than others. She idealises him far too much – he was after all a hardened veteran of the Comintern.)

After the war, Miss Xuan's brother-in-law, a decorated military officer, wrote to the then party leader, Le Duc Tho, to demand an investigation, threatening to sue the Party for killing his wife and sister-in-law. There was no response. The children were not harmed. The boy was adopted by Vu Ky, Ho's old friend and personal secretary when he became president in 1954. The girl was farmed out to a family in the countryside. The first job the son, Tung, was given was as doorman of the Ho Chi Minh museum in Hanoi. I wonder which joker on the Politburo thought that one up. There he remained till his half-brother, Nong Duc Manh, the son Ho had with his housekeeper, helped him join the army. Nong, who led the party from 2001 to 2011, has publicly denied that Ho is his father, but all the circumstantial evidence suggests otherwise. Tung's sister works for the public broadcasting system.

Duong is a gifted storyteller, and her earlier novels were well translated by Nina McPherson with Vietnamese help. *The Zenith* suffers by comparison. McPherson has been replaced with three translators (which of them thought it sensible to describe a Vietnamese woman as having a 'peaches and cream complexion'?). The finished work doesn't appear to have been properly edited, which is a pity given that the story itself is so powerful. But it's hard for a translator to damage Duong's descriptions of food.

In *Novel without a Name* the starved soldiers can't believe their luck when in the depths of the jungle they are served 'sautéed papayas and wild chillies marinated in shrimp sauce on warm rice'. Less enticing, on paper at least, is a pig's vagina stuffed with chillies, dipped in egg powder and fried. In *Beyond Illusions*, the journalist who has sold his soul tries to win his wife back via her stomach. Instead of writing a hack piece, 'Nguyen went to Dong Xuan Market and bought a crab to make fried *nem* spring rolls and sautéed crab with vermicelli.' The attempt is unsuccessful. His wife visits a soup vendor in Ly Quoc Su Street whose hot snail soup is the best in town: 'the rice noodles were always pearly white and the snails deliciously plump. Their famous chillies fried in oil and vinegar drew Hanoi women like a magnet.'

A painter in the same book is fed up but will not leave for Canada because he enjoys 'snake liqueur and grilled cobra' far too much. And in *The Zenith*, Ho remembers a Vietnamese New

Year's Day in a war zone near the Chinese border when there was a cooking competition. A dish of 'congealed duck's blood with pig intestines' was the winner. Perhaps the soldier cooks and their comrades should have been allowed to run the state.

The short-lived experiment *Doi Moi*, the political and economic reforms that followed the Party Congress in 1986, suggests they couldn't have been any worse than the incumbents. Delegates (many of them war veterans) stood up one after the other and denounced the corrupt generals who had looted the South and built their own fortunes. Three generals were removed from the Politburo. The citizens of Hanoi rejoiced, hoping that this might lead to the democratisation of the country. But the security forces denounced 'excessive democracy' and brought the process to an end. The Chinese road to state-sponsored capitalism was the alternative they chose: corruption enveloped the entire country and the dollar became a parallel currency. Many asked why the war had been fought, given what followed.

And Ho? In his three testaments (stolen and kept in the private safe of the man who had killed his lover) Ho had insisted that his body be cremated and his ashes scattered. He did not want to be mummified. The party he had led for forty years ignored his wishes. His testament is still censored, so the Vietnamese people cannot read about his hostility to the idea of the grotesque mausoleum in Ba Dinh Square where his embalmed remains are now on display.

14

At M-K's

Arranged marriages are hardly a novelty in any culture. They work or fail just like any marriage. It was not until early 1993, however, that I received a proposal for an arranged friendship. On this occasion Mary-Kay Wilmers rang, suggesting lunch. I had no idea what she wanted. A date was fixed. I selected a venue. We met.

I had met her at the odd party in the sixties. The only conversation we had back then was when she, an editor at Faber, invited me to lunch. A well-typed letter arrived in which she suggested date, time and location – the Trattoria Terrazza in Soho. The reason for this 1967 meeting was to discuss a book. 'I thought you might be interested in writing a novel and we could discuss the possibility.' I was taken aback by the very thought. Writing fiction had never entered my mind. She put it there. It gestated for several decades.

Now, a quarter of a century later, in 1993, it was different. M-K wanted to discuss the *London Review of Books* and related matters. Given my own involvement in editing left-wing magazines and later writing regularly for *Time Out* and the *Guardian*, I only had time in those days to read the *New Statesman* and the *TLS*. I was not hugely attracted to either Leavisite or deconstructionist notions of English literature. Francis Mulhern and Terry Eagleton were stronger influences. When in October 1979 Bob Silver's *New York Review of Books* incubated and launched the *LRB* in its pouch, I rarely read it. I started reading it regularly during the Falklands/Malvinas War that, to its credit, it opposed.

Karl Miller, the founding editor of the *LRB*, was tough-minded but also generous. He was flanked by M-K and Susannah Clapp, both of whom had worked with him at the *Listener*. Strong spirits were brought in to review books: Angela Carter and Lorna Sage were in my top ten, inimitable and unmissable. They always had something to say, avoided deceit, did not conceive of writing as a milepost to career promotion, never sought to please, and did not name-drop or gush over celebrities. Would Karl have permitted such tabloid priorities? I doubt it.

Leaving the paper's own political proclivities aside (it was centre-social-democratic) it had promised in its first and last statement of intent to be democratic, permit debate and encourage different voices. The *Guardian* already did this, but the new paper had reams of space for more. What they wanted was well-written review essays and a style that was all their own. This included the cover, leaning on the watercolours created by Peter Campbell. It gave the *LRB* an attractive quality that all the other papers and weeklies in Britain lacked.

It was Karl who initially commissioned E.P. Thompson, Edward Said and Paul Foot to write in the paper. They continued to do so until they dropped dead. He was less accommodating to Harold Pinter, who was always far more radical than his plays suggested. For example, in 1991 he had been enraged by the Gulf War, especially by the 'turkey-shoot' on the Basra Road where a retreating Iraqi army had been massacred by US bombers. Tony Harrison's equally vicious attack had been published across a page in the *Guardian*. Harrison read it aloud for a 1991 programme I edited for Channel 4, *Reflections on the New World Order* (the poem is now on the *LRB* blogsite).

In contrast, Pinter's poetic rage was rejected by every paper and magazine. He had sent it to the *New Left Review* as well, but we did not publish poetry. Had *Black Dwarf* still been in existence, I later said to him, it would have been a poster-cover. A quizzical smile was the only response. He got over it.

The poem was not to everyone's taste.

American Football
Hallelujah!
It works.
We blew the shit out of them.

We blew the shit right back up their own ass
And out their fucking ears.

It works.
We blew the shit out of them.
They suffocated in their own shit!

Hallelujah.
Praise the Lord for all good things.

We blew them into fucking shit.
They are eating it.

Praise the Lord for all good things.

We blew their balls into shards of dust,
Into shards of fucking dust.

We did it.

Now I want you to come over and kiss me
on the mouth.

As an editor Karl was not without his defects, and it was this that brought about his fall. He could be charming, witty, generous but also a rude, bad-tempered, arrogant bully. Even his close friends found this difficult to deny. Reading the *LRB* was usually a pleasure, but working with him was not. His tantrums hit his colleagues like thunderbolts and the target of his attacks could often be M-K. He would walk out of the office in a rage and wait till a pleading voice rang to get him back from his other office at UCL where he was a professor.

The inevitable finally happened in 1992. There had recently been a slough of books attacking feminism, written by slightly creepy ageing men. One of these contained an unpleasant and libellous denunciation of M-K. She was in the process of consulting a lawyer. Miller noticed the book lying on the table and inquired aggressively why it had not been sent out for review as he had instructed. No debate; simply an assertion of power. As it became obvious that most people were against publishing a review of yet another third-rate work of misogyny, a row developed.

The defiance surprised the editor. Gripped by a bout of office rage he flung the proofs on the table and walked out: 'You know where to find me if you need me to look at the proofs.' Supported, on this occasion, by some of her closest colleagues – John Lanchester, Jean McNicol, Andrew O'Hagan – M-K decided they did not need him. And that was how it ended. Sadly, Susannah Clapp, who I had met often at Angela Carter's or Carmen Callil's tea parties, and who I liked, also left. Karl was a comrade-in-arms and she was expressing her solidarity. What I am recounting is M-K's version, but many close to Karl have confirmed the essential details. The atmosphere in the office was often terrible, but after Karl's departure M-K became the new editor and began to make changes.

Karl was taken aback at not being asked to resume the editor's chair. It is never a good idea to imagine that you are indispensable. Had he been offered the *TLS* or a new magazine he might have taken a few contributors with him (Frank Kermode and Neal Ascherson come to mind), but no such luck. Only one major contributor stopped writing altogether for the *LRB*, Karl's brother-in-law, Dr Jonathan Miller.

When, at the thirtieth anniversary party, M-K asked me to say a few words, I started by proposing a toast to the founding editor, Karl Miller. Shock and horror, but most people joined me. Ascherson was the most thrilled and came up to thank me. I pointed out that it would be good if Karl and Susannah mended the breach and started writing for the *LRB* again.

On a train to Edinburgh for the Bookfest some months later I ran into Susannah. We sat next to each other and chatted for the whole journey, mostly about the *LRB*. 'If I were still there,' she said, 'I would encourage you to write about literature and other things as well as politics.' I raised the question of her writing for the paper again. 'It's so grand now.' When I pushed, she said 'Karl might, but I never will.' In the event both did. The feud was finally over.

Reports also began to infiltrate back to the effect that Perry Anderson was 'helping out'. This came home to me at a dinner party at the philosopher Ted Honderich's pad opposite Keats's house in Hampstead. Heated debates were taking place on the subject of the Yugoslav civil war. Karl was present, as were Michael and Jill Foot, together with the host and his new lady-friend, and Susan and me.

It was too small a party to ignore anyone. Ted set the tone by denouncing the war and forced a debate by turning to me first. I said it was a civil war, encouraged by the German state to break up Yugoslavia as their greedy eyes devoured central Europe. Michael muttered: 'Outrageous'.

Our host turned to another guest. 'What do you think of all this, Karl?'

Karl didn't bother to reply. The question was repeated verbatim. Karl said it was 'an interesting debate' and left it at that. As the party began to wind down, he took me aside.

'How well do you know Perry Anderson?'

'We've been colleagues and friends for decades. Of course I know him well.'

'Obviously I know his work, but how would you describe his defining quality?'

'A very brilliant editor. Second to none.'

We exchanged smiles.

M-K felt she needed a *consiglieri* outside the paper. She did not feel that anyone could replace Karl just like that, so she decided to approach a university contemporary who had started writing for the *Review* under Karl – Perry Anderson. I knew that Perry was offering advice when asked, but till M-K told me I had not realised the scale of the aid being provided. He suggested pieces that should be commissioned and gave detailed advice on how texts could be improved and strengthened regardless of their politics. I was familiar with Perry's editing style from the *NLR* and Verso, but the time he was spending on the *LRB* astonished me. She appreciated it much more than I did, thinking of the needs of our own mag and the publishing house. Her nickname for him was appropriate: '*der uber editor*' or simply 'the Uber', as in 'Is the Uber in London or LA at the moment?'

Back to our arranged meeting. Finally coming to the point, M-K said: 'Given the role [PA] plays in helping the paper, I find it odd that I don't know anyone else from his circle. It might be nice if we met regularly?'

'Regularly or clandestinely?'

She laughed. I understood her problem. She was surrounded by swarms of people including some if not all her colleagues who saw most things in a different light from Perry and the *NLR*. These were, after all, not favourable times for a left intelligentsia in decline throughout the world. Perry's ideas across a wide range of problems, political and cultural, and even his humour, could not be appreciated without equipment of a different sort that was rapidly going out of fashion.

This included his polite yet firm way of conversing, and not conversing, often by asking other people questions to avoid saying anything himself. I was sharing a TV panel discussion with Francis Fukuyama on one occasion. Afterwards he asked after Perry. They had met for lunch in LA after Perry had reviewed *The End of History*, but without stiffening the tone. 'Professor Anderson, a Marxist, understood the book perfectly and I appreciated his criticisms. At lunch he deluged me with questions of every sort. My background, my formation, Japan, etc. They were interesting questions, but it was not till lunch was over that I realised he had not given me a chance to ask him anything. Is this normal for him?'

M-K and I became friends quickly, proving that arranged friendships can be more successful than casual encounters. There were few matters, whether personal, political or cultural, that we did not or do not discuss.

M-K's attitudes to the left and to feminism were not too difficult to decipher. As far as the left was concerned her own view is best summarised in her own words: 'Neither communist nor anticommunist, captivated by the left but never quite of the left ...'

This was spotted early on, as was told to me by Dorothy Thompson. Dotty was a tough and determined person. While interviewing candidates for a new secretary for the *NLR* office in 1961, she was looking for someone like her younger self who could make sure there was discipline and hygiene and a sense of order. She gave short shrift to one of the applicants, who had been recommended by Denis Butt, a member of the editorial committee. His over-the-top praise did not tally, in Dorothy's eyes, with the young person sitting in front of her. 'And your name is ... ?'

'Mary Wilmers.'

Dorothy looked her up and down. 'Your CV is a bit on the skimpy side.'

'Oh. I forgot to put in that I'm fluent in Russian.'

The response was a sarcastic laugh. 'We're not looking for a teacher!'

A few more desultory exchanges of this sort sealed Miss Wilmers' fate. 'I don't think you're what we need.'

Decades later, a year after Edward passed away, the two women met at an *NLR* summer party at our house. I asked Dorothy whether she regretted not having employed Mary-Kay.

'Not at all,' she laughed. 'I think she's found her niche.'

Alan Bennett had once taken her to a Downing Street reception when a fellow Yorkshireman was prime minister. She liked Wilson, who remained her favourite Labour leader of all time. This left a taste for the dead-centre, even after its more gifted journalists, MPs and ministers were long gone. Benn and Corbyn were not popular in the *LRB*. There was a semi-silence on Blair till the Iraq War except for one very strong piece by Seumas Milne, who never repeated the performance.

'Never quite of the left' would become, more or less, the philosophy of the paper, except on one issue: British social-democratic politics. M-K once proudly read out a description of the *LRB* in some daily or the other as being 'left-of-centre'. She liked that.

I disagreed: 'I think "dead-centre" would be more accurate. Since the post-Thatcher centre is permanently shifting rightwards.'

Her response was to stick out her tongue.

Eventually, in the late nineties, M-K asked me to write for her paper more than once, but I was still caught up in too much television work. The first article I wrote was a Diary piece after a trip to Pakistan in 1999. I reported that the most popular name for newly born boy-babies in Pakistan that year was Osama.

Sunday night dinner together became a ritual for decades. Table-talk varied. There were relaxed evenings during the early years when it was just us or Jenny Diski or Andrew O'Hagan (a retailer of high-class Tory gossip) or Jeremy Harding, not to mention John Sturrock, who I really liked.

Perry had warned me that M-K had an instinctive dislike of couples, but not in this case, or at least not most of the time. She liked Susan as well and despite political differences that occasionally unbalanced the conversational rules of the kitchen table, ties of friendship were never torn asunder. Soon after the invasion of Iraq Susan had published a signed *NLR* editorial 'Vichy on the Tigris' defending the idea of resistance. The following weekend, as we entered the kitchen, M-K greeted her warmly: 'Ah. Here's Rosa Luxemburg. I thought you would be in khakis.'

M-K had just started researching a book on her family, concentrating on her three remarkable Eitingon great-uncles: Leonid, Motty and Max. The first was a Bolshevik, later charged by Stalin with organising the assassination of Trotsky, which he did using Ramon Mercader as the killer. The second was a furrier whose trade links with the Soviet fur import organisation made him a multimillionaire with offices in New York at a time when it was not easy to become one. And the last was a psychoanalyst, a friend and funder of Freud and, like his two siblings, also a product of the 1917 revolution.

One Sunday evening, M-K had over a few old Russians who she had got to know while researching the book. One of them was Zoya Zarubina. She had worked with Leonid Eitingon and there was little she did not know about the inner workings of the NKVD. She had, for a brief period, also been Beria's girl-friend. This did startle me. Her description of when she first met Stalin's notorious police chief was diverting, painting a picture of a twenty-something young woman dressed in a glistening white blouse and regulation skirt standing on a staircase at HQ. I thought she was a bit old for Beria, whose penchant for thirteen-to-fifteen-year-olds was well known, but my lack of Russian prevented me from asking the babushka about that and related questions such as 'Was he fun in bed?'

15

Richard Gott and the *Guardian*

Early, too early, on a December morning in 1994, I was woken by a phone call. It was Richard Gott. 'Comrade,' he said in distraught tones, 'have you seen the *Spectator*?'

I hadn't.

'They've accused me of being a KGB agent.'

I jumped out of bed and began to get dressed, Susan muttering 'Why are they ringing so early?' To Richard I said: 'I'm going to the Bandung offices. Just stay calm. And a lawyer's letter should be despatched to Dominic Lawson [the *Spectator* editor] today! I'll read the piece asap. What are your movements?'

'I'm going into the offices to see Preston [the *Guardian* editor].'

'Do not agree to anything till we've spoken.'

As I gulped down my coffee, I told Susan what was happening.

'I know it's one of your jokes. Richard a KGB agent! Very weak. I'm not that gullible. You're usually better than this...'

I left the house without further argument. Richard was one of my oldest friends in this country. As I've described in *Street Fighting Years*, our relationship went back to the mid-'60s, when Richard ran as a radical anti-war candidate against Wilson's Labour Party. The *Guardian*'s Latin America correspondent in the '60s and '70s, he became features editor in 1981, then the literary editor, a mainstay of the paper.

On my way to the *Bandung File* office I picked up the *Spectator*. Rubbish. Based on the memoirs of a Russian double-agent, trying to earn a crust from Murdoch's papers (in this case *The Sunday Times* bought the serialisation rights) by peddling sensationalism. I rang John Gittings (NUJ rep at the *Guardian*) and also spoke at length with Seumas Milne and others on the paper. Richard was still ensconced in Peter Preston's office. They had all told him not to do anything without consulting the union, which should deal with all matters related to employment. We waited. Finally, Richard rang: 'I've resigned.'

I shouted at him, as did his colleagues. He had not been asked to resign, he just offered to, as he felt that he should have told his editor that he was flying to Cyprus to meet the KGB guy in charge of Latin America, purely for purposes of getting information. The agent was banned from entering Britain, and the only way to meet him was to accept a ticket to Cyprus. Richard should have told Preston, but since he had informed the paper's go-to person connected to MI5, what was the big deal? To Richard's surprise, Preston accepted his resignation with immediate effect. No attempt to set up an internal inquiry. Richard had shot himself in the foot by this stupid gesture and his dear friend and editor amputated it without mercy.

I insisted, as did Seumas, that he should sue the *Spectator*. Once again, he refused on the perfectly honourable, but apolitical, grounds that journalists should not sue each other. Our opinion was that the magazine might have to close, since the evidence did not exist.

Without a job, his reputation was in tatters. His friends being both angry with him but also hugely sympathetic, we decided we should act in concert. I suggested that I be allowed to see if some of those who had been commissioned by Richard to write articles for the *Guardian* might sign a letter to the paper. On my list were Ian Gilmour, Alan Clark and Enoch Powell from the Tory side; Martin Gilbert, Ben Pimlott and Dorothy Wedderburn from establishment Labour and Tony Benn from the Labour Left. Eric Hobsbawm was annoyed by what had happened and asked me after I'd read out the letter to him: 'Are you signing it?' I told him I thought that it was best signed by mainstream folk. 'Very good thinking,' said Eric, 'I'll follow you in that...'

The draft letter, containing the most moderate sentences I've ever written, read as follows:

We have read with dismay the news of Richard Gott's resignation from the *Guardian*. We have known Richard Gott over a number of years and recognise him as an independent and creative editor who always encouraged pluralism across the political spectrum.

Gott's resignation should not be regarded as an admission of guilt, rather a quixotic display of loyalty to his paper and his editor, at a time when both are under attack from other sources. We hope that Gott's loyalty will be reciprocated and urge the *Guardian* to continue to grant full scope to his obvious talents.

Here's what happened after I'd read the draft to Enoch Powell and Alan Clark. Powell: 'I won't sign. If you play with fire, you get burnt.' It could have been a description of his own career. Alan Clark got cross with me: 'I'm really surprised you've left out all reference to the CIA. That bastard on the *FT* [he named him] has been working for the Americans for ages. Fleet Street is full of US agents. C'mon Tariq. Get your bloody act together.'

Back to the drawing board, I typed an additional paragraph and inserted it between the existing two:

The notion that he was a 'KGB agent of influence' is just as absurd as the equivalent charge of being a CIA agent which could, on exactly the same basis, be levelled at so many other journalists of distinction in the broadsheet press.

I sent a messenger to get the signatures. I got two phone calls. The first from Ian Gilmour asking why I'd added the extra para. 'Pressure from Alan Clark'. A chuckle from Ian: 'He's so contrarian.' The other was from Martin Gilbert, a close friend of Richard's from university days. They'd both written a book together on appeasement. Martin: 'Tariq, I don't know why you decided to add that para. Now I can't sign it.' And that was that. All the others signed. The final version was published on 12 December 1994.

Elated by its success, the *Spectator* next had a go at Fred Halliday, Professor of International Relations at the LSE. He, sensibly, warned them of legal action and they gave him three pages to state his case. In a rash mood, the jokers at *The Sunday Times*, using the same tainted source, accused Michael Foot, the former Labour leader, a member of Callaghan's Labour Cabinet and a staunch supporter of Thatcher on the Falklands War, of having been a KGB 'agent of influence'. This backfired dramatically. Most papers rushed to Foot's defence. He sued and obtained damages from Rupert Murdoch. Many felt that Richard Gott should be exonerated as well and at least given a column. Foot had made clear that Thatcher had offered to let him see the intelligence reports on the Falklands, but that he had declined.

Richard could not compete on this level! He would recover, however, and produce three very good books, on Chávez, Cuba and the British Empire. That December, though, he told me that what was depressing him the most was spending Christmas with his wife Vivien's posh family in Northamptonshire. Vivien herself was very radical, as was her sister, but the whole charade created some tension. When they got back home he said it hadn't been too bad and that the very cheery vicar collecting money after midnight mass had whispered: 'We accept rubles too.'

When I arrived in the UK in 1963, the *Guardian* was still a serious liberal newspaper uncomfortably straddling the establishment and the soft-left intelligentsia. Every self-respecting capitalist democracy has one such paper. Ours was never as good as *Le Monde* in Paris or the *Süddeutsche Zeitung*, but it was much better than the Roman *Repubblica* and the Turkish *Cumhuriyet*. And yet ... there was a marked shift in the late eighties. The paper moved bodily along the spectrum in tow to the Thatcherite dynamic. The advertising and marketing men took control. Increasingly there was a collision between the desire of the *Guardian* grandees to be accepted and respected by the establishment and the needs of important chunks of the paper's readership.

These contradictions were played out painfully in the behaviour and personality of the man who edited the *Guardian* between 1975 and 1995: Peter Preston.

An East Midlands boy, crippled by polio and a shyness so

overwhelming that it might have been considered an automatic disqualification for the job, Preston was the archetypal out-sider. He yearned to be an insider, but knew he never would be. A cynical, anti-collectivist radical by instinct, he disliked the English upper classes and yet wanted them to take him seriously. Hardly surprising, then, that he had a soft spot for Thatcher.

The first ten years of Preston's ascendancy went well for the *Guardian*. It cornered the local government and teaching markets, it successfully wooed the social workers and, feeding off the revulsion among the liberal intelligentsia against the early years of Thatcherism, it doubled its circulation. The various strands of the paper's readership were catered for by an odd melange of writers and editors. On the left there was the eccen-tric figure of Richard Gott, whose political mischief-making was littered across the features pages. Victoria Brittain gave no quarter to Eurocentrism or sub-colonial nostalgia on her Third World page. Liz Forgan ran a paradigmatic women's page and Chris MacLean's letters page resembled a picket line, causing offence internally to the grandees and externally to the rest of Fleet Street. W.L. Webb produced a highbrow literary page that was unmatched. The late James Cameron provided a regular column: his was the only voice permitted to defend CND on a regular basis in the whole of Fleet Street. Not long afterwards Steve Bell made his appearance, winning over young readers who might otherwise have never picked the paper up.

In another part of the forest, as Peter Preston might say, were the *Guardian's* very own Gang of Four. Chris Huhne (econom-ics correspondent), Malcolm Dean (social affairs leader writer), columnist Peter Jenkins and his wife, prolix Polly Toynbee. With the Labour right split in 1981, all four stood as SDP candidates. Despite the Gang's presence, the vast majority of journalists remained Labour supporters, a fact reflected in the overall cover-age of the paper. Gott was a Bennite, Ian Aitken supported the Foot–Kinnock axis, younger journalists were much influenced by Ken Livingstone's refreshing populism.

The event which caused the greatest internal confusion and disorientation was the launch of the *Independent* in 1986. For

Preston, understandably, it became an absolute obsession. He realised that the new newspaper might appeal to a section of *Guardian* readers, but instead of meeting the challenge head-on and fighting the *Independent* with improvements in the quality of writing, analysis and news coverage, Preston decided to move the *Guardian* downmarket. The newspaper he had always admired from afar was the *Daily Mail*, a middle-brow, ideologically coherent tabloid, which helped the Conservative Party to communicate with its grassroots supporters and activists.

Preston could appeal to no such base, but he caved in to the empty cant of the enterprise culture. In 1988, he hit back with a new-look *Guardian*. The paper's radical redesign was, unsurprisingly, popular with advertisers. They were, after all, given pride of place in the new *Guardian*. The paper's journalists loathed the disabling 'grid' system and many readers were dismayed. But the more serious changes concerned the content. Preston pushed through a shift towards a consumerist, leisure-oriented, 'people-centred' apoliticism born of the Thatcher boom years. His reading of the *Independent*'s success was that it was in part a reaction to the *Guardian*'s lefty image. He decided that it was time for a change.

Bill Webb was removed as literary editor and replaced by the paper's art critic, Waldemar Januszczak. In keeping with the times, his first action on changing desks was to dump Webb's files in the dustbin. Valuable correspondence over twenty-five years with William Golding, Raymond Williams, J. G. Ballard, Angela Carter, Christa Wolf, etc., etc., was thrown onto the bonfire. Webb established the obituary page, which began to read like a samizdat by internal exiles, and then took early retirement. Januszczak himself couldn't stomach the new conformism and moved on to *The Late Show*. His replacement, Tim Radford, introduced publishers' handouts thinly disguised as literary gossip on the books pages under his own byline. The soundbite mentality had penetrated Webb's old empire.

Richard Gott's decade-long rule in the features department was ended by Preston. Gott was replaced by former diarist, Alan Rusbridger, who boasted to a former editor of the *Spectator*,

Alexander Chancellor, that his task was to obliterate most traces of the Webb–Gott school of journalism. Victoria Brittain's Third World review page was first gutted and then suppressed. A succession of woman's page editors were considered too radical or insufficiently pliant and duly disposed of.

The nadir of Preston's drive to blot out the *Guardian*'s traditional concerns and image was reached in 1989. An uncharacteristically blunt memo from the editor landed on the desks of the editorial staff. It was based on a survey of *Guardian* readers, lapsed *Guardian* readers, *Independent* readers and floating readers of no fixed daily paper. To nobody's surprise the survey revealed that lapsed and non-readers of the *Guardian* thought the paper more biased than did *Guardian* readers. By now Thatcher had been in office for over a decade and Preston was beginning to panic. Perhaps, he thought, this one is going to be with us forever. She will grow old in Downing Street and I on Farringdon Road. He decided on a peace offering and wailed to his staff:

> They [a reference to lapsed readers] don't automatically want to be told every five seconds how awful the government is. They don't want, I reckon, the personalisation of every issue into Thatcher this and that. They don't want slanted headlines. They don't want slanted intros. And they want a broader range of views.

The message was clear. In the opinion of its editor, the *Guardian*'s attitude to Thatcher was far too negative. Old staffers were shocked. After all, it was hardly the case that readers in search of a less hostile view of Thatcher were deprived of choice. Preston clearly felt isolated from the establishment. The problem was that his turn to Thatcher was badly timed. The week after his memo hit the desks, Labour swept to victory in the elections to the European Parliament. Thatcherism was not invincible after all and the more astute gurus of *Marxism Today*, like Stuart Hall and Eric Hobsbawm, began to see the writing on the wall. She would be ousted by her own MPs in 1990.

Nonetheless, Preston's missive had the desired effect. It was widely perceived in the newspaper as a signal for a shift to the right. One of the results was the hiring of two new groups of journalists. The first of these consisted of unashamed right-wing hacks from the tabloids. Quite separate from the Preston levy, but even more pervasive, was the new-model *Guardian* intake. In their late twenties, these were Thatcher's children: Oxbridge-educated for the most part, lacking even the rudiments of a liberal political culture, self-regarding, cynical and, above all, ambitious. Most of them would have felt at home at *The Sunday Times* or the *Daily Mail*. Andrew Rawnsley was hired as a funny boy and told to write a column that treated politics as a spectator sport. Jocelyn Targett was appointed deputy editor of the Weekend *Guardian*. This was, no doubt, a reward for his intelligence. In his first blockbuster feature for the new *Guardian* he had described Aneurin Bevan as 'an important trade union leader'. Targett proved to be an ideal accompaniment to the Weekend *Guardian*'s editor, Roger Alton. Together they produced a bland and characterless mix, popular with advertisers and the culture industry. It did not really matter since both the editor and the marketing department were happy.

Preston's drive to uproot the *Guardian* from its social and political moorings would have been a total success had it not been for a bizarre coincidence. As part of the change there was an attempt to marginalise and pigeonhole the usual suspect radical writers on the paper. To defend themselves, some of the latter began to meet regularly and organise counterattacks. But where once features and home news had been the most troublesome departments, it was now the foreign department. It was lucky for some of us that Jonathan Steele was stationed in Moscow to provide more than impressionistic nonsense on the events in the former Soviet Union.

It was the Gulf War, alas, which forced the *Guardian* to confront its past and permit the old voices back on to its pages. The paper had opposed Suez vigorously. Preston had supported the Falklands escapade editorially but permitted opposition in the rest of the paper. The same method was adopted for the Gulf conflict, with one major exception, Edward Pearce. Once a *Daily Telegraph* parliamentary sketch-writer, Pearce had no radical past. He was meant to be part of the *Guardian*'s recantation. Without him the paper's letters page and a weekly diet of Chomsky, Pilger, Fadia Faqir, Avi Shlaim, among many others, would have kept dissent flowing through the pages, but the opposition would have been restricted to outsiders. Pearce's savage hostility to the war provided a structural balance and temporarily brought the *Guardian* back to life.

A *Guardian* that could be brought back to life is now dead. This is upsetting in some ways. Regardless of my criticisms, it was good to have a paper with a regular space for dissenters of all sorts. I wrote most of my pieces during Alan Rusbridger's editorship and was *never* censored. This is not because he agreed with me. Far from it. He understood what a newspaper needed.

After he left something strange happened. A sly and unpleasant self-censorship took hold and a Zionist grip on the paper became pretty evident. I was told that Jonathan Freedland became the de facto censor of all material concerning Israel/Palestine. Kath Viner, the new editor, seemed powerless. Did she have any regrets, scruples, second thoughts? If so, she kept them to herself. The paper's decline continued. With the worst ever leader of the opposition at the helm of Labour, I felt strongly that an oppositional paper was necessary. No such luck. Bad things happened. Steve Bell, the most gifted political cartoonists of recent decades was first censored and then banned altogether. He was accused of 'anti-Semitism' for a strong anti-Netanyahu cartoon. Criticism of Israel virtually disappeared from the paper and its tabloiditis got worse. A handful of serious journalists hung on, but the editor was living in a bubble. I had no desire to write for them again. They asked a couple of times, but I was not tempted. It had become a soulless rag. I don't read it now. Anything useful in its pages reaches me on Facebook or X. That's enough.

16

A Burial at Père Lachaise

20 July 1995. A sad call from Berlin. It was my old friend and comrade, Winfried Wolf, with bad news. Ernest Mandel had died in Brussels that day. He was seventy-two. Ernest was one of the more creative and independent-minded revolutionary Marxist thinkers of the postwar world. His writings on political theory, world history and Marxist economics were translated into thirty languages and in every continent. In a series of specialist works – *Late Capitalism* (1975), *The Second Slump* (1978), *The Long Waves of Capitalist Development* (revised and reissued in 1995) – he analysed the functioning of capitalism in the West.

Mandel had been a prominent leader and theoretician of the Trotskyist Fourth International from the late 1950s onwards, but even those on the left who were not sympathetic to his Trotskyist politics – and there were many – acknowledged his influence and respected his razor-sharp intelligence.

He was born in Belgium and educated at Brussels University and the École pratique des haute études in Paris. His father Henri, a left-wing socialist, had opposed the First World War and fled from Belgium to Holland to avoid conscription. Here he met the German communist Wilhelm Pieck, and both men rushed to Germany after the fall of the Kaiser.

Henri Mandel worked in Berlin for several months as a journalist for the newly organised Soviet Press Agency. He also became a close friend of Karl Radek, the Bolshevik emissary despatched by Lenin to speed up the German revolution. Stefan Heym's last novel, *Radek*, published in Munich in 1995 and translated into English in 2022, captures the spirit of the times and Radek's character and role in that period extremely well. Had he lived another six months, Ernest would have liked it very much and probably reviewed it.

Demoralised by the repression which followed the execution of Rosa Luxemburg and Karl Liebknecht, Henri Mandel remained a member of the German Communist Party for only a few more years. Then he dropped out of active politics and moved to Antwerp. It was here that his second son, Ernest, was born. Ernest was ten years old when Hitler came to power. Years later he told me: 'My father made some very sharp comments at the time on the incapacity of the social democrats and the communists to resist fascism. I remember him saying, "This will end very badly. It could be the end for our people, the Jews."'

In 1939, when he was sixteen, he joined a small Trotskyist group in Antwerp and a few years later became active in the Belgian Resistance. His close friend and mentor, Abram Leon, was five years older. Leon was captured and executed by the Gestapo, but left behind a brilliantly original study, *The Jewish Question: A Marxist Interpretation*. When it was published in many languages after the war, Mandel wrote the introduction. Its tone was emotional, the anger and sense of loss palpable on every page. When I discussed it with him, he told me that he regarded Leon as a brother and that he had learnt more from him than almost anyone else. Both Leon and Mandel had been disgusted by the total capitulation of the Belgian Socialist Party, whose leader, the deputy prime minister, made a public appeal to collaborate with the Nazis and was supported by a significant section of the trade union apparatus. The official communists published a newspaper under the Occupation, basking in the deadly rays of the Stalin–Hitler pact.

Ernest was arrested for distributing seditious leaflets to the occupying German soldiers, calling on them to desert and fight fascism. He had hidden behind a wall to observe the effect of anti-fascist propaganda on the uniformed Germans, and that's how he was caught. There was little doubt as to his fate. He was a revolutionary and a Jew. The Nazis sent him to a transit camp for prisoners en route to Auschwitz. Astonishingly, he escaped.

The circumstances in which he freed himself are revealing and left a permanent mark that fuelled his optimism about the capacity of ordinary people to emancipate themselves however bad the conditions.

Always a strong believer in his own capacity to convince anyone of the merits of socialism, Mandel started talking to the warders. The other Belgian and French prisoners treated the warders, veteran employees of the German state, as subhumans, but Mandel discovered that some had been members of the now-banned social-democratic and communist parties in Germany. The warders, impressed by the precocity of the sixteen-year-old boy in their charge, actually helped him to escape. Even though he was soon re-arrested the experience had made him an internationalist. He steadfastly refused to write off a whole nationality because of the crimes of its leaders.

After the war, Mandel devoted most of his energies to building the Fourth International as a world party for the socialist revolution. He genuinely believed that conditions might favour the rebirth of a movement not tarred with the crimes of Stalinism or the capitulations of social democracy. But here he encountered a problem. After the fascist triumph, Trotsky, who till then had advised his followers to see themselves as an internationalist left faction inside the Comintern, now declared the same body to be counter-revolutionary.

This did not, however, mean abandoning the Soviet Union, since the economic class structure there had abolished capitalism. But the idea of a counter-revolutionary workers' state was bound to cause confusion. The postwar Napoleonisation of Eastern Europe created more states on the Soviet model. This led to splits and confusions within Trotskyism. In private, Ernest never denied this problem, but he did not acknowledge it in public. Isaac Deutscher, unattached to any group, came much closer to explaining the realities of the day, arguing that the very expansion of the 1917 revolution to China, Yugoslavia and Cuba would lead to structural reforms in the Soviet Union.

During the late sixties and seventies, Ernest's polemical and oratorical skills (he spoke all the major languages of his continent) together with government paranoia led to him being barred from entering the US, France, West Germany, Switzerland and Australia. He was deemed a threat to 'national security'. We often joked as to which of us was banned from more countries. I was banned from the US, France, Bolivia, Turkey, Pakistan and Thailand. I won easily, since neither of us regarded Switzerland, a bourgeois El Dorado, as a historic nation. More a foreign exchange.

The restriction on his movements sent him back to his old typewriter. Pamphlets and books emerged at an amazing speed. He was a great educator. His pamphlet, *An Introduction to Marxist Economics*, sold half-a-million copies. And yet a great deal of his life was spent on dealing with the views of rival Trotskyist groupings. When I rang him during the seventies and asked politely 'How are you?', the reply was never the same: 'I'm just finishing off a draft reply to the sectarians in Ceylon on the Tamil question,' or 'Fine. Have you read my reply to the IS Group on state-capitalism?', or 'Those sectarian idiots in Argentina have caved in to Peronism. Crazy people. Don't they understand?' They never did, but Mandel never stopped trying to convince 'crazy people' to tread the true path. I always regarded most of this as a phenomenal waste of time.

I was very close to him for the most important years of my life. Even after I left the movement in 1981, we remained close friends. Friendly relations were abruptly broken off for just under a year in 1990, after the appearance of *Redemption*, my fictional satire on Trotskyism. It was my first novel and I had written it in a fortnight, in a rage after reading that two factions of a particularly sectarian Trot group had come to fisticuffs when their totally discredited leader had died. They were fighting over which of them would get to bury his putrefying body. He had been accused of raping young women and had been expelled from the party. The factions fighting for burial rights had disagreed with the expulsion in the first place.

The novel's storyline was simple. The leader of world Trotskyism, realising the game is almost up, convenes a liquidationist World Congress. They must dissolve, adopt an entryist mode and enter the monotheistic religions to ultimately take power in the Vatican, Jerusalem, al-Azhar, Qom and Canterbury. The first two people to read the manuscript, apart from Susan who read it as I finished each chapter, were Carmen Callil at Chatto and Francis Mulhern, the Irish socialist literary critic and friend, who worked at *NLR*/Verso. I trusted his judgement on these matters and, had he asked me to, I would have dropped the idea. Despite being critical of certain sections, he enjoyed it. That was that.

The central character in *Redemption*, Ezra Einstein, was loosely based on Ernest and was written with warmth and affection. But the FI leadership, or many of them, were not pleased and some suggested at a Secretariat meeting that I should be denounced as a renegade and anathematised. Daniel Bensaid, who passed this on to me, said that the French delegates burst out laughing. He suggested that those who really knew me could tell them that I would be delighted at being publicly denounced, would reply in kind, and book sales would take a leap upward.

Ernest agreed strongly with Bensaid, while complaining to my friend Winfried in Berlin that a few of the things I'd written recently were worrying. 'Like what?' asked Winny. 'Oh, he's become too pessimistic. He wrote that after the defeat in Portugal, a new revolutionary wave in Europe was off the agenda for a very long time.' Winnie pointed out that many still inside the FI (including himself) agreed with that assessment. Sadly, the idea of publicly denouncing me was dropped.

A few pages from Ezra's journal, excerpted from *Redemption*:

4 January 1990: I have had to stop all work on my memoirs. I find it difficult today to summon the ghosts and spirits of my past. The voices are there and the sounds, some of them only too painfully acute. So much has passed before my eyes that at times like these they refuse me the power of recall, reducing my memory to a blank wall. It is the noises of time present which keep intruding, and even I begin to wonder whether the price being paid for what we have gained means that much of what we thought we had gained was nothing but illusion. Mirages in our minds and a living hell for those who supposedly gained. Surely this can't be so, for the gains of 1917 were spread all over the world: decolonizations which otherwise would have been delayed or bloody or both. The welfare states in the West would probably have been far less effective had it not been for the 'barbarians at the gate'.

This morning, for instance, a long letter from Otto in Berlin and the German translation of Igor Shagarevich's article. There is no doubting that it is an effective piece of writing, like some of Goebbels' filth in the early Thirties. It is a horrible little essay. Reading it has depressed me a great deal. It was first published during the last days of the old Brezhnevite regime, but it's become a sacred text for the nationalists. It's grotesque, unbelievable. This great Soviet mathematician is a vulgar anti-semite. The Soviet Union is not in crisis because of the crimes and disasters of Stalinism, but because of the 'criminal intrigues' of the 'lesser people'. First the 'lesser people' were Zionists. Then they became Yid-Masons and now they are the Jews. Poor Shagarevich! But why are the songs of the Black Hundreds finding a new audience? Have all the gains of the Revolution disappeared? I suspect that this might be the case, but I cannot believe that the USSR will slowly lapse into capitalism. That is the sinister side of Shagarevich and his slavophile friends. They are hostile to modernity. Hence, too, their nostalgia for Stalin and the Tsar. I fear that Gorbachev could be overthrown if and when elements in the party and army link up with the slavophile intelligentsia. All this talk about love for Russian culture is nothing but a mountain of shit. And all this on the eve of the third millennium. Poor Russia! Are Pasternak and Mandelstam and Grossman not part of this Russian culture?

Otto's letter was a tonic. What an excellent comrade he is! And yet even Otto doubts if we can salvage something from the wreck. I am very late with my new book answering the German revisionist historians on the origins of fascism. Unfortunately all this proto-fascist material in the Russian papers, *Molodave gvardia, Nash sovremennik* and *Moskovsky literator,* will help their thesis and not mine.

Last night Maya asked me to explain how it was that despite all its crimes, its inquisitions, its wars and its present backward positions on the liberation churches in Brazil, the Roman Catholic orthodoxy and its Pope have held out much better than Marxism. My answer was simple. We never were a religion. She laughed in my face. It was impossible to convince her. But I must confess the question has been bothering me since 1979.

7 January 1990: Long phone call today from the British comrades early in the morning. I hope they didn't hear Maya being sick in the background. It would be awful if they think she pukes every time they ring up. This would be the third time it's happened. Want me to go to London immediately. They say that my proposal for an emergency Congress without preconditions has created a problem for them. They are still a tiny group. They fear they'll be totally swamped by the Rock and Burroughs organisations. The whole business is ridiculous, but part of the wretched English disease. For a country whose bourgeoisie has rarely split and whose labour movement remains the most unified in Europe, the continuing factionalism and splits in our movement is perplexing. Hood's old empire has splintered dramatically and there are three groups even within our own ranks. It would be ridiculous if Rock and Burroughs turned up but our comrades stayed away. Points in favour of going to London: (a) Maya likes the town. I could show her the Cemetery at Highgate and the Zoo. (b) I could meet Jemima Wilcox and the *New Life Journal* comrades. Find out why the *NLJ* publishing house is not reprinting my last three books. I wonder whether this tardiness is due to the fact that I referred to them as centrists and compared them to Kautsky and *Die Neue Zeit?* Perhaps I was too harsh! (c) Meeting with the RSG and LSD comrades to be restricted to two hours. (d) A nice hotel.

There is no way I can go this week. Warsaw gets priority.

'Tell me something,' Ernest said when peace had finally been restored, 'why did you make me out to be so obsessed with sex?' I tried to explain that a true political utopian would also be a sexual utopian and that in fiction one had the right to imagine anything. He shook his head in disapproval. He was capable of theorising on any subject under the sun, but not sex. This divide with the generation of '68 was never overcome.

He had complained about two minor scenes in the novel, both set in Brazil. During the first I had depicted him and his much younger Brazilian girlfriend, Maya, cavorting naked on a deserted beach, making love and swimming restfully to recover in the calm sea. His complaint here was this was clearly meant to ridicule. I tried to convince him to the contrary, but failed.

His second objection was more biological and philosophical in character: 'I cannot understand why you had the character based on me lactating and nipple-feeding his newborn son. Even for you it's a bit crazy.' I explained that I had thought about this quite seriously. Some of the best utopian (in the best sense) feminist novels express a desire for men to lactate to reduce biological and psychological inequalities. I recommended a Marge Piercy novel. He refused. I then pointed out that Francis Mulhern had told me that male lactation is possible *in extremis*. 'But he is a serious comrade.' I agreed. 'Now perhaps you should be serious and consider making male lactation a transitional demand in the programme, but only *in extremis*.' He laughed.

A letter from another veteran socialist, Edward Thompson, expressed some misgivings when the book first came out, but also included warm-hearted comments that moved me greatly. I thought of him as we sang the Internationale and laid Ernest to rest. I dug out the letter from EPT only recently. Dated 17 December 1990, he wrote:

I have taken a long time to send my thanks [for *Redemption*]. I am still slowly recovering from serious illness, and the medication (steroids) have got my eyes in a blurry state (not to mention my morale so that I am generally slowed down). I didn't like the first few chapters of *Redemption* but I really got into it around Chapter 5 to Chapter 23 or so. I found all this long middle part of the book was very successful, witty, even sad as well as provocative – and often just not satire, but also challenging in its philosophical and political quest.

I'm not quite sure why I didn't so much like the last few chapters. I think there was an uncertainty of tone. I liked the book best when the satire was not too implausible, when some kind of belief was possible, and I thought you changed your own rules at the end, and allowed satirical slapstick. However, I could well be wrong. I don't know your targets very well. I felt sad about the considerable intelligence and dedication to lost causes which you demonstrated. Despite the putrid factionalism there were some very gifted people in the Trotskyist *milieu*. They won't thank you …

They didn't, but most who mattered forgave me. I was saddened by the end of Edward's letter. I had no idea that he had been so ill, thinking of death and what he would be able to write in the time left.

Ernest had suffered a serious heart attack a few years earlier, which left him extremely frail, but up to the last he was thinking of new projects. 'I can't decide what book to write,' he told me the year before he died. 'A history of the European workers' movement or the permanent and eternal links between capitalism and crime.' In the event he wrote neither.

Like many of his generation he was shaken by the restoration in Russia, though he tried to mask the fact with heady rhetoric. He knew the game was up for another four or five decades or even more, but fearful of 'demoralising the cadre' a pretence was maintained that nothing fundamental had really happened. Life and the struggle went on just as before The truth was that In the changed mood of present times his optimism had ceased to be infectious.

Perry, Robin and I went over to Paris for the funeral. My diary entry for that day:

30 September 1995: Ernest's funeral. We gather at the Place Gambetta and march to the Père Lachaise where the old revolutionary will be buried, together with the Communards and numerous others of the Left. Am told that a committee decides as to whether a person deserves to be buried here or not. What if sectarians captured the committee and excluded their opponents? Technically it's possible. Try to overthrow the committee or split the cemetery?

Lots of old and ex-Trotskyists. Very few young people. A dispiriting assembly, in keeping with the times. I run into Michel Pablo [Diablo in *Redemption*]. Ultra-friendly, he waves his finger at me. '*Roman* very mischievous,' he whispers and laughs. Adolfo Gilly has flown over from Mexico City. We embrace. He whispers: 'Read your book on a plane to Montevideo. I laughed all the way, sometimes so loudly that the stewardess thought I was mad. Sad day.'

The arrangements are bad. We move off slowly to Père Lachaise. It's moving to see various old comrades but, nonetheless, a strange reunion for me. The Sardinian comrade who proposed a public denunciation of me looks away as we pass each other. Then I remembered why. The single line in which he was mentioned didn't go down too well. All I had written was that, obsessed with football as a teenager, he had wanted to become a professional, but failed and football's gain was the FI's loss. Oh well.

Afterwards, an unimaginative meeting with boring and predictable speeches. Ernest deserved better. Anne, his wife and a proficient pianist, should have played a Beethoven Sonata. Poor Ernest. Our *NLR* delegation left the meeting early. Jonathan Steele from the *Guardian* joined us in the search for an eatery. Robin zipped off to pick up a promised article for the *NLR*. He returned with a new text by Jacques Bidet. 'Whatever the content,' I suggested, 'let's title it "Sanitary Marxism".' It was destined to be an unlucky day. The food was truly appalling.

17

NLR: Saving the Review

Over lunch in 1992, Peter Wollen asked how the 'old firm' was doing. He meant *New Left Review*, of course. I said that attempts to enlarge the Editorial Committee for the new era had not been very successful. Robin had been working on his books on slavery and a vacuum had been created which micro-factions were taking advantage of to try and corner him. Added to this was the fact that the collapse of the Soviet Union and its consequences – the Gulf War and the breakup of Yugoslavia – had created a serious political divide. Peter listened carefully. What he said next startled me.

'I don't want to panic you too much, but I think it's even more serious than you think. The micro-factions are going to try and take over the magazine.'

'How do you know?'

'They're going to demand shares for the new EC members, outvote you and appoint a new editor. I gather the most serious candidate is called Ellen Wood. I don't know her at all. I'm not joking. You better do something.'

I had been so completely immersed in producing *Bandung File* and subsequently *Rear Window* for Channel 4 that I had semi-withdrawn from the *NLR* and let Robin and others get on with it. After speaking with Peter, I went over to the journal's Meard Street offices in Soho. There was undoubtedly tension in the air. After speaking with a few people and having a long talk with Robin, it became obvious that Wollen was correct.

Fred Halliday and Norman Geras had publicly supported the Gulf War. Ellen Wood was slightly embittered because she was desperate to edit the *NLR*. Quintin Hoare's and Branka Magas's understandable sympathy and support for Bosnia had led them to jump into bed with Croatian nationalism (which they denied but was obvious to the rest of us), which to many of us was no different to the Serbian variety and in any case was also guilty of anti-Bosnian actions and propaganda. The break with them, for me at least, was both political and emotional. They had, until then, been very close friends. Our children grew up together. We went on family holidays and I had a learnt a great deal of Yugoslav history from Branka, for which I will always be grateful. These memories are unforgettable.

I was seriously shocked when at an EC meeting, Patrick Camiller, disagreeing mildly with Branka, cited an article by Misha Glenny to prove a point. 'He's married to a Serb' was her response. I had never heard talk of this sort at any left gathering leave alone the *NLR*, and said so angrily. Later there was an attempt to stop Robin publishing a very measured text on the break up of Yugoslavia, though ultimately the article did appear.

The third micro-faction was the office bureaucracy trying to replace Robin. I have no idea what their positions were on the Middle East and Yugoslavia, but since one of this crew was a disciple of Terry Eagleton and since Terry was solid on both the Gulf and the impending NATO bombing of Yugoslavia, I doubted that this staffer's positions would be too different. But ...

The balance of forces on the EC amounted to two micro-factions becoming softer and softer on US imperialism, the office bureaucracy planning a mini-coup, and the rest of us, with a tiny number of nature's weaklings, not wishing to take sides on the issue of the editor. At stake, of course, was much more than that. As I told Perry at the time, with the tectonic plates shifting after the Berlin Wall fell and the Soviet Union disintegrated, followed by the wars in the Gulf and the Balkans, it would have been surprising had the *NLR* remained completely unaffected. But to become uncritical supporters of the US in Iraq and in Israel and of the NATO intervention in Yugoslavia was unacceptable.

When the *NLR* was founded every EC member had two shares; this was later reduced to one as Robin expanded the committee to two dozen members. New shares to the latest entrants had not yet been approved, but their presence had been destabilising. Especially when all the micro-factions agreed to unite and vote Robin out. This, Norman Geras triumphally announced, was 'a brute fact' and there is 'nothing you can do about it'. Perry was teaching at UCLA at the time. I rang him with the whole story, emphasising Peter Wollen's insistence that we act immediately to save the journal.

That would not happen if we accepted Norman's 'brute fact' and let the micro-factions run riot. Apart from anything else, they simply could not have agreed on a political formula to guide the *NLR*. There would have been a reader's revolt had the journal backed the Pentagon and NATO over two issues, opposed them over the next two, with culture/metaculture filling the space. Colin Robinson, embedded in Verso at the time, told me later that the office bureaucracy gang had reassured him that a new dispensation was under way, that they would soon be in charge and that everything would be different. Colin wasn't totally convinced.

What was to be done? It was obvious that new structures were needed. It was also obvious that sooner or later we would have to map a new political agenda in response to the changed global realities. In the meantime, we needed to set up a Trust as the majority shareholder and, as such, the ultimate decision-maker for both journal and publishing house. This entailed appealing to all shareholders past and present to agree to the new plan. The micro-faction shareholders were, unsurprisingly, not in favour. We decided to move forward without them. Perry, Robin and I divided up the list of shareholders we would approach.

The affection and respect in which the old guard held Robin became obvious early on. Most of those who had left the magazine when Robin first became editor handed over their shares to the Trust and their proxy votes for the Board meeting that would confirm Robin in office. Even for those further removed from Robin the question was depersonalised. Which other team of people could maintain the journal at the same level? Two early editors, Raphael Samuel and Stuart Hall (two shares each), declared for Robin. As did much of the next generation: Ronald Fraser, Peter Wollen, Juliet Mitchell, Tom Nairn, Gareth Stedman-Jones, Roger Murray and Anthony Barnett (who, in return, demanded a life sub to the *NLR* and Verso books of his choice).

I was assigned to speak with, amongst others, Edward and Dorothy Thompson (two shares each). How would they decide? Might their votes be split? My trip to Wick Episcopi, an old vicarage near Cheltenham, turned out to be memorable. I had fixed the date so that we could also film separate interviews with them for *Rear Window*. Sheila Rowbotham, who knew Dorothy's work well, conducted that interview. I recorded a conversation with Edward. The film, *A Life of Dissent*, was later shown on Channel 4.

After the filming and while the house was being cleared of our equipment, Edward disappeared to rescue a bottle of fine claret he had been saving 'for a special occasion'. It was time to discuss the *NLR* and we talked for several hours. What struck me at the time was how warmly he spoke of the journal as if he were still part of the project. There had been many arguments and rows in the past but he never stopped reading it. He had remained a comrade. He spoke warmly of Robin: 'I buggered off. Perry buggered off. Robin stayed on. Our great helmsman. The ship is still seaworthy. Perhaps a lick of paint here and there, but it doesn't need repairs, leave alone throwing the captain overboard. What is really going on? There must be something political behind all this.'

I gave him my version of the three micro-factions. His position on the breakup of Yugoslavia was very tough, much more so than that of the *NLR*. For him it was a crime, a tragedy, a civil war engineered by the Western powers for their own 'bloody purposes'. Milosevic and Tudjman were, of course, utter rogues, but the demonisation of Serbians was unacceptable. NATO bombing made him recall the Second World War. He wondered whether the Luftwaffe had made use of their old maps. His most emotional moment (including tears) during our TV interview had come while he was discussing the Yugoslav partisans who fought the Nazis and the stories he had heard from them when he went to help in the reconstruction, rebuilding the railways, soon after the war.

The Balkans held a special place for Edward, in any case. His brother Frank, a communist and a British army officer, had been sent by the SOE as part of a unit to establish contact with the Bulgarian partisans, who were effectively staving off the fascists, and to report their situation. The partisan group with which the unit were embedded was captured by the Bulgarian fascists. The partisans were executed on the spot but there were instructions not to kill British officers. Frank Thompson was twenty-four years old and spoke nine European languages, including Serbo-Croat, Greek, Bulgarian, Czech and Polish. He was asked for his name, rank and serial number. He had just witnessed the execution of his comrades. He replied, 'I'm a communist.' They executed him. The SOE radio-operator provided his own details (understandably so) and was spared. The trauma stayed with him. He wept when he met the family on his return. They reassured him. They wished Frank had done the same.

After the war the Bulgarian resistance leaders (now in power) erected a statue in honour of Frank Thompson near the spot of the executions. The last time I enquired it was still there, but not looked after, and the annual remembrance ceremony was no longer held there. Times have changed. Edward and Dotty used to attend the event as regularly as they could. Together with other British socialists, Edward had gone to Yugoslavia to reconstruct the railways, the experience recorded in a slim volume he edited. We talked about all this as well, but the memory of Frank kept intruding that day. 'He was the genius of the family,' he told me at one point. 'I was the duffer. My parents never got over his death.' Difficult not to wonder in which direction Frank might have gone had he not died. Many possibilities were open to him. He had been engaged to Iris Murdoch. Postwar, would either have returned to the other? Who knows. All that can be said with some certainty is that with Frank's heroic death, Britain lost one of its most brilliant communist intellectuals.

Edward went to take a phone call. I speculated aloud to Dorothy that we should explore the possibility of a low-budget movie.

Working title: *A Peculiar English Family*. Thompson *père* in India, his friendship with anti-imperialist politicians and intellectuals and his later fall out with Rabindranath Tagore; Frank and Iris Murdoch and the war; Edward at Monte Cassino, the historian, the anti-war activist. Many possibilities. She laughed. 'Our family has already discussed Peter O'Toole playing EPT.' He heard that, muttered 'enough frivolity' and, when we resumed the discussion, took it back firmly to the *NLR*.

In 1980, Perry had published what I still consider to be his best book after the histories of the ancient world and of the transition to feudalism. *Arguments Within English Marxism* was both an act of comradeship and a critique on a very lofty level of some of Thompson's recent work. In particular, it was an objective attempt to discuss *Poverty of Theory*. It worked. The opening paragraph of *Arguments* established a crystal-clear style and a carefully controlled tone, pointing at how differences and agreements would be discussed in the rest of the book. That is why it deserves to be quoted in full:

> Edward Thompson is our finest socialist writer today – certainly in England, possibly in Europe. Readers of *The Making of the English Working Class*, or indeed *Whigs and Hunters*, will always remember these as major works of literature. The wonderful variety of timbre and rhythm commanded by Thompson's writing at the height of his powers – alternately passionate and playful, caustic and delicate, colloquial and decorous – has no peer on the Left. Arguably, too, the strictly historical achievement of the series of studies that extends across the 19th and 18th centuries, from *William Morris* to the rich group of recent essays whose collection is promised in *Customs in Common* is perhaps the most original product of the corpus of English Marxist historiography to which so many gifted scholars have contributed. Setting aside any other consideration, it is rare for any researcher to become equally at home in two such contrasted epochs. Whatever comparative estimate is made in this respect – where doubtless no final judgement is attainable – two distinctive characteristics of Thompson's practice as a historian stand out. Throughout, his has been the most

declared political history of any of his generation. Every major, and nearly every minor, work he has written concludes with an avowed and direct reflection on its lessons for socialists of his own time. *William Morris* closes with a discussion of 'moral realism'; *The Making of the English Working Class* recalls our debt to the 'liberty tree' planted by the early English proletariat; *Whigs and Hunters* ends with a general revaluation of the 'rule of law'; an essay like 'Time, Work, Discipline, and Industrial Capitalism' speculates on the possible synthesis of 'old and new time-senses' in a communist society of the future that has surpassed the 'problem of leisure'. Each of these texts has been in its own way a militant intervention in the present, as well as a professional recovery of the past. The massive consistency of their direction, from the mid 50s to the late 70s, visibly attested in the long Postscript to the new edition of the study of Morris (1977), is profoundly impressive. At the same time, these works of history have also been deliberate and focused contributions to theory: no other Marxist historian has taken such pains to confront and explore, without insinuation or circumlocution, different conceptual questions in the pursuit of their research. The definitions of 'class' and 'class consciousness' in *The Making of the English Working Class*; the critique of 'base and superstructure' through the prism of law in *Whigs and Hunters*; the reinstatement as disciplined imagination of 'utopianism' in the new edition of *William Morris* – all these represent theoretical arguments that are not mere enclaves within the respective historical discourses, but form rather their natural culmination and resolution.

The claim on our critical respect and gratitude, then, is one of formidable magnitude and complexity. Some appraisal of Thompson's central ideas and concerns is, however, long overdue...

We were speaking thirteen years after the publication of *Arguments* but Thompson remained struck by 'Perry's extraordinary generosity, the economy of words, the high level of debate of the sort that can educate an entire generation.' Both the Thompsons liked the book a great deal and it had the desired effect. It brought Edward back to the *NLR*, debating issues of war and peace and insisting that nuclear proliferation produced the threat of 'Exterminism'. The weapons, he warned, would be used in some shape or form. I vividly recall Edward speaking at a giant anti-war rally in Hyde Park in the 1980s protesting against the stationing of cruise missiles in Britain. His voice urgent and passionate, his grey hair blowing in the wind, he had the appearance of an Old Testament prophet. 'Exterminism' started life as an essay in the *NLR* where it was widely debated, later becoming the cornerstone of a Verso book. Now he feared that the new US dominance would become a magnetic force and he feared for the peace movement.

'What do you think of Perry's essays in the *LRB*?' He was referring to the pieces on conservative thinkers. Before I could respond, Dorothy spoke up. 'I like them very much. Very necessary.' Edward looked thoughtful. 'Tell him to stiffen the tone. Oakeshott was a scoundrel.' Dorothy and Edward then signed the form transferring their two shares each to the New Left Trust.

By now, Edward was looking tired. It had been a long day. During a recent visit to the US he had been taken ill and, though he recovered, had picked up a hospital infection that resisted treatment. We kept in touch, exchanged novels. I got an appreciative note from him after he finished reading *Shadows of the Pomegranate Tree* in hospital, regretting that he had only managed one novel himself. 'You will write many more, I hope. Too late for me.'

Both of them appreciated *A Life of Dissent*, the Channel 4 documentary I had produced in 1993. Edward saw it going out live in July that year while he was still in hospital and viewed it more carefully once when he was back at home. 'I'm glad we said everything that needed to be said,' he confided to Dorothy afterwards. I was planning to go and see him again in August when she rang to say he'd died. I felt a huge sense of loss, regret that I had not known him long and anger at the time I had wasted on far less important matters.

The funeral was restricted to the family. A fortnight or so later I drove down to the wake with Sheila Rowbotham. The old vicarage in Upper Wick, where they had spent their last decades, was crowded. Representatives of different political clans had assembled: shadows from the fog of time. Edward's youthful association with the Communist Party and work for the WEA had always given him a real sense of community that also incorporated 'self'. This absence of pure individualism helped exclude the need for constant affirmation, so common amongst academics. In *A Life of Dissent* he described a spontaneous history lesson he once got from a factory worker on the role of machines and factory conditions. Nobody else but a worker engaged in actual production could have spoken like that, he marvelled.

The atmosphere at the wake was not atypical. Laughter and tears. Trevor Griffiths had been very attached to Edward and we discussed a possible play: Brothers. Frank and Edward. He sighed. The theatre was too far gone. Thompson's ideas, his conversations, his humour, his poetry, his politics could only be appreciated by those who possessed equipment of a different order. Richard Eyre, Nick Kent at the Tricycle? He was not optimistic. I pointed out that Eisenstein once had plans to film *Capital*. A stage version of *The Making of the English Working Class* could be very dramatic. Juliet Stevenson as Joanna Southcote? We kept being interrupted and, like so many others, this discussion was never resumed.

Dorothy wanted a chat. I informed her that Channel 4 wanted to repeat the programme and follow it with a discussion chaired by me and a few well-considered guests. Given Edward's leading role in helping to found END (European Nuclear Disarmament) we might get a European colleague. She named one possibility: 'Try Luciana Castellina at *Il Manifesto* in Rome. Intelligent, attractive, staunch ENDer, speaks English and was besotted with him.' 'A powerful combination,' I agreed. We laughed. It was done. Luciana agreed. The programme's viewing figures doubled when it was re-shown after his death. Dorothy's comment: 'She always did dress well.'

The next day Dorothy rang again. 'Do you think we need a public event?'

'Definitely. For all those who wanted to attend the funeral and many others. We need a memorial meeting.'

'Can you take charge. I mean organise it and select the speakers and everything. I'm tired. I will attend but not speak.'

'Are you sure you don't want to suggest anyone?'

'No. Leaving out people is the problem. Now I can say truthfully that it was your choice. I wasn't consulted.'

I warmly agreed to Dorothy's request, and was touched to be asked. It was another step forward in bringing the real and imagined disputes of the past to an end. Perry's book had been the first leap on to this path. The organisation of the memorial took it further. Bandung Productions was still in existence. We had a progressive staff and those who had worked on *A Life of Dissent* were keen to help. I booked the large hall at the Institute of Education in Bloomsbury and began to get a speaker's list and some poetry and music together.

Quite a few people were abroad (Perry, Robin, Eric Hobsbawm). Those who agreed immediately were Christopher Hill, Sheila Rowbotham, Trevor Griffiths, Rodney Hilton, Raphael Samuel, Penny Corfield, John Saville and Jean McCrindle. There was no published list of speakers, and I can't remember whether Stuart Hall spoke or not. He was certainly invited. Ben Thompson recalls him speaking. I'm cursing myself for not having filmed the event.

Trevor Griffiths had a surprise for the thousand-plus people who attended. Few could remember Edward's lecture on Blake's 'London' that had been directed by him and shown on BBC2 in the 1970s. It was a WEA-style talk on TV. The BBC's own tape had been wiped and re-used as was often the case in those days. Trevor kept his own copy and gave it to Bandung for safe keeping. The memorial was its premiere. Edward was mesmerising. His screen presence dominated the evening.

A week earlier I had asked Dotty which poem was his favourite during these last few years. 'Yeats,' she replied. 'Sailing to Byzantium'. I rang Juliet Stevenson to see if she would read it. She would. She appeared slightly nervous before the event. Why, I asked.

'Tariq, I don't like reading aloud when I'm not sure what the words mean. They're beautiful but what is he saying?'

'Many interpretations,' I said, 'and what exactly Edward found in it I don't really know. But the simplest explanation lies in the first verses. This (our country or our city) "is no place for old men". I read it as a poem about old age, about old people wanting to run away from desires and passions that they still feel but that can no longer be fulfilled. Yeats and Hardy both wrote wonderful poetry about the closeness of death. Edward must have felt that too. He was no mean poet himself.'

Needless to add, Juliet did a wonderful job. Most important was that Dorothy, temperamentally a stern critic of people and texts and events, sent me an appreciative postcard. The sting was in the tail. Under Sheila's pressure, I had allowed another woman to speak, someone who had been intimate with Edward a long time ago. Her speech was not great, which didn't help. Hence the PS on DT's postcard: 'Had you consulted me, I would have found you a much better ex-girlfriend.'

Back to the coup of the *NLR* committee. I had one more share-holder to meet. This was Tommy Wengraf, now a lecturer at Enfield College. It was a terrible November evening. Thunder and lightning followed by continuous rain. I had never met Tommy or exchanged words with him but he agreed to see me. His bedsit near Finsbury Park was austere. His opening salvo was straightforward.

'Before you say anything, I need to tell you that in my opinion Perry and Robin are shits.'

I had a hard time keeping a straight face. 'We could discuss this for a long time, Tommy, and I might even agree with you, but it's not a very constructive start. The question posed is not their character, but who else could run the mag?'

There was a to and fro on this issue, but he admitted that they were good editors.

'In that case,' I suggested, 'why not hand over your share to the Trust?'

'Well,' he said, 'I don't really know you well, but I totally trust Mike Rustin and Ronnie Fraser. Let me ring them for their opinion.'

Mercifully, Mike's phone was engaged non-stop. After fifteen minutes Tommy rang Ronnie and got a friendly but firm lecture. Ronnie, one of my closest friends, later told me what he had said, which had had the desired effect. Tommy signed the share transfer form and handed it over to me and was generally more friendly. Just before I left he asked who the Trustees were. I told him: Ronald Fraser, Benedict Anderson, myself and, of course, Perry and Robin.

'Nice to meet you, Tariq.'

My task was done. We had a comfortable majority. Alexander Cockburn and I were appointed secretary and chair of the *NLR* respectively. The gnashing of teeth and wailing and legal threats came to nought. Raphael rang that night for a lengthy chat and post-mortem on the whole wretched business and suggested I write a summary of what I had told him and send it out to the shareholders who had supported creating a New Left Trust. This I did.

To all whose Christmas has been enriched this year by the flow of *NLR* internal documents

I'm now in receipt of a letter from Q&E, threatening legal action, innumerable letters from N, Q, E, and, most recently, a coherent, yet specious, account of recent events from Mike Rustin and Doreen Massey.

If one were to take everything in these documents at face value, we would assume that while there had been some problems in the past, the EC now had everything under control, and all was proceeding smoothly. In other words, those of us who acted in the way we did are either mad or victims of misinformation, or both. The shareholders who handed over their proxies, according to this logic, are naive or foolish, easily swayed by imagined conflicts. All that is needed is a bit of marriage counselling and soon everything will be alright again.

If I believed even half of what has been written in the above material, I would not have wasted valuable time and energy over the last month in a last ditch attempt to ensure the political and financial stability of the magazine. The volatility of world politics and the economic recession (and sometimes downright inefficiency) have led to the collapse of many journals on the left in recent years. Those that remain are under threat. It would be foolish to imagine that the NLR is immune from this process. So my thoughts on the matter were and are as follows:

1. For some years there has been an irregular network on the EC, which was hostile to Robin Blackburn, tried to remove him, failed and voted against him, even in the absence of another candidate. Since that time, Robin has felt his authority being constantly undermined. Even those out of sympathy with Robin now know full well that relations have been anything but amicable. It is worth reminding ourselves that, unlike all of us, Robin has devoted the bulk of his adult life to this magazine. Most of us went our separate ways. He stayed on. I know for a fact that he turned down a number of part-time job offers in North America because of his commitment to the *Review*. As far as I'm concerned, that outweighs his weaknesses, of which he has a fair share. Add to this the fact that he is more pluralistic than his predecessor, much more willing to publish ideas at variance with his own, and constantly attempting to broaden the appeal of the *Review*, and for these reasons is, at the moment, irreplaceable. I have to say that it was not thus in 1983. Of that EC, almost anyone could have edited the *Review*. I do not see a successor to Robin on the present EC. For the last 3–4 years this editor's life has been made miserable by the various goings-on. I myself witnessed an odd incident at the last EC meeting I attended. The production editor had taken a unilateral decision to cut the print run of the *Review*. The editor complained, but not a single member of the EC thought this unusual.

2. Since 1987–88 I have felt that the time had come to end, once and for all, the 'romance' of the EC as a quasi-Leninist Politburo, which is a hangover from the past. For that reason, I was opposed to the enlargement of the old-style EC. I said so at the time, and in private I tried to persuade Robin that the time had come for a revised structure. My own view was and remains that the *NLR* is a magazine and should be run like one. It is not a sect or a party. Nor is it a substitute for either. After the bungled attempt to remove Robin, I was even more convinced of the need for a change of structures. The notion that democratic legitimacy lies with an appointed and co-opted collective, responsible and answerable to nobody but themselves, while the editor with a 30-year track-record of work for the *Review* is marginal, is ridiculous.

3. Instead, the EC was polarised and the editor, effectively, isolated. On the one side, a hostile minority, on the other a Chairman and a subcommittee who saw themselves as permanent conciliators. It is to Mike Rustin's credit that he rarely loses his cool. But he also seems to think that everything can be solved through mediated counselling. Even in the real world, this is unusual, but in the rarefied atmosphere of a factionalised committee, where everything becomes magnified, it is virtually impossible.

4. The conciliation technique, when applied to politics, can paralyse a magazine. The discussion on Yugoslavia was interesting, but Mike Rustin knows full well that a determined attempt was made by Quintin to prevent Robin from writing anything on Yugoslavia for the *Review*. True, it didn't succeed, but it is bizarre that the discussion of the subject has been dominated by two members whose political sympathies are now so close to those of Croatian nationalism. If NATO were to bomb selected targets in Belgrade, how would the *NLR* react? Who would speak publicly for it?

5. Add to all this a financial crisis, which alas is only too real. Factional logic leads to saying either that there is no crisis at all, or it is all the editor's fault. The time I spent with the *NLR* accountant left no room for doubt. He told me bluntly that unless something drastic was done, the *NLR* would cease to exist within the next eighteen months. He pointed out the two major costs: salaries and print costs. For him it was obvious that the magazine was top heavy. Something had to be done. The subcommittee's report, as I read it, was, largely, a critique of the editor, an attempt to give powers to the secretary above the head of the editor, and a financial proposal, which was unsatisfactory to all concerned ...

6. We did feel that doling out shares to the present EC and making them all Directors would be both politically and financially unsound. Perry expressed these views in a letter to Norman Geras last September and was informed that the 'existing EC was a brute fact which could not be overridden'. Now, after the event, it is easy to say: 'If only you had come to the EC you would've won them over,' but the change in perceptions that has occurred is a direct result of our reaction.

7. The manner of our intervention is open to criticism, but let's not overblow the rhetoric. For me, what we did is no more regrettable than the constant harassments of the editor, and much less so than would have been handing over the title deeds of the *Review* to the present EC. In these troubled times, it was best that the legal ownership no longer be a contentious issue. Not even Perry Anderson's bitterest opponents could deny his continuing intellectual and financial commitment to the *Review*. The question I asked myself was this: Would I rather the *NLR* was in the hands of Perry and Robin or some combination of the present EC? I chose the former as did most the shareholders despite their own previous disputes with one or both of the parties concerned.

T.A.

In February 1993 all the micro-factions accepted it was pointless carrying on. I got a phone call from Robin: 'They've all left.'

A few weeks later the *Guardian* commissioned a piece by journalist Patrick Wright describing the *NLR* blow-out. Its tone, unsurprisingly, was friendly to the dear-departed and the borderline-racist reference to me did not win him too many admirers. I checked in the weeks that followed to see whether there had been a Gadarene rush to cancel subscriptions as a protest against our decision to take firm action. Not one!

Walking up Dean Street in Soho that same week, I heard my name shouted by voices in unison. I looked up to see three grinning faces. My three favourite people from the *Eye*. Richard Ingrams, Paul Foot and William Rushton raising their arms in a red fist salute and smiling. I walked over.

Foot was livid. 'Who are these people? Total madness. Trying to get rid of Perry and Robin!'

Ingrams asked whether it was worth replying in the *Eye* to the dreadful *Grauniad* piece? Best to ignore, I said.

Rushton changed the subject: 'We might need your help. [Peter] Cook passing away with his wife now owning his shares is posing a problem. We should have sorted this out when he was alive just like you've done now.'

He meant creating a Trust. I suggested they buy her off. A friendly lawyer had suggested the same.

18

Collateral Damage

The collapse in Moscow took place almost in tandem with the beginning of the multi-sided civil wars in Yugoslavia and the subsequent NATO intervention. A war the US entered in order to expand and control NATO even further was portrayed as 'a human rights intervention'. Accompanied by massive TV coverage given to one side in the civil war, the phrase was used to maximise support at home. Bill Clinton's address to his people explained that they had to go in since 'US interests were being threatened'. A section of the left agreed, marking the beginning of a shift to the right that continues to this day, from supporting the war to supporting the system that wages it.

When I arrived in Leeds for a debate on the war, my pro-war opponent was Denis McShane, till then a progressive Labour MP. 'Sorry I'm on this side comrade, but times have changed...' They certainly had.

At an *Observer* party, the son of very old and dear friends, who I had known since he was a kid and who was now a factotum at No. 10 and a Blair speechwriter, walked up to me, hand proffered, and said: 'I hear you're giving New Labour a hard time...' I put my hand behind my back and replied: 'Can't shake a hand with blood on it.' As I walked away, David Miliband said: 'Milosevic is a very evil man.'

As if Tudjman was any better. Or as if the appalling massacre in Srebrenica was morally worse than the brutal murders and ethnic cleansing of the Krajina. This kindergarten-style propaganda of good and evil was common during the Blair years. The fact that so many were taken in by this rubbish always enraged me.

Some months later I began to compile a volume on Yugoslavia for Verso. Colin Robinson (then publisher) and Gavin Everall (then marketing supremo) made sure we got it out quickly. The fact that it had to be reprinted rapidly was an indication that the British left was still present and strong and that others not on the left at all were interested in debate and discussion.

Masters of the Universe? NATO's Balkan Crusade included important contributions from Susan Woodward, Harold Pinter, Oskar Lafontaine (who had resigned as German finance minister over his country's role in the war), Regis Debray, Yevgeni Yevtushenko, Noam Chomsky, and four *NLR* essays by Robin Blackburn, Gilbert Achar, Peter Gowan and myself. In the world at large, Eric Hobsbawm and Claude Lanzmann (the producer and director of *Shoah*) strongly criticised the concept of 'humanitarian intervention'. Lanzmann wrote at the time: 'I am revolted by this total lack of respect for the gravity of history ... These perpetual references to the Holocaust are a way of muzzling all discussion. Talking forbidden! Argument over!'

A *strong* supporter of the war, Michael Ignatieff, also indulged in some plain talking. Without the help of Yeltsin's Russia, he said, NATO would have been defeated by the Serbs – referring to the Russians denying their state-of-the-art anti-aircraft weaponry to Yugoslavia and threatening to stop the oil unless the country surrendered. The Russian prime minister, Yevgeni Primakov, on his way to Belgrade to reach an agreement to help the country, had to turn his plane back on orders from the Kremlin. Yet another example of White House pressure, with Yeltsin abjectly doing the Americans' bidding. NATO itself was deeply divided. Germany and Italy were compliant, but unhappy. Ninety per cent of Greece was opposed to the war and parties and unions there threatened a general strike if NATO troops were permitted to use Thessaloniki airport. They weren't.

All the essays published in the NATO volume shared a common approach. We regarded the breakup of Yugoslavia as a huge tragedy that could have been averted. Slavoj Žižek was very keen to be included. He supported the NATO bombing, and was a symbol in some ways of Slovene national egoism. Had the book been conceived as a debate he would certainly have been in it, but that wasn't the case and I said, 'Nyet.' I think he forgave me.

Asked in July 1999 to take part in a BBC World Service debate with Robert Nye (Harvard), Dame Pauline Neville-Jones (former chairwoman of the Joint Intelligence Committee) and a former US ambassador to Yugoslavia speaking from Washington, I thought that a 3–1 balance against me was a bit much even for the BBC, but surprises were in store. Nye could not deny that the NATO intervention was a humanitarian disaster. Dame Pauline was not in a mood to defend Blair's gung-ho bluster and it was obvious she found it distasteful. When I argued that NATO's first real war had paved the way, sooner or later, for adventures by other big powers – mentioning specifically India/Kashmir and China/Taiwan – they both agreed that this was a real possibility and potentially the most dangerous outcome of the war. I should have added Russia/Chechnya as well. Later, Pauline Neville-Jones said to me: 'Even you underestimate the divisions within NATO. I don't think this sort of war will ever happen again.'

The NATO assault in Yugoslavia divided Britain and there was a reasonable amount of debate in the press and on the networks. In the realm of culture, there was sadly no poetic intervention from Tony Harrison, whose Gulf War poem in the *Guardian* had struck a real chord. In *The New World Order*, a *Rear Window* cabaret filmed for Channel 4, Tony had electrified the audience with his rendering of it some years later.* We missed him in this moment. In desperation, over lunch with Howard Brenton one day, I scribbled a spoof Harrison poem. Howard did not participate but smiled. 'Some will undoubtedly be taken in,' was all he said.

The Luftwaffe Digs Out Old Maps
(An Unfinished Poem by Tony Harrison)

General Wesley Clark,
Searching for his dick in the dark

---

* It can be found on the *LRB* blog.

Collateral Damage

Decides,
Time to degrade
The 11.30 from Belgrade.
Let the man-of-war bird soar.
'Only ten killed?
We need a few more.'
Chinese embassy in the way?
Let them feel NATO's sway.
Its our fiftieth today.
More orders arrive:
Tomorrow hit Novi Sad
Collateral damage
To make Mad Albright glad.

The poet sees something glowing on the leaves,
Encrusted, depleted uranium tears from other wars
That rained terror on Yugoslav shores.
The Luftwaffe in the lead
Panders now to NATO's need.

I see armies in a dream,
Blood flowing in every Balkan stream;
Let NATO rage, let NATO fall,
Future writing on the wall?
What good's a poet in a Yorkshire pub?
Giving his conscience too soft a scrub?

It's time to call a halt
This war's also our fault.
And if you sight Blair or Cook
Challenge them with an ethical upper hook.
...

This was distributed at various meetings, and rejected by the *Guardian* (I heard they rang Tony) and the *LRB* (M-K rang and asked: 'Is it you?' I said: 'Yes'). Tony Harrison never wrote an anti-war poem like 'A Cold Coming' (1991) again.

But there was a side effect. Harold Pinter, after reading the spoof, got in touch to ask: 'Aren't you and Brenton doing something on the war?' Howard and I spoke and agreed it would be a good way to mark NATO's fiftieth. Nicholas Kent at the radical theatre in North London, the Tricycle (today no longer radical and no longer the Tricycle), said the stage was available, but the theatre had no money. Andy de la Tour, who had agreed to direct, informed Harold of the situation. Like an eighteenth-century patron, he decided to fund the play.

We called it *Collateral Damage*, and wrote it in two weeks as a double hander. A middle-class couple in London are marking the husband's fiftieth birthday. The guests are due in a few hours. The table is being laid, the cake is ready and the candles are lit. Suddenly the husband realises that his wife does not agree with his support for NATO's war. A huge argument erupts and ends with crockery being thrown. Angered by his failure to convince his wife through political argument he assaults her sexually. While he's raping her the guests outside press the bell singing 'happy birthday'.

Harold read and liked the script, suggested a few additions, and gave the director a note: 'The rape must be depicted brutally. It's NATO bombing...' What touched us all throughout the run of the play was the sizeable number of Yugoslavs (Serbs, Croats, Bosniaks and Slovenians) who came to see it and discussed the show in the bar most nights. And despite our strong criticisms of Milosevic, the play did transfer to a radical venue in Belgrade and to theatres in Germany, Estonia and Turkey.

Harold ticked off Andy for not depicting the rape more harshly. Susan Wooldridge, who played the wife, was also Andy's wife, and stood firm on how she wanted the scene enacted. The German version fulfilled Harold's demand.

After one of the performances in London a student from Zagreb asked me whether I had heard of their satirical magazine, *Feral Tribune*. I confessed my ignorance, whereupon she took an old copy out of her bag. It was the iconic cover with Milosevic and his Croatian equivalent, Tudjman, together in bed. At a time when *Private Eye* was backing the Croats and criticising the

Foreign Office from an ultra-pro-NATO position, courageous Croat journalists were doing the opposite and being denounced by Tudjman for being 'ultra-leftist and anti-Croatian'. The *Feral Tribune*'s satires were often accompanied by serious and lengthy investigations of political corruption in all the old-new states.

In bombed Belgrade, opposition to the government came from the broadcasters at the dissident B92 radio station, who kept a flow of alternative news going despite the station being state-owned. Eventually, banned from broadcasting news, they filled the empty slots by playing Public Enemy's 'Fight the Power' on repeat. They kept an internationalist flag flying. I admired them greatly and met some of them when I visited the former Yugoslavia many times in the years after the war. One year I spoke at literary festivals in Sarajevo, Belgrade and Zagreb in the same month; audiences laughed when I thanked publishers in all three cities for publishing my books thrice in the same language. On one occasion I mediated a deal between Belgrade and Sarajevo publishers so that a novel could be published in time for the event in Belgrade.

While our play was being performed, the *Guardian* asked me for a piece on the war. It was published on 26 May 1999. The opening paragraphs were as follows:

> Outside Natoland, the situation about the war is extremely serious. Ukraine was the only country in the world to renounce nuclear weapons and unilaterally disarm. A few weeks ago, its parliament voted unanimously to revert to its former nuclear status. The deputies claimed that they had foolishly believed the United States when it had promised a new norm-based and inclusive security system. NATO's war on Yugoslavia had destroyed all their illusions.
>
> If Kiev is angry, Moscow is incandescent. The military-industrial complex is one of the best-preserved institutions in the country. Its leaders have been arguing with the politicians for nearly two years, pleading that they be allowed to upgrade Russia's nuclear armoury.
>
> Until March 24 this year they had not made too much headway. On April 30, a meeting of the National Security Council in Moscow

approved the modernisation of all strategic and tactical nuclear warheads. It gave the green light to the development and manufacture of strategic low-yield nuclear missiles capable of pin-point strikes anywhere in the world. Simultaneously the defence ministry authorised a change in nuclear doctrine. First use is no longer excluded.

In the space of several weeks, Javier Solana and Robin Cook, veterans of European Nuclear Disarmament, have re-ignited the nuclear flame. In Beijing, too, the bombing of the Chinese embassy has resulted in a shift away from the no-first-strike principle. The Chinese refuse to accept that the bombing of their embassy was an accident ... The bombs on Belgrade may well come to be seen as the first shots of a new cold war.

19

The Art of Spying

I have been fascinated by espionage from a very young age till now. The skills of the three top Soviet spies of the twentieth century – Richard Sorge, Leopold Trepper and Ignace Poretsky/ Reiss (better known as Ludwik) – remain unmatched. Sorge has always attracted particular attention. Ian Fleming called him the 'most formidable spy in history'; other admirers included John le Carré, Tom Clancy and General MacArthur, several Japanese notables, and his many colleagues in the Fourth Department in Moscow. What a department that was!

Spying always accompanies war, peace, revolution and counter-revolution. Civil wars in particular make it an absolute necessity. For centuries, the methods of obtaining and transmitting vital information barely changed. 'Cromwell', Pepys wrote in his diary, 'carried the secrets of all the princes of Europe at his girdle.' The man who got them for him was a civil servant called John Thurloe. The son of an Essex vicar, Thurloe became head of intelligence in 1653, with access to all state papers and secret documents. He pioneered a spy network which long outlasted the English Commonwealth. Documents and reports brought back by couriers from the Continent (still available in the British Library) were analysed in detail by a group that included John Milton and Andrew Marvell. Among other things, they helped support the operations of a navy engineered to extend British interests.

Thurloe tended to overreact to any threat of dissent at home. He dealt harshly with Leveller factions and with the apprentices and joiners of the Fifth Monarchy Men, proto-anarchists based in

Mile End who were allegedly preparing to assassinate Cromwell and unleash an insurrection. A silk-weaver from Whitechapel had revealed the plot. Some of the accused did not deny the main charge but pointed out that mass uprisings cannot be ordered like a jug of water. The House of Commons thanked Thurloe for his vigilance. All this and much else was meticulously recorded in the seven volumes of Thurloe's state papers.

After the Restoration, the Earl of Clarendon was forced to negotiate with Thurloe to acquire his spy network for the post-revolutionary regime. In return, Thurloe was given a list of the people Clarendon planned to arrest (the regicides in particular), which gave him time to warn them to flee the country. Most went to Holland, but under heavy political pressure (and probably with financial inducements) the Dutch betrayed them and handed over as many as they could catch to Clarendon, who had them executed and their heads displayed on pikes in Whitehall. Thurloe's Europe-wide spy network was, however, preserved intact.

I once made notes for a possible fictional work on Thurloe. But, unsurprisingly, there was very little material related to his wife, family, etc. that I could lay my hands on. There was some information on Cromwell's mistresses, and Thurloe must have threatened those circulating the stuff, but in the end I gave up. I once suggested the idea to Hilary Mantel, but she felt one Cromwell was enough for a lifetime. Instead, I began reflecting on the dedication of the Red Orchestra spies, a way of thinking through the commitment – and betrayals – of the short Soviet century, after its defeat. This reading would inform my 'fall of communism' novel, *Fear of Mirrors*.

Instead, I put my efforts into studying the origins of the Soviet greats in this field, and the Latvian genius who welded them into one of the most effect spy networks of the last century. Yan Karlovich Berzin (born Pēteris Ķuzis in 1889) recruited the first generation of Soviet spies. From a Latvian peasant family, he participated in the 1905 Revolution that swept the country soon after the crushing defeat inflicted on the Tsarist navy by imperial Japan, and in 1906 he was elected secretary of the St Petersburg branch of the Russian Social Democratic Labour Party. He was arrested by the Cossacks and sentenced to death, but spared because of his young age. He served two spells in Siberia and escaped. After the October Revolution he was given the task of organising Red Guards to defend the Bolshevik leaders. Following Fanny Kaplan's assassination attempt on Lenin in August 1918 he set up a bodyguard composed of Latvians, Finns, Russians and Chinese migrant workers, who joined the Bolsheviks in large numbers.

All the major achievements of the Fourth Department, as Soviet military intelligence came to be known, were planned in detail by Berzin (including penetration of the British Foreign Office and intelligence services in the 1920s; the creation of the Red Orchestra, which had spies in the highest echelons of the German military both in Germany and Nazi-occupied Europe; and Sorge's astonishing successes in Japan in the 1930s). In *Great Game*, his memoir of the period, Leopold Trepper, who coordinated the Red Orchestra network in Belgium and France, writes that Berzin was 'universally respected': he 'never left his men in the lurch, never would he have sacrificed a single one ... To him, the agents were human beings and, above all, communists.' He recounts a conversation between Berzin and Sorge, as reported to him by the latter (all of them were taught how to memorise messages and conversations). Berzin had summoned Sorge from China just after Hitler's triumph in 1933. Berzin had no doubt as to the consequences of that victory. He cut to the chase:

Berzin: What, in your opinion, is the greatest danger the Soviet Union faces at this time?

Sorge: Even if we grant a confrontation with Japan, I think the real threat comes from Nazi Germany.

Berzin: Well that's why we sent for you. We want you to take up residence in Japan.

Sorge: Why?

Berzin: Rapprochement between Germany and Japan is coming; in Tokyo you will learn a great deal about military preparations.

Sorge: What? Go to Japan and become a spy? But I'm a journalist!

> Berzin: You say you don't want to be a spy, but what's your idea of
> a spy? What you call a 'spy' is a man who tries to get information
> about the weak points of the enemy so that his government can
> exploit them. We aren't looking for war, but we want to know
> about the enemy's preparations and detect the cracks in his
> armour so we won't be caught short if he should attack. Our
> objective is for you to create a group in Japan determined to
> fight for peace. Your work will be to recruit important Japa-
> nese, and you will do everything in your power to see that their
> country is not dragged into a war against the Soviet Union.
> Sorge: What name will I use?
> Berzin: Your own.

Sorge was stunned. Even Berzin's assistants were taken aback,
reminding their chief that Sorge had a police record in Germany.
He had been a member of the German Communist Party at the
end of the First World War before moving to the Soviet Union.
Berzin knew it was risky to make Sorge play a German Nazi, but,
as he argued:

> A man always walks better in his own shoes. I'm also aware that
> the Nazis have just inherited the police files. But a lot of water will
> flow under the bridges of the Moskva before Sorge's file comes to
> light ... Even if the Nazis find out sooner than we expect, what's
> to keep a man who was a communist 15 years ago from changing
> his political opinion?

Then he turned to an assistant: 'Arrange to have him hired as
the Tokyo correspondent of the *Frankfurter Zeitung*.' 'You see,
this way you'll feel at home and not as if you're playing a spy,' he
told Sorge.

Sorge went to Berlin in May 1933 and spent the next three
months fulfilling the tasks set for him. He joined the Nazi Party,
obtained a German passport – his profession declared as 'journalist' – and was accredited as the Tokyo correspondent of the
Frankfurter Zeitung. He made a favourable impression on the
publisher and editor of *Zeitschrift für Geopolitik* and from them

got letters of introduction to key figures in the German embassy in Tokyo and other useful Germans living in the city.

Similar instructions were given by Ludwik, the third of these Soviet spies (who probably recruited Kim Philby), to Philby, Anthony Blunt, Guy Burgess and Donald Maclean. Philby dropped all his communist contacts and joined the pro-Nazi Anglo-German Fellowship, which made it easier for him to get access to Franco's forces in Spain as a 'journalist'.

Berzin and Ludwik were both in Spain in 1936, in the hope that a victory for the Spanish Republic might weaken the Axis powers. It was not to be. Berzin was recalled to Moscow in June 1937 and resumed his post as head of military intelligence. To his enormous credit he confronted Stalin with the realities of the Spanish Civil War and registered strong complaints against the NKVD's murders of dissident communists such as the POUM leader, Andrés Nin, and others on the left.

He must have known what lay ahead. Arrested by the NKVD later that year, Berzin was shot in the cellars of the Lubyanka in July 1938. He was posthumously rehabilitated in 1956. Ludwik wrote to Stalin in July 1937, returning his medals and condemning the purges and the NKVD's killings. He then went into hiding in Switzerland, but was tricked into a meeting with a fellow agent and murdered a few weeks later. Twenty years ago I met his son, who showed me his father's bullet-pierced wallet.

Sorge avoided returning to Moscow, where he might well have met a similar fate. As a disciplined cadre he continued with his mission: whatever the cost, the Japanese Empire must be prevented from joining the coming war against the Soviet Union. The German embassy in Tokyo became a second base of operations for him. It was in the ambassador's safe that he later discovered details of the plans for Operation Barbarossa – Hitler's invasion of the Soviet Union. He sent the information to Filipp Golikov in Moscow.*

At around the same time, Sorge found out from his Japanese contacts that Japan was not going to invade the Soviet Union and

---

* For a detailed account of this episode, see my *Winston Churchill: His Times, His Crimes* (London, 2022), pp. 243–4.

was instead targeting the United States. This enabled Moscow to withdraw crucial divisions from the Far East, helping to frustrate the German attack on Moscow. Sorge had got much of this information from Ozaki Hotsumi, a journalist close to the Japanese prime minister. 'Considered simply as spies,' Chalmers Johnson wrote in *An Instance of Treason: Ozaki Hotsumi and the Sorge Spy Ring*, 'Ozaki and his partner, Richard Sorge (PhD, Political Science, University of Hamburg, 8 August 1920), were possibly the most intellectually overqualified spies in modern history. Neither was a spy for financial gain; their motivations were political.'

Ozaki's influence was based on his knowledge of Chinese politics and culture: he lived there for several years and wrote a number of sympathetic books and numerous essays on post-Sun Yat-sen China. For a while he had supported the notion of a Japanese–Chinese alliance that might drive the European empires out of Asia, but a closer look at the nationalists of the Kuomintang and the Japanese military leadership cured him of his illusions. Ozaki saw the KMT as clannish and corrupt, and predicted that the Chinese communists would ultimately defeat them. When Sorge suggested to Ozaki that he should argue for the entire Japanese Army to be sent to China, where they would sooner or later be defeated, he presented this hallucinatory notion as allowing three victories: Japan's defeat would open up the country to a revolutionary uprising; only the Chinese communists were capable of defeating the Japanese Empire; the Soviet Union's eastern border would be secured. Ozaki said bluntly that it was a bad idea, not worth the risk.

Neither was aware that the hardcore military faction in Japan, backed by the emperor, was planning an attack on Pearl Harbor, a decision that meant restricting the number of armed forces they sent to China, ignoring the Soviet Union and concentrating on weakening American power in the Pacific.

Even without the Japanese opening a second front on the USSR's eastern border, the Germans almost pulled off a victory. Sorge's messages had been ignored, the best Soviet military leaders, including Mikhail Tukhachevsky, had been executed, and despite the military superiority of the Soviet Union, the Wehrmacht and Luftwaffe almost took Moscow and Leningrad in the first-wave attack. According to the historian of the Red Army John Erickson, Tukhachevsky had carried out manoeuvres that predicted the lines of a German attack as early as 1933. In his last off-the-record question and answer session, restricted to senior Red Army officers, he again insisted that the Germans were preparing a military assault. They would strike suddenly, he said, and deploy everything available on land, sea and air to take the Red Army by surprise. He was accused of treason and shot in June 1937.

Unlike the Germans, who saw the Nazi–Soviet Pact as necessary but temporary, Stalin had illusions that it might be lasting. In a 1966 interview with Zhukov, conducted by Lev Bezymensky, a Soviet historian and war veteran. In January 1941, Zhukov and others had warned Stalin of ominous German troop movements. Stalin wrote to Hitler, asking politely whether these reports were true. Hitler replied that they were, but he swore 'on my honour as a head of state that my troops are deployed ... for other purposes'. Stalin believed him.

It was Molotov who broke the news of the invasion to Soviet citizens. For a fortnight, Stalin made no public appearance. Finally, he addressed the nation. His speech was leaden at the start, but improved as he went on, even if its ideology and language were reminiscent of 1812 rather than 1917. He pledged fierce resistance and a scorched-earth policy.

Arming the people in Moscow and Leningrad prevented the fall of the two key cities of the Revolution; in Stalingrad and Kursk the Red Army broke the backbone of the Third Reich. Soviet resistance was decisive in defeating Hitler. The price was 27,000,000 dead and countless numbers disabled. Many who had tried their best to ensure a victory at a lesser price had been killed before the Nazi invasion even began – murdered, in the words of Ludwik's widow, 'by our own people'.

Sorge had sent Golikov the details of Operation Barbarossa, but he was slandered and ignored. In October 1941, after the Japanese had become suspicious that a spy ring was in operation and had succeeded in intercepting some of Sorge's messages, he and Ozaki were arrested. He spent two years in prison. The Japanese offered to exchange him three times but Stalin refused. He was hanged in Sugamo Prison in Tokyo on 7 November 1943, a few hours after Ozaki. It was the anniversary of the Russian Revolution.

A few months after Chalmers Johnson's book was published in 1964, Sorge was rehabilitated and made a Hero of the Soviet Union. A Post-Constructivist statue of him was erected in his native Baku, and a postage stamp issued. When Yuri Andropov was head of the KGB and a member of the Politburo in the early 1980s, he called in a popular thriller writer called Julian Semyonov and gave him access to some of the files on Trepper and the Red Orchestra. In the resulting novel, *The Red Mole*, the hero Issaev penetrates the highest levels of the Nazi hierarchy. Leonid Brezhnev was so taken by the book that he wanted Issaev to be honoured posthumously. Andropov had to explain that he was a fictional character. Ludwik alone was left to bask in obscurity. That was one reason why I wrote *Fear of Mirrors*.

Ludwik was the inspiration for that book. In Paris in 1991, I managed to track down his son, who was very helpful. The novel was completed in 1992 but not published till 1998. My mainstream publishers felt it was too close to the fall of the Berlin Wall and that I should wait before returning to the subject. I did, but still they weren't keen. Arcadia Books, a small fiction house run by Gary Pulsifer, sent it to Malcolm Bull for a reader's report. Malcolm, who I had not met till then, was enthusiastic and the book was published six years after I had finished it. It was later translated into French, Spanish, Arabic and Turkish, and, I was told, pirated in China.

The Turkish edition, to my surprise, became a bestseller. It was translated by my editor Osman Akinhay for Everest. He understood it perfectly. He had been imprisoned during the dictatorship and boycotted in prison by Stalinist leftists who wanted to punish him for translating Isaac Deutscher and Eric Hobsbawm and other 'revisionists'. He was targeted even after his release. Walking in Ankara one day, he pointed out a spot 'where I was brutally attacked by our Stalinist friends. They left me for dead outside a morgue. I was saved by a passing taxi driver, who took me to hospital. So, I understood your novel very well. I felt its importance in my bones. So did many others, including ex-Stalinists.' Once upon a time the Turkish left, though varied, was huge. Osman felt that *Fear of Mirrors* appealed to them because it explained that past and was not anti-communist. 'Today,' he told me, 'the Turkish left continues to divide and shrink, struggling against extinction.'

I had sent Roman Bernaut, Ludwik's son, an English edition. Bernaut was the false name taken by his mother after his father was murdered. He rang and invited me to visit him and his family in France. It was a joyous July weekend, as millions of people danced on the streets, commemorating the sensational success of their 'blanc, bleu et noir' football team in winning the 1998 World Cup. For a few precious days, cynicism was banished and the interminable baying of the French far-right ('This was not a *French* team') silenced by the dazzling performance of a new, multicultural France. It was difficult not to be slightly infected by the mood as I boarded a train for Fontainebleau to meet one of history's orphans.

An hour later, I was sitting in a beautiful country garden in a tiny village nestling in an ancient forest, sipping a glass of wine with my host. This was my second meeting with Roman Bernaut. He was in his seventies, but his eyes were as sharp and blue as when I first met him almost a decade earlier. He was clearly enjoying his retirement.

He liked the book. 'What amazed me was how you reconstructed that world.'

'Have you anything here that belonged to your father?' For a moment, pain crosses his eyes. He walks indoors, returning with a faded, brown leather wallet. It is pock-marked with bullet holes. He puts it on the table in front of me. We look at each other in silence.

'I had his camera, as well, a Leica. To my eternal regret, I exchanged it many decades ago for a new one.' It was more than sixty years ago, on 4 September 1937, that the body of Roman's father, a youngish, well-dressed man, was discovered on a road a few kilometres from Lausanne. He was thirty-eight. The autopsy revealed that dozens of machine-gun bullets had been fired into his body, most of them after he was already dead. The killers had continued to fire in a frenzy. A few grey hairs were found in the clenched fist of the victim.

The dead man possessed many identities. He had travelled on several passports and was fluent in a number of European languages, among them Polish, Yiddish, Russian, German, Czech, French and English. The day after his assassination, his widow revealed his 'true' identity. He was Ignace Reiss, one of the heads of Soviet military intelligence in Western and Central Europe. In June of that same year, he had sent a letter to the Central Committee of the Communist Party of the Soviet Union denouncing Stalin and his associates as criminals. He resigned from his duties and returned his Order of the Red Banner. For him, the Moscow Trials – in which the old Bolshevik leadership, including Zinoviev and Kamenev, had been convicted on preposterous charges and executed – had proved to be the last straw; he, better than most, knew how the confessions had been obtained. He had signed the letter to Stalin with his old Bolshevik pseudonym, Ludwik.

In Moscow's eyes, much more serious than the letter to the Central Committee were the anonymous warnings Ludwik had despatched to independent anti-Stalinist socialist groups in Spain, alerting them that 'the decision by Stalin to employ every means against you has just been taken. Understand me well, I am saying every means. All your militants are thus at risk.'

This warning had coincided with the kidnapping of the independent socialist leader Andrés Nin, in Barcelona, in June 1937. The Civil War had begun the previous year, but Franco was not yet in the ascendant. Nin had been arrested by the Spanish Republican police, headed at the time by the communist Burillo. He was kept in a private prison controlled by the Spanish Communist Party, which remained pro-Stalin, and was taken to a Soviet-controlled aerodrome in Alcalá de Henares. He disappeared without trace. It was later discovered that he had been tortured and killed by the NKVD.

This was one of the incidents that inspired George Orwell's anti-Stalinist outrage in *Homage to Catalonia*. Ludwik's warning had come too late to save Nin. Others were luckier, and lives had been saved. Stalin acknowledged Ludwik's letter in characteristic fashion, ordering his immediate execution. Another noble life was to be brutally truncated.

There is a photograph of Ludwik's son Roman, Norah and Ira, the two daughters of Andrés Nin, and Seva, Trotsky's grandson. The unknown photographer has labelled it 'Stalin's Orphans'.

I first encountered the case of Ludwik over fifty years ago, when a book by his widow, Elisabeth K. Poretsky, was published. *Our Own People: A Memoir of Ignace Reiss and His Friends* was haunting, a beam from a distant lighthouse that revealed a group of people whose lives were shaped by history and who had seen the decade following 1917 as a marvellous destiny. They had experienced the carnage of the First World War, which had swept away human lives like rotting leaves.

Ludwik and his friends refused to be mere spectators. The fall of the Kaiser and the Tsar filled them with hope. Rosa Luxemburg and Lenin appealed to their intellects. They saw themselves as bearers of a new idea. In their minds and hearts, they carried the vision of a world without oppressors and oppressed.

The idealism of this generation appealed greatly to those of us who were politically engaged in the 1960s, for, along with much else, it provided evidence to justify our assertion that Stalinism was not preordained. It was not the inevitable outcome of communism. Other alternatives had existed. Elisabeth Poretsky's book had moved me deeply, but on a second reading I noticed the gaps. A great deal had been left out. There were virtually no personal reflections, no details of the operations in which Ludwik had been involved, no descriptions of his character. I scoured libraries for accounts of the period, but the results were disappointing. Mentions of Ludwik were always complimentary, but there were too few of them. Only his wife's testimony, like a flute at a silent funeral service, mourned the loss.

Slowly, Ludwik became an obsession with me. For many years, and over dozens of lunches in seedy Soho restaurants, the late Maurice Hatton and I discussed a film based on his life, but nobody was interested, not even in the seventies. By the time I realised I should go and speak to Elisabeth Poretsky, it was too late. She died in 1976. Interest began to wane.

Then, in 1987, came Peter Wright's *Spycatcher*, which described Ludwik as one of the 'great illegals' and a spymaster based in the West. More importantly, Wright referred to his interrogation of the late Anthony Blunt and described how Blunt's mask had slipped only once. This was when Wright had deliberately provoked him, taunting him that he had been seduced by a sordid enterprise. Blunt's eyes flashed fire as he turned on his interrogator: 'Our generation was won over by the finest minds in Europe.' Even though Blunt himself had not been recruited by Ludwik, that single sentence in *Spycatcher* revived my interest, and I began to make notes for a fictional reconstruction of Ludwik's life.

Soon after I'd completed the first draft, I was told by a French friend that Ludwik's son, aged twelve when his father was killed, lived and worked in Paris. I got in touch with Roman Bernaut and he agreed to see me. He was delighted that his father was being rescued by history – and not simply in my novel. A Swiss filmmaker was preparing a documentary and a French historian was trying to penetrate the military archives in Moscow. Nothing Bernaut told me was to alter my own imagined version of his father's life.

'Any photographs?' I enquired nervously. He nodded. Poring over the family album was an eerie and moving experience. So this was what the real Ludwik looked like. As I studied the fifty-year-old photographs, I found everything I had wanted. The rare moments of joy during a family holiday. A photograph of Ludwik and the young Roman with pain written on both faces, a pain that is clearly visible, despite the fact that Ludwik's eyes are hidden by dark glasses.

'Before a parting?' I asked.

'I think so,' he replied. 'It may even have been the last time.'

How distant that world seemed now. I wondered aloud what it

must have felt like to have one's life burdened by the weight of history. The smile returned and he shrugged his shoulders.

'It was a very long time ago. I have lived my own life, but there are ironies. For instance, in this little village there is someone else who knows about history. Leah Andler. She's now nearly ninety. Her father was the Menshevik leader Boris Abramovich. She's a wonderful woman. It reminds me of how, during the dark days, my parents used to talk about the way the Mensheviks, the defeated factional opponents of the old Bolsheviks, had always preserved their dignity. I remember Father saying once that, taken one by one, the human qualities of the Menshevik leaders greatly outweighed those of their Bolshevik counterparts.'

Did he remember the actual day his father died?

'Yes, very well. Someone rang my mother. She was stunned, but what I remember really well is that she didn't panic at all. She told me what had happened, and who had done it, but she never lost her composure in front of the Swiss or French police. She told them it was no ordinary crime. She advised them to look for the killers in the Soviet embassy in Paris. Of course, nothing happened. The actual killers were never apprehended. Many years later, the French inspector in charge of the inquiry told my mother he'd been warned to lay off. The government of the day did not wish to offend Stalin.'

To this day, Roman has no idea of the real name of his father. It was certainly not Eberhard or Reiss or Ludwik or ... he names other aliases. It might be Poretsky but – he shrugs his shoulders – it might not. Why had he never asked his mother?

Roman smiled, as if to imply that it was not easy to get his mother to part with information against her will. After her husband's murder, Elizabeth felt she was being suffocated by the stifling walls of Europe. She was desperate to escape. They needed new passports and an identity change to reach America. They were helped by a young Belgian Socialist MP, Paul-Henri Spaak, but Roman has no idea why the name Bernaut was chosen.

'My earliest memory is of Moscow in 1931. I was six years old, and it was the first time all three of us had lived a normal life together. Ludwik had an office routine. I remember being very proud of him for not using his military position to jump to the front of a queue. Later, in Berlin, I was usually alone with mother. He would arrive, stay three or four days, then leave again. He never talked about his work, except to say it was "for the world revolution", and conditions were such that kids my age knew instinctively not to push one's parents.'

The first Soviet spies were not technicians or trained killers. In the twenties, spies were above all political people, chosen for their ability to grasp, analyse and connect events that appeared to be unconnected. Above all, Soviet spies in those days of hope saw themselves as foot soldiers of the world revolution. Utopia was very firmly inscribed on the maps of Lenin and Trotsky. Both leaders believed and wrote that, without a revolution in Germany, the backward Soviet Union might not survive. This desperate belief determined their whole outlook, and early Bolshevik military strategy, under Marshal Tukhachevsky, was premised on going to the aid of other successful revolutions. It was this idea that fired Ludwik and five other boys from his native village in Polish Galicia to become communists and, later, spies.

The Fourth Department of the Red Army was created to gather intelligence abroad. Headed by Berzin, the department looked for people with a broad culture, intellectual qualities, linguistic skills, a capacity to think strategically and meticulous powers of observation. There are accounts of Berzin's boys sitting in the bar of the Hotel Lux in Moscow during the twenties, conversing in thirty different languages with visiting revolutionaries of hugely different backgrounds, drawn from all over the globe. Many of them were won over to Moscow by the cadres of the Fourth Department. Few other countries in this century have fielded such a devoted group of agents, imbued with a disciplined idealism and the conviction that they were working to transform the world. They risked their lives repeatedly, and many of them were finally killed by Stalin.

Ludwik, Sorge and Trepper were three of Berzin's most gifted operators. It was Trepper who, after Ludwik's death, established the Red Orchestra (possibly the most effective spy network ever created) at the very heart of the Nazi war-machine, which supplied valuable information to the Allies throughout the second half of the war. Trepper had an agent in the very office of the German High Command. Arrested by the Gestapo, Trepper was one of the very few communist prisoners of Jewish origin to escape. After the war, he was rewarded for his services with a few years in the gulag, accused of being a Gestapo agent.

Hitler's victory in Germany had meant that young Roman and his mother had to leave Berlin in a hurry. Ludwik organised their transfer to France. They lived in a furnished flat in Paris for the first two years and then moved to a slightly larger apartment, in Rue Raffet in the 16th Arrondissement, from 1935 to 1937. In Berlin, Roman had barely seen his father.

'I saw him more often in France. There were times he would stay with us for a whole three weeks. It was always fun when he was at home. He was very warm, very outgoing, laughed a lot and loved nice things. He never lost an opportunity to admire a nice fountain pen or a watch. He ate well. This I have inherited from him. Mother didn't care a damn about what she or I ate. She had a stern, puritanical, ascetic side. Always ultra-generous to her friends or comrades in trouble. Nothing was too good for them. At home, the regime was strict.'

'But surely, you must have had some idea of what they were up to ...'

He laughed. 'They were often changing names and nationalities, and so I was aware of the extraordinary nature of their work, but my mother ensured that we led as normal a life as possible. Of course, I knew that they were working for Moscow. I knew my father's work involved danger. To this day, I'm not sure how much my mother really knew. He kept many things secret from her, so as not to endanger her. I remember once, as a cover, they ran a stationery shop in Holland. The shop did rather well, and there was much amusement when a Dutch friend announced that they had made a profit.'

'Did your father recruit Philby?'

Bernaut shrugs his shoulders. 'That is what people say, but who knows? Father was in Vienna a great deal in 1933–34, reorganising the network after Hitler's victory. He knew Britain well. It was he who had recruited a cipher clerk in the Foreign Office so that Berzin in Moscow read many secret documents a day before they were seen by Lord Curzon. Once the Spanish Civil War began in 1936, Ludwik was in charge of placing spies at the heart of Franco's operation. That is where Philby won his spurs. So, all the circumstantial evidence suggests that he would have had to approve Philby's recruitment. The truth lies in the archives of Soviet military intelligence in Moscow. These are still unavailable. Untouchable. Even money can't buy them. At least not yet.'

Ludwik belonged to the generation that had made the Russian Revolution, won the civil war between the Reds and Whites and founded a Soviet Union stretching from the Baltic to the Pacific. A Polish Jew who had given his life to a political cause, he had studied law in Vienna, joined the clandestine Polish Socialist Party, suffered imprisonment and torture as a militant in Warsaw and Vienna, and had been headhunted by Berzin for the Fourth Department. From 1923–26, he worked for the German Communist Party in the Ruhr. He established the first Soviet contact with Sinn Féin in London and Dublin during the Black-and-Tan wars of the twenties. He knew virtually every country in Europe.

Then the dark years arrived. In Moscow, the old party was being transformed into a pitiless, bureaucratic machine, peopled by bandwagon careerists and informers. Old Bolsheviks were being identified and exterminated. The new Bolsheviks, recruited after Stalin had established his total grip on the party apparatus in 1927, tended to be temperamentally mean, intellectually insipid, politically brutal and hostile to all manifestations of 'rootless cosmopolitanism' – a code-word for the old Bolsheviks of Jewish origin, who, the cruder Stalinists (and, we might add, their modern successors) alleged, never understood the needs of Russia.

Ludwik was hoping that the Republic would win in Spain. He carried on serving with clenched teeth. In his Dantean moods, all he thought of was Hell and devils and death. In a more optimistic frame, he dreamt of a victory in Spain reigniting Europe and isolating Stalin within the Soviet Union. Increasingly, he was overcome by a desire to escape, knowing it could mean instant death. He had been paralysed by his own powerless disgust, but the anger grew; finally, he broke away and ran.

He made one crucial mistake. One of his agents, a veteran German communist, Gertrude Schildbach, had been suicidal ever since the Moscow Trials. Ludwik felt that if he disappeared without letting her know, she might take her own life. He informed her of his hiding place. It was an act of humanity that led to his own death. The NKVD assassins sent a young Italian agent to seduce Schildbach and recruit her to their cause, telling her that Ludwik had gone over to the Nazis. Schildbach, dazed, believed them and agreed to betray her lifelong friend and mentor.

At first, like a character in a third-rate thriller, she was sent on her own with a box of poisoned chocolates to Ludwik's safe cottage in the Swiss mountains. But just as Roman went to sample one, Gertrude panicked. She could not bear to see him die. She retrieved the box clumsily and put it away in her handbag. Ludwik was used to her eccentric behaviour and thought nothing of the incident. When she rang him the next day, he agreed to the fatal meeting. This was the ambush planned by the killers. It was Gertrude's grey hairs that were found in his hand when Ludwik's body was discovered.

Bernaut and his mother fled to America, where she was a target of the intelligence services. 'She was questioned at great length by the FBI and, after the war, by the CIA, who wanted her to identify agents of Soviet military intelligence. She could not help.' He chuckles. 'One of Elizabeth's friendly interrogators turned out to be Jim McCord, later famous as a Watergate burglar.'

During the last year of the war, Bernaut, now a student of economics at Columbia, was called up. 'When they discovered I could speak German, Russian, Polish and French, they smiled and sent me straight to the OSS [US military intelligence]. It was a hotbed of ex-communists and ex-Trotskyists, run mainly by Austrian ex-communists, all of them dissidents. They only wanted to hire confirmed anti-fascists. It was a very sympathetic outfit in those days. I appreciated the paradox. My father had started the century with Soviet intelligence, and here, in the middle of this same century, I was now a wartime agent for the United States.'

How might Ludwik have reacted to this development? 'I don't know. But if Ludwik had stayed alive, we would never have gone to the United States. When he and Walter Krivitsky used to speak about the horrors of what was happening in Moscow, my father always said that they could never go over to the West. Never. Krivitsky, as you know, did defect to Washington and was miserable. My mother was convinced that his suicide was real. He was an obsessive neurotic, and I think the awful book, *I Was Stalin's Agent*, which the FBI made him write, depressed him greatly.'

So, eight years after the death of Ludwik, his son, in US military uniform, found himself in liberated Berlin. His task: to act as a liaison with Soviet military intelligence. Bernaut frowns at the memory. He was dealing with the men whose organisation killed his father. He lightens up at another memory:

'Once I was in a US Army jeep going to work. On the road ahead German POWS were being walked along the road and loaded into trucks. Suddenly someone shouted my name. I parked, got off the jeep and walked over. The POW was weeping. Then I recognised him. We were the same age. He was the child of a German communist family that had fled to the Soviet Union after 1933. We used to play together. After the Stalin–Hitler Pact, to show good will, Stalin handed over many, too many, German communists to Hitler. I asked what happened and gave him my details. "Nothing much", he said. "My parents were taken to a camp and executed. I was sent to an orphanage and joined the Luftwaffe. I was sent to bomb Moscow, but please tell our friends I never did. I used to fly just outside and dump my bombs in the fields."'

There was a tear in Roman's eye as he finished the story.

After the war, Bernaut returned to Columbia and finished his studies, but his mother was desperate to return to Paris. 'She was always being visited by intelligence agents from Britain. Like you, they wanted to know if Ludwik had recruited Philby and, more pertinently, who else had been recruited. They were constantly in search of old names. My mother knew little and told them nothing. I remember her anger after Peter Wright's visit. He was engaged in completing his *Spycatcher* and was desperate for information about my father's activities. She was really alienated by him and, after his very short stay, she described him to me as a "fascist fool".'

In New York and Paris, Elizabeth Poretsky had developed close ties with Menshevik families. She visited England to establish contact with Isaac Deutscher, the Polish-born historian of communism, whose biography of Trotsky remains a modern classic, admired by Michael Foot and, yes, even Tony Blair. 'You are our conscience,' Elizabeth told Deutscher. 'We depend on you.' Bernaut remained aloof from politics. He got a job at the OECD, where he worked as an economist for twenty-five years. Now, in retirement, he wonders whether the Russians might have the dual honour of having destroyed both dirigiste socialism and laissez-faire capitalism.

At long last, his curiosity has been aroused as to what his father's real name might have been. Ludwik's elder brother was decorated by the Poles. He had fought and died on the Polish side during the ill-fated Soviet advance on Warsaw in 1921. 'There are bound to be records of him. If I get round to finding out the real name, I'll let you know. In your novel, a Vietnamese millionaire buys the Ludwik archive from the Russians. If that happens in real life, please let me know.'

20

Renewals

The collapse of the Soviet Union and its peripheral states was a huge boost for global capitalism. In a stroke, any real mass alternative to the system evaporated. New social movements arose, first in Seattle in 1999 (a radical US initiative very well described by Alexander Cockburn in his short book on the subject), and some months later in Porto Alegre in Southern Brazil, a city where the local left was in power and had been experimenting with popular and democratic budgets and encouraging citizen assemblies to discuss and vote on how local funds should be spent. Initiatives such as these were attracting attention in a world where nothing grander seemed possible. The Porto Alegre annual conferences became the venue for radicals of every sort for some years.

In Meard Street, Soho, the *New Left Review* was facing different problems. As described earlier, the civil war in the Balkans divided and split not only the *NLR* but the left intelligentsia throughout Western Europe. The journal had to readjust and renew itself if it was to survive. Longevity alone was no guarantee of future existence. Perry and I had several lengthy conversations about what needed to be done politically and in terms of literary presentation to effectively relaunch the magazine. While politically solid on all the key issues that now confronted us, the *NLR* style itself had become too academic, a bit repetitive, loosely edited, and with too many self-referential footnotes. There was a danger of it becoming dull and predictable.

I said all this to Robin as well, without belittling in any way his own intellectual and editorial contribution. Unsurprisingly, he became a bit defensive, but understood very clearly that a political/design relaunch was necessary. He agreed, too, that the best person to take charge and push it all through was Perry. The latter took a sabbatical from UCLA and returned to London. The minutes of a meeting attended in Fall 1998 by 'RB (Editor, NLR), TA (Chair NLR/Verso), PA (Chair NLT)' record the decision to reappoint PA as editor. At a subsequent meeting, Perry, in a mode similar to that of 1962 (as described in Edward Thompson's letter quoted in Chapter 12), demanded and obtained the following:

(e) PA vested with mandate to

> reorganise office
> setting up efficient and transparent systems of recording and
>   registering material sent to the office
> constructing an archive
> a map of how the *Review* is actually run
> charged with organising the re-design of the magazine
> an up-to-date copy inventory
> office integration/installation of Verso/NLR answerphone

At two successive editorial committee meetings we all spelt out in turn what each of us would like to see in the relaunched *NLR*. I stressed regular book reviews and cultural coverage, on which we once had a very good record. Also possibly satire (the looks on some faces suggested this would not get through) and experiential writing.

Ronald Fraser had once used his skills as an oral historian in an old series called 'Work', interviewing workers of 'hand and of brain', that had gone on to become a much-referenced Penguin collection. We couldn't repeat that. Instead, I suggested a series inspired, in some ways, by Karl Kraus and his magazine *Die Fackel* during the interwar years in Vienna. Our title should be 'In These Great Times', reflecting the eccentricities and moods of the present but without a trace of whimsy. We later published Georgi Derluguian's amazing account of moving from Moscow to

Chicago and building a house close to Northwestern University. A description of a party given by a nouveau riche Chinese billionaire appeared soon afterwards. But then other needs of the magazine took over and there was no time to commission articles like this on a regular basis. A great pity, since these essays had begun to attract attention.

The central and defining piece in the relaunch of the journal was Perry's essay entitled 'Renewals' (*NLR* Jan/Feb 2000). It was, as he put it, a 'lucid registration of political defeat'. It's no-nonsense analysis startled quite a few people and all sorts of dire predictions were floated. The essay may have been over-pessimistic but by and large it got things right. 'Renewals,' I thought on reading a first draft, marked a break with fantasy politics of every variety.

It's interesting that John Lloyd of the *Financial Times* was keen to promote it, and even asked for a 'Lunch with Perry Anderson' interview. But it was clearly indigestible to his bosses. When I inquired years later as to why, all he would say was that he was ashamed and should have written to Perry to apologise. Obviously what irritated them was the editorial's clear statement of what our political priorities were: continuous analyses and critiques of capital and empire and the defenders of both. We were never tempted to loot the *Communist Manifesto* for quotes to justify neoliberal capitalism as a stepping stone to socialism.

In later years, Meghnad Desai, professor of economics at the LSE and an erstwhile Marxist, chaired a talk by me on the Islam Quintet (by this time he was a New Labour Lord) and afterwards semi-whispered: 'So glad you and the NLR still carry on. I've just become a prostitute.' I nodded in agreement with both statements.

When the first draft of 'Renewals' was completed in June 1999, Perry sent it to the editorial committee for comments, but also to a few contributors and friends. Where there were criticisms, Perry's responses were meticulous. Fred Jameson was reassured that there was 'no question of deserting the political battlefield for *Kulturkritik*'. The historian Carlo Ginsburg – who wrote essays for the *NLR* and books for Verso and whose work we valued (and still do) – was the sharpest interlocutor, demanding self-criticism and an exorcising of all the ghosts from the past. He explained that:

> When I said that your proposal struck me as 'sectarian', I should have said 'surprisingly sectarian', since I never considered you a sectarian. Sectarian is not necessarily a synonym of 'radical' ... Self-criticism ... should be an antidote to this. Why don't you write an essay entitled 'Why we have been defeated'? ('We' meaning, of course, the Left). Self-criticism is – must be – a bitter medicine. But I cannot see any alternative to this.

Perry's response to this was on the sharp side:

> I do feel there is something amiss in just a blank reiteration – unaccompanied by any positive editorial suggestion – that the journal should confess the error of its ways, as if this were its only salvation. It smacks too much of the figure of the *pentito* for which too few Italian intellectuals can bring themselves to express aversion. Actually, most of the European Left has spent a decade in much the kind of sackcloth and ashes you recommend, as any number of organisations, titles and authors in Italy indicate ... Self-flagellation is today not a recipe for editorial novelty ...
>
> Given this, your insistence that 'self-criticism must be a bitter medicine' – worthy of some album of Flaubertian *poncifs*! – strikes me as out of character. Perhaps I can put this with a counter-factual parable. Let us imagine, all too easily, that the Japanese had made the logical decision in December 1941 and – as so many of their strategists wanted – attacked the USSR across Siberia rather than the USA in the Pacific. Caught between the two axis powers, the Soviet Union would certainly have collapsed, without America being drawn into the war, leaving Hitler the uncontested master of Europe. Should we imagine you, from some redoubt in the Abruzzi, telling contemporaries that their first task, faced with the victory of the enemy, was to practice self-criticism and learn lessons from the Third Reich? Obviously not. For the two cases are not comparable, you will say, quite reasonably.

But this is just the point. I would have expected a response more straightforwardly, along these lines: 'My dear Anderson, haven't you realised. No left could ever be new again – that story is finished. Close down your journal, and rejoin the rest of humanity.' In other words: liberal capitalism is not such a bad thing, one should settle down and improve it where one can...

It was a rich debate with many constructive and useful contributions from existing members of the editorial committee. From the outside, Benedict Anderson had some very useful comments, suggestions and corrections. He pointed out that:

> one thing that anyone comparing early *NLR* with late *NLR* will see at once is the movement of *NLR* people to universities and university jobs. Rise of footnote culture, as well as mandarinal styles of communication. Also, self-absorption. (Jim Scott's famous claim, said to be based on statistics, that the average readership of any single article in an academic magazine is 2.4 people.) This should be formally recognised as a problem or a plus. In any case, it denotes something of structural importance. The Right is perfectly happy to have the Left corralled on campus.

Ben went on to criticise the text for 'what is perhaps some over-statement' regarding classical thinkers:

> Gramsci, for example, has far from disappeared, he is wildly popular with my students. Let alone Benjamin, and not just a depoliticised Benjamin. Raymond Williams is still there. I suppose what is in the end needed is a kind of inventory of what 'deserves' to survive. There is also the historical fact that it is rather rare for people to disappear fully. They 'go down' soon after their political or physical death, but are sooner or later recuperated in some form or another.

This sage advice was certainly followed by Verso in its publishing programme as well as the *NLR*.

Perry had asked M-K to peruse the draft editorial with a 'critical eye'. She certainly did that but refused to comment in writing like the rest of us. Instead, she insisted on a tête-à-tête. She informed him that the editorial was dull, arrogant and reactionary. Perry's report of the exchange was also sent to M-K, who verbally stamped the seal of accuracy.

M-K's argument:

– dull: your picture of the current scene presents a completely uniform world, in which nothing new or interesting makes any appearance. Everything is reduced to a boringly flat geopolitical diagram. You pay little or no attention to, for example: genetically modified foods, human rights, immigration, Nationalism, fundamentalism, women's emancipation (Internet could, of course, be added). These are the kind of political issues young people care about. If you want to gain new readers, they are what you should be addressing.

– arrogant: waste space talking about *NLR* in the 60s, as if anyone under pensionable age knew or cared less about these old tales. The assumption anyone would be interested in them is complacent introversion. As for tone: you say the editorial is personal and so not binding, but actually you lay down the law as to what your journal should or should not publish in the most peremptory manner.

– reactionary: you reject or ignore nearly everything young people find attractive in present day culture – a typically rearguard attitude. No American movies, no Afro-Caribbean novels, no cable TV. You invent imaginary dangers even in traditional areas: for example, deconstruction is a back number on the critical scene. Basically, this is the outlook of someone quite out of touch with what's going on. Politically, you don't seem to notice that not everything in the world is on the slide. Feminism has made a huge difference for the better. But all you talk about is capitalism.

My reply was this:

– youth: mistake to imagine young people move in droves. Every generation is more varied than this. There's always a minority that resists what the majority likes. So jazz. Peer pressures produce very high levels of conformity in adolescence, but by the time of university they tend to weaken. A journal going against the stream isn't automatically ruled out for everyone under 25. More generally, youth as such is anyway not a credible test of progress. Historically, some generations are mostly apolitical or conservative, others are radical or insurgent. One needs to discriminate.

– hauteur: there's probably some ineradicable vice there. Still, it makes no sense to kick off a new or relaunched journal in too diffident a way. The 'manifesto' is a literary form with its own rules. It has to be somewhat declamatory to work at all. The same goes for an element of self-reference, when the journal has already existed for 40 years. One can't write as if these hadn't existed; a minimum retrospect is unavoidable. But it's true that further disavowal of authoritative position-taking would be an improvement.

– politics: agenda of new 'hot' issues hasn't exactly been overlooked in *NLR* – Cockburn on food/forests, Hobsbawm/Gowan on torture/human rights, Keddie on fundamentalism, Nairn/(B) Anderson on nationalism, extensive series on women's movements. But the deeper point is valid. The premise of the editorial is that *NLR* belongs to an intellectual and political tradition that rejects capitalism. But it doesn't argue for the premise.

So someone is entitled to say: 'I am much more concerned about feminism. Why should I care about capitalism? Actually, things have been looking up under it.' This is a reasonable position. The editorial allows for it. (Sexual minorities could say the same.) But the question addressed by the editorial is another one. All such progress has so far been compatible with the spread of neoliberalism across the world. One can bracket that, if one wishes, and just pursue issues of choice within the system. There are plenty of publications that do so to good effect. But there will be limits to what can be said about them if the system is intellectually sidestepped in the name of practical improvements. *NLR*'s job is to keep the system as the general framework of all politics in sight.

The new *NLR* was duly launched in January 2000. That month I received many phone calls and messages from friends. A majority were favourable, some were disturbed by the tone, others expressed sadness that the *NLR* had abandoned its past. Mis-readings were common. A reluctance to accept that the US had triumphed was expressed in different registers. Yet we entered the twenty-first century with a sense of renewal, not knowing what was waiting for us there. We soon found out. In order to preserve and buttress its global hegemony, the United States unleashed a new set of wars. These were followed by the crash of 2008, the emergence of China as a new player, which shifted the world market eastwards, and the sensational backfiring of the attempt to isolate the new Russia. Added to all this was a shift to the right in the EU countries, the UK referendum that took Britain out of the EU, and the actual and virtual collapse of social democracy. A new opposition emerged against the new wars in the US and UK but outside parliamentary structures. The relaunched and renewed *New Left Review* had a great deal to write about.

BOOK II

A FAMILY INTERLUDE

21

The 'Noble and Warlike' Khattars of Wah

In 1993, when my father died, I received some very moving letters of condolence from friends in the UK, especially after a warm obit in the *Independent*. One of them was from Raphael Samuel. Apart from other things Raph had a request: 'The obituary notice of your father made a fascinating read, but it needs the special tenderness that comes through in your own *obita dicta* to make him real to those who did not have the privilege of knowing him. It sounds so representative a life, even if also of one who walked courageously alone, and I do hope one day you will find occasion to let us have more glimpses of it.'

Raph wasn't the only one to suggest this, but he was the most persistent. When I showed my mother this letter, her immediate response was: 'What about my life?'

'This might be difficult to believe,' I replied, 'but you're still alive.' She's gone too now so I can write about both.

Both my grandfathers belonged to the Khattar tribe from the village of Wah in North-Western Punjab. The village was close to the Indus at Attock, a day's journey by bullock cart to Peshawar. It was a few miles from the ancient city of Taxila and very close to Hasanabdal, a settlement noted by a visiting Chinese scholar in 7 AD and given its present name seven or eight centuries later to honour the Sufi saint Baba Hassan Abdallah. Later, Hasanabdal became a key small city during the Mughal period and a holy place of worship for Sikhs all over the world.

Sons of the murdered Karam Khan. My two great-grandfathers, Muhammad Hyat Khan and Gulab Khan (second right and right), circa 1875.

Who were the Khattars, and where did they originally come from? To this day their origins, unlike that of virtually all the other tribes in Northern Punjab, remain mysterious. A family historian informed me that it is now more or less agreed they came from Ghazni (now in Afghanistan), but I'm not sure how accurate this is. My late father's rule of thumb was that most of India's Muslims were likely converts from different varieties and castes of Hinduism and that it was a total waste of time searching for other ancestors.

This is probably the case for much of the old country, but North-Western Punjab was the gateway to India. The first entrants were the Indo-European immigrants in ancient times; however, no evidence of their presence exists. Sanskrit was created in the Swat–Northern Punjab areas and a version of Farsi in the Attock region. Mixed with the local dialects, they enriched the culture. They were followed centuries later by invading armies: Persians, Greeks, Afghans and Central Asians who, like unstoppable torrents, expanded the mountain passes on the edge of the subcontinent. All these migrations and conquests created the ethnic heterogeneity that has characterised the region. All this

278

at a time when the Indus was the natural and accepted border between India and what later became Afghanistan. The border regions were always popular as trading centres and as places to gather information on what lay ahead. They were also the first port of call for numerous marauders and conquerors on their way southwards. This was the pathway – a meeting point for trade routes, by land and river – traversed by the Aryans, Alexander, the Mughals and sundry others.

If several hundred of Alexander's soldiers and a handful of his generals settled here after his own hurried departure, there is no logical reason why this pattern should not have preceded or continued after him. What is now known as the Khyber Pass was used by the Macedonian conqueror in 326 BC. In this region he built an alliance with the ruling tribes of Taxila. Taxila was the capital city of a sizeable kingdom, extending from the Indus to Kashmir. Its rulers collaborated with Alexander and helped him defeat the powerful local Raja Poros (our childhood hero) on the banks of the large Hydaspes River.

My paternal grandmother, Yusuf Sultana, with her younger brother, Masud Hyat, later head of the family, circa 1902.

The contributions from the rulers of Taxila to Alexander's conquering army were significant. The ancient Greek historian Eratosthenes wrote that as well as building a bridge over the river they gave 200 talents of silver, 3,000 oxen fattened for the shambles, 10,000-plus sheep, thirty elephants and a cavalry unit consisting of 700 armed auxiliaries. Alexander was also gifted Taxila to use however he wished, as a military base or a 'rest-and-recreation' centre.

The Khattar tribe may have first arrived in the region on one of Sultan Mahmud of Ghazni's seventeen excursions – terror raids, tourist trips, however one wishes to describe them – to India in the early eleventh century. Mahmud set up a kingdom, modestly renaming Lahore as Mahmudabad. However, no written account of the Khattars' migration exists. Had they, like falling stars on a silent night, dropped out unnoticed during one of Mahmud's journeys from Ghazni to Delhi and back? Not impossible. Were they exclusively warriors or traders, or a mixture of both, as was not uncommon in those times?

Of only one fact are we sure. Remnants of Mahmud's armies did settle in the Punjab and intermarry. However, none of the family storytellers or regional historians – nor the authors of the remarkable Gazetteers produced for administrators during the British Raj, which mapped the then recent histories of different regions – have any idea when the Khattars moved here. The region was known for its fertile soil, flowing streams, lakes big and small, fruit gardens and flowers in abundance. I still remember my mother insisting that I regularly munch on the watercress growing wild on the banks of large streams. It was, she insisted, very good for the eyesight. When the Mughal king Jehangir first encountered these streams five centuries ago, he quoted from a Persian verse: 'The water is so transparent that a blind man in the middle of the night could count the particles of sand at the bottom.' It was the same in my childhood. We used to drop to the ground, lie flat on our stomachs and drink from the stream.

An alternative story, accepted by some genealogists, traces the tribe's origins back to the eleventh-century Rajputs, whose large-scale conversion to Islam began a century or so later. One such account is contained in *Khattars of Wah: Full and Proper Historical Background and Authentic Pedigree* (1866–67) by Col. C.H. Hall:

> About the noble and warlike Khattars, there are many stories and tales, and many later embellishments and strange fictitious accounts, etc. Some say they are 'Arabs' (relatives of the Awan tribe of Punjab), some say they are 'Afghans' or 'Pashtuns' (Pathans in India), some say they are Jatts, like many indigenous races of this Land of Five Rivers, and some even claim they are 'Turkish' people. The ancient history is covered in many veils and sagas and the saga is very very long and ancient. However, briefly, in truth, as all pedigrees and genuine old records show and prove to us, the Khattars are in fact Rajputs by origin, descended from 'Chauhan' or 'Chohan', a major branch or clan of the Rajputs.

Hall quotes from Mullah Sarwar, the genealogist attached to my great-grandfather Sardar Muhammed Hyat Khan's household. In a period where most historians were oral genealogists, over-reliant on Chinese whispers, tradition played an important role, and figures like Sarwar often posed as literate and reliable scholars. More than a few were charlatans in search of employment. Sarwar's genealogy has its merits. It is mercifully brief. It does, however, regularly miss out several generations.

For example, he is blissfully unaware that the area where the Khattars settled had once been a centre of Buddhism. Before their arrival, Buddhist learning and culture dominated the region as a whole and many Brahmins converted, regarding their own religion as having degenerated into castes and meaningless rituals. It was far removed from customs established during Vedic times. A huge university and three or four cities existed in the region around Taxila when it was a Buddhist principality. Some ancient Greek historians, Strabo and Megasthenes in particular, have attested to this.

As did my mother in her own fashion. She often recalled her surprise one day while walking from Wah to a neighbouring Khattar village, when she decided to use a stone bridge across a shallow stream to shorten the journey. She paused on the smooth shiny surface and was struck by the quality of the ancient construction. Village women accompanying her asked: 'Do you know what's underneath the bridge? It's Baba Buddha.' My mother discarded her sandals, slipped into the stream and went underneath the bridge to have a look. She was stunned. It was as near perfect a life-size statue of the Buddha as she'd ever seen. She got back on the bridge and sat there in silence, immersed in contemplation.

'You can take it back to Lahore if you want,' her companions laughed. 'Here we sometimes use it to frighten the children, saying it's a punishing demon.' Now my mother was a fanatical – I use the word advisedly – collector of Gandhara art and sculptures, and of children's toys from archaeological finds that pre-dated Buddhism, so it is a surprise that she didn't take the statue, especially since a close family friend in Mardan had found one (or rather, the peasants ploughing the land had). It too was life-size and adorned the hallway in their house. How did my mother, quite competitive on this front, manage to resist the temptation? 'It would have been a sacrilege,' she later explained. 'I somehow liked the idea of the Buddha being utilised for the local people, so let's not spread the word.' I wonder whether it's still there.

A similar excitement gripped her several years before she passed away. I could sense it on the phone: 'A dealer has just arrived from Bamiyan with something you'd like. It's a head in white marble. The price is very reasonable. He's waiting. Should I buy it?'

The head belonged to Sokrati (Socrates). I suggested she buy it. Even if it were a fake, it would be nice to have. When I saw Sokrati's head for the first time in Lahore it was still covered with layers of mud, some of them probably new, added to enhance its value. I had it thoroughly washed till the white marble emerged gleaming in the sun. The laws on taking antiquities out of the country without permission were now very strict. But of course this did not apply to fakes.

I photographed it for a Greek friend in London, a very serious, scholarly dealer in antiquities. He could not give a verdict. 'On balance, I would guess it's a fake. Socrates' face is too handsome.

Ancient Greek depictions present him as a very ugly man.' He showed me some images. This did not convince me. Since there was an exaggerated view of all male Greeks as being tall, handsome and fair, with godlike bodies, how could ancient Pakhtun sculptors have portrayed the great philosopher as the opposite? Sokrati still sits in my sister's house in Lahore, but I've given up and instructed her to give it as a house-warming present to two young friends. They'll keep him safe.

As I write, I feel my mother is getting impatient. She wants to make a grander entry than this, but will have to wait until the next chapter.

Back to the story of the tribe. I will have to miss out a few centuries, which is fine, since I have no way of determining whether a genealogy is imagined or otherwise. I also have a slight aversion for those who get obsessed with this side of family history.

In 1026, Sultan Mahmud of Ghazni raided the Hindu temple of Somanatha (Somnath in the colonial textbooks). The story of the raid has reverberated through Indian history. The equally exaggerated triumphalist accounts in Turko-Persian chronicles became the main source for most eighteenth-century historians. It was first depicted as a trauma for the Hindus, not in India, but in the House of Commons. It suited everyone and helped the British to divide and rule a multi-millioned subcontinent.*

In the thirteenth century, just before the Mughals arrived, Islam was the dominant culture in the region. The head of the Khattar clan was also the commander of a warrior army that

---

* The story of the raid has been revived under the democratic-fascist RSS/BJP combination that rules India today. Romila Thapar, the doyenne of Indian historians, has reconstructed what took place by studying other sources, including local Sanskrit inscriptions, biographies of kings and merchants of the period, court epics and popular narratives that have survived. The result is astounding and undermines the traditional version. Inconveniently, her findings also contest the current Hindu nationalist version of this history. My penchant for huge digressions is well known and I am tempted again, but Romila's book-essay *Somanatha* deserves to be read to gain a full account of this. It reveals among other things how often historical events are decontextualised to serve the needs of the present. First the British, now Modi.

numbered in the hundreds. Early opposition to the Mughals – refusing a newly imposed tax – ended some months later, after a few Khattar chiefs served a short spell in prison for non-payment, together with others of the regional nobility.

Here I must offer retrospective critical support to the state. After a reconciliation, the Khattar chief was ranked a *mansabdar* (apart from other duties, one of his key tasks was to collect tax in the region) and granted the right to maintain 3,000 men under arms. In *Passages from Antiquity to Feudalism*, Perry Anderson defined a key feature of early feudalism as 'parcelized sovereignty': each baron his own master and negotiations (usually involving bags of gold from the ruler) essential before forces could be committed to wars at home or abroad. The Mughal state did not encourage sovereignty. It kept a tight grip, crushing any illusions regarding shared power, frequently and forcefully. This was one major reason for its instability and the fall of the dynasty.

In short, the version that is now agreed by most local and family historians goes like this: Sometime in the eleventh century, the Rajput Raja Kaidamath (known as Kaidu or Khaddar), together with a sizeable section of his followers, converted to Islam and took the name Khattar Khan. This followed a period of inter-marriages with Afghan, Persian and Central Asian migrants and these grew in number following the conversion. Others remained Hindu and later some became Sikhs.*

Khattar Khan's tribe spread to different parts of the country. The largest segment moved a bit further up the banks of the

---

* This mixture was brought home to me recently when my younger brother, Mahir, revealed that he had been seduced by a cheap offer on the internet and had gone in for a heritage hunt. The results did confirm some of the oral accounts. He wrote: 'Just did it for a lark, as there was a heavily discounted offer. The results were mainly predictable, slightly intriguing on the margins: 82% South Asian, 5% West Asian, 4.5% Central Asian, 6% Irish, Scottish and Welsh, and about 1% each Ashkenazi Jewish and Baltic. They correctly pinpointed Shahid as a first cousin, with a 13% DNA match.' I was delighted that there was a Celtic infusion. It reminded me of how once, in the seventies, while sharing a platform with the Provo leader Seán Mac Stíofáin in Dublin, he informed the audience to much laughter and applause that Sinn Féin had an Irish version of my name: Terry Kelly.

Indus. The leader of this migration from one section of the Indus to another was Sardar Sarbuland (Head Held High) Khan. It was under him that the tribe occupied huge tracts of land in what is now the Attock District. One of Head Held High's direct descendants, Jamal Khan, settled in 'little paradise', and named the village Jalalsar after his son Jalal. It was in this large village, surrounded by streams and greenery of every sort, that wild fruit trees grew, bearing the 'curved fruit' unseen before by the Macedonian warriors. Could it be that the curved fruit that Alexander banned his soldiers from consuming (because so many Greeks had been felled by the resulting constipation) was the same wild and unripe banana usually preferred by monkeys? Quite possibly.

The Mughal emperors who first set eyes on Jalalsar never made such a mistake. They were great fruit experts: Babur, the founder of the empire, had a passion for orchards and fruits of all varieties which he expressed with delicacy in his memoirs. Jalalsar was renamed Wah after a Mughal king visited the village on a stopover during one of his journeys in the region. There is some controversy here. Architectural evidence suggests that it was the Emperor Akbar's architects who laid the foundations of the astonishing Mughal Gardens at Wah. This does not mean that we must credit Akbar for the change of name. It was more likely his son, the sybaritic emperor Jehangir, who fell in love with the spot, as he writes in his memoirs:

> Stayed at Baba Hasanabdal on 12th Muharram, 1016 A.H. At about two miles on the eastern side of this place there is a water-fall. The water falls with great speed. The center of the pond has the main exiting of the waterfall. Raja Maan Singh has made a very little building. There is a lot of fish in the pond having a length of quarter yard. I stayed at this beautiful place for three days. I put the net in the pond and caught about 10 to 12 fish. These fish were again dropped in the water after sewing pearls in their noses.

Raja General Maan Singh, Akbar's chief of staff, had a rest house constructed on the banks of the lake for Akbar, and when we

A segment of the Wah Gardens where my cousins and I played and picnicked during childhood and youth.

visited Wah over the years we often stayed there. But it was Jehangir, according to most accounts, who was so overcome by the beauty of the location that he admired it in silence for a while and then, surrounded by the Khattar chiefs, spoke a single word: 'Wah'.

Head Held High's descendants did not waste time. They changed the name of the village to Wah on the spot. The literal equivalent would be 'Wow'. Might the English 'wow' be derived from the Persian 'Wah'? In any event, the Khattar chiefs had offered Raja Maan Singh all the land he needed to build a garden. The architects thought that twelve acres was sufficient and the village itself was shifted slightly northwards. Plans were made and the building process started. It was continued by Akbar's son and then completed by his grandson Shah Jehan.

The original architects chosen were a much-admired father-and-son team from Herat. Mirak Mirza Ghiyas and Saiyyid Mohammed were Persians and had demonstrated their skills to Akbar in the construction of his father Humayun's tomb in Delhi, which surpasses the icy cold Taj Mahal. Both the design of the tomb in Delhi and the materials used – red sandstone with white marble used only to enhance certain features – make it a much more attractive, popular construction than the Taj with its gleaming white marble that gives an impression of aloofness.

The poet Sahir Ludhianvi conveys this alienation in his 1930s poem 'Taj Mahal', a reproach to his lover for wanting to meet at an inappropriate location, a tomb of the rich, whose construction had cost hundreds of poor lives. She got an earful:

> My love, let us meet somewhere else.
> An emperor, flaunting his wealth, mocks thus the love of the
>   poor.
> These structures and sepulchres, these ramparts and forts,
> These relics of the mighty dead are, in fact, no more
> Than the cancerous tumours on the face of earth,
> Fattened on our ancestors' very blood and bones.
> They too must have loved, my love, whose hands had made
> This marble monument, nicely chiselled and shaped
> But their dear ones lived and died, unhonoured, unknown,
> None burnt even a taper on their lowly graves.
> My love, let us meet somewhere else.

The Herat architects brought to Mughal India a Persian tradition not previously incorporated in its architecture. The vaulted masonry almost universal in Mughal architecture was a vital contribution. Akbar laid the foundations of the gardens, and Jehangir indulged his architects, but the most decisive intervention was that of Shah Jehan. On his way to Kabul, he broke his journey at the rest house in Wah. Expressing strong displeasure at the unfinished character of the gardens, he instructed his department of constructions to inspect the place and come up with a new plan. His favourite architect was, as his name suggests, resident in Lahore but of Persian extraction: Ustad (Master) Ahmed Lahori, who had built the Taj Mahal as well. Lahori's final plan for the expanded gardens visualised little palaces, twelve-door structures with running hot and cold water (baradaris), overlooking canals, waterfalls and large ponds. Shah Jehan made four visits after the gardens were completed and expressed his pleasure, nodding his head forcefully when Lahori claimed the mandate of heaven for the garden. It was heaven's garden on earth.

Many rooms were decorated with murals depicting trees, flowers, fruits and petals. There were still traces of them even after the buildings had become total ruins following a century of Afghan and Sikh rule. As children we explored them endlessly in search of Mughal treasures. As a teenager I picnicked in the moonlight with cousins who lived there, imagining Jehangir threading the trout with pearls. Apocryphal stories multiplied. Ghosts and demons, too, were ever present, reducing us to a fearful silence as we walked back home in the dark.

The gardens were wrecked by the Durrani invaders from Afghanistan (1747–1826) and by the Sikhs from the Punjab who took the province and made Ranjit Singh their Maharaja. One of my uncles often moaned that under the *Sikhashahi* (Sikh despotism of 1826–49) the officers stabled their horses in the Mughal rest house. My riposte, which never went down well, was that it was not a mosque, it was not destroyed and horse dung was always useful for the soil.

Before long, the British were heading in this direction. Determined to take the Punjab, they sensed an opportunity after Ranjit Singh shuffled off. Two wars were fought. The Sikh armies were defeated, and the Sikh chiefs who swore loyalty to the pink-faced conquerors kept their word and were duly rewarded with lands and titles.

The Khattar clan united under the military command of my great-great-grandfather, Sardar Karam Khan of Wah; his makeshift cavalry, over a thousand strong, fought on the British side. It was this act of farsighted opportunism on the part of my forebears that sealed Khattar–British relations till 1947. But it also created a rift in the family that ran down the generations, culminating with my parents, a few stray uncles and, a little later, myself.

22

Family Origins

The origins of the family feud between two brothers in the mid-nineteenth century lay, I'm pleased to say as a Marxist, in a dispute over land. Property, not some rift over concubines, was the principal cause. The historian of the family informed me a few years ago that it was very likely the head of the family, Sardar Karam Khan, had denied his younger brothers some of their share of the land, which encompassed many thousands of acres and numerous villages.

Ostensibly to resolve this dispute, in September 1846 Karam Khan was invited by his younger half-brother Fateh Khan to a private meeting without retainers or hangers-on. They met near a stream, on horseback. Without warning, Fateh drew his sword and with a single blow severed his older brother's head from his neck. Not so easy to execute – perhaps he'd been practising for weeks in advance? The mare on which the slain man was riding galloped back with the decapitated body to the stables on his estate. Family lore suggests that, after washing the body and preparing it for burial, a special dish was prepared for the loyal mare that had brought the headless corpse home. This was how the feud started.

The widow immediately sent an appeal for help to the local British administrator, James Abbott, at his encampment about forty miles away. She was seriously worried, and for good reason, that her four boys might be massacred by their uncle. In the meantime, armed retainers loyal to Karam Khan kept guard all night, but no attempt was made by Fateh Khan to abduct the women and kill the children. Further tragedy was averted.

Abbott and his troop arrived promptly and he assured her of his support. He took the children under his care. Investigations revealed that Fateh had been aided by his Khattar namesake from Dhrek, a neighbouring village. This fellow was arrested by British soldiers and threatened by Abbott that unless he captured and executed the actual assassin, his own neck would be severed and his lands confiscated. The man from Dhrek needed no further convincing and did as he was asked.

The feud between the two sides continued for a while, but the annexation of the Punjab by the British after the rout of the Sikhs meant that British allies were favoured, so Karam Khan's side of the family prospered. His oldest son, Sardar Muhammed Hyat Khan, was trained up and, being fluent in both Persian and Arabic, regularly promoted within the new administration. He maintained armed retainers and fought on the side of the new masters in the Afghan wars and in the Great Uprising of 1857.

Muhammed Hyat Khan became a fanatically loyal servitor of the British. As a teenager I was always envious of the other side of the family, which I was led to believe was anti-imperialist. My father, however, advised caution: 'Best not to have too many illusions; the anti-imperialists may not have been as solid as you think.' He was right. A handful of Fateh Khan's descendants did join the uprising, but most remained loyal. I used to think, cynically, that the top echelons of the family did this deliberately: support both sides so that whichever faction of the ruling class wins, the family never loses. That was often the case. Not this time.

The Neapolitan saying *fratelli/coltelli* (brothers/knives) has other versions that pre-date even the Cain and Abel story in the Old Testament. Reasons for fraternal conflicts are varied, some more dramatic than others. In the case of my forebears, their property dispute was rooted in the fact that Islam does not authorise primogeniture. This is much fairer than under feudalism proper, but it often leads to conflict. Fateh Khan was angered by what he saw as his older brother's unfair division of property and insisted he was also acting on behalf of a younger brother. This was, unsurprisingly, denied by the other side. They believed it was a straightforward land grab that threatened the whole family. That is why the widow sent for James Abbott.

By tradition, in the absence of primogeniture, land was divided up, with each generation splitting a large estate into smaller and smaller portions. As a consequence, by the mid-nineteenth century the family had become a classic example of a decaying aristocracy, quarrelling over property. Absentee landlordism further complicated matters. My parents, for instance, had no idea how much land they owned, but it was a hell of a lot since its sale kept them going for a long time. My father's share was not inconsiderable when he died (and he was the youngest brother in the family). It was automatically put in my name and that of my brother. We granted power of attorney to my mother so she could carry on indulging her fondness for Gandharan artefacts. Islam does not forbid women owning property or trading. Had European women had a similar ration, they would have been delighted. In India this had to be specified in the will of the deceased. Since both my grandfathers did so, my mother and aunts had shares of land and their own bank accounts, long before this became the case in Britain.

One genealogist ends his version by listing the sons of Muhammed Hyat Khan and giving pride of place to my maternal grandfather:

CAPT SARDAR SIR SIKANDAR HAYAT KHAN, KBE, KCSI etc., former Premier of the Punjab (1892–1942) – the noblest and most distinguished of the sons of his notable father and the most brilliant of the scions of the Khattar race, the true pride of all Punjabis, Hindu, Muslim or Sikh.

With this side of the story completed, I can now turn to my parents.

I turned thirty in October 1973. My mother, usually unsentimental about birthdays except her own (she sulked whenever I forgot), had pressured me to go to Lahore and spend the hallowed date at home. That proved impossible, but I promised to visit

in December and spend their thirty-first wedding anniversary –
23 December – with them. This was never a big occasion, not
regularly marked, and I was about to find out why.

The pollution in Lahore had been getting steadily worse over
the years. Endless traffic jams, unregulated factories and rising
smoke from cow dung burned for fuel had wrecked the ecology.
The fogs had got worse and the sky rarely cleared till midday, if
then. It took me a day or so to recover from the jetlag. On the
afternoon of the 23rd, while we were pacing up and down in the
garden, my mother remarked without any throat-clearing: 'Today
is not our real anniversary.'

I was taken aback. Until then I had thought I knew all her
early life stories. My father was discreet and reserved, but my
mother was incapable of keeping big secrets. As children, my
sister Tauseef and I (and later my much younger brother Mahir)
had heard all about how her boarding school days had come to a
premature end in 1940 when she was sixteen. She was expelled
from the elite Queen Mary College in Lahore for insisting at one
morning assembly that Jawaharlal Nehru, then a dashing nationalist leader, be invited to address the college. The principal, Miss
Cocks, was livid: 'You will apologise immediately, Tahira Hyat!'

My mother, wilful and impulsive from a very young age, asked
why. 'For daring to suggest that a male politician holding such
odious views be invited to a purdah college,' came the response.
Tahira refused to say sorry point blank. 'If that was the case,' she
argued back, 'how come a purdah college invited Uday Shankar,
the famous male dancer with suggestive body language, to
perform in front of the girls? Is it gender or nationalist politics
that's the problem?' And if the former, she could have added, was
it appropriate to have a principal whose very surname threatened
the ethos and moral stability of the elite purdah school. Might
she not have used an alternative spelling, for example, Cox?
When, much later, I pointed this out to my mother, she laughed
and said: 'What a pity you weren't around to advise me.'

Tahira Hyat was asked to leave the assembly. She refused to
apologise in private as well. My pro-British grandfather, then
the elected Premier of the Punjab, was contacted and asked to

The official wedding, 23 December 1942. My father, Mazhar Ali Khan (third from left in Indian Army uniform) and his father, Nawab Muzaffar Khan (centre in white turban), at the wedding reception that went on all day.

My mother, Tahira Hyat, on her wedding day.

remove her from the school. That same afternoon, a chauffeur duly arrived with a maid in tow to pack her clothes and books. And that was that.

My mother was different from the other women in Queen Mary College (though a few close friends were sympathetic) and constantly challenged their submissive romanticism. Imagined happiness via an arranged marriage, she used to tell them, meant selling your freedom. But she was not so different from young women in normal schools and colleges and 'good homes' – who were excited by the new breeze blowing through the country and· the world – and she was becoming politically active.

While at school she had corresponded with Nehru, who was then in prison. He had explained Indian history to her and told her what a good thing it was that she was being radicalised. Scared that her father might discover his letters to her, she destroyed them. Her own schoolgirlish questions to him are preserved in the Nehru Memorial Library in Delhi. When, after his release, Nehru came for tea to discuss British intentions with my grandfather, my mother was invited to join them. She was thrilled that her father wanted her to be present. He introduced her to Nehru: 'My young daughter, alas, is a great admirer of yours.' Nehru smiled but, to her great relief, did not reveal they were already correspondents! A week later, on her father's advice, she went to see Jinnah, who was good-natured but much more patronising. He scolded her. She was 'very naughty' for backing his 'big rival', Nehru.

The British decision in 1931 to hang Bhagat Singh, a revolutionary activist who promoted violent struggle, unsettled many who, till then, had not been actively anti-British. Throughout India, radical nationalist students publicly attacked Gandhi for refusing to plead for Bhagat Singh's life during his many meetings with the Viceroy, Lord Irwin, and other senior members of the administration.

A new generation was in motion. Young people from most social classes were defying tradition and the conservative hostility to the new. For some women, the necessity of emancipation from colonial rule encouraged freethinking. They began to understand

and challenge the iron grip of patriarchy. Widow-burning had been illegal since the mid-nineteenth century, but widow remarriages were still frowned upon. Pre-colonial traditions that had persisted, like the caste system, were now being questioned. Fresh voices were beginning to break through. The country's youth was rushing headlong to embrace the politics of the freedom movements. My parents came of age during this political tumult.

My mother was nineteen when she gave birth to me, and given the small age gap between us, we became close friends, sharing many secrets that, if revealed, would be damaging to 'the family honour'. Why, then, did she confect a fake wedding anniversary and keep it a secret for so long? Parental hypocrisies and double standards, of course, must never be underestimated, but waiting till your eldest child was thirty? It was puzzling. Happiness, after all, generally loosens the tongue.

The story unfolded as we continued walking in the garden. After her expulsion from school, her father took her aside and said that, with her reckless behaviour, she had ruined her educational career. Like Miss Cocks, he was not too keen on Nehru either. The only other avenue left was marriage. My mother bit her lip on this occasion but asked him to promise that she would never be forced to marry someone against her will. To this he agreed happily, at the time. News of her availability spread. It was a niche market and proposals began to arrive from different parts of the country. A shortlist of suitors followed. She and any sisters at home on visiting days inspected them collectively from behind a screen.

One poor guy, the first in line, Oxford-educated and mildly radical (in reality he was the only son of a filthy-rich landowner whose father was one of my grandfather's closest friends and a staunch political ally), was mortified when he heard my mother whisper loudly to her siblings, 'Impossible! Chest and waist the same,' followed by a lot of giggling. One suitor had oily hair, another purple gums, misshapen teeth, etc. There was no shortage of excuses. The sisters giggled and thought they had seen off any imminent threat. My mother did not realise that she was about to move from a small battlefield to a much larger one.

The fact was that she had developed a huge crush on my father. And it was reciprocal. They were second cousins. But it almost didn't happen. In 1939 my father had applied and obtained admission to study at Wadham College, Oxford. Wartime Britain would certainly have distracted him from goings-on at home. He was literally about to board a vessel from Mumbai in early September when, worried by the impending war, his parents panicked. Retainers were despatched to drag him off the boat, by force if necessary, and get him back to Lahore. And so fate kept them close.

My mother had confessed to an older married sister (her closest friend for life) that she wasn't interested in anyone else. The sister advised extreme caution, but she too knew my father well. They all met regularly at family lunches and gatherings, and both sisters liked him. He, in turn, was bowled over by Tahira's good looks, her growing interest in politics and the fact that for a seventeen-year-old she was delightfully self-willed. Once my aunt had ascertained that my father felt the same way, she became a crucial ally, a strategic adviser, but because her husband's job entailed a lot of travel, she was rarely in Lahore for long periods. During her absences my mother's wilder instincts came into play. At some stage she and my father decided that they would brook no parental restrictions and that marriage was the only way out. His own parents were not opposed, but had told him firmly that the decision lay with their relation, my maternal grandfather.

My father's political views seemed to be the only obstacle. He had become a communist while at university in the thirties, and was very active in the Indian Students Federation that had united the Indian left. His college days were dominated by the anti-imperialist struggle. At one stage, both he and his older brother (also very radical but not a member of the CPI) were taken into custody and placed under house arrest on the orders of a government led by their uncle and in which their father was a leading figure.

This created a sensation in the province. Their mother, totally apolitical, was livid. The nerve of these men, she is supposed to have said, daring to imprison my boys. The men concerned tended to avoid her company till her beloved sons were released. Both the women's colleges in Lahore had come out on strike, demanding they be freed, as they soon were. All this had a huge impact on my mother. But her admiration extended further. My father's waist and chest were definitely not the same. Apart from his political activities, he was also the All-India backstroke champion and had been selected as part of the Indian swimming team for the 1936 fascist Olympics in Berlin. Here, he nursed a fantasy should he have won a medal. When mounting the platform to receive it, he would have knifed Hitler or Goering or any other Nazi dignitary and cut his throat. Sadly, short of funds, the Indian sports federation had to make economies and the swimmers were dumped, as they stood the least chance of winning anything. My father, though, never allowed his Olympic blazer to be thrown away. It was my mother who later took that decision. *Too much clutter*, she said. The row resounded through the house.

It was not that my father was completely innocent. He denounced his uncle and future father-in-law at public meetings. At one of these gatherings, as the young couple were planning to ask for permission for their future happiness, my father was much quoted in the national press for his critical remark: 'When Sir Sikandar Hyat Khan stands on his hind legs and barks the latest instructions from his British masters...' This was a very clear case of putting politics above blood ties, something he believed in throughout his life. My mother recalled that when her oldest brother, who had been present at the meeting, reported the remark at the dinner table that evening, a grim silence descended. A shiver of fear crawled down her back, but she recovered rapidly. That same week, she made up her mind: regardless of the consequences she would confess all to her father. It took some courage on her part.

By now, her father had begun to worry at her rejection of every potential bridegroom and her apparent lack of interest in marriage, and summoned her to his study for a pep talk. It ended with a direct question. 'Is there anyone else you like and who hasn't yet sent his family to propose?'

'Yes.'

'Who?'

'Elder cousin Mazhar.'

Not too difficult to imagine his response. His face went pale. The clichés piled up: 'Over my dead body', 'Never', 'Impossible', 'My daughter can never marry a communist.'

Like Miss Cocks before him, he ordered her out of the room. She ran to her mother and stepmother (whom she adored) and wept. They hugged and kissed her, but neither of them could offer much hope. The extended family, branches and twigs combined, was divided. A large majority thought my father had exceeded the bounds of political decency with his 'hind legs' utterance and thus forfeited any right to marry my mother. Others, largely apolitical, took a different view. If the kids loved each other, and were determined to take all these risks to get their way, might it not be easier to get it over and done with quickly? But my grandfather would not budge. Numerous family conclaves failed to secure an agreement. The young couple were forbidden to see each other. Such foolish injunctions usually spur the couple concerned to become even more stubborn and then openly defiant, and so it was with my parents. They met in secret, exchanged letters and occasionally managed to speak on the phone to keep their spirits up.

'When you met secretly,' I interrupted my mother, 'did you do anything or just gaze at each other? Was there any action at all?'

'Shut up.'

'Did you not even hold hands?'

I finally managed to get her to admit that at times their hands touched, her sleeve brushed against him, and once he stroked her face. The overwhelming feelings were those of embarrassment, yearning, curiosity. Once or twice their feet touched and that was exciting. He made her laugh a lot. My father put pressure on his own father, who responded kindly, if a bit on the cold side, writing back: 'As for the other matter, I'm doing my best but impossible to rush this business.'

My maternal grandfather must have been relieved when summer hit the plains and the Punjab government shifted to the cooler, summer capital at Simla. This annual three-month sojourn usually released tensions for young and old. My parents were distraught at being apart, but letters were exchanged. In July 1940 my mother wrote informing my father that she was coming under heavy pressure to get engaged. Both were fed up. My father's friends in Delhi and Mumbai told me years later that he was in a terrible state that whole summer. 'Going mad like Majnun in Layla's absence,' one of them remarked. This explains the admirable recklessness that followed.

My father wrote back saying he was on his way to rescue her. On a specified date, when the guards on duty were fast asleep, she was to leave her house and meet him at a designated spot. She agreed. My father was accompanied to Simla by his brother Mahmood, his foster brother Gulab and the 'Red Mullah', Nizam Din, a warm-hearted and knowledgeable political activist and an expert on Islamic law.

'Why have you brought him along?' my mother asked, trying to restrain a giggle.

'We need a witness and someone to marry us. Who better than him?'

And so, the first step of the elopement was set in motion. They had no money, no place to hide, but the contract was signed.

I ask: 'Now that you were formally married, no restrictions applied. Were you not tempted to ditch the others and rapidly consummate the marriage?'

'Shut up. You have the mentality of a loafer.'

She returned to the official residence while my father and his group drove back to Lahore. Nobody was told except my mother's elder sister, who was relieved, but nervous. They were not returning to the plains until early September. Tahira Hyat was now a married woman, but her parents were unaware of the fact. Her father continued to press her into seeing more suitors.

Finally, as the pressure on her mounted, my father told his parents. They were taken aback, but my grandmother gave him permission to collect his wife and bring her to their house. He did so that very night. Surprisingly, neither of his parents warned their cousin's household. That same evening, my mother wrote a letter to her father informing him that 'Mazhar and I are married', provided him with sharia details and the name of the witness, and made it clear there would be no going back. She asked a younger sister to hand him the letter at breakfast. As the household slept, my mother slipped out to a waiting car with my father at the wheel. She was warmly welcomed in her new home and sent to bed in the guest room.

I interrupted her once again: 'Now did you consummate the marriage?'

Before she could say 'shut up', I explained that had they done so and however angry it had made my grandfather, the loss of virginity would have been definitive. There is no way he could have insisted on her marrying someone else. Not even Nizam Din. She said that she was too nervous waiting for the official reaction from her father's house to think of anything like that. She did not have to wait too long. The rapid response team was on its way.

Tasked with handing over the letter, Tahira's younger sister, all of thirteen years old, was scared witless at the thought of concealing it till breakfast. Fearful that she would be punished too, she could not sleep at all. At 4 am she knocked on her father's bedroom door and woke him up. With trembling hands she handed him the missive explaining that 'Tari said to give it to you in the morning.' She then promptly ran out of the room.

He refused to accept the marriage as legal. He woke up my grandmother and told her he was treating this as an abduction and would have my father locked up. He ordered a full-scale assault. The full paraphernalia of power was deployed: motorcycle outriders and a jeep filled with cops, his personal bodyguard flanking the official car flying the Union Jack.

My paternal grandfather's household was rudely woken up as Sardar Sir Sikandar Hyat Khan stood at the front door: 'My daughter has been illegally abducted. I've come to take her back.'

My parents came downstairs in defiant mood, but were advised to keep calm and let her return till the issue could be properly settled. Tahira simply informed her father that they were married. He grabbed her by the arm and dragged her back to his car, followed angrily by my father. As the car door was opened, he pushed her in. My father looked my grandfather in the face: 'If you harm a single hair on her head, I'll see you in court.' The response was violent. He was slapped hard on the face and pushed to one side. The car then drove off.

As my mother reached this section of her story, my father, back home from the *Viewpoint* office, joined us in the garden. She fell silent. I stood in front of my mother to shield her and block his path. He was puzzled. With uplifted chest, I stood in front of him and aggressively acted out the lines: 'If you harm a single hair on her head, I'll see you in court.' He made as if to slap me. 'I knew you were many things,' I teased, 'but a Bollywood style-hero? Allah protect us!'

'So now you know. I'll go inside and rest a while. Let her finish the story.'

It was still dark when she got back home and her mothers were waiting anxiously. The lights were on. The siblings were wide awake, peeping from their bedroom windows. My grandfather instructed the servants to make up a bed in his dressing room. He took my mother upstairs and, once the bed was prepared, went to his own bedside table next door and came back with a revolver in his hand. She was terrified, imagining that he was going to kill her. But all he said was: 'Look carefully at this weapon. If you try and run away again, I'll first kill you and then myself.' My mother burst into tears, first with relief that nothing was going to happen right away, and then at the thought that he would take his own life.

She adored her father, and she was his favourite too: a love child with a wife who produced five others. His first wife, Zubeida, had died prematurely, an early victim of the killer flu brought back to India and Africa by soldiers after the First World War. Her favourite and most experienced maid was isolated by the doctor, who assumed she must be infected. During the sunny winter days, the maid lay on a *charpoy* underneath the lime tree at a distance from the house. When she ran out of fresh water she would pluck the fresh limes and drink their juice. She survived. Zubeida did not. A hurriedly convened conclave of women elders in the family married my grandfather off to her younger sister,

Amina, so she could help bring up her blood-sister's children. He never had much of a say and never became attached to her. Her affection ran deep but remained unrequited. A son was dutifully produced, the wittiest of all my aunts and uncles, but physical contact between the couple ceased immediately afterwards.

He met my grandmother by pure accident, at a feudal wedding in Amritsar in 1922. She was helping her mother, the cook-housekeeper of the household, serve the food and drinks to the guests. She was eighteen years old, ten years younger than my grandfather. He fell for her. He wanted her. He could have had her. But he insisted on marriage. He demanded that the senior women in the family immediately send a proposal to the girl's mother. His eldest brother-in-law, however, tried to sabotage any such development. He offered huge sums of money to the bride-to-be's mother as long as she took her daughter away and hid in some obscure village in Kashmir from where they originally hailed.

My grandfather, in his ardour, sent a very firm warning. He knew perfectly well that if all financial inducements failed (which they did), his in-laws might try to have the object of his affection kidnapped and disappeared. The head of what I refer to as the 'assassins wing' of the family (usually deployed to resolve inter-feudal conflicts of one sort or another) was summoned, apprised of the situation and instructed to warn the recalcitrant brother-in-law that any nonsense on his part would be dealt with firmly. Very firmly.

All opposition ceased and a formal but quiet wedding ceremony followed. Knowing this family history only too well, my mother had thought her father would be more understanding in her own case. She underestimated the fact that, for him, politics overrode the problem of contradictory class locations.

This time, nevertheless, the family elders began to negotiate a deal. A great-uncle scolded my grandfather: 'Whether you like it or not, according to the sharia, Tahira and Mazhar are lawfully wedded. Meet the boy. Impose some conditions if you must. Everyone's miserable, you have a war to manage, the country is falling apart.'

He had more than enough to concern himself with. It was

December 1940, and Congress, the main nationalist party, had resigned from the provincial governments. The British-backed Unionist Party, with Sikandar Hyat Khan as its leader, had been elected to office in Punjab in 1937, fronting a union of Muslim, Sikh and Hindu landlords, but now a strange and unpredictable chaos was beginning to envelop British India. The Punjab, both the 'sword-arm' and the 'granary' of India, became a crucial province. If the Punjab was lost to the nationalist rabble, if terrorism spread, British control of the country might be seriously destabilised.

Over the following summer, both my grandfathers, preoccupied by the war, embarked on a tour of Punjabi villages on a recruitment drive. It would have been odd had they not discussed their wayward children. Soon afterwards my father was summoned by my maternal grandfather. There was some excitement in both houses. He laid down a single condition. Mazhar had to join the British Indian Army and fight against the fascist powers.

My father came out of the meeting depressed. The CPI line loyally followed that of Moscow. The Stalin–Hitler pact was still in force and, however critical some party members were, they would never express different views in public. Add to this the realities of Indian politics. The Congress opposed any Indian participation in the war and Gandhi was about to launch the Quit India movement. The left-wing Congress leader, Subhas Chandra Bose, even argued for armed struggle against the British as the main enemy. The Muslim League opted to support the war effort. Jinnah saw it as an opportunity to outflank Gandhi and Nehru.

In June 1941, however, history intervened in a fashion that favoured my parents when Hitler unilaterally abrogated the German 'non-aggression' pact with the Soviet Union. His armies crossed the frontier and unleashed Operation Barbarossa. Stalin had a nervous breakdown and went missing for a fortnight. The Communist Party leaders in Europe who had, in the main, uneasily followed Moscow now heaved a collective sigh of relief and declared it was their war too. In India the CPI called on its upper- and middle-class members to join the army and defeat fascism.

Soon afterwards, my father was despatched to the Dehra-dun Military Academy, modelled on Sandhurst. Early reports declared him to be capable and diligent. He appeared courteous to his superiors, but the mask concealed a silent arrogance and occasionally pure hatred. Simultaneously, his official engagement to my mother was publicly announced. A photograph of him in uniform a year later, at the wedding reception hosted by Nawab Muzaffar Khan, reveals him in a cheerful mood. Congratulated by all sides, including his most diehard opponents on this matter, my father smiled through the event with undiluted pleasure. As did my mother. They felt all the personal injustices they had suffered were now embedded in the past.

Three siblings were all married on the same day in defiance of the advice from Master Kale Ram, the Hindu manager of the family estate. According to Hindu tradition, he warned Sikandar Hyat, marrying three of your children on the same day invariably brings bad luck. My two uncles, Shaukat and Azmat Hyat, in the cavalry and infantry regiments respectively, and my father, about to be assigned a regiment (the 4/16th Punjab), were all in military uniform.

The wedding was a significant social event. My mother was deluged with presents, mainly jewellery, from the landed gentry and princely families who attended. The evening before, my father had invited CPI comrades and an 'underground cell' to briefly discuss maintaining cross-regimental contact in wartime Europe. Minutes of the meeting were taken with the location registered as 'Prime Minister's House, Lahore, Punjab'. Or so CPI veteran Harkishan Singh Surjeet, who was present, told me when we first met. A bunch of uniformed CPI members also attended the wedding. All's well that ends well was the sentiment of most of the guests.

Alas, not. A tragedy awaited the whole family.

My parents left before all the guests had departed. They had a train to catch. They boarded a reserved compartment at Lahore station, on their way to Shillong for their honeymoon. The train suddenly stopped at a tiny station where local officials were waiting outside their compartment. They informed Mazhar that his father had unexpectedly died that night, and that they had orders to halt another express train and send them back.

However, both parents decided not to interrupt their honeymoon. Even I was slightly taken aback by this piece of information. My mother explained: 'Your father's relations with him weren't that good. And he was a bit of a cold fish, really.'

The train moved on. Half an hour later it made another unscheduled stop. A different set of officials had arrived with a telegram for my mother. It was Sikandar Hyat Khan who had died, not Muzaffar Khan. My grandfather had been suffering from undiagnosed angina pectoris. My mother was in a state of total disbelief. How could this be so? She broke down completely, ran out weeping and wailing on to the platform. It was a cold December night she would never forget. Even now, so many years later, as she told me the story a sadness overcame her. We sat down on the bench for a few minutes in silence. She dragged me up and the walk resumed. I had glimpsed this look many times before in the preceding decades. Now I understood. She continued.

They were put on another train heading back to Lahore. They missed the funeral but were driven straight to my grandfather's freshly prepared grave at the Badshahi Mosque. She wept uncontrollably for most of that day in her mother's arms, and with her siblings. She wept, overpowered by a feeling of guilt that never totally disappeared. Had she not defied him, he might have been less stressed. He might not have died. Many similar thoughts crossed her mind. In vain did my father, her siblings and later I, try to explain that her feelings of guilt were irrational. She was never completely convinced.

Stray remarks and actions in later years fell into place. Traumatised by Sikandar's sudden death she felt that love was more like a punishment. This, I'm pretty sure, led for a while to a partial aversion extended to my father and, ten months later, to her newly born son (me). When, in my late teens I asked why she hadn't breastfed me, her reply seemed too well prepared: 'I had all those romantic ideas of how babies are so sweet and enticing, but you were so ugly that my milk dried up.'

It used to make me laugh and may even have been true, but the real reason, I think, was a combination of vanity and memories that refused to recede: of the one whole year she had proudly and courageously defied her father. My birth was part of the inner pain she felt, a pain connected to the entire episode that, so she thought, had helped send my grandfather to an early grave. And that too, it was now obvious, was the reason she didn't want to discuss the first wedding at Simla, nor the flight from her father's house months later.

23

Family Life

The mark was never, and nor could it be, erased. I would sometimes catch her talking to herself. When I looked enquiringly,
she would shake her head, but the conversation that invariably
followed concerned her father. 'Abaji would always insist that we
ate carefully.' 'We should leave the table while still feeling slightly
hungry.' 'We must drink so many glasses of water every day.' 'We
must exercise. Walking and biking were very important.'

She once wondered aloud: 'I was wondering what Abaji would
have made of you.'

'Why?'

My mother (seated first on right) with her five brothers, four sisters, two
mothers and father (middle top right).

'Oh, I don't really know why.'

'I doubt very much that he would have approved of my activities. He would have seen me as he saw my father.'

'Hmm. I'm not sure about that. You're quite different from your father in many ways. When your grandfather was in England studying medicine he went through a phase of getting very close to a dangerous anti-British terrorist group.'

'What?'

I wanted details.

While studying medicine at King's College in 1912, Sikandar had come across the remnants of a terrorist group based in Highgate, in an office opposite the first Indian Students' Hostel to be built in the imperial capital. Its members were few but spread all over the city. Some key members were housed in digs at 109 Ledbury Road in West London.

This was what became the India Home Rule group. It was a strange mixture of theosophists (Annie Besant, Charlotte Despard, Madame Cama from Paris), secular Muslims and Hindutva nationalists such as V.D. Savarkar, a BJP icon today, then in his twenties, whose justifications for violence came from the Hindu scriptures. The founding conference was attended and supported by H.M. Hyndman of the Social Democratic Federation, a precursor of the British Communist Party, who had walked over from Hampstead to Highgate for the event.

The Home Rule League was under permanent surveillance and no doubt infiltrated by a few strategically placed informers. Its martyr was Madan Lal Dhingra, a courageous if slightly confused anti-imperialist, who had been encouraged by others in the group to become a member of a shooting gallery at 92 Tottenham Court Road, where he learnt how to aim and fire a revolver. As he became more proficient, he formulated a ritual where he named the targets as he fired. The names changed but Lord Curzon was a constant and Dhingra 'shot' him many times. As Viceroy, Curzon had stirred communal tensions by partitioning Bengal in 1911, and was hated by many Bengalis for this outrage.

Dhingra regarded the struggle to get the British out of India as a permanent war. They were killing Indians. The British atrocities after the defeat of the Great Uprising in 1857 remained embedded in his mind. He would kill the British. He did so in July 1909. Two men were shot dead at a meeting in the Imperial Institute in South Kensington. The first, Sir W.H. Curzon Wyllie, was a British civil servant in India, the other was an innocent. Dhingra had intended to kill himself, but the revolver did not click. To his immense regret, he never became Britain's first suicide terrorist. Instead, he was tried, found guilty and hanged in Pentonville Prison. Dhingra's sacrifice was impressive on a personal level, but quite useless politically. Did any good come of it at last? None, but it was a famous martyrdom. And years after India became independent a postage stamp with Dhingra's image was issued by the government.

Remnants of the terrorist group survived, but the assassination of Curzon Wyllie had alarmed the state. Informers were recruited. Was V.D. Savarkar one of them? Unsubstantiated rumours to this effect still fly around India. What is impossible is that he was not subjected to an interrogation. Two of his brothers had been arrested in India and sent to the Andaman Islands, often the equivalent of a death sentence.

My grandfather, like others, attended some terrorist meetings in 1913–14. This news was telegraphed back to India and his family was informed. The elders in Wah sent him a telegram

My father (standing) with Sir Stafford Cripps in Lahore meeting young leftwing representatives to discuss the war, July 1942.

309

The Cairo summit, August 1942: Churchill, my grandfather and Field-Marshal Wavell confer after the fall of Singapore.

concocting a story that his eldest sister-in-law, who had mothered him after his own mother died, was terminally ill, and asking him to return home immediately. He left by the next boat. My mother told me this story to stress that biographies of individuals are not written in the stars. And, who knows, her father could have become a radical.

Strange, therefore, that in 1942 Churchill decided that the only Indian politician he could trust completely was Sikandar Hyat Khan, and summoned him to a wartime summit in Cairo. Wavell and other senior British officials gave Sikandar a secret pledge that, Churchill or no Churchill, they would leave India after the war. This was the message that SHK conveyed to the Congress leaders, Gandhi, Nehru and Maulana Azad, on his return from Cairo. Gandhi was unconvinced. He had launched the Quit India movement in August 1942, following the Japanese advances against British colonies in Asia, which led to London abandoning Malaya and Burma after the fall of Singapore. (The Dutch and the French did the same in Indonesia and Indochina.) Like many others, Gandhi assumed that he might be negotiating Indian independence with Hirohito rather than Churchill.

My grandfather was only fifty when he died, late on the night of 25 December 1942. When my grandmother came to bed that night, he appeared to be fast asleep, which seemed slightly odd. It was a bit too early for him. She thought he might be teasing her and shook him, saying: 'I know you're joking. Open your eyes.' He didn't move. When she realised he wasn't breathing, she screamed. The family servants told my mother later that week that the house had echoed with her heart-rending cry summoning the elder wife: 'Elder sister Amina, please come here.' Both women were in a state of shock. Grandmother Amina took charge and summoned the family.

The temporary structures that had been erected for the three weddings during the day were hurriedly transformed early next morning to service the funeral. When my mother got back, the house was in turmoil. Loud wailing went on throughout the night. The public funeral was huge. The family wanted Sikandar to be taken back and buried in the family graveyard in Wah, but the provincial government, the city authorities and Muslim cultural and educational bodies insisted he be buried in Lahore.

His contribution to raising and allocating the funds needed to repair the seventeenth-century Badshahi Masjid (Royal Mosque) meant it offered the perfect resting place. The mosque, the last great edifice constructed by the Mughals in India (the Emperor Aurangzeb in this case), had been the heart of the old city. The repairs necessary to restore it to its pristine splendour took some years and were supported by the entire Unionist government. It won my grandfather enormous popularity among the entire Muslim population in Northern India. He was buried in the garden of the mosque. The only other person so honoured was the Urdu poet and philosopher Muhammad Iqbal.

The British, on their part, were nervous that none of SHK's successors could manage the Punjab. My paternal grandfather was asked if he could take over. Wise old man: he refused. Two days after Sikandar's death, Viceroy Lord Linlithgow – in a despatch to Leo Amery, the secretary of state for India in London – analysed what it meant for British imperial interests:

The real tragedy of the last couple of days has been the sudden death of Sikandar. He had his faults, as you and I well know. He was a rather difficult person to rely on in a really tight corner, and on more than one occasion he had caused me serious embarrassment. But he had a really remarkable record of achievement, and his services both to the Punjab and to India were very great indeed … I always felt … that he had an extremely difficult hand to play in the Punjab and that was the most probable explanation of his apparent weakness. He has with great skill for a number of years kept together a delicate political mosaic and I am by no means [untroubled] as I write at the thought of what may happen, for Sikandar was well-known to be very non-communal in temper and outlook, and he had conciliated a far greater degree of general support in that most important Province than anyone whom I can think of as a possible successor is likely to manage to do.

The Unionist Party as a whole and its leaders individually regarded all talk of a confessional Partition as extremely dangerous. They foresaw much more clearly than Gandhi, Nehru or Jinnah that rivers of blood would flow in the Punjab.

My grandfather had been a staunch defender of the Punjab as a unified, autonomous, multicultural/multi-religious province located within an Indian Federation where the centre was only responsible for defence and foreign policy. He believed that a multi-national federation was the real solution and that an independent India with a combination of democratic structures and economic development would be a success. His document spelling out the plan for a strictly non-communal zonal federation was published and widely discussed in 1942.

He had a concluded a pact with Jinnah whereby Unionist Party Muslim MPAs could simultaneously be members of the Muslim League. Had either the Congress Party or the Muslim League favoured a zonal federation it might have been better for all. But the Congress's commitment to a majoritarian outcome meant an India run along the lines of the departing empire: the preservation of old political, judicial, administrative and military structures created by the British, with nearly all power concentrated at the centre.

Jinnah's response was separatism. He decided to push for an independent Pakistan, a homeland for Indian Muslims concentrated in Muslim-majority or near-majority regions: Punjab, Pakhtoonkhwa, Kashmir, Sindh and Baluchistan, and Bengal. This meant the division of the Punjab and Bengal. It meant bloodshed on a massive scale. Nehru and Jinnah were both shaken by the scale of the Partition killings and the rapes and massacres and refugees. How could they not have foreseen this?[*]

In January 1947, my mother, pregnant with my sister, heard a knock on the front door. She was, unusually, alone. She unlocked the door to see a large, burly Sikh man standing there. She thought this might be the end, since killings were commonplace elsewhere in the city. Seeing the fear on her face, the Sikh smiled and stepped back. 'Please don't worry, madam. I just wanted to know where road X is located.'

She pointed out the direction, he thanked her politely and went on his way. She was ashamed of herself that the very sight of a Sikh had scared her. But Lahore was burning. A civil war had engulfed the city. When telling me this story she wondered aloud whether her father, had he not died, might have been able to keep the Punjab united. 'Had he been alive still,' she once said, 'seeing all this would have killed him.'

My grandfather's death seriously destabilised his immediate family and the Khattar clan as a whole. The younger daughters and sons were unmarried. His wife was pregnant again (she had an abortion the week after his death). My mother once asked her, why so many children? How could she be so fertile? 'All your father has to do is sneeze and I get pregnant,' she replied. I think it was a bit more than that.

---

[*] I have revisited this episode at length in my Pakistan trilogy: *Pakistan: Military Rule or People Power?* (1970), *Can Pakistan Survive?* (1982) and *The Duel* (2008), and in the last novel of the Islam Quintet, *Night of the Golden Butterfly* (2010).

The oldest son, Shaukat, left the army and went into politics, but was not as gifted as his father. He became a leader of the post-Unionist Muslim League and a sidekick of Jinnah. Most of the League leaders were second-generation Unionists. Whatever else, the party of rural grandees, created and patronised by the British, continued to rule the Punjab after independence. Buttressed by state and local power, they resented the intrusion of political refugees from India who had worked with the Muslim League. Pakistan's first prime minister, Liaquat Ali Khan, appointed by Jinnah, appointed many of his own cronies to office, thus antagonising some of the more gifted administrators who had also shifted to Pakistan to service the structures of the new country.

Observing that Liaquat was becoming too self-important, the very top layers of the ruling Muslim League in the Punjab decided to bump him off. The Inspector-General of Police, a very close friend of both my grandfathers and always regarded as a member of our family, was asked to organise the affair as neatly and cleanly as possible. And so, on 16 October 1951, four years after the birth of Pakistan, an assassin, Said Akbar Babrak, shot the prime minister dead while he was addressing a large meeting in the Company Gardens in Rawalpindi (named to honour the East India Company, now named Liaquat Gardens, where, incidentally, Benazir Bhutto was killed many decades later). In a Lee Harvey Oswald moment, Babrak in turn was immediately executed by Najaf Khan, a police officer acting on instructions, who was standing a row behind the assassin.

When my mother next met the police chief, she asked him point-blank: 'Happy now? Liaquat despatched. The whole world knows Najaf Khan only obeys your orders.' He laughed in her face and denied the charge, but unconvincingly. He issued a serious warning. She shouldn't involve herself in state matters and spread 'wild rumours'.

Scotland Yard was hired to help track down the conspirators, but there was little evidence. It was reported at the time that a local politician had seriously suggested that, if the Yard was incapable, 'we should hire Sherlock Holmes'. The murder itself remained a 'mystery'. Liaquat's widow shared my mother's views on the matter. She was convinced that a coterie of politicians in the Punjab had organised her husband's removal. It later emerged that the hired assassin was an Afghan national but had been expelled from that country for being a British agent. He was on a Pakistani government pension of 455 rupees a month.

In the years after Sikandar's death, his five daughters, in their different ways, proved to be more resilient and tough-minded than their five brothers. When I said as much in an interview with a Karachi magazine in the last decade of the preceding century, my oldest aunt, Mahmooda, whose effigy we had burnt as students when she was education minister, sent me a message: 'On this we can agree.' She was a tough old thing. After widowhood (her husband died young) and three children, she was not in the least bit shy of being seen in public with her women friends, a pioneer in many ways.

Writing all their stories would require a volume on its own, though some of these filtered through the subconscious and made an appearance in the novels of my Islam Quintet. I wanted to challenge the notion that because women were denied equal rights in much of the Islamic world this made them empty-headed creatures of the harem. This has never been the case in the world of Islam. Women have managed to assert themselves in many ways. No doubt compared to some twenty-first-century examples – Afghanistan, Iran, Saudi Arabia – women in medieval Islam had fewer restrictions (from this point of view *The Thousand and One Nights* should also be read as an anthropological account), but even here resistance bubbles underneath the surface and explodes now and again.

A few months after I was born, my father, now a lieutenant in the 4/16th Punjab regiment, was on a troop ship taking Indian soldiers to fight in Italy. He hated weapons and uniforms. In a postcard to my mother he wrote, 'only in battle do we find our allotted part', which did not sound like him at all. His allotted part was the freedom struggle in India, not as cannon fodder, supposedly defending the Soviet Union.

The British Indian Army played a decisive part for the British in the war. In 1939 Indian soldiers numbered 200,000. By 1945 this had risen to 2.5 million. They fought in Asia, in Africa and in Europe. Without Indian soldiers (whose presence could not avert the disasters at Singapore and Tobruk) it's difficult to imagine a single British military victory. Up to 90,000 Indians died fighting for the empire. My mother, like innumerable other wives and mothers, wondered whether she would see her husband alive again. She almost didn't.

Just before his departure my father had formally recruited my mother to the CPI. Ajoy Ghosh, later the party general secretary, signed the card himself. After my father left, Ghosh called on my mother again to ask for a donation. In her eagerness, and short of cash, she handed over the box containing most of her jewellery, heavy in weight and value thanks to her wedding presents. When my father returned after the war, she proudly informed him of the gift. He was not impressed. 'If ever I see Litto (Ajoy Ghosh's wife and a CPI member) sporting one of your necklaces or earrings at some wedding, comrade Ghosh had better watch out.'

In this highly politicised time, CPI membership distracted my mother somewhat from sadder memories. With her father dead and her husband on his way to the front in Europe, she felt abandoned, and political activism seemed the best possible therapy. For a while some of the family moved back to the old house in idyllic Wah. While my mother gallivanted around the family estates, my maternal grandmother took complete charge of my upbringing.

My father meanwhile found himself caught up in one of the bloodiest and probably least necessary battles in the later stages of the war. The Battle of Monte Cassino lasted four months. My father fought in all four assaults against the German defences that were holding up the march towards and capture of Rome, only sixty miles away. Only. The Allies lost 50,000 men, the Germans 20,000.

My father never talked to me in any detail about his personal experiences in Europe. A few times he let slip that on two occasions it was pure luck that he did not die. His metal suitcase with his name, rank and regiment painted on it, and his uniform and several medals secure inside, was in our attic for a long time. In my early teens I would look at the medals, imagine what it must have been like and wonder why he got them. He was never that interested in recounting the past and, when the moths finally won the battle against the uniform, the trunk was thrown away. I saved the medals at the time, but have no idea what happened to them.

What he did talk about was the camaraderie with both English soldiers and young officers. During one gathering in the officers' 'mess' (a battlefield tent), he had got into a serious argument with Tom Mitford, the brother of the famed Mitford sisters. Of the sisters, Decca was a communist, Diana a fascist, Nancy a novelist, and Deborah, the Duchess of Devonshire. I always meant to tell the three of them that I met about the chance battlefield encounter of my father and their brother, but always forgot.

A staunch imperialist, Tom made the mistake of attacking Indian nationalist leaders and arguing that India did not deserve 'any freedom whatsoever'. My father lashed out at him and, just before a bout of fisticuffs, a senior officer stepped in to remind them that early next morning they would be fighting the fascists. 'That is what I am doing,' my father told him. 'Except this one's in our camp.'

What pleased my father enormously was that most of the other British officers present had applauded him. Two of them became good friends, and one of them wrote me a very touching letter when my father died. He remembered well 'your dad and me running through a vineyard, breaking off branches heavy with grape and eating them greedily till we reached the sea, stripped, and swam a long way out. Your dad was confident that India would never be partitioned … Seeing you so often on television over the years always reminded me of him.'

I was later to discover that British communists and others on the left were also present at Monte Cassino. More than I had imagined. The most memorable account by one of them was published by E.P. Thompson in his collection *The Heavy Dancers* (1985), in an essay titled 'Overture to Cassino'. It depicts the chaos that had left my father semi-speechless on the subject. When I suggested to Edward that if, somehow or the other, a caucus of Cassino communists had been summoned, the numbers might have surprised everyone, he replied 'coincidence, not conspiracy'.

Many of my father's friends were part of the Congress left and teased him and other communists of the time for having betrayed the struggle at home, but he never regretted the decision to fight. He explained to me that, for him, internationalism superseded nationalism and, had the Congress delayed a bit, the unity of India might not have been threatened. On his return to India in 1945 he discovered an altered landscape. Both the Muslim League and the CPI had grown during the war, since, as British and Soviet allies respectively, they faced no restrictions whatsoever. As the demand for two separate states grew louder, politics became completely polarised. The bulk of the Muslim Unionists in the Punjab blew with the wind. They joined the Muslim League, citing the Sikandar–Jinnah Pact. The CPI leadership passed a resolution defending the right of the Muslims 'as a nationality' to become a separate state. They meant North Indian Muslims. South India remained immune.

My father was unhappy with the decision but did not breach party discipline. His view was that Punjabi, Bengali and South Indian Muslims had nothing in common apart from their faith, and here too the rituals and practices, influenced by dominant local cultures, varied somewhat. The CPI now instructed a band of selected and trusted Muslim members to join the Muslim League and provide it with some intellectual ballast. Danial Latifi, a talented if loquacious CPI lawyer, drafted the League manifesto for the Punjab (approved by Jinnah) for the 1946 elections to provincial assemblies and a Constituent Assembly that would select a national interim government. The manifesto pledged drastic land reforms, nationalisation of all public utilities, progressive taxation, public control of private industry, and so on.

Out of the 503 members of the Muslim League National Council, there were 163 landlords and 145 lawyers, some of whom worked for the landlords. Sindh had twenty-five members on the Council: fifteen were landlords. Most of them declared the manifesto to be 'un-Islamic'. Three princely states in the mountains – Dir, Chitral and Swat – were effectively slave-states, their royal families rotten to the core, their existence overlooked by the manifesto. The radical agenda, however, helped the Muslim League mobilise a section of the people and become the dominant party in the Punjab.

My father had still not been released from the army and was posted to Sialkot, a sleepy old cantonment town. My mother and I went with him. For the next year, he was under three conflicting pressures. His radical Congress buddies and Nehru urged him to work with them for a united progressive India. The CPI asked him to join the Muslim League as a CPI mole. From the British side, Major Bill Short of military intelligence was still very much present and active. He had a very lengthy meeting with my father and tried to persuade him to stay in the army. His arguments were certainly logical and turned out to be prescient, but my father was not the right person. The war, the heroic role of the Red Army in defeating fascism, the rising tide of revolution in China, Vietnam and Korea, the birth of anti-colonial movements around the globe, all served to reinforce his political views.

In response, Bill Short argued that Partition was unavoidable. The new state (Pakistan) needed strong-minded and trustworthy people. Jinnah was ill; his lieutenants were mediocre and determined to keep out more gifted Muslim leaders. The Raja of Mahmudabad was mentioned in this regard. The Muslim League was effectively run by landlords and a claque of bandwagon careerists. The communists too would perforce split and would become marginalised in the new state. The only solid institution would be the army, 'so just stay in there and you'll climb very quickly'. From a conservative point of view this was sage advice, though the major tended to equate the Punjab with Pakistan, a mistake that proved costly later on. When in 1958, under US guidance, the army did take over the country, I teased my father: 'Had you accepted Bill Short's advice you might well have been *our* military dictator and linked up with Nasser!'

Instead, he decided to build a peasant league in Wah and surrounding villages, conceived as an organisation that could break
the iron grip of local landlords and help educate the peasants
and their families. It was a good idea, but it undoubtedly created
serious tensions within the family. My grandfather stepped in to
pre-empt a major clash, suggesting that the idea of a peasants'
organisation was not wholly bad, that educating their children
was necessary, but that my father was not necessarily the right
person to organise all this. He should, instead, be active on the
political front, and participate in the forthcoming 1946 elections
from one of the family seats in the area. Far more important to be
in a decision-making Constituent Assembly than fooling around
in the local villages, raising hopes among the peasants that could
not be fulfilled.

No doubt my father argued back, but his father was a very
intelligent person who himself favoured educating peasant families and donated generously to create scholarships for talented
poor students. My father laid down a basic condition: 'I will not
stand as a Muslim Leaguer.'

'You can stand as an Independent.'

'What if I stand for the CPI?'

'Not advisable, but not impossible.'

My father reported this suggestion to the CPI leadership.
They, too, were tempted but decided, wisely, that to accept a
safe feudal seat, a rotten borough, was not a great idea; and in
those times political principles were considered important. My
father, torn but tempted by his father's offer, agreed with the
party decision. The CPI candidate, Fazal Elahi Qurban, a solid
working-class cadre, did contest the seat and got a few hundred
votes, including those of my parents. My father's first cousin, a
dim, smalltown lawyer with chambers in Attock, sleepwalked
into the 1946 parliament. Largely abandoned by now in the
home country, rotten boroughs were another English import
that appeared to work reasonably well in the subcontinent both
during the Raj and after.

For my father, another offer was in the pipeline. His closest
friend and comrade, Mian Iftikharuddin (MID), was the

Congress leader in the Punjab Assembly and a friend of Nehru. On the party's advice, he had shifted gears to reverse course and join the Muslim League. I have fond memories of him. Our families were very close and virtually in everyday contact. For my father, political friendships mattered more than blood ties, a trait I have inherited. *Ifty chacha* (uncle) meant more to us than some blood uncles.

The Iftikharuddin family home at 21 Aikman Road in Lahore was located on the edge of the GOR (Government Officers Residences) – elegant bungalows constructed by the British for white-skinned civil servants in the mid-nineteenth century. It soon became the venue for political salons that sprang up whenever Jawaharlal Nehru or Ghaffar Khan were staying, and for the weekly gathering of comrades to discuss the succession of crises that were shaking the subcontinent before and after independence. With Partition approaching and the CPI's Muslim cadres entering the Muslim League, MID became a very significant figure in Punjab politics, but he was thinking broader.

In 1946 he cabled my father to announce that he was on his way to Wah and that my father should sit tight until he arrived. He stayed for two days to discuss a brilliant new idea. It was now clear that nothing could stop Partition. The British had agreed to divide the subcontinent and Congress majoritarianism had

The *Pakistan Times'* first home on the Mall, Lahore (circa 1946), in the same building where Kipling first worked for the *Civil and Military Gazette*.

become the Great Wall of Indian politics. Given that there was a de facto Muslim League/CPI agreement for creating Pakistan, MID had met several times with Jinnah and the leading Unionist families who had by now joined the League, including Naurab Muzzafar Khan. In fact, a unity conference to discuss the mechanisms of bringing old rivals together was also held at Aikman Road, presided over by my fudge-loving grandfather.

Here MID proposed to Jinnah that the new state needed a chain of independent newspapers that were not attached to any party. The Delhi weekly *Dawn*, for instance, was a party paper created by Muslim League partisans, moving to Karachi as a daily in 1947. *The Civil and Military Gazette* in Lahore, for which Kipling had worked, was a relic of the past, and my tenure of little more than a year as its pseudonymous student correspondent (where I was given Kipling's desk and quite possibly his typewriter) did not help revive its fortunes. Might Jinnah agree to give his blessing to such a project and might some of his wealthy supporters agree to buy shares to help launch the new enterprise? Jinnah agreed to be named on the masthead of the new papers: 'Founded by Mohammed Ali Jinnah.' Once that was secure, his Punjabi sidekicks queued up to buy shares.

When my twenty-nine-year-old father frowned at this proposal, MID, a generation older, scolded him: 'Let me finish, I know what you're thinking. We'll be prisoners of the Muslim League. Wrong. I will be the largest shareholder and Chairman of the Board. Others not in the League are also buying small amounts of shares. We have found a very good managing director in Amir Hussain Shah. Once we've established the papers, we will gradually buy the shares of the League men so we will have majority control.'

My father was initially sceptical, not at all sure that he wanted to get involved. But as the discussion continued he warmed to the idea. Both men agreed that the 1946 Muslim League Manifesto, drafted by the CPI's Danial Latifi, was the perfect document to serve as a guide. It established a line the papers should take on domestic issues.

'What do you think we should name the company?' asked MID.

'Progressive Papers Limited.'

'Faiz should be the editor, you the first assistant editor, of the *Pakistan Times*. Faiz is suggesting Chiragh Hasan Hasrat as the editor for *Imroze*, the Urdu daily.'

Faiz, of course, was the (even then) highly regarded poet Faiz Ahmed Faiz, whose politics, like those of Pablo Neruda in Chile and Nazim Hikmet in Turkey, had been moulded by the Russian Revolution. Hasrat had no links with the CPI or any front organisation but was a distinguished Urdu writer and essayist with a pungent pen and dry wit. He established very high standards for *Imroze*. If the papers were a success, there were plans to launch an Urdu cultural weekly, *Lail o Nahar* (Night and Day). The editor being discussed was Syed Sibte Hassan, a leading CPI intellectual from Lucknow, waiting with his comrade Sajjad Zaheer to be despatched to Pakistan to help the fledgling Communist Party of Pakistan, now depleted after its Sikh and Hindu members had no option but to flee to the new India.

Hassan and Zaheer were both high-powered literary critics. Zaheer hailed from a landed family in Allahabad, very close to the Nehrus. Neither man was too keen to shift to Lahore, but their Muslim origins determined the issue. I grew very fond of the 'Uncles from India'. They were frequent visitors to our apartment and often stayed with us. I can still hear them: Sibte's voice, ever alert and clear; Sajjad Zaheer, puffing a 555 fag, languid and laidback. Both Faiz and my father were insistent that none of the PPL editors, whatever their sympathies, should be members of *any* party. Faiz was never a formal member of a party but was a leading light of the Progressive Writers' Association that spanned the subcontinent. Both Sibte and my father left the CPI. Neither joined the CPP.

So, it seemed that neither a radical peasant organisation, nor parliament, but the creation of a progressive newspaper chain was to be the priority of the Pakistani left. Contrary to later government propaganda, the vast majority of working journalists were not communists in any sense of the word. MID, Faiz, Sibte and my father were all agreed that the aim should be the production of very high-quality newspapers. The hiring of journalists

1949 May Day meeting in Lahore where the Chinese Revolution dominated the proceedings. My parents and I attended. My first public meeting.

Lahore 1956. Seven years later, victorious Chinese leaders Prime Minister Chou En Lai and Marshall Ho Lung visit Pakistan and spend an afternoon at 21 Aikman Road. 'Be careful of the Marshall,' Chou En Lai whispered to me, 'he was a very dangerous bandit leader.' Pakistan's prime minister, Feroz Khan Noon, was asked to stand at the back.

Chinese leaders with senior journalists of Progressive Papers Ltd. Kneeling front row, first and second right, my father and Mian Iftikharuddin.

should be largely based on merit and talent. The fact-checking and subbing should be of the highest standard. And that is what happened. As a result, the newspapers became the most popular left-wing force in the country, educating an entire generation of students as well as young civil servants, and they were not banned in all the army messes immediately. They exposed the plight of unlawfully evicted peasants, of working conditions in the factories, corruption, and so on.

For example: when a Commission of Inquiry was established by the government to investigate the conditions of the peasantry in the province of Sindh, two of the members were landlord stooges. The third was a supposedly pliant government official,

ADW:jg-264

THE FOREIGN SERVICE
OF THE
UNITED STATES OF AMERICA

AMERICAN CONSULATE GENERAL
LAHORE, PAKISTAN

January 27, 1956

Mr. Mazhar Ali Khan,
    Editor,
        The Pakistan Times,
        Lahore.

Dear Mazhar:

    I cannot deny having read the Pakistan Times editorial today with considerable resentment. Your personal opinion of Ambassador Hildreth is not a matter of great concern to me, nor are your criticisms of what he chooses to say in his public addresses in Pakistan. I find your unwarranted attack on the United States, however, couched as it is in vicious, unfair and irresponsible langauge, personally offensive to a large degree.

    In view of your expressed opinion of my country, you will understand if I find it difficult, in conscience to accept your hospitality this evening. My apologies to Tahira. In view of the friendly feelings which my wife and I hold for both of you, I can only express my hope that it was not you yourself who authored this regrettable article.

Very sincerely yours,

Alan D. Wolfe
American Vice Consul

Encouraging democracy in Pakistan: A letter.

M. Masud, who wrote an incendiary dissenting report that shook the bureaucracy. They immediately banned it from circulation and most of the press were quiescent in their silence. However, one day without warning, Masud dropped into the PPL editorial offices and handed over a copy to my father. It appeared that same week as a special weekend supplement in the *Pakistan Times*. Masud was sacked from the civil service and found it hard to obtain employment. Despite this, his friends and admirers helped him out. As a consequence of the report's publication, there have been changes in Sindh, but not as many as one might think.

On world politics, the PPL papers argued strongly for a non-aligned Pakistan, citing India's example and denouncing Pakistan's membership of US security pacts set up as instruments of counter-revolution. On Kashmir they insisted very strongly on the right of national self-determination. When the Anglo-French-Israeli coalition invaded Egypt in 1956 and the Pakistan government supported its former colonial master, the tone of the newspapers registered a sharp criticism. Their lead was followed by hundreds of thousands who marched in Lahore, Karachi and other large cities in support of Nasser and Egypt.

On a trip to Delhi in 1957, my father, by then editor of the *Pakistan Times*, had a long session with Nehru. After an exchange of pleasantries that included news of friends, MID and Aikman Road, my father pressed the Indian prime minister on Kashmir. Nehru sounded sympathetic, but equivocated: 'Tell me, Mazhar, who in Pakistan can I speak with? The politicians are a waste of time. In one day, out the next. Your country is effectively run by *daftaris* [office boys/bureaucrats].'

24

A Family in Jeopardy

Nehru got his answer a year later when the Pakistan Army took over the country with US backing. The first military dictator, General Ayub Khan, was a Sandhurst-trained officer with nothing to recommend him. At the very first Cabinet meeting in October 1958, as Zulfikar Ali Bhutto later informed me, Ayub pronounced a sophisticated one-liner on foreign policy: 'As far as we are concerned, there is only ONE embassy in the country and that is the United States'.' On this, he was a tiny bit ahead of Britain.

The coup was carried out to prevent the country's first ever general election from taking place. Washington feared that a coalition of parties opposed to its military and security needs in the region might form the next government; an accurate assessment. What neither MID nor my father realised was that it would affect the PPL as well.

Well before 1958, MID had become the principal shareholder of the media bloc and was unchallengeable. Military Intelligence had kept an eye on the newspapers ever since the Rawalpindi conspiracy case of 1951, when Faiz, then still editor of the *Pakistan Times*, was arrested for being part of the organisation planning a coup. In his absence my father took charge. The conspiracy was a bizarre affair. Its mastermind was the Chief of Staff, General Akbar Khan, a hugely popular figure inside the army who had, as 'General Tariq', led the 'unofficial' Pakistani guerrilla assault to take Kashmir in 1948. Had they captured Srinagar airport that would have been that, but Akbar was let down by a severe outbreak of indiscipline on his own side, with the Pashtun tribesmen wasting time by looting and sexually assaulting men and women.

By 1951 General Akbar was angered by the weakness and corruption of the prime minister and the domination of the Pakistan Army by British officers and their native stooges, who had sabotaged his Kashmir assault. This was not an inaccurate assessment of the situation, and the embryonic coup of 1951 can be interpreted as a proto-nationalist attempt to topple a pro-Western government and nationalise the army by getting rid of the British officers and their influence. Akbar knew it could be a long and dangerous journey but was determined to have a go. Aware that he needed a sociopolitical programme, he consulted progressive intellectuals such as Faiz and Sajjad Zaheer.*

This red-khaki alliance could not agree on a programme, but both sides did agree on the preparation of a list of those who had to be immediately executed after the takeover. My mother said later that 'evidently our comrades had been very eager to help prepare this list'. It included the army Commander-in-Chief, General Ayub Khan, the prime minister, Liaquat Ali Khan, the Inspector-General of Police, etc. This list, I gather, was destroyed and is not in any government archive, but it was used in the court trials of the 'top' conspirators, Akbar and Faiz.

I was not old enough to appreciate the finer points but was upset that a much-admired family friend, Faiz Ahmed Faiz, the country's greatest living poet, was handed a long sentence after

---

* Much later, when Sajjad Zaheer came to London in 1967, he invited me to lunch. I asked about the origins of the conspiracy case. His very first sentence had me in fits: 'Well you see son, I was at a cocktail party in Lahore and General Akbar Khan took me aside.' That was the level and totally believable. He continued: Akbar had said at this very party that he was planning a coup to topple the government and needed help from left intellectuals. My parents were forever grateful that they had not been approached. Was MID in the know? If he was, there was no proof, and the newspapers were protected. The few communist intellectuals who did have meetings were jailed alongside two generals, a dozen colonels and a handful of majors together with a few naval and air force guys who were compromised. A number of majors, as well as Air Commodore M.K. Janjua, having served their sentences, became part of the left on their release.

Lahore, 1957. Faiz Ahmed Faiz is welcomed back after his release from prison.

a year-long trial and sent to Montgomery jail. His daughters –
Saleema and Moneeza – were dear friends at the time, and his
anti-imperialist English wife Alys was one of my mother's close
friends and comrades.

One of Akbar's colleagues was clearly an informer from the
outset. And a round-up of CP leaders began. A week before the
conspiracy was made public, a heavily disguised Sajjad Zaheer
was staying with us when one evening, totally unannounced,
my grandfather and an old and very close family friend, Khan
Qurban Ali Khan, who happened to be the Inspector-General
of Police, came in and sat at the dining table. Sajjad Zaheer was
introduced as a visiting professor of Urdu literature from Aligarh
University. A brilliant conversationalist and a literary critic to
boot, he charmed the two old men for a few hours, then pleaded
exhaustion and retired to bed. 'I wish all your friends were like
that,' said the I-G, and my grandfather nodded vigorously. Three
days later the police chief was shown the list of those to be executed. His name was on it. A few hours later the underlings
showed the chief pictures of the underground CP leaders; the
first photo was a very striking image of the 'Professor of Urdu

Literature', described here more accurately as the secretary-general of the CPP. The I-G rang my mother, shouted a Persian abuse – 'badzat' (bad caste) – down the phone, and threatened to deal with her after 'all your red friends' had been arrested and charged.

When the army took over the country in 1958 it was welcomed by most of the press. The *Pakistan Times* ran an editorial on 'Soil Erosion'. The involvement of Faiz and a few others from the PPL newspaper chain meant that the papers were now on blacklists and, gradually, vital income from advertisements from the armed services diminished (although never completely stopped). But with the US embassy in charge of the country from October 1958 onwards, pressures grew on the military government to ban all left media.

On occasion my parents would be disinvited from a formal US consulate party in Lahore to which my father had been invited as the editor of the country's largest paper. One of these rejections from the Consul-General read as follows: 'Dear Tahira and Mazhar, this is to regretfully inform you that I have decided to disinvite you from our party this week. The editorial in today's *Pakistan Times* left me with no other choice …' My mother heaved a sigh of relief.

We all giggled, but the last laugh was in preparation. General Ayub Khan and his Cabinet that included two civilian lawyers of repute (Manzur Qadir and Zulfikar Ali Bhutto) decided to nationalise the PPL, frame MID with charges of 'illegal trade with China', and accuse his newspapers of being 'strangers in the house'.

In January 1959, my father received a phone call from the minister for commerce, Z.A. Bhutto. He was in Lahore, and wanted to meet up. It was a secret and confidential meeting at the Faletti's Hotel. 'The government is going to do something horrible to your newspapers,' Bhutto confided. 'You better tell Mian Iftikharuddin to fly to Karachi and ask for a meeting with Ayub Khan. Offer some compromise to the army.' He wouldn't say more than that. He had already taken a huge risk by breaching Cabinet secrecy.

My father drove straight to 21 Aikman Road and conveyed the message. Both men were puzzled. They could not fathom what these 'horrible' plans could be. As a consequence, MID refused to go and see Ayub. 'Let the army do its worst.' Two months later as spring hit the country and as I was getting ready for school, I heard loud knocks on the front door. The day before – though none of us knew it – had been the last day in the life of the independent Progressive Papers Limited. Two Cabinet ministers now stood outside our front door. Bhutto was one of them, the other was General Khalid M. Sheikh, minister of the interior and married to my father's sister, Bilquis. They patted my head and asked me to get my father. I seated them in the living room and woke up my father, who, on hearing who the guests were, shaved and dressed hurriedly. They were closeted for well over an hour. I was blissfully biking to school, unaware of what was going on.

When I returned for lunch my mother's shell-shocked face startled me. I thought someone had died or been arrested, but slowly the story came out. It had been a 'courtesy' call. The ministers had come to inform my father that the military government had seized the PPL but it had no desire to sack him. On the contrary, they wanted him to stay on as chief editor of the whole enterprise. It was MID that they did not trust. He was not a patriot. My father responded: 'This was, of course, not Jinnah's view.' As for the job offer, he refused. No ifs or buts, just 'No'.

Nonetheless, the government ordinance nationalising the papers was being published. Bhutto said: 'We could force you to stay in your office under the Essential Services Act.' My father replied: 'You could try but you'll have to send me to prison because I'll defy the order. There are no circumstances under which I can work for a military government.' Instead, he was allowed to go to the office and collect his personal papers.

The PPL building on Nisbet Road was surrounded by police jeeps. Despite opposition from the government bureaucrat in charge, my father insisted on calling a staff meeting. He informed them that the charges were a pack of lies, MID's lawyers were going to challenge the government and that he was resigning with immediate effect, instructing his deputy that he did not want his name as editor in tomorrow's paper, simply a small item informing readers that he had resigned. It was an emotional scene. He was aware, he said to them, that they all had family responsibilities and should not behave rashly. It was pointless. (He never entered the editorial office again. When he did return to the PPL building many years later, it was as the chief guest at a trade union function held outside the huge print shop. His relations with the print union had always been close.)

After the staff meeting he went to visit MID at 21 Aikman Road. By the time he returned home, my mother had told me the whole story. I hugged him tight and wept. It was a huge blow. I knew what it meant for him on both personal and political levels. Later that evening he sat me down and explained to my mother and me: 'Our success went to our heads. We became too complacent. We thought that because of our huge circulation and influence, we were untouchable. The lesson is obvious. Never trust the state.'

Rarely has the Pakistani press been so disgusting as they were when they collectively celebrated the fall of the PPL. MID died in 1962, a broken man. Throughout the dictatorship, my father was blacklisted, allowed neither to write nor teach. Faiz was in and out of prison until he went into voluntary exile. It was great seeing him in London and receiving instructions to attend this funeral or that meeting. He ordered me to accompany him to the last World Peace Conference organised by the world communist movement, in Helsinki in 1965. He and I were the Pakistan delegation, although we split on the Sino-Soviet dispute. My parents reprimanded me on the grounds that 'Faiz was the leader of the delegation'. My only response was laughter; I replied: 'My leader was Mao Zedong.'

When we arrived at Moscow airport en route to Helsinki via Leningrad, Faiz was met by leading Soviet poets, including, to my surprise, Anna Akhmatova. In Helsinki he was cross with me for not voting in favour of the Soviet declaration, but neither did the Vietnamese, whose lead I had followed by remaining neutral in the Sino-Soviet debate. When the Chinese were denied the right to move a counter-resolution, the leader of their delegation announced that they were leaving the gathering and flying back to Beijing – a dramatic occasion I've already recorded in *Street Fighting Years*.

In 1969, a popular insurrection toppled the dictatorship, but the PPL papers were never returned to the MID family. Bhutto was prepared to make General Akbar his head of National Security, appoint Faiz to head the National Arts Council, and grant official permission and a declaration to my father enabling him to set up a liberal-left weekly, *Viewpoint*. But the PPL papers remained government rags, dreadful propaganda sheets.

The best journalists had left. Those who remained could shift from supporting military dictatorships to elected civilian politicians. Panegyrics had by now become an art form. Cynicism prevailed. A decade or so later, the PPL died a natural death. Neither the government which had sold the papers off nor the rich businessmen who bought them were capable of or wanted to keep them alive at all costs. When they were taken over, the other proprietors and editors had celebrated or held their tongues. They were cowards, and one of the more decent of them admitted to my father that 'everybody's afraid...'

In 1965, Steven Lukes, David Caute and I organised the first teach-in (a debate open to all) on Vietnam at Oxford. It was a huge success, televised selectively by the BBC programme *Gallery*. General Ayub, Pakistan's first military ruler, and his foreign minister, Zulfikar Ali Bhutto, were on a state visit at the same time. I tried very hard to get Bhutto to speak at the event. I knew he was extremely hostile to the US presence in South-East Asia. He turned us down with genuine regret. A year later during a private visit (Ayub had since sacked him), we had tea at Claridge's. 'I was desperate to speak at the teach-in, as you can imagine, but Ayub vetoed it, no doubt on the advice of our hosts.' Before I could respond, he continued: 'And, oh yes, during our lunch while we were pleading our case for more exports to the UK, the British prime minister [Harold Wilson] said with a smile: "There is one Pakistani export we'd like you to take back with you. He must have been delivered by mistake. Tariq Ali."'

I was a bit surprised since I'd hardly done anything. According to Bhutto, General Ayub laughed and said: 'We know the family well.' An anonymous civil servant seated next to Bhutto whispered to him: 'We know them well too, but that's not the point.'

25

My Father

Given my mother's strong personality and the fact that, as I grew up, she treated me as a friend and confidante, I was much closer to her emotionally than to my father. She found this convenient too, since she could use him as a figure of authority when I needed to be reprimanded or punished. As a result, I tended to downplay my father's life and story even though, in many ways, he had a much larger impact on my own evolution than my mother, especially in the realms of radical politics and world literature and history. I learnt more from his library than I did at school. Urdu poets – Ghalib, Iqbal, Faiz – were read aloud, followed by explanation and interpretation. Cousins coming to visit were roped in for readings of Shakespeare's plays. Some of them moaned in despair. And there were times when my father went over the top, pressuring me to read Hardy when I was twelve, and his all-time favourite writer, Tolstoy, when I was sixteen.

Among non-fiction writers, he saw no one who stood above Edward Gibbon. His words, his verbs, the varied shadings in his speech, his rousing challenge to the Church and official historians, and the splendour of his intellect. It was a treasure house, but, despite repeated attempts, I was not up to it. I tried but failed. Difficult to get a grip on Gibbon if you have no idea of ancient history or Latin. And the art of sentence arrangement has never been one of my strong points. My father read and reread the master. Often he would read a paragraph to me. It had nil impact. When, finally, I did read Gibbon at the tender age of twenty-four, I understood my father's obsession. It is an amazing work of history on practically every level. And it still has the capacity to excite the mind. Gore Vidal's novel *Julian* could not have been written without Gibbon, a good example of the impact of history on literature.

I came to Thomas Hardy's works at Oxford and read all of them, including his poetry, and, once again, I was glad I'd waited. The local countryside certainly made them more enjoyable.

My father was born in Wah in 1917, the youngest of my grandfather's four children, three boys and a girl. On his passport, however, his birth year was recorded as 1918, a mistake that pleased him in later life. It was auspicious, he would say, and he never bothered to have it corrected. So, he was a year older when he died in 1993.

During his last visit to London in 1992, my father and I spent a few days on our own. I tried to get him to talk a bit about his past but, as ever, he was extremely reluctant. He did admit to several regrets, mistakes he'd made and not rectified. None of these were political. He admitted that his feudal household (unlike that of my mother) was not a happy one. His parents had never got on, and tensions, instead of dying down, went in the other direction. That is why he tried to spend as much time as he could with friends, immersed himself in extra-curricular activities at college, became the all-India swimming champion (backstroke) and was selected for the 1936 Olympics. He fell silent when I asked why the household was so divided, so unhappy. He did not want to discuss that with me. I already knew. Long mountain walks usually loosened my mother's tongue. I took full advantage. The story she told me regarding Yusuf Sultana, my paternal grandmother, helps in understanding my father's character, in particular his acceptance of women's equality and rights, but also his determination and refusal to just sit back and accept what life offered. There was a sharp contrast between his life inside and outside the family houses in Lahore and Wah. Inside he tended to be bottled up, silent, always polite. At school and college and in the cafés he patronised he was energetic, high-spirited, loquacious, witty, and had something to say on every subject under the sun. That's how I knew him at home and abroad, except when he was sulking with me, quite unnecessarily. In the fourth form I forged my school report with the help of a friend before bringing it home and was found out. He didn't speak to me for a week. Once I was caught stealing English novels at the Punjab Religious Book Society on The Mall in Lahore, which had the best collection. They saw my overstretched trousers but instead of apprehending me they were mean-spirited and rang my father. For some reason this really did annoy him and it was one of the few occasions he used violence. My mother thoughtfully handed him her hairbrush, the weapon used to spank me. 'Have I ever denied you funds for buying books?' he asked me. It was difficult to explain why that was not the problem. Had this rare assault on my dignity anything to do with his own past? I doubt it.

My grandfather Nawab Muzaffar Khan's first wife had died soon after childbirth, leaving behind an infant son. There was no shortage of staff, but he felt, understandably, that the infant needed a mother and so started looking around for a replacement. He found one. A cousin over two decades younger than him and whose father was head of the Wah Khattar family. At first, she refused point blank, informing her mother that she was interested in someone else, also a cousin but closer to her in age, a wit and bon vivant and, more to the point, there was strong mutual attraction.

At this point my grandfather should simply have retired from the fray. Instead, he upped the pressure and young Yusuf Sultana (aged seventeen) capitulated unhappily to her mother's unending pleas. The fact that her mother was terminally ill and wanted her married while she was still alive made it urgent. Why did Yusuf not insist on the cousin she liked? Did family hierarchies play a role? Or was it that he was slightly louche and drank too much? She did her duty, helped look after the motherless boy, who she liked a lot, and produced four children in rapid succession. And there the story might have ended.

That Yusuf was unhappy in her marriage was hardly a secret. She would often leave the Lahore house on Davis Road and return to her home in Wah, where her brother Masud, who she adored, was based. More importantly for her, he was totally supportive and indulgent. He, too, was a great wit and japester, and friends with the cousins she had been forced to abandon. She was much happier in Wah than in Lahore, but she never left her children alone for too long. Sometimes they accompanied her to Wah as well. At some stage she re-encountered the cousin she would have really liked to marry. He and her brother often drank and joked together. The cousin was not yet married. At some point they started having an affair, which – so I was informed – remained a secret. I doubt this very much. There are very few secrets in households with large numbers of servants. To survive psychologically she must have confided in a woman friend or cousin. It was not that common for married women on these social levels to take such a big risk.

There was another factor. Women often travelled accompanied by their maids. It was almost impossible not to do so. In my father's household there was an added complication. Since his parents were semi-estranged, there were two separate sets of servants with competing loyalties. My grandmother's closest and senior maid was also my father's wet nurse, and looked after me (and years later my brother) throughout my childhood and youth. My father had gifted her a very attractive plot of land in Wah and the family had helped with funds to build a very tasteful little house on the edge of a stream. She would retire there at times to look after her own grandchildren, but always came back whenever she felt bored. Her husband was my grandfather's butler. Between them this couple knew everything that went on. I cannot imagine she did not know about the affair. Sometime in 1924, the dormant volcano erupted. My grandmother discovered she was pregnant. Primitive abortions usually performed by midwives were not uncommon but they were dangerous; the herbal concoctions didn't always work. Or perhaps she was in a reckless mood, and simply wanted to have at least one love child. Suicidal sentimentalism. I could never find out.

When my grandfather found out that he had been so openly cuckolded, he went berserk. This usually very calm and considerate man asked his wife to leave the house immediately. Whatever else she had expected it was certainly not banishment. She left as soon as she could for Amritsar, twenty miles from Lahore, and was given refuge and affection at the home of the Kashmiri segment of our family that had intermittently intermarried with the Khattars to enlarge the gene pool. And there she remained.

My father, not yet eight, was severely shaken by her departure. He was very close to his mother and must have picked up what had happened from the comings and goings of the Khattar elders and servants' gossip. Having discovered where she was, he got hold of some money, walked out of the house, got a *tonga* to the railway station, bought a ticket for Amritsar and hopped on the train. He found the house. His mother nearly fainted as she hugged him. 'Did you tell anyone you were coming here?' He shook his head. The lady of the house rang Lahore to inform them he was safe. They all stared at him in amazement. He clutched his mother's hand.

'I've come to take you home.' Tears greeted this remark. They fed him well, bathed him and arranged for a car to drive him back to Lahore. Both parents must have been alarmed by this development and it was undoubtedly used as an argument when the family elders sat down with my grandfather to negotiate a settlement. He allowed Yusuf back but they barely spoke to each other. When the child (a daughter) was born that same year, my grandfather agreed that she could be part of the family and bear his name. My grandmother gave her a female variant of her own brother's name.

As he grew up, my father remained very close to his mother and this continued till she died. Even before he became political, he never had time for notions of 'honour' or many other patriarchal rituals based on hypocrisy and double standards. Nor did he ever have any sympathy for those who argued that cheating in bed should be punished with lead. There are few 'honour killings' in the Khattar family tradition – more cases of the Khattar armed wing (the 'assassins') helping friendly clans when their women were abducted.

It must have been terrible living in a house divided, and it was here that my father first developed feelings bordering on hatred for feudal customs and rituals, feelings that eventually pushed him away from all this and into the arms of the Communist Party of India. The best years of his life were those spent helping to set up Progressive Papers Ltd and edit its publications. I often pleaded with him to write books. His knowledge of Pakistan and pre-Partition India was enormous. He explained once that he simply did not have what it took to write a whole book. He preferred the short form. I never found that convincing. Blacklisted by the county's first dictator, and imprisoned briefly on two occasions by the third, he thought of essays rather than books – but even these were not completed. Two of his close friends died relatively young. He was lonely. *Viewpoint*, the magazine he founded and edited for almost two decades, was his last contribution to the country's political culture. It served throughout the Zia dictatorship as a singular source of measured but consistent dissent and a refuge for otherwise unemployable journalists. He stopped because he ran out of funds.

There is an entertaining footnote. Among those shocked by the closure of *Viewpoint* was the ISI (the country's premier intelligence agency). The reason? It was the only Pakistani publication read seriously by Indian civil servants and the agencies attached to them. The ISI approached Nadira Alvi, a freelance journalist in Lahore, and offered to fund the magazine secretly through her in order to keep it going and read in India. She told me she respected my father too much to act as a conduit for the ISI and did not dare approach him. She later met and married V.S. Naipaul of her own volition.

I spoke to my father in Lahore the day before he died. He was about to drive to Islamabad to a reception at the Indian High Commission, an event that was being officially boycotted. 'Why tire yourself unnecessarily?' I asked him. 'Only to show that not all of us follow government instructions.' He was exhausted by the journey and passed away the next day.

I pleaded with my mother to delay the funeral till I got there. She refused. 'In our tradition, as you know,' she said in tears, 'an early morning burial the day after is compulsory.' I arrived a day later and helped deal with the steady stream of visitors for the next few days. I didn't weep then.

My Father

Years later, finishing off *The Stone Woman*, my third novel of the Islam Quintet, at a writer's retreat, I was describing a funeral and found myself crying. I was reminded of my father. The tears I had not shed when he died were now flowing.

26

Aftermath

When I arrived in the UK in October 1963, I never imagined that the family past would catch up with me so quickly. Soon after I graduated, I was buttonholed by Guy Wint, masquerading as an *Observer* journalist but an old Intelligence hand who had made several trips to Pakistan. He used to mingle with the Oxford left and became an imbiber of marijuana. He insisted he had started smoking in Pakistan, but Steve Abrams, a postgraduate American resident in Oxford, claimed the credit for the addiction. Guy took me aside and asked: 'Well, what are you going to do now?' I shrugged my shoulders: 'I've applied to join the National Liberation Front in Vietnam to help accelerate your side's defeat. But no reply so far.'

He snorted. 'Dear boy, I don't like the war either. I have a more creative alternative. Why not do a postgraduate degree at St Anthony's?'

'Because they specialise in counterrevolutions.'

Exasperated, he gave up on me, but my bedraggled archive contains two letters from him, written probably before he had lit another joint. He insisted that I meet Sir Penderel Moon (a truly wonderful name that should have featured in Conan Doyle as an intimate of Mycroft), who would be in touch. 'Uncle Pendy', as his nephew Richard Gott referred to him, had been my grandfather's 'private personal (read: political) secretary'. Everyone praised his intelligence, including my father. He had to be taken seriously.

He did get in touch a month or so later, but only after Michael Heseltine had offered me a critic's job on *Town* magazine, as described in *Street Fighting Years*. My mother wrote instructing me that I must not prevaricate – I should meet Moon, not be rude, listen politely and agree to think hard about whatever he suggested. Did my father dictate the letter? It was so out of character for her.

Uncle Pendy invited me to the Atheneum; the reception desk provided a tie. We settled down to lunch. It was a pleasant occasion. We discussed Partition at length. He disagreed with my assessment and said it was unavoidable. The Congress leadership (Nehru and Patel in particular, more so than Gandhi) were simply not in any mood to compromise with the Muslim leaders. (As I write, I smile. Perry Anderson's book-essay *The Indian Ideology* [2012] brought him into tandem with Uncle Pendy.)

He went on to explain the reason why he had invited me to lunch: 'Opposing the American war in Vietnam is fine. The Yanks can't win and sooner or later they will realise that and move on. But you will have to settle down ... I have an idea for you. Why not decide on a postgraduate project, publish it with OUP and get a job at a university?'

'My only postgraduate project is teaching Vietnam wherever I can.'

'Very childish of you. I have a better idea. Why not do a comparative survey of three armies: post-Ottoman Turkish under Atatürk, Egyptian under Nasser, and Pakistan under Ayub. You might enjoy that, and Marxist categories could even help you out.'

'How?'

'The class locations of the officer corps in all three armies, for instance.'

'I only got a Third. Who would fund me?'

'I think you would be accepted by All Souls.'

I burst out laughing.

'Commuting from Hanoi wouldn't be easy.'

He smiled. It actually was an intelligent idea and I thanked him sincerely and profusely for it.

'I could do that project as a book and I might, but you want to intern me in the All Souls torture camp under Warden Sparrow.'

He smiled despairingly.

A few years later, in 1968, my parents came over for a brief holiday. They went to Devon to spend a few days with Major Bill Short (retired). I was barely out of the news that year and I wasn't surprised when they reported his anger. My father had not got into an argument, simply saying that they had no influence on me. But what had the Major said? My mother reported in detail:

'Instruct the boy to grow up. There will never be a revolution in this country again. The first one alerted us for ever. You must be mad to believe that English working men are interested in any Marxist nonsense. They don't even know the words of the Red Flag but they can all sing Rule Britannia. Tell Tariq that Harold Wilson is the farthest left this country will go ...'

Hearing this, I suddenly remembered Michael Foot's words at the Oxford Socialist Club in early 1966, when I suggested he should bring the Labour government (it had a majority of three) down on Vietnam. He railed at us: 'You imbeciles, don't you realise this is the most left-wing government we'll ever have. Wait till he [Wilson] has a majority and then we'll tackle him on Vietnam.' He did get a large majority a few months later but he was never seriously tackled on Vietnam by the PLP. However, it might well be the case that he was the most left-wing prime minister that Britain ever had. It certainly seems so now.

Later that year, I received a very long handwritten letter from Sir Olaf Caroe, the last British Governor of the North-West Frontier Province (now Pakhtunkhwa) and an extremely well-educated civil servant, fluent in Pashtu, Persian and Urdu. His translation of Khushal Khan Khattak's poetry is better than that of most locals. The basic points underlined in the Caroe missive were as follows:

1. I was abusing the hospitality of the British by calling for an overthrow of the state. In fact, I never did quite that, as became obvious in my evidence to the Spy Cops tribunal in 2021 and their preliminary judgement.

2. This was particularly shocking to him since 'your grandfather Nawab Muzaffar Khan and I were very close friends. Seeing your image repeatedly on television reminded me of him, but alas, you are not him and that angers me. He was a wonderful

person and a good friend. Please stop behaving like the wild man from Borneo.' This last made my English friends laugh a lot.

3. I was out of control and, for the sake of the noble Khattar clan if nothing else, I should get a proper job, get married and settle down, preferably in Wah, which he had visited as a guest and whose 'beauty, I'm sure, still enchants'. I shouldn't get involved in British politics. 'You and your types only know how to speak nonsense. You have no ethics or principles, unlike both your grandfathers.' That was clear.

4. If I wanted to go and have tea with him, I would be 'most welcome'. I was not in the mood for cucumber sandwiches on the lawn.

When I read the letter out to my mother, she was livid: 'He has no right to say these things. Did you reply?'

'No. I couldn't be bothered.'

'You're wrong. You should have replied and said *he* was abusing Khattar hospitality by seducing your aunt, breaking up her marriage and trying to persuade her to elope with him to Canada.'

'But that's quite sweet, Ma. Were they in love? Anyway, I'm not opposed to that. You did the same.'

'Please be serious for a minute. She had children.'

'But mother, did she enjoy the affair. Was it in enchanting Wah? Moonlit breezes in the night, the aphrodisiacal scent of *raat-ki-raani* ('queen of the night') enhancing the passion.'

'If that's your attitude, don't bother replying to this dolt.'

I didn't.

BOOK III

THE PROLONGED
TWENTIETH CENTURY

Part 1: Wars Old and New

27

A New Millennium

In March 2000 a book landed on my desk in the Verso/*NLR* offices in Meard Street where I was Editorial Director and Chair of Verso at the time. The author was Chalmers Johnson, a former CIA consultant and cold warrior, now teaching at Berkeley. Fluent in Mandarin and Japanese, he was a sharp critic of the falling standards of intellectual life in his country. The book was called *Blowback*, a CIA coinage denoting the unintended consequences of US global military interventions on four continents. I read it over the next few weeks, liked it very much and cursed that it had not been offered to us but to Henry Holt and Co.

The book was almost completely ignored in the United States in its first year, with no mainstream review at all. Chalmers later told me that an erstwhile hanger-on in Bush the Elder's court, an egocentric mediocrity by the name of Philip Zelikow, had written in the Council of Foreign Relations' house mag that *Blowback* 'reads like a comic book'. One of many striking sentences in the book read: 'World politics in the 21st century will in all likelihood be driven primarily by blowback from the second half of the twentieth century – that is, from the unintended consequences of the Cold War and the crucial American decision to maintain a Cold War posture in a post–Cold War world.' Poor Zelikow.

Johnson's *Blowback* became the master work for many critics of US policies after the hits of 9/11 on the World Trade Center and the Pentagon. These events changed the political landscape. The citizens of the 'indispensable nation' wanted to know why and how they had happened and whether they might happen again. *Blowback* and its author, now in great demand on radio and

TV, had already informed them that the attacks were a response to US foreign policy:

Blowback is shorthand for saying that a nation reaps what it sows, even if it does not fully know or understand what it has sown. Given its wealth and power, the United States will be a prime recipient in the foreseeable future of all the more expectable forms of blowback, particularly terrorist attacks against Americans in and out of the armed forces, including within the United States.

The 'foreseeable future' turned out to be only eighteen months away from the book's publication date. Small wonder that the author was treated as a semi-prophet and his book prescribed as necessary homework for the more serious journalists writing in the *New York Times*, the *LA Times* and the *Washington Post*. One of the three (I think it was the *LA Times*) ran a special supplement listing every US military intervention since the Second World War to explain the blowback.

10 February 2001

I was at the World Social Forum in Porto Alegre, in the deep south of Brazil, for the second annual gathering of progressives. It was more than a symbolic counter to Davos. The aim behind it was serious: to unite a new generation inspired by the anti-WTO protests in Seattle, and to think about alternatives to neoliberalism. The rising Latin American left was now demonstrating what could be achieved in practice. Together, they proved a magnet for global activists everywhere.

The polar contrast between cold, isolated Davos, besieged by demonstrators and protected by the Swiss Army (and its knives), and the tropical warmth and openness of Porto Alegre highlighted the gulf between the two events. The province of Rio Grande do Sul and the town itself were at the time run by the left-wing of the PT (the Brazilian Workers' Party), with participatory democracy as their guiding principle. The local state was active. The mayor of Porto Alegre, a self-confessed devotee of Antonio Gramsci, was confident that the PT's project had hegemonised much of the population in the Brazilian south. This industrial port, the sixth largest city in Brazil with a population of 1.5 million, demonstrated that resistance to globalisation, however modest, was possible. The budgets were limited by the central government, but the PT local government involved the local population at every level in determining how the money was spent – what came to be known as participatory budgeting, with a focus on investment in schools, hospitals and infrastructure projects.

It was an ideal setting for such a conference. Yet it greatly annoyed Brazil's president, Fernando Henrique Cardoso (a onetime leftist and contributor to the *NLR*, but now a great admirer of Tony Blair, Bill Clinton and the 'third way'), whose own neoliberal solutions were currently under attack from all sides. Cardoso denounced the PT for using taxpayers' money to fund the Porto Alegre bash, but the taxpayers I met seemed very happy that their town was the centre of world attention. The local Chamber of Commerce denounced Cardoso for his remarks, claiming that the out-of-season guests were benefiting the local economy.

What worried Cardoso was that the example might spread in Brazil itself, thus propelling the PT to national power. In the recent mayoral elections in São Paulo, and against all predictions, a leading PT intellectual, Marta Suplicy, had defeated the right and taken the city. During the dictatorship, clandestine PT leadership meetings had been held in her luxurious apartment (workers' leader Lula was forced to enter through the servants' entrance). Outside Brazil, the conference was also a nightmare gathering for pro-globalisation pundits in the US press, typified by Daniel Yergin and Thomas Friedman of the *New York Times*. These writers spent their lives promoting the message that the new economy was 'cool' and state intervention was totalitarian – exactly what was being challenged at the Porto Alegre conference.

We had all come to discuss opposition to the neoliberal status quo. There were delegates from 122 countries, attending a dozen plenary sessions and nearly 400 workshops to discuss the alternatives in more detail. The importance of Cuba to Latin America was demonstrated at the opening session when the conference applauded wildly the presence of delegates from the tiny island. There were loud cheers when the eighty-four-year-old veteran of the Algerian liberation struggle, Ahmed Ben Bella, the leader of the FLN and a former president, announced that Che Guevara was the most amazing person he had ever met and a fine figure of a man. Much to our amusement this last was mistranslated into English as: 'and Che had a beautiful body'. At the airport a few days later, I asked Ben Bella whether he had ever sighted Che naked. Were there any photographs? He burst out laughing when I described the translation, but his wife replied: 'No to both questions, I can assure you.'

There were forty mayors from South American cities at the conference. Mariano Arana described the steady growth of misery in his own city, Montevideo. He was here to find ways of regulating and controlling the brutality of the free market. The strongest European presence was from France. Two ministers from the French Cabinet, dozens of MPs and Euro-MPs, and behind them the remarkable organising skills of *Le Monde diplomatique*. London's Ken Livingstone was invited but failed even to respond.

The tension between the Cardoso government in the centre and the PT government in Rio Grande do Sul reached breaking point on the last night of the Forum. The federal police arrested the French farmer José Bové on the orders of the minister of interior in Brasilia and served him with an expulsion notice. Bové had joined the Landless Workers Movement that was occupying a field on which Monsanto was experimenting with genetically modified crops. The local government had declared it illegal to plant GM crops in its province, but Monsanto obtained permission from the federal government. Bové's arrest was a spectacular own goal by Cardoso. It enraged much of the media and gave incredible publicity to the Forum. It also helped to defuse the tension between the two currents in the Forum: the social movements and the politicians.

Many activists from the social movements had been annoyed by the opening session, dominated by PT leader Lula and former

French Cabinet minister Jean-Pierre Chevènement. The latter's presence had irritated me as well. The closing session restored the precarious balance. Bové and the social movements dominated it, with everyone chanting: WE ARE ALL JOSÉ BOVÉ. Bové was in a cheerful mood when I spoke to him over breakfast the following morning. He was planning to leave the country that day in any case, but had decided to defy the expulsion order.

Bové was a very interesting and courageous character and a witty raconteur. When I met him again in Istanbul (we were on different missions) he regaled me with his views on French cheeses and why any EU attempt to standardise them could lead to a new French revolution. 'Dantonist or Robespierrean?' I asked. He insisted that Robespierre was incorruptible, but also a foodie where cheeses were concerned. Every meal was accompanied by a plate of the sacred object. 'Strange Escoffier never mentioned that in his book.' He snorted.

What I felt was missing at the conference was the presence of Russians, Eastern Europeans, Chinese, Vietnamese and Koreans – these were the citizens suffering the worst effects of US-led 'shock therapy'. The figures on public education, health and employment in all these countries showed a sensational decline since 1990. There were hopes that they might come to the next Forum in a year's time. But in the interim, the world changed.

11 September 2001

As news travelled around the world that planes had crashed into the Twin Towers in New York and the Pentagon in DC, the al-Qaeda leader, Osama bin Laden, attending a wedding in Kabul, led the applause. I was glued to a dilapidated TV set in Meard Street that day. Three phone calls came early. Seumas Milne from the *Guardian* with an instruction to start thinking about an article. From New York, Robin Blackburn, teaching at the New School during that period, rang to ask whether we knew what was going on. I told him. 'My God,' he replied. 'So those were the planes we heard flying really low over our apartment building this morning.' We discussed the US response. I thought

Afghanistan might become a likely target. And Pakistan would get centrally involved in helping the US get the Taliban out of the way. This would create havoc in Pakistan itself.

The third call came from Mary-Kay Wilmers at the *London Review of Books*, informing me that they were planning several short – very short – pieces from their regular contributors for the next issue. I groaned. I hate this vox-pop style journalism and tried to chicken out. How could one say anything in 400 words? 'Just get on with it,' she said, and 'don't be provocative.' I did try. The last two paragraphs weren't too bad:

The terrorists who carried out the killings in the US were not bearded illiterates from the mountain villages of Afghanistan. They were educated, middle-class professionals from Egypt and the Hijaz province of Saudi Arabia, two key US allies in the region. What made them propagandists of the deed? The bombing of Iraq, economic sanctions, the presence of American forces on Saudi soil. Politicians in the West have turned a blind eye to this, as they have to the occupation of Palestine and the crimes of Israel. Without profound change in the Middle East, Osama bin Laden, dead or alive, is of little significance.

In the West, Saudi Arabia is simply a source of oil. We prefer not to notice the scale of social and religious oppression, the widespread dejection and anxiety, the growing discontent among Saudis. The Wahhabi Islam practised there has been the inspiration of the Taliban. It was the Saudi monarchy that funded fanaticism in South Asia; it was they (and the CIA) who sent bin Laden to fight the Russians in Afghanistan. Islam was seen by all the experts as the main bulwark against Communism. Denied any secular openings, dissenting graduates have turned to radical Islam, accusing the Saudi royal family of hypocrisy, corruption and subservience to America. These are clever tacticians, open in their admiration of bin Laden and the regime headed by his father-in-law, Mullah Omar, in Kabul. When they blow up bases or foreigners in the Kingdom, the security forces round up a few Pakistani or Filipino immigrants and execute them to show the US that justice has been done, but the real organisers are untouchable.

Their tentacles reach into the heart of Saudi society, and it's debatable whether they can now cut them off, even at the request of the United States.

A day after the *LRB* issue appeared I got a phone call from a friend belonging to the upper reaches of Saudi society. She insisted on a private lunch. When I arrived at her pad she was in a state. She had rung her sister in Riyadh to find out what was going on. Her niece had answered the phone. After salaams were exchanged she asked: 'Where's your mother?'

'My dear aunt,' came the reply, 'not a word for me? Not even a simple mubarik [congrats] for what we did?'

My friend was shaken, as were the CIA operatives listening in to the conversations of princes and reporting back on the joy and laughter they heard at Osama's triumph.

The *LRB* piece that caused a storm in a coffee cup, however, came from a very mainstream academic figure: Mary Beard, Professor of Classics at Cambridge and a regular contributor to the *TLS*. This caused the *LRB* to be universally rubbished in the mainstream press, including in weasely articles by John Lloyd in the *Financial Times* and Ian Jack in the *Guardian*, and a few others. What did Mary Beard write to create the hysteria? Her strong piece included the following:

> But when the shock had faded, more hard-headed reaction set in. This wasn't just the feeling that, however tactfully you dress it up, the United States had it coming. That is, of course, what many people openly or privately think. World bullies, even if their heart is in the right place, will in the end pay the price.

What the ideological censors picked on was the phrase 'the United States had it coming'. Mary was clear enough that this is what most people thought. I strongly defended her right to write these words, at various literary festivals and elsewhere. Not too many others did.

Several weeks later at M-K's, Beard told us that very few – in fact hardly any in the circles in which she moved, nor citizens stoked by the manufactured anger of the tabloids – had reproached her. 'In fact,' she said, 'the very week my *LRB* article appeared I was at dinner at All Souls. When I entered the dining room, all of them, without exception, raised their glasses. I recommended Chalmers Johnson as further reading.'

Over lunch the next day with Paul Foot and Richard Ingrams at the Gay Hussar in Greek Street, I handed over a few paragraphs I had written on the appalling campaign by liberals and conservatives alike against the *LRB* in the media. Both liked it, but Foot said: 'I will pass it on but there's no way Hislop will publish this. They've really moved to the right.' Ingrams agreed, muttering 'disgraceful'. In vain did I point out that this was attacking blatant censorship, nothing to do with left or right as such. It would soon become a pattern, with Francis Wheen and Nick Cohen dominating the 'Letters From ...' and other foreign news in the *Eye*, sometimes to the right of the Foreign Office, as they had been on Yugoslavia.

Meanwhile, old promises had to be kept. I had been invited to a Toronto book festival that fall, followed by a conference at the CUNY postgraduate centre in New York. To go or not to go? I did wonder whether delaying my trip might be more sensible, given the 'secret' deportations of Muslims and an ugly atmosphere in parts of America. But my Canadian friends would not have it and were annoyed by the implication that Canada was no different from the US. I flew to Toronto. The literary gatherings were transformed into huge political assemblies with only one subject: 9/11, its impact, its consequences.

CBC had a show called *CounterSpin* that debated current affairs seriously and invited critics to discuss them with the show's intelligent presenter, Avi Lewis. The latter had moved on but not the programme. They set up a debate on 9/11 between me and Charles Krauthammer from the *Washington Post*. I gave him the full Chalmers Johnson. When I suggested that the war on Afghanistan was a 'crude war of revenge', he agreed: 'So what?' He then tried changing the subject: 'How are your bearded friends next door?' It took me a few seconds to realise he'd moved on from Afghanistan. This was a reference to Fidel and the Cubans. 'He's fine,' I assured him. 'All your attempts to kill him failed. Pity you were chasing the wrong beards.'

I was due to fly to La Guardia the next day. Some close friends accompanied me to the airport in case I was turned back by US Customs. The burly African-American customs officer stared at me as I entered. As I got closer, he grinned: 'Are you the guy who was debating that asshole on television last night?'

I nodded. He stamped my passport and shook hands. A life-enhancing moment.

At the time, Susan Sontag was being hounded on US TV for having challenged the description of the suicide terrorists as 'cowards'. Whatever else they were, she said in public, they were not cowards. How was it possible to disagree? But many did. A fear stalked the country, and friends in the academy – Giovanni Arrighi at Johns Hopkins, Robert Brenner at UCLA and others – informed me that the atmosphere was toxic. Too few people were prepared to speak out.

Flying to the US, I thought how I would now have to rewrite my book on the secular history of Islam. Over the last fifteen years I had been working on my novels – the Islam Quintet – and thinking of mullahs and heretics and the bulging veins of dissent and eroticism in the history of Islam. This next book was going to be titled *Mullahs and Heretics*, but I decided that a slightly different approach was needed. An important question had been raised in public by the US president, George W. Bush. At a press conference on 12 October 2001, the leader of 285 million American people stated: 'How do I respond when I see that in some Islamic countries there is vitriolic hatred for America? I'll tell you how I respond: I'm amazed. I just can't believe it because I know how good we are.'

This is a fundamental belief shared by many US citizens. Nor is it unusual. Powerful empires have never understood the wrath of their subjects. Why should the American Empire be any different? I scribbled an alternative title in my notebook: *The Clash of Fundamentalisms*. The book was to be an attempt to explain why much of the world doesn't see the US Empire as 'good'. In the clash between a religious fundamentalism – itself the product of modernity – and an imperial fundamentalism determined to 'discipline the world', it was necessary to oppose both and argue for a space in the world for Islam and the West in which freedom of thought and imagination could be defended without fear of censorship (or cancellation), persecution or death.

While the Arab people had been careful in any demonstration of support for the violence of 9/11, this was not the case elsewhere. Many in non-Islamic parts of the world were unmoved by what took place and some publicly celebrated – in the chilling phrase of Osama bin Laden – an 'America struck by almighty Allah in its vital organs'. In the Nicaraguan capital, Managua, people hugged each other in silence. In Porto Alegre, a large concert hall packed with young people erupted in anger when a visiting Black jazz musician from New York insisted on beginning his performance with a rendering of 'God Bless America'. The kids replied with chants of 'Osama, Osama!' The concert was cancelled. There were celebrations on the streets in Bolivia. In Argentina, the mothers who had been demonstrating for years to discover how and when the military had 'disappeared' their children refused to join the officially orchestrated mourning. In Greece the government suppressed the publication of opinion polls that showed a large majority actually in favour of the hits, and football crowds refused to observe the two-minute silence.

In Beijing the news came too late in the night for anything more than a few celebratory fireworks, but in the week that followed the reaction became clearer. While the Politburo dithered for over twenty-four hours, Xinhua, the official Chinese news agency, put out a short video of the 9/11 footage complete with Hollywood music. A second video mixed images of the events with footage from *King Kong* and other disaster movies. Beijing students interviewed by the *New Yorker* reminded the shocked journalist of the lack of response in the West when NATO planes had bombed the Chinese embassy in Belgrade.

As we landed at La Guardia, I put away my notebook. Purely by chance the taxi I got to my hotel was festooned with the Stars and Stripes – mass sales of the US flag only made possible by Chinese workers working overtime shifts. The driver was a Latino. To make conversation I asked what I thought was an innocent question: 'Where were you on 9/11?'

He stiffened. 'Where are YOU from?'

'London.'

'Stop joking. Where are you really from?'

'Pakistan.'

He laughed. 'Oh good. I can talk to you.' He proceeded to tell me that he had not been near the World Trade Center on the fateful day. 'It was a great day. I was overjoyed that someone had hit them. I wouldn't have minded if I'd died as well.'

I was taken aback by this degree of hatred. His explanation was straightforward. He was from Costa Rica. The Yanquis had screwed his country and 'our continent'.

'I hope you don't mind my asking but if you hate them so much, working here must be a daily torture.'

'I only do it to put my kid through school. He wants to be a doctor. Nowhere can he do that in my country. If that had been possible, I would never have come here. We'll both return when he's finished.'

'And the Stars and Stripes?'

'To avoid foolish talk. Did you know several Sikh Indian people driving taxis have been badly beaten by passengers for speaking in Punjabi on their cells?'

I did not, but I would get first-hand reports very soon.

At the CUNY postgraduate centre, the audience was sophisticated enough, except for two questions that surprised me so much I wrote them down in my notebook while on the platform. The first from a much-respected feminist who sadly passed away a couple of years ago: 'Hi Tariq, my daughter is holidaying in the Middle East. Do you think she's safe? I mean, I don't want her raped by some towelheads.' I replied coldly to the effect that I hoped she was never raped by anyone anywhere. In this question lay the seeds of Islamophobia. I had words with her afterwards and expressed my shock and anger.

The second question, also from a feminist of sorts, I at first thought was purely satirical: 'Hi. As we all know the Twin Towers were a phallic representation of male superiority. But given that they were hit by Arabs, does this suggest that Islam's male-dominated sexual urges were insulted by their size and that this was the real cause rather than what you've been saying?'

Doug Henwood in the audience began to laugh ('It was the look of incredulity on your face. You obviously had no idea we have crazies of every sort in this city.') To the questioner I replied: 'I have no idea but if ever I run into those who ordered the attacks, I'll ask on your behalf.' While others were trying to conceal their mirth, she said, 'Thanks'.

This was the first of many talks I was to give in the US in those post-9/11 years where I was always asked a conspiracist question. A plaintive voice from the back row: 'I agree with much of what you said, but you ignored one possibility. Are you sure we didn't do this ourselves? I mean we're in Afghanistan and Condy's already saying we've got to remodel the world ...'

I heard him out. I understood that it was the total lack of trust in anything their government did at home and abroad that had made some Americans search for conspiracies. But I was sharp in my response, explaining why I thought it was very unlikely. At future events I had no patience at all for these theories. They simply distracted from discussing real events taking place even as we spoke. Alex Cockburn later told me that when he came out definitively against publishing conspiracy theories in *Counterpunch* the magazine lost a quarter of its readership.

I was really pleased to be in New York, the US city I like the most and where I have many friends of every nationality. Chicago is a close second and LA is not the third. Invitations to speak were pouring in after I had been on *Democracy Now!*, but they had to be put on hold. I wanted to finish *Clash of Fundamentalisms* and I had to return to London, where a handful of us had decided to launch the 'Stop the War' campaign in opposition to the 'Operation Enduring Freedom' invasion of Afghanistan. It had been voted for by all the permanent members of the UN Security Council and virtually everyone else. But you can't please all. Given the talk in Washington, we knew this would not be the last war waged by the US.

The first Stop the War committee included Lindsey German, Jeremy Corbyn, John Rees and me. On the first march we packed Trafalgar Square and demanded the withdrawal of all foreign troops from Afghanistan. At an earlier meeting, thousands filled the Friends Meeting House in London. As I came out to debate Michael Gove on Channel 4 News they joined in with boos and cheers. I called Gove 'an ignorant oaf' as the show ended and then gave a short talk to those waiting outside. By any standards this was a huge success.

In November 2001 I went to speak at a surprisingly large anti-war meeting in Glasgow and was heckled as an apostate by some young Muslims. They were energetic and I chatted to them afterwards. Their knowledge of their own faith was sadly limited. But they impressed me with their desire to debate. On the train back I made some detailed notes for *Clash of Fundamentalisms* that constituted a reply to them. This was a layer that could not be ignored.

Letter to a Young Muslim

Dear friend

Remember when you approached me after the big anti-war meeting in Glasgow? I have not forgotten the shock you registered when I replied 'no' to your question as to whether I was a Believer, or the comment of your friend ('our parents warned us against you'), or the angry questions which the pair of you in particular then began to hurl at me like poison darts.

All of that made me think, and this little book is my reply for you and all the others like you who have asked similar questions elsewhere in Europe and North America. It's heavily intertwined with history, but I hope it will suffice. When we spoke, I told you that my criticism of religion and those who use it for political ends was not a case of being diplomatic in public. Exploiters and manipulators have always used religion self-righteously to further their own selfish ends. It's true that this is not the whole story. There are, of course, deeply sincere people of religion in different parts of the world who genuinely fight on the side of the poor, but they are usually in conflict with organised religion themselves. The Catholic Church victimised worker or peasant priests who organised against oppression. The Iranian Ayatollahs dealt severely with Muslims who preached in favour of a social radicalism.

If I genuinely believed that this radical Islam was the way forward for humanity, I would not hesitate to say so in public, whatever the consequences. I know that many of your friends love chanting the name 'Osama' and I know that they cheered on 11 September 2001. They were not alone. It happened all over the world, but had nothing to do with religion. I know of Argentinian students who walked out when a teacher criticised Osama. I know a Russian teenager who emailed a one-word message – 'congratulations' – to his Russian friends whose parents had settled outside New York and they replied: 'Thanks. It was great.' We talked, I remember, of the Greek crowds at football matches who refused to mourn for the two minutes the government had imposed and instead broke the silence with anti-American chants.

But none of this justifies what took place. What lies behind the vicarious pleasure is not a feeling of strength, but a terrible weakness. The people of Indo-China suffered more than any Muslim country at the hands of the American government. They were bombed for fifteen whole years and lost millions of their people. Did they even think of bombing America? Nor did the Cubans or the Chileans or the Brazilians. The last two fought against the US-imposed military regimes at home and finally triumphed. Today, people feel powerless. And so, when America is hit, they celebrate. They don't ask what such an act will achieve, what its consequences will be and who will benefit. Their response, like the event itself, is purely symbolic.

I think that Osama and his group have reached a political dead-end. It was a grand spectacle, but nothing more. The United States, in responding with a war, has enhanced the importance of the action, but I doubt if even that will rescue it from obscurity in the future. It will be a footnote in the history of this century. Nothing more. In political, economic or military terms it was barely a pinprick.

What do the Islamists offer? A route to a past which, mercifully for the people of the seventh century, never existed. If the 'Emirate of Afghanistan' is the model for what they want to impose on the world then the bulk of Muslims would rise up in arms against them. Don't imagine that either Osama or Mullah Omar represent the future of Islam. It would be a major disaster for the culture we both share if that turned out to be the case.

Would you want to live under those conditions? Would you tolerate your sister, your mother or the woman you love being hidden from public view and only allowed out shrouded like a corpse? I want to be honest with you. I opposed this latest Afghan war. I do not accept the right of big powers to change governments as and when it affects their interests. But I did not shed any tears for the Taliban as they shaved their beards and ran back home. This does not mean that those who have been captured should be treated like animals or denied their elementary rights according to the Geneva Convention, but the fundamentalism of the Empire has no equal today. They can disregard all conventions and laws at will.

The reason they are openly mistreating prisoners they captured after waging an illegal war in Afghanistan is to assert their power before the world – hence they humiliate Cuba by doing their dirty work on its soil – and warn others who attempt to twist the lion's tail that the punishment will be severe. I remember well how, during the Cold War, the CIA and its indigenous recruits tortured political prisoners and raped them in many parts of Latin America. During the Vietnam War the US violated most of the Geneva Conventions. They tortured and executed prisoners, raped the women, threw prisoners out of helicopters to die on the ground or drown in the sea, and all this, of course, in the name of freedom. Because many people in the West believe the nonsense about 'humanitarian interventions' they are shocked by these acts, but this is relatively mild compared to the crimes committed in the last century by the Empire.

I've met many of our people in different parts of the world since 11 September. One question is always repeated: 'Do you think we Muslims are clever enough to have done this?' I always answer 'Yes'. Then I ask who they think is responsible, and the answer is invariably 'Israel'. Why? 'To discredit us and make the Americans attack our countries.' I gently expose their wishful illusions, but the conversation saddens me. Why are so many Muslims sunk in this torpor? Why do they wallow in so much self-pity? Why is their sky always overcast? Why is it always someone else who is to blame? Sometimes when we talk I get the impression that there is not a single Muslim country of which they can feel really proud. Those who have migrated from South Asia are much better treated in Britain than in Saudi Arabia or the Gulf States. It is here that something has to happen.

The Arab world is desperate for a change. Over the years, in every discussion with Iraqis, Syrians, Saudis, Egyptians, Jordanians and Palestinians, the same questions are raised, the same problems recur. We are suffocating. Why can't we breathe? Everything seems static. Our economy, our politics, our intellectuals and, most of all, our religion. Palestine suffers every day. The West does nothing. Our governments are dead. Our politicians are corrupt. Our people are ignored. Is it surprising that some are responsive to the Islamists? Who else offers anything these days?

The United States? It doesn't even want democracy, not even in little Qatar, and for a very simple reason. If we elected our own government they might demand that the United States close down its bases. Would it? They already resent Al Jazeera television because it has different priorities from them. It was fine when Al Jazeera attacked corruption within the Arab elite. Tommy Friedman even devoted a whole column in praise of Al Jazeera in the *New York Times*. He saw it as a sign of democracy coming to the Arab world. No longer. Because democracy means the right to think differently, and Al Jazeera showed pictures of the Afghan war that were not shown on the US networks, Bush and Blair put pressure on Qatar to stop unfriendly broadcasts. For the West democracy means believing in exactly the same things that they believe. Is that really democracy?

If we elected our own government in one or two countries people might elect Islamists. Would the West leave us alone? Did the French government leave the Algerian military alone? No. They insisted that the elections of 1990 and 1991 be declared null and void. French intellectuals described the Front Islamique du Salut (FIS) as 'Islamo-fascists', ignoring the fact that they had won an election. Had they been allowed to become the government, divisions already present within them would have come to the surface. The army could have warned that any attempt to tamper with the rights guaranteed to citizens under the constitution would not be tolerated. It was only when the original leaders of the FIS had been eliminated that the more lumpen elements came to the fore and created mayhem. Should we blame them for the civil war, or those in Algiers and Paris who robbed them of their victory? The massacres in Algeria are horrendous. Is it only the Islamists who are responsible? What happened in Bentalha, ten miles south of Algiers, on the night of 22 September 1997? Who slaughtered the 500 men, women and children of that township? Who? The Frenchman who knows everything, Bernard-Henri Lévy, is sure it was the Islamists who perpetrated this dreadful deed. Then why did the army deny the local population arms to defend itself? Why did it tell the local militia to go away that night? Why did the security forces not intervene when they could see what was going on?

Why does M. Lévy, a creature from a polluted world, believe that the Maghreb has to be subordinated to the needs of the French republic, and why does nobody attack this sort of fundamentalism? We know what we have to do, say the Arabs, but every time the West intervenes it sets our cause back many years. So, if they want to help, they should stay out.

That's what my Arab friends say, and I agree with this approach. Look at Iran. The Western gaze turned benevolent during the assault on Afghanistan. Iran was needed for the war, but let the West watch from afar. The imperial fundamentalists are talking about the 'axis of evil', which includes Iran. An intervention there would be fatal. A new generation has experienced clerical oppression. It has known nothing else. Stories about the shah are part of its prehistory. These young men and women are sure about one thing if nothing else. They don't want the Ayatollahs to rule them anymore. Even though Iran, in recent years, has not been as bad as Saudi Arabia or the late 'Emirate of Afghanistan', it has not been good for the people.

Let me tell you a story.

A couple of years ago I met a young Iranian documentary filmmaker in Los Angeles. He came from a poor muezzin's family in Tehran. His name was Moslem Mansouri. He had managed to escape with several hours of filmed interviews for a documentary he was making. He had won the confidence of three Tehran prostitutes and filmed them for over two years. He showed me some of the footage. They talked to him quite openly. They described how the best pickups were at religious festivals. I got a flavour of the film from the transcripts he sent me. One of the women tells him:

Today everyone is forced to sell their bodies! Women like us have to tolerate a man for 10,000 Toomans ... Young people need to be in a bed together, even for ten minutes ... It is a primary need ... it calms them down. When the government does not allow it, then prostitution grows ... In the parks, in the cinemas, or in the streets, you can't talk to the person sitting next to you. On the streets, if you talk to a man, the 'Islamic guard' interrogates you endlessly. 'Who is this guy? How are you related to him? Where are your documents? ...'

Today in our country, nobody is satisfied! Nobody has security. I went to a company to get a job. The manager of the company, a bearded guy, looked at my face and said: 'I will hire you and I'll give you 10,000 Toomans more than the pay-rate.' I said: 'You can at least test my computer skills to see if I'm proficient or not ...' He said: 'I hire you for your looks!' I knew that if I had to work there, I had to have sex with him at least once a day. I thought to myself it's not worth it! If I work for myself, I can make more money. Wherever you go it's like this!

I went to a special family court – for divorce – and begged the judge, a clergyman, to give me my child's custody. I told him 'Please ... I beg you to give me the custody of my child. I'll be your *Kaniz* ...' (Kaniz means a servant. This is a Persian expression which basically means 'I beg you, I am very desperate'). What do you think the guy said? He said I don't need a servant! I need a woman! What do you expect of others when the clergyman, the head of the court, says this? This guy had 50 kilos of beard and hair on his face! And he says I want a woman! I asked him don't you have a wife? He said: I need many!

I went to the officer to get my divorce signed, instead he said I should not get divorced and instead get married again without divorce, illegally. Because he said without a husband it will be hard to find a job. He was right, but I didn't have money to pay him ... These things make you age faster ... you get depressed ... you have a lot of stress and it damages you. Perhaps there is a means to get out of this ... In Western countries, prostitutes have welfare and governmental insurance. They get medical check ups and so forth. Here we don't have a right to exist ... Why? We are workers too, you know ...

A second woman forced to sell her body tells him:

The men who come for my services are all kinds: ranging from bazaari [shopkeepers], students, doctors, old, young, illiterate ... Basically anyone who has money to buy a woman for some time. Most of them treat us really badly ... Because they give us money, they think they have the right to do anything with us ... and we tolerate it.

Today in our society no one is financially secure. I can't pay my rent ... You tell me what should I do? If I don't sell my body tonight, I don't have money tomorrow ... In a society where there is no job, no security, and no rights, what can a person do? You go to the streets and you're always afraid that Islamic guards might arrest you for any reason; a wisp of hair showing from your *hejab*, a faint lipstick, anything goes ... If I was living in a society where I could work and support myself independent of anyone, I would have never gone after selling my body. Then maybe I would have had a physical need to be with someone, and I could choose ... I would have been able to live with my feelings, as I wished ... with joy ... But in this situation, the government has made men the buyers and people like me the sellers ...

Moslem was distraught because none of the American networks wanted to buy the film. They didn't want to destabilise Khatami's regime! Moslem himself is a child of the Revolution. Without it he would never have become a filmmaker. He comes from a very poor family. His father is a muezzin and Moslem's upbringing was ultra-religious. Now he hates religion, and with a passion that even I can't reproduce. Moslem refused to fight in the war against Iraq. He was arrested. This experience transformed him, as he told me:

It was 1978–9 when I started a little newspaper stand on the corner of a crowded street in Sangsar. Every week I would get books and newspapers of political groups and sell them in the newspaper stand. After a while it became a spot for interested youth to discuss the political situation.

One night the Islamic guards which called themselves 'Hezbollah' attacked the newspaper stand and burned the place. I took the burned books and put them in front of the stand every day for a week. Then they arrested me and took me to the prison.

The prison was a hard but good experience for me. It was in the prison that I felt I am reaching a stage of intellectual maturity. I was resisting and I enjoyed my sense of strength. I felt that I saved my life from the corrupted world of clergies and this is a price I was paying for it. I was proud of it. After one year in prison, they told me that I would be released on the condition that I sign papers stating that I will participate in Friday sermons and religious activities. I refused to sign. They kept me in the prison for one more year.

When I was released from the prison, my birthplace seemed too small for me. I felt suffocated in there. So I came to Tehran. I worked in the mornings and went to the 'Free' university at nights. [Free university is a private university with high tuition.]

In the early Eighties, I was not interested in cinema. My inner thoughts and struggles would not allow me to pay attention to cinema or have any long-term plan. I kept thinking that I can never adapt to the situation in Iran. The whole social and political atmosphere bothered me seriously.

After the war ended [1989], the government made a law that required people to change their old birth certificates into new ones. I knew that if I went to change my birth certificate, I would have to give up my fake documents. It would become clear that I was a drafted soldier who did not go to war. On the other hand the cost of university was very high. So I decided to do my military service. After I came back, I looked for a job and accidentally I found a film magazine that was looking for a reporter. I took the job. Even though I tried to interview the non-governmental filmmakers and literary figures, I knew well that if I write anything – even if critical – the regime would still be able to take the credit by saying that they allow criticism and therefore they are democratic! Cinema was in total control of the state and filmmakers were bound by the limitations of the system.

If I interviewed filmmakers such as Mehrjui, Makhmalbaf or Kiarostami, it would ultimately benefit the political system. But I told myself that I would allow the regime to take such advantage of me temporarily … I thought my work in the media would serve as a cover for my own projects, which were to document the hideous crimes of the political regime itself. I knew that I would not be able to make the kind of films I really want to make due to the censorship regulations. Any scenario that I would write would have never got the permission of the Islamic censorship office. I knew that my time and energy would get wasted. So

I decided to make eight documentaries secretly. I filmed my footage in the period between 1994 and 1998 and I smuggled it out of Iran. Due to financial problems I've only been able to finish editing two of my films. One is *Close Up, Long Shot* and the other is *Shamloo, the Poet of Liberty*.

The first film is about the life of Hossein Sabzian, who was the main character of Kiarostami's drama-documentary called *Close-Up*. The latter is the story of a guy who tries to present himself as Makhmalbaf, whom he resembles physically, to a family. The family buy his story and try to sponsor one of his movies, thinking he is the famous Makhmalbaf. He lives with the family for four days and ultimately the family realise that he is making the whole thing up. They get him arrested. A few years after Kiarostami's film, I went to visit Sabzian. He loves cinema. His wife and children get frustrated with him and finally leave him.

Today, he lives in a village on the outskirts of Tehran and has come to the conclusion that his love for cinema has resulted in nothing but misery. In my film he says: 'People like me get destroyed in societies like the one we live in. We can never present ourselves. There are two types of dead: flat and walking. We are the walking dead!'

We could find stories like this and worse in every Muslim country. One thing more and then I'll stop. There is a big difference between Muslims of the diaspora, those whose parents migrated to the Western lands and those who still live in the House of Islam. The latter are far more critical because religion is not crucial to their identity. It's taken for granted that they are Muslims.

Moslem Mansouri did not speak English or Urdu and I did not speak Farsi. We communicated through an Iranian exile of Jewish origin, Elham Ghetaynchi. In Europe and North America things are different. Here an official multiculturalism has stressed difference at the expense of all else. Its rise correlates with a decline in radical politics as such. 'Culture' and 'religion' are softer, euphemistic substitutes for socioeconomic inequality – as if diversity, rather than hierarchy, were the central issue in North American or European society today.

I have spoken to Muslims from the Maghreb (France), from Anatolia (Germany), from Pakistan and Bangladesh (Britain), from everywhere (United States) and a South Asian sprinkling in Scandinavia. Why is it, I often ask myself, that so many are like you? They have become much more orthodox and rigid than the robust and vigorous peasants of Kashmir and the Punjab, who I used to know so well.

The British prime minister is a great believer in single-faith schools. The American president ends each speech with 'God Save America'. Osama starts and ends each TV interview by praising Allah. All three have the right to do so, just as I have the right to remain committed to most of the values of the Enlightenment. The Enlightenment attacked religion – Christianity, mainly – for two reasons: that it was a set of ideological delusions, and that it was a system of institutional oppression, with immense powers of persecution and intolerance. Why, then, should I abstain from religious criticism?

Why should we abandon either of these legacies today? Who would imagine that religions have become less of an illusion since the days of d'Holbach or Gibbon? I have never liked relativism or special pleading. What I want to know is why there is never a single Muslim name when the Nobel Prizes for Physics and Chemistry are announced each year. Are intelligence, talent and inspiration absent from Muslim genes? They never were in the past. What explains the *rigor mortis*?

Sweet irony: did you know that the only Muslim to win the Nobel Prize for Physics was someone I knew? A Pakistani citizen, Professor Abdus Salam. Alas, he was a member of the Ahmadi sect which had been deprived of its status as Muslims. While he was a Muslim when he got the prize, a few years later he was informed by law that he was not. He used to joke with a sad expression that although he was not a Muslim in Pakistan, he was still one in India, Europe and East Africa.

I don't want you to misunderstand me. My aversion to religion is by no means confined to Islam alone. And nor do I ignore the role which religious ideologies have played in the past in order to move the world forward. It was the ideological clashes between two rival interpretations of Christianity – the Protestant Reformation versus the Catholic Counter-Reformation – that led to volcanic explosions in Europe. Here was an example of razor-sharp intellectual debates fuelled by theological passions, leading to a civil war, followed by a revolution. The sixteenth-century Dutch revolt against Spanish occupation was triggered off by an assault on sacred images in the name of confessional correctness. The introduction of a new prayer book in Scotland was one of the causes of the seventeenth-century Puritan Revolution in England.

The refusal to tolerate Catholicism sparked off its successor in 1688. The intellectual ferment did not cease and a century later the ideas of the Enlightenment stoked the furnaces of revolutionary France. The Church of England and the Vatican now combined to contest the new threat, but ideas of popular sovereignty and republics were too strong to be easily obliterated.

I can almost hear your question. What has all this got to do with us? A great deal, my friend.

Western Europe had been fired by theological passions, but these were now being transcended. Modernity was on the horizon. This was a dynamic that the culture and economy of the Ottoman Empire could never mimic. The Sunni–Shia divide had come too soon and congealed into rival dogmas. Dissent had, by this time, been virtually wiped out in Islam. The Sultan, flanked by his religious scholars, ruled a state Empire that was going to wither away and die. If this was already the case in the eighteenth century, how much truer it is today. Perhaps the only way in which Muslims will discover this is through their own experiences, like Iran.

The rise of religion is partially explained by the lack of any other alternative to the universal regime of neoliberalism. Here you will discover that as long as Islamist governments open their countries to global penetration, they will be permitted to do what they want in the socio-political realm. The American Empire used Islam before and it can do so again. Here lies the challenge. We are in desperate need of an Islamic Reformation that sweeps away the crazed conservatism and backwardness of the fundamentalists but, more than that, opens up the world of Islam to new ideas which are seen to be more advanced than what is currently on offer from the West. This would necessitate a rigid separation of state and mosque; the dissolution of the clergy; the assertion by Muslim intellectuals of their right to interpret the texts that are the collective property of Islamic culture as a whole; the freedom to think freely and rationally and the freedom of imagination.

Unless we move in this direction we will be doomed to re-living old battles, and thinking not of a richer and humane future, but of how we can move from the present to the past. It is an unacceptable vision. I've let my pen run away with me and preached my heresies for too long. I doubt that I will change, but I hope you will.

After the book was published, I received a letter:

Hello Tariq.

My friend and I are on a bus, on our way to the anti–Iraq War demo. We've been reading your book and couldn't believe you'd taken the trouble to write us an open letter. Thanks. Both of us have joined the Scottish Socialist Party!

28

Iraq at the Centre
of the World

Where injustice speaks with the voices
of justice and of power
where injustice speaks with the voices
of benevolence and of reason
where injustice speaks with the voices
of moderation and of experience
help us not to become bitter
And if we do despair
help us to see that we are desperate
and if we do become bitter
help us to see that we are becoming bitter
and if we shrink with fear
help us to know that it is fear
despair and bitterness and fear
So that we do not fall
into the error
of thinking
we have had a new revelation
and found the great way out
or the way in
and that alone had changed us.

Erich Fried, 'Prayer at Night'

After 9/11 my life and activities registered another shift. From 1984 to 1999 I had largely concentrated on a cultural resistance, making films, writing novels and plays and giving the odd political lecture in different parts of the world, but now the publication of *The Clash of Fundamentalisms* in over a dozen countries in 2002–3 had resulted in a near total immersion in the political crisis. 'When are you going to finish your Islam Quintet?' I was asked at a press conference during a visit to Australia in 2002 (the first of many to that country, which I like immensely) to speak at the Sydney Writers' Festival. 'Ask George Bush,' I replied. 'It depends on how many wars they wage.'

After the US/NATO 'success' in Afghanistan – where the Pakistan Army advised the Taliban to disappear, shave their beards if necessary and bide their time – the US began to plan the invasion and occupation of Iraq. The reason? They wanted to topple the regime and divide the country. Why? Because they could. It was in their regional interests.

How else can one explain the mass conversions that marked the end of the twentieth century as hordes of politicians, academics, intellectuals, novelists and journalists, not to mention bandwagon careerists, collectively ingested the Washington Consensus? Their sharpened instincts told them that the decisive trend in political and cultural life was conformity. They metamorphosed, hoarding all their ideas into a single enclosure. The pillars of the new global order were viewed as almost divine institutions whose authority derived from the mere fact of their existence.

In reality, this logic was underpinned by NATO's eastward expansion and a network of US military bases in 121 countries. The crisis and collapse of all non-capitalist alternatives coupled with the end of the cold and hot wars between the United States and the communist world had a profound impact on many who had, till then, been broadly aligned with the left. In contrast to Europe, Australia and the US, there were fewer penitents in South America. A substantial layer of activists and intellectuals there refused to turn their backs on the Cuban Revolution. More importantly, even those sharply critical of Castro refused to applaud his would-be assassins in Washington or Miami.

The two principal ideas of the New Order were: (a) the new model capitalism as the sole way of organising humankind from now on till the planet imploded, and (b) the West's right to flagrantly violate national sovereignty in the name of imposing its own brand of 'human rights'. These ideas and the domestic and foreign policies based on them have spread like a contagious fever over the last decades. Betrayed promises and discarded hopes led to an embittered view of the past, fuelling personal ambitions. The individual took precedence over the community.

The result of the first idea has seen a hollowing out of democratic institutions and the continued decay of the political party system. While this was more pronounced in the West, it could also be seen in India, Brazil and South Africa. Drained of political differences, the parties became empty shells, mechanisms designed to help the political elite share both power and money. The parties had fewer and fewer members but were kept going by a tiny network of professionals, the political equivalents of their peers in the advertising industry. In the last century Herbert Marcuse was widely mocked for predicting that trends in modern capitalism were creating a consumerist culture in which humans too were being mass-produced and which was leading inexorably towards a passive and atomised society. The collapse of the Soviet Union in 1991 turbo-charged the process.

Quite a few old friends became new versions of the empire loyalists of yore. In 2002 I described the literary types in the *Guardian* as the *belligerati*. It annoyed them greatly. Salman Rushdie, Martin Amis, Ian McEwan and their hangers on were inspired by the US neocons. Rushdie posed naked for the cover of a French magazine, draped only in the Stars and Stripes – the sole occasion on which I felt grateful for the existence of the flag.

The mass converts were men and women who were once intensely involved in left-wing activities. It was a short march for some of them: from the outer fringes of radical politics to the antechambers of the State Department. Like many converts, they displayed an aggressive self-confidence. Having honed their polemical and ideological skills within the left, they now deployed them against their old friends. This is why they became the useful idiots of the empire.

They had, nonetheless, to pass the David Horowitz test. Horowitz, the son of old communists and a biographer of the late Isaac Deutscher, underwent the most amazing self-cleansing in seventies America. Today he remains a leading polemicist of the right, constantly denouncing soft liberals as a bridge to the more sinister figures of the left. Compared to him, Christopher Hitchens continued to appear to his new friends as a marginal and slightly frivolous figure, though his sidekick in the run up to the Iraq War, the Anglo-Iraqi writer, Kanan Makiya, would certainly pass the test.

Unlike Hitchens, who was strongly opposed to the 1990 Gulf War, Makiya, who became a favourite of the Richard Perle wing of the State Department, chose that very same year to defect. He is, at least, consistent. He was in favour of a Japanese-style US occupation of Iraq even then and pretended to be shocked when Bush *père* refused the role, acting instead in what he regarded as vital US interests by keeping Saddam in power. Makiya regarded Bush 1's refusal to occupy the country and push through regime change as an act of betrayal, but he was respectful of Bush 2.

He was paraded on transatlantic TV talk shows and news programmes as the voice of Iraq. Given an outing in the *Guardian* as 'Iraq's most eminent dissident thinker', he declared: 'September 11 set a whole new standard as to what could be achieved, and if you're in the terrorism business you're going to start thinking big, and you're going to need allies. And if you need allies in the terrorism business, you're going to ask Iraq.'

Far from being an eminent thought, this was a pure fabrication of which most self-respecting intelligence officers on either side of the Atlantic would have been ashamed. But Makiya had become a reckless operator. So keen was he to fly alongside the men of the 82nd Airborne that his capacity to spin extraordinary spirals of assertion based on no empirical facts whatsoever knew no bounds. When he was received by Bush Jr in the White House he advised him to invade Iraq: 'People are waiting to welcome US soldiers with sweets and flowers.'

Hitchens started off with a thoughtful piece on 13 September 2001, in the London *Standard*, in which he stated that the 'analytical moment' had to be 'indefinitely postponed', but nonetheless linked the 9/11 hits to the past policies of the United States and criticised Bush for confusing an act of terrorism with an act of war. What happened to make him a Bush apologist? There was talk that Graydon Carter, his editor at *Vanity Fair*, had warned that he should think very carefully because if he maintained the sub–Chalmers Johnson position his career and bank balance might suffer. From then on he and I debated in public but we never spoke. During our last confrontation on Al Jazeera I pointed out yet again that the balance-sheet on Iraq was a disaster: over a million dead, democracy a joke, Iran catapulted into becoming a major force in the region. He muttered: 'difficult to disagree'.

The permanent shift was his position on Palestine when he became an Israel apologist. A few years before he died, I ran into him at the Paraty book festival in Brazil. 'Greetings, General,' I nodded. Israel had launched another war and my friends Mourid Barghouti and Radwa Ashur, as well as Susan and myself, decided we should make a public statement. We got a draft together that Susan edited. The first signatory was Toni Morrison, despite Hitchens's attempt to prevent her from doing so. 'Don't follow him,' he said, pointing at me. Her snub to him was brutal. Once she'd signed, many other writers did so as well, and I read the statement and the names of signatories out from the platform before beginning my keynote. Unsurprisingly it divided people, but there was little doubt that the handful of Zionists there had little support. I never saw Christopher again.

Hitchens soon moved on to denounce those who made similar but much sharper criticisms than him of 9/11 hysteria, and began to talk of the supposed 'fascist sympathies of the soft left' – Noam Chomsky, Harold Pinter, Gore Vidal, Susan Sontag, Edward Said et al. In post-conversion television appearances he began to sound more like a saloon-bar bore than the fine critical mind that had once blown away the halos surrounding Kissinger, Clinton and Mother Teresa or, for that matter, Isaiah Berlin. Sounding increasingly like the pompous neoconservatives he once derided, he hitched himself to the bandwagon of the Pentagon's most favoured Iraqi exile and the darling of US oil interests, Ahmed Chalabi.

What united the New Empire loyalists was an underlying belief that, despite certain flaws, the military and economic power of the United States represents the only emancipatory project and, for that reason, it has to be supported against all those who challenge its power. What they forget is that empires always act in their self-interest. The British Empire exploited the anti-slavery campaigns to colonise Africa, just as Washington uses the humanitarian hand-wringing of NGOs and the *bien pensants* to fight its new wars today. They laugh in Washington when they hear European politicians talk of revitalising the United Nations.

I argued this at length with the empire loyalists and their apologists. Their response was usually to accuse me of 'anti-Americanism'. But I was not alone. A substantial number of US citizens had opposed the war in Vietnam and its sequels. Without the courage and heroism of the American anti-war movement (especially its retired and serving GIs) the Vietnam War might have been prolonged. On the day when the world marched to try and stop the Iraq War, the turnout on the streets of New York, Chicago, Los Angeles and every state capital was impressive. I spoke at later anti-war demonstrations in the US and came to know the country better and replenished the old friendship cupboard.

There was a certain innocence too that I liked. Once in Madison I was returning to my hotel after a PBS interview when the doorman stopped me. 'Did I hear you on the radio just now?' I nodded. 'Is it true what you said, that Israel has nuclear weapons?' I nodded again. 'How come I didn't know that?' It was a good question and we chatted for almost half an hour.

On my return to Britain I spoke a great deal on radio and TV, denouncing the coming invasion of Iraq. There was little doubt that the country was seriously divided, more so than during the

Suez war in 1956. The foreign secretary, Robin Cook, resigned his post and was replaced by the toadying Jack Straw. (In 2023, he confessed that the war had been a mistake.) Former members of the Blair Cabinet (Mo Mowlam comes to mind) publicly attacked the government and over fifty MPs said they would vote against it. Invited by Foreign Office civil servants to address them one lunchtime, bearing in mind the 'Chatham House Rule' (no reporting of who said what), I did so, making the case against the war. Some vigorous questioning followed. As they returned to their offices, I asked: 'Going back now to prepare the dodgy dossiers?' Sheepish laughs.

At roughly the same time sixty former UK ambassadors wrote a letter to *The Times* opposing the war. I was asked if I would be prepared to give a lecture to currently serving ambassadors to the region and answer questions. I regarded all this as a slightly unusual 'building the demonstration' activity. Both the BBC at the time and the liberal press reflected the divisions in the country. When the US secretary of state Colin Powell lied to the United Nations that Iraq possessed 'weapons of mass destruction', the *New York Times* quoted US pilots as saying they'd bombed the country for years. 'There are no targets left.' Asked to respond to Powell's assertion by US radio stations, I said it was a totally false claim that revealed the bankruptcy of the Bush administration. This turned out to be the case and some years later Powell confessed that he had been 'misled'.

Speaking to the ambassadors, I referred to the various Western-backed regimes in the Arab world as 'Wahhabi kleptocracy' (Saudi Arabia), 'upgraded petrol stations' (the Gulf States), 'moth-eaten dictatorship' (Egypt), etc. The first to ask a question introduced himself thus: 'As Her Majesty's ambassador to the moth-eaten dictatorship, could I ask ...'

15 February 2003

In London it seemed that everyone was going to the Stop the War demo in Hyde Park. As I walked into the park I was greeted by senior Scotland Yard officers with smiles. One of them said: 'For the first time in my life I agree with you lot. Terrible.' That was the mood in many places and it is why the turnout was 1.5 million. None of us had predicted such a huge crowd, and multi-class and multi-generational at that. It was much, much larger than the Suez, CND and Vietnam War demonstrations.

Apart from disgust at the horror of war itself, the scale of the turnout showed that large numbers of people globally did not trust their politicians. They did not believe their lies and were withdrawing their consent. Eight million people marched that day across 600-plus cities, but all of Rupert Murdoch's titles (with the exception of his paper in Tasmania) supported Bush. Particularly pleasing were the very large crowds in US cities. In New York, the city targeted by the suicide terrorists on 9/11, there were close to 200,000 people, and every state capital had large turnouts. Over two million marched in Rome and Madrid. Yet very few in Paris, where the Socialist Party leader visited the US embassy to express his support and inform the ambassador that had he been president, they would have sent troops! Pauvre France.

When I spoke in London I started with: 'We desperately need regime change in London.' Most people got the message, but after I finished speaking, Michael Foot, who was in the queue of speakers, came up to me: 'That's the worst speech you've ever made. Calling for a Labour prime minister to be overthrown. Shocking.' I felt reassured.

ABC TV from Australia was more sympathetic (they reported that the march in Sydney was very large as well) and quoted me as saying that 'there's no doubt' that 'the overwhelming mass' of demonstrators, among them many who had never demonstrated before, felt the march could achieve its objective: 'These were citizens, marching, genuinely believing that what they did could affect politics and when they realised that it couldn't, that was it ... It had very little effect on mainstream politics and I think this fact – that the politicians don't listen – played a big part in alienating young people from politics.'

To an Italian journalist who asked me to explain my remarks about 'toppling' Blair, I replied: 'In Britain the Blair regime is on the defensive regardless of the spin and the rhetoric. Even loyalist Labour MPs were shaken by the size and composition of the demonstration and the strength of feeling. The key fact here is whether they will display the ruthlessness of the Tories who ditched their leader Margaret Thatcher when she had become a liability. Labour MPs of left and right tend to be far more sentimental towards their leadership, but Blair isn't really a traditional Labour leader. So it should be easier for the junior rats to push the big rat off the sinking ship first, in the hope that they might save the ship. Blair is hoping that it will be a quick war and happy Iraqis will welcome him to Baghdad, and that these images on TV will dispel the anger – I think he's wrong. He will never outlive this crime. People have seen through him and the fake reasons given for waging this war.'

A month later, on 20 March 2003, the US and Britain invaded Iraq. I got a morning phone call from the Stop the War office: 'Hundred and probably more schools have walked out and are heading for Parliament Square. Can you go and speak please?' I did and was delighted to see my younger daughter, Aisha, present and accounted for and singing with her mates: 'Who let the bombs out? Bush, Bush, Bush, and Blair.' Many young people had been chanting 'This is what democracy's all about' on the big demo itself. Now they began to grasp some realities about the new world order.

A week before the invasion, purely by chance I ran into a group of Arab friends near Westminster Bridge. Meeting them was a real relief, something they could not have realised. I had come straight from participating in a slightly claustrophobic BBC television debate on Iraq. As a giant image of Richard Perle smiled cynically from a Washington studio, the British foreign secretary Jack Straw (a weasel of many years' standing) had insisted that the only purpose of invading Iraq was disarmament and not regime change. In another corner, two Peninsular potentates from the Hashemite and Al Saud dynasties exchanged mild insults. While Prince Hassan of Jordan insisted that Islam was not incompatible with democracy, Prince Turki bin Faisal, the Saudi ambassador to Britain and former head of intelligence, stated the opposite and reminded the audience that Osama bin Laden had played a glorious role fighting the Russians in Afghanistan with the complete approval of the West.

After all this, encountering a few 'street Arabs' was pure ozone. We talked of the coming war, its likely impact, whether there would be a resistance, and so on. I was undecided whether to accept an invitation to dinner till the friend inviting me said: 'We've just bought two videos with old footage of Nasser.'

I was happy to be dragged back to watch Nasser in Knightsbridge. It was an eerie and moving experience. Eerie because of the timing. Nearly half a century after the Suez war, another Arab country was being targeted for invasion by two imperialist powers backed by Israel. This time the United States had replaced France. Moving because the documentaries concentrated on Nasser's rapport with the Arab street, and his 1956 defiance of the ageing British lion ('Let the imperialists choke in their rage') as he announced the nationalisation of the Suez Canal – there were scenes of a population wild with delight. Here was an Arab leader who, despite all his weaknesses, was genuinely popular with his people, unlike the freaks and monsters that came later.

The depiction of the mass mobilisations throughout the Arab world was stunning. The refusal by the people to accept Nasser's resignation after the 1967 defeat; the genuine displays of grief at his funeral as they instinctively realised that an important period of their history had come to an end. Not much was said after the films ended. What was there to say? And yet all of us were thinking how much the world had changed.

In 1956 when Britain, France and Israel invaded Egypt, it was seen as a pre-emptive assault on the entire Arab nation. In response, the Suez Canal was blocked; oil pipelines and pumping stations in Iraq and Syria were blown up; the Saudis refused to pump any oil that might be loaded onto French or British tankers, and the flow from Saudi oilfields to Bahrain came to a total halt. Explosives were even planted underneath oil installations in Kuwait – then and now, little more than an imperial petrol station. And this time? Would the Arab states do anything remotely similar to punish the invader of Iraq? It seemed unrealistic even to pose such a question.

The second pre-emptive strike, this time from Israel alone, came in 1967. It took the Egyptians by surprise and was a body blow against Arab nationalism, which never recovered. A decade after Gamal Abdel Nasser's death, his successor Anwar Sadat had sold himself and the state to the American Empire. It was to be neoliberalism at home and the recognition of Israel. Sadat paid the price with his own blood. Islamist soldiers substituted real bullets for blanks at a ceremonial parade and executed him in full public view. This made every dictator nervous. Soldiers are now carefully watched before and during these events.

Another pre-emptive strike, this time a direct one, led to the occupation of Iraq. The plan was to install a market-fundamentalist regime that would recognise Israel 'within three months', but the process was delayed by the refusal of most Iraqis to collaborate. The consequences of the occupation would mark the twenty-first century. As I write, two decades after the occupation, there is no continuous electricity in Iraq.

Poets with an understanding of history are often filled with a deep foreboding. They never allow themselves to become submerged in despair; they continue to hope, while recalling misdemeanours from the past as a caution to the criminals of today; they alert their readers to the punishments that befall those who remain silent and become accessories to murder.

The Hebrew poet Aharon Shabtai appeals to his fellow countrymen not to think of the past only from the perspective of the oppressed, but to look inside themselves and ask if they have, even subconsciously, inherited something from those who once oppressed and slaughtered them. History is unpredictable. The colonial horrors being inflicted on the Palestinians might one day confront Israelis in the dock:

> And when it's all over,
> My dear, dear reader,
> On which benches will we have to sit,

Those of us who shouted 'Death to the Arabs!'
And those who claimed they 'didn't know'?*

For most of the twentieth century, poetry – if not the poets –
enjoyed some freedom in the Arab world and in South Asia,
regardless of who ruled there. Sometimes dictators became
addicted to poetry and wrote very bad verses themselves. In
Bangladesh, General Ershad attended a poetry reading and his
sycophants insisted that he honour the event by reciting the
first poem. As shameless bureaucrats applauded, Ershad went
to the podium and recited a terrible poem ('A stinking fart after
Eid lunch' was how an old Dhaka friend described it to me).
A real poet followed him and decided to extemporise: 'Today,
every motherfucker thinks he can write poetry ...' Before he
could continue, he was dragged off the platform and taken to
prison.

The popularity of poetry was often linked to ongoing political crises – like Milton in England, Keats and Shelley after him
and Burns in Scotland. In the Arab world, a poem, easily learnt,
could be recited in a café; it could be recorded on tape and posted;
it could be sung by a diva and could cross any frontier, travelling from city to city without fear. This helped to relieve the
intellectual and spiritual hunger of the Arab nation. As for the
poets, they suffered. Their lives were ruled by forced departures, by undesired exile. Once public truth is outlawed, the
hour of the timeserver arrives – the jackal poet (or journalist or intellectual) who decorates official platforms, mocks all
notions of the poet-as-tribune, mouths only the virtues of the
intellectual-as-entertainer. But dictators, even the less intelligent ones, prefer the real thing. They are contemptuous of the
jackals who can be bought and sold by the Mukhabarat (secret
police) of any country. The leader who wields absolute power
(and sometimes this can be an elected politician without an
opposition) believes he also possesses absolute wisdom and, naturally, absolute goodness, and consequently wants the poets who

---

* Aharon Shabtai, 'Nostalgia', in *J'Accuse*, New York, 2003.

are respected by the people to write verses that deify and honour his regime.

The week Baghdad fell, I rang Saadi Youssef to suggest a meeting and, if he was agreeable, lunch. Widely regarded as one of the great Arab poets of the modern period, he lived in temporary exile in Uxbridge, a London suburb close to Heathrow airport and a long way from the village of Abulkhasib, near Basrah, where he was born in 1934, and from Baghdad, where he spent his formative years. I smiled when he told me he lived near the airport.

The next day we met in the Soho offices of the *New Left Review*. 'Where would you like to eat?' 'Oh,' and then with a nonchalant shrug, 'anywhere'. As we walked through the streets inspecting one local eatery after another, my offers of Chinese, Vietnamese, Japanese and Thai restaurants were systematically rejected. 'Let's not eat Far Eastern.' After another futile search for something else I suggested he should decide on the cuisine. 'Is there an Arab café or something?' There was one on Greek Street. It was empty and that's where we ended up having lunch. He recognised the Algerian accent of the waiter. The music was loud and we asked them to turn it down. 'That was a Nizar Qabbani poem being sung,' he told me. 'You like his work, don't you?' I did, but it was still too loud.

We talked of Qabbani for a while and of the Pakistani poet Faiz, whom Youssef had met in Beirut a quarter of a century earlier, when both were in exile. He liked Faiz and asked about his impact on Pakistani culture. 'For many of us growing up under a dictatorship,' I told him, 'Faiz was Pakistani culture.' Qabbani and Faiz were both dead but the poetry lived on.

Youssef talked of poets he had translated into Arabic: Whitman, Cavafy, Ritsos, Ungaretti and Lorca. When I asked about his own work and reputation, he insisted that he was not alone. Iraq had been blessed with poets: 'There were three of us from an older generation: al-Jawahiri, Muthaffar al-Nawab and myself. All of us ended up in exile. I think al-Jawahiri was a hundred years old when he died a few years ago [in 1997] in Damascus. Never saw Baghdad again. Saddam was always sending his emissaries to plead with us. He wanted all three of us to return for a public poetry reading in Baghdad. He knew and we knew that if this happened there would be at least half a million people at the event, if not more. Through his messenger he told us: "I know you're all communists and you attack me, but understand that you're also part of our national heritage. Please return. The blood on my neck will guarantee your safety." Somehow this was not a very reassuring message. In any case too many of our friends and comrades had been tortured and killed by him. That's the deal he made with the Americans at the time. He would wipe us out, and not just us. There were some very committed and decent people in the Ba'ath Party as well. They, too, perished. So, we did not return to Baghdad. And now it's occupied again.'

Exile had not tamed these poets. Their poetry circulated inside a country where their acidic verses were much appreciated. Their experience of the regime and its Western backers had not made them embittered and disillusioned old renegades, speaking in a servile and self-deprecating idiom as they queued for Saudi largesse. In his yearning for home, Muthaffar al-Nawab had spoken for a whole generation of exiles:

> I have accepted my fate
> Is like that of a bird,
>
> And I have endured all
> Except humiliation,
> Or having my heart
> Caged in the Sultan's palace.
> But dear God
> Even birds have homes to return to,
> I fly across this homeland
> From sea to sea,
> And to prison after prison after prison,
> Each jailer embracing the other.

The poem narrates its author's experiences in the early sixties. Muthaffar was imprisoned after the first Ba'athist coup of 1963 and tortured. Together with other prisoners, he managed to escape; they crossed the Iranian border into Ahwaz in Khuzestan, an ethnic Arab province. Their presence was soon discovered by SAVAK, the Shah's secret police. They were arrested, tortured and returned to Baghdad.

Saadi Youssef paused as he lit another cigarette. We were both depressed. He had not seen his two sisters, who lived in Basrah, since 1978. Were they still there?

Under the Anglo-American occupation the memory and history of the Iraqis were being looted. The Baghdad Museum contained antiquities that dated back to early Mesopotamian civilisation (writing was invented there in 3500 BC). Thieves and some GIs (according to photographs circulated on the internet) ransacked the building after a tank shell had destroyed the front door. The Baghdad Library was set alight yet again, under the watchful eyes of the occupying soldiers, and priceless documents of the Ottoman period lay scattered and burnt on the pavements outside. The ziggurat on the ancient site of the royal city of Ur was graffitied by triumphant US soldiers. Further south, a unit of British soldiers were photographing themselves torturing and sexually assaulting Iraqi men and women. It was the unchanging face of colonial history.

Every few minutes Saadi Youssef would shake his head in despair and disbelief: 'Who would have thought the West would be back again.' And then he expressed an unshaken confidence in his people. 'We have a long history of resistance. Did you know that al-Jawahiri's brother was badly wounded during the 1948 uprising against the British? He died in al-Jawahiri's arms, not far from the Jisr al-Shuhada [The Bridge of Martyrs] on the Tigris where the bullets had felled him. How could the bloodstains be erased? This occupation will not be accepted for too long. Nor will their puppets.'

Al-Jawahiri had commemorated the 1948 anti-British uprising with a poem whose opening lines were recalled by many Iraqis the week that Baghdad fell:

I see a horizon lit with blood,
And many a starless night.
A generation comes and another goes
And the fire keeps burning.

Saadi Youssef had composed a new poem, addressed to his exiled
fellow poet in Damascus and titled 'The Jackals' Wedding'. He
read it to me, first in Arabic, later in English.

O Muthaffar al-Nawab,
my life-long comrade,
what are we to do about the jackals' wedding?
You remember the old days:
In the cool of the evening
under a bamboo roof
propped on soft cushions stuffed with fine wool
we'd sip tea (a tea I've never since tasted)
among friends ...
Night falls as softly as our words
under the darkening crowns of the date palms
while smoke curls from the hearth, such fragrance
as if the universe had just begun
...
Then a cackling explodes
from the long grass and date palms –
the jackals' wedding!
...
O, Muthaffar al-Nawab –
today isn't yesterday
(truth is as evanescent as the dream of a child) –
truth is, this time we're at their wedding reception,
yes, the jackals' wedding
you've read their invitation:
For tho' we trudge past Dahna empty-handed
We depart Dareen our purses lined with gold.
'While the townsfolk attend to their affairs
Now, Zuraik, fleece them, quick as a fox!'

...

O, Muthaffar al-Nawab,
let's make a deal:
I'll go in your place
(Damascus is too far away from that secret hotel ...)
I'll spit in the jackals' faces,
I'll spit on their lists,
I'll declare that we are the people of Iraq –
we are the ancestral trees of this land,
proud beneath our modest roof of bamboo.

Via email the poem reached Baghdad and Basrah within minutes of being completed and from there it travelled everywhere in occupied Iraq. Many who read it nodded their heads in amusement. They understood the poet just as he understood them.

The jackals, incapable of competing with the poem, began to hurl hate-filled darts at the poet. Their venom was spat out in public. Saadi Youssef was denounced regularly in the jackal press produced by those who wanted to impose themselves on Iraq not by appealing to the people who live there but by standing on the shoulders of the occupying armies and shouting that they were the rightful rulers. A few cursed jackals even began to harass the poet at home: threatening emails and anonymous phone calls were received every day. His life-comrade in Damascus also began to be vilified.

Could anyone have asked for a better demonstration of the power still enjoyed by poetry in the Arab world? From Damascus in March 2003, observing the war preparations and the plans to recolonise his country, Muthaffar al-Nawab penned a sober warning:

Would you ever forgive a lynch mob
Because they pulled your stiff corpse
From the gallows?
And never trust a freedom fighter
Who turns up with no arms –
Believe me, I got burnt in that crematorium.

> Truth is, you're only as big as your cannons,
> While the crowds who wave knives and forks
> Simply have eyes for their stomachs.
> O my people in love with our homeland,
> I'm not scared of barbarians gathered at our gates.
> No, I'm afraid of the enemies within –
> Tyranny, Autocracy, Dictatorship.

Saadi Youssef and I embraced as we parted. 'I wonder how long this occupation will last?' 'I wonder whether there will be an Iraqi resistance.' 'Will they divide Iraq into three units: Kurds (like now), Shia and Sunni?'

The following week Perry rang. 'Your next task is to sit down and write a text for the *NLR*.' I did. 'Re-Colonizing Iraq' ran in the May–June 2003 issue:

On the one side, a vast popular outcry against the invasion of Iraq. On the other, a US administration coolly and openly resolved on it from the start. Between them, the governments of the rest of the world. How have they reacted? London, as could be expected, acted as a blood-shot adjutant to Washington throughout. Labour imperialism is a long tradition, and Blair had already shown in the Balkan War that he could behave more like a petty mastiff, snarling at the leash, than a mere poodle. Since Britain has been bombing Iraq continuously, wing-tip to wing-tip with America, for as long as New Labour has been in office, only the naive could be surprised at the dispatch of a third of the British Army to the country's largest former colony in the Middle East; or the signature paltering of House of Commons 'rebels' of the stamp of Cook or Short, regretting the violence but wishing godspeed to its perpetrators.

Berlusconi in Italy and Aznar in Spain – the two most right-wing governments in Europe – were fitting partners for Blair in rallying such lesser EU fry as Portugal and Denmark to the cause, while Simitis offered Greek facilities for US spy planes. The East European states, giving a new meaning to the term 'satellite', which they had previously so long enjoyed, fell as one into line behind Bush. The ex-communist parties in power in Poland, Hungary and Albania distinguished themselves in zeal to show their new fealty – Warsaw sending a contingent to fight in Iraq, Budapest providing the training-camps for Iraqi exiles, even little Tirana volunteering gallant non-combatants for the battlefield.

France and Germany, on the other hand, protested for months that they were utterly opposed to a US attack on Iraq. Schroeder had owed his narrow re-election to a pledge not to support a war on Baghdad, even were it authorized by the UN. Chirac, armed with a veto in the Security Council, was even more voluble with declarations that any unauthorized assault on the Ba'ath regime would never be accepted by France. Together, Paris and Berlin coaxed Moscow into expressing its disagreement too with American plans. Even Beijing emitted a few cautious sounds of demurral. The Franco-German initiatives aroused tremendous excitement and consternation among diplomatic commentators. Here, surely, was an unprecedented rift in the Atlantic Alliance. What was to become of European unity, of NATO, of the 'international community' itself if such a disastrous split persisted? Could the very concept of the West survive? Such apprehensions were quickly to be allayed. No sooner were Tomahawk missiles lighting up the nocturnal skyline in Baghdad, and the first Iraqi civilians cut down by the Marines, than Chirac rushed to explain that France would assure smooth passage of US bombers across its airspace (as it had not done, under his own Premiership, when Reagan attacked Libya), and wished 'swift success' to American arms in Iraq. Germany's cadaver-green Foreign Minister Joschka Fischer announced that his government too sincerely hoped for the 'rapid collapse' of resistance to the Anglo-American attack. Putin, not to be outdone, explained to his compatriots that 'for economic and political reasons', Russia could only desire a decisive victory of the United States in Iraq. The parties of the Second International themselves could not have behaved more honourably.

Farther afield, the scene was very similar. In Japan, Koizumi was quicker off the mark than his European counterparts in announcing full support for the Anglo-American aggression, and promising largesse from the beleaguered Japanese tax-payer to help fund the occupation. The new president of South Korea, Roh Moo-hyun, elected with high hopes from the country's youth as an independent radical, disgraced himself instantly by offering not only approval of America's war in the Middle East, but troops to fight it, in the infamous tradition of the dictator Park Chung Hee in the Vietnam War. If this is to be the new Seoul, Pyongyang would do well to step up its military preparations against any repetition of the same adventure in the Korean peninsula. In Latin America, the PT regime in Brazil confined itself to mumbling a few mealy-mouthed reservations, while in Chile the Socialist president Ricardo Lagos – spineless even by the standards of sub-equatorial social democracy – frantically cabled his ambassador to the UN, who had irresponsibly let slip the word 'condemn' in chatting with some journalists, to issue an immediate official correction: Chile did not condemn, it merely 'regretted' the Anglo-American invasion.

In the Middle East, the landscape of hypocrisy and collusion is more familiar. But, amidst the overwhelming opposition of Arab public opinion, no client regime failed to do its duty to the paymaster general. In Egypt Mubarak gave free passage to the US Navy through the Canal and airspace to the USAF, while his police were clubbing and arresting hundreds of protesters. The Saudi monarchy invited cruise missiles to arc over their territory, and US command centres to operate as normal from their soil. The Gulf States have long become virtual military annexes of Washington. Jordan, which managed to stay more or less neutral in the first Gulf War, this time eagerly supplied bases for American special forces to maraud across the border. The Iranian mullahs, as oppressive at home as they are stupid abroad, collaborated with CIA operations Afghan-style. The Arab League surpassed itself as a collective expression of ignominy, announcing its opposition to the war even as a majority of members were participating in it. This is an organization capable of calling the Kaaba black while spraying it red, white and blue.

The reality of the 'international community' – read: American global hegemony – has never been so clearly displayed as in this dismal panorama. Against such a background of general connivance and betrayal, the few – very few – acts of genuine resistance stand out. The only elected body that actually attempted to stop the war was the Turkish parliament. The newly elected AKP regime performed no better than its counterparts elsewhere, cravenly bargaining for larger bribes to let Turkey be used as a platform for a US land attack on Northern Iraq. But mass pressures, reflexes of national pride or pangs of conscience prompted large enough numbers of its own party to revolt and block this transaction, disrupting the Pentagon's plans. The Ankara government hastened to open airspace for US missiles and paratroop drops instead, but the action of the Turkish parliament – defying its own government, not to speak of the United States – altered the course of the war; unlike the costless Euro-gestures that evaporated into thin air when fighting began. In Indonesia, Megawati pointedly drew attention to the Emperor's clothes by calling for an emergency meeting of the Security Council to condemn the Anglo-American expedition. Naturally, after months of huffing and puffing from Paris, Berlin and elsewhere about the sanctity of UN authority, the response was complete silence. In Malaysia, Mahathir – not for the first time breaking a diplomatic taboo – bluntly demanded the resignation of Kofi Annan for his role as a dumb-waiter for American aggression. These politicians understood better than others in the Third World that the American Empire was using its huge military arsenal to teach the South a lesson in the North's power to intimidate and control it.

29

So Was It Worth It?

An exchange with Mike O'Brien, UK minister for trade, invest-ment and foreign affairs, in October 2003 that was initiated by Rusbridger's Guardian.

Dear Mike,

The difference between Britain and Afghanistan, of course, is that in Afghanistan there is a strong opposition. Karzai is so confident of his popularity in Kabul (his writ does not extend beyond the capital) that no Afghan is permitted to guard him. Elsewhere the various factions of the Northern Alliance and remnants of the Taliban control the country.

The aim of the war and occupation was to capture and kill Osama bin Laden and Mullah Omar and shackle al-Qaeda. The result has been a dismal failure. The video earlier this year of Osama and his deputy wearing their Chitrali hats and strolling cheerfully in the Hindukush was a cheeky reminder of this.

Removing the Taliban from power was always a secondary aim. The condition of the population is certainly not better today than before the war. The reconstruction has turned out to be a joke. The women's liberation talked about so eagerly at the time by the first ladies of Bush and Blair has come to naught. More money is being spent on feeding and housing Western troops than on the war-weary citizens of Afghanistan. And it will end badly, just like the Soviet intervention did in the eighties. I fear another civil war is waiting in the wings.

Yours,
Tariq

So Was It Worth It?

Dear Tariq,

So scathing, so cynical, so wrong. When I drove through the suburbs of western Kabul, every building I passed had been damaged by twenty years of civil war. You impressively described those wars in your book, *The Clash of Fundamentalisms*.

But I saw a lot of people in those derelict homes making bricks and rebuilding. They were building because they had hope that the future could be better. I talked to people who were so glad that the Taliban were gone that they had tears in their eyes; women who no longer had to wear the burqa and who could send their daughters to school. I went to a school for the blind to present the children with some braille machines because the Taliban had destroyed them all. 'Failure,' you say. It's not what they say.

Those who opposed intervention in Afghanistan would have denied hope to these people. But you are right on one thing. There are still mega-problems. There are drug warlords and poverty and injustice. There are terrorist incidents. The government needs the ability to better enforce its writ outside Kabul. Yes, it will take years to sort out the mess created over decades. But there is today a hope that defies any hard-bitten cynicism. Those people impressed me with their determination to rebuild. Karzai is an ordinary man trying to do an extraordinary thing, to create a democracy from devastation. There are no guarantees that he will succeed, but we should do all we can to help.

The UN and the world have not turned their back. There is a lot of money going in there. Rebuilding will be hard and will take time, but it is worth it.

Best wishes,
Mike

Dear Mike,

You sound like a *Pravda* man I argued with in the early 1980s. He too accused me of cynicism when I denounced the Soviet intervention as something that would end badly. In reality the Russians did push through an effective modernisation in the towns that provided an educational system for all (including women), and the number of women working in schools and hospitals multiplied rapidly. That was the time when Reagan and Thatcher welcomed the bearded mujahideen and introduced them to the Western media as 'the equivalent of our founding fathers'. They certainly were the founding fathers of the Taliban.

I doubt whether the current bunch can do anything that remotely resembles the Soviet modernisation. How can Western regimes busy dismantling the welfare state and privatising everything at home create a social democratic paradise in Afghanistan?

The burqa is back in business, I'm afraid, enforced by the men who rule the country with Washington's blessing. Human Rights Watch has spoken to women who said they veiled themselves to avoid violence and harassment. Add to that the fact that ministers are busy demolishing homes (possibly not the ones you visited) to grab land, and that senior Afghan military commanders and officials are involved in corruption and violence on a daily basis. This is reality for the majority of Afghans.

There has been little reconstruction. Very little of the $4.5bn (£2.7bn) pledged in Tokyo in 2002 has come through. The World Bank estimates that a minimum of $13bn is needed to reconstruct Afghanistan. It was no problem finding $11bn to fight the war and occupy the country, but it's virtually impossible to raise funds to repair the infrastructure. This is the pattern of all the recent wars. In most cases foreign interventions create more problems than they can solve. The Western states act to defend their own interests.

As for poor Hamid Karzai, he is a longtime worker for the US intelligence agencies, like his friend Zalmay Khalilzad who put him there. But he seems to represent nobody inside Afghanistan. I fear he might be bumped off despite the all-American bodyguard.

There are two choices. Either he could be put on a Paris catwalk to model shawls, or the Dear Leader could find him a safe New Labour constituency. It would be mean-spirited, having used him as a filter, to let the brutes of the Northern Alliance flush him down.

Yours,
Tariq

So Was It Worth It?

Dear Tariq,

I doubt that many Afghans would share your charitable view of Soviet occupation. But let's not let political prejudice get in the way of the facts, eh? $4.5bn was pledged at Tokyo but you missed out that it was pledged over five years, not all in one year. Much of that money is now flowing and will continue over the next five years.

Schools have opened, hospitals operate and a road is to be built from Kabul to Jalalabad. Some $1.8bn in foreign aid was spent last year and the UK alone provided £45.5m at the start of last year. We are committed to spending £322m over five years – £122 million more than we pledged at Tokyo.

Okay, so all this will not create a social democratic paradise. I think Afghans, like the rest of us, are prepared to wait for paradise if they could get peace and a reasonable standard of living now. And things are not as bleak as you portray. Four million children are now back at school, 37 per cent of them are girls and the numbers are rising; eight million children have been vaccinated against measles, preventing 30,000 deaths; over six million children have been immunised against polio; and more than two million refugees have voted with their feet and returned to Afghanistan because they now have hope. In addition, more than 400,000 internally displaced persons have also been able to return home.

Not paradise, but Hamid Karzai will not have to go looking for a New Labour constituency. He will have a few remarkable achievements to put before his own people in the presidential election due in 2004.

Best wishes,
Mike

Dear Mike,

My only point about the Soviet occupation was that, like Washington, they believed their modernising reforms would do the trick. Now the arguments you deploy are virtually the same. The difference is that the Russians did achieve much more. Incidentally, the figures you supply are already being challenged by all sides.

Many refugees who went back have returned to Pakistan. Law and order does not exist, not even in parts of Kabul. The barons of the Northern Alliance control the country and are biding their time. That's why I would urge you again to get Karzai out while you can. He would make a good politician in this country and surely Hartlepool beckons ...

The imposition of a puppet regime, propped up by NATO troops, thousands of miles away from base, is untenable. It might have helped to build the image of the Dear Leader as a War Leader. But no amount of cluster-bombs and daisy-cutters can solve the problem. Very few Afghans support this occupation. Sooner or later you'll have to pull out the Marines. Then what? A Northern Alliance bid for power and a new forward thrust by the Pakistan Army. This time their boys will be clean-shaven and attired in modern dress. It could go down well on the networks and Fox TV. The modern soldiers of our closest ally sweeping the bearded men of the Northern Alliance out of the way and retaking Kabul. It could happen.

I hope, Mike, that you will soon emerge as the leader of the anti-war faction in New Labour, but beware the Hoon example. He, too, was once a junior minister at the Foreign Office and prone to wild exaggerations. In reality, and I'm quite serious, I think you should resign from the government and use your talents to win the party over for the future. New Labour will probably win the next election, but it has already lost the argument.

Best,
Tariq

Dear Tariq,

Thanks for your email and your solicitations for my future. I will stick with this government and this government will stick by the Afghans in reconstructing their country.

You attack my figures with vague references to challenges from 'all sides'. Name them, I say! You use the fact – which I readily agree with – that there are problems in security. But to suggest what? That we should leave Afghans to another civil war? Perhaps we are the anti-war faction in Afghanistan now.

So Was It Worth It?

Like Private Frazer in *Dad's Army* you seem to say: 'We're all doomed!' I accept that we need to tackle the security problem. Some 300 British troops are doing just that, alongside Germans, Canadians and others. Provincial reconstruction teams have recently been established to address the problems of the warlords. For the first time in twenty-three years there is an Afghan government and an army which is representative of all Afghans. We must continue this work.

And it is not just idealism. Ninety per cent of the heroin in Britain originates in Afghanistan. The security problem means opium production will go up before it comes down, but if we stick with it and eliminate poppy growth by 2013 we will have helped both Afghanistan and Britain.

We are funding the Afghans to produce sustainable crops to eat and sell instead of poppies. We cannot create paradise there but we can help reduce the suffering. By the way, if the Afghans don't want Karzai – the current choice of their traditional parliament, the Loya Jirga – then in 2004 they can vote him out. Votes, not bullets, I say!

Best wishes,
Mike

Dear Mike,

It will not work. First, because there is no representative government (even in the broadest sense of the term) in the country. And I would urge you not to treat the Loya Jirga as anything but a collection of tribal leaders who are bought in the open market.

The Foreign Office where you sit has all the documentation. The British Empire played the same tricks for over a century. The fact that your chum Karzai is a puppet of Washington is hardly a secret.

The 2004 'elections' will be just like the ones the British Empire pushed through in Iraq during the early colonial period. What that produced according to a subsequent British intelligence assessment was 'an oligarchy of racketeers'.

Idealism, my dear Mike, has nothing to do with any of this. The Afghan adventure was a crude war of revenge. The fact that Europeans are involved doesn't make it any better. If New Labour intends new colonisations then these should be openly discussed and argued. They didn't work before. Why should they now?

As for the figures, just look at the Human Rights Watch reports on refugees and women. They are lying on my desk in London and I'm sending this last one from New York. Or follow the time-honoured Downing Street method: type out Google.com, write 'Afghan Refugees' and then see what hits the fan. On the crucial question of your own future and that of Karzai, let's continue to talk. I am concerned.

Best,
Tariq

Dear Tariq,

You present no alternative policy, merely rhetorical fireworks, sparkling but fleeting. As a minister I have to work out how Britain can help the Afghans to reconstruct their country.

The era of colonialism is dead and any Western leader who does not realise this is a fool. The West cannot run Afghanistan but we must empower the Afghans to run it for themselves, then we must get our troops out. Our best long-term guarantee is a genuine democracy in Afghanistan.

Yes, the Loya Jirga wasn't perfect but it was the best we could do at the time. Next year's election will be better. The measure is whether things are improving, not whether they are perfect.

At least we are looking to give the Afghans all the help they need. Tony Blair promises it and we are delivering. The figures I quoted are real British taxpayers' money flowing to help the Afghans.

The difference remains that my responsibility as a minister is to deliver, while your responsibility as a writer is to criticise. My record will be measured in the improvements in the lives of Afghans, yours in influencing public opinion about Labour.

I still believe government driven by idealism can do good things, you don't. So, I will get on with helping the Afghans and you will keep on knocking our policy. Even so, I enjoyed our exchange – a bit of healthy criticism can improve ministerial performance!

Best wishes,
Mike

30

Mojitos in Pyongyang: A Flashback

As well as Iraq and Iran, Bush had declared North Korea to be a member of the 'axis of evil' in his 2002 State of the Union address. Pyongyang TV responded in kind. Bush was a 'nuclear maniac' and his speech 'tantamount to a declaration of war'. I wondered how my friends there were doing. It had been a long time.

I first visited North Korea in the summer of 1970. I was in Pakistan when the invitation reached me, researching my first book. As I've written, Pakistan's military dictatorship had just been toppled after a three-month insurrection and the country was in the throes of its first ever general election campaign. I was travelling to every major town and many smaller ones, interviewing opposition politicians, workers and students who'd taken part in the uprising for *Pakistan: Military Rule or People's Power?* I was still there, my work unfinished, when the mysterious invitation arrived. North Korea was even then a country apart.

The letter came via a local communist known as Rahim 'Korea-wallah', secretary of the Pak-Korea Friendship Society. Short, paunchy, loquacious and full of beer, he was out of breath as he handed me the letter from Pyongyang. I had to leave straightaway, he said. Why? Because the North Koreans were convinced that the US was preparing to invade and needed global solidarity. In January 1968 the Koreans had captured the USS *Pueblo*, a naval intelligence vessel, and arrested its crew. Relations between the two countries remained tense. Could I leave next week, Koreawallah asked? I laughed and said no.

I was on my way to what was then East Pakistan. North Korea was a distraction. Koreawallah was both angry and insistent, but his argument was weak. There was no evidence that Washington was preparing for war. I had experience to back me up. A few years earlier I had spent six weeks in North Vietnam and, as well as crouching in air-raid shelters during US bombing raids on Hanoi, I sat through several military briefings by senior Vietnamese officers who made it clear that they would eventually win the war. For the Americans, already overstretched in Indochina, a new war in Korea would be suicidal.

I had other reasons not to go. I considered Kim Il-sung a ridiculous leader, his regime a parody of Stalin's Russia. I turned down the offer again, this time more forcefully. But my parents, both of them communists, thought I should take advantage of the opportunity to see the country (they had never been). And Koreawallah would not be deterred. With a sly smile, he let drop that I could go via China, taking a train from Beijing to Pyongyang. That decided the matter. I was desperate to visit Beijing and this seemed my only chance. I just said I couldn't go until mid-June.

When I returned to Dhaka after two gruelling weeks in the countryside, a problem had arisen. The East Pakistan trade unions had called a one-day general strike – a show of strength against General Yahya Khan's transitional regime in Islamabad – on the day I was due to get an early morning flight from Dhaka to Canton. I took it personally. Friends asked the communist leaders of the taxi and rickshaw drivers' unions for a thirty-minute exemption so I could get to the airport. Their pleas were rejected. I said to one of them that it was a political decision, but never said so in public, where I defended the unions. When the activist local student leaders stepped in, the unions relented. There could be no motorised traffic on the streets, but I could travel by cycle rickshaw.

My suitcase and I were too much for the emaciated driver. After ten minutes of huffing and puffing we'd got nowhere. Worried I might miss the flight, I asked him to get in the back and pedalled like crazy for the five or so miles to the airport. Apart from stray animals, there was nothing else on the road. When we got to the airport the rickshaw-wallah, seeing me bathed in sweat, grinned broadly and refused to accept my money. I stuffed it down his dry vest and ran to the plane. Soon after it took off, the strike committees closed down the airport. I had predicted that Pakistan was about to break up, but I didn't think as I watched the sun rise over the paddy fields that it would be my last glimpse of East Pakistan.

In Beijing posters decorated the streets, loud music blared from speakers and groups of children bowed before portraits of the Great Helmsman. A stream of bicycles flowed along unpolluted thoroughfares. How lucky they were, I thought, not to fetishise the car. I wandered away from the hotel, managed to find Tiananmen Square, discovered a cheap and good restaurant, then headed back to the hotel, where two Korean embassy officials were waiting to take me on a low-key tour of the Forbidden City. We appeared to be the only foreign visitors. Sin Hyen Chil spoke and wrote reasonable English. He was the embassy's interpreter as well.

Later that afternoon, I packed for the two-day train journey to Pyongyang and we set off for the station. There was no phrasebook in the hotel. The only Chinese I knew was 'Mao Chu Shi Wansui' – 'Mao Zedong will live ten thousand years' – which wasn't much help in ordering a meal or finding the lavatory. More reprehensibly it was an updated version of the slogan that courtiers chanted every morning in olden times when the Emperor arrived at court. Mercifully a Sikh courier from the Indian embassy came into my compartment before the train left the station. By chance, I think. After we had exchanged greetings in Punjabi, he told me he was fluent in Mandarin and, much more importantly, that his wife had cooked food for the journey, and he hoped I would share it with him. Not being a Brahmin, I replied I would be delighted.

Just before the train began to move, two PLA officers also entered the compartment. No, they laughed, they were not going to Pyongyang. My efforts to draw out their thoughts on the Cultural Revolution failed, but they were eager to discuss Pakistan and surprised to hear my criticism of its military dictators:

Chinese propaganda portrayed them as 'anti-imperialist allies'. They hadn't heard about the recent uprising. The jollier of the two warned me about the 'personality cult' in Korea and my Sikh friend roared: he never stayed more than a night at the embassy in Pyongyang. The PLA men got off at Beidaihe, a seaside resort east of Beijing. Once frequented by emperors, their wives and concubines, it had become a favourite spot for Communist Party leaders. 'If these two are holidaying here,' my Sikh fellow traveller muttered, 'they must be important or related to someone who is, just like in our part of the world.' Unlike me, he found this thought reassuring.

Colonised by the Japanese between 1910, when they annexed the country, and the end of the Second World War, Korea experienced both 'modernity' and extreme brutality and repression. The country's mineral wealth was used to buttress Japanese militarism; local workers were paid starvation wages; tens of thousands of women were treated as prostitutes by the occupiers but not paid for their services. The Japanese aimed at total integration: Korean was forbidden in schools, Korean-language newspapers were banned and people were to use Japanese names. Agriculture met imperial needs – thousands of farmers were expelled from the land and the bulk of the rice and wheat produced was sent to Japan – leading to mass starvation. A Japanese proconsul admitted that every spring half of Korea's farmers lived off grass and bark. The two million Koreans transported to Japan as slave labourers were lucky in one sense: they were fed.

All this, unsurprisingly, led the Koreans to develop strong nationalist feelings, though fear limited the number who joined clandestine groups. Indigenous communists were active in these groups: they worked alongside the nationalists and were widely seen as heroic figures. During the Second World War a resistance movement gradually took shape, at its strongest in the South. Its members – students, intellectuals and peasants – faced the usual penalties of occupation: torture, rape, mass killings and burial in unmarked graves.

The defeat of Japan in 1945 was greeted joyously, and popular committees sprang up in a number of cities. The future of Korea wasn't discussed at Yalta, where the division of Europe was decided, but Moscow and Washington privately agreed on a similar division of the Korean peninsula. The Red Army marched into North Korea, with Kim Il-sung reportedly in one of its tanks; the United States took the South. General MacArthur flew into Seoul with a valuable piece of hand luggage: Syngman Rhee. Rhee had little support, however, so MacArthur used the Korean members of the Japanese occupation army to keep control of the new state. This in itself was enough to alienate the people. Dissent was crushed, people were imprisoned en masse, communists and anti-American nationalists were disappeared or openly assassinated. 'The jails in Seoul are overcrowded with political prisoners,' Frank Baldwin, an adviser at the US embassy, reported:

> Six weeks ago I inspected a police jail in Inchon. The prisoners there were living under conditions which I hesitate to describe in this letter. It reminds you of a sense of the *Divina Commedia*. Goya could have painted what we saw there. What is going to happen to the almost 10,000 political prisoners in case the capital is to be surrendered? It is hard to imagine the acts of vengeance and hatred which people will commit if they survive the conquest of Seoul by their 'liberators'.

The involvement of the US and the Soviet Union had put an end to any chance of Korean autonomy, but Soviet prestige was still high and many believed that the Russians would help liberate and reform the whole country. Few believed partition was permanent. Kim Il-sung, installed as leader of the People's Committee by the Soviets, was barely known, but local communists had no reason to doubt him.

Growing popular anger in the South and an overwhelming desire for reunification triggered the invasion of the South by the North in 1950. Lacking popular support, the Rhee government collapsed and had to be rescued by US troops. The Soviet Union boycotted a Security Council session at which it could have vetoed America's war, conducted under the UN flag. The

Chinese revolution had panicked Washington. It couldn't be allowed to spread.

US troops and their allies (including the Japanese Navy) pushed the North Korean Army back. The Chinese revolution was less than a year old and its leaders saw the war in Korea as an attempt to reverse events in China. A Politburo meeting determined to save the Koreans. Chinese troops under the command of General Peng Dehuai crossed the Yalu River in droves. The Americans and their allies were driven back to the 38th parallel. General MacArthur declared that it might be necessary to nuke Chinese air bases; President Truman sacked him. In 1953 a truce was signed at Panmunjom on the 38th parallel. Around a million soldiers and two million civilians had died (there are many different estimates). One of them was Mao's oldest and favourite son.

Nearly twenty years later I was about to cross the Yalu River on a Chinese train. At Sinuiju, I was welcomed onto the sacred soil of the DPRK with a bunch of flowers. Standing in front of a life-size statue of Kim Il-sung, my host told me that he was a bit disturbed by the scale of the personality cult in China. In Pyongyang a Young Pioneer gave me another bouquet of flowers. I was shocked at what I saw as we drove through the city: we could have been in Eastern Europe after the Second World War. Then I remembered that what General Curtis LeMay had threatened to do to North Vietnam had already been done to North Korea: it had been bombed into the Stone Age. There were no protests in the West against the heavy bombing of Pyongyang at only fifteen minutes' notice: 697 tons of bombs were dropped on the city, 10,000 litres of napalm; 62,000 rounds were used for 'strafing at low level'.

Three years earlier in Phnom Penh the Australian journalist Wilfred Burchett had told me that what I had seen in Vietnam was 'nothing compared to what they did to Korea. I was there. There were only two buildings left standing in Pyongyang.' It was alleged that the US had used germ warfare, and although the Americans dismissed these claims as 'outrageous', on 9 August 1970 the *New York Times* reported that chemical weapons had been considered after 'American ground forces in Korea were overwhelmed by Chinese communist human wave attacks near the Yalu River'. Pentagon policymakers wanted to 'find a way to stop mass infantry attacks', so 'the army dug into captured Nazi chemical warfare documents describing sarin, a nerve gas so lethal that a few pounds could kill thousands of people in minutes if the deadly material were dispersed effectively'. Was it used in Korea? Probably not, though germ warfare tests were conducted in US cities. In one test 'harmless' bacteria were introduced into the Pentagon's air-conditioning system.

I asked to see the foreign minister to discuss the tensions with the United States, but, to my minders' surprise, I didn't ask to meet Kim Il-sung. My first few days in Pyongyang were spent visiting museums with my excellent interpreter and a minder – 'the chief of protocol'. They both accompanied me everywhere. At the war museum I asked why there was no sign of the Chinese 'volunteers' without whom the war would have been lost. No reply. Finally the guide went upstairs and returned with the museum director. I repeated my question. 'We did have the display but those rooms have been closed for repairs and painting. The photographs have been removed to safe places.' I asked to see where they had been, but the man's embarrassment was so painful I gave up. We moved on to the museum of art. After seeing four rooms filled with bad paintings of Kim Il-sung, his mother and other relatives, I lost my cool and asked to see something from earlier centuries. After a hurried consultation with my minder, the director asked us to follow him, making it clear that he was doing me a huge favour.

Locked away in the underground vaults were the most stunning tomb paintings I have ever seen. Some dated back 2,000 years, others were from the eleventh and twelfth centuries. They depicted soldiers, hunters, scenes of wealth, exquisitely beautiful women. I thanked the director profusely and said I hoped that Koreans would one day be able to see these treasures. He smiled and shrugged. He was the only person I met there who didn't mention Kim Il-sung once, let alone refer to him as the 'great and beloved leader' – GBL – of forty million Korean people. One day

I was driven to Mangyongdae, where I was promised a real treat. It turned out to be Kim's birthplace and virtually the whole city was a shrine to him, with all the same stories I had heard dozens of times about his heroism repeated yet again.

Back at the hotel in Pyongyang I saw Kathleen Cleaver in the lobby, who was heavily pregnant with Joju Younghi, her daughter with the Black Panther leader Eldridge Cleaver. We spoke briefly. She handed me Bobby Seale's latest book, before she was whisked away and I never caught sight of her again. Later I discovered that her husband had met Kim Il-sung and pledged the support of the Black Panther Party. That no money changed hands in return for this is inconceivable. American friends told me afterwards that Kathleen had been kept in her room in Pyongyang for four months, a punishment her husband had decreed after discovering that the baby wasn't his. Kim had obliged his new friend. Useful to know, I thought.

It was still early evening. There was no bar in the hotel so I went to the billiard room to bash balls. Three tall men I hadn't seen before were at the table. Two of them spoke English. They were students from the University of Havana, in Pyongyang on a three-year course in exchange for the hundreds of Korean students who were sent to Cuba to train as doctors. Why them? They laughed. Protocol demanded that someone be sent.

They thought I would get on with the Cuban ambassador and so we left in the embassy car for tamarind juice and mojitos followed by a very good meal. The ambassador was a veteran of the revolution. Sending him to North Korea had not been a friendly act: 'I'd got a bit critical of Fidel and the way things were being done in Cuba. I talked to many others about this and Fidel got angry. I would have preferred prison but they sent me here instead. It's worked. Havana's a paradise and Fidel is god. Just get me out of here. I'll never open my mouth again.' It was the most enjoyable evening I spent in the DPRK.

The next week was spent in trains and cars. The car would often stop in the middle of nowhere. We would get out and I would be shown a site where 'GBL Comrade Kim Il-sung gave on-the-spot guidance to peasants on the wheat harvest.' At one point, in the middle of nowhere, I asked them to stop. My bladder was full. As I got out of the car I said: 'I'm just going to give on-the-spot guidance to that tree.' The interpreter and minder convulsed with laughter. It was the most reassuring sight of my trip. Nothing was said when I returned to the car, but we never stopped again.

At Panmunjom on the 38th parallel the loudspeakers were blaring out cliché-ridden propaganda. American soldiers were lounging around, occasionally pointing at the speakers and laughing. I asked the Koreans if I could use a loudhailer. When they finally agreed, I asked the Americans why they were hanging around in Asia given that their own country was on fire. They woke up a bit. I gave an account of the Kent State shootings – the Ohio National Guard had fired on and killed four students for protesting against Nixon's invasion of Cambodia – which had taken place only a few weeks before. Four million US students had gone on strike. I asked the soldiers to join me in a minute's silence in memory of the dead students, at which point a senior officer came and shepherded them all back to barracks.

The Koreans were amazed. I resisted the temptation to point out that my 'on-the-spot guidance' had been more effective than GBL's propaganda. My diary of later that day reads:

> In the afternoon, visited a breath-taking waterfall and climbed the mountain to see it in full flow. We spent an hour and a half just relaxing and chatting. I had a dip in the pool created by the waterfall. It was too cold to swim, but the water tasted lovely. In the evening a lavish dinner in my honour with endless toasts thrown to and fro. I tried not to laugh when the Colonel proposed a toast 'to the great revolutionary paper *The Red Mole*'. They demanded and I promised a hundred copies of the next issue. The promise was fulfilled.

Back in Pyongyang I was granted my appointment with the foreign minister, who gave me the official North Korean position on the world. I listened politely. As I was about to leave he said: 'We appreciated your talk at Panmunjom, but there is one thing

411

you don't seem to understand about our country. You do not appreciate the role that Comrade Kim Il-sung played in liberating and creating the DPRK.' I couldn't deny this so stayed silent. He gave me an odd smile.

Two years later I was asked back, to give a speech at a conference on the 'role of US imperialism in Asia'. I was reluctant but the Vietnamese persuaded me. They hadn't been invited and wanted their position on the subject defended. This time the journey took even longer. We were flown first to Prague, where the Russian military plane that was to transport us to Pyongyang was five days late. I stayed a few days with Jiri Mucha in his lovely house in Hradcany that once belonged to his father, the painter Alphonse Mucha. I saw Karel Kosik briefly, but he was too tense to have a conversation. I was pleased I was in Prague.

When the plane finally arrived, it was filthy and rank; in the middle of the night it stopped to refuel at Omsk in below-freezing conditions, and a few of us rushed out to breathe in some fresh air. In Pyongyang, each delegate was assigned a chauffeur-driven Mercedes. I'd been hoping to be assigned the same interpreter, but my luck was out. He'd asked me for an English dictionary: I gave the one I'd brought to the new team and asked them to pass it on to him. They said he'd been transferred to a small town. Had he been too open with me on my last trip?

At the hotel a senior party apparatchik was meeting with each delegate or delegation separately. The subject of the conference had been changed, he told me. It was GBL's sixtieth birthday and they thought we should discuss 'Comrade Kim Il-sung's contribution to Marxism–Leninism'. I refused point blank, said I wasn't qualified, and demanded a flight back home. The apparatchik left the room in a nervous state.

Over dinner that night an affable Algerian professor and a representative of Frelimo from Mozambique couldn't believe what I'd done. The Algerian said he had sold himself for $5,000, the friend from Frelimo was too ashamed to name the sum he'd accepted. The next morning, I was offered $10,000, which would have come in extremely handy for *Red Mole*. I was tempted to

accept and then make a purely satirical speech, but I declined.
They still wouldn't let me leave. There was no flight to Europe for
a week. I said I'd fly to Pakistan. They told me that was difficult,
too. The Vietnamese ambassador came to see me. He pleaded
with me not to leave. 'The personality cult is bad here,' he said.
'Very, very bad.' That much I knew.

At an official reception the day before the conference began we
were all introduced to GBL. Never in my life had I felt such an
aversion to a political figure on the left. His bloated neck seemed
to bc inviting a bullet. I wished I'd been a Decembrist. The only
words he addressed to me were distinctly odd: 'London, yes? "The
Red Flag". They still sing it?'

They made the mistake of seating me on the plenum. I didn't
applaud a single speech, but I did keep notes. The Politburo star
who opened the conference – the subject was 'the task of social
science to thoroughly defend the great leader Comrade Kim
Il-sung's revolutionary thinking and propagate it extensively' –
quoted a GBL speech. 'There is a revolutionary song which says:
"Let cowards flinch and traitors sneer. We'll keep the Red Flag
flying here." This expresses our unvarying determination.' I wondered who in Moscow had introduced him to the anthem of
British social democracy. His appalling speech was interrupted
143 times for applause, standing ovations, etc. My table in the
hotel restaurant expanded each day as more and more despera-
does came to joke about our situation. Our codename for GBL
was Peterson.

The reason for the absurdly narcissistic cult was obvious. Who
the hell was Kim Il-sung? Where did he come from? Had he
ever operated as a guerrilla leader? There had been other well-
known Korean communists, including a female general. Kim
Il-sung killed some of them. Others had fled to China during
the Japanese occupation and fought alongside Mao's partisans.
Many veterans of the Long March were Koreans. It is possible
that Kim Il-sung operated as a guerrilla in China and then fled
to Russia. We don't know for sure. What we do know is that the
Red Army freed the country in 1945 and the Chinese saved it
during the Korean War. But these facts were never mentioned

in DPRK propaganda. 'Juche', an aggressive form of self-reliance, was the word coined to designate this xenophobia. When I asked the interpreter on my first trip whether he had read any Marx or Engels or Lenin, he looked puzzled. 'No,' he told me. 'Everything is interpreted by Comrade Kim Il-sung.' He wasn't sure whether any of the classic texts were available in libraries.

Soon my last day in the country had arrived and I scribbled a blow-by-blow account:

At 10.15 a.m., two bureaucrats from the newspaper *Reunification* arrived with two huge packets of documents in Korean. I had already asked my interpreter to tell them that that I had read all the reunification documents. Repetition should be avoided. Needless to say, this request was ignored. After an hour of speeches whose content I knew, I interrupted the senior bureaucrat and said I knew all this and could we just save some time. He was a bit disconcerted because he was not used to the truth from visiting foreigners.

At 11.45 they departed and I am told the deputy prime minister (also foreign minister) will see me later at 3.30. He has received my questions. I doubt whether he'll answer them, but let's see. At 12.50 I'm taken off to lunch. Yesterday the Korean strawberry harvest materialised and I've been eating them with every meal.

At 3.30 I met the deputy prime minister, Pak Chul Song. He answered the three most important questions over an hour and a half. Another fifteen minutes telling me the comrades in Panmunjom had greatly appreciated my speech to the US marines, but I must try and understand the role of comrade Kim Il-sung in the Korean revolution. I remained silent and he said: 'We shall explain some more to you next time.' He looked at my face and grinned. A canny customer he was. We said our farewells.

Then the Director of Propaganda called on me and made an amazing request. I could hardly believe my ears. What he wanted to know was whether the *Red Mole* printshop could publish the collected works of Comrade Kim Il-sung. Did they have no idea I was a Trot? Perhaps they didn't care! I said I would have to discuss this with colleagues and we would get back to them. All he specified was that the paper should be glossy and photographs very high quality. When he left, I lay on the bed and laughed.

In the evening a farewell banquet in my honour laid on by the Union of Journalists. I asked where the Red Army Faction Japanese students were being kept after they hijacked a Boeing to Pyongyang. Embarrassed looks. I said I was worried that they might be handed back to Tokyo, which would greatly discredit the DPRK regime. A silence fell. As I was leaving a senior figure from the union came up to me, shook hands as if he were saying farewell and whispered: 'That will never happen.'

Message waiting in my room. The First Secretary at the Vietnamese embassy had rung to say he would call on me at 8.15 a.m. tomorrow to say farewell. He did. We laughed about various things. 'Colonel Ha Van Lau said to tell you that another year at the most before our flag flies over Saigon.' We embraced. He muttered warm regards to *Red Mole* and VSC [Vietnam Solidarity Campaign] comrades and soon I was flying to Moscow.

At one stage it appeared that the United States was going to buy out the North Koreans. Bill Clinton despatched Madeleine Albright to Pyongyang in 2000 to do a deal – loadsamoney for the Kims, denuclearisation of sorts, followed by a soft reunification with the South – but it didn't go through. George W. Bush had no interest at all in contact. Why? I got an answer of sorts after a public debate on the Iraq War in Berlin in 2003.

My opponent was Ruth Wedgwood from Yale, an adviser to Donald Rumsfeld. Over lunch I asked her about their plans for North Korea. She was cogent. 'You haven't seen the glint in the eyes of the South Korean military,' she said. 'They're desperate to get hold of the North's nuclear arsenal. That's unacceptable.' Why? 'Because if a unified Korea becomes a nuclear power, it will be impossible to stop Japan from becoming one too and if you have China, Japan and a unified Korea as nuclear states, it shifts the relationship of forces against us.'

31

The Boulder Interview: Palestine and Israel (2004)

Explain why Palestine is so central to Muslim consciousness.[*]

The question of Palestine evokes anger, despair, sadness and bitterness because it was a very important part of the Arab world. The Palestinians were regarded as amongst the oldest inhabitants of that world. The crude, brutal way in which the state of Israel was created, with mass expulsions of Palestinians, the destruction of Palestinian villages, ethnic cleansing, the rape of Palestinian women – the exact numbers of which are yet to be revealed – left its mark. It was in some ways as much of a cultural and political shock as the entry of the Crusaders in the eleventh century had been. The nature of the shock was exactly the same: we had been violated, our world entered and taken away from us, and a new state created in its place – without our permission, without collaboration, without discussion – by a major imperial power: Great Britain. That's what most Arab people thought.

To that shock can be added the total failure of the Arab armies to take back the territory, and the fact that the armies were under the control of corrupt kings and officers who sabotaged the 1948 war. The Arab defeat was not merely due to Israeli superiority or fanaticism – which were there – it was a deliberate failure on

---

[*] This chapter is extracted from an interview conducted by David Barsamian, in Boulder, Colorado, in 2004, later included in *Speaking of Empire and Resistance: Conversations with Tariq Ali* (New Press, 2005).

the part of the Arab elites, who did not really want to win the war but needed to make a show of it. The depth of this shock is illustrated in the work of one of the greatest Arab writers of the twentieth century, Abdelrahman Munif, in his book *Story of a City: A Childhood in Amman*, where he describes the importance of Palestine, even to young children. Munif recounts that at school, when the teachers in class used to say, 'Name ten Arab cities,' the first six names were always those of Palestinian cities, which are still with us today, in the news every single day. This failure went very deep. It was this failure that led to the birth of Arab nationalism. The establishment of Israel in the Arab world created a new wave of radical Arab nationalism, whose principal leader, Gamal Abdel Nasser, became probably the most popular leader in the Arab world since Saladin.

Since then we have seen the systematic crushing of the Palestinians; the wars waged, beginning with the 1967 war; and the continuing expansion of Israel's frontiers. The Zionist leadership attempted to wipe out the Palestinians as a political force, to crush their spirit so that they would forget who they once were. Like the slaves who were once brought to the United States, they hoped that these people, too, would develop new identities, new personas, and forget the past. But that failed miserably and led us to the situation we are in today, where every single attempt by the Palestinians to make concessions in order to get something has collapsed.

Today we are here in the United States of America discussing Israel and Palestine at a time when George Bush has given the Israelis the green light to take whole chunks of Palestine – he says it is utopian to return to the 1967 borders, that the settlers should remain, and that Gaza should be turned into a prison camp, a large ghetto, like the Warsaw ghetto, permanently supervised by Israel. In this situation, what can one say? It is, therefore, unsurprising that Palestine remains central in the minds of large numbers of Arab people, if not among the corrupt, venal elites who rule that world.

Given the daily breach of all human rights laws and the daily violations of elementary human decency, why is the liberal conscience of the West blind to Palestinian suffering? It is because, in the United States in particular, the Palestinians as a people are widely regarded as terrorists, to a person. This term is now used to describe anything that opposes imperial interests or the interests of imperial satrapies, and the Palestinians have been given this image in the mainstream American media. The liberals here are incredibly weak on this subject – in the US, the world's dominant power, public opinion follows whatever the government says regarding the Palestinians: they're *Untermenschen*, subhuman; they're terrorists.

The degree of anti-Palestinian and anti-Arab racism is deeply shocking. If you compare what has been done to the Palestinians with what Milosevic did to the Kosovars, the crimes being committed in Palestine are of a totally different nature. Every single day the Israel Defense Forces, as they call it, targets children – young boys in particular. During the last three years, a week has rarely passed without the deaths of young boys in Palestine. This is approaching, not in terms of scale but in terms of intent, a genocidal war, to try and wipe out future generations of Palestinians. They justify it, disgustingly, by saying 'We're destroying the terrorist bombers of tomorrow.'

If the United States is blind to this, the Europeans are partially blind as well. They know what's going on and they are unhappy about it, but the Israelis have got them in a bind. The Germans are unwilling to speak against Israel because of the Judeocide of the Second World War. But the present generation of Germans is not responsible for that any more than the present generation of Belgians is responsible for the atrocities and genocide in the Congo. You cannot make guilt retrospective by blaming current generations for what happened in the past. But that is what they say to the German governments. And very few German politicians dare to speak on this. Without Germany, the rest of Europe is embarrassed and shamefaced – they know what is going on but remain too scared to speak.

I have said this before and I will repeat it: the Palestinians have become the indirect victims of the Judeocide of the Second World War. The Jews were the direct victims and the Palestinians are

Checking focus during the Bandung years.

London, 1982, the Indian actress Shabana Azmi, a dear friend, was complaining that no one recognised her in London. So Susan and I took her to Southall, where she was mobbed.

Bandung File marks the bicentenary of the French Revolution with a short dramatisation by Tariq Ali, 'Liberty's Scream', which stresses the unity between black and white Jacobins in Haiti and France.

Catalogue featuring C. L. R James, Indian actress and dancer Zohra Sehgal. A still from 'A Licence to Kill'.

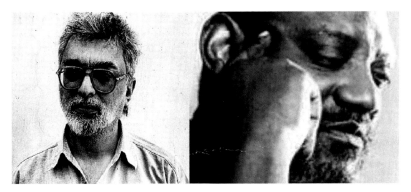

Farrukh Dhondy and Darcus Howe, the latter a colleague at *The Bandung File* and the former a writer and commissioning editor at Channel 4. A strong team.

born 1985
died 1989

cause of death – execution

YOU ARE INVITED TO
A WAKE

ON TUESDAY 19th DECEMBER AT 7.45PM
(doors will close at 8.15pm)

at Bandung Productions, Block H
Carkers Lane, 53/79 Highgate Road
London NW5 1TL

TO HAVE A BITE AND
WATCH
THE FINAL PROGRAMME

Dress	**RSVP Sandra Smith**
All Black	**Tel 482 5045**

Present

THE BANDUNG FILE
a series of six programmes
for Channel 4's Autumn Season

A Licence to Kill — *TX 12 September 8pm*
Too Many Questions — *TX 19 September 8pm*
Till Death Us Do Part?: Labour and
the Black Vote — *TX 26 September 8pm*
Linton Kwesi Johnson
in Concert — *TX 3 October 8pm*
The New East Enders — *TX 10 October 8pm*
President Nyerere in Conversation with
Tariq Ali and Darcus Howe — *TX 17 October 8pm*

Bandung Production 82 Wardour Street London W1V 3LF

The Wake Card for Bandung when it finally was shut down in December 1989.

With Benazir Bhutto a few weeks after the first time she was elected as prime minister of Pakistan, 1988.

With Murtaza Bhutto, speaking at a rally a few weeks after the assassination of his father, 1979.

Dear Tariq Ali,

   I wanted to write to you earlier but did not know how to reach you. Our Comrades hear of your Political Activities, and we are glad that you are consistantly keeping alive the struggle.

   It is our firm opinion that no " In Flight Folly " took place. For those who had been severely tortured the Hijacking was an act of pure Liberation. We feel that the Political and Armed struggle must co-exist.

   I hope that we may be able to keep in more regular contact so as to further our common cause and to prevent sabotage of it.

   Please convey my best regards to all our friends.

       Sincerely,

       (MIR MURTAZA BHUTTO)

When Murtaza's outfit hijacked a PIA plane in 1981, demanding the release of political prisoners, I assumed it was a provocation by the military regime that had hanged his father. A mass movement for the restoration of democracy had been launched, and this was a perfect terrorist diversion. I suggested as much in the *New Statesman*. I was wrong. One of Murtaza's rogue minion's hand-delivered this letter.

With Hugo Chávez and his chief of staff, Maximilien Arvelaiz, at the Venice Film Festival, for the launch of *South of the Border*, 2009.

INTELECTUAIS SE UNEM Participantes do Fórum de Porto Alegre associam a rejeição a uma possível invasão do Iraque à batalha travada contra o modelo neoliberal

CONTRA BUSH

Porto Alegre, 2002.

With Oliver Stone and Chávez in Venice, 2009.

On the set of *Wittgenstein*, 1993, with director Derek Jarman. The photographer, Howard Sooley, shouted: 'Derek, how should I shoot you two?' Jarman: 'Make us look like the Kray twins.'

the indirect victims. They are not responsible for what happened; the responsibility rests firmly on the shoulders of Christian 'civilisation', which wiped out six million Jews, not on the Arabs, the Muslims or the Palestinians. I blame not just the fascist states that committed these atrocities, but also Roosevelt and Churchill, who declined to bomb the railway lines and the concentration camps where Jews were held. They knew the locations and they knew what was going on, but they refused to send bombers to destroy the railway lines and the concentration camps. Why? It wasn't a priority. The priority was to win the war; the priority was not to save the lives of Jews. Contrary to mythology, the Second World War was not fought to save the Jews.

Many Israeli dissidents, who are disgusted by what their own government is doing, are much sharper in criticising that government than anyone in the United States. In September 2003, more than two dozen Israeli pilots signed a public statement announcing that they refused to bomb Palestinian towns and villages. It was a very sharp statement, saying 'We were recruited to join the Israeli Air Force, not the Mafia; not to go out and carry out revenge killings.' This created a big debate in Israel, and it is not a minor matter. No American pilot ever refused to bomb Iraq or Vietnam. Some soldiers finally stopped fighting, but no US bomber pilot ever refused to carry out the orders of the government. These Israeli pilots who refused have a very heightened political consciousness. They were denounced and viciously attacked by politicians and the press.

This reaction angered some decent liberal journalists in Israel. One of them, Yehuda Nuriel, published an article in a Tel Aviv weekly owned by *Maariv*, the daily tabloid newspaper, attacking the pilots and defending the Israeli government; he signed the article with a false name, A. Schicklgruber, which was Hitler's real name. No one at the newspaper knew this. Under the name of A. Schicklgruber he attacked the pilots for what they were doing, but the whole article – every single sentence – was taken from *Mein Kampf* and Hitler's speeches. The article got printed, and the editors were not troubled by its contents – until someone with a historical memory said, 'Oh my God. Schicklgruber is not

some old Jew in Jerusalem. It's the real name of Adolf Hitler.'
Nuriel was fired, naturally. But the fact that an Israeli journalist
had the guts to do this is remarkable. As I often say to mainstream journalists in the United States and in Europe: follow the
example of some of your Israeli peers. They are more courageous
than you.

I think this is the worst period for the Palestinians since 1948.
The Israelis are now talking about killing Arafat, assuming in line
with the colonial mentality that if you chop off the head of the
leaders or imprison them, the resistance will wither – the British
did this throughout the history of their empire. They even had a
phrase for this absurd notion: nipping rebellion in the bud. Cut
off the bud and the flower won't grow.

But this is politics, not botany. You can nip things in the bud,
or leave them to mature and then decapitate them – as the
Israeli did with the Hamas leaders Ahmed Yassin and Abdel-
Aziz Rantisi – but there are always new generations coming up.
The children today can see clearly the conditions in which they
and their families live and the daily humiliation they face; they
will mourn for Yassin and Rantisi, but tomorrow they will do
the same thing. Killing off Arafat will have a similarly negligible
impact; people will carry on the struggle. Any notion that it will
stop is crazy – it is not going to stop at this rate. And the war
against terror has become a war of terror, a war of state terror
waged against people trying to fight for their freedom.

*Talk more about the intersection of racism in terms of framing
attitudes towards not just Palestinians but Arabs and Muslims
in general. Let me just read you a few comments, one from a
British TV talk-show host, Robert Kilroy-Silk, who wrote: 'We
owe the Arabs nothing. Apart from oil – which was discovered, is
produced, and is paid for by the West – what do they contribute?'
Arabs, he says, are 'suicide bombers, limb-amputators, women
repressors'. On this side of the Atlantic, you have people like the
bestselling author and TV pundit Ann Coulter recommend-
ing that 'we' – that is, the West, America – 'should invade their
countries, kill their leaders and convert them to Christianity'.*

You have people like Paul Weyrich and William Lind, members of the conservative establishment, saying 'Islam is, quite simply, a religion of war'; or Billy Graham's son Franklin saying that Islam is 'a very evil and wicked religion', and on and on.

The diatribes by conservatives everywhere, not just in Britain and the United States, are unending. You can find similar things in France; this French popinjay, Bernard-Henri Lévy, one of the leading official state intellectuals, wrote a book about Daniel Pearl that is filled with the most disgusting stuff about Pakistan, because he doesn't know the country. He doesn't speak the language, he doesn't know the people, but he writes a 500-page book, which is a pile of garbage. The Italian journalist Oriana Fallaci comes out with similar stuff. It's a sign of total intellectual and moral bankruptcy that this is all these people have to say. In the case of Coulter and Kilroy-Silk, it's vulgar beyond belief that they can even get away with talking like this.

Just imagine if anyone said such things about Jews. You would have the Israeli embassies going berserk denouncing them. If Coulter had made these remarks against Jews or even African Americans, in this day and age, there would have been hell to pay. But after September 11, it's open season as far as Arabs and Muslims are concerned.

The Arab regimes, or most of the Muslim governments, are utterly incapable of defending themselves or their culture against this imperial verbal onslaught. Force and awe doesn't work on ordinary people, but it certainly works on the elites who run the Arab world – because behind the force and awe are the IMF, the World Bank and the US Treasury. Kilroy-Silk did actually get fired from the BBC for his remarks, but his company retained the contract.

Talk more about Palestine and the hold it has on people's imagination. For example, would a merchant in Multan in Pakistan, or a dockworker in Chittagong in Bangladesh, or a rice farmer in Java in Indonesia care about Palestine?

It is not necessarily because of a common religion – the cultures you cite, after all, are totally different. What they can see in Palestine under Israeli occupation is the most grotesque display of double standards. Another Arab country has been invaded, virtually dismembered, and occupied by foreign armies, supposedly because its leaders possessed weapons of mass destruction. But at the same time, they see a neighbouring country that indisputably has such weapons of mass destruction, the only country in the region that might even use them – and they see this country, Israel, denying basic, elementary human rights to the Palestinian population, in Israel and in the occupied territories. It angers people, and it leads naturally to anger with the imperial power for acting on false premises in the case of Iraq while turning a blind eye to the obvious in Israel, since it is a long-standing ally. If the United States or the West were imposing sanctions on Israel, cutting off all subsidies to Israel, putting it under siege until it withdrew back to the 1967 borders, this anger would not exist. In fact, some of the kids attracted to terrorism would lose interest, having seen evidence that someone in the world is working to help them.

There is a movement of solidarity with Palestine, though not among states or the political classes; many young people in the United States and Europe are very angry about the situation. The name of Rachel Corrie has become immortal in Palestine.

She is the young American woman who was crushed to death by an Israeli bulldozer in Gaza.

She was deliberately crushed to death by an Israeli bulldozer. It was no accident. This was Israel's way of sending a message to Western kids who come to Palestine: We will not treat you any differently. You come and stand by the Palestinians, and you will be crushed. Rachel Corrie was not the only victim; Tom Hurndall, a young Briton, was shot in Gaza and died after a long time in a coma. This is how they operate – they murder the kids who come from the West to stand side by side with the Palestinians to prevent their houses from being demolished.

They have turned the Israeli embassies into total propaganda machines for the Zionist state, touting a new, big wave of anti-semitism sweeping the world, which is nonsense. Antisemitism exists in certain parts of the world – genuine antisemitism – but they confuse this deliberately with hostility towards Israel. If you are critical of what Israel is doing to the Palestinians – the punishments it's inflicting, the kids it's killing, the lands it's occupying – if you're hostile to the settlers in Palestinian land, you are an antisemite. And if you are a Jew, then you are a self-hating Jew. Israeli embassies all over Europe are devoted to this propaganda effort – they are concerned because the Europeans are sceptical about Israeli actions in the territories. In the US, they don't need to worry, because the House and the Senate essentially passed a blank cheque of support to Israel. It's unheard of – they don't give that sort of support to their own government, but they're prepared to give that support to Israel. There is an Israeli offensive against dissent, abroad and at home ...

Talk about how elements of the Palestinian national movement have themselves internalised the sense of being colonised. In particular, their consistent appeals to the principal patron of their adversary to somehow liberate them, to do right by them.

Edward Said described Oslo as a Palestinian Versailles, where, in return for a few crumbs, they basically agreed to surrender. The Palestinian leadership thought they might get a tiny state out of this, a state that would at least be functional – but they didn't even get that. Instead, all the Israelis were prepared to offer them was tiny Bantustans. Instead of using the Oslo period to mobilise their population and the rest of world public opinion by saying, 'This is what we expected, and we're not getting it,' Arafat and his entourage were busy making money, recycling the money being donated for lots of decent projects in Palestine. They started eating up this money, looting their own country.

The second intifada was not just an uprising against the Zionist occupation of Palestine; it was also a protest against the corruption of the Palestinian leadership. I think the Palestinians themselves might have deposed Arafat had it not been for Sharon's new offensive against him. When the Israelis cut off his electricity, they made him into a hero again, just by attacking him. Those images of Arafat, photographed in the candlelight, made him look like a Rembrandt painting; after this attack on Arafat, people gave him a break.

The question you pose is an important one. We have paid a terrible price for the decision of the secular Palestinian leadership to cave in to the United States. It means that the radical opposition is in the hands of the religious group Hamas, whom I defend despite disagreeing with many of their tactics because they are the only people defending the Palestinians against daily brutalities. But, to be honest, it's not in the interests of the Palestinian people to be led by a group which is so deeply religious, because – leaving aside all the other reasons – Palestine is not simply composed of Muslims. There are many Christian Palestinians as well, and we don't want to drive them out; they've been very active in the struggle.

But the PLO made the fateful mistake of agreeing to Oslo, and then participating in the farce that took place at Camp David. When I look at the pictures from that summit, the paternal familiarity with which Clinton and Barak treated Arafat reminds me of the way feudal lords used to treat their favourite servants – that's the way they were treating Arafat. They even tried to restrain him physically to prevent his leaving Camp David after he realised that he was being offered no more than the status quo. The Palestinian leaders saw this happening, but they were not capable of devising any alternatives.

When the Israelis agreed to negotiate at Oslo, they insisted it be with the PLO – then in exile in Tunis – and not with the local leadership of the first intifada. The local leadership, which essentially forced the Israelis to Oslo to try and negotiate a settlement, were honest and incorruptible. Even the PLO leaders in the West Bank were very different from those in exile. There was a deliberate decision to negotiate with the PLO in exile and to force the internal leaders, PLO and non-PLO, of the first intifada, to accept Arafat's sovereignty. When you see Arafat's spokesmen on television today, on CNN or whatever, their body language is pathetic, trying to please the imperial masters: Look how reasonable we are. Look how we crawl on our knees in front of you. We are on our knees, and the Israelis still come and kick us down. That's what they've been reduced to.

Palestine desperately needs national leadership which is going to pursue the struggle for this century. I hope by the end of this century we will see a Palestinian state that is meaningful – a proper state with contiguous borders and at least half of the old state of greater Israel – or, if that does not happen, that Palestinians win the struggle to become equal citizens in a unified state of Palestine–Israel. The Zionist establishment is against both, and that is their great weakness – they can't prevent both forever.

When Sharon came to Washington in April 2004, the United States essentially signed off on the annexation of large swaths of the West Bank and its very precious aquifer. Let's not forget the water resources that are involved. Curiously, there was no mention of the annexed Golan Heights of Syria – that's completely disappeared from any kind of public scrutiny – or East Jerusalem, for that matter, which was annexed by Israel in violation of international law.

We have to be very careful when we talk about international law. You are, of course, absolutely right – there are UN resolutions denouncing all this. But international law only functions when the largest, most powerful state in the world wants it to do so. It cannot function unless that state accepts it. The United States has always been cavalier in the enforcement of international law – in the wars they've fought, with the people they've killed, in what they continue to do in Iraq. So I'm afraid it's not international law that is going to come to help the Palestinians. What they will have to do at some point is make that part of the world ungovernable unless they get their rights.

There has historically been a notion of a united front. What if there were a real coalition of nations and peoples coming together to resist the empire? Could that not have an effect?

Absolutely, but only if at least one bloc emerged that was hostile to the American empire, whether in the Far East or elsewhere, which could provide some support, and some cover to the beleaguered populations of Palestine and Iraq. If the Latin American states and the Asian and South Asian states began to say, 'We don't care what the United States says or does, we're going to help the Palestinians; we're going to send volunteers; we're going to help them with arms; we're going to help the struggle,' that would also make a great difference. Why would they do that? Because this is the last remaining colonial struggle of the twentieth century. Obviously, if that were to happen, it would change the situation in the Middle East.

But even the wretched Arab governments that surround the Palestinians don't support the struggle, which creates a very bad impression for the rest of the world. If the Arab League had some muscle and made these appeals to the rest of the world, it would help, but they do not. I sometimes get very depressed when I consider this situation, and then I think the only way forward is for a wave of democratic revolutions – democratic in the sense that they reflect the will of the people in that region – to sweep aside the corrupt imperial satrapies that dominate the Middle East.

That would transform the situation overnight. Washington would then face an interesting problem: they would have to make a choice between establishing relations with these new regimes and continuing to back Israel – quite a test for the imperial leadership.

But this is a time when the Palestinian struggle should be *the* central cause in world politics, alongside Iraq. For many people, of course, it is. The dual occupation of the Arab East is increasingly being taken up as a rallying cry. But many liberals in Europe and in the United States who are very hostile to the occupation of Iraq will not mention Palestine at all. As I mentioned earlier, this is largely the result of guilt for what was done to the Jews by the Third Reich. For others it's purely cynical – Israel is a close ally of the United States, and we'd better not offend the United States. In the United States itself, the stranglehold of pro-Israeli sentiment is so strong that l think there has only been one op-ed piece in the *New York Times*, by Noam Chomsky, denouncing the wall. Otherwise, no one gives a damn.

It's not simply due to the might of the Zionist lobby, though that is very strong. l don't think that's the only reason. In the United States, they feel that Israel is the oasis of Western interests – it's a country like ours. In some ways that's true, because the original emigrants came from Europe, and many of the settlers are actually from the United States. When they appear on American television, people can identify with them, because many of them speak with American accents.

There are other people who refuse to denounce Israel because that would mean denouncing the United States – indeed, you can hardly denounce Israel without denouncing the US, and the policies of Clinton and Bush alike. The population of the United States, as with many other issues, is blissfully unaware of the realities on the ground; the bulk of the political, cultural and media elite is staunchly pro-Israel, as we can see so clearly in the election campaign under way at the moment. On the question of Israel, John Kerry, the Democratic presidential contender, says he is 100 per cent in agreement with George W. Bush. He went even further than Bush by defending, where Bush had been a little less strident, the killing of the Hamas leaders. Kerry released a statement describing how proud he had been to visit Israel, and his joy at riding in an Israeli jet bomber, which he had flown for a bit to see for himself what the ground looked like underneath. The Palestinians – and the basic human rights violations that take place every day – didn't rate a mention. When the world's most powerful state is run by such politicians, why should the Palestinian leadership pin its hopes on them? In time, a leadership will emerge that will break from the United States, and when that begins to happen, the struggle will commence in earnest, and we will see portions of American public opinion shift as well.

There does exist a formation called the Palestine National Initiative. Mustafa Barghouti is active in it. Edward Said was one of its founders. The PNI is a democratic, secular movement. But I am interested in discussing the fact that even people with our views use the terms of propaganda – for example, calling these colonies 'settlements' and calling colonisers 'settlers', which has a very benign resonance, particularly in the United States. We're in the American West right now – it was settled by brave pioneers who came and conquered the savage Indians.

We are all partially guilty of that, it's true. When I use the word 'settler', however, the image I have is not of the United States, because I don't live here, but of the French settlers in Algeria or the Dutch settlers in South Africa, who were defeated. Many of us in Europe use that word in the hope that they will suffer the same fate as the Boers – after hundreds of years in South Africa – and the French in Algeria.

The big difference between the Israelis and the other colonial enterprises is that the French in Algeria, and even the Dutch in South Africa, if they had been pushed or driven out, had places to go back to. The French went back to France; if the Dutch had been driven out, they would have gone back to Holland, and probably then been used to police Indonesia. In any event, they had a place; but for many Israeli Jews, there is no such thing anymore. These Brooklyn guys who go and impose themselves on the Palestinian lands can always come back to Brooklyn, of course. But for large numbers of Israelis, there is nowhere to return. The Palestinian leaders have accepted this, as has the Arab world. No one talks now about driving the Israelis into the sea, as they used to in some of the belligerent rhetoric of the 1950s, which the Zionists invoke constantly: 'We are a small, beleaguered little country. They want to drive us into the sea.' No one says that anymore – no one serious, that is – because people have accepted that these guys are going to be with us. All that is at stake is a way of living together. They can't even accept that – they don't seem to accept it, at least. They're still posing as the offended party; that's what is disgusting. If the Israeli leaders stood up and apologised for what they did, just one public apology – 'We are sorry for what we did' – it would make a world of difference. But they will not make that apology.

The revisionist Israeli historian Benny Morris, who is without any doubt a serious historian, did an interview with *Haaretz*. Morris essentially said, 'Yes, there were ethnic cleansings; yes, we expelled nearly a million people; yes, there were rapes. But so what?' Others deny that this happened. But Morris can't deny it, because he has seen the papers. And he doesn't want to deny it. He defends it as necessary to build the Israeli state and goes on to say the pity is that they didn't kick out all the Palestinians when they had the chance. He compares Israel's actions to what the early Protestant fundamentalist settlers in the Americas did to the Native Americans – compares them with no shame at all. A superior civilisation; a colonial project. Benny Morris's parents are English Jews, so presumably the legacy of the British Empire had some effect on him. This is one of Israel's most prominent and senior historians. He's been denounced by left-wing Israeli historians, and even the Zionist establishment is embarrassed by his statements. But at least he has said it; he's laid it all down on paper. It's very significant that he's done this, comparing the fate of the Palestinians to that of the Native Americans. People like myself used to invoke this comparison, and the Israelis protested that this was slander: 'What an outrageous comparison; we've been so kind to the Palestinians, but they won't listen to us – they're the ones who fight us, who bomb us. What have we ever done to them? All we wanted to do was live in peace.' That argument no longer holds any water.

How would you respond to the traditional Zionist argument that there is only one state for the Jewish people while there are more than twenty Arab states? Why don't those Arab states absorb the Palestinian population and integrate them into their societies? Only Jordan has offered citizenship to the Palestinians.

The question is this: Why should the Palestinians be forced to settle anywhere else? Why shouldn't they have the right, like other people in the world, to live in their villages, to live in their lands? They don't want to move out of their homes – they were forced out. They're quite happy to be citizens with equal rights in an Israeli state, provided they are not permanently mistreated, maltreated, punished, locked up or humiliated. What is wrong with that? Coexistence has played a very strong part in the liberal cultural tradition of Judaism – it's the combination of Zionism and some Jewish fundamentalists that has created this monstrosity.

None of the Arab states were ever purely Muslim states. They had Christian populations, and there were Jewish populations in Cairo and Baghdad – very large Jewish populations. What happened to them? Nothing, until Israel was formed and the Israelis sent in people to drive those Jews out – they bombed cafés in Baghdad to frighten the Jews there into emigrating to Israel. I think a state created on this basis, quite honestly – leaving aside the fact that it's wrong or immoral – it's not even in the interests of the majority of Jews to live in a ghetto state. All your life you've been put in ghettos; you've been trying to get out of these ghettos, trying to integrate. Now you want to build a ghetto state in a part of the world which isn't yours.

I think we have to argue, on principle, for the right of all states to be multicultural. The only reason to create an ethnic, racist state in that part of the world is to drive out the remaining Palestinians; the wall that is being built is partially designed to do that. But it will not work. Sooner or later even the majority of the Jews of Israel will rebel against this life, because it's not a very nice life for them.

In Palestine, there is a great asymmetry of force and military might – you have a clear preponderance on one side and very little on the other. It mirrors, to some degree, the situation in India at the time Gandhi launched his nonviolent resistance movement – against a colonial power with liberal pretensions about the rule of law. Israel, like the British, embraces liberal rhetoric about law and human rights – could the Palestinian trump card in this situation be nonviolent resistance? Eqbal Ahmad, for one, proposed that the refugees in the surrounding Arab countries march on the borders of Israel and say 'We want to go home.'

It would be an event that would dominate the news for no more than four days. It's a nice idea, but one has to take into account that the Zionist leadership is not the British Empire in India. The British Empire in India could only maintain its rule with the support of large sectors of the local elite – the empire only functioned because the feudal lords in India, the princes who controlled both the land and the peasants, cooperated. But when the national movement emerged and began to affect the peasants – Gandhi's greatest appeal was to the Indian peasantry – then the empire became untenable.

The situation in Israel is totally different. This is a state with nuclear weapons and the fifth-largest army in the world, a very effective and brutal fighting force. It is conceivable that they would permit demonstrations – they probably would – but if these coalesced into a large nonviolent resistance movement, they would crush it. They would crush it brutally.

But don't you think, for example, that suicide bombers play right into the hands of the Israelis?

They do and they don't. It's not a tactic I particularly favour, but consider what some senior Zionist leaders have been saying: let's look again at Avraham Burg, the former speaker of the Knesset and former head of the Jewish Agency, who wrote that Israel, having ceased to care about the children of the Palestinians, should not be surprised when they come washed in hatred and blow themselves up in the centres of Israeli escapism. They consign themselves to Allah in our places of recreation, because their own lives are torture. They spill their own blood in our restaurants in order to ruin our appetites, because they have children and parents at home who are hungry and humiliated.

He said this because he realises that you cannot dissociate the suicide bombings from the reality of the occupation – all the reporting, however, separates the two. You must understand the realities of the occupation of Palestine, the daily realities – forcing people to stand for hours at checkpoints while you search them and humiliate them; refusing to allow pregnant women to be taken to the hospital, which has caused miscarriages – all of these things breed desperation.

Do you think that Israel was a factor in the US attack on Iraq?

It was a factor, but I don't accept that it was the dominant factor or that the Israelis organised the war, or anything like that. The Israelis wanted to end the regime in Iraq because they saw it as the only regime with the potential to take them on, if it so wished; they had never liked the Iraqi regime, precisely because it was an independent Arab state. During the Iran–Iraq War, even as the US and Britain were backing Iraq, the Israelis were actually giving spare parts for Chieftain tanks to the Iranians. Menachem Begin was asked, 'What is your position on the Iraq war?' And he said, 'When goyim fights goyim, all I can do is sit back and applaud.' But they were very nervous about Iraq – don't forget that they bombed Iraq's nuclear reactor in 1981, with US permission. There is no doubt at all that the Israelis wanted the invasion of Iraq. What the Israeli ambassador to Washington said was, 'Don't stop now – go and finish the job with Syria and Iran.' There is no doubt about where they stand.

There is also no doubt that senior Israeli officials met with Ahmed Chalabi before the invasion of Iraq, and Chalabi promised them that Iraq would recognise Israel within a few months of his taking charge. Today, Chalabi himself isn't recognised by anyone, so he's in no position to deliver for the Israelis, but his promises certainly made them happy, and they obviously backed the invasion.

The American occupation of Iraq could have followed the old, time-honoured British formula: find a layer of the local elite, real natives, and make a deal to secure their support and cooperation. For that, of course, you need time, which the British had in their day. But the Americans could have adapted this scheme – by leaving the Iraqi army intact, perhaps, and making use of it. This might not have worked, but the Americans didn't even try it; they opted for the Israeli methods of colonisation: hit hard; punish towns, villages and families. Destroy the villages of resistance fighters or the homes of their families.

Where did Israelis learn this? They learned it from their German oppressors; this is what the Germans did in the Second World War: punish whole towns at once. Power based on brutality, force and occupation always remains precarious, unstable.

Collective punishment?

The Germans imposed collective punishment. The United States took it to new heights during the Vietnam War. The Israelis did it to the Palestinians. And now the Americans are doing it to the Iraqis and to sundry others – they chose the Israeli model but are less precise. That is how they want to run Iraq: keep their own bases there, stay in those bases to reduce US casualties, and go out in big numbers with air cover to hit the Iraqis when they have to. It's not going to work. There will be chaos in the region.

32

Remembering Edward Said

Whenever Edward Said and I tried to remember when we had first met, our recollections differed. Ultimately, we agreed to agree on a date: 1972, at a conference on Bangladesh and Pakistan at Columbia University in New York. Even in those turbulent times, one of the features that distinguished Edward from the rest of us was his immaculate dress sense: everything was meticulously chosen, down to the socks. It is almost impossible to visualise him any other way. At a conference in his honour in Beirut in 1997, he insisted on accompanying Elias Khoury and me for a swim. As he walked out in his swimming trunks, I said it was a disgrace that the towel did not match. 'When in Rome,' he replied, airily. But that evening, as he read in public for the first time an extract from the Arabic manuscript of his memoir *Out of Place*, his attire was faultless. It remained so till the end, throughout his long battle with leukaemia.

Over the years one had become so used to his illness – the regular hospital stays, the willingness to undergo trials with the latest drugs, the refusal to accept defeat – that one began to think of him as indestructible. Around 2002, purely by chance, I met Said's doctor in New York. In response to my questions, he told me that there was no medical explanation for Edward's survival. It was his indomitable spirit as a fighter, his will to live, that had preserved him for so long.

Said travelled everywhere. He spoke, as always, of Palestine, but also of the unifying capacities of the three cultures, which he insisted had a great deal in common. The monster was devouring his insides but those who came to hear him could not see the process, and we who knew preferred to forget. When the cursed cancer finally took him in September 2003, the shock was intense.

His quarrels with the political and cultural establishments of the West and the official Arab world were the most important feature of his biography. It was the Six-Day War of 1967 that changed his life; prior to that event, he had not been politically engaged. His father Wadie, a Palestinian Christian, had emigrated to the United States in 1911, at the age of sixteen, to avoid being drafted by the Ottomans to fight in Bulgaria. He became an American citizen and served, instead, with the US military in France during the First World War. Subsequently he returned to Jerusalem, where Edward was born in 1935.

Said never pretended to be a poverty-stricken Palestinian refugee as some detractors later alleged. After the family moved to Cairo, where Wadie set up a successful stationery business, Edward was sent to an elite English-language school. His early teenage years were lonely, dominated by a Victorian father, in whose eyes the boy required permanent disciplining, and an after-school existence devoid of friends. Novels became a substitute – Defoe, Scott, Kipling, Dickens, Mann. He had been named Edward after the Prince of Wales but, despite his father's monarchism, was despatched for his further education not to Britain but to the United States, in 1951. Said later wrote of hating his 'puritanical and hypocritical' New England boarding school, describing his time there as 'shattering and disorienting'. Until then, he thought he knew exactly who he was, 'moral and physical flaws' and all. In the United States he had to remake himself 'into something the system required'.

Nevertheless, he flourished in the Ivy League environment, first at Princeton and then Harvard where, as he later said, he had the privilege to be trained in the German philological tradition of comparative literature. Said began teaching at Columbia in 1963; his first book, on Conrad, was published three years later. I asked him about it in New York in 1994, in a conversation filmed for Channel 4 in his Riverside Drive apartment. That day was so humid that Said removed his jacket and tie as the cameras began to roll, creating much merriment in the household. He described his early years at Columbia between 1963 and 1967 as a 'Dorian Gray period'. We could just as well have called it Jekyll-Hyde:

T.A. So, one of you was the Comp Lit professor, going about his business, giving his lectures, working with Trilling and the others; yet at the same time, another character was building up inside you – but you kept the two apart?

E.S. I had to. There was no place for that other character to be. I had effectively severed my connection with Egypt. Palestine no longer existed. My family lived partly in Egypt and partly in Lebanon. I was a foreigner in both places. I had no interest in the family business, so I was here. Until 1967, I really didn't think about myself as anything other than a person going about his work. I had taken in a few things along the way.

I was obsessed with the fact that many of my cultural heroes – Edmund Wilson, Isaiah Berlin, Reinhold Niebuhr – were fanatical Zionists. Not just pro-Israeli: they said the most awful things about the Arabs, in print. But all I could do was note it. Politically, there was no place for me to go. I was in New York when the Six-Day War broke out, and was completely shattered. The world as I had understood it ended at that moment. I had been in the States for years but it was only now that I began to be in touch with other Arabs. By 1970 I was completely immersed in politics and the Palestinian resistance movement.

Said's 1975 work *Beginnings* – an epic engagement with the problems posed by the 'point of departure', which synthesised the insights of Auerbach, Vico and Freud with a striking reading of the modernist novel – and, above all, *Orientalism*, were the products of this shock. Published in 1978, when Said was already a member of the Palestinian National Council, *Orientalism* combines the polemical vigour of the activist with the passion of the cultural critic. Like all great polemics, it eschews balance. I once told him that, for many South Asians, the problem with the early orientalist British scholars was not their imperialist ideology but, on the contrary, the fact that they were far too politically correct: overawed by the Sanskrit texts they were translating. Said laughed, and insisted that the book was essentially an attempt to undercut the more fundamental assumptions of the West in relation to the Arab East.

Orientalism spawned a vast academic following. While Said was undoubtedly touched and flattered by the book's success, he was well aware of how it was misused and often disclaimed responsibility for its more monstrous offspring: 'How can anyone accuse me of denouncing "dead white males"? Everyone knows I love Conrad.' He would then go through a list of postmodernist critics, savaging each of them in turn for their stress on identity and their hostility to narrative. 'Write it all down,' I once told him. 'Why don't you?' came the reply. What we recorded was more restrained:

T.A. The 1967 war radicalised you, pushed you in the direction of becoming a Palestinian spokesperson?

E.S. Arab, at first, before Palestinian.

T.A. And *Orientalism* grew out of that new commitment?

E.S. I started to read, methodically, what was being written about the Middle East. It did not correspond to my experience. By the early seventies I began to realise that the distortions and misrepresentations were systematic, part of a much larger system of thought that was endemic to the West's whole enterprise of dealing with the Arab world. It confirmed my sense that the study of literature was essentially a historical task, not just an aesthetic one.

I still believe in the role of the aesthetic; but the 'kingdom of literature' – 'for its own sake' – is simply wrong. A serious historical investigation must begin from the fact that culture is hopelessly involved in politics. My interest has been in the great canonical literature of the West – read, not as masterpieces that have to be venerated, but as works that have to be grasped in their historical density, so they can resonate. But I also don't think you can do that without liking them; without caring about the books themselves.

Culture and Imperialism, published in 1993, extended the core arguments of *Orientalism* to describe a more general pattern of relationships between the metropolitan West and its overseas territories, beyond that of Europe and the Middle East. Written in a different political period, it attracted some vituperative attacks. There was a celebrated exchange in the *Times Literary Supplement* with Ernest Gellner – who thought Said should give 'at least some expression of gratitude' for imperialism's role as a vehicle of modernity – in which neither side took prisoners. Later, when Gellner attempted a reconciliation of sorts, Said was unforgiving; hatred must be pure to be effective and, here as elsewhere, he always gave as good as he got.

But by now debates on culture had been overshadowed by events in Palestine. When I asked if the year 1917 meant anything to him, he replied without hesitation: 'Yes, the Balfour Declaration.' Said's writings on Palestine have a completely different flavour from anything else he wrote, passionate and biblical in their simplicity. This was his cause. In *The End of the Peace Process, Blaming the Victims* and some half-dozen other books, in his *al-Ahram* columns and his essays for the *NLR* and the *LRB*, the flame that had been ignited in 1967 burned ever brighter. He had helped a generation to understand the real history of Palestine and it was this position, as the true chronicler of his people and their occupied homeland, that won him respect and admiration across the Arab world. The Palestinians had become the indirect victims of the European Judeocide of the Second World War, but few politicians in the West seemed to care. Said pricked their collective conscience and they did not like him for it.

Two close friends whose advice he had often sought – Ibrahim Abu-Lughod and Eqbal Ahmad – had died within a few years of each other, in 1999 and 2001. Said missed them greatly, but their absence only made him more determined to continue his political fight. Though he had served for fourteen years as an independent member on the Palestinian National Council, and helped to polish and redraft Arafat's address to the UN General Assembly in 1974, he became increasingly critical of the lack of strategic vision that typified most of the Palestinian leadership.

Writing in the *LRB* in October 1993, in the immediate aftermath of what he termed the 'fashion-show vulgarities' of Arafat and Rabin's handshake on the White House lawn, Said described the Oslo Accords – imposed on the vanquished by the United States and Israel after the Gulf War of 1991 – as 'an instrument of surrender, a Palestinian Versailles', offering only shrivelled Bantustans in exchange for a series of historic renunciations. Israel, meanwhile, had no reason to let go as long as Washington supplied it with arms and funds. (Arafat's lieutenant Nabil Shaath, echoing *Orientalism*'s more reactionary critics, responded: 'He should stick to literary criticism. After all, Arafat would not deign to discuss Shakespeare.')

History has vindicated Said's analysis. One of his most scorching attacks on Arafat's leadership, published in the *NLR* and in *al-Ahram*, denounced Oslo as a mere repackaging of the occupation, 'offering a token 18 per cent of the lands seized in 1967 to the corrupt, Vichy-like authority of Arafat, whose mandate has essentially been to police and tax his people on Israel's behalf':

> The Palestinian people deserve better. We have to say clearly that with Arafat and company in command, there is no hope ... What the Palestinians need are leaders who are really with and of their people, who are actually doing the resisting on the ground, not fat cigar-chomping bureaucrats bent on preserving their business deals and renewing their VIP passes, who have lost all trace of decency or credibility ... We need a united leadership capable of thinking, planning and taking decisions, rather than grovelling before the Pope or George Bush while the Israelis kill his people with impunity ... The struggle for liberation from Israeli occupation is where every Palestinian worth anything now stands.

Could Hamas provide a serious alternative? 'This is a protest movement against the occupation,' Said told me:

> In my opinion, their ideas about an Islamic state are completely inchoate, unconvincing to anybody who lives there. Nobody takes that aspect of their programme seriously. When you question

them, as I have, both on the West Bank and elsewhere, 'What are your economic policies? What are your ideas about power stations, or housing?' they reply: 'Oh, we're thinking about that.' There is no social programme that could be labelled 'Islamic'. I see them as creatures of the moment, for whom Islam is an opportunity to protest against the current stalemate, the mediocrity and bankruptcy of the ruling party. The Palestinian Authority is now hopelessly damaged and lacking in credibility – like the Saudis and Egyptians, a client state for the US.

Behind the reiterated Israeli demands that the Authority crack down on Hamas and Islamic Jihad, he detected 'the hope that there will be something resembling a Palestinian civil war, a gleam in the eyes of the Israeli military'. Yet, writing in the *LRB* in the final months of his life, he could still celebrate the Palestinians' stubborn refusal to accept that they were, as the IDF Chief of Staff had described them, 'a defeated people', and saw signs of a more creative politics in the Palestinian National Initiative led by Mustafa Barghouti: 'The vision here is not a manufactured provisional state on 40 per cent of the land, with the refugees abandoned and Jerusalem kept by Israel, but a sovereign territory liberated from military occupation by mass action involving Arabs and Jews wherever possible.'

With Edward Said's death, the Palestinian nation lost its most articulate voice in the northern hemisphere, a world where, by and large, the continuous suffering of the Palestinians is ignored. For official Israelis, they are *Untermenschen*; for official Americans, they are all terrorists; for the venal Arab regimes they are a continuing embarrassment. In his last writings, Said vigorously denounced the war on Iraq and its many apologists. He argued for freedom from violence and from lies. He knew that the dual occupation of Palestine and Iraq had made peace in the region even more remote. His voice is irreplaceable, but his legacy endures. He has many lives ahead of him.

33

Was Hugo Chávez Murdered?

The United States, which seemed predestined by Providence to rain down misery on the Americas in the name of liberty ...

Simón Bolívar, 'Letter to Patrick Campbell' (1829)

During an oil summit in Qatar, just after the US occupation of Iraq, Hugo Chávez, then leader of Venezuela, was interviewed for an hour by Al Jazeera TV, his voice dubbed in Arabic. On one of my visits there, the head of the station said to me: 'It's the most popular interview we have ever done. It was watched by over a million people. We had to hire new employees to reply to the mountain of emails.'

Fan mail?

'A bit more than that,' he replied. 'Most of them, in one way or another, asked the following question: When will the Arab world produce a Chávez?'

'Why haven't you been to Venezuela?' he had asked me during the World Social Forum in Porto Alegre in 2001. I did, the following year, soon after the military coup instigated by Washington and Madrid had failed. What appealed was his bluntness and courage. What often appeared as sheer impulsiveness had been carefully thought out and then, depending on the response, enlarged by spontaneous eruptions on his part. At a time when the world had fallen silent – when centre-left and centre-right had to struggle hard to find any differences and their politicians had become desiccated machine men obsessed with making money – Chávez lit up the political landscape.

He appeared as an indestructible ox, speaking for hours to his people in a warm, sonorous voice, with a fiery eloquence that made it impossible to remain indifferent. His speeches were littered with homilies, references to continental and national history, quotes from the nineteenth-century revolutionary leader and president of Venezuela Simón Bolívar, pronouncements on the state of the world, and songs.

'Our bourgeoisie are embarrassed that I sing in public. Do you mind?' he would ask the audience. The response was a resounding 'No'. He would then ask them to join in the singing and shout, 'Louder, so they can hear us in the eastern part of the city.' Once before just such a rally he looked at me and said: 'You look tired today. Will you last out the evening?' I replied: 'It depends on how long you're going to speak.' It would be a short speech, he promised. Under three hours.

The Bolivarians, as Chávez's supporters were known, offered a political programme that challenged the Washington Consensus. This was the prime reason for the vilification of Chávez. Politicians like him had become unacceptable. What he loathed was the contemptuous indifference of mainstream politicians in South America towards their own people. The Venezuelan elite is notoriously racist and regarded their elected president as uncouth and uncivilised, a *zambo* of mixed African and indigenous blood who could not be trusted. His supporters were portrayed on private TV networks as monkeys. Colin Powell had to publicly reprimand the US embassy in Caracas for hosting a party where Chávez was portrayed as a gorilla.

Was he surprised? 'No,' he told me with a grim look on his face. 'I live here. I know them well. One reason so many of us [non-whites] join the army is because all other avenues are sealed.' No longer.

He had few illusions. He knew that local enemies did not seethe and plot in a vacuum. Behind them was the world's most powerful state. For a moment he thought Obama might be different. The military coup in Honduras disabused him of all such notions.

He had, however, a punctilious sense of duty to his people. He was one of them. Unlike European social democrats, he never believed that any improvement in humankind would come from the corporations and the bankers, and said so long before the Wall Street crash of 2008. If I had to pin a label on him, I would say that he was a socialist democrat, far removed from any sectarian impulses and unimpressed by the self-obsessed behaviour of various far-left sects and the blindness of their routines. He said as much when we first met.

I questioned him on the Bolivarian project in Caracas in 2003. What could be accomplished? He was very clear; much more so than some of his over-enthusiastic supporters:

> I don't believe in the dogmatic postulates of Marxist revolution. I don't accept that we are living in a period of proletarian revolutions. All that must be revised. Reality is telling us that every day. Are we aiming in Venezuela today for the abolition of private property or a classless society? I don't think so. But if I'm told that because of that reality you can't do anything to help the poor, the people who have made this country rich through their labour – and never forget that some of it was slave labour – then I say: 'We part company'.
>
> I will never accept that there can be no redistribution of wealth in society. Our upper classes don't even like paying taxes. That's one reason they hate me. We said: 'You must pay your taxes.' I believe it's better to die in battle, rather than hold aloft a very revolutionary and very pure banner, and do nothing ... That position often strikes me as very convenient, a good excuse ... Try and make your revolution, go into combat, advance a little, even if it's only a millimetre, in the right direction, instead of dreaming about utopias.

I remember sitting next to an elderly, modestly attired woman at one of his public rallies. She questioned me about him. What did I think? Was he doing well? Did he not speak too much? Was he not too rash at times? I defended him and she was relieved. It was his mother, a village teacher, worried that perhaps she had not brought him up as well as she should have done: 'We always made sure that he read books as a child.' This passion for reading stayed with him. History, fiction and poetry were the loves of his life: 'Like me, Fidel is an insomniac. Sometimes we're reading the same novel. He rings at 3 a.m. and asks: "Well, have you finished? What did you think?" And we argue for another hour.'

It was the spell of literature that in 2005 led him to celebrate the 400th anniversary of Cervantes's great novel in a unique fashion. The ministry of culture reprinted a million copies of *Don Quixote* and distributed them free to a million poor, but now literate, households. A quixotic gesture? No. The magic of art can't transform the universe, but it can open up a mind. Chávez was confident that the books would be read, now or later.

The closeness to Castro has been portrayed as a father–son relationship. That was only partially the case. When Chávez was meant to be recuperating from cancer treatment, a huge crowd had gathered outside the hospital in Caracas, and their chants got louder and louder. Chávez ordered a loudspeaker system on the rooftop. He then addressed the crowd. Watching this scene on Telesur in Havana, Castro was shocked. He rang the director of the hospital: 'This is Fidel Castro. You should be sacked. Get him back into bed and tell him I said so.'

Above the friendship, Chávez saw Castro and Che Guevara in a historical frame. They were the twentieth-century heirs of Bolívar and Antonio José de Sucre. They tried to unite the continent, but it was like ploughing the sea. Chávez got closer to that ideal than the quartet he admired so much. His successes in Venezuela triggered a continental reaction: Bolivia and Ecuador saw victories. Brazil under Lula and Dilma did not follow the Chavista social model but nonetheless refused to allow Washington to pit them against Venezuela. It was a favoured trope of Western journalists: Lula is better than Chávez. Later Lula publicly declared that he supported Chávez, saying that his importance for 'our continent' should never be underestimated.

By 2004, the image of Chávez most popular in the West was that of an oppressive *caudillo*. Had this been true I would wish for more of them. The Bolivarian constitution – opposed by the Venezuelan opposition, its newspapers and TV channels and the local CNN, plus Western supporters – was approved by a large majority of the population. It is the only constitution in the world that affords the possibility of removing an elected president from office via a referendum triggered by collecting sufficient signatures. Consistent only in their hatred for Chávez, the opposition tried to use this mechanism in 2004 to remove him. Regardless of the fact that many of the signatures were those of dead people, the Venezuelan government decided to accept the challenge.

I was in Caracas a week before the vote. When I met Chávez at the Miraflores Palace he was poring over the opinion polls in great detail. 'It might be close.' 'And if you lose?' I asked. 'Then I will resign,' he replied without hesitation. He won.

Did he ever tire? Get depressed? Lose confidence? 'Yes,' he replied. But it was not the coup attempt or the referendum. It was the lock-out organised by the corrupt oil unions and backed by the middle classes that worried him, because it would affect the entire population, especially the poor: 'Two factors helped sustain my morale. The first was the support we retained throughout the country. I got fed up sitting in my office. So, with one security guard and two comrades I drove out to listen to people and breathe better air. The response moved me greatly. A woman came up to me and said: "Chávez, follow me, I want to show you something." I followed her into her tiny dwelling. Inside, her husband and children were waiting for the soup to be cooked. "Look at what I'm using for fuel ... the back of our bed. Tomorrow I'll burn the legs, the day after the table, then the chairs and doors. We will survive, but don't give up now." On my way out the kids from the gangs came and shook hands. "We can live without beer. You make sure you screw these motherfuckers."'

What was the inner reality of his life? For anyone with a certain level of intelligence, of character and culture, his or her natural leanings, emotional and intellectual, hang together, constitute a whole. He was a divorcee, but his affection for his children and grandchildren was never in doubt. Most of the women he loved, and there were a few, described him as a generous lover, and this was long after they had parted.

Once I asked whether he preferred enemies who hated him because they knew what he was doing or those who frothed and foamed out of ignorance. He laughed. The former were preferable, he explained, because they made him feel that he was on the right track.

The death of Hugo Chávez on 5 March 2013 was mourned by the poor throughout South America and in other parts of the world. He had put his country on the world map, visited every continent and inspired a new generation.

I recalled a conversation with some Cuban leaders I had met in Caracas in 2003. Over supper, one of them asked: 'Do you think the Americans will try and kill Chávez?'

I nodded.

'How?'

'I have no idea. It would be too stupid to have him assassinated. Everyone will immediately say it's the CIA and that could set off a continental civil war.'

I had another idea. 'They could revert to older fashions. Poison? He's a bit loose with his choice of women.'

They laughed and then one of them said: 'As you can imagine this is an important question for us. Fidel thinks it might be via a well-trained US woman agent who infiltrates his bedroom, and has warned him about this.'

I asked Max Arvelaiz about this several times. He usually shrugged his shoulders. 'We don't know, Tariq. No evidence at all.' Max was a French-Venezuelan intellectual and a good friend of mine. He worked with Chávez as a political chief of staff and promoted the idea of Caracas becoming the headquarters of an unofficial International – an idea Chávez liked very much. It was Max who had explained the origins of the Vietnam War to the Comandante in great detail, and when Chávez was informed that General Giap was still alive he flew to Vietnam on a hurriedly organised state visit to meet him.

A year after Chávez's death, Max was in London and came for supper. A tiny bit of evidence had emerged. 'There was a woman who aroused the suspicions of the Comandante. She didn't last long. After being diagnosed with cancer, he confessed to intimates that his instincts warned him that there was something odd about her.'

'Why did X [I named the Venezuelan intelligence boss] not investigate?'

'She had disappeared.'

I asked a US friend of mine, a top-ranking surgeon, whether it was possible to inject a person with a killer-cancer.

'Yes,' she replied, 'but I would have to closely inspect his X-rays to venture an opinion. It is possible. Almost anything is possible these days.'

We still don't know, but someone does.

After he had died, I was invited to Caracas to give a set of lectures to Telesur journalists and producers on investigative journalism, and to meet the new president, Nicolás Maduro. On a free day I went to the Comandante's tomb, watched the soldiers on guard duty parading up and down, and the memories flooded back. It was more upsetting than I had expected.

We had lost one of the political giants of the post-communist era. Venezuela, its elites mired in corruption on a huge scale, had been considered a secure outpost of Washington. Few thought of the country before Chávez's victories. After 1999, every major media outlet in the West felt obliged to send a correspondent. Since they all said the same thing (the country was supposedly on the verge of a communist-style dictatorship) they would have been better advised to pool their resources.

What of the country he left behind? A paradise? Certainly not. How could it be, given the scale of the problems? But he did leave behind a very changed society in which the poor felt they had an important stake in the government. There is no other explanation for his popularity. Venezuela is divided between his partisans and detractors. He died undefeated, but the big tests lay ahead. The system he created, a social democracy of sorts based on mass mobilisations, needs to progress further. Might his successors be up to the task? In a sense, that was the ultimate test of the Bolivarian experiment.

Of one thing we can be sure. His enemies will not let him rest

in peace. And his supporters? His supporters, the poor throughout the continent and elsewhere, will see him as a political leader
who promised and delivered social rights against heavy odds;
as someone who once fought for them and won. The US tried
to topple him three times and his successor twice. Then they
imposed sanctions to punish the Venezuelan people who had
voted for Maduro. They appointed an imaginary president who
looked and behaved like the total creep that he was and is. The
EU countries backed the US, with ghastly Britain in the lead.
The Bank of England stole Venezuelan gold on the grounds that
Juan Guaidó and not Maduro represented the country. Then,
realising that they had blundered yet again, the Americans got
rid of Guaidó.

34

Havana Diary

25 November
The first thing one notices on arriving in Havana from almost anywhere in the world today is the pleasing absence of ugly skyscrapers and giant billboards advertising global products. Whatever happens in the future, I hope the Malecón isn't wrecked by the global coastal architecture that masquerades as modernity in so many parts of the world, not least South America.

On the long flight from London, I had finished reading Richard Gott's stirring and educative history of Cuba. It had revived many memories, but also raised some uncomfortable questions. This was my first trip to the island, a fact that surprises many people, including myself. A few of us had been invited to visit Havana in 1968, to meet and discuss with Fidel. In the meantime, the Soviet Union had invaded Prague that August, to change the popular reformist 'socialism with a human face' government led by the Communist Party under Dubcek. We were hoping that Cuba would, at least, stay neutral, but Fidel was pressured to endorse the invasion, which he did, lukewarmly.

I cancelled the trip and wrote an 'Open Letter to Fidel' in the *Black Dwarf* explaining why. The Cuban ambassador, a very staunch socialist herself, pleaded with us to go and argue with him face-to-face. We refused. It was a mistake. She was correct and we were very young. I was thinking of all this on the journey. I had been invited to give a lecture at the University of Havana on *Clash of Fundamentalisms* – which had been recently published in Cuba – and related issues. Anything else I would like to do? I named some Cuban intellectuals, including the former editor of *Pensamiento Critico*, Fernando Martinez, who had written for the *NLR* in the past and translated some of our texts for his magazine before it was closed down. 'And,' I had added, 'if Fidel has time I would like to meet.'

Despite all the attempts by the US Empire and its newfound allies in Eastern Europe to suffocate Cuba, it is still here and that is also pleasing. Not because it is a perfect state or a paradise or anything remotely resembling that, but because despite everything it is better than what might replace it if Miami moved back to Havana. We know this because we have been here before and even Hollywood issued a health warning: Francis Ford Coppola provided us with a few memories in *Godfather II*, with its images of 1950s Havana as a Mafia-infested brothel and the Mafia bosses fleeing the country along with the defeated Fulgencio Batista as the Revolution moved closer to the capital on New Year's Eve 1959. Their heirs will be back if Cuba falls, and that would be a tragedy for most Cubans.

The legitimacy of the regime still derives from that Revolution, which remains one of the single most important events of the twentieth century for Latin Americans of every hue. It affected the politics of both right and left in North and South America. Questions are still asked about whether disaffected Cuban exiles might have been involved in Kennedy's assassination. After the Bay of Pigs disaster he had refused to authorise a full-scale assault. Every US president since has been careful to continue the blockade of the island, while staid histories of relations between the North American giant and its tiny opponent frequently record that 'US–Cuban relations continued to deteriorate during ...' – one can fill in the blank with every year following 1959.

Cuba's Revolution affected every left current on the continent. Thinking back one is reminded of the impact it had on Salvador Allende's socialism, and of the openness with which he spoke of it with one of his interlocutors, Régis Debray. Allende's meeting with Guevara was particularly poignant. How could they have known that soon, within years of each other, both of them would be executed by officers acting on imperial instructions, and mourned on more than one continent:

Debray Comrade president, you were one of the first politicians to arrive in Cuba after the victory?

Allende Yes ... I arrived, and there was Che ... he was lying in the hammock, stripped to the waist, and when I arrived he was having a violent attack of asthma. He was using an inhaler, and, waiting for him to recover, I sat down on the bed and said to him, 'Comandante', but he broke me off, saying: 'Look, Allende, I know perfectly well who you are. I heard two of your speeches during the '52 presidential campaign; one very good, and the other very bad. So, we can talk in complete confidence, because I have a very clear opinion of who you are.' ... We had dinner, and then we went into a room with Fidel to talk. There were peasants playing chess and cards, lying on the floor, machine guns and all ...

Debray You were talking about Fidel. How did the two of you become friends?

Allende In fact, from the first moment. I was impressed by his immense intelligence – an incredible phenomenon that sweeps all before it like a sort of human cataract – and by his candour ...

Debray Differences of opinion?

Allende Yes, fundamental and violent ones.

Debray But always frank.

Allende Always.

Debray How did Fidel react when he heard of the victory of Popular Unity in Chile?

Allende He sent me a copy of *Granma*, the official organ of the Cuban Revolution, which had the news of our electoral victory splashed across the front page. He had been at the offices of the newspaper waiting for the news from Chile, and he sent his congratulations on the front page proclaiming that ours was a victory against imperialism, signed it and had it signed by everyone around him. I keep it as a souvenir.

Castro and Guevara had come after Zapata and Villa in historical time and for that reason their impact was greater in the continent as a whole. Though, through no fault of their own, they never reached the epic grandeur of Bolívar and San Martín. Fidel and Che both dreamed of liberating continents. But the empire they fought was on the ascent, unlike decrepit old Spain.

The twenty-first century might, however, be different. It has begun well in South America. The change in Caracas has brought badly needed relief. The Old Man used to become irritable when yet another visiting foreign journalist sprang the cliche: 'After Fidel, who?' Now he replies: 'After Fidel, Chávez, and after Chávez, Morales, and after Morales our continent will throw up others who will take over the revolutionary baton.'

From the beginning of the Revolution, its leaders emphasised the continental aspect of the struggle. There was a real charge to the Second Declaration of Havana (1962), an angry call to arms that still resonates:

> What is Cuba's history but that of Latin America? What is the history of Latin America but the history of Asia, Africa and Oceania? And what is the history of all these peoples but the history of the cruellest exploitation of the world by imperialism?

Over lunch with Eduardo Galeano in Porto Alegre, we had discussed whether things were getting better in the continent or worse. 'They appear to be getting better,' he said. 'Cuba is less isolated than ever before. The new socialist leaders we've produced – Lula, Chávez, Morales and others – fly in and out of Havana. He lectures them on the change of epoch and avoiding any ultraleft stupidities.'

I make notes on the plane a few hours before it lands. Usually I do this before the actual talk. Historic circumstances permitted certain European countries and the United States to attain a high industrial development level that enabled them to subject and exploit the rest of the world. The Latin American nations were systematically pauperised. The value of their per capita income fell. The dreadful percentages of child mortality grew. Illiteracy exploded. People lacked employment, land, adequate housing, schools, hospitals, communication systems and the means of subsistence. On the other hand, North American investments in Latin America exceeded ten billion dollars. Latin America, moreover, supplied cheap raw materials and paid high prices for manufactured articles. Like the first Spanish conquerors, who exchanged mirrors and trinkets with the Indians for silver and gold, so the United States traded with Latin America. To hold on to this torrent of wealth, to take greater possession of the continent's resources and to exploit its long-suffering peoples: this is what is hidden behind the military pacts and missions and Washington's diplomatic lobbying.

How to construct a counter-hegemony? Not easy. And slightly different from the blandness of 'another world is possible', a slogan that has become too much of a cliché and is especially irritating when mouthed by 'NGO' bureaucrats who desire to change very little, excepting their apartments. The real question is 'After Fidel, what?' Or to put it another way: is the Bolivarian victory in Venezuela simply having an effect on an ageing Cuban Revolution, or might it help repair and build on the existing foundations so that new institutions can be developed to take the process forward?

Cuba must not be left to the tender mercies of the demolition squads waiting patiently in Miami. That would be a political defeat for the entire continent. Miami may not be the same as it was a few decades ago, containing as it does many economic migrants from Cuba, but nests of Cuban fascists are still occupied.

That is not a word I apply loosely, but how else to categorise the radio hosts who spread hatred? In 1994, a discussion on one of these shows elicited the following comments on the topic 'What to do with the leftover communists' after the triumph of the market. The replies from callers included remarks such as 'burn them alive' and 'open the incinerators and throw them all in – men, women and children'. The enlightened compere thanked them politely for their contributions.

28 November

My host is the Cuban Book Institute. As well as a lecture in the Great Hall of the University of Havana, I have been invited to participate in a public tribute to Jean-Paul Sartre, who visited

Havana forty-five years ago. To commemorate the event, the Institute has just reprinted *Nausea*, and there is a moving exhibition of photographs of Sartre and Simone de Beauvoir during their visit in 1960. They spent a month here and I have rarely seen that couple looking so happy in photographs. They appear relaxed, their faces soft and joyful. A few mojitos with Fidel Castro and Che Guevara (who also seem very cheerful) appear to have worked wonders. But it is a revolutionary excitement on Sartre's face that shines through the photographs. Back in Paris, he writes:

What surprises me here is that the troubles began so abruptly. Nothing announced them, not the slightest visible catastrophe. Four years earlier a coup d'etat had brought Batista to power. Few people had protested – they were resigned to the dictatorship by disgust with their prattling and corrupt assemblies.

One day, all the same, July 26, 1953, a young lawyer, Fidel Castro, launched an attack on the Moncada barracks with a handful of comrades. But he was taken, imprisoned, condemned. Public opinion did not give him much support. 'Who is this blusterer? There's an escapade for you! And which leads to nothing. If Batista were angry he would have taken it out on us!'

The opposition parties were quick to blame this rash man who had failed. The Cuban Communist Party spoke of adventurism. The Authentic Party threw up their hands; the Orthodox Party was more severe. Castro was a member of it when he attempted his coup.

'We need a left wing,' said all these mature and reflective men. 'It carries the hopes of the country. On his side, by demagoguery, in order to persuade America that there is freedom of opinion in Cuba, the president tolerates it on condition that it doesn't so much as raise a little finger. Very well! Let's do nothing except be here. Time is working for us! But we don't need an irresponsible kid to risk breaking this equilibrium by an escapade ...'

The Cuban masters of the island, lazy and morose tyrants, were suspicious of knowledge because it led to subversion. The shabby state of higher education was premeditated. To protect the

underdevelopment of the Cuban economy, they tried to produce
in Cuba only underdeveloped men ...

Later, in 1971, like García Marquez and others, Sartre was
angry at the treatment accorded to a homosexual poet Heberto
Padilla, and signed an open letter; the signatories later divided
further into those who remained supportive but critical, and
those who were already on the move to staler pastures and used
Padilla as 'the last straw'. There were to be other 'last straws' in
the years to come. In Latin America, all that was required to
impress Washington was a public denunciation of Cuba as an
evil, authoritarian dictatorship. This was the first hurdle, after
which tickets to a different future became freely available.

Some of us who were or are critical did not feel any urgent
need to desert the Revolution. It is important to restate this
in a world dominated by 'human rights' – as if 'rights' were an
anthropological rather than a juridical norm – in which a majority of human needs are ignored. The West blithely disregards
the rights of others because it is inconvenient to acknowledge
them – the US and Britain in Guantánamo, Abu Ghraib, Falluja,
Basra, Haditha; Israel in its own country as well as occupied
Palestine and Lebanon; France in Haiti and its colonial posses-
sions in Africa.

The human rights industry is, naturally, sympathetic to their
collective dilemma. The hastily appointed professors attached
to US campuses in this new industry have a great deal to say in
defence of 'humanitarian wars', but very little about the horrendous violations of existing laws by those whose largesse led to
their appointments in the first place.

30 November

An informal meeting with Cuban writers and intellectuals at the
Casa de las Américas. A few familiar faces are present, including Lisandro Otero, whose novel *The Situation* is an incredibly
strong evocation of the torpor that gripped bourgeois society in
pre-revolutionary Cuba. Lisandro has just returned from exile
in Mexico City. Here, also, is a gifted veteran of the Revolution,

Fernando Martinez, editor of *Pensamienta Critico* ('Critical Thought') in the sixties – probably the most intelligent political magazine in the Americas, which was 'discontinued' in the early seventies for attempting to live up to its name. The result was a monochrome media, little different from its counterparts in Moscow or East Berlin: predictable, dull, dreary, dry and dead. This was one of the tragedies of the Revolution. Before we can exchange memories, I am asked by a sprightly white-haired woman to explain 'your attitude to our revolution'. I reply: 'It was our revolution, too. We grew up together. My generation fell in love with the Cuban Revolution. It was the lyrical element that appealed to us. The element that conditions the psychology and morals of any society. We read your books, those amazing posters you produced were up on our walls, we reprinted speeches of Fidel and Che in our magazines, we defended you against dogmatic Marxists who did not believe you had made a revolution and against the liberals who believed you had … and because we loved you, we trusted you. Then you betrayed us by going to bed with a fat, ugly, bureaucrat named Brezhnev and you defended the Warsaw Pact invasion of Czechoslovakia and this turn affected your culture and the lyrical element almost disappeared. And so we had to separate.'

There were a few sad smiles and then silence, till my interlocutor spoke again: 'And now?' 'Now,' I replied, 'we are both old. We need each other. It's love in the time of cholera.' After this, the discussion became animated. Questions were asked about the *New Left Review*, and two women present who had known a close friend and colleague when he had spent a year in Cuba in 1962 wanted an explanation as to why his hair had turned white when he was still a twenty-something. I have a number of theories on this, but resisted the temptation.

The colleague they were referring to was Robin Blackburn, and it was appropriate in the circumstances. Political affinities are often the basis of long friendships. I had read Blackburn's seminal essay on Cuba in the *New Left Review* some weeks after arriving in Britain in 1963, and a few years before I first met him. He had started off modestly:

Like other great revolutions, Cuba's is a proclamation that man can make his own history. But this history can only be made within certain material and social conditions. This essay will study these. At this stage, any attempt will inevitably suffer from many limitations and failings. But with this reservation, a historical and theoretical analysis is possible. This essay will, it is hoped, contribute towards one.

He then proceeded to explain the specific circumstances that had delayed the independence of Cuba in the nineteenth century, compared to Venezuela and Bolivia, and suggested that the reason the Creole elite was not too keen to get rid of the Spaniards was because of race more than class: 'The white population was outnumbered by the black: 291,021 to 339,959 by the census of 1817. By comparison, only 2 per cent of the population of mainland Spanish America was African in origin at this date; there were fewer negroes in all the mainland colonies of Spain put together than in Cuba.'

Cuba overflows with history. Its own and that of the rest of South America. José Martí and Simón Bolívar are points of reference for everyone, but the future of the island is uppermost in many people's minds today. The worst may be over, but the 'special period in peacetime', a euphemism for the privations the Cubans had to endure after 1990, has left many traumatised. During a dinner hosted by Fernando Martinez, we discuss frankly the mistakes that were made. If, three or four decades ago, I say to them, any voice had prophesied that by the turn of the next century, the USSR will have collapsed, capitalism will have taken China and Vietnam and Cuba too, and that our dear comrades will have to re-examine the principles for which they fought and made their Revolution, it would have been drowned in hoots of derisive laughter. On this we could agree, and then we talked of bad times.

All were agreed that 'the special period in peacetime' that followed the collapse of the Soviet Union was the worst period in recent Cuban history. Dependent on cheap oil from the Soviet Union, the economy collapsed when the Russians demanded payment in dollars and the Cubans responded 'can't pay, won't pay'. Despite everything, there were no famines (as in North Korea) or mass unemployment (as in East Germany). But some in leading positions who had been so used to following Moscow were quite prepared to ape their Russian and Eastern European counterparts and become the new entrepreneurs, buying the state assets they supervised and amassing private fortunes.

For them, the logic was simple: Let's Miami-ise ourselves to keep Miami out. They even forgot capital's laws of motion, imagining they could deal with their Cuban-American cousins as equals. It was not to be. And it is hardly a secret in Havana that it was the Old Man who stood up and refused to surrender any of the basic gains of the Revolution, insisting that what had been achieved was incompatible with what was being demanded by global capitalism. He won. The 'international community' responded by continuing to punish the country.

In 1993, the Cuba Lobby in the United States (otherwise known as the Cuban American National Foundation) believed that this was the time to tighten the noose and bring about regime change in Cuba. They went on the offensive, with the full backing of President Clinton, then in need of cash and support for his re-election campaign. Clinton obliged the hardliners in the Cuban exile fraternity, as the *Miami Herald* triumphantly explained:

> The decision to punish Castro directly – by cutting off the flow of dollars brought in by families and by limiting the number of charter flights, among other steps – came straight from Clinton. Indeed, the president all but discarded a set of milder options prepared by his advisers in favour of a tougher plan advocated by many exile hard-liners, including Jorge Mas Canosa. That decision was taken at a late-night White House meeting attended by several Cuban-American leaders in Miami … Clinton did more to squeeze the Cuban dictator in a few days than either Republican [president] accomplished during the 1980s.

1 December

I have always been allergic to heritage culture and Potemkin villages. So when I was shown a tiny garden in downtown Havana dedicated to the late Princess Diana, I was taken aback by the surreality of it all. I was also curious. Why in Havana? Simply a desire to appear normal by infecting themselves with the celebrity disease? Or had the Princess turned on the Old Man? My guide smiled but did not venture an explanation. All he said was: 'So I suppose you don't want to see the statue the Church here built to commemorate Mother Teresa?' He was lucky I wasn't driving. It was true that the Albanian nun had been a dear friend of the Duvaliers, *père et fils*, in neighbouring Haiti, but even Baby Doc, when in power, had only honoured her with a medal, not graced her with a statue.

As a result of this, I was slightly apprehensive when invited to visit a brand new showpiece university. Might it be a Potemkin village? Here I was in a total minority. Everybody, including the cynical, insisted I had to go and see it for myself. I did. The site was about fifteen miles outside Havana on the road to Pinar del Río, which I'd already visited, sampling the delights of Cuban eco-tourism. Driving out of the city again, it was difficult not to compare Cuba with its sister Caribbean islands and poor countries in other parts of the world. Despite all the problems, the progress made is visible, and nowhere more so than in this remarkable IT university – designed as a modest leap forward to bridge 'the digital divide' between South and North.

We entered the long driveway and the sculptures came into view; later I saw the giant murals on the walls. The aim is to create an environment in which the appreciation of art in the real world encourages creativity in its virtual counterpart. Sighting some of the older buildings on the campus, I wondered aloud whether it might not have been possible to find a better architect. I was told with a smile that the eyesore was military in origin.

The university had once been the location of the largest Soviet surveillance centre in the Americas. 'From here,' they said, 'the Russians could observe the US president travelling everywhere in his own country and listen in to the conversations between him and his entourage.' The facility had been kept on after the Soviet collapse, with the Cubans now insisting (as the Russians had done in relation to oil) on a high rent payable only in dollars. On a visit to the island in 2000, the Russian president had pledged a long lease on the base, but following 9/11 the US pressured Moscow to close down the station and Putin had agreed, probably in return for some trade-offs in Chechnya and elsewhere. Whether he got what he was promised, the consequences for Cuba have certainly been beneficial.

The Universidad de las Ciencias Informáticas (UCI) – with 3,500 students, half of whom are women, and a staff consisting of 250 lecturers – is ringed by a multi-gigabit fibre-optic cable that provides high-speed capacity to the entire campus. The aim is to create a layer of software innovators and facilities that could service the whole of Latin America. What the Cubans have achieved in medicine is about to be replicated in information technology. 'In connecting to the future we are ensuring the future of the Revolution.' I made this note in my diary, but without specifying whether someone had said this to me or if it was a slogan on a wall. In either case it's a nice thought.

GNU/Linux is the favoured system, which reminds me of Richard Stallman, a free-software guru, who I last met in Caracas several months ago. He was in Venezuela to help Linux the country and had spoken of doing the same in Cuba. 'And China?' I asked. 'Oh,' he said, 'they invited me to Beijing and I told them what we could do. They got quite excited but when I insisted that the GNU/Linux system was free and that they could not charge users, negotiations came to a rapid conclusion. They were just not interested.'

Some weeks prior to this trip, I had been in Pakistan when the massive earthquake had struck. The figures released after the first week (which later turned out to be an underestimate) had indicated the scale of the catastrophe: 50,000 dead, 74,000 injured and at least 3.3 million – far more than after the tsunami – left homeless, virtually all of them in the mountains, where snow begins to fall in November. In Islamabad a relief worker told me 'there is a stench of rotting corpses everywhere. In their midst survivors are searching for food. Local people say that 50,000 have died in this town alone. And more will follow if medicines and food are not equitably distributed.'

The president of Pakistan appeared on state television bemoaning the shortage of helicopters to carry food and sup-plies. In neighbouring Afghanistan, where there was a glut of helicopters, NATO was reluctant to release too many from the war zone. But what about the doctors?

By the time I had left Pakistan the Cubans had sent over a thousand medics, half of them women, which was more than all those despatched by the 'international community'. The Cubans came with their field hospitals and medicines. The women doctors were immediately permitted to treat the peasant women, and conversations between the Cubans and the locals, conducted no doubt through interpreters working for the local intelligence agencies, could sometimes take on a surreal air.

'Where are you from?'

'Cuba.'

'Where is that?'

The Cuban explained the location of the island.

'So you've come a long way. Who is your leader?'

'Fidel Castro.'

'Never heard of him.'

'Would you like to see a photograph?'

It's shown and the beard is greatly admired: 'He could be from near here. They have beards like that in a village twenty miles away.'

In Havana, I was told that some of the doctors had been shaken by the levels of poverty they had observed in the mountain regions of my country. The experience was educative for both sides. Peruvian and Bolivian peasants would have been more familiar with Pakistani conditions.

Cuban medicine is the envy of most continents and the best advertisement for what can be achieved under different social conditions. There are 69,000 doctors in Cuba, tending a population of twelve million. The Latin American School of Medicine (ELAM) established in 1999 is situated in a stunning location on the sea, a former training facility for naval cadets. This site – there are twenty-one others on the island – is for foreign students only. It takes several thousand from every Latin American country and from some in Africa and Asia. And Cuban medicine is a notable export: in Venezuela 17,000 medical students are trained by Cuban doctors, while some 2,000 Cuban doctors work throughout Africa.

During my 2005 visit, I spoke with some students from the Dominican Republic, all of whom were from poor families just like their Afro-American and Hispanic peers from the United States. Earlier that year the first 1,600 doctors had graduated from a six-year course, including Cedric Edwards from New Orleans. I read an interview with him in which he spoke of how he 'loved the fact that regardless of a person's economic situation, he or she can see a doctor and get preventive care, free of charge', and how his studies, like those of his fellow students from Latin America and the Caribbean, were completely free: his modest room-and-board, textbooks and tuition were all paid for by the Cuban state.

In 2004, the US secretary of state, General Colin Powell, aware of the economic plight of Afro-American kids at home, had ensured that when the Bush administration intensified its anti-Cuba policies, an exception clause was written into the economic blockade and travel ban. The seventy-six young people from the United States studying medicine at ELAM could continue to do so, as could future students. The Cubans refer to the university graduates of their country as 'human capital'. What would happen to all this if Miami returned?

'So this is your answer to the School of the Americas,' I muttered to a young Cuban functionary as we left the university. He smiled, but I wasn't totally confident he had understood the reference. I explained. The School of the Americas was a school in Panama, later shifted to Fort Benning in Georgia. Here US instructors, some of them veterans from imperial wars in Korea and Vietnam, educated Latin American policemen and intelligence agents in the most effective forms of torture. The graduates went on to demonstrate their skills in Brazil, Argentina, Chile, Uruguay and Central America.

In the realm of foreign policy, the Cubans usually tread their own path. I met a staggering number of veterans from the Angolan war, the high point of Cuban internationalism, which helped to bring down the apartheid regime in South Africa. In 1975, Fidel Castro decided that the South Africans had to be stopped from pushing through regime change in Luanda, which was their declared aim. The Cubans decided to act. He declared in a powerful speech that in the past many slaves had been transported to Cuba from the Angolan coast and revolutionary Cuba had a debt to honour. It would not allow the Afrikaners to enslave a newly independent Angola.

Contrary to reports at the time, the Russians were not at all pleased by this decision and refused to allow Soviet transport planes to be used. The first Cuban soldiers were flown to Angola on hired British transport planes, which took off from Trinidad and Tobago, whose prime minister, Eric Williams, supported the effort. Later, under US pressure, Williams reluctantly stopped the flights, but by that time other avenues had been found. The Carter administration sent an envoy with a Mafia-style offer to the Cubans: if they withdrew their troops from Angola, the US might lift the embargo. Castro's response was characteristic:

> There should be no mistake – we cannot be pressured, impressed, bribed or bought ... Perhaps because the US is a great power, it feels it can do what it wants and what is good for it. It seems to be saying that there are two laws, two sets of rules and two kinds of logic, one for the US and one for other countries. Perhaps it is idealistic of me, but I never accepted the universal prerogatives of the US – I never accepted and never will accept the existence of a different law and different rules ... I hope history will bear witness to the shame of the United States, which for twenty years has not allowed sales of medicines needed to save lives.

For over a decade, 50,000 Cubans played a decisive role in helping Angola defeat the armies of the Apartheid state. On 23 March 1988, the South Africans launched their last major attack against Cuito and failed. Castro mocked them: 'One should ask the South Africans: 'Why has your army of the superior race been unable to take Cuito, which is defended by blacks and mulattoes from Angola and the Caribbean?'

The Cuban presence accelerated the independence of Namibia as well, and Nelson Mandela's first port of call in Latin America after his release was an emotional visit to Havana in 1991 to pay homage to Cuban internationalism: 'We come here with a sense of the great debt that is owed the people of Cuba ... What other country can point to a record of greater selflessness than Cuba has displayed in its relations to Africa.'

There were some unpleasant side effects, however, which should not be ignored or downplayed. They included the trial of General Ochoa and the de la Guardia brothers (from the elite unit of the ministry of interior). They were charged with corruption, drug-trafficking in league with the Colombian barons, and endangering the security of Cuba. This was the first and, mercifully, the last time that the Cuban Revolution devoured its own. There was much talk that the de la Guardias had been turned by the US during their frequent visits to Miami. If so, the evidence should be made public.

But Ochoa? A veteran of the revolutionary movement, he had fought with the Venezuelan guerrillas during the heyday of armed struggle in South America. He was extremely popular with his soldiers. In his public trial broadcast live on Cuban TV, he pleaded guilty and admitted that drug money had been used, but insisted it was to fund the war against the South Africans rather than for personal gain. It was the executions that angered many inside Cuba and led to another set of defections abroad.

When I raised this subject with a few Cuban veterans of the Angolan war, their eyes became sad. The US press had speculated that Ochoa's popularity (at a time of big changes in Russia) had led to his fall. He was perceived as a successor to Fidel. I did not get the impression that this had much to do with it. Why then the executions? They remain a mystery. Whether or not one supports capital punishment (and I don't), in this case it definitely did not fit the crime.

And what of Cuban culture? The continent as a whole has a rich and vibrant culture stretching back to Bolívar, whose prose had a powerful literary ring and helped to create a tradition that was not easy to repress. There have always been strong links between art and politics – of both right and left – in South America. Mexico's muralists decided on that particular form in order to de-privatise works of art. The giant murals they painted could not be bought and were freely visible to all. Diego Rivera's mural depicting the history of Mexico on the walls of the ministry of education is one of the most remarkable.

Cuba's struggle for independence against Spanish rule was led by a gay poet, José Martí. Domingo Faustino Sarmiento, author of *Facundo*, and Rómulo Gallegos, who wrote *Dona Barbara* and *Canaima*, became the respective presidents of Argentina and Venezuela. More recently, the Peruvian novelist Mario Vargas Llosa unsuccessfully contested the presidential elections in his country on behalf of the respectable right. Poets, too, have been politically engaged, usually on the left – Pablo Neruda, Ernesto Cardenal, Nicolás Guillén, Aimé Césaire, for example. The Uruguayan essayist and critic Eduardo Galeano invented a form of non-fiction storytelling (in *Memory of Fire* and *Open Veins of Latin America*) that took both the Americas by storm. And even Bolivia, where literature was overdetermined by politics, produced its poets and writers, less well known than those elsewhere in South America, but important in the part they played in the political culture of the country.

Brazil, though separated from the rest of the continent by colonial history and language, was no exception in this regard. It produced a rich crop of writers, poets, critics and, later, film-makers. Linguistic unity (barring Brazil) provided Latin America with an intertwined yet diverse political culture that could not be matched by Asia or Africa, and was far more alive than most of what North America had to offer.

Cuba, the last Spanish colony in South America, got rid of its old colonial rulers in 1898 and their US-backed replacements in 1959, but the oppositional function of culture had been in evidence since the last decades of the nineteenth century. Even though the country was largely illiterate, the slaves and free blacks developed their own combination of religion and culture, creating a separate world in which they felt free. That this was not simply escapist was evidenced in the large proportion of black Cubans who led rebellions and participated in the wars of independence, often continuing to struggle after the Creole leaders had accepted a compromise. A number of leading black musicians were executed after black-led uprisings.

The entry of printing presses into the colony in the early years of the nineteenth century provided the basis for a culture independent of the metropolis, and the press (even under Spanish rule), while censored, displayed a vibrancy that reflected the wider culture of the island.

Some of the worst effects of Soviet literary life and norms during the stagnant Brezhnev period were to be deeply felt in Cuba, more in the realm of literature and sexuality than cinema, which fared better. Under the prudent but creative leadership of Alfredo Guevara, the Cuban Institute of Cinematographic Art and Industry (ICAIC) provided a shelter in which a few dozen flowers could bloom.

The presence of a cinematic giant like Tomás Gutiérrez Alea, flanked by colleagues of high calibre, Octavio Gómez and Humberto Solás, helped to defeat the cruder attempts at censorship, and all suggestions that implied rigid, formal, aesthetic criteria were openly defied. At the same time, Santiago Alvarez was developing a documentary film art whose poetry impressed friend and foe. Alvarez utilised the scarcity enforced by the US blockade to great effect: his use of photographs, television clips and old newspapers gave a new life to collage as an art form. Chris Marker and Joris Ivens marvelled at *Now*, *Hasta La Victoria Siempre* and *Hanoi, Martes 13* (Hanoi, 13 March). A stray visitor from Hollywood, Francis Ford Coppola, saw Alvarez's work in the late sixties and commented: 'We do not have the advantages of their disadvantages.'

These days, the ICAIC largely concentrates on organising the Havana Film Festival. I met with some filmmakers during my visit, and while it would be unfair to judge them on the basis of a rushed meeting, the impression I got was that they were working under the constraints of the global market, searching for commercial projects that could get funding from outside and suffering from an over-obsession with producing soaps for the Latin American market. Perhaps there are a few auteurs hidden away somewhere and they will suddenly emerge like the old mole and surprise us all.

Many Cuban novelists, too, challenged the notion that imaginative literature was frivolous or superfluous. The dead weight of Russian bureaucratic and critical traditions could be felt behind some of the criticisms. But the cultural commissars were on permanent watch to weed out all 'anti-state' sentiments or any 'gloomy or filthy' poetry or fiction that portrayed homosexuality. The rationale was borrowed from Tsarist and Stalinist Russia, and even though anti-gay prejudices were the global norm at the time, they were marginally worse in Latin America, where macho culture was especially strong and movements for sexual liberation had not accompanied the growth of far-left or armed struggle groups. Homosexuality was tolerated in its most repressed and secret form, though Alejo Carpentier was known to have suggested in private that homoeroticism was integral to the culture of the Revolutionary Armed Forces.

Much of this has changed. The novelist Abel Prieto, currently the minister of culture, has publicly criticised the persecution of a few poets and novelists in the seventies. He recognises that the artificial world of culture is dominated by mediocrity, and creativity is either submerged or heavily disguised. The novels of Cabrera Infante and Reinaldo Arenas have now been published in Cuba and there is a real attempt to draw a line underneath a past that many regret.

It would be beneficial to the country and its people if a similar attitude was extended to the print media and television. I have always been of the view that revolutions can enhance democracy in a way that is (especially today) forbidden in the capitalist world. Public debate, criticism and the exchange of conflicting opinions will strengthen Cuba and empower and arm its citizens, already amongst the best educated in the world. This is now a political necessity and should not be indefinitely delayed.

The choice in neoliberal times is between the destruction through privatisation of the remarkable system of health, education and culture that has been constructed in Cuba, and the strengthening of the Revolution by preserving its gains and creating an effective internal mechanism that makes the leadership accountable to the people. This will not happen overnight, but it is worth working for.

35

Al Jazeera,
Al Bolivar, Telesur

On 12–13 April 2002 the United States greenlighted a military coup against Hugo Chávez, the elected president of Venezuela. He had obtained almost 60 per cent of the popular vote. Not a single opposition personage challenged the result. Nor did the State Department or the Pentagon. After 9/11, however, Chávez had rejected the whole concept of 'if you're not with us, you're against us' and sharply opposed the invasion and occupation of Afghanistan in 2001. That was enough for him and his country to become targets. Three well-known war criminals based in DC – Elliott Abrams, Otto ('Third') Reich and Charles Shapiro, all Cold War apparatchiks specialising in the political torture of Latin America – set to work, plotting a coup to topple Chávez.

The Creoles in East Caracas started to make more and more noise in the two weeks preceding the coup. The opposition-controlled private TV networks and attached print media began to accuse Chávez of planning to make Venezuela a 'Cuban-style dictatorship'. The reality was, if anything, the opposite. The Bolivarian leadership was promoting a referendum on a new constitution that Chávez had carefully edited to include universal healthcare and free education as social rights due all Venezuelan citizens, in addition to cultural and political rights for all women, indigenous peoples, workers and peasants. Most important, in some ways, was the right of citizens to recall an elected president via a referendum if they obtained a percentage of the popular vote.

A political polarisation was taking place. Chávez was hugely popular. So why not get rid of him? Not by assassination, as with Allende in Chile, but by a massive use of private media, big business and right-wing collaborationist trade union bureaucrats working with the oil industry. The largest private network, Venevision, began to openly agitate for a military coup. A senior general was put on air the day before to demand Chávez's immediate resignation. If he did not do so voluntarily, they might have to use force. They did, but failed. The masses poured down from the mountains, the soldiers refused to accept orders, and within forty-eight hours Chávez was back at the Miraflores Palace, stronger than before. The mechanisms of the attempted coup had been laid bare.

I first raised the idea of setting up a station to counter the Washington Consensus networks at a mass public meeting in 2003, marking the first anniversary of the defeated coup. It was seized on quickly, but the name I suggested – Al Bolivar – was firmly rejected. It was inappropriate, Chávez told me, since it would exclude the largest continental state, which had no links to the Liberator. In the event, Brazil excluded itself. 'Why won't you support Telesur?' Chávez asked Lula. 'I don't know,' he replied, shamefaced. The reason was obvious: he didn't want to antagonise the Brazilian media or annoy Washington.

In 2005, I was back in Caracas for the Telesur launch. The new studio was ready. Everything had been tested and was functioning. We were a few hours away from the press conference announcing the new channel. The minister of information, Andrés Izarra, was a former CNN correspondent who had left the channel after the Chávez electoral triumph and become a media adviser to the radical government. He had risen and was now running the ministry. I asked casually who was going to lead and run the new channel. 'I am,' he replied with a smile. I was taken aback. 'Andrés,' I said, 'you can't be minister for information AND run Telesur.' He was unconvinced. I rushed off to see Chávez. On my way I was buttonholed by the Cubans. They, too, were baffled and pleaded with me to convince Chávez.

He didn't need too much convincing. He had realised it was

a mistake. Izarra was given a choice. The ministry or Telesur? He chose the ministry, then grabbed hold of me and insisted that as the originator of the idea and a member of the advisory board I should announce the new channel to the media and 'please could we have an early breakfast tomorrow?' I spoke to the press, explaining the ideas behind Telesur. Our agenda was to provide an alternative to the globalised networks in terms of both content and images. I repeated what Chávez had said to me: 'If you ask most citizens of our continent they will know the name of their capital city but hardly any of another South American republic. If you ask them what is the capital of the United States they all know the answer. One of our tasks is to explain their continent to them.'

I explained the concepts of Bolivarianism and liberating the air waves. 'Will Telesur be a propaganda network?' asked a Miami radio journalist. I was statesmanlike: 'No more – and I hope less – than CNN, the BBC and the Cisneros private channels.'

At breakfast the next day, Andrés Izarra asked whether I would be amenable to the idea of shifting to Caracas for a few years and running Telesur. I was touched, but it was impossible. My Spanish was primitive. I had too much else on. On this he said: 'You can write books here and travel to wherever you have to go. Just a shift in location.' It was tempting but unrealistic. An Armenian-Uruguayan broadcaster did the job but left after a year or thereabouts. The station moved on and acquired an audience in most parts of the continent.

When I visited again in 2007, the 1960s skyscrapers of Caracas seemed uglier than usual. The Hotel Gran Melia wasn't very appealing either. The kitsch ceiling in the giant lobby was reminiscent of the Dubai School (why does oil wealth seem to result in such bad architecture?), and I wished I was staying, as I normally did, at the shabby, bare, miserable but atmospheric Hilton.

I was in Caracas to speak at a conference on global media networks and to attend a meeting of the Telesur advisory board. The channel had been a modest success, with between five and six million regular viewers. While the privately owned Western channels devoted hours of coverage to US Congressional results or a murder on a US campus, Telesur would announce such events briefly and then devote the rest of the bulletin to, say, live coverage of elections in Nicaragua, or a referendum in Ecuador on the drafting of a new constitution.

The conference centre was packed for Chávez's speech. We exchanged a few pleasantries beforehand. 'You must be happy now that Blair is going,' he said. I pointed out that my happiness was somewhat circumscribed by the succession. 'Long live the Revolution,' he replied, practising his English. Then we settled down for his three-hour address, which was being broadcast live. Occasions like this always make me wish I'd brought a picnic basket.

The speech was not untypical: some facts (for example, that the increase in oil revenues brought about by charging more royalties amounted to a few billion dollars); some homespun philosophy; a bit of autobiography; an account of his most recent conversation with Castro, together with a rough estimate of the total length of time the two men have spent talking to each other (well over a thousand hours); his pride that the Venezuelan government was funding Danny Glover's film about Toussaint L'Ouverture and the Haitian slave uprising; the horrors of occupied Iraq; and a sharp attack on the Pope for suggesting in the course of his recent visit to Brazil that the indigenous population had not been badly treated and had willingly embraced Christ.

An impromptu song, which normally indicates that the speech is nearing its end, followed the denunciation of the Pope, but this time the speech continued. There was a shortish (thirty-minute) historical detour, much of it to do with Bolívar and how he had been let down by men in the pay of the local oligarchy: 'The history books at school never taught us about these betrayals.' Then there was a discussion of planetary survival before the speech ended with a slogan borrowed from Cuba in bad times: 'Socialism or Death'. It's a truly awful message. When I pointed out to one of Chávez's aides how threatening this sounds, he explained that the president was in Rosa Luxemburg mode. What he really meant was 'Socialism or Barbarism'.

Chávez had seemed slightly subdued, and I wondered whether

the audience he'd really been addressing was the army rank and file. The next day, the former vice-president, José Vicente Rangel, told us that there had been a US–Colombian plot to infiltrate Colombian paramilitaries, including snipers, into Venezuela. The aim, he said, had been to create a national emergency: government members and leaders of the opposition would be assassinated and each side would blame the other. A plot to assassinate Chávez involving three senior army officers was uncovered around the same time. Two of the would-be assassins were imprisoned; the third reportedly fled to Miami.

Chávez's military studies had taught him that the enemy must never be reduced to desperation, since this only makes them stronger. His strategy was to offer escape routes. He and his supporters were not vindictive, and the Western media chorus that portrayed his regime as authoritarian was wide of the mark. It was in full voice when I was in Caracas. The cause this time was a privately owned TV station (RCTV) whose twenty-year licence the government had refused to renew. In common with most of the Venezuelan media, RCTV was involved in the 2002 coup against Chávez's (democratically elected) government. The station had mobilised support for the coup, falsified footage to suggest that Chávez supporters were killing people, and when the coup failed didn't show any images of Chávez's triumphant return. A year later they made lengthy appeals to citizens to topple the government during an opposition-engineered oil strike. Again, they were not alone, but their appeals actively encouraged violence.

Asked by a *Guardian* reporter whether I supported the decision, I said I did. He was shocked: 'But now the opposition is without its TV channel.' I asked whether the opposition in Britain or anywhere else in Europe or America had 'its TV channel'? Which Western government would tolerate any of this? Thatcher had refused to renew Thames TV's franchise, when all it had done was show one critical documentary on Northern Ireland. Blair sacked Greg Dyke and neutered the BBC because of Iraq. Bush had the luxury of uncritical news channels and Fox TV as a propaganda network.

At the conference I warned against an obsession with the power of the media. After all, Chávez won six elections despite near-universal media opposition. Evo Morales in Bolivia and Rafael Correa in Ecuador also won despite unremitting opposition. And this wasn't true only of South America. The French had voted against the European Constitution without the encouragement of a single daily newspaper or TV station.

I was booked to leave Caracas on an early morning flight. An Indian, his back bent, a brush in each hand, was cleaning the streets. While waiting at the airport I flicked through the guest book in the VIP lounge. Two messages summed up the contradictions. The first was from the president of Samsung in South America: 'Venezuela is one of the core markets for Samsung. We will continue to invest here and contribute development to this market.' A few entries later: 'Dear President Chávez and Venezuela. Thank you for the love and hospitality of your people. In love and peace. Cindy Sheehan, USA.'

Over the next few years, we discussed an English-language Telesur. The plans were ambitious. A global news centre based in London, etc. Then Chávez died. A pall of gloom descended but the Telesur team were determined to go ahead with the English version. Patricia Villegas, the Colombian broadcaster put in charge, was sharp and determined.

We launched Telesur English in Caracas in July 2014. I flew over to interview President Maduro on various issues. We filmed in Simón Bolívar's house in the old centre of the city. He spoke about the legacy of Hugo Chávez, the Venezuelan opposition, the economy and the most recent world developments. Maduro stressed the importance of recognising democratic rule. 'In 15 years of revolution, we have won eighteen out of nineteen elections, we have built a solid majority based on our projects and on national and international values. The oligarchy ... has a "superiority" complex and has not been able to respect this new majority that was built by Comandante Hugo Chávez.' There was an Israeli massacre going on in Gaza at the time, and Maduro was sharply critical of the Arab leaders for failing to stop the onslaught or help the Gazans.

Patricia had asked me to plan a current affairs/culture show that could go out three days a week. I said once a week would be enough and we should get some other programmes, especially from the United States. This was done and in 2015 Abby Martin took charge of US feature coverage with a striking programme, *The Empire Files*.

I put out *The World Today*, including a revived *Rear Window* as a cultural slot. Some of our old Channel 4 documentaries had been shown on Venezuelan state television and Chávez had particularly liked Galeano's take on South America in *Memory of Fire*. It did feel as if we had revived the *Bandung File* on another continent, and some veterans from the C4 version came to research, direct and edit, together with a new, younger team provided by Christopher Hird and Sandra Leeming at Dartmouth Films, who produced the show. Jenny Morgan, a Bandung stalwart, returned to team up with art historian Julian Stallabrass for two arts series in our *Rear Window* slot, both highly regarded in South America.

On the main part of the show we had a counter-explanation to world politics as viewed by the Western media. I would deliver a thirty-minute talk direct to camera, later changing the format to interviewing activists, intellectuals and writers from all over the world and establishing a unique record of lives not often seen on Western networks. We were not shy of subjecting mainstream documentaries to sharp criticism. When PBS in the States broadcast their over-hyped series by Ken Burns on the Vietnam War, three of us (former C4 editor Rod Stoneman, a South Korean anthropologist and myself) carried out an effective deconstruction that pleased some of those associated with the PBS documentary.

We carried on for nearly five years, until US economic sanctions against Venezuela eventually sabotaged the hiring of US and UK companies. I'm very proud of the work we did for Telesur.

36

Fellow Traveller:
Oliver Stone

In summer 2008, I received a phone call from Paraguay. It was Oliver Stone. He had been reading *Pirates of the Caribbean: Axis of Hope*, my collection of essays on the changing politics of Latin America. He asked if I was familiar with his work. I was, especially the political films in which he challenged the fraudulent accounts of the Vietnam War that had gained currency during the B-movie years of Reagan's presidency.

Stone had actually fought in that war as a US marine, which made it difficult for others to pigeonhole him as a namby-pamby pacifist. Many of his detractors had avoided the draft and were now making up for it by proclaiming that the war could have been won had the politicians not betrayed the generals. This enraged Stone, who detested the simplistic recipes being offered on every aspect of American domestic and external politics. In the original *Wall Street* (1987), for instance, he had depicted the close links between crime and financialised capitalism that ultimately led to the crash of 2008.

The Vietnam War played a large part in shaping Stone's radical take on his own country. One of the most striking scenes in *JFK* (1991), almost ten minutes in length, portrays a talking-heads duo: Jim Garrison (Kevin Costner) and an unidentified military intelligence officer (Donald Sutherland) are walking by the Potomac River in Washington DC, discussing who killed Kennedy. The Sutherland character links the president's execution to his decision to withdraw US troops from Vietnam some months previously. For me, this scene is one of the three finest in political cinema – together with the depiction of French officers calmly justifying torture in Gillo Pontecorvo's classic *Battle of Algiers*, and the Greek far-right plotting to kill the left-wing deputy Lambrakis in Costa-Gavras's *Z*.

A steady flow of critics on the left and the right denounced this scene in *JFK* as pure fantasy. Later research, however, including a biography of one of the Kennedy administration's leading hawks, McGeorge Bundy, has overwhelmingly vindicated the director's approach. The evidence suggests that Kennedy had indeed decided to pull out – largely on the advice of retired General Douglas MacArthur, who told him the war could never be won.

Stone's refusal to accept establishment 'truths' is the most important aspect of his filmography. He may get it wrong, but he always challenges imperial assumptions. That is why he was now in Paraguay, talking to the new president – a defrocked bishop weaned on liberation theology, who had succeeded in electorally toppling the long dictatorship of a single party. Fernando Lugo had become part of the new Bolivarian landscape, one that included Hugo Chávez in Venezuela, Evo Morales in Bolivia and Rafael Correa in Ecuador, flanked by the Kirchners in Argentina and defended by Lula in Brazil.

Stone asked whether we could meet to discuss his most ambitious project, a nine-hour documentary series entitled *The Secret History of America*. A month later, we met up in Los Angeles. He explained why he felt this project was so necessary. There was a shocking lack of information in the country about its own past, he said, let alone in the rest of the world. The receding memory of US citizens was not an accident. 'For decades now the kids are either being taught rubbish pre-packaged as history modules or nothing,' he told me. He regarded this television history as being, in some ways, his most important work. It would present a historical narrative of the United States and how it became an empire. He interviewed me on film for seven hours with a few breaks for water (both drinking and passing). Some of my books were by his side, heavily underlined. It was a stimulating experience, devoid of melancholy or sentimentality on either side. He had a job to do and got on with it.

Until then, I had assumed that Stone's recent tour of South America was part of the *Secret History* project, but this turned out not to be the case. Angered by the crude assaults on the new leaders by US television networks, as well as the print media (the *New York Times* was a serial offender), Stone had decided to offer the much-traduced elected politicians a voice. But he and his producers, Robert Wilson and Fernando Sulichin, now felt the film had become too bogged down on US media terrain.

They asked me to view a rough cut. It was a well-meaning but confusing effort; it simply did not work. Given the scorn Stone's enemies were likely to heap on the film, regardless of its quality, it was best to reduce the number of hostages to fortune. Could it be rescued, Wilson wanted to know? I suggested that the existing structure be discarded; I also suggested the valuable archive and a few interviews should be retained and reinserted in a new version.

In the new commentary they asked me to write, I concentrated on the strengths of the footage Stone had amassed on his whirlwind two-week tour. In contrast to the mesmeric *Comandante* (2003), Stone's filmed interview with Castro, and its follow-up *Looking for Fidel* (2004), this film could be much more playful. *South of the Border* was re-edited as a political road movie with a straightforward narrative. A radical and legendary Hollywood filmmaker, angered by what he is watching on his TV screen, decides to hop on a plane. In moving and simple terms, the documentary stated the case for the changes taking place in South America.

It did not set out to be an analytical, distanced, cold-blooded view of leaders desperate to free themselves from the stranglehold of the Big Brother up north. The film is sympathetic to their cause, which is essentially a cry for freedom, the interviews with the seven elected presidents forming its spinal cord. Chávez was given centre stage, because he was the pioneering leader of the radical social-democratic experiments then underway in the continent. 'If the film convinces people that Chávez is a democratically elected president and not the evil dictator depicted in much of the Western media,' Stone said, 'we will have achieved our purpose'.

It was a tall order but worth a try nonetheless. A typical gringo criticism is that Stone can't even pronounce Chávez's name (he says SHAH-vez, not CHAH-vess). Interesting that this barely ruffled a feather in Latin America. A mispronounced name is the least of their problems. I have yet to meet a gringo (friend or enemy) who can pronounce my name properly, but it's not a reason to regard the person as intellectually impoverished.

There was another view of the film that we encountered from some Latin American academics working in the US – that it was too simple. Here we plead guilty. It was never intended to be a tract or a debate. Stone knows his country and its citizens and their viewing habits: *South of the Border* was designed to raise a few questions in their minds. Not that Europe is a great deal better: the hostility to the Bolivarian leaders was pretty universal in the European media as well, with a few partial exceptions. Strange that a world that bleats on endlessly about democracy has become so hostile to any attempt at economic and political diversity.

Venezuela's late great novelist Rómulo Gallegos wrote in 1935 of Venezuelan history as 'a fierce bull, its eyes covered and ringed through the nose, led to the slaughterhouse by a cunning little donkey'. No longer. What impressed Stone was that the cunning oligarchs of the two-party system had been defeated and that the bull was free.

More than 3,000 people, mostly poor and indigenous, attended the film's premiere in Cochabamba, Bolivia, and cheered their side without restraint. 'They knew instinctively who the baddies were,' Stone told me in New York. 'Unlike here.' The *New York Times* assigned a veteran hack from Reagan-time – a staunch supporter of the Contras – to interview us. Perhaps it was tit-for-tat: they wanted to punish us for the disobliging references to the 'paper of record' in the documentary. At times it felt as if we were being questioned by a Cold War spook after a trip to a forbidden country.

What next? Over dinner at Stone's house, with his Korean partner Sun-jung, their intelligent fourteen-year-old daughter (the real inspiration for *Secret History*) and his feisty eighty-seven-year-old French mother, Jacqueline Goddet, the director asked jokingly whether there were any strong characters left to consider for a movie.

'Lenin or Robespierre?' I inquired hopefully. He turned to his mother, a staunch and devout Gaullist, who couldn't believe her ears. 'Robespierre?' she repeated. 'Assassin!' That in itself would never be sufficient reason for Oliver not to embark on such a project. An old sinner can't be stopped from casting the penultimate stone.

37

In War There Is a Need for Translators

In 2003, I was invited to give the first W. G. Sebald lecture, in memory of the novelist and political thinker, Max Sebald, who ran the translation centre at the University of East Anglia. He had died tragically in December 2001 in a car accident, just as the world was starting to appreciate his unique fiction. The lecture took place at the Royal Festival Hall on a Sunday evening in September.

I last met Max Sebald at a conference of translators organised by the British Centre for Literary Translation at the University of East Anglia in Norwich. It's rare these days for universities in the age of market dominance to encourage such departments and I hope this doesn't stop. Max was a defining figure at that Centre and we met at a conference packed with translators. I had to speak first and I paid tribute to the translators. Many of my own works have been translated and, in some cases, have done much better in foreign languages than in English, which I thought was a tribute to the translator and said so, assuming that this is what the conference had been organised in aid of: to pay tribute or homage to the great translators of the world.

Not a bit of it. Max took the floor and – I can't remember his first sentence – it wasn't exactly 'I hate translators', but it came close. And then we got a riveting account of how bad the translations of his own work had been. Of how, in the case of one of his books, which had been translated into Dutch, the translation was so appalling that he had insisted the entire book be pulped and a new translator hired. He then went on to berate translators for being lazy and not working hard enough. I don't know what the discussions were like in the dining room afterwards, as I had to leave early.

English is not my first language. Until I was about seven or eight I spoke my mother tongue, which is Punjabi. In parts of the subcontinent this is now a written language, but for a long time it was a language that was only spoken and it spawned a rich culture, a rich history, a rich tradition: popular ballads and short songs, poetry of a very high quality, later the Sikh holy book, which was written in Punjabi and incorporated some of the Sufi poems. Soon after I had to learn another language, Urdu, which was imposed on us and became the national language of my country, Pakistan. The new rulers and especially the dominant bureaucracy perceived Punjabi as a threat.

Urdu, a confected language, began to be spoken in the last years of the eighteenth century and the beginning of the nine-teenth in India. A camp language – a language of the military encampments of the great Mogul Empire already in its decline. When Persian was the court language they invented a new lan-guage for commoners, a mixture of Persian, Arabic, Hindi and Sanskrit. Words of every sort were thrown into this language and it became an incredibly potent mix, but to prove you were really adept at speaking and writing it you had to make sure you got in as many Persian words as you could manage. The result was that many of our great poets wrote whole verses in Persian, which few ordinary citizens could understand but which had a tremendous resonance when recited.

We were not allowed to speak Punjabi at school or at univer-sity, because a new state needed a new language and Urdu was to be this language. In the other part of Pakistan where they spoke Bengali, Urdu couldn't be imposed because the Bengalis resisted, saying 'our language is a better language'. There were language riots. What is it about language that excites so much anger, so much fervour? I think the reason for the anger was that people who don't speak the particular language and have it imposed on them or see it becoming a dominant language feel that this is the way power will be exercised. By and large, this is the case in many parts of the world.

If you look at the whole history of which languages have been globally dominant there is the paradox of Chinese, which is the language spoken by the world's most populous country and has been a continuous language in written and spoken form for well over 3,000 years. Chinese made very few inroads anywhere else, but in China it is the language which, I think, will never be displaced. Elsewhere, languages went with empires. As we know, following the displacement of the Greeks and the victory of the Romans, and after the long existence of the Roman Empire, Latin became the dominant language. With the decline of the Roman Empire, the eruption of various warring tribes and, subsequently, the emergence of the Arabs in the early Islamic period as a dominant military presence and later a cultural force, Arabic became the principal language of learning in the Mediterranean lands. It was this language and this Arab culture that produced, probably in the eleventh and twelfth centuries, the first real, organised, systematic school of translators – the school in Toledo where translators from all over the world were brought together and every known work was translated into Arabic. Many of the ancient works of Greek and Roman civilisation, which were no longer being read by anyone since most of Europe was in the Dark Ages, were retranslated. First into Arabic and subsequently into Latin and later vernacular languages from the Arabic.

Prior to the period of Arab rule in the Iberian Peninsula, for 200 years the Arabs ruled Sicily. It's very interesting that even after the Normans took over the island and ruled it for a few hundred years more, Arabic remained a court language for most of the period. The tuition of the princes, the language of learning, the language in which many of the property registers were compiled, remained Arabic. Its influence lasted a long time after those who had brought it to Sicily had lost political power. So languages can drift on longer than power.

That's what we saw with Arabic and subsequently Turkish, which displaced Arabic during the Ottoman period. But interestingly enough the Ottoman Empire could never impose, nor did it seek to impose, Turkish on all the regions and kingdoms of the empire, which were vast. Most local languages survived because this was a very centralised empire. Since everything was done centrally, the rulers felt no fear, no threat, from people speaking Arabic in what is now the Arab world, or speaking many of their native dialects in what are now the different countries in the Balkans. Modern Greek also survived, even though the official language remained Turkish. This is probably one of the few episodes in human history where an empire has not sought to impose a language.

By the time the nineteenth- and twentieth-century empires came around, the French and the British were very careful because language by then had become a very rare commodity. It was a route to power and to further education, so it was rationed. During the whole period of the British Empire in India, language was very carefully restricted. The famous 'minute' of Lord Macaulay – the 1835 minute on education – said that English could only be provided to a small, elite layer in the country. And for good reason. They feared that if English was made available to the entire population of a multi-millioned subcontinent, the end of the Empire would come much sooner. This was quite rational, logical imperial thinking. If everyone can read and write, and study, say, the works of John Stuart Mill, who was very popular in the nineteenth century, then ideas of liberty and freedom and the greatest happiness of the greatest number begin to spread – and once that happens it's very difficult to keep a whole population down. Educating the elite in that sense happened, but later and under imperial control.

The reason English, unlike French, did not go into decline after the fall of the British Empire was because another empire had been waiting in the wings for a long, long time. Once this empire became dominant, which it began to do after the Second World War, English became a crucial language. Of course, in Eastern Europe, Russian was the main second language, but secretly, here too, people learnt English – as they did in East Germany, despite the fact that they could tune in to West German radio stations and later television. Here as elsewhere in the world the feeling was that the United States was the dominant empire and the language this empire spoke had to be understood. Many people wanted to hear and understand it to make up their minds for themselves, without being told that the empire was doing right or wrong. And so large numbers of people began to learn English secretly – even in remotest North Korea in the 1970s.

French, however, having once been the diplomatic language par excellence, went into very sharp decline, so that now we have a strange situation that many of you who work in or are associated with publishing houses will recognise. There has been a deep shift in French culture. Whereas thirty or forty years ago, French intellectuals of right and left were not very interested in whether or not they were translated into English, today there is a permanent queue of French authors desperate to be translated into the dominant imperial language. They want to be read in the United States because that is where power lies.

This relationship between language and power confronts us today as we stand at the crossroads of an unusual epoch in world history where not only is one empire dominant but it is the only empire. All the main rivals have been defeated, scattered to the winds, submerged like Atlantis. Capital is triumphant everywhere, and there is only a single powerful empire, with a military presence in 121 countries in a world that only has 191 member states in the United Nations. The domination of this empire has meant a new wave of English spreading. So those of us who were fortunate enough to be colonised by the British are now giggling at the Algerians and the Senegalese. In fact, when we were growing up, this used to be the big joke amongst some of us. We used to say, 'God, I wish the French had colonised us rather than the British.' And people used to say 'why?' Well, we would have had wonderful wine, wonderful food, Napoleon rather than the dreaded Wellesley – it would all have been different, you know, the language of Baudelaire, we would have all have been speaking like that, etc. But that debate is over. Nobody can think it anymore.

I was also wanting, in this lecture, to discuss a different side of language. The language which was formative in developing English culture, especially the art of understatement, which Anthony Powell once wrote affects all social classes on this island. What are the origins of the lack of flourishes that differentiates modern English from the Latin languages and even German? A seventeenth-century pamphlet might provide a clue. The decades between 1640 and 1663 saw pamphleteering on a massive scale in England. Twenty-five thousand pamphlets were produced on various subjects and one bookseller in the London actually stocked them all because they were bought and sold out very quickly. One of them was a wonderful 1646 pamphlet written by John Wilkins titled 'Ecclesiastes or a Discourse concerning the gift of preaching as it falls under the rules of Art'. I do feel all our politicians and academics would benefit if they put Wilkins's precepts into practice:

> It [preaching] must be plain and natural!, not being darkened with the affectation of Scholasticall harshnesse, or Rhetoricall flourishes. Obscurity in the discourse is an argument of ignorance in the minde. The greatest learning is to be seen in the greatest plainness. When the notion is good, the best way to set it off, is in the most obvious plain expression. And it will not become the Majesty of a Divine Embassage to be garnished out with flaunting, affected eloquence. How unsuitable it is to the expectation of a hungry soul, who comes unto this ordinance with desire of spiritual comfort and instruction, and there hear onely a starched speeche full of puerile worded Rhetorik? Tis a sign of low thought and designs when a man's chief study is about the polishing of his phrase and words. Such a one speaks only from mouth and not from his heart.

This tradition of English, as a striving for immediacy and direct contact through an easy style, was fairly common and pronounced during the monarchy-free period of the English Commonwealth. You see it in John Bunyan's great work *A Pilgrim's Progress*, in the best possible way. By and large, I think this tradition has lasted. You have Byron and you have Sterne, who can get away with long, never-ending, very brilliant sentences, but by and large the English spoken in the seventeenth century and discussed then has come to play a big role, and a good thing it is too. Many, many years later, Chekhov in a letter to Gorky said exactly the same thing as this seventeenth-century pamphleteer was saying to his contemporaries: 'forget the flourishes, just stick to the basics, avoid the adjectives and bad language'.

The key point in terms of translation, and its importance, doesn't need to be stressed. It is that it's the only way in a culture increasingly dominated by English that you get to hear or read what people are writing or making in their countries. Films with subtitles are one example, novels are another. How many great novels are there in other cultures that we do not know about because they have not been translated into English?

Increasingly, the effect of this even on other cultures, whether it's Brazil or Taiwan or Japan, India or Africa, is exactly the same. There's a desire to aim for the same success, to mimic that success, and I know publishers, very good ones, in different parts of the world who each week, each month, look at the bestseller list in the *New York Times*. Whether the books on that list are of any interest to their local readers is beside the point. They decide whether they can make an offer for these books and it's assumed that if they sell in the United States they will automatically sell in countries A, B, C, D, E, X, Y, Z. Do they? We don't know, statistics on this delicate matter aren't often published, but I would doubt it. I mean, some things obviously are universal but there are others which are very particular to the cultures that produced them.

This absolute desire to mimic success leads to the translation of many works of indifferent quality. They are translated simply because they happen to be on the best-seller list of the principal organ of the United States, which is the *New York Times*. I think this is a dangerous route. It's not a good way of developing a world literature and a world culture in which we learn from each other, as world literature and world culture have always allowed us to do.

This brings me to a subject very dear to my heart, which is the delight of poetry. Even though I don't write it I enjoy it enormously. We all know how difficult it is to translate a poem from another language. I've often failed when I've tried to do it, but you sometimes have to because poetry for many cultures represents their heart and their soul if you like. In many countries, to understand the people and their culture you still have to understand their poetry.

I remember when, many years ago, I was just starting university in Pakistan and we used to have massive poetry readings where you would have six or seven big poets, respected poets, and ten thousand people gathering to listen. The poetry reading would start after nine or nine-thirty in the evening, and go on until the early hours, and then everyone went and had breakfast and discussed what they had heard. Then a military dictatorship established its grip on the country and suddenly critical poetry went into decline. Some of the poets were arrested, others were scared. I remember going to a poetry reading some months after the dictatorship was imposed in 1958 to hear a very great Punjabi poet, Ustad Daman. He was busy reciting love poems and poems about animals and some of us were fed up; we were very young, and a few in the audience heckled him with an appeal to 'say something, just say something'. He lost his temper, because poets, like anyone else, don't like being heckled; he finally recited an extemporary poem, as they often did at these big events. After a certain time all the poems were extemporaneous – it almost became a poetry competition where the masses were the judge; the loudest applause meant this poet was very successful. So when we shouted 'say something' Daman lost his temper. But he recited a wonderful couplet in Punjabi, which went like this – in Punjabi first, just to give you the rhythm of the words:

> Hun ho gyan maujan hi maujan,
> jidr tako, faujan hifaujan

I see that a few Punjabi speakers in the audience are smiling. Translate this into English, which I did, and it's not as good. Even though I understand the poem perfectly, it translates much softer than in the original. Listen to it:

In War There Is a Need for Translators

> Now each day is sweet and balmy
> Wherever you look it's the army.

Which is quite funny and nice but the word *maujan* means more than sweet, it goes deep, it's pleasure/ecstasy, and *maujan* rhymes with *faujan* which means 'armies'. So, I know from personal experience how difficult translating poetry is and yet people do it. I think the great translations of poetry written in non-English languages come largely from people who are poets themselves. It's poets working together with literal translators from that language who sometimes produce the best translations.

The best translations of Faiz Ahmed Faiz (the greatest of Pakistani poets) were not those produced by my old comrade, Victor Kiernan, a great English scholar of Urdu and Persian, but those by Agha Shahid Ali, a Kashmiri poet resident in the United States who died tragically in 2001. Shahid understood the rhythms of the poetry in Urdu and was successfully able to transmit as much of that rhythm as possible into English. That is what one constantly looks for, and when the magic works the results are exhilarating, inspiring the translator to new heights of creativity.

In a stunning essay, the Peruvian scholar Efrain Kristal has recently reminded us of a classic case: the translation of the Latin American poet César Vallejo's work into English. And the translator? He once described himself as 'a paid hack for UNESCO' – a man called Samuel Beckett. It was Beckett who translated Vallejo's amazing poems into English, a translation that later found a reflection in the character of Lucky in *Waiting for Godot*. How did this happen? Simple. It was while he was working on *Godot* that he was translating Vallejo. It left its mark on him. It's not just the poetry; it's almost as if the tender and compassionate pessimism of the Latin American poet found an echo deep inside Beckett himself, because that's what *Waiting for Godot* is, a very tender and compassionate, but also pessimistic and bleak, view of the world and of the infinite capacity of human beings to do mischief to each other. This is Lucky's philosophical speech in *Waiting for Godot*:

Given the existence of a personal god who from the heights of divine apathy loves us dearly with some exceptions and suffers with those who are plunged into torment – and considering that as a result of labours left unfinished that man in spite of strides in alimentation and defecation is seen to waste and pine and shrink and dwindle and considering that in the plains and the mountains the air is the same and the earth, the earth a bode of stones, the tears, the stones so blue so calm on the skull alas abandoned unfinished the skull the skull alas the stones.

The metaphor of the human skull as a blue suffering stone comes straight out of Latin American poetry. César Vallejo's most celebrated poem starts like this, translated by Beckett:

Considering, coldly, impartially that man is sad and coughs.

And when, later in *Godot*, Lucky is taken with a rope and beaten by others who punish him for no rhyme or reason, you also find an echo in Vallejo's poetry, translated by Beckett:

– they beat him, everyone,
without him doing anything to them;
they gave it to him hard with a stick and hard

also with a rope. Witnesses are
the Thursday days and the humerus bones, the loneliness, the
    rain, the roads –

Kristal insists that many of these gifted Latin American writers and poets were the pupils – not directly, but in a literary sense – of the great Nicaraguan poet, Ruben Dario. Dario was the first poet in the Spanish language to break with all the codes and traditions of that language and produce modernist poetry on a very high level, putting Latin American Spanish way ahead of Spanish as it was written in Spain itself. Vallejo nourished himself on Dario's work and Beckett learned from Vallejo, and that's the best way for a cultural synthesis to take place. It's this synthesis that we enjoy and that takes creativity to a higher level and which helps us to live in a world that is otherwise quite bleak. The power exercised by poetry came back to me when I was writing my two non-fiction books, *The Clash of Fundamentalisms* and *Bush in Babylon*, and I want to explain why.

The conflict between the Arab world and the West arguably would not exist had it not been for a geological and geographical accident – the fact that the bulk of the world's cheap oil lies underneath lands that are inhabited by Muslims. Had it not been for this I don't think Islam would have played much of a part in the culture of the modern world, whether as inspirer or bogey. What has kept Western interest in Islam alive throughout the twentieth century has not been the religion but the oil. And this goes on.

I get very fed up when I hear pundits who should know better – people like Bernard Lewis who actually reads Arabic – saying that the Arabs as a people are incapable of subjecting themselves to criticism. Now this could apply to politicians who are mainly there because the West put them there or keeps them there, but as far as the writers and poets of the Arab world go, nothing could be further from the truth. I want to beg your indulgence and read to you a poem just to show that sometimes poetry works wonderfully well in translation even if it's not an exact replica of what was written and even if the translation cannot replicate its rhythms. One can still get part of the way. The poem is by the great Syrian poet Nizar Qabbani, who wrote it after the defeat of 1967 – the biggest defeat suffered by Arab nationalism. Qabbani was exploring why this had taken place and the poem is one of the most vivid and imaginative pieces of self-criticism in modern Arab literature. It's very critical, that's why I want to quote it at length. So here is 't):

1

Friends,
The old word is dead.
The old books are dead.
Our speech with holes like worn-out shoes is dead.
Dead is the mind that led to defeat.

2

Our poetry has gone sour.
Women's hair, nights, curtains and sofas
Have gone sour. Everything has gone sour.

3

My grieved country, in a flash
You changed me from a poet who wrote love poems
To a poet who writes with a knife.

4

What we feel is beyond words:
We should be ashamed of our poems.

5

Stirred by Oriental bombast,
By boastful swaggering that never killed a fly,
By the fiddle and the drum,
We went to war
And lost.

6

Our shouting is louder than our actions,
Our swords are taller than us,
This is our tragedy.

7

In short
We wear the cape of civilisation
But our souls live in the stone age.

8

You don't win a war
With a reed and a flute.

9

Our impatience
Cost us fifty thousand new tents.

10

Don't curse heaven
If it abandons you,
Don't curse circumstances.
God gives victory to whom He wishes.
God is not a blacksmith to beat swords.

11

It's painful to listen to the news in the morning.
It's painful to listen to the barking of dogs.

12

Our enemies did not cross the border,
They crept through our weakness like ants.

13

Five thousand years
Growing beards
In our caves.
Our currency is unknown,
Our eyes are a haven for flies.
Friends,
Smash the doors,
Wash your brains,
Wash your clothes.
Friends,
Read a book,
Write a book,
Grow words, pomegranates and grapes,

Sail to the country of fog and snow.
Nobody knows you exist in caves.
People take you for a breed of mongrels.

14

We are thick-skinned people
With empty souls.
We spend our days practising witchcraft,
Playing chess and sleeping.
And we the 'Nation by which God blessed mankind'?

15

Our desert oil could have become
Daggers of flame and fire.
We're a disgrace to our noble ancestors:
We let our oil flow through the toes of whores.

16

We run wildly through streets
Dragging people with ropes,
Smashing windows and locks.
We praise like frogs,
Swear like frogs,
Turn midgets into heroes,
And heroes into scum:
We never stop and think.
In mosques
We crouch idly,
Write poems,
Proverbs
And beg God for victory
Over our enemy.

17

If I knew I'd come to no harm,
And could see the Sultan,
I'd tell him:

In War There Is a Need for Translators

'Sultan,
Your wild dogs have torn my clothes
Your spies hound me
Their eyes hound me
Their noses hound me
Their feet hound me
They hound me like Fate
Interrogate my wife
And take down the names of my friends,
Sultan,
When I came close to your walls
And talked about my pains,
Your soldiers beat me with their boots,
Forced me to eat my shoes.
Sultan,
You lost two wars.
Sultan,
Half of our people are without tongues,
What's the use of people without tongues?
Half of our people
Are trapped like ants and rats
Between walls.'
If I knew I'd come to no harm
I'd tell him:
'You lost two wars
You lost touch with children.'

18

If we hadn't buried our unity
If we hadn't ripped its young body with bayonets
If it had stayed in our eyes
The dogs wouldn't have savaged our flesh.

19

We want an angry generation
To plough the sky
To blow up history

To blow up our thoughts.
We want a new generation
That does not forgive mistakes
That does not bend.
We want a generation of giants.

20
Arab children,
Corn ears of the future,
You will break our chains.
Kill the opium in our heads,
Kill the illusions.
Arab children,
Don't read about our windowless generation,
We are a hopeless case.
We are as worthless as watermelon rind.
Don't read about us,
Don't ape us,
Don't accept us,
Don't accept our ideas,
We are a nation of crooks and jugglers.
Arab children,
Spring rain,
Corn ears of the future,
You are a generation
That will overcome defeat.

This was written in 1967 and the poem was immediately memorised. Every taxi driver, every tea café knew it. It was banned. The great Egyptian singer Um Kalthoum, who used to sing Qabbani's poetry, wasn't allowed to sing this one until many years later. For a while Qabbani himself was banned and his work wasn't published. But then he came back again. The poem lived, the poetry lived, because it didn't need official transmission channels. It went from country to country, it crossed borders, and that is how poetry has affected not just the Arab world but also for a long time the Indian subcontinent, China, the former Soviet Union and Russia still, where you know the joke used to be that poetry was so highly regarded by Stalin that the punishment for a really good poem was execution for the poet.

And the American translator of the great Arab novelist, Abdel-rahman Munif, can't translate any more fiction because he's been seconded to the Pentagon.

In times of war, you see, there is a great need for translators.

Part 2: Politics and Literature

38

The Case against
Tony Blair

On 7 July 2005, the murderous chaos of Blair's war in Iraq came home to London in a lethal series of suicide bombings. I made this point in a piece in the *Guardian* the following day, and got more flack than usual. Two weeks later, with apparent impunity, security forces shot dead Jean Charles de Menezes, a young Brazilian electrician on his way to work. The terror attacks in London, and the descent into apparently endless war in the Middle East that sparked them, marked a watershed in British political culture. How many of the Labour voters celebrating victory on that beautiful spring morning in May 1997 anticipated that it would come to this? On BBC Radio 4's *Any Questions* the week after, I denounced the Menezes killing as a public execution designed to create fear. The police said it was a mistake, and that they thought Menezes was a Muslim. But would killing a Muslim have been any better? A 'shoot to kill' policy had backfired.

New Labour's socioeconomic trajectory had been predictable. The plan was laid out with bullet-point clarity in *The Blair Revolution*, put out by Peter Mandelson and Roger Liddle in 1996: the free-market Thatcherite model would be maintained, ameliorated by a few low-cost anti-poverty measures. The revolution of 'choice' would be pushed through in the health and education services. The criminal justice system would be toughened up.

In 1994 I predicted in the *New Statesman* that Blair's project would transform Labour into a British version of the US Democratic Party. Shortly after the 1997 Labour victory, Blair suggested that it was time 'elections fought on the basis of ideology and politics' were brought to an end. This was not a case of betrayal; if anything had been betrayed it was the illusions others had about Blair. He never claimed to be a supporter of Nye Bevan or Anthony Crosland. Reviewing Sir Geoffrey Howe's memoirs in the *Financial Times* a year or so before the 1997 election, Nigel Lawson concluded: 'Mrs Thatcher's true successor is currently Leader of the Opposition.'

The pretence of 'no politics' and 'no ideology' was nonsense. In his first days in office Gordon Brown had sent a clear message to the City by handing command over interest rates to the Bank of England. As Seumas Milne pointed out, in one of the sharpest and most prescient critiques of the Blair project (published in the *LRB* while much of the country was giddy with euphoria), there was a very clear political goal:

> Within three weeks of the Party's election victory, four prominent businessmen had been appointed or approached to join or advise the Government: Sir David Simon, Chairman of BP, to become European Competition Minister; Martin Taylor, chief executive of Barclays Bank, to lead a Whitehall task force on tax and benefits; Lord Hollick, chairman of United News and Media, to advise on industrial policy; and Peter Jarvis, Whitbread Chief Executive, who was asked to head the Low Pay Commission, charged with setting the rate for the planned legal wage ... There is no question that the crowning of New Labour represents a historic break ... For the New Labour advance guard – Blair, Peter Mandelson and their closest supporters – that means an unconditional embrace of the new rules of the globalised economic game, with its privatised, deregulated, free-fire zones for multinational business, along with the new balance of power that goes with it, both at home and abroad.

Blair's hyper-militarism was not so easy to foresee – though there was a premonition of it in the whipping of the Labour Shadow Cabinet to produce unanimous support for Clinton and Major's 1996 air strikes on Iraq. In office, Blair's first blooding was again in the skies over Iraq. Operation Desert Fox, unleashed in December 1998 as Clinton faced impeachment charges, blasted a hundred targets in southern Iraq over the course of seventy hours; it was just the start of the bombing campaign that would continue more or less uninterrupted until Operation Iraqi Freedom.

Mere months later, in the spring of 1999, Blair would be baying for a full-scale military invasion of Yugoslavia. At this point it became clear that he was excited by war. He liked being surrounded by military men. He liked the smell of blood. But the driving force was political. I am often asked by anti-war activists – leftists and liberals in the United States especially – what explains Tony Blair. How can a Labour prime minister adopt the position of a neoconservative Bushite so rapidly, and with such fervent conviction? Is there a psychological explanation? Is it religion? My response is that though character and religion may play a part, the answer lies in politics.

That analysis has certainly passed the test of time. Blair believes in the dogmas of the Washington Consensus. He sees the Atlantic Alliance as the cornerstone of British foreign policy and as vital to preserving Britain's position in Europe and the world. There is no radical streak in his political make-up. A manipulator of public opinion, he would trample on the popular mood if it did not accord with his views. Religion may have helped to provide the burning eyes and fake humility that served him well in speeches, but Mammon is a worldly god. Blair is a natural pander, and will always make up to those richer and more powerful than he. Politically, that means Washington. Financially, anyone willing to pay.

The key to Blair's foreign policy was very simple. It was revealed in words of one syllable to Christopher Meyer, Blair's new ambassador to Washington in 1997, by Jonathan Powell, the prime minister's Chief of Staff. On his appointment, so Meyer explained to Blair's biographer, Powell gave him the following advice: 'Your job is to get up the arse of the White House and stay there.'

Maintaining this cosy, even intimate position was the lodestar of Blair's strategy. 'Whither thou goest, I will go,' he is famous for having vowed to Clinton during an after-dinner speech at the height of the Lewinsky affair. But as he packed his bags, Clinton made clear to Blair that this was not just personal. It was the British premier's duty to forge an equally close relationship with the 44th president, whoever it might be.

Blair had some rocky moments initially, as the Bush administration made clear that it had little interest in this middle-ranking Atlantic state. In 2001, Britain was anyway convulsed by petrol protests and foot-and-mouth disease. But as the B52s stuffed with daisy cutter bombs revved up for Operation Enduring Freedom, Blair went into hyperdrive. The war on terror was his war. He would see it through to its apocalyptic end. A secret Downing Street memorandum from 23 July 2002, leaked to *The Sunday Times*, revealed more about Blair's real thinking on Iraq than anything his speechwriters had been able to confect.

It confirmed that, by July 2002, Bush had decided to go to war and had confided in Blair. Both these rogues set about devising plans to do so effectively. There was a perceptible shift in attitude. Military action was now seen as inevitable. Bush wanted to remove Saddam through military action, justified by the conjunction of terrorism and WMD. But the intelligence and the facts were being fixed around the policy. Blair's main concern was how to manipulate the situation so the White House could get what it wanted. His government would 'work on the assumption that the UK would take part in any military action'. But the key issue was to have 'the political strategy to give the military plan the space to work'.

It's clear that God had little part to play in these calculations. Far more central was the need to remain embedded in the president's nether regions. This was the level of strategic thinking that lay behind the invasion of Iraq and the bloody military occupation that followed – and which blew back in the tragic events of 7 July 2005. This disastrous foreign policy was pursued against the background of a hollowed-out national political life, and the solidification of a government–media consensus that precluded serious public debate about the country's direction. By 2005, a 'model' neoliberal economy reigned supreme. An unrepresentative, unreformed electoral system; a foreign policy whose loyalty to Washington was comparable, in the novelist John Lanchester's memorable phrase, 'only to the coital lock which makes it impossible to separate dogs during sex'; the right to a jury trial and the presumption of innocence under heavy attack; an authoritarian social agenda; a conformist media, shamelessly used as a propaganda pillar for the new order – these became the principal characteristics of Blair's Britain.

To these can be added the broader homogenisation of national culture, with BBC managers desperately aping their commercial rivals; the virtual death of an indigenous cinema; the market-realist transformation of British publishing by global conglomerates; the ghettoisation of all thought that does not produce quick profits; and the takeover of the universities by assessment-driven management dogma, in which academics are encouraged to refer to their students as 'customers'. Political life in Britain had increasingly come to resemble that of a banana monarchy.

The transformation of the Labour Party was part and parcel of this. Thatcher's electoral successes had first traumatised and then hypnotised her supposed Labour opponents. She had transformed the Conservative Party, marginalising its patricians and pushing it in a Poujadist direction from which it never recovered. Tired of being defeated by Thatcher, Labour's leadership decided to mimic her success. In Blair they found the perfect cross-dresser. Awestruck by Thatcher, the Blairites aped her achievements within their own party. The party conference, once a reflection of a vigorous internal debate that permitted ordinary members a voice, was totally recast. Presentation drowned what little politics still prevailed inside the party and journalists were reduced to recording the exact time of standing ovations. The trade unions, promised a few stale crumbs, went along with the great transformation.

Thatcher's abrasiveness alienated the liberal intelligentsia. Astonishing to recall now, but in those days a majority of Oxford dons had deemed themselves independent enough to vote against giving the prime minister an honorary degree. The Blairites had no desire to reverse any of Thatcher's measures, but they saw her style as too harsh, too divisive. One had only to think of Norman Tebbit. New Labour, however, produced its own Tebbit in the shape of David Blunkett. Obsessed with pleasing *Daily Mail* and *Sun* readers, he soon became narcissistic about his own tough-guy image. He would show criminals and asylum seekers who was master. The tabloids built him up as the strongman of the junta.

Presentation and spin became a central feature. Labour's metamorphosis into a party whose programme was virtually indistinguishable from the Conservatives (and in some respects – wars, arts, tuition fees – worse than that of the Major government) did not provoke any rebellion within its ranks. The left had been crushed in the early 1980s. The trade unions had been brought to heel and the party itself was ready for any kind of Faustian pact, as long as Blair could get them into office. Some, no doubt, genuinely believed that the shift was merely cosmetic. Once in power, Labour would revert to its old Keynesian ways. Others, including converts from the old left, were in more 'realistic' mode. Capitalism was the only game in town and the rules had to change accordingly. The same dogma that had once characterised their Trotskyism or other isms was now put in the service of capital; former Cabinet ministers Milburn and Byers spring immediately to mind, but they were not alone.

There was some initial recoil. In the summer of 1997 I encountered a senior Cabinet minister, a genial old Labour frontbencher, in a bookshop on Museum Street in Central London. 'What's it like?' I inquired. In response he held his nose. 'That bad?' 'Worse,' he said, 'worse than even people like you could imagine.'

Slowly, the Blairites helped their colleagues to squeeze the old ideas out of themselves, drop by drop, until they woke up to find that the blood coursing through their veins was that of the living dead. They happily went along with everything that was done. Accepting donations from Bernie Ecclestone to the party coffers and, as a consequence, delaying the ban on tobacco advertising? Fine. Private Finance Initiatives in the public services? Fine. Selling off schools suffering from financial undernourishment? Fine. The same applied to the war on Yugoslavia and the invasions of Afghanistan and Iraq.

The Parliamentary Labour Party, with few exceptions, swallowed every bitter and nauseating pill that Blair and Alastair Campbell forced down its collective throat. If government ministers felt angry and humiliated, a combination of timidity and prudence sealed their lips. They knew full well that the knacker's yard beckoned, yet virtually none resigned. Most would only leave when pushed. Afterwards the rage poured out, but it was too late to be of any use.

Presiding over this constellation was the Dorian Gray–like figure of Tony Blair; the heavy make-up no longer concealed the cracks and fissures. 'New, new, new, everything new,' the Boy Leader is reported to have said, soon after taking office. It's true that, if Labour's socioeconomic agenda was essentially an unpleasant amalgam of Thatcher and Clinton, there was something genuinely new in the degree of control over governmental processes. Blair's grip on state, media, church and party was unprecedented. Thatcher's Cabinet had included some heavyweights, who ultimately brought her down. From the beginning, Blair's Cabinet – with the exception of Gordon Brown – was a weak and enfeebled outfit. It became even more so once Cabinet ministers or their civil servants had to clear everything with Alastair Campbell or Jonathan Powell.

Thatcher had always had a substantial section of the media and the intelligentsia against her. She was anathema not just to the Oxford dons but to most of the country's writers and academics as well as the programme-makers at Channel 4 and the BBC. Though she had the backing of the Murdoch and Rothermere empires, the *Guardian, Mirror, Observer* and *Independent* were always hostile. Blair, by contrast, enjoyed virtually unanimous support from the *Sun* and the *Economist* leftward. In the 2001 election he had the backing of the whole Murdoch stable – *The Times, Sunday Times, Sun, News of the World* – as well as the *Economist, Financial Times, Independent, Guardian, Express* and *Mirror*. The *Daily Mail* stayed silent. The *Telegraph* alone called for a Tory vote. This consensus only hardened as the Blair government lurched from one war to the next.

'Christianity is a very tough religion,' wrote Blair in 1993. 'It is judgemental. There is right and wrong. There is good and bad. We all know this, of course, but it has become fashionable to be uncomfortable about such language.' Under his aegis, it became fashionable to be entirely comfortable about it. Religion does not explain Blair's warmongering, but it helped to characterise its tone. Blair was undoubtedly the most religious prime minister that Britain had thrown up since Gladstone. Not only does the deity exist, but a muscular Christianity was needed to fight on His behalf. A Republican in the United States, a Christian Democrat in Europe – on this side of the Channel the divine being was definitely New Labour.

Blair's inner circle was deeply tinged with the New Christianity. Thrusting young careerists, dreaming of a safe parliamentary seat when the old codgers died off, soon began to discover a deep spiritual gap in their lives which could only be filled with some form of Christianity. British society remained thoroughly secular, however, and Blair's advisers kept a wary eye on the packaging of his faith. When, in the run-up to the Iraq War, Blair wanted to conclude a TV address to the nation with the words 'God bless you,' there was a revolt from the assembled aides – Powell, Campbell, Mandelson, Hunter, etc. He ended his speech with a limp 'Thank you'.

Unlike Thatcher, Heath or Wilson, Blair deliberately tried to abandon a political vocabulary. In its place there was a great deal of vacuous moralism and, of course, religion. As prime minister, Blair had some thespian talent and could perform in a range of different registers, from the blokeish 'I'm just an ordinary guy', to the army chaplain speeding the troops to their death, to his trademark 'I honestly believe'. Hard truth, always difficult for politicians, was replaced with the facile simulacrum of sincerity.

In 1997, some 13.5 million voted Labour (already fewer than the fourteen million who had cast their ballots for John Major in 1992). In 2001, the Labour vote was down to 10.7 million. In 2005, it sank still further to 9.5 million – barely a fifth of the overall electorate. Thanks to the winner-takes-all electoral system, however, these falling votes continued to deliver overwhelming parliamentary majorities for Labour. In 2001, with turnout down to 59 per cent, Labour was allocated 413 seats, the Conservatives 166 and the Liberal Democrats 52. In 2005, with turnout little better, the system awarded Labour 356 seats for 35 per cent of the vote, the Tories 198 seats for 30 per cent of the vote, and the Liberal Democrats a mere 62 seats for 22 per cent of the vote. Nearly three million Labour voters in the old industrial heartlands of Northern England and the West Midlands decided to abstain. The entry of Starbucks into the old city centres had, alas, failed to override the deep sense of alienation and despair. Blair had long been insulated from the diminishing popularity of his policies by the parliamentary system and by the media bubble. Increasingly though, he alienated a substantial section of the population. Inside the bubble, many were incredulous. 'A foreign policy issue helping to decide the election? Preposterous.' But it was true. The grammar of deceit employed by Blair and his ministers to support Washington's drive to war in the Middle East had alienated millions. These were by no means confined to traditional Labour voters but extended to 'middle England'. More than once I heard people of moderate sensibilities use words to the effect that 'I used to approve of his politics, I admired his eloquence, ignored his reverence for the Church. But then came Iraq. He lied. I will never forgive him for the deception.'

The Iraq War would not go away. The savage chaos of the occupation was visible each day on the internet, even though the extent of it was regularly underplayed by the bulk of the print media as well as the BBC and commercial broadcasters. The 2005 election campaign was one of the most dismal in British history. On all the issues that mattered, the Conservatives supported their opponent – Tory leaders being awestruck by Blair just as he had once been by Thatcher. The Liberal Democrats did not make Iraq the central issue in the campaign, even though they had initially opposed the war and favoured withdrawing all British troops by December 2005. They were cursed with a weak leader incapable of even looking in the direction of the New Labour jugular. The Green Party and the recently formed Respect alliance did focus their campaign on Iraq, as did some individual

Lib Dem candidates and Military Families Against the War. Of these groups, Respect alone triumphed. George Galloway, expelled from the Parliamentary Labour Party because of his strong stand on Iraq, now won a safe Labour seat in the East End of London.

Blair won the 2005 election, but with a rock-bottom popular vote and a reduced parliamentary majority. A poignant moment on election night was when one of the prime minister's rival candidates, Reginald Keys, who had lost a son in Iraq, denounced the war and Blair's inhumanity, while a pale-faced victor looked on, compelled to stay still and take the rough music. It was then that I thought of him as Dorian Gray. What a contrast there was between the 'everything new' face we were shown in 1997, surrounded by Mandelson's Union Jacks, and the war-ravaged features of this much-despised politician in 2005. A number of British military families were consulting lawyers to see if Blair and Straw could be prosecuted according to international law. The war had gone badly wrong. The country was awash with propaganda, but the bloody images refused to go away.

39

The Family Miliband

Ralph Miliband and his wife Marion Kozak were close friends over many decades. He died in 1994. In my obituary for the *Independent* I wrote of his family background and political formation, but it was only afterwards that Marion told me that his original name was Adolphe. His father had changed it on the advice of a landlady in South London after they arrived as refugees from Belgium in 1940. 'Better for the lad if you give him a new name, dear.' I asked Marion why this information had been kept a secret. She smiled. 'He said that you, Tariq, should never find out. First because you would tease him and secondly you were quite capable of calling him that name in the middle of an argument when other guests were present and then correcting yourself.' This was only a slightly exaggerated fear.

In the late 1980s, I was due to spend the weekend with the Milibands in a cottage near Banbury. Ralph asked whether I could drive David down and have a career discussion with him. I was very fond of both the brothers (and remained so to some extent until contacts virtually ceased). I spoke with David. There were three options: the academy here, the academy in the United States, or the academy somewhere else. He had obtained a first at Oxford and later a master's at MIT. He would be a good teacher.

He laughed and said: 'No. Definitely not the academy. I don't want to be a professor. It's either journalism or politics.' I understood that following in his father's footsteps might be off-putting, but persisted, suggesting that he would acquire a reputation in the academy very rapidly and then, like A.J.P. Taylor in history or Keynes in economics, would be able to write in different newspapers here and in the States on different subjects. Apart from all else, such a direction would permit a certain independence. Why not go for the *Financial Times*?

What about politics, he asked. I was harsh. 'There is absolutely nothing positive you can do in politics today. The tiny space that existed for reforms has gone. Don't go near it.' He said, 'You're too cynical.' I remembered Ralph telling me that David as a university student would sometimes come into his study, watch him on the computer and mutter: 'Scribble, scribble, scribble, Dad. You must *do* something...' But Ralph was very obstinate and, in this instance, correctly so.

Another thing that bothered him and Marion would later have a bearing on British politics. One evening, after supper in Edis Street and apropos of nothing in particular, Ralph suddenly said to me: 'I'm a bit worried about Eddy. Why do you think he mimics and follows David so blindly?' We'd discussed our children many times but this concern was new to me.

'Explain.'

'OK. They go to the same state school. Fine. Can't be helped. Then Edward applies for Oxford. Why not Cambridge? I press him. He refuses. OK. In Oxford why the same college as David, the same subjects as David and the desire to be taught by the same tutor: Andrew Glyn? Why? What do you think?'

'What worries you about all this, Ralph?'

'It's unhealthy. Obsessive.'

Marion was less harsh, but she did say that Eddy being so unconcerned about his own independence as an individual worried her.

I pointed out to them that Edward's freelancing as a critic on LBC and his first published work – a letter to the editor (me) of *Socialist Challenge* in July 1980, criticising C.L.R. James for demanding that Geoff Boycott be sacked from the English cricket team – were hardly signs of subordination to big brother. I said to them if you're really worried, suggest an analyst. They had considered it. Susan said it could be as simple as admiration for an older brother. Ralph's view was not that. To put it at its lightest it was probably competitive. I sang a few lines from the Irving Berlin ditty: 'Anything you can do, I can do better ...' I never thought of this again.

One day, Marion rang: 'David is Blair's speechwriter and part of the team. And Edward is now doing the same for Brown. Where will all this end?'

'They'll both become New Labour Cabinet ministers.'

'At the same time?'

'Possibly.'

David entered Parliament in 2001, aged thirty-six, as MP for South Shields. Edward followed in 2005. In 2007, he joined his brother in Cabinet. And then came the big bang. Brown went down to electoral defeat in 2010. Both Miliband brothers stood for the leadership, creating a huge family crisis. I spoke regularly to Marion at the time. She was in a state, and understandably so. 'What would Ralph have done?' she would ask. I said that as a parent it was very difficult to take sides and she should just stay out of it. As socialists we didn't believe in primogeniture. She was under pressure from David to persuade Edward to withdraw. This she would not do. Edward, she said, is convinced that David will win.

Asked by Radio 4 on the BBC, I repeated my response to Marion on primogeniture and added that it would be decided by how much of a change Labour wanted from Blair and Brown. Here Eddy had an advantage. He had opposed the Iraq War and reminded me of this when I ran into him in Harvard outside a bookstore where I was speaking on *Bush in Babylon*. David had supported Blair. On other matters their views, in my opinion, were not so different.

The trade union vote gave Edward the victory. The family were split. Marion rang, clearly delighted. What did I think? I said: 'Had David won you could have explored Downing Street. You quite enjoyed weekends at Chevening when David was foreign secretary.'

'How do you know?'

'You rang from there and it was evident.'

'You mean Eddy won't win the next election?'

'No. The media proprietors will not like or trust him even if he goes to kiss hands on one of Murdoch's estates.'

When Edward Miliband became Labour leader the *Daily Mail* decided to go on the attack, falsely denouncing Ralph. This created a furore. Ralph's politics were very different to those of both his sons. Once, Marion told me, she and Ralph were returning from supper at our place and as they entered Edis Street they could hear the boys engaged in New Labour talk. 'I wonder what they're saying,' said Marion. 'I don't want to know,' replied Ralph as they sped up the stairs.

The only purpose of the assault on Ralph's reputation was to punish and undermine his son. The operation backfired sensationally. It was designed to discredit the son by hurling the 'sins of the father' at his head. Instead, Edward Miliband's spirited response united a majority of the country behind him and against the tabloid. Ralph, had he been alive, would have found the ensuing consensus extremely diverting.

The Tories and Lib Dems made their distaste for the *Mail* clear; Jeremy Paxman on BBC's *Newsnight* held up old copies of the paper with its pro-fascist headlines ('Hurrah for the Blackshirts', the best remembered); two former members of Thatcher's Cabinet defended *père* Miliband, with Michael Heseltine reminding citizens that it was the Soviet Union and the Red Army that made victory against the Axis powers possible in the first place; and an opinion poll commissioned by *The Sunday Times* revealed that 73 per cent supported Ed Miliband against the once pro-fascist Rothermere rag.

The demonisation of Ralph Miliband raised a few issues avoided by both the Tory and the liberal press. These relate to his views on Britain and its political institutions, as well as the world at large. It also raised the question of the first Lord Rothermere's addiction to Mussolini and Hitler and their English offspring (Oswald Mosley and gang, but not them alone) right up until September 1939, and the issue of patriotism and its compatibility with left-wing views.

The popularity of fascism amongst the interwar elites was not confined to the Rothermeres or the Mitfords. The class confidence of European conservatism had been shaken by the 1917 Revolution in Russia. Fear stalked the corridors of power and the presence of large numbers of Marxists of Jewish origin in both the Bolshevik and Menshevik parties was used to fuel anti-semitism throughout Europe.

The British politicians – Chamberlain, Halifax, Butler and co – who would later be denounced as 'appeasers' were, in fact, far more representative of the Anglo-European elite than those who hurriedly changed their minds at the last moment when they realised that Hitler would neither agree to an equitable sharing of the continent or its colonies or oblige London by attacking the Soviet Union before taking the rest of Europe. This made war inevitable.

This was the atmosphere in which the *Daily Mail* and other tabloids (not to mention Geoffrey Dawson at *The Times* and the former King, Edward VIII) demonstrated varying degrees of sympathy for the Third Reich. It was this context that explains the attraction of many British intellectuals and workers (including comrades Philby, Burgess, Maclean, Blunt and others) to communism as the only force capable of defeating the Nazis. In this, as Heseltine reminded the country, they were not so wrong. Curiously enough, Ralph, contrary to Tom Bower's slurs in *The Sunday Times*, was never attracted to the communist parties or the groups to their left. Nor was he a partisan of the armed-struggle line in South America, even though he was ferociously hostile to the US-supported military dictatorships in the region.

Like many anti-fascists, Ralph joined the armed forces during the Second World War. He opposed the wars in Korea and Vietnam, and spoke loudly and clearly against the Falklands expedition. Even a cursory glance at *Socialist Register*, the annual magazine he founded in 1964, reveals the strong internationalism that was at its core. Ralph was always grateful (his word) that Britain offered him and his father, Jewish refugees fleeing occupied Belgium, asylum in 1940. Despite that, he remained an outlier, a stern critic of the British ruling elite and its institutions as well as the Labour Party and the trade union knights and peers. He was a socialist intellectual of great integrity.

He belonged to a generation of socialists formed by the Russian Revolution and the Second World War, a generation that dominated left-wing politics for almost a century. His father, a leather craftsman in Warsaw, was a member of the Jewish Bund, an organisation of militant socialist workers that insisted on preserving their ethnic autonomy. Poland, after the First World War, was beset by chaos, disorder and a foolish incursion by the Red Army, which helped to produce the ultra-nationalist military dictatorship of General Piłsudski. There were large-scale migrations. One of Ralph's uncles had gone eastwards and joined the Red Army, then under Trotsky's command. His parents had left Warsaw separately in 1922. They met in Brussels, where they had both settled, and were married a year later. Ralph was born in 1924.

The years that lay ahead would be bleak. Hitler's victory in Germany in 1933, followed by Franco's triumph in the Spanish Civil War, radicalised politics throughout the continent. It was not possible for an intellectually alert fifteen-year-old to remain unaffected. Ralph joined the lively Jewish-socialist youth organisation Hashomer Hatzair (Young Guard), whose members later played a heroic role in the Resistance. It was here that the young Miliband learned of capitalism as a system based on exploitation, in which the rich live off the harm they inflict on others. One of his close friends, Maurice Tran, who was later hanged at Auschwitz, gave him a copy of the *Communist Manifesto*. Even though he was not yet fully aware of it, he had become enmeshed in the business of socialist politics.

In 1940, as the German armies began to roll into Belgium, the Milibands, like thousands of others, prepared to flee to France. This proved impossible because of German bombardment. Just as well. Vichy France, with the complicity of large swathes of French citizens, would later send many Jews to the camps. So Ralph and his father walked to Ostend and boarded the last boat to Dover, which was already packed with fleeing diplomats and officials. The family was divided. Ralph's mother and younger sister, Nan, remained behind, and only survived the war with the help of the Resistance.

Ralph and his father arrived in London in May 1940. Both worked, for a time, as furniture removers, helping to clear bombed houses and apartments. It was Ralph who determined the division of labour, ensuring that his main task was to carry the books. Often he would settle on the front steps of a house, immersed in a volume. His passion for the written word led him to the works of Harold Laski. He discovered that Laski taught at the London School of Economics (then exiled in Cambridge) and became determined to study there. His English was getting better by the day and, after his matriculation, he finally found his way to the LSE. Laski became a mentor, never to be forgotten.

Miliband interrupted his studies for three years from 1943 to serve as a naval rating in the Belgian section of the Royal Navy. Aware of the fact that many of his Belgian comrades were engaged in the war against fascism, and traumatised by the absence of his mother and sister, he had volunteered, using Laski's influence to override the bureaucracy. He served on a number of destroyers and warships, helping to intercept German radio messages. He rose to the rank of chief petty officer and was greatly amused on one occasion when his new commanding officer informed him how he, Ralph, had been rated by a viscount who had commanded the ship on which he had previously served: 'Miliband is stupid, but always remains cheerful.'

After the war, he graduated from the LSE with a PhD and embarked on a long academic career. He taught first at Roosevelt College in Chicago, then became a lecturer in political science at the LSE, later still a professor at Leeds. This was followed by long stints at Brandeis and New York. In the late 1960s and '70s he was in great demand at campuses throughout Britain and North America. He winced at some of the excesses ('Why the hell do you have to wear these stupid combat jackets?' I remember him asking a group of us during a big meeting on Vietnam in 1968), but remained steadfast.

A Miliband speech was always a treat: alternately sarcastic and scholarly, witty and vicious, but rarely demagogic. At a teach-in on Vietnam in London in 1966, he roared in anger: 'Our left-wing friends in the Parliamentary Labour Party tell us that they cannot force a vote on the Labour government's shameful support for the imperialist war in Vietnam because Labour only has a tiny majority. They do not want to bring the government down. Bring it down and let honest politicians arise.' Everyone knew the Conservatives would back the government on Vietnam, but it was the mendacity of some on the Labour left that angered him.

The student uprisings of 1968–9 found him at the LSE. His initial reaction, similar to that of Adorno in Germany, was to describe (in a private letter) the occupation of the LSE by radicals as 'fascism of the left'. He strongly disapproved of the notion that students should elect their professors, and when it was pointed out that he would win by a large majority, he was not amused. He changed his mind after the mass arrests and the sacking of Robin Blackburn, writing that 'sophisticated Oakeshottism is a fairly thin crust; when it cracks, as it did here, a rather ugly, visceral sort of conservatism emerges'.

His key work on Britain was *Parliamentary Socialism* (1961) where he referred to the 'sickness of labourism', leaving no doubt as to where he stood. And later he was prescient on what the future might hold given the collapse of the broad left, writing in 1989:

We know what this immense historic process is taken to mean by the enemies of socialism everywhere: not only the approaching demise of communist regimes and their replacement by capitalist ones, but the elimination of any kind of socialist alternative to capitalism. With this intoxicating prospect of the scarcely hoped-for dissipation of an ancient nightmare, there naturally goes the celebration of the market, the virtues of free enterprise, and greed unlimited. Nor is it only on the Right that the belief has grown in recent times that socialism, understood as a radical transformation of the social order, has had its day: apostles of 'new times' on the Left have come to harbour much the same belief. All that is now possible, in the eyes of the 'new realism', is the more humane management of a capitalism which is in any case being thoroughly transformed.

His political views were far removed from those of his sons and pretending otherwise is foolish. Ralph was not a one-nation conservative who believed in parcelised 'social justice'. He remained a staunch anti-capitalist socialist till the end of his life. He was extremely close to both his sons and was proud of their success, but as any other migrant refugee would be – kids have done well in a foreign land – rather than in any political sense. He loathed New Labour and in one of our last conversations (when he was dying in hospital) described Blair as 'Teflon man'. Neither he nor Marion (an equally strong-minded socialist and feminist) ever tried to inflict their politics on the kids. Given his short temper I wonder whether this self-denying ordinance would, in his case at any rate, have survived the Iraq War. I doubt it.

And what of patriotism? Is it any different to national chauvinism, jingoism, etc.? Does it have the same connotation in an occupied nation as in the occupying power? Many decades ago I was being grilled by three journalists on *Face the Press*, a TV show that included Peregrine Worsthorne, editor of the *Sunday Telegraph*. Annoyed by what I was saying, he interrupted me:

'Does the word patriotism have any meaning for people like you?'

'No,' I replied. 'In my eyes a patriot is little more than an international blackleg.'

Taken aback, he muttered, 'Rather a good phrase.'

In fact, I had pinched it from a speech by the German socialist Karl Liebknecht, explaining his vote against war credits in the German parliament in 1914.

Ralph's death on 21 May 1994 left a gaping void in a time difficult for socialists everywhere. And there we might have left it, privately bemoaning the fact that the Miliband name is now known largely because of the political fame acquired by his sons. As things turned out, it was the election of Ed Miliband as leader of the Labour Party that revived a discussion on his father's political philosophy.

❧

Edward Miliband lost the 2015 elections and resigned as Labour leader, ironically paving the way for Jeremy Corbyn to take the post. He is currently supporting the Starmer regression. David Miliband left politics and obtained a sinecure at the International Rescue Committee, an international NGO with historic links to the CIA. He has been critical of the West's handling of the war in Ukraine and has come out in favour of an 'immediate ceasefire' in Palestine. And one more thing: Before becoming a full-time Labour speechwriter, he applied for a job at the *FT* as their social affairs leader writer. At the job interview, as far as the committee was concerned, there was only one Miliband. David was asked about that and replied accurately that his own politics were very different. Then came the next question: 'What are your views on Marxism?' Once again, he was straightforward. He was not a Marxist, but (oh that fatal but) there were things Marx wrote that demanded respect. I have no idea who the pink'uns took on as their leader writer.

Ralph, who told me all this, was very pleased and even proud that David had not rubbished Marx. Ralph had always wondered where the Milibands came from originally. During an official Miliband trip to Moscow, someone saw the British foreign secretary on television and sent a message. It was a Russian Miliband. Mystery solved.

40

The *New Left Review* at Fifty

In 2010 the *NLR* marked its fiftieth anniversary. Its editors had been Stuart Hall (1960–62), Perry Anderson (1962–83), Robin Blackburn (1983–99), Perry Anderson (2000–2) and Susan Watkins (2003–). In 1999, Perry asked what I thought about taking Susan on at the *NLR* to work with him in bringing out the relaunched magazine. I said perhaps we should miss a generation. When Perry asked who from the current generation, I didn't have a candidate. Susan had been working as a freelance writer and copy-editor, and had already written for *NLR* and the *LRB*. Robin and Perry both thought that since she had a strong political background, was a good editor and wrote well, she should be taken on. I agreed. She worked as a deputy for a couple of years and was appointed editor by the New Left Trust in January 2003. Francis Mulhern pointed out to me recently that Susan is now the longest continuous editor of the journal.

The general view, which I share, is that she does a very good job. At the same time, I should confess that, though I write for the *Review* and for its blog, *Sidecar*, and take part in editorial committee discussions, my own very close relationship with the journal from the 1970s to 2002 became less so after Susan became editor. Why?

Several months after Terry Eagleton's 'kill the father' essay on Raymond Williams had shaken the editorial board in 1976, the *NLR* conducted a long series of interviews with Raymond, published as a book, *Politics and Letters*, that remains a classic in its field to this day. When Robin later asked Raymond what his wife Joy had thought of Terry's text, he replied: 'I hid that issue of the *NLR*. I hate it when couples who are also comrades stoke each other up.'

This had happened only once before at the *NLR*, but we got the message. In fact our experience of couples has been the opposite. After Perry published an article comparing the outcomes of the Russian and Chinese revolutions, his wife Wang Chaohua wrote a sharp response in a subsequent issue, challenging him on a number of fronts. I tended to agree with her and, so far, there has been no response from Perry.

What interested me was their way of looking at events. Perry, as a historian, tends to wait till history has settled the issue. Chaohua comes from a different tradition altogether. The Chinese past is ever present for her on a number of levels: literary, historical, political. In her youth she was a Red Guard during the Cultural Revolution and later one of the leaders of the Tiananmen Square uprising in 1989, on which she has written a book and several essays. She was on the wanted list and had to flee the country via Hong Kong. As a result, her thought processes are partially moulded by having been active in two important events and by her exile. Ernest Mandel said once that Isaac Deutscher and the *NLR* tended to worship accomplished facts. Chaohua could never be accused of this heresy.

As for me, I moved sideways and let Susan alone, unless she had a specific question. (This was helped by my non-stop travels once *Clash of Fundamentalisms* and later *Bush in Babylon* were published; there was a point during that period when I counted almost fifty invitations per month to different continents.) It's not how I would have edited the journal, making it near perfect as a literary-political product, but also, and for that very reason, too predictable. Too little polemic (Ben Anderson's savage assault on Kapucinski and James Fenton comes to mind) and no satire at all (save perhaps for *Sidecar*). Enough said.

The response to *NLR*'s fiftieth in 2010 surprised us a bit. A *Guardian* leader by Aditya Chakraborty and an essay the same week by the intellectual historian Stefan Collini were generous in tone and content. *Le Monde* in Paris carried a friendly review, noting our affinities with Sartre's *Les Temps moderne* and European political culture. John Lloyd at the *Financial Times* wrote that when people abroad sarcastically asked in which field Britain was ahead of anyone else these days, he replied: 'We produce the best Marxist magazine in the world.' Collini was more expansive:

> When so much of even the so-called 'serious' media is given over to celebrity-fuelled ephemera and the recycling of press releases and in-house gossip; when the academic world is struggling to mitigate the worst effects of funding-driven overproduction and careerist modishness; and when national and international politics seem to consist of bowing to the imperatives of 'the market' while avoiding public relations gaffes – then more than ever do we need a 'forum' like the *NLR*. It is up to date without being merely journalistic, scholarly without being scarred by citation compulsion, and analytical about the long-term forces at work in politics rather than obsessed by the spume of the latest wavelet of manoeuvring and posturing.

Despite its self-description in its guidelines for contributors, the journal is not in any obvious sense 'lively'. It is downright difficult (but none the worse for that) because what it tries to analyse is complex and its preferred intellectual tools are often conceptually sophisticated. It is difficult where being easy would be no virtue, difficult where aiming to be 'accessible' would mean patronising its readers, difficult where ideas need to be chewed rather than simply swallowed. That is what I admire above all about the journal: its intellectual seriousness – its magnificently strenuous attempt to understand, to analyse, to theorise.

So, no balloons, and definitely no party lines. No cheap consolation, either. But hey, respect, no question …

Collini left behind a question: 'Can a left intellectual project hope to thrive in the absence of a political movement? That remains to be seen.' Fourteen years later, I think it's fair to respond with a firm, if modest, 'yes'. The wars (Ukraine and Gaza being the latest) and crises that afflict the American-led order have received a very firm response from the *NLR*. And the addition of a successful blog, *Sidecar*, has helped to bridge a general gap, partially by a rapid political response to events in all five continents.

At our party that year, I missed one person in particular. Peter Gowan had died six months before, on 12 June 2009. I was holed up in Sardinia at the time completing *The Night of the Golden Butterfly*, the last novel of my Islam quintet. We had spoken a number of times, but I had no indication that he might go so quickly. When she realised this, his wife Halya was going to ring me so I could come back, but Peter stopped her. It was more important, he said, that I finish my book. For that reason he never rang to say farewell. With his passing, the international left lost one of its most astute political analysts, and the *NLR* the most generous and steadfast of comrades. Eight years later, in 2017, Adam Tooze paid this homage on his blog:

> Interested in global political economy? US power? The crisis of 2008 and after? If you have a few minutes today read a short but brilliant essay by the late Peter Gowan that appeared in *New Left Review* in February 2009, 'Crisis in the Heartland'.
>
> Sometimes when reading one stumbles on a piece that is like a kindred spirit. In this case it seemed to me, reading Gowan a few weeks ago, that I had found a Doppelgänger, or rather the better double that I wish I was. Finishing a manuscript on the genesis of the 2008 crisis and its aftermath, I found that I was not just in agreement with Gowan, not just in agreement on ideas and sources, but in agreement at the level of which particular passages from which particular sources to quote. It was like reading a condensed, edited and improved version of my own draft chapters, written by somebody else 9 years ago who did not have the benefit of hindsight that we enjoy but saw the world with what, at least to me, seems like brilliant clarity ... The poignancy of reading the essay is increased by the knowledge that Gowan finished it under the shadow of terminal illness.

Peter was a socialist intellectual of the highest calibre, combining enormous energy and independence of mind with a truly collective spirit. A contributor to *NLR* from the 1970s, he joined the editorial committee in 1984. His interventions in the journal made up a substantial body of analysis in their own right. His work was translated into many languages and he had readers on every continent; unlike some, he was incredibly patient in replying to their emails. He loved a good argument, although he was always extremely courteous to his critics. For me the loss was deeply personal. He had been a close friend and comrade since we first met as activists in the Vietnam Solidarity Campaign in 1967. There is little that we did not discuss over the next four decades.

Peter was born in 1946, three years after his sister Philippa, another close friend. They were war babies in the classic sense: their father, a Canadian officer of Scottish ancestry stationed in wartime Glasgow, was already married. Their mother, Jean MacDonald, came from a well-off Glaswegian family who were stunned when she broke her engagement to a local and opted for her mysterious Canadian. The two children were born in her father's house in Glasgow. When it was hurriedly sold after his death, she moved to Belfast and brought up the children as a single parent, with occasional 'unofficial' help from her brothers which paid for Peter's education.

Young Gowan was sent to Orwell Park prep school and later to Haileybury College, an institution that had initially been set up in 1806 by the East India Company to educate civil servants destined for the colonies. After 1858 its doors were opened to all, and the school developed a reputation for liberal scholarship. Clement Attlee had been a pupil and a pride in the reforms of his government permeated the school in the 1950s. Peter became a committed supporter of the Labour Party while at Haileybury. It was primarily his sister's influence that pushed him to the left: then a Christian socialist, she was active in CND (led by Canon Collins) and the Anti-Apartheid movement (led by Bishop Ambrose Reeves).

At the University of Southampton, one of his more inspirational lecturers was Miriam Daly, an independent-minded

Irishwoman who radicalised him further. She encouraged him to study the Russian Revolution and its legacy, which soon became an obsession for many of our generation. Peter was never satisfied until he had read everything he could possibly lay his hands on, and in this case the literature was enormous. He embarked on postgraduate work at the Centre for Russian and East European Studies at the University of Birmingham, where the staff included the formidable scholar R.W. Davies. But revolution was in the air and he did not finish his PhD; something I never heard him regret.

Philippa and Peter were never to meet their father, and this undoubtedly left a deep mark on him; he discussed it with me at various times over the years. He once managed to track him down in Toronto and rang him at work. The fear in his father's voice was so palpable that Peter was disgusted rather than sad and never tried again. The arrival of his own children helped, but he could never forget the issues raised by his missing parent. He himself was a wonderful father to his four sons and spent enormous amounts of time with them and their friends, discussing each and every problem with the same energy that he applied to questions of politics and theory and, in more relaxed moments, to gardening.

From 1968 until 1976, Peter was deeply involved as a militant in the International Marxist Group. What had attracted a number of us to this tiny group was both its considered anti-Stalinism and, more importantly, its internationalism: it was the British section of the Fourth International, not a mass organisation by any stretch of the imagination, but one which had activists in every continent, including many who functioned in clandestine conditions under the dictatorships of Latin America and southern Europe, above all in Portugal, Greece and Spain.

Party loyalties never impeded Peter's independence of mind. In 1967 *NLR* inaugurated a debate on 'Trotsky's Marxism' with a powerful critique by Nicolas Krassó, one of the left leaders of the Hungarian uprising of 1956 and a member of the *NLR* editorial committee. The de-Stalinisation process in the Soviet Union had semi-rehabilitated Bukharin and other Old Bolsheviks by the mid-sixties. Trotsky alone remained anathema, and this was the first serious attempt to discuss his legacy within a broader left. Krassó was a former pupil of Lukács, well-versed in the theory and the practice of the communist movement. He made some effective criticisms of Trotsky's writings.

Ernest Mandel despatched a defensive reply. Krassó challenged him once again. Mandel's second reply was more effective. I remember well Peter's first response to the initial exchange. 'I agree with Krassó,' he told me. 'Ernest's response is unconvincing.' He forced me to re-read the Krassó text carefully and, while I could see he had a case, *partiinost* prevented me from admitting it to anyone except Peter. He developed a growing friendship with the Hungarian. In an interview conducted with Krassó shortly before his death, Peter asked how he would sum up the meaning of the Hungarian events of 1956. With characteristic mordancy, Krassó replied:

> I have often remembered the 19th Party Congress in the Soviet Union in 1952. Stalin kept silent throughout the Congress till the very end when he made a short speech that covers about two-and-a-half printed pages. He said there were two banners that the progressive bourgeoisie had thrown away and which the working class should pick up – the banners of democracy and national independence. Certainly, nobody could doubt that in 1956 the Hungarian workers raised these banners high.

In February 1968, a group of us in London had decided to launch a new radical newspaper. The poet Christopher Logue was despatched to the Reading Room of the old British Library to research names. He returned with detailed notes on a nineteenth-century paper, *The Black Dwarf*, whose editor Thomas Wooler had been imprisoned for his scathing attacks on the state perpetrators of the Peterloo Massacre. We decided to revive it on 1 May 1968. A week later the barricades went up in Paris and one of our correspondents, Eric Hobsbawm, situated them in the continuum of French history. I offered Peter his first job, as distribution manager. He moved to London immediately, found a squat, and took to his task with gusto, delivering copies of the paper to bookshops in a beat-up van.

My fondest memory of him from that period is his returning to our Soho offices at 7 Carlisle Street (a floor below the *New Left Review*) one day and laughing with delight. That issue had carried an acerbic piece by Robin Blackburn defending Herbert Marcuse against Alasdair MacIntyre, who had written an ultra-critical political biography of the US-based German Marxist for Fontana Modern Masters. We found a photograph of Marcuse, his fist raised as he stood on a platform with Black Panther members. The piece was titled: 'MacIntyre, The Game is Up'. Peter had just delivered the issue to Collets, the radical bookstore on Charing Cross Road that took a hundred *Dwarfs* each fortnight.

As he was about to leave he saw the great philosopher stride through the door. MacIntyre went straight to the pile, lifted a copy and began to flick through it until he came to the offending headline. Peter described watching him as he pored over Blackburn's assault, turned puce, threw the paper back on the pile and walked out. We were thrilled. It was rare to witness the immediate impact of a text on its target.

One day a volunteer helper arrived in the *Black Dwarf* offices in Soho. He was a friend of Peter's. They had been at school together. John Weal subsequently revealed himself to be a reasonably wealthy heir to a family bequest. He took on the responsibility of paying all the bills and later bought a printing press when we moved to King's Cross.

By 1968 Peter had started teaching, moving from Barking College to the Polytechnic of North London, then London Metropolitan. He remained deeply engaged in solidarity work with left dissidents in the Soviet Union and Eastern Europe, partly through contacts with the Ukrainian socialist, Bohdan Kravchenko. It was through this circle that he got to know Halya Kowalsky, whom he married in 1975. I was always worried by the amount he smoked and started hassling him at an early stage. We hoped Halya didn't smoke. We were disappointed.

From the mid-1970s Peter was increasingly convinced that the West European left should be intervening more effectively in the underground debates that were taking place in the East. This was the starting point for *Labour Focus on Eastern Europe*, a magazine launched in 1977 with the support of broad sections of the left, including social-democratic and euro-communist MPs, and a talented editorial board including Patrick Camiller, Günter Minnerup and Gus Fagan.

Halya was an indispensable part of the operation, both politically and technically; 'her integrity, sensitivity and generosity', Peter wrote in *The Global Gamble*, 'have been an inspiration as well as a great support'. Her no-nonsense approach was often brought to bear when Peter let his imagination run away with him. In the early days Halya used to lay out the whole magazine. I retain a warm memory of her walking into the IMG headquarters in Upper Street, Islington with her newborn son, Ivan, going straight down to the awful basement where the print-shop was located, parking her baby on the table and sitting down to typeset an entire issue of *Labour Focus*.

Through Peter, the magazine tracked the hollowing out of the Soviet bloc regimes without losing hope that more democratic forms might arise there on the basis of socialised economies. The transformation of Eastern Europe into satellite states of Washington and the disintegration of the Soviet Union, pushed into socioeconomic free fall by American shock therapy, represented a historic defeat for all those who had hoped that something better might arise from the ashes.

Unsurprisingly, a few of the team around *Labour Focus* were unsettled. It was in this period that Peter's steadfastness won the day. We had many discussions on what the impact on friends and colleagues would be. He predicted that the trauma would go deep and many would fall by the wayside. This began to happen as early as 1990, when the United States geared up for the attack on Iraq, having first given Saddam Hussein the green light to go into Kuwait. Some on the left chose to see the first Gulf War as the indication of a new and refreshing cosmopolitanism. More clear-sightedly, Peter saw the war, which secured a huge new US military presence in the Gulf, as a drive to forward imperial interests, wrapped in a liberal humanitarian flag.

Soon after came the breakup of Yugoslavia. I have rarely known Peter – an incredibly generous-spirited human being, always ready to see the best in people, including a few who were walking disasters – as angry as he was during the assault on Yugoslavia. He would write more on this single theme than on any other conflict past or present: in the *NLR*, *Socialist Register* and his 140-page essay 'The Twisted Road to Kosovo' in *Labour Focus*. While the Western media portrayed the events in Yugoslavia as exclusively the outcome of internal forces, 'inflamed nationalists' pushing for disintegration, Gowan pointed to the crucial role played by the Atlantic powers. He fiercely condemned a 'system of Western power-politics' which could 'casually and costlessly make a major contribution to plunging Yugoslavia into turmoil and wars, use these wars to further their geopolitical ends, and then seek to make political capital out of war crimes tribunal judgements of perpetrators of atrocities, while themselves refusing all responsibility'.

From 1990, Peter's work focused on the strategic goals of the American and European elites in restructuring the post–Cold War world. His starting point, as always, was that since policy-making in state executives and multilateral institutions is largely closed to public scrutiny, understanding how state power is being wielded requires 'mapping back' onto the *cui bono* of policy outcomes. He insisted, too, on the highly political nature of financial and economic institutions, and the statecraft they entailed. His 1999 book *The Global Gamble* took issue with the notion that 'globalisation' was the outcome of organic economic processes, and set out a compelling case for viewing the transformation of the world economy in the 1990s as crucially driven by the highly political moves of operatives of the 'Dollar–Wall Street Regime' in Washington and New York.

Talk of a 'global financial market' obscured the fact that, since the 1980s, the vast bulk of international financial activity has been centred in Wall Street or its 'satellite', the City of London. 'Those who believe the adjective "American" is redundant', he argued, should ask themselves what difference it would make if the international financial system were dominated by markets and operators in China, let alone Iran.

Gowan's writing emphasised the role of human agents: strategic policy elites, high state functionaries, military planners, actively pursuing particular class or national interests. If his approach runs the risk of overstating intentionality and understating structure, as was sometimes suggested in *NLR* internal discussions, in this depoliticised age the overcorrection was invaluable. His work was always addressed to an audience of potential activists, movers and shakers in a project of world reform. He wrote to reveal – to denaturalise – the workings of contemporary capitalist power. His last essay, 'Crisis in the Heartland', in *NLR* 55, is a bravado analysis of the 2008 meltdown, ending with a call for a public-utility credit system.

Tall and broad-chested, with a full-bodied laugh, Peter was a strong man who could have had another twenty years if he had not been struck down at the age of sixty-three by mesothelioma, an asbestos-related cancer impossible to detect before the final implosion (probably contracted in the ramshackle postwar building that housed Barking Tech). When he dropped in to give me the news, he shouted: 'It wasn't the fags, Tariq.' On holiday in Canada in the summer of 2008, the month before he was diagnosed, he was running six miles a day. He faced up to his death with extraordinary calm, good cheer and courage. A Leninist to the last, he planned his funeral in meticulous detail with his family, and went out to Country Joe's Vietnam song – 'Gimme an F!'

'I'm so glad I'm a materialist,' he told me, as he lay dying. No nonsense to believe in. We all have to go sometime, and the only difference was that he knew when. It was too soon – he had books to write and promises to keep; but death held no fears. In the last phone conversation I had with him we talked about Afghanistan, comparing the current war to its equally appalling predecessors. I read him a verse from a Kipling poem, reflecting the mood in the late nineteenth century when Winston Churchill had been a young officer in the region:

> When you're wounded and left on Afghanistan's plains,
> And the women come out to cut up what remains,
> Just roll to your rifle, and blow out your brains.
> And go to your God like a soldier.

Peter roared with delight. It is a sound I will treasure.

41

The *Charlie Hebdo* Massacre

In January 2015, I wrote the following in the *London Review of Books* in response to recent events in Paris:

It was a horrific event. It was condemned in most parts of the world and most poignantly by many cartoonists. Those who planned the atrocity chose their target carefully. They knew that such an act would create the maximum horror. It was quality, not quantity they were after. The response will not have surprised or displeased them. They don't care a damn for the world of unbelievers. Unlike the medieval inquisitors of the Sorbonne they do not have the legal and theological authority to harass booksellers or printers, ban books and torture authors, so they go one step further and order executions.

What of the foot-soldiers? The circumstances that attract young men and women to these groups are creations of the Western world that they inhabit – which is itself a result of long years of colonial rule in the countries of their forebears. We know that the Parisian brothers Chérif and Saïd Kouachi were long-haired inhalers of marijuana and other substances until (like the 7 July bombers in the UK) they saw footage of the Iraq War and, in particular, of the torture taking place in Abu Ghraib and the cold-blooded killings of Iraqi citizens in Fallujah.

They sought comfort in the mosque. Here they were radicalised by waiting hardliners for whom the West's war on terror had become a golden opportunity to recruit and hegemonise the young, both in the Muslim world and in the ghettoes of Europe and North America. Sent first to Iraq to kill Americans and more recently to Syria (with the connivance of the French state?) to topple Assad, such young men were taught how to use weapons effectively. Back home they got ready to deploy this knowledge against those who they believed were tormenting them in difficult times. They were the persecuted. *Charlie Hebdo* represented their persecutors. The horror should not blind us to this reality.

Charlie Hebdo had made no secret of the fact that it intended to carry on provoking Muslims by targeting the Prophet. Most Muslims were angry about this, but ignored the insult. The paper had reprinted the Danish daily *Jyllands-Posten*'s cartoons of Muhammad in 2005 – the ones that depicted him as a Pakistani immigrant. The Danish newspaper admitted that it would never publish anything similar depicting Moses or the Jews (perhaps it had already done so: it certainly published articles supporting the Third Reich), but *Charlie Hebdo* sees itself as having a mission to defend republican secular values against all religions. It has occasionally attacked Catholicism, but it's hardly ever taken on Judaism (though Israel's numerous assaults on Palestinians have offered many opportunities) and has concentrated its mockery on Islam.

French secularism today seems to encompass anything as long as it's not Islamic. Denunciations of Islam have been relentless in France, with Michel Houellebecq's recent novel *Soumission* (the word *Islam* means 'submission') the latest salvo. It predicts the country being ruled by a president from a group he calls the Muslim Fraternity. *Charlie Hebdo*, we should not forget, ran a cover lampooning Houellebecq on the day it was attacked. Defending its right to publish, regardless of consequences, is one thing, but sacralising a satirical paper that regularly targets those who are victims of a rampant Islamophobia is almost as foolish as justifying the acts of terror against it. Each feeds on the other.

French law allows freedoms to be suspended under the threat of unrest or violence. Before now this provision has been invoked to forbid public appearances by the comedian Dieudonné (well known for making antisemitic jokes) and to ban pro-Palestinian demonstrations – France is the only Western country to do this. That such actions are not seen as problematic by a majority of the French people speaks volumes.

It isn't just the French, though. We didn't see torchlight vigils or mass assemblies anywhere in Europe when it was revealed that the Muslim prisoners handed over to the US by many EU countries (with the plucky Poles and Labour-run Britain in the forefront) had been tortured by the CIA. There is a bit more at stake here than satire.

The smugness of secular liberals who talk of defending freedom to the death is matched by liberal Muslims who waffle endlessly about how what happened had nothing to do with Islam. There are different versions of Islam (the occupation of Iraq was used deliberately to trigger the Sunni–Shia wars that helped give birth to the Islamic State); it is meaningless to claim to speak in the name of a 'real' Islam. The history of Islam from its very beginnings is replete with factional struggles. Fundamentalist currents within Islam as well as external invasions were responsible for wiping out many cultural and scientific advances in the late medieval period. Such differences continue to exist.

Meanwhile, Hollande and Sarkozy have announced that they will lead a march of national unity (Cameron's going along and Netanyahu is likely to fly over too). A French friend wrote to me, 'The idea of *Charlie Hebdo* provoking a "union sacrée" has to be one of the ironies of history that even the most cynical post-'68 libertarian anti-establishmentarian would have choked on in disbelief.'

In response, letters poured in, and M-K was irritated enough to reply to the first and defend her contributor.

As a devoted reader of the *LRB* I am deeply disappointed by your immediate response to the *Charlie Hebdo* attack. No message of solidarity, no support for freedom of expression. I would have thought that the execution of the editorial staff of a magazine a few hours' journey from your own office would provoke a more heartfelt response.

Simon Hammond
London E1

Mary-Kay Wilmers writes: I believe in the right not to be killed for something I say, but I don't believe I have a right to insult whomever I please. Those – and there are many – who insist that the only acceptable response to the events in Paris is to stand up for 'freedom of expression' are allowing people the freedom to say 'Je suis Charlie' but nothing else.

In the next issue, I followed up:

In the week following the atrocities, a wave of moral hysteria swept France. 'Je suis Charlie' became almost obligatory. The Hollande/Valls message was simple: either you were for the magazine or for the terrorists. Quite a few, now as in 2001, were for neither. These included Henri Roussel, the 80-year-old founder of *Hara-Kiri*, the title under which *Charlie Hebdo* was published before it was forced into a name change – it was banned by the French government for insulting the corpse of Charles de Gaulle. In a remarkable essay published in the *Nouvel Observateur*, Roussel made two essential points. The first concerned French foreign policy:

I don't much like it when a head of state speaks of the dead as heroes. It usually happens because citizens have been sent to war and not come back, which is rather the case with the victims of the attack on *Charlie Hebdo*. The attack is part of a war declared on France, but can also be seen in the light of the wars France has got itself involved in: conflicts where its participation isn't called for, where worse massacres than that at *Charlie Hebdo* take place every day, several times a day, where our bombardments pile death on death in the hope of saving potentates who feel threatened and are no better than those who threaten them ... If Obama had not held Hollande back, he would have gone after Assad in Syria, just as Sarkozy went after Gaddafi in Libya ... with the result we're familiar with.

The second was personal. Roussel knew all the victims well and this made him both angry and sorrowful. He denounced Charb [the director of *Charlie Hebdo*] for his recklessness:

He was the boss. Why did he need to drag the whole team into it? In the first attack on *Charlie Hebdo* in November 2011, the offices were torched after an issue was called 'Charia Hebdo'. I quote what I said ... in the *Obs*: 'I think we're ignorant and imbeciles who have taken a pointless risk. That's all. We think we're invulnerable. For years, decades even, we do provocative things and then one day the provocation comes back at us. It didn't need to be done.'

It didn't need to be done, but Charb did it again. A year later, in September 2012, after a provocation that put France's ambassadors in Muslim countries in a state of siege ... I asked Charb in the pages of the *Obs*: 'To show, with the caption "Muhammed: A Star is Born", a naked

Muhammed praying, seen from behind, balls dangling and prick dripping, in black and white but with a yellow star on his anus – whatever way you look at it, how is this funny?'

I was sick of it. Charb told a journalist from *Le Monde*: 'I have no kids, no wife, I prefer to die on my feet than to live on my knees.' Cavanna, who feared death, wrote when he was Charb's age: 'Rather red than dead.' The reds are no longer red, the dead are still dead. Everyone has seen Charb's last cartoon: 'Still no attacks in France?' And the jihadist in the cartoon, armed like the one who killed Charb, Tignous, Cabu, Honoré and the others, replies: 'Wait! We've got until the end of January for New Year's greetings.' ... Have you seen Wolinski's last cartoon? It ends: 'I dream of returning to Cuba to drink rum, smoke a cigar and dance with the beautiful Cuban girls.'

Charb who preferred to die and Wolin who preferred to live. I blame you, Charb. Peace on your soul.

Roussel's was a lonely voice and in response to complaints, including one from the publisher of *Charlie Hebdo*, the editor of *Nouvel Observateur* replied that after serious discussion it had been agreed that freedom of speech was best preserved by not denying it to those who disagreed with the mainstream narrative. Elsewhere three publishers who refused to display 'Je suis Charlie' on their websites were subjected to persistent questioning and bullying. It was reminiscent of the post-9/11 mood in the UK (remember Mary Beard?), leave alone the States.

And what of the huge Sunday crowd convened by the president at the place de la République? The photo-op brigade at the front turned into a disaster when Netanyahu, waving triumphantly to onlookers, crashed his way to the front. The dignitaries he was so keen to join weren't all that impressive: the puppet president of Mali; Angela Merkel, the Mother of Europe (her hands held in a way that suggested a mysterious Masonic signal); Donald Tusk, the Polish president of the Council of Europe; and – hurriedly summoned at the last minute to balance the presence of the Israeli leader – Mahmoud Abbas, the PLO leader, holding hands with the king of Jordan (both are Israeli supplicants). Sarkozy, placed in the fourth row, quickly began his own long march to the front, but by the time he got there the cameras had disappeared and the celebs soon followed suit. How many turned up in all? A million was the official figure. Eric Hazan, the waspish historian of Paris, used different criteria:

> It was as big as the one on 28 April 1944, when Marshal Pétain attended the funeral service for the victims of Allied bombings at the Hôtel de Ville. War fever apart (the shouts of 'To Berlin!' in 1914), the great moments of unanimity have taken place at public funerals – like those of Victor Hugo, Pierre Overney, Jean-Paul Sartre or Edith Piaf. Sunday's demonstration is of the same order, the crowd is moved by sentiment and satisfied by coming together to express a vague desire for unity and reconciliation. As if the strength of the crowd was enough to mitigate the lack of a society that takes our common well-being as its goal.

Slowly, a more critical France was beginning to speak up. An opinion poll two days after the big march revealed a divided country: 57 per cent were 'Je suis Charlie', but 42 per cent were opposed to hurting the feelings of minorities. Some of the latter might have been thinking of the blanket publicity for Michel Houellebecq and his new novel on TV and in print in the week preceding the attack on the magazine. Those with longer memories might have recalled Houellebecq's statement in 2001, which laid the basis for the title of his latest offering: 'Reading the Quran is a disgusting experience. Ever since Islam's birth it has been distinguished by its desire to make the world submit to itself. Submission is its very nature.'

Replace the Quran with the Old Testament and Islam with Judaism and you would be locked up in France today, as some have been, including a sixteen-year-old schoolboy who parodied *Charlie Hebdo*. A satirical magazine, it appears, cannot be satirised. The double standards prevailing in France were made clear yet again when the Jewish Defence League, modelled on its US counterpart, was allowed to organise a demonstration under a banner – immigration: referendum – which aligned it firmly with the extreme right in France and the rest of Europe.

In the Muslim world, responses were varied. Even as Niger's president, Mahamadou Issoufou, was marching in Paris, forty-five Christian churches in his country were being torched and pastors' homes targeted – the Boko Haram leader, Abubakar Shekau, was born in Niger and was an influential presence there, if only on video. Public funerals for the slain terrorists were held in Pakistan and Turkey (even though Islam expressly forbids funerals without a body).

Two distinct narratives competed in Turkey. The president and his prime minister, just back from the Paris march, entered the realm of conspiracy satire by implying that the terrorist attack had been carried out by the French themselves, possibly aided by Mossad. The mayor of Istanbul backed them. The Turkish republican followers of Kemal Atatürk supported *Charlie Hebdo* unconditionally. Their daily paper, *Cumhuriyet*, published four pages from the new issue of *Charlie Hebdo* as an insert, but not the cover or drawings portraying the Prophet Muhammad. However, two columnists on the paper reproduced the cover beside their pieces, enraging the government and its followers. Vans carrying the paper to distribution outlets were seized and President Erdoğan also used the crisis as an excuse to crack down on local dissidents who had been rubbishing him on various websites.

Elsewhere the Sunni–Shia divide was highlighted when Sayyid Hassan Nasrallah, the leader of Hezbollah, used a TV address marking the anniversary of the Prophet's birth to denounce extremists within Islam (*takfiris*) who behead and slaughter their captives, claiming that their actions were much more dangerous for Islam than for anyone else. He had had no such compunctions when the Ayatollah Khomeini pronounced a fatwa sentencing Salman Rushdie to death, and was still going on about it in 2006 on Al Jazeera: 'If the faithful had carried out Ayatollah Khomeini's injunction and killed the apostate Rushdie,' he said on that occasion, 'the Danish newspaper editor would never have dared to publish these cartoons.' A naive view, but times had changed and the battle with Sunni extremism was now at its peak.

On the question of images there has always been a debate

within Islam. The Quran itself contains warnings against the worship of idols and graven images, but this is taken straight from the Abrahamic tradition and the Old Testament. It's a stricture on forms of worship. After all, images of the Prophet were embossed on early Muslim coins to replace Byzantine and Persian potentates. A number of paintings by Muslim artists in the late medieval period depict the Prophet with loving care.

The Shia tradition has always ignored the supposed ban on images, and portraits of Shia imams have never been forbidden. The different schools of Sunni jurisprudence don't agree on the question. It has only become a big issue since Saudi money pushed Wahhabi clerics onto the world stage to fight communism during the Cold War (with the total backing of Washington). Wahhabi literalism misinterprets the Quran, and its hostility to images led the Saudi government to destroy the graves of the Prophet, his companions and his wives in Mecca. There were no protests except from architects and historians who denounced the vandalism. One can only imagine the response in the world of Islam had the destruction of the graves been carried out, whether deliberately or accidentally, by a Western power.

We now know that the assault on *Charlie Hebdo* was the outcome of intra-Wahhabi rivalry. The attack was claimed by Ayman al-Zawahiri as an al-Qaeda initiative, organised by its section in the Yemen. There is no reason to doubt his assertion. His organisation had been outflanked and partially displaced by the Islamic State and a global act of terror was needed to restore its place as the leading terror group. As in other suicide-terrorism outings by al-Qaeda, the act itself was well planned and predictably successful, and those who carried it out were duly sacrificed.

Western leaders insisted, as they do after every outrage, that the problem is radicalised Islam and therefore the responsibility lies with the religion. (Why was Catholicism never blamed for the IRA offensive?) The real problem is not a secret: Western intelligence services regularly tell their leaders that the radicalisation of a tiny sliver of young Muslims (more of whom probably work for the security services in Britain and France than for al-Qaeda or ISIS) is a result of US foreign policy over the last two decades.

42

With Satyajit Ray

Twice in the late 1980s and once in 1990, I spent several hours with Satyajit Ray. I was very struck by his appearance when I first met him. Six-foot three, looking very relaxed in a *kurta pajama*, with a deep sonorous voice and a very firm hand grip. His eyes had a touch of mischief. Not a prelude to laughter, but quizzical, sceptical, mocking. His laughter was infectious. His intelligence usually revealed itself casually. The Japanese master Akira Kurosawa once said: 'Not to have seen the cinema of Ray means existing in the world without seeing the sun and the moon.' What he meant was that Ray was a foundational genius of the new art form that swept the twentieth century. I often wonder how many cinema-lovers in the West (or for that matter even in India) know his work today. Not many, I would wager.

What did we discuss? Everything. Cinema, of course, but also politics, literature, food, language. In the early eighties, he had received a phone call from the prime minister, Mrs Gandhi, who wanted his advice. Sir Richard Attenborough was pressing her for government funds to help film *Gandhi*. 'I am fond of Dickie, but how could I recommend throwing money down the drain? I said no. She disregarded my advice. The film was awful, but a huge financial success. It made a lot of money and our government made a handsome profit. This remark is not to be repeated.'

Earlier that month in Delhi I had, together with other friends, teased one of the Indian producers of the film. Finally he revealed: 'When we started filming, Attenborough told us "There's only one reason we're making this film. I don't want anyone in the West to make the mistake of thinking that Mrs

Gandhi is Mahatma Gandhi's daughter."' Back in London, I asked Attenborough whether he had actually said this. He replied: 'I did but I failed. After the film was shown in the White House, Reagan came up to me: "Congratulations, Sir Richard. Great man. Just like his daughter."'

Ray and I discussed the differences and contrasts between Western and Indian classical music, his training as a painter, and his great teacher, the muralist B. B. Mukherjee. He explained that Tagore's novellas, much more than his poems, had a Bengali rhythm. 'My more classical films based on them totally transcend the original work and on many levels.' He spoke casually but in the language of a true auteur. For his critics to really understand him they must understand, as Geoffrey Nowell-Smith argued,

> that the defining characteristics of an author's work are not necessarily those which are most readily apparent. The purpose of criticism thus becomes to uncover behind the superficial contrasts of subjects and treatment a hard core of basic and often recondite motifs. The pattern formed by these motifs ... is what gives an author's work its particular structure, both defining it internally and distinguishing one body of work from another.

I see in my diary notes that I read this passage out to him. He agreed with a laugh. 'This would suggest that with the occasional exception of Philip French in London and Pauline Kael in New York, there are no critics at all in the UK or US. France, Germany and Italy are a different case altogether.' We discussed his films. The three sets of trilogies depicting three different movements in Indian history: pre- and post-independence; dissent, despair and anger post-independence; and the sinister emergence of Hindutva-type currents that he began to tackle in his last phase.

Pather Panchali (Song of the Open Road), made in 1955, was acclaimed by all. It centred on a poor family in a Bengali village. The scene where the two children watch their first train on its way to the big city was stunning, expressing as it did, in a minute, the desire to get out, the possibility of doing so, and modernity, at last. Then he surprised me: 'I know this is a crass question and

I hate it when I'm ever asked it, but I must ask since you appear to know my work very well.' He paused. I nodded. 'Which work of mine do you like best?' I was taken aback.

I thought back to a 1964 masterpiece with a stunning soundtrack. 'It is difficult. I suppose if I had to choose it would be *Charulata* (The Lonely Wife). I could watch Sharmila Tagore once a month if not more.' He laughed. 'Good judgement. I thought you might have preferred the Calcutta trilogy. Those films are more political.' Seen by too many critics as a turn to romantic fiction, *Charulata* is based on a Tagore novella and is about something very different. At its very heart is the domination of women – by culture, by tradition and even by the kindest of husbands. So the tiniest and most trivial of happenings makes the heroine leap for joy. The birdsong is a call to freedom. The hooves on the road signify a moving outside world. Ray wrote the music for this one. It melds without any fuss into the main concern of the movie.

We moved on to other subjects. I noted his lack of sympathy for younger filmmakers. Eyebrows were raised. A weary look. 'I know they groan and moan, my dear. But how could I possibly help them? The best help I can give them is by remaining silent. Mrinal [Sen] would be better at that than me. He's a very good teacher. Have you seen his latest?'

In fact, I'd seen *Khandhar* (The Ruins) a few days before and it was fresh in my mind. Mrinal Sen, a tremendous filmmaker himself, was an unabashed Marxist but hated it when he was referred to as a Marxist version of Ray. Both directors disliked the description. *Khandhar* was compulsory viewing for me since the lead was one of India's best actresses and a dear friend of mine, Shabana Azmi. It was not Sen's best work; a bit mystical and the cinematographer slightly out of control. I said this to Satyajit. He claimed not to have seen it, but several minutes later returned to the subject. 'The problem with Mrinal's latest is that there is only one hero: the ruins. Nothing else of note. Nothing. Correct me if I'm wrong. And you're not to publish this.' I laughed. I had noticed the cinematic obsession. The ruins dominate. They are striking, but the story of emotional transience didn't grab me.

Derek Malcolm, the film critic at the *Guardian*, had written a snarky review of one of Ray's recent films, *Ghaire Baire* (Home and the World), also based on a Tagore novella. Malcolm, usually an astute critic, didn't fully understand the political and historical context (Lord Curzon's 1911 partition of Bengal, considered by many as a dress rehearsal for 1947) or Tagore's deep hostility to crude nationalist demagogy. His fiction explored complexities. There were inner contradictions. In this work, he explained why so many Bengali Muslims didn't object as strongly to the partition as the Hindus did. In fact, secretly, some poor Muslims favoured it for a combination of economic and existential reasons. Ray understood each sensitivity in the Tagore story and *Ghaire Baire* is a very fine movie.

I reviewed it in *Time Out* and received an appreciative note from him a few weeks later. I've since misplaced the note, but my response was neatly filed away. It reminded me that he had suffered a debilitating heart attack while filming *Ghaire Baire*. This, for him, added another layer to the film. I suggested in my response that some of his critics at Cannes were possibly settling accounts with their recent radical past:

> What is far more disturbing is that these reactions to your work and that of others reflect an undoubted cultural and critical decline in the West. It's almost as if the fact that too many mainstream filmmakers in Hollywood are making movies for 9–15-year-olds and making pots of money as a result has scarred the faculties of many critics as well. I have yet to read a polemical blast against Hollywood infantilism by Derek M and will remind him of this fact when I next see him ... I'm glad that the Houston operation was successful. I'm now an expert on these operations. My father had one two years ago and is in very good heath as a result. His energy is back and he's swimming regularly again. So it moves. Don't permit too many wasteful intrusions. I'll be in Cal in December and will come and see you if you're up for it ...

Tagore and Ray were liberal humanists but much sharper in understanding that how you fought the British would help determine the new India you wanted to create. In a world where traditional nationalists couldn't think of moving beyond the Indianisation of existing colonial institutions, and their communist rivals couldn't think of moving beyond the Stalinist structures established in Moscow, independent-minded thinkers and artists were sometimes more incisive simply because of the lack of competition.

Satyajit Ray's parents were close friends with the Tagores and both families had participated in the late-nineteenth-century Bengal renaissance that took on the British in the realm of culture. As a young filmmaker, Ray had studied at Santiniketan, a school and cultural centre founded by Tagore that celebrated the Bengali language and culture in all its forms. It was here that he learned how to paint, write, read and play music and become an auteur in the real sense of the word. He often wrote both the music and the script for his films, and designed the posters, especially for his early movies. They are displayed still on slightly kitsch Victorian streetlamps in Kolkata as a permanent tribute to his work.

The model of Santiniketan inspired Leonard and Dorothy Elmhirst (she had the dosh) to recreate a much more idyllic version in Dartington, Devon, restoring a neglected and decaying fourteenth-century estate. The college's annual summer schools included music, art and literature as well as farming, forestry and educational projects. Ray once asked me if I'd been there. 'Yes,' I replied. 'To explore the 1,200-acre estate, and have a dip in the river, but mainly to speak at their literature festivals.' When I described the place, he smiled. 'Much grander than our Santiniketan.'

When he died in 1992 the entire city of Kolkata came to a standstill. His funeral was huge. It's not often that this happens for an artist. It happened in Paris when Sartre died and in Damascus when the poet Nizar Qabbani passed away. It would have happened in Lahore for Faiz and in Santiago for Neruda, had the two countries not been under brutal military dictatorships.

43

The Bhuttos of Larkana

The Bhuttos were family friends going back to my grandfather's time. As I described earlier, Zulfikar Ali Bhutto started his political life as a Cabinet minister in the government of the country's first military dictator, General Ayub Khan. The post-Partition story of this wing of the family has been akin to a Greek tragedy. In 1979, Zulfikar Ali Bhutto was hanged by the army with the support of the US. His oldest son Murtaza was shot dead outside his house in Karachi in 1996. Earlier his younger brother Shahnawaz had been poisoned to death by his Afghan wife, and in 2007 his daughter Benazir, campaigning against Musharraf, was assassinated in Rawalpindi after addressing a large rally. This is their story. I knew them well. The frequency of disagreements never led to a break in friendship.

I first met Benazir at her father's house in Karachi in the 1960s when she was a fun-loving teenager, and then again in the 1970s at Oxford, where she was studying. She was not a natural politician and had always wanted to be a diplomat, but history and personal tragedy pushed in a different direction. Her father's death transformed her. She became a new person, determined to take on the military dictator of that time. She had moved to a tiny flat in London, where we would endlessly discuss the future of the country. She agreed that land reforms, mass education programmes, a health service and an independent foreign policy were constructive aims and crucial if Pakistan was to be saved from the vultures in and out of uniform. Her constituency was the poor, and she was proud of the fact.

She changed after becoming prime minister from 1988 to 1990, and then between 1993 and 1996. In the early days, in response to my numerous complaints, all she would say was that the world had changed. She couldn't be on the 'wrong side' of history. But she was hemmed in by the army and the bureaucracy and virtually paralysed during her first spell in office. Many a time I pleaded that some elementary reforms were necessary. Schools for girls in town and country; access to water and electricity in all the villages; medical centres in every village and proper hospitals in the towns. Her response: 'Why don't you come back and take charge of all these projects?'

She was serious but also knew that it was impossible. She needed at least fifty good people and true to start the process. She was convinced they wouldn't let her do even this. 'In that case,' I said, 'go on the offensive. Institute a weekly broadcast to the nation and tell people what is being sabotaged and by whom and what you want to do.'

During her second term the priorities had shifted markedly and corruption was rife. Her husband, Asif Ali Zardari, was discredited. In 1996, I got a phone call from Farooq Leghari, the president she had appointed: 'I am about to take action. The situation is very serious and her husband is behaving as if though he runs the country. It's no longer tenable. I have seen the evidence of his misdemeanours. I just wanted you to know.' That same night, Leghari dismissed the government. Effectively the ground was laid for the army's return, though a transition was agreed that brought the Sharif brothers – a powerful Punjabi political clan – back to power.

The elder Sharif (Nawaz) then tried to remove General Musharraf, the military chief, via a palace coup and a few paid-off generals. They tried not to let the army chief land in Pakistan as he was returning from an official visit to Sri Lanka in October 1999. This backfired, to put it mildly. The plane landed at Karachi airport, which was sealed off by the local army commander, and that same night commandos scaled the walls of the prime minister's house to pick up Nawaz Sharif. By morning, Pakistan had a new military dictator.

In his death-cell, Benazir's father had mulled over similar problems and come to slightly different conclusions. *If I Am Assassinated*, Zulfikar Ali Bhutto's last will and testament, was written in semi-Gramscian mode, and its meaning was not lost on his colleagues:

> I entirely agree that the people of Pakistan will not tolerate foreign hegemony. On the basis of the self-same logic, the people of Pakistan would never agree to an internal hegemony. The two hegemonies complement each other. If our people meekly submit to internal hegemony, a priori, they will have to submit to external hegemony. This is so because the strength and power of external hegemony is far greater than that of internal hegemony. If the people are too terrified to resist the weaker force, it is not possible for them to resist the stronger force. The acceptance of or acquiescence in internal hegemony means submission to external hegemony.

After he was hanged in April 1979, the text acquired a semi-sacred status among his supporters. But when in power, Bhutto *père* had failed to develop any counter-hegemonic strategy or institutions, other than the 1973 constitution drafted by the veteran civil rights lawyer Mahmud Ali Kasuri (whose son Khurshid later became foreign minister under Musharraf). A personality-driven, autocratic style of governance had neutered the spirit of the Pakistan People's Party, encouraged careerists and finally paved the way for Bhutto's enemies. He was the victim of a grave injustice; his death removed all the warts and transformed him into a martyr. More than half the country, mainly the poor, mourned his passing.

The tragedy led to the PPP being treated as a family heirloom, which was unhealthy for both party and country. It provided the Bhuttos with a vote-bank and large reserves. But the experience of her father's trial and death radicalised and politicised his daughter. Her two brothers, Murtaza and Shahnawaz, were in London, having been forbidden to return home by their imprisoned father. The burden of trying to save his life fell on Benazir and her mother, Nusrat, and the courage they exhibited won them the silent respect of a frightened majority.

They refused to cave in to General Zia's military dictatorship, which on top of its other brutalities was invoking Islam to claw back rights won by women in previous decades. Benazir and Nusrat were arrested and imprisoned several times. Their health began to suffer. Nusrat was allowed to leave the country in 1982 to seek medical advice. Benazir was released from prison a little more than a year later – thanks, in part, to US pressure orchestrated by her old Harvard friend Peter Galbraith. She later described the period in her memoir, *Daughter of the East* (1988), which included photo-captions such as: 'Shortly after President Reagan praised the regime for making "great strides towards democracy", Zia's henchmen gunned down peaceful demonstrators marking Pakistan Independence Day. The police were just as brutal to those protesting at the attack on my jeep in January 1987.'

Her Barbican flat in London became the centre of opposition to the dictatorship, and it was here that we discussed a campaign to take on the generals. Benazir had built up her position by steadfastly resisting the military and replying to every slander with a cutting retort. Her brothers had been operating on a different level. They set up an armed group, al-Zulfikar, whose declared aim was to harass and weaken the regime by targeting 'traitors who had collaborated with Zia'. The principal volunteers were recruited inside Pakistan and in 1980 they were provided with a base in Afghanistan, where the pro-Moscow communists had taken power three years before. It was a sad story with a fair share of factionalism, show trials, petty rivalries, fantasies of every sort and death for the group's less fortunate members.

In March 1981, Murtaza and Shahnawaz Bhutto were placed on the Pakistan security services' most-wanted list. Their collaborators had hijacked a Pakistan International airliner soon after it left Karachi (a power cut had paralysed the X-ray machines, enabling the hijackers to take their weapons on board) and it was diverted to Kabul. Here Murtaza took over and demanded the release of political prisoners. A young military officer on board the flight was murdered. The plane refuelled and went on to Damascus, where the Syrian spymaster General Kholi took charge and ensured there were no more deaths. The fact that there were American passengers on the plane was a major consideration for the generals and, for that reason alone, the prisoners in Pakistan were released and flown to Tripoli.

This was seen as a victory and welcomed as such by the PPP in Pakistan. For the first time the al-Zulfikar group began to be taken seriously. A key target inside the country was Maulvi Mushtaq Hussain, the chief justice of the High Court in Lahore who, in 1978, had sentenced Zulfikar Ali Bhutto to death and whose behaviour in court had shocked even those who were hostile to the PPP. (Among other charges, he had accused Bhutto of 'pretending to be a Muslim' – his mother was a Hindu convert.) Mushtaq was in a friend's car being driven to his home in Lahore's Model Town area when al-Zulfikar gunmen opened fire. The judge survived, but his friend and the driver died. The friend was one of the Chaudhrys of Gujrat: Chaudhry Zahoor Elahi, a dodgy businessman who had ostentatiously asked General Zia to make him a present of the 'sacred pen' with which he had signed Bhutto's death warrant. The pen became a family heirloom.

Benazir first returned to Pakistan in 1986 and was greeted by large crowds who came out to show their affection for her and to demonstrate their anger at the regime. She campaigned all over the country, but increasingly felt that for some of the more religious-minded having a young unmarried woman as a leader was not acceptable. She once asked me how she could visit Saudi Arabia without a husband. An offer of marriage from the Zardari family was accepted and she married Asif in 1987. She had worried that any husband would find it difficult to deal with the periods of separation her nomadic political life would entail, but Zardari was perfectly capable of occupying himself.

A year later, on 17 August 1988, General Zia died in an aircraft crash. In the elections that followed the PPP won the largest number of seats. Benazir became prime minister, but was squeezed by the army on one side and the president, the army's favourite bureaucrat, Ghulam Ishaq Khan, on the other. She told me at the time that she felt powerless. But being in office, it seemed, was satisfaction enough. She went on state visits, met and liked Mrs Thatcher, and later, with her new husband in tow, was received politely by the Saudi king. In the meantime there were other plots afoot – the opposition was literally buying off some of her MPs – and in August 1990 her government was removed by presidential decree. Zia's protégés, the Sharif brothers, were back in power.

By the time Benazir was re-elected in 1993, she had abandoned all idea of reform. This period marked the complete degeneration of the party. All that shamefaced party members could say, when I asked, was that 'everybody does it all over the world', thus accepting that the cash nexus was now all that mattered. In foreign policy Benazir's legacy was mixed. She refused to sanction an anti-Indian military adventure in Kargil on the Himalayan slopes, but to make up for it her government backed the Taliban takeover in Kabul – which makes it doubly ironic that Washington and London were promoting her as a champion of democracy.

Benazir's brother, Murtaza Bhutto, had contested the 1993 elections from abroad and won a seat in the Sindh provincial legislature. He returned home and expressed his unhappiness with his sister's agenda. Family gatherings became tense. Murtaza had his weaknesses, but he was not corrupt and he argued in favour of the old party's radical manifesto. He made no secret of the fact that he regarded his brother-in-law Zardari as an interloper whose only interest was money. Nusrat Bhutto suggested that Murtaza be made the chief minister of Sindh; Benazir's response was to remove her mother as chairperson of the PPP.

Any sympathy Murtaza may have felt for his sister turned to loathing. He no longer felt obliged to control his tongue and at every possible opportunity lambasted Zardari and the corrupt regime over which his sister presided. It was difficult to fault him on the facts. The incumbent chief minister of Sindh was Abdullah Shah, one of Zardari's creatures. He began to harass Murtaza's supporters. Murtaza decided to confront the organ-grinder himself. He rang Zardari and invited him round for an informal chat, *sans* bodyguards, to try and settle the problems within the family. Zardari agreed. As the two men were pacing the garden, Murtaza's retainers appeared and grabbed Zardari. Someone brought out a cut-throat razor and some warm water and Murtaza shaved off half of Zardari's moustache, to the delight of the retainers, then told him to get lost. A fuming Zardari, who had probably feared much worse, was compelled to shave off the other half at home. The media, bemused, were informed that the new clean-shaven consort had accepted intelligence advice that the moustache made him too recognisable a target. In which case why did he allow it to sprout again immediately afterwards?

Some months later, in September 1996, as Murtaza and his entourage were returning home from a political meeting, they were ambushed just outside his house by some seventy armed policemen accompanied by four senior officers. A number of snipers were positioned in surrounding trees. Murtaza clearly understood what was happening and got out of his car with his hands raised, instructing his bodyguards not to open fire. The police started shooting nevertheless and seven men were killed, Murtaza among them. The fatal bullet was fired at close range. The trap had been carefully laid, but as is the way in Pakistan, the crudeness of the operation – false entries in police logbooks, lost evidence, witnesses intimidated, the provincial PPP governor (regarded as untrustworthy) dispatched to a non-event in Egypt, the killing of a policeman who they feared might talk – made it obvious that the decision to execute the prime minister's brother had been taken at a very high level.

While the ambush was being prepared, the police had sealed off Murtaza's house. The family inside felt something was wrong. A remarkably composed Fatima Bhutto, Murtaza's fourteen-year-old daughter, decided to ring her aunt at Prime Minister's House. The conversation that followed remained imprinted on her memory and some years ago she gave me an account of it. It was Zardari who took her call:

Fatima I wish to speak to my aunt, please.
Zardari It's not possible.

Fatima Why? [At this point, Fatima says she heard loud wails and what sounded like fake crying.]

Zardari She's hysterical, can't you hear?

Fatima Why?

Zardari Don't you know? Your father's been shot.

Fatima and her stepmother Ghinwa found out where Murtaza had been taken and rushed out of the house. There was no sign that anything had happened on the street outside: the scene had been wiped clean of all evidence. There were no traces of blood and no signs of any disturbance. They drove straight to the hospital but it was too late; Murtaza was already dead. Later they learned that he had been left bleeding on the ground for almost an hour before being taken to a hospital where there were no emergency facilities.

When Benazir arrived to attend her brother's funeral in Larkana, angry crowds stoned her limo, and she had to retreat. In another unusual display of emotion, local people encouraged Murtaza's widow to attend the actual burial ceremony in defiance of Islamic tradition. According to Fatima, one of Benazir's hangers-on instigated legal proceedings against Ghinwa in a religious court for breaching Islamic law. Nothing was sacred.

Anyone who had witnessed Murtaza's murder was arrested; one witness died in prison. When Fatima rang Benazir to ask why witnesses were being arrested and not the killers, she was told: 'Look, you're very young. You don't understand things.' Perhaps it was for this reason that the kind aunt decided to encourage Fatima's blood-mother, Fauzia, whom she had previously denounced as a murderer in the pay of General Zia, to come to Pakistan and claim custody of Fatima. No mystery as to who paid her fare from California. Fatima and Ghinwa resisted and the attempt failed. Benazir then tried a softer approach and insisted that Fatima accompany her to New York, where she was going to address the UN Assembly. Ghinwa Bhutto approached friends in Damascus and had her two children flown out of the country.

A judicial tribunal was appointed by Benazir's government to inquire into the circumstances leading to Murtaza's death.

Headed by a senior judge, it took detailed evidence from all parties. Murtaza's lawyers accused Zardari, Abdullah Shah and two senior police officials of conspiracy to murder. Benazir (by now out of power) accepted that there had been a conspiracy, but suggested that 'the hidden hand responsible for this was President Farooq Ahmad Leghari': the intention, she said, was 'to kill a Bhutto to get rid of a Bhutto'. Nobody took this seriously. Given all that had happened, it was an incredible suggestion.

The tribunal found there was no legally acceptable evidence to link Zardari to the incident, but noted that 'this was a case of extra-judicial killings by the police' and concluded that it could not have taken place without approval from the highest quarters. Nothing happened. Eleven years later, Fatima Bhutto publicly accused Zardari; she also claimed that many of those involved that day had been rewarded for their actions. In an interview on an independent TV station just before the emergency was imposed by Musharraf on 3 November 2007, Benazir was asked to explain how it happened that her brother had bled to death outside his home while she was prime minister. She walked out of the studio. A sharp op ed piece by Fatima in the *LA Times* on 14 November elicited the following response: 'My niece is angry with me.' Well, yes.

Musharraf withdrew the corruption charges against Zardari, but three other cases were ongoing in Switzerland, Spain and Britain. In July 2003, after an investigation lasting several years, the Geneva magistrate Daniel Devaud convicted Mr and Mrs Asif Ali Zardari, in absentia, of money laundering. They had accepted $15 million in bribes from two Swiss companies, SGS and Cotecna. The couple were sentenced to six months in prison and ordered to return $11.9 million to the government of Pakistan. 'I certainly don't have any doubts about the judgments I handed down,' Devaud told the BBC.

Benazir appealed, thus forcing a new investigation. On 19 September 2005 she appeared in a Geneva court and tried to distance herself from the rest of the family: she hadn't been involved, she said; it was a matter for her husband and her mother (by now afflicted with Alzheimer's). She knew nothing of the accounts. And what of the agreement her agent Jens Schlegelmilch had signed, according to which, in case of her and Zardari's death, the assets of Bomer finance company would be divvied out equally between the Zardari and Bhutto families? She knew nothing of that either. And the £120,000 diamond necklace in the bank vault, paid for by Zardari? It was intended for her, but she had rejected the gift as 'inappropriate'.

In Britain the legal shenanigans concerned the $3.4 million Rockwood estate in Surrey, bought by offshore companies on behalf of Zardari in 1995 and refurbished to his exacting tastes. Zardari at first denied owning the estate. Then, when the court was about to instruct the liquidators to sell it and return the proceeds to the Pakistan government, he came forward and accepted ownership. Lord Justice Collins ruled that, while he was not making any 'findings of fact', there was a 'reasonable prospect' that the Pakistan government might be able to establish that Rockwood had been bought and furnished with 'the fruits of corruption'. A close friend of Benazir told me that she was genuinely not involved in this one, since Zardari wasn't thinking of spending much time there with her.

By 2007, Benazir had been in exile for some years, but her political role was not over. Now, she was being used as a chess piece within the larger great game of the 'war on terror'. The time came for her to return to Pakistan. Arranged marriages can be a messy business. Designed principally as a means of accumulating wealth, circumventing undesirable flirtations, or transcending clandestine love affairs, they often don't work. Where both parties are known to loathe each other, only a rash parent, desensitised by the thought of short-term gain, will continue with the process knowing full well that it will end in misery and possibly violence. That this is equally true in political life became clear in the attempt by Washington to tie Benazir to General Pervez Musharraf.

The single, strong parent in this case was a desperate US State Department – with John Negroponte as the ghoulish go-between and Gordon Brown as the blushing bridesmaid – fearful that if it did not push this through both parties might soon be too old for recycling. The bride was certainly in a hurry, the groom less so. Brokers from both sides engaged in lengthy negotiations on the size of the dowry. Her broker was Rehman Malik, a former boss of Pakistan's Federal Investigation Agency, who had been investigated for corruption by the National Accountability Bureau and served nearly a year in prison after Benazir's fall from power, then became one of her business partners and was later under investigation (with Bhutto) by a Spanish court for making questionable payments to Saddam Hussein.

Both parties made concessions. She agreed that the general could take off his uniform after his 're-election' by parliament, but it had to be before the next general election. (Musharraf did so, leaving himself dependent on the good will of his successor as army Chief of Staff.) He pushed through a legal ruling – yet another sordid first in the country's history – known as the National Reconciliation Ordinance, which withdrew all cases of corruption pending against politicians accused of looting the national treasury. The ruling was crucial for Benazir since she hoped that the money-laundering and corruption cases pending in three European courts – in Valencia, Geneva and London – would be dismissed.

Many Pakistanis – not just the mutinous and mischievous types who have to be locked up at regular intervals – were repelled, and coverage of 'the deal' in the Pakistan media was universally hostile, except on state television. The 'breakthrough' was loudly trumpeted in the West, however, and a whitewashed Benazir Bhutto was presented on US networks and BBC TV news as the champion of Pakistani democracy, with reporters loyally referring to her as 'the former prime minister' rather than a fugitive politician facing corruption charges in several countries.

She had returned the favour in advance by expressing sympathy for the US wars in Iraq and Afghanistan, lunching with the Israeli ambassador to the UN (a litmus test) and pledging to 'wipe out terrorism' in her own country. In 1979 a previous military dictator had bumped off her father with Washington's approval, and perhaps she thought it would be safer to seek permanent shelter underneath the imperial umbrella. Harper-Collins paid her half a million dollars to write a new book. The working title she chose was 'Reconciliation'.

As for the general, he had begun his period in office in 1999 by bowing to the spirit of the age and titling himself 'chief executive' rather than 'chief martial law administrator', which had hitherto been the norm. Like his predecessors, he promised he would stay in power only for a limited period, pledging in 2003 to resign as army Chief of Staff in 2004. Like his predecessors, he ignored his pledge. Martial law always begins with the promise of a new order that will sweep away the filth and corruption that marked the old one; in this case it toppled the civilian administrations of Benazir Bhutto and Nawaz Sharif. But 'new orders' are not forward movements, more military detours that further weaken the shaky foundations of a country and its institutions. Within a decade the uniformed ruler was overtaken by a new upheaval.

Dreaming of her glory days in the 1980s, Benazir wanted a large reception on her return. The general was unhappy. The intelligence agencies (as well as her own security advisers) warned her of the dangers. She had declared war on the terrorists and they had threatened to kill her. But she was adamant. She wanted to demonstrate her popularity to the world and to her political rivals, including those inside her own fiefdom, the Pakistan People's Party. For a whole month before she boarded the Dubai–Karachi flight, the PPP had been busy recruiting volunteers from all over the country to welcome her. Up to 200,000 people lined the streets, but it was a far cry from the million who turned up in Lahore in 1986 when a very different Benazir had returned to challenge General Zia. The plan had been to move slowly in the Bhuttomobile from Karachi airport to the tomb of the country's founder, Muhammad Ali Jinnah, where she would make a speech. It was not to be. As darkness fell, the bombers struck. Who they were and who sent them remains a mystery. She was unhurt, but 130 people died, including some of the policemen guarding her. The wedding reception had led to mayhem.

The general, while promising to collaborate with Benazir, was coolly making arrangements to prolong his own stay at President's House. Even before her arrival he had considered taking drastic action to dodge the obstacles that stood in his way, but his generals (and the US embassy) seemed unconvinced. The bombing of Benazir's cavalcade reopened the debate. Pakistan, if not exactly the erupting volcano portrayed in the Western media, was being shaken by all sorts of explosions. Only firm action could 'restore order' – i.e. save the general's skin. The usual treatment in these cases is a declaration of martial law. But what to do when the country is already being governed by the army Chief of Staff? The solution was simple. Treble the dose. Organise a coup within a coup. Which is what Musharraf decided to do. Washington was informed a few weeks in advance, Downing Street somewhat later. Benazir's patrons in the West told her what was about to happen and she, foolishly for a political leader who has just returned to her country, evacuated to Dubai.

On 3 November 2007, Musharraf, as chief of the army, suspended the constitution and imposed a state of emergency: all non-government TV channels were taken off the air, the mobile phone networks were jammed, paramilitary units surrounded the Supreme Court. The chief justice convened an emergency bench of judges, who – heroically – declared the new dispensation 'illegal and unconstitutional'. They were unceremoniously removed and put under house arrest. Pakistan's judges have usually been acquiescent. Those who in the past resisted military leaders were soon bullied out of it, so the decision of this chief justice took the country by surprise and won him great admiration. Global media coverage of Pakistan suggests a country of generals, corrupt politicians and bearded lunatics: the struggle to reinstate the chief justice had presented a different picture.

Aitzaz Ahsan, a prominent member of the PPP, minister of the interior in Benazir's first government and president of the Bar Association, was arrested and placed in solitary confinement. Several thousand political and civil rights activists were picked up. Imran Khan was detained, charged with 'state terrorism' (for which the penalty is death or life imprisonment) and taken in handcuffs to a remote high-security prison. Lawyers were arrested all over the country and many were physically attacked by policemen. 'Humiliate them' was the order, and the police obliged.

In the evening of that first day, and after several delays, a flustered General Musharraf, his hair badly dyed, appeared on TV trying to look like the sort of leader who wants it understood that the political crisis is to be discussed with gravity and sangfroid. Instead, he came across as a dumbed-down dictator fearful for his own political future. His performance as he broadcast to the nation, first in Urdu and then in English, was incoherent. The gist was simple: he had to act because the Supreme Court had 'so demoralised our state agencies that we can't fight the "war on terror"' and the TV networks had become 'totally irresponsible'. 'I have imposed emergency,' he said halfway through his diatribe, adding, with a contemptuous gesture: 'You must have seen it on TV.' Was he being sarcastic, given that most channels had been shut down? The English-language version put the emphasis on the 'war on terror': Napoleon and Abraham Lincoln, he said, would have done what he did to preserve the 'integrity of their country' – the mention of Lincoln was obviously intended for the US market. In Pakistan's military academies the usual soldier-heroes are Napoleon, De Gaulle and Atatürk.

What did Benazir, now outmanoeuvred, make of the speech as she watched it on TV in her Dubai sanctuary? Her first response was to say she was shocked, which was slightly disingenuous. Even if she had not been told in advance that an emergency would be declared, it was hardly a secret – for one thing, Condoleezza Rice had made a token public appeal to Musharraf not to take this course. Agitated phone calls from Pakistan persuaded Bhutto to return to Karachi. To put her in her place, the authorities kept her plane waiting on the tarmac. When she finally reached the VIP lounge, her PPP colleagues told her that unless she denounced the emergency there would be a split in the party. Outsmarted and abandoned by Musharraf, she couldn't take the risk of losing key figures in the PPP. She denounced the emergency and its perpetrator, established contact with the beleaguered opposition, and, as if putting on a new lipstick, declared that she would lead the struggle to get rid of the dictator. She then tried to call on the chief justice to express her sympathy but wasn't allowed near his residence.

She could have followed the example of her imprisoned colleague Aitzaz Ahsan, but she was envious of him: he had become far too popular in Pakistan. He'd even had the nerve to go to Washington, where he was politely received by society and inspected as a possible substitute should things go badly wrong. Ahsan had advised her against any deal with Musharraf. When generals are against the wall, he is reported to have told her, they resort to desperate and irrational measures. Others who offered similar advice in gentler language were also batted away. She was the PPP's 'chairperson-for-life' and brooked no dissent. The fact that Ahsan was proved right irritated her even more. Any notion of political morality had long ago been dumped. The very idea of a party with a consistent set of beliefs was regarded as ridiculous and outdated. Ahsan was now safe in prison, far from the madding hordes of Western journalists whom she received in style during the few days she spent under house arrest and afterwards. She made a few polite noises about his imprisonment, but nothing more.

The go-between from Washington arrived at very short notice. Negroponte spent some time with Musharraf and spoke to Benazir, still insisting that they make up and go through with the deal. She immediately toned down her criticisms, but the general was scathing and said in public that there was no way she could win the elections scheduled for January. No doubt the ISI was planning to rig them in style. Had she remained loyal to the general she might have lost public support, but he would have made sure she had a substantial presence in the new parliament. Now everything was up for grabs again. The opinion polls showed that Benazir's old rival, Nawaz Sharif, was well ahead of her. Musharraf's hasty pilgrimage to Mecca was probably an attempt to secure Saudi mediation in case he had to cut a deal with the Sharif brothers – who had been living in exile in Saudi Arabia – and sideline Benazir completely. Both sides denied that a deal was done, but Sharif returned to Pakistan with Saudi blessings and an armour-plated Cadillac as a special gift from the king. Little doubt that Riyadh would rather him than Benazir.

Even those of us sharply critical of Benazir Bhutto's behaviour and policies – both while she was in office and after – were stunned and angered by her assassination in December 2007. An odd coexistence of military despotism and anarchy created the conditions leading to her death in Rawalpindi. In the past, military rule was designed to preserve order – and did so for a few years – but this soon degenerated into disorder and lawlessness. It was assumed that Benazir's killers were jihadi fanatics. This may well be true, but were they acting on their own? She survived the bomb blast but was felled by the bullets fired at her car. The assassins had taken out a double insurance this time. They wanted her dead.

What happened was a multilayered tragedy. It was a tragedy for a country on a road to more disasters. And it was a personal tragedy. The house of Bhutto lost another member. A father, two sons and now a daughter all died unnatural deaths.

44

A Painter of His Time

In October 2017, just a few months after the seventieth anniversary of Indian independence and the partition of the subcontinent, the Pakistani painter Tassaduq Sohail died in Karachi. The anniversary was celebrated with dazzling military displays: the centrepieces in both Delhi and Islamabad were nuclear missiles. Partition was history now, we were told, but for Sohail and others who experienced it first-hand, the memories had never lost their force.

In January 2000, after forty years in Britain, Sohail had decided to return to Pakistan. A week or so before he left, I got a call. He spoke, as always, in Punjabi and by common agreement we avoided using any English words – a common practice that enraged him. It was a test I sometimes failed. Sohail was seventeen years older than the country he sometimes called home and sometimes hell. Usually when he rang, he would recite a few lines from the Sufi poets with gaiety in his voice, and occasionally he even laughed at my attempts at Punjabi double entendres. But this time his tone was sombre.

'I'm going back.'

I was taken aback. There had been no hint of this in recent conversations. 'Why?'

'To die.'

'Why?'

'Everyone has to. I thought it best to be close to my final destination.'

I laughed. His laugh was forced. He didn't have too many plans, or hopes. After forty years, he had no family and few real friends in Britain. The decision to return had been taken with very little consultation. Among the few people with whom he felt a sense of camaraderie were three Jewish elders in Golders Green ('my three fathers') who had posed for him and become friends. They look quite jolly in his depiction. He had not discussed his decision with them because one of them was always thinking about moving to Israel, the other two were strongly opposed, and it would have provoked a row between them.

Suddenly he fell silent, then spoke in a very abrupt tone. 'Tell me something. Be honest. Do you think any of my paintings would encourage anybody to fight back? I mean anyone. Even a single person? You, for instance?'

It was a puzzling question from someone who had never shown any interest in politics. I said as much. It turned out that he had recently returned from Berlin where he had heard some English people ('white people from here', as he put it) in the Käthe Kollwitz museum say that about her work. He was equally happy for people to dislike his work or like it very much. What he hated was eliciting no response at all. That was really why he was going back. Whatever else, in Pakistan there would be a reaction. I worried that the response might be fatal. His head might be blown off. I did not say this because he knew it better than I did.

On a previous trip to Karachi, he had sold erotic paintings to what he described to me as 'rich begums left alone by their husbands during the day'. They bought his paintings in secret and a few of them commissioned new work, giving detailed and 'shameless' instructions on what they required him to paint. 'For the first time I realised the function of a eunuch in the harem,' he told me. I asked for names. He declined. 'Pity the poor eunuch caught revealing secrets.'

He had made a fair bit of money and thought that he could always repeat the process when he got back to Karachi. I'm not sure he did. The atmosphere had changed and the combination of philistinism and piety meant that Sohail was no longer received in polite society, not even in secret. His phone calls became less frequent, then stopped altogether. The last time I had a conversation with him was after he'd read *The Night of the Golden*

Butterfly, the final novel in my Islam Quintet. The painter in it was loosely based on Sohail.

He was not finding it easy in Karachi. Hell was lonely too, just like England. Too many of his friends were dead. The city had become a network of competing protection rackets. Culture was disintegrating. Nobody paid him much attention. 'I feel a python has wrapped itself around my heart.' Depictions of his inner life weren't selling. Piety was so widespread that he had become very cautious: he stopped painting beards and penises. More and more animals began to appear in his work (including the odd unicorn) as well as mermaids in different shapes and sizes. Both safe. The colours became more vibrant: a lot of turquoise and sea green. It was obvious that he was painting to please. He admitted this, saying he was returning to his street artist years in London. I reminded him that that was not the way he had begun. 'We are all driven by our destinies, friend. Mine is to spend the few remaining years sinking slowly in this wasteland.'

Of all my friends and acquaintances from the subcontinent, Sohail was the most traumatised by Partition and, also, the least political. His imagination was haunted by the horrors of 1947. The images grew misty, but he never got over it. One result was his aversion to all religions, to which he attributed the tragedy: several million refugees and well over a million dead bodies. On this he never softened. All my attempts to explain the 1947 divide as the result of global events, how they were refracted in India and used by politicians, were greeted with a snort.

I first met him in 1987. He had managed to raise the money to fund an exhibition in a small gallery on a tiny street on the fringes of Bloomsbury. A friend rang to insist I go and see it without telling me too much about it. I had never heard of Tassaduq Sohail, which was an added inducement. Sohail rang too and suggested he could have the gallery opened for me on a Sunday if that made it easier. It did.

A short, thin, prematurely bald, middle-aged Asian man in a light-blue supermarket security guard's uniform let me in. I suppressed a smile at the incongruity between his uniform and his stature. He switched on the awful neon lights. We were on the ground floor and I could now see that the walls were covered with miniatures painted in black ink. Each etching was crowded with strange figures, both male and female, each face agonised, almost paralysed by the brutalities being inflicted. The intensity was astonishing. What was disconcerting, as I inspected each of the sixty or seventy works in turn, was being followed by the security guard in his ghastly uniform. I was sorely tempted to ask him to wait outside, but it was raining. Just as well. It turned out he was the painter.

It was June 1947. He and his parents were leaving everything behind except for a few clothes and some heirlooms. All the Muslims in his village in the Punjab were waiting for a bus to take them to Jalandhar, from where they would be transported in larger buses and trucks to Lahore, now in Pakistan. A number of Sikh neighbours, he recalled, came to embrace them, but they did not hang around, not wanting to be seen by their more fanatical brethren.

In Jalandhar, Sohail ran to the first vehicle in the convoy of buses and trucks, but his parents called him back and told him to let the elderly and those with very young children on first. Instead, they got on the second bus, which was already overfull, and then they were delayed waiting for stragglers. The first bus moved off. Their convoy caught up with it thirty miles later. Every single person had been dragged out and killed. He remembered the blood, the naked bodies of women of all ages, violated before their throats were slit. Dead babies beside dead mothers.

The convoy came to a halt. People rushed out screaming as they recognised friends and relations. The drivers checked to see if anybody was alive. Nobody. The convoy now moved at great speed, the drivers ignoring all attempts to stop them. There was no time for burials. A few bullets were fired at them, but they reached Lahore safely. 'Everyone went crazy,' Sohail muttered. 'Each side massacred innocents. The whole of the Punjab was an inferno. We left one hell and arrived in another, but we were alive.'

His parents moved to Karachi in 1952, but he was not happy there, never found a partner. He wrote a few short stories. Nothing ever worked out. Witnessing the aftermath of the massacre made him extremely pessimistic, apolitical and bitter. He remained alienated on every level. Two years after the 1958 military coup in Pakistan, he left for Britain. In those days no visas were needed for Commonwealth citizens and five years of permanent residency entitled us to UK citizenship.

Sohail got a factory job in Ealing, and shared a room with other immigrants. Shift work meant that the landlord (usually a fellow South Asian) could charge four lots of rent per room per day, a very primitive accumulation of capital that led in due course to many medium-sized fortunes and a few supermarket empires. It was the first time since 1947 that he had met, eaten and conversed with Sikhs, some of whom were from Jalandhar. He hated the work itself but one thing stuck in his mind. His fellow Asians got very agitated at the reluctance of the white shop stewards of the Transport and General Workers' Union to give them union cards. Sohail didn't care at all.

The high point of his social life, he told me, was to save up a few shillings, visit a strip-joint in Soho and then, while the memory was strong, indulge in some fist-fucking. I was never convinced by the stories he sometimes told me (usually when others were present) stressing his virility and his conquests. He told me more than once that he preferred living on his own. The women he sometimes turned up with were for the purpose of showing off. All the ones I met were his models, who were very fond of him because no sexual favours were demanded. Two of them, at least, were sex workers. They told him their stories and he painted them with a real anger at their circumstances.

He changed jobs frequently. After the West London factory, he moved to Golders Green, rented a room and got work in a newsagents at the Tube station. He started sketching in notebooks or on blank paper to pass the time. One day an Englishman who regularly bought *The Times* from him asked what he was drawing. The man told him he should take up painting seriously and bought a few pages of the notebook.

Soon after that he left his job, abandoned his black ink drawings and concentrated instead on pastels and acrylic and watercolours. He sold his work on the pavement outside Hyde Park. He said that the worse the painting was, the more likely it was to sell. He started putting in a few naked women and sales rocketed.

On the first floor of the Bloomsbury gallery the work was entirely different: paintings in exuberant colours, full of humour. They were viciously satirical, with religion and its hypocritical clergy as the target. Sex had all of them in thrall. Here was a mullah walking with his wife but thinking of two naked women and watched by an all-knowing crow. Sohail regarded animals as more refined in many ways than humans and they began to dominate his work. There is a watercolour of a Hindu or Buddhist monk having a wet dream, an arc of sperm rising from his penis and descending on the backside of a distant doe.

Partition had convinced him that the capacity of humans to do mischief to one another was limitless. My attempts to give him explanations for the violence were shrugged off. For a while his paintings became more and more vicious, with the penises of clergymen or the priests of ancient Egypt often depicted as oppressive weapons. I was worried someone might issue a fatwa. He was unconcerned. 'All the humans in my work are anonymous. They have no identity. What could be the content of such a fatwa? That I'm blaspheming against a particular penis? I don't think any mullah anywhere is going to self-identify to such an extent. And what you don't know is that more than a few religious-minded scholars buy these paintings.'

When I asked if he'd ever had any formal training his explanation was not out of kilter with the rest of his life.

'When I was working as a bus driver I used to go past the art school on Charing Cross Road every day. It was a busy road and slow. It was summer. On the pavement, leaning against the fence or sitting on the steps, I would see very beautiful young men and women, joking and laughing. I wondered what happened inside that building. I didn't think they could be artists. They looked too happy.

On one of my days off I went to investigate. There was a long queue. They told me they were painting nudes that day. I joined them and was given pastels and paper. I sketched a female nude in black, with two red dots as her nipples, very restrained work.

A teacher standing behind me and looking over my shoulder, smiled and said: "You have a good sense of colour." Two red dots were enough for her! She had a good sense of humour, I thought, but she encouraged me to return. For the next six months, I went once every week, probably the most valuable days in my life as an artist.'

That was the extent of his training.

Sohail once asked me whether Partition could have been avoided. To which my answer remains yes. Trotsky's view that history shares commonalities with biology, and that causality works through a 'natural selection of accidents', is a pretty good description of what happened in India.

He once told me that he adored Ibsen and had seen all his plays. His favourite was *Ghosts*. He liked the portrayal of the severely disabled son, Oswald, a painter. Sohail underlined the passage in which Oswald wants his mother to help him die:

Oswald: You'll have to help me now, mother.

Mrs Alving: I?

Oswald: Who better than you?

Mrs Alving: I? Your mother?

Oswald: For that very reason.

Mrs Alving: I, who gave you life!

Oswald: I never asked you for life. And what kind of life have you
given me? I don't want it! You take it back!

45

Casteism

Caste was never discussed as such in our household. There were odd fleeting references, usually related to how the caste system had survived in the new religions that came to India. In my teens I discovered two books that had been written within months of each other during the 1930s. The first was a novel by Mulk Raj Anand, *Untouchable*, a social-realist depiction of the Dalit condition. The second was Ambedkar's *Annihilation of Caste*, the transcript of a speech he was not allowed to read at a conference of anti-caste Hindu reformers in Lahore in 1936: the text was too much for the organisers and the event was cancelled. In his collection *Vindication of Caste*, Gandhi wrote that while the ban had been a misjudgement, Ambedkar's 'utopian' hostility to Hinduism was unacceptable.

I met Anand in 1965 at the World Peace Conference in Helsinki. He was born in Peshawar, but Lahore – where I grew up – had been his favourite city, though he had not returned there since Partition. After discussing mutual family friends, he asked whether I'd read any of his novels. I had, all of them. My favourite was *Untouchable*. He smiled. 'That one will last as long as untouchability. Eternal.'

He had read Ambedkar's essays and journalism and met the man himself. The extract below is a fictionalised version of a real event. Ambedkar's father worked for the British Indian Army, but even in army schools, untouchable children were not permitted to study in the same classroom as other Indian children. They sat outside in the heat of the dusty courtyard. Anand offers a memorable account:

The outcastes were not allowed to mount the platform surrounding the well, because if they were ever to draw water from it, the Hindus of the three upper castes would consider the water polluted. Nor were they allowed access to the nearby brook as their use of it would contaminate the stream. They had no well of their own because it cost at least a thousand rupees ... Perforce they had to collect at the foot of the caste Hindus' well and depend on the bounty of some of their superiors to pour water into their pitchers ... So the outcastes had to wait for chance to bring some caste Hindu to the well, for luck to decide that he was kind, for Fate to ordain that he had time to get their pitchers filled with water. They crowded round the well, congested the space below its high brick platform, morning, noon and night, joining their hands with servile humility to every passer-by, cursing their fate and bemoaning their lot if they were refused the help they wanted.

Anand asked me many questions about northern Pakistan. We shared a love of what was then a tiny hill station called Nathiagali that served as the summer capital of the North West Frontier Province, usually administered from Peshawar. I told him of my first encounter with the Christian untouchables there. There was no sewage system, and excrement was collected from wooden thunder-boxes by these Christians three times a day.

We went to Nathiagali for two months every summer and I got to know some of them reasonably well. In June 1962 all the other local council workers were given a pay rise, but not the shit-collectors. They were despondent. I asked their leader, Abdul, the reason. He said they had not received a pay rise the year before either, unlike everyone else. I suggested a strike. 'Listen,' I said to him. 'Most of the people whose toilets you clean are senior civil servants, government ministers and the like. Let them smell their own shit for two days. You'll win.' The strike was a huge success. Within forty-eight hours they got a backdated pay rise. Anand laughed. 'If only it was so easy all the time.'

I shouldn't have been, but I was taken aback by a forwarded news item from an Indian newspaper during the Tokyo Olympics in August 2021. The Indian women's hockey team had lost to Argentina in the semi-final. The team contained a Dalit player, Vandana Katariya. Outside her family house in a small village near Haridwar, India, a handful of casteist bigots celebrated India's defeat by letting off crackers and dancing in mock celebration. Why? Because, like many others, including other members of the Indian team, they blamed the Dalits for the defeat and expressed pleasure because they hoped this would force the Indian sporting authorities to get rid of all Dalits from national teams.

I spoke to Indian friends. 'Oh, Tariq, this is nothing. Much worse things happen.' True, but it was this event that haunted me. Similar things happen in cricket, but only when India plays Pakistan and the Muslim players in the Indian team are watched by the Islamophobic hawks in the squad (there are a few) and pitilessly abused online. Given that Islamophobia is official government policy, the state encourages this prejudice.

But casteism remains deeply embedded in the sociocultural system. Four years prior to the targeting of Vandana, I had come across a remarkable book by Sujatha Gidla, *Ants among Elephants: An Untouchable Family and the Making of Modern India*. I had read Ambedkar and Arundhati Roy and essays on the subject before that, but Gidla's work was unusual. The account stayed with me. I went back for a re-read. It's a family biography encompassing a history rarely told: despite its longevity, caste, and caste oppression, is not a popular theme in India. Sujatha Gidla writes of poisoned lives, of disillusionment, betrayed hopes, unrequited loves, attempted escapes through alcohol and sex. What distinguishes her book is its rich mix of sociology, anthropology, history, literature and politics.

Gidla writes of her great-grandparents, born in the late nineteenth century in the Khammam district of what is now Andhra Pradesh. They belonged to a clan of pre-agricultural, forest-based tribal nomads. Hunting and gathering supplied necessities; they worshipped their own forest gods. When the occupying British cut down forests and replaced them with teak plantations, the clan was forced out. They found a large lake with no villages nearby and settled on its shores. The soil was rich. They took to agriculture and produced much more rice than they needed. They found a market for the surplus, which meant that they caught the attention of local landlords and their agents: they were forced to pay taxes and dragged into the caste-based Hindu world. As landless agricultural labourers they were the lowest of the low, classed as untouchables, 'outcastes'. They carried on as normal, until one day they provided shelter, as was their custom, to a fugitive from the Yanadi clan who was on the run from the police. He was a burglar: the Yanadis traditionally rejected all private property rights, but went a few steps further. They regarded it as a 'sacred duty' to violate them. An early example of the 'unity of theory and practice'. When a few policemen arrived the villagers drove them away. But then Gidla's clan encountered modernity in the shape of a hundred baton-carrying colonial policemen, who destroyed their goods and food, harassed the women, and took every male into custody. 'The villagers did not know what to do,' Gidla writes.

> They did not know about jails, bail, courts or lawyers. But fortuitously, some Canadian missionaries active in a nearby town learned what had happened. They sent a white lawyer to defend the villagers and win their release. In gratitude, the villagers started to give up their old goddesses and accept baptism. They began sending their children to attend the schools set up by missionaries.
>
> Untouchables had long been forbidden from learning to read or write. But when the missionaries arrived, they opened schools that, to the horror of the Hindus, welcomed even the untouchables ... caste Hindus often refused to send their children, unwilling to let them sit side by side with untouchable students.

The stigma extended to animals. Gidla's uncle K. G. Satyamurthy, later one of the founders of the Maoist People's War Group, was startled at the age of ten to discover that 'untouchable buffaloes were not allowed to graze in the same meadows as the caste buffaloes'.

Gidla's maternal grandparents, Prasanna Rao and Maryamma, lived after their marriage in a village called Adavi Kolanu, where they taught in a mission school. But they moved to the city after Maryamma was insulted by some local upper-caste men who had seen her wearing a new sari the missionaries had bought her as a Christmas present. The two groups – untouchables and caste Hindus – had gathered in the village square when a brahmin intervened: 'Kill me first before you kill each other,' he challenged them. To kill a brahmin is the sin of sins. First the untouchables backed down, then the caste Hindus. The nonviolent brahmin then counselled the untouchables to never again try anything that might provoke the caste Hindus. This was the way his idol, Gandhi, always resolved caste disputes. Symbolism that left the real problem unsolved.

When they arrived in Visakhapatnam (Vizag in British shorthand), their two sons, Satyamurthy ('the wise one'), henceforth known to all as Satyam, was five and his brother, William Carey, was two. Their sister, Mary Manjulabai, Gidla's mother, was born in Vizag. The parents got jobs as teachers in Christian schools and earned enough to rent a modest apartment. The landlord was a caste Hindu and so they lied, claiming they had converted to Christianity from middle-caste Hinduism. The landlord was suspicious, but their status as teachers clinched the deal.

The intersection of their lives with British withdrawal from India and the eruption immediately after Independence of a huge peasant uprising in the state of Telangana, which borders Andhra Pradesh, helped shape all their lives. In Telangana, which had its own feudal ruler, 'every untouchable family in every village had to give up their first male child as soon as he learned to talk and walk. They would bring him to the *dora* [landlord] to work in his household as a slave until death.' Other castes suffered too. This wasn't, as Gidla writes, 'a traditional system', but one instituted in the late nineteenth century to allow the large-scale cultivation of tobacco and cotton. The peasants, aided by the Communist Party, rose up and fought this servitude.

By now the brahmins were in power in Delhi. No untouchable or low-caste Hindu harboured too many illusions. Some even feared that after the British withdrawal things would get worse for them. They did. The Indian Army invaded the city of

Hyderabad in Telangana, deposing its rulers, but then turned its guns on the peasants, detaining, torturing and raping thousands and evicting them from the land. The more progressive elements in the Congress Party may have believed that with industrialisation and modernisation the problem of caste would solve itself. It never did. Capitalism itself may be caste, colour and gender-blind but the dominant classes utilise these divisions to preserve their own rule. As Gidla recounts, the 1928 general strike in Bombay was defeated thanks in part to caste divisions within the workers' movement. This isn't the only example.

Christianity could not provide social upward mobility, but it ensured that Satyam and his siblings received a proper education, despite taunts from caste Hindus. Because they were educated, Gidla's relatives could get jobs in Christian schools and hospitals. But a brown-skinned Christian was still treated very differently from a white-skinned one, and brahmin converts to the imperial religion refused to marry untouchable Christians. Conversion didn't erase the stigma of untouchability. As a teenager, Satyam was hostile to Nehru and Gandhi – he saw them as products of British rule and tied to it in too many ways – but sympathetic to the militant, secular nationalism of Subhas Chandra Bose.

From here, Satyam moved the short distance to the Communist Party, inspired by the accounts that student CP members gave him of the Telangana peasants' struggle. Until a few years before his death in 2012, Satyam was engaged in the peasant resistance in Andhra Pradesh. After the Communist Party split in 1967 he became involved in the Naxalite, Maoist wing of the party, backing an armed revolt. After its failure, and the killing of many Naxalite leaders, he cofounded the People's War Group, which Gidla describes as the 'most notorious, famous and successful Naxalite party, a thorn in the side of the Indian rulers'. He was eventually expelled from it after complaining about the party's treatment of untouchables. 'Talk of caste feeling within the party had always been taboo,' Gidla writes, but young untouchables were beginning to see it as a political issue.

They told Satyam that 'when they joined the party, they were not given a gun. Instead, they were handed a broom and told to sweep the floors.' For a long time, too long, he'd preferred to believe that caste prejudice was false consciousness and would disappear in time. It never did. Even in the People's War Group, members of the barber caste shaved their comrades, washer-caste members washed the clothes, and the untouchables 'were made to sweep and mop the floors and clean the lavatories'. This was life in a revolutionary group committed to an armed struggle to liberate the poor.

Satyam can't have been too surprised by this. He had suffered many insults from upper-caste members of the party, some of whom would leave money in the lavatory in order to see if he pocketed it.

Feeling that the question of caste had now reached a new stage (there had been massacres of untouchables and angry responses), he confronted his comrades on the Central Committee. Their response was 'swift and ruthless. He was expelled on the spot for "conspiring to divide the party".' The news of his expulsion became public when Gidla's mother wrote a letter to a newspaper explaining what lay behind it. That was when most people found out that the founder of the People's War Group, whom they knew as a revolutionary and a poet, publishing under the pseudonym Siva Sagar, was also an untouchable.

Gidla, born in appalling conditions in an untouchable ghetto in the city of Kazipet in Telangana, now works as a conductor on the New York subway (she lost her job as a software programmer in a bank after the 2008 financial crash). Her experiences in the United States pushed her to write the book – an attempt to explain to her new friends and colleagues the difference between caste and race. Race is visible. Caste is a hierarchy established more than 2,500 years ago. 'What comes by birth and can't be cast off by dying – that is caste.' Arundhati Roy describes it in an essay introducing B.R. Ambedkar's 1930s classic, *The Annihilation of Caste*:

> What we call the caste system today is known in Hinduism's founding texts as *varnashrama dharma* or *chaturvarna*, the system of four varnas. The approximately four thousand endogamous castes and sub-castes (*jatis*) in Hindu society, each with its own specified

hereditary occupation, are divided into four varnas – Brahmins (priests), Kshatriyas (soldiers), Vaishyas (traders) and Shudras (servants). Outside of these varnas are the *avarna*castes, the Ati-Shudras, subhumans, arranged in hierarchies of their own – the Untouchables, the Unseeables, the Unapproachables – whose presence, whose touch, whose very shadow is considered to be polluting by privileged-caste Hindus ... Each region of India has lovingly perfected its own unique version of caste-based cruelty, based on an unwritten code that is much worse than the Jim Crow laws.

Unsurprisingly, Gidla's tone in her portrait of everyday social and political life in India over the late nineteenth and twentieth centuries is defiant, sometimes angry: Gandhi is portrayed as a hypocrite, Nehru as a conscienceless Kashmiri brahmin who was happy to send troops to crush the Telangana peasant uprising and remained unaffected by the resulting thousands of deaths. Unlike his many apologists, Gandhi never concealed his views on the caste system. He was opposed to treating untouchables badly, but defended the system itself: 'I am one of those who do not consider caste to be a harmful institution,' he wrote in the journal *Young India* in 1920. 'In its origin, caste was a wholesome custom and promoted national wellbeing. In my opinion, the idea that inter-dining or intermarrying is necessary for national growth is a superstition borrowed from the West.'

Contrary to the radical slogans of the late 1940s, India's wasn't a 'fake independence'. Self-rule was achieved at a high price and it meant something, but it incorporated many colonial practices. The new masters benefited, but for the untouchables, tribals and others, conditions remained the same or got worse. According to recent estimates by India's National Crime Records Bureau, every sixteen minutes a crime is committed by caste Hindus against an untouchable – or Dalit, as they prefer to be called. The figures are horrific: every month fifty-two Dalits are killed and six kidnapped; every week almost thirty Dalit women are raped by caste Hindus. These are probably serious underestimates. Most victims of caste violence don't report the crime for fear of reprisals, notably death by burning.

In 2012 the Indian and Western media extensively covered the gang rape and murder of a single woman in Delhi, largely because students and feminist groups had protested on the streets and made it an issue. That same year 1,574 Dalit women were raped and 651 Dalits murdered. Add to this the regular mob punishment of Dalit and low-caste women, who are forcibly stripped, then paraded through villages to humiliate them further. Politically a democracy, constitutionally secular, India has, since 1947, been a caste Hindu dictatorship. During the run-up to independence, B.R. Ambedkar pinpointed the futility of 'rights': 'If the fundamental rights are opposed by the community, no law, no parliament, no judiciary can guarantee them in the real sense of the word ... What is the use of fundamental rights to the Negro in America, to the Jews in Germany and to the Untouchables in India?'

He also advised the leader of the Muslim League, Mohammed Ali Jinnah, not to place any trust in the brahmin-dominated Congress and to fight hard for a Muslim state. Ambedkar considered demanding a separate status for untouchables, slicing them away from Hinduism. This would have given them separate electoral representation, as was the case with Muslims and other minorities. Gandhi talked him out of this by flattery, and by arguing that since Ambedkar would be drafting the new Indian constitution he could write in all the safeguards he wanted. This did happen, but had little impact. 'Implement the Constitution' remains a Dalit demand to this day.

The evolution of caste in India remains a subject of heated debate. In its earliest forms it must have been in existence at least 2,500 years ago, when Siddhartha Gautama (the Buddha) began a reform movement to purge the brahminical religion of its impurities. The hierarchical caste system was a principal target. After he failed, his followers were driven out of India to Sri Lanka and further east. The untouchables, pushed out of the officially designated caste system, remained silent. There isn't a single recorded account of a Dalit rebellion. The repression was systemic: worse and more effective than that imposed by slavery and making the latter unnecessary. Three medieval mystic poets spoke for them. In the fifteenth century, Ravidas, a tanner (hence low-caste), imagined Be-gham-pura, the city without sorrow, a place with no caste segregation, 'where there is no affliction or suffering, neither anxiety, nor fear, taxes nor capital, no menace, no terror, no humiliation. One who shares with me that city is my friend.' Kabir, a weaver, writing in the same period, was more aggressive. His poems (indifferently translated into English by Rabindranath Tagore) are still sung in many parts of India. One of them, not a Tagore translation, reads:

> Cow dung's impure,
> The bathing-square is impure
> Even its curves are impure
> Says Kabir: Only they who have cleansed their minds
> Are pure.

A century and a half later, the Punjabi Sufi poet Bulleh Shah lamented:

> Come Bulleh, let us go
> to the land where all are blind
> where none can recognise our caste
> or a sage in me find

And later speaks on behalf of an untouchable cleaner:

> I'm a sweeperess,
> I'm untouchable,
> They avoid me,
> I don't care.
> My pay after a long day's work?
> A stone pillow and what you leave behind.
> My life?
> Cold and sickness and scorn
> Empty stomach,
> Clothes always torn.
> The straws of my broom are all I own.
> I'm a sweeperess.

These poems are still sung at rural concerts, especially those marking the anniversaries of the poets' deaths. It's difficult to believe (and I don't) that the oral culture of the Dalits did not produce laments and vicious anti-brahmin songs and satires or jokes. Some of these must survive. But in Satyam's era, poets and short-story writers didn't write about caste: it was considered divisive. Muslim progressives ignored the theme, as did many leftist intellectuals of Hindu and Sikh origin.

The far-right BJP government led by Narendra Modi deliberately misinterprets and distorts India's ancient history to justify its cultural offensive against Islam and other minorities, aiming to create a monolithic Hindu narrative and an official Hinduism. School textbooks, university education, what is and what should not be stocked in public libraries, are all policed. The Hindu epics, long read and appreciated as literature, are now being characterised as history. When asked to explain the elephant god, Modi responded: 'We worship Lord Ganesha. There must have been some plastic surgeon at that time who got an elephant's head on the body of a human being and began the practice of plastic surgery.' The new monolithism confronts a giant obstacle in the shape of the caste system. In 2018, at a huge gathering of the party faithful in Meerut, Mohan Bhagwat, the leader of the RSS – effectively the BJP's parent organisation, a movement influenced by European fascism that was founded in 1925 to preach the superiority of Hinduism – stressed the importance of Hindu unity:

> Say with pride that you are a Hindu. As Hindus, we have to unite because the responsibility of this country is upon us ... The roadblock to being united is that we are fighting on the lines of caste. We have to say that all Hindus are brothers irrespective of their community. Those who believe in Bharat Mata, her culture, and are progeny of India's forefathers are Hindus. There are Hindus in this country who do not know they are Hindus.

Here, Bhagwat is referring to those whose forebears converted to Islam many centuries ago.

The message that all Hindus are brothers hasn't percolated very far. Rohith Chakravarti Vemula, a PhD student at Hyderabad University, was the author of a well-regarded book called *Caste Is Not a Rumour*. He was active in the university's Ambedkar Students' Association, formed by untouchable students in 1993. In July 2015 the university authorities abruptly suspended him. It emerged that an investigation had taken place and he had been found guilty of 'raising issues under the banner of Ambedkar Students' Association'. Punished for defending Dalit students against caste Hindus he felt completely isolated and committed suicide on 17 January 2016.

How the BJP will create a single Hinduism without abolishing the caste system is unclear, but the party should not be underestimated. In 1989 it formed an alliance with socialists and the CPI(M) which, its key organiser claimed, 'increased our legitimacy in the eyes of backward communities'. Simultaneously, the party claimed to represent Hindus 'hurt' by the 1981 Meenakshipuram conversion, when several hundred Dalits publicly converted to Islam. The aim of winning the support of Dalits and low-caste Hindus wasn't supported by senior brahmins in the BJP leadership, who were publicly critical of the 'social engineering' envisaged by their opponents. The upper-caste Hindus won the day, but the BJP suffered badly in subsequent elections, failing to win Uttar Pradesh (the most important state in the country) in 2007, 2009 and 2012.

Enter stage further right, Narendra Modi and Amit Shah, the BJP party president. The upper-caste rebels were sidelined and Shah renewed the appeal to lower castes and Dalits by setting up social programmes and opening schools, health clinics and so on. The model here was the Muslim Brotherhood in Egypt, with its commitment to provide to the poor what they were denied by the state. A decade earlier, when Modi was chief minister of Gujarat, he had effectively justified the massacre of more than a thousand Muslims in 2002. Many thought this would finish him off as a politician, but his support of the rioters was used by Amit Shah to make him seem a plausible national leader. In 2017 the BJP won a huge majority in Uttar Pradesh and a spectacular victory in the Indian parliament. For the first time in thirty years, a single party had triumphed. No need for coalitions.

Satyam would be horrified by the number of Dalits voting for the BJP. He decided to work in the countryside not simply out of Maoist convictions. He used to explain that two-thirds of the population is rural and a quarter landless, a majority of them not Dalits. A firm believer in cross-caste alliances of the poor, he argued for the creation of new movements and parties to embody this reality.

46

Come Dancing

In 2001 I received a phone call from Ferdinand Mount, then editor of the *TLS*. Would I like to review Anthony Powell's *A Writer's Notebook*? It was a peculiar book. It consists of fragments, random and discontinuous scribblings, 'erratic juxta-positions' of names, book titles, aphorisms, situations, quotations, plot outlines – 'Two men share a flat, one reads the other's diary, it becomes a vice.' 'A is having an affair with B's wife, and tries to teach her habits of punctuality, so that B too shall profit in some way from the situation.' And many entertaining one-liners: 'The eponymous nourishment of the Earl of Sandwich.' 'We thought of the FO, or the BBC. You know there is no exam for the latter.' 'Some women seem to imagine that one has nothing better to do than to sit up all night listening to anecdotes about their first husband.' 'She wrote badly, even for a lesbian novelist.' The overall tone is relaxed. The jottings are witty and light in style.

Reflections of a literary, political, military or personal nature are absent. The brief introduction provided by the author tells us very little. Begun in 1930, when Powell was twenty-five, this notebook – so the internal evidence suggests – continued throughout the war years and long after he had finished choreo-graphing and crafting *A Dance to the Music of Time*.

No dates are attached to the entries, strengthening the impression that *A Writer's Notebook* was never intended for publication. Its appearance was timely nonetheless, and greatly amused Powellites of every stripe. It contains many anticipa-tions of the masterwork whose fiftieth anniversary was marked with a conference at Eton. This choice of location was somewhat unfortunate (the museum in Manchester Square where the Wallace Collection is housed would have been far more appropriate). It is the interrelationship of history, culture and comedy that makes the *Dance*.

The changes in focus and subject, from a coming-out ball in Belgravia to a bohemian assembly in seedy Fitzrovia and thence to a desolate Welsh-dominated army camp in Northern Ireland, are both rapid and exhilarating, the descriptions vivid and funny. The time span covers half a century, and in this period the material processes of life – being born, working, drinking, dining, quarrelling, falling in love, producing children and dying – affect people in different ways. The portraits of writers, painters, dons, musicians, left-wing intellectuals, army officers, literary critics, businessmen, bohemian women, mystics and fading aristocrats are so varied and vigorous that, when social barriers are breached and characters from different walks of life appear in a single scene, the result is hugely diverting. The psychology, behaviour, morals, dress, manners, language and customs of the men and women in the *Dance* spring from social requirements. Chance throws them together. History and the laws of the heart do the rest.

A Powellism from the *Notebook*: 'You can't be a creative artist if you are in any restrictive sense an intellectual snob.' A return to the text, necessitated by the emergence of the *Notebook*, was even more joyful. A second reading of a novel can in some ways be much more fruitful. Since the narrative no longer holds any mysteries, the architecture of the work can be appreciated more fully. It is not the lives of 'toffs' that drive the novel forward. At its heart is the creative process itself.

The *Dance* remains a work of literature without equal in modern English letters. The only projects equivalent in scope were crafted during the first decades of the last century in Paris and Vienna. Proust, Musil and Powell all shared an aversion to cultural Fordism. They could not write to please. Commercial gain was subordinated to a passionate seriousness and a strong belief in their respective literary projects.

Despite the differences in tone and style, one can easily imagine a George Grosz sketch in which three self-absorbed characters – Charlus, Diotima and Widmerpool – are captured peering eagerly into the same trough. The *Notebook* is littered with names. These include choices made by other novelists which stimulated Powell's curiosity. There is a note of triumph in the following entry: 'Chatterley a name in Surtees? Lawrence got it from there. cf. 'Game Keepers', Mr Romford's Hounds, Chapter 1, page 161.' And irritation: 'Henry James's inability to invent good proper names, and his country house names particularly inept.' Powell himself took names very seriously, often searching as far afield as the Domesday Book to find a name that could be matched to a character.

This fixation is visible in the *Dance*. Thus the narrator: 'The name "Sunny Farebrother" struck me as almost redundant in its suggestion of clear-cut straightforward masculinity.' Or again, Widmerpool to narrator: 'I thought it might be you, Jenkins. Only yours is such a common name that I could not be sure.' Rosie Manasch's surname is derived from the Baron Manasch with whom Swann fought a duel. But what about the freelance violinist Carolo, who plays the Wigmore Hall in *Casanova's Chinese Restaurant*? Just as we are wondering whether this was concocted in an Italian restaurant after a concert and is a cross between Caruso and Barolo, we are casually informed that the name is a pure fantasy and that his real name is 'Wilson or Wilkinson or Parker – a surname felt to ring too much of plain common sense.'

And what of the name Widmerpool, which makes its first appearance in the *Notebook*? The *Journals* 1982–86 reveal that Powell lifted it from Lucy Hutchinson's account of the English Civil War: Widmerpool was one of Cromwell's captains. One can only hope that Captain Widmerpool of the New Model Army, unlike his fictional reincarnation, agreed with the Protector's maxim to the effect that 'A man never rises so high as when he does not know where he is going.'

While on the subject of the monster, a confession is in order. After reading the *Dance* again, another impression was confirmed. I was not convinced by the final volume. Widmerpool's evolution seemed to be out of character. If in the immediate postwar period the author's political inclinations were to the right, he tended to veer to a leftish bohemianism socially. Was the unconvincing transformation of Widmerpool into a Dickensian grotesque, and his awful death, the literary outcome of this shift? The *Notebook* offers a clue on p. 110: 'The whole series ends with Jenkins looking out of a window at the men working in a street from a room in which some incident has been taking place. Possibly Widmerpool walking away, as he walked in out of the fog.'

Well, exactly. This would have encouraged readers to imagine different futures for Widmerpool. I could see him becoming a founder member of the SDP. And then one day, thinking himself unobserved, he bends down to tie a shoelace in the lobby of the House of Lords and finds himself being whacked on the bottom with a folded copy of the *Daily Telegraph*. As he looks up and realises it is the prime minister herself in a jovial mood, a look of adoration disfigures his face.

Subsequent to this life-enhancing event, he changes allegiances once again, becoming a much-sought-after platform speaker for the Poujadist wing of the old party. And as he approaches his ninety-eighth birthday in January 2001, his face is once again flashed on the TV screens. He is the oldest millionaire supplier of soft money to the New Labour apparatus.

The week after publication I received a warm and appreciative note from Ferdy, but most important was the sentence: 'I quite agree with you about Widmerpool's unconvincing end.' A few days later a note from the author's son, Tristram Powell, a friend. Here the sentence that I appreciated most was: 'My mother was absolutely delighted with your review of the notebook in the TLS and your sympathetic homage to Dance.'

Over lunch a few days later I asked Tristram whether Lady Vi had said anything about Widmerpool's end. The reply was vigorous: 'She agreed completely with you and also agreed that AP's shift to the Bertorelli Right had affected his writing adversely.' After this, lunch became jollier. Tristram said that his mother was quite a sharp critic of AP's work and that he was quite dependent on her for tales and gossip re the aristocracy, since he had never had much direct access to that layer. At various stages, both

Tristram and I had stressed Violet Powell's part in the enterprise to Hilary Spurling, who wrote AP's bio. She regretted she had waited too long and never thought Violet would die so soon.

Someone else keen to discuss AP with me was Auberon Waugh. We met for a drink at his wine club. There were a few stray questions such as 'How much would you pay for a bottle if only you and your wife or a close friend like Foot were going to drink it?' I gave a non-committal response. I didn't want to read my reply in one of his columns. Then he cut to the chase: 'I hear that you're a great fan of the horse?' I had no idea who he meant. 'Anthony Powell'.

'Oh yes, I am. No big secret.' He frowned. In fact, I had no idea either that Bron had done a gratuitously savage review of one of AP's books in the *Telegraph* which had resulted in AP walking out as the paper's chief literary critic forever. Bron then asked: 'Do you like my father's books.'

'Yes,' I replied. 'Very much so.'

'But you don't think he's as good as Powell?'

'I don't but many others do.'

'Why?'

And then I explained why this was so, much along the lines of what I've written above.

'Are you thinking of writing a book on him?'

'No, but someone from the left should.' And two decades later Perry did exactly that in *Different Speeds, Same Furies*, comparing and contrasting Powell to Proust rather than Evelyn Waugh. Just as well Bron wasn't around to review this work. (One last point: if a vote was taken on the *Dance* on the *NLR* editorial board, I think Perry, Susan and I would be in a tiny minority. But don't despair, dear Dancers, *La Lutte Continue*.)

I was touched when asked by the Wallace Collection and the Anthony Powell Society to deliver the inaugural annual lecture on him in 2007. First because they clearly rejected the thought that someone holding my views might be an incongruous choice, but secondly, and much more importantly, because we need to get away from the blinkered view that regards *A Dance to the Music of Time* as a novel that can only be enjoyed by 'toffs' or readers of the *Daily Telegraph*, not that the two are identical these days by any means. It is, however, a prejudice that has dogged Powell's great novel sequence for far too long.

What is on offer to those coming for the first time to the twelve novels that constitute the *Dance* is not the nuances of class snobbery, but a fictional reflection on the social history of five crucial decades of the last century, beginning with the end of the First World War and ending with the turbulence of the sixties. History, culture, comedy and the interrelationship of each to the other form the centrepieces of this novel. It is the work of an extremely intelligent novelist and one who, unlike many of his peers, was deeply steeped in European culture. His knowledge of that culture – not just his admiration for Proust, which is well known, but also his fondness for Stendhal – had a deep impact on his own work. I was very struck by his liking for Stendhal (my own favourite French novelist), because it revealed an admirable literary openness. Despite his own conservative political opinions, he could appreciate the work of a writer whose worldview was far removed from his own. And the Stendhal that Powell liked the most is *The Life of Henri Brulard*, a thinly disguised autobiography that pours bucketfuls of scorn on French conservatism. His favourite year, Stendhal calmly informs the reader in a footnote, is not 1789 (the beginning of the Revolution), but 1793 ... the year the French king and queen were beheaded.

The 'ultras', as Stendhal refers to the supporters of the *ancien régime* and its latter-day successors, include his own father and the local priests, who have betrayed every single ideal that he believes in – it is a very spirited and lively piece of writing. Powell's favourite novel, he tells us time and time again, is Dostoevsky's *The Devils* (or *The Possessed*). All this is a far cry from the style of the *Dance*. Neither Proust nor Stendhal, leave alone Dostoevsky, influenced the way Powell wrote, just as Proust was not influenced by his favourite literary work: *The Thousand and One Nights*.

Powell was, in some ways, the most European of English writers and that is why it is worth repeating that the literary project that became *A Dance to the Music of Time* has no equivalent in English letters and is better seen in the same framework as Proust or Musil. Powell, though from a younger generation, is nonetheless not so far removed from them. Proust grew up during the belle époque; Robert Musil fought in the First World War. Powell was born in 1905, but was still haunted by the memories of that war – he came from a military family, he knew a whole generation that had been wiped out, and he himself served in the Second World War. There is a moving passage in *The Military Philosophers* (volume 9 of the *Dance*) when the narrator in uniform is going through Normandy and suddenly:

> 'Just spell out the name of that place we stopped over last night, Major Jenkins,' said Cobb. [I've always wondered whether this was a name inspired by Richard Cobb, who was one of the history tutors at Balliol College, Oxford.]
>
> 'C-A-B-O-U-R-G, sir.' As I uttered the last letter, scales fell from my eyes. Everything was transformed. It all came back, like the tea-soaked madeleine itself, in a torrent of memory. Cabourg – we had just driven out of Cabourg, out of Proust's Balbec. Only a few minutes before, I'd been standing on the esplanade along which, wearing her polo cap and accompanied by the little band of girls he had supposed the mistresses of professional bicyclists, Albertine had strolled into Marcel's life. Through the high windows of the Grand Hotel's dining room, conveying to those without the sensation of staring into an aquarium, was to be seen SaintLoup, at the same table Bloch, mendaciously claiming acquaintance with the Swanns. A little farther along the promenade was the casino, its walls still displaying tattered playbills just like the one Charlus, wearing his black straw hat, had pretended to examine, after an attempt at long range to assess the narrator's physical attractions and possibilities.

There's a very funny scene earlier on, where, during a bombing raid, the narrator finds himself under the table with General Liddament, who asks, 'What do you think of Trollope?', to which the reply comes, 'Not very much.' They then turn to a discussion of what he really likes, and while this is taking place he's holding a copy of *Swann's Way* that he was reading before the bombs fell.

Despite the chronological gaps between Proust, Musil and Powell, their literary projects, while different in style and preoccupations (Proust and ambivalent sexuality, Musil's Kakania), are nonetheless analogous in terms of scale and ambition, and the problems each confronted in developing their own early writing styles. The early short stories penned by the Austrian are brisk and entertaining, very different in style from *The Man Without Qualities*. Powell's early novels are also very witty, but in his first fiction, *Afternoon Men*, for instance, you can see the seeds of the *Dance*. The dialogue between Atwater and Lola at a sordid bohemian party is incredibly funny, and operates by way of a minimalism that foreshadowed Beckett and Pinter.

By the time he began to write the *Dance* – a project that took him twenty-five years to complete – his style had changed. No doubt his immersion, between 1951 and 1975, in Burton's *Anatomy of Melancholy*, and the impact of working on a book on John Aubrey, had something to do with it. The style is almost baroque – which actually lifts the comedy to a far higher level than one finds in the early novels. And that is what makes the *Dance* such a fine work of literature.

Powell was lucky. He was a survivor. His European counterparts never finished their work. Proust died relatively young, at fifty-one, and the complete *In Search of Lost Time* had to be published posthumously, the author's proofreading and rewrites still incomplete. Musil's pencil of creation snapped with him: *The Man Without Qualities* remained an unfinished masterpiece. Powell was well aware of all this, and was determined to complete his work. He said himself he brought the *Dance* to a close when he did because he understood the dangers of going on for too long.

Also, times had changed. His own political sympathies had always been on the right, but his bohemian friends (and Orwell) tended to veer towards the left. By the time he concluded the *Dance* with *Hearing Secret Harmonies*, all this had changed. The book is dedicated to Robert Conquest. Charlotte Street in the late sixties was no longer a bohemian haunt. Bertorelli's had become the regular meeting place of a virulently anti-left, cold warrior group of writers, Powell among them, who like Conquest supported the wars in Indo-China. It was this, in my view, that adversely affected the tone and structure of the last novel.

When did I first *Dance*? It was either 1979 or 1980. I was travelling from London to Mexico to attend a left-wing conference with Perry Anderson. He was sitting next to me and re-reading some volumes from the *Dance* throughout the flight (it's an eleven-hour hop). One of them was definitely *Casanova's Chinese Restaurant*. At one point his laughter became so infectious that an American passenger came up to him and said: 'Hey, guy, what's that you're reading? It must be really funny.' My friend held up the book briefly, said, 'It certainly is,' and carried on as before.

My own reading matter was comparatively dull, which made me envious. Several months later, back in Britain, I bought the whole collection with Mark Boxer's amazing covers and read the entire work. Sometimes one hears people explaining how they started off with *A Question of Upbringing* when it first came out and stopped there, because they had no idea how this could go on and become what it became. They didn't like that first one and never read the rest. I loved the first one, but it was useful to have them all stacked up on the bedside table, so that the reading could be systematic and continuous. I'm sure that's the reason the *Dance* had such an immediate impact on me.

Some years ago I encountered one of our leading literary critics at an Xmas party, and the following conversation took place:

'What do you think of the *Dance*?'

'Oh, you've read it?'

'Yes, I have.'

'Well, I didn't like it. You obviously did?'

'I did, but why didn't you?'

'Closed world.'

That's all he would say, and I resisted asking whether he had actually read it all. I confess I've only read the *Dance* twice, but a closed world it definitely is not. It contains the most entertaining accounts of bohemian life in London from 1920 to 1958, decades during which Powell not only mingled with that world, but often enjoyed it more than the coming-out parties in Belgravia.

What then is the central theme of this novel? It is creativity: Moreland composes, Barnby paints, X Trapnel writes, Quiggin, Members and Maclintick criticise, and the narrator, having first been a publisher, then becomes a writer. What excites the novelist is music and painting, literature and criticism. Creativity together with the comedy of everyday life sustains the *Dance*. It is also remarkable for its astonishing characterisations. Most obviously, Widmerpool.

The late Lord Longford often claimed that Widmerpool was based on him. There's an entertaining entry in one of the journals where Powell is at a college reunion at Oxford and runs into Denis Healey. The former Labour deputy leader greets him like a long-lost friend, and then: 'I've always wanted to ask you this: did you base Widmerpool on Edward Heath?' The first time one finishes reading the *Dance*, there is a natural curiosity to discover who particular characters could have been based on. It can become an obsession, like trainspotting, and should be resisted.

Powell has written somewhere that no character in fiction is ever based on any other single character, they are always composites: different aspects of people you've met can be synthesised in one particular creation. This is even more true of him than of Proust, as we know from George Painter's excellent biography of the latter: many of the 'vices' that he ascribes to Charlus are actually his own; and the person on whom he most based Charlus, an aristocratic popinjay named Montesquieu, certainly understood what was going on, saying to a friend: 'Perhaps I should now change my name to Montproust.' Widmerpool is, in some ways, a more inspired creation than Charlus, a universal character. After all, thrusting mediocrity rises to the surface in almost every sphere. Virtually every government has its Widmerpools – and not just in Europe.

The *Dance* is set over five decades and coincidence plays an important part in the characters' many encounters. How many times, since I've read the books, I've run into someone not seen for twenty years or so and muttered inwardly 'It's the *Dance*' – and it is. Yet structured as art, the coincidences also build up into the greater patterning of the dance. Friendship is another crucially important theme. There are moving passages in the novel about friendship, what it means and how important it is, and what you feel when you lose a friend – usually, but not always, during the war. That leaves a deep impact, so that the friends who survived become even more important and, when they behave badly, more hurtful. Powell can be witty, waspish, patronising and even vicious, but not malicious. He writes about many people generously – some would say too generously. So what is to be said about some of the remarks that have been made about him since his death in 2000? They are related to the question of friendship. V. S. Naipaul was regarded as a friend. The Powell journals are full of him. Too full. Naipaul's *The Writer and the World*, not his best by any means, indeed probably his worst, contains an essay on Powell. What is astonishing is his claim – I assume it must be true – that he had never read the *Dance* in all the years that he was a close friend of Anthony and Violet, visiting them regularly and often playing the court jester by mouthing remarks about race and class that were being discouraged in polite society. If he hadn't read the *Dance*, why not? You don't have to like a friend's work, but surely to read it is obligatory. Be that as it may, let's accept that he hadn't read the books but possibly pretended that he had, at numerous gatherings.

When he did read them, after Powell's death, he didn't like them, thought they were overrated, with no narrative worth speaking of, and so forth. This was then followed by tittle-tattle picked up from X and Y who also disliked the novels and the man. It was the unpleasantness of the tone that surprised me – even if he hadn't read the books when Powell was alive, what caused him suddenly to sit up now and urinate on his friend's grave? I know that getting the Nobel Prize can have a strange effect on people, but one always hopes they rise above it. So the ill will remains a bit of a mystery.

Or does it? In *Books Do Furnish a Room*, the novelist X Trapnel, besotted with Lady Pamela and dominated by her, is slowly losing his grip: 'In the street his incoherent, distracted state of mind was much more apparent. He was certainly in a bad way. All the talk about writing, its flow not greatly different from the termination of any evening in his company, was just a question of putting off the evil hour of having to face his own personal problems.'

Or to put it another way, as the great eighteenth-century Chinese novelist Cao Xueqin wrote:

> Truth becomes fiction, when the fiction's true
> Real becomes not-real where the unreal's real.

47

The New Adventures of Don Quixote

The following is a tiny extract from a play I wrote, *The New Adventures of Don Quixote*, which was performed in 2013 in theatres in Germany, the next year in Croatia, and in 2022 in Turkey, but never in the UK. The lines are intended as a warning in case the next Peace Prize is given to Netanyahu:

NOBEL COMMITTEE MAN: I've come on behalf of the Nobel Peace Prize Committee.

PRIVATE X: I think you've got the wrong man. Surely you want Don Quixote?

NOBEL COMMITTEE MAN: Certainly not. He's never killed anyone. This prize is awarded only to those who help peace by making war. It's a lot of money. Millions of dollars.

PRIVATE X: (*smiles*) Just for killing children? Or adults as well?

NOBEL COMMITTEE MAN: For preserving the peace.

This section led to the only 'aesthetic' argument between me and the very fine director, Jean-Claude Berutti, who I first met in 2012 in Brussels. Between 1997 and 2011, he was the artistic director of the most emblematic French public theatres: the Théâtre du Peuple in Bussang and the Comédie de Saint-Etienne. We got on well on that occasion and discussed possible projects we could do together. We agreed that bringing Cervantes's characters into the twenty-first century might be interesting. Our differences on the Nobel scene were summed up by Jean-Claude as follows:

As for the play's structure, I eliminated two scenes: the one called 'The Angel of History' and the second called 'The Military Hospital Revue'. Let me explain these cuts ...

The case of the second cut scene is different. It was written at the beginning and turned the place of death – the military hospital of Landstuhl – into a joyful hospice, upon the occasion of the arrival of CNN and an ambassador to bestow the Nobel Peace Prize. The whole scene constituted an essentially attractive 'number', but Tariq had placed it after Sancho and Don Quixote had left the hospital. Because the two protagonists were not present at the festivities, the scene became superfluous. Indeed, since the subject of the play is Don Quixote's view of the contemporary world, and since he is not there to convey his thoughts on the scene, something didn't work ... This was the main reason for cutting it. The second had to do with the scene's tone. The previous scene showed soldiers in bed singing that they were the envoys of the devil and that they were aware of what they had done in Afghanistan and Iraq. Based on the script, Arturo Annecchinno wrote music that was part moving and part ironic, that transports the audience into a nightmarish world (in any event, I hope so) that is perfectly in tune with the description of the surgical butchery that follows the war. But all of this unfolds at a slow pace in an atmosphere like that in which one finds oneself when emerging from a nightmare (I must have been thinking of the famous chapter in Malraux's *Man's Fate* that unfolds in a military hospital in Spain). It very quickly occurred to me that it was a shame to follow this important scene with one of simple political satire [the Nobel Prize scene], and I have no regrets that I cut it ...

I won't say anything more here since we are right in the middle of rehearsals, but I wanted to give this example to provide a sense of how difficult yet secretly coherent Tariq's kaleidoscopic writing truly is – you can't unravel its difficulties except by attempting to put together a stylistic puzzle, for which he obviously provides no clues. And this stylistic puzzle (which I associate with the one set up in *Night of the Golden Butterfly* in which painting is constantly at issue) is also a puzzle of meaning for each scene in that it asks the audience to find coherence in the relationships of complementary images. This is perhaps what makes Tariq Ali's plays so original when compared to other contemporary theatre (which he knows extremely well but isn't interested in joining, that is, compared to which he feels independent and free in a manner rare enough to be noticed). He prefers to work 'through images', a bit like Peter Weiss, a German writer whom Tariq and I often discussed during our long conversations.

What had inspired me was the latest English translation of Cervantes's masterpiece. What a joy it must be to read this book in Spanish. Those of us not adequately versed in the language have no option but to grit our teeth and seek refuge in a translation. I was in my late teens when I first read the book. Far too young, alas, to understand what had been written and incapable of reading beyond the words. I enjoyed the cruel jokes, sided with the wrong people, laughed in the wrong places, totally ignored the tragic landscape, and skipped a great deal. In other words, I never really read the book. The two principals I regarded with utter contempt, perhaps – no, definitely – because they were far too chaste. I had no problems with Boccaccio's *Decameron*, which I devoured eagerly at roughly the same time and which was much more to my taste, as confirmation that it was probably the lack of sex that put me off Cervantes.

I cannot remember the name of the translator and when, in 2009, I tried to recover the book in my late father's library in Lahore, it had disappeared. Might I have understood it better if the introduction (was there one?) had made some attempt to contextualise the work? I doubt it. I'm convinced that this is a novel that should be read by people later in life, perhaps after they have reached thirty, preferably even later.

The new 980-page English version published to commemorate the book's 400th anniversary turned out to be a soul-saver. Some translators are haunted by earlier translations. Not Edith Grossman. Her footnote references are spare, but a treat, and of real use to any serious reader. The only spoiler in the book is Harold Bloom. It is a limiting and lazy introduction that he has written. It does not contain a single sentence that might help the reader contextualise the world that produced Cervantes and in which he struggled against adversities of every sort. Bloom could have done a little homework. The attempted profundity of his first two sentences is revealing: 'What is the true object of Don Quixote's quest? I find that unanswerable.'

Why? Did he even attempt to search for an answer? That would have meant immersing himself for a few weeks in Spanish history. It's obvious he has never read Américo Castro or Juan Goytisolo or Miguel Asín, but was he too lazy even to glance at a biography of Cervantes published by a fellow American, William Byron, in 1978? It would appear so. This is a pity. He would have found it helpful. Instead we are told of the impact the novel had on Melville, among others, and reminded that Nabokov found the cruelty repellent, amid trivial details of a similar sort that might be handy for compilers of middlebrow crossword puzzles, but are useless to a reader who wants to know more about the novelist and the culture that spawned him.

Bloom's problem is his lack of humility. He can't bring himself to confess that the drama contained in *Don Quixote* is enacted within a historical frame too large for his comprehension. Without that knowledge, it is impossible to discern the fragments that offer clues to the object of Cervantes's quest. For Bloom the realm of meaning is confined to literature alone – and the Western canon at that – but this is totally insufficient to understand the novel. Cervantes, like the rest of the population in the region, is a creature of the tragic drama that constituted the history of the peninsula in the fifteenth and sixteenth centuries.

These were times when the very act of living had become a colossal effort for the poor. The silver ingots from South America only exacerbated the structural economic crisis. Inflation was rampant, there was mass hunger in Andalusia, bubonic plague in Castile, brutal repression of vagrants everywhere (reminiscent of how a crisis-racked Catholic Italy is treating gypsies and other minorities today), corruptions of church and empire, against a background of growing depopulation and a severe crisis in agriculture. The decay of Spanish society was visible at the time to most of its inhabitants. The French historian Pierre Vilar, writing in 1956, stressed this historical context against those who were beginning to reduce history to 'a discontinuous series of singular totalities':

> It is often said that it would be pointless to search in Cervantes for an interpretation of the 'decadence' of his country, 'because he could not have foreseen it'. This is to have a singular disregard for chronology. For if the word *crisis* rightly describes the passage from an ascending conjuncture to one of collapse, it is surely between 1598 and 1620, between the 'grandeur' and the 'decadence', that we must situate the decisive *crisis* of Spanish power, and much more surely still, the first great crisis of confidence for the Spaniards.

Well: the two parts of *Don Quixote* are dated 1605 and 1615. And there was always the ever-present Inquisition. For these were also times when the torment of individuals attached to a defeated civilisation had become unbearable. How to keep calm while evil, like polluted rain, covers all in darkness? It is all around them. Injustice flourishes as never before. Spanish Muslim rebellions in the Alpujarras are the harbingers of guerrilla wars and resistance in centuries yet to come. Critical thought is abolished. A secret police spies on suspect citizens and a vicious censorship is imposed by state and Church ... Juan Goytisolo has argued that all the features of the modern totalitarian state had already been configured in post-1492 Spain. It's difficult to disagree.

Philip II had unilaterally annulled the agreements reached by his forebears with the Moriscos, as the Spanish Muslims were known at the time. The few rights they had left were withdrawn, and a humiliating code of conduct was imposed: it became a crime to read, write or speak Arabic, and to visit the public baths – which would soon be destroyed throughout Spain (cleanliness being considered by the Church as a licentious Moorish habit) – while the use of Morisco surnames or the wearing of Morisco clothes was also banned. A whole people was thus criminalised. They were the enemy within, soon to be converted, expelled or killed. This was the Spain into which Cervantes was born in September or October 1547, in the town of Alcalá de Henares, to which his family had moved from Córdoba. It is this that explains the writing of a book so rich in fantasy, imagination, poetry, mysticism, satire, joy and grief, as well as a degree of political and psychological perception that is astonishing.

The Catholic Church had spearheaded a long campaign – the *Reconquista* – to ethnically cleanse the Iberian Peninsula of alien influences. In 1492, several hundred years after a tiny Arab force had fought and defeated the Visigoths and established a political and cultural hegemony over the peninsula, the last Muslim kingdom of Granada fell to the Catholic monarchs, Ferdinand and Isabella. Almost simultaneously, Columbus 'discovered' the New World. The two events became intertwined in many Christian minds as a show of divine support for the Catholic Church and retribution against the Muslims and Jews, who should be driven into the sea.

This was Spain after the fall of Granada, the final victory of the 'Reconquest' – but it turned out to be not quite as final as had been thought. As church bells rang everywhere to mark the triumph, an edict signed by the monarchs expelling all Jews from Spain unless they converted was posted on church doors in most cities. A century later, the Muslims would suffer the same fate: there were too many to expel in 1492, and the state feared a prolonged armed conflict.

Under Philip II, the entire peninsula was in the grip of Catholic monarchs, flanked by zealous prelates and obsessed with preventing 'New Christians' (recent converts) from becoming part of the empire in the New World. Catholic, monocultural Spain was determined that the single Christian identity forged by means of torture, blood and the burning of books and people should be extended to all Europe. They were determined to ethnically cleanse Spain of its past. Philip II would use his power without scruple, and the Church would defend every atrocity on the grounds that the unanimously desired end – a paradisiacal Kingdom of God on earth – justified all the means used. Any measure adopted in this good cause was automatically virtuous.

Religious and political fundamentalisms share this feature in common. The victims have to contend with the hard silence of justice. Not that the Spanish Muslims passively accepted the new order. They fought back and defended their historical rights to their lands and villages. There were three important rebellions in Granada and countless incidents of non-cooperation, expressions of anger (hurling excrement at the Holy Sacrament) and even the odd act of terror.

Philip II was an effective, if paranoid, monarch. He saw rebellions everywhere, and almost triggered one in Catalonia by imagining that Protestant subversives were mounting an insurrection against him. He was hostile to compromises with either Muslims or Protestants, on the grounds that tolerance was a sign of weakness and would only encourage apostasy.

Laughter in Cervantes is never innocent. It is usually linked to fear and cruelty, which for him was symbolic of the transition – from three cultures to one – that he was experiencing. The dominant culture in terms of language and learning had for more than half a millennium been Arabic. Ultimately it gave way to Castilian, but here too the traces would never disappear. As the second part of the novel nears the end, Cervantes has the knight explaining this fact to his squire, who does not understand the use of the word *albogues*, as in: 'Well, and what if in the midst of all this music albogues should resound!'

'What are albogues?' asked Sancho, 'I've never heard of them or seen them in my life.'

'Albogues', responded Don Quixote, 'are something like brass candlesticks, and when you hit one with the other along the empty or hollow side, it makes a sound that is not unpleasant, though it may not be very beautiful or harmonious, and it goes well with the rustic nature of pipes and timbrels; this word *albogues* is Moorish, as are all those in our Castilian tongue that begin with *al*, for example: *almohaza, almorzar, alhombra, alguacil, alhucema, almacén, alcancía*, and other similar words ... I have told you this in passing because it came to mind when I happened to mention albogues.'

There is nothing in these stories that is told 'in passing'. The treasure chest is full of fine-cut diamonds. Everything has been carefully considered before the commitment to paper. It could not have been otherwise during the Inquisition. What intrigues is what Cervantes thought could not go into the book at all, and here the tragedy of his own people must have been paramount in his mind, even in the midst of composition.

The choice given to the Jewish community in 1492 was simple: convert or get out. Many decided to leave. In most cases they sought and were granted refuge in the lands of the Ottoman Empire. Till the end of the twentieth century, scholars had to travel to Istanbul to hear *ladino* being spoken as it was in medieval Spain. (The old community has died out, and since the rise of Turkish Islamism many of their descendants have left for other lands, including Israel.)

Others, understandably reluctant to be uprooted, were prepared to sacrifice their past for their children's future. They became *conversos* and stayed on as New Christians, their loyalty ever suspect. Some belonging to merchant families, or the Jewish physicians who served the court and the nobility, rose to high positions in the land – on occasion proving their loyalty to the Church with a vengeance that stunned former co-religionists. Tomás de Torquemada was one such. He became the first Grand Inquisitor, and a living example of the adage that the fanaticism of the convert knows no bounds. From a *converso* family, he became a byword for cruelty. Torquemada authorised the burning of at least 2,000 Jewish 'heretics' – Jews who had converted to Christianity but whose motives were considered suspect, and who had been spied on and reported to the Inquisition. The terror of the Inquisition was implemented by its own secret police, the Holy Brotherhood.

It was not enough for Jewish silversmiths in Majorca to convert. They had to prove it by sitting outside their shops on the Jewish Sabbath, ostentatiously eating pork. All the circumstantial evidence suggests that Cervantes belonged to a family of Jewish *conversos*, a *mala casta* for life. There is no documentary evidence because such families took care to destroy every trace (as Jews would again do under the Third Reich), so that when they applied to the relevant tribunal for a certificate testifying that they were Old Christians, no incriminatory material could be produced. Nonetheless Cervantes was denied permission to go to the New World on a number of occasions. He did get the 'certificate of purity' and, as a result, obtained a menial job at the home of a church dignitary in Rome. Back in La Mancha, however, it was generally known that he was of Jewish origin and his literary rivals, Lope de Vega for one, used this against him during heated exchanges. There is the odd clue in the master-work as well.

One of the many conceits Cervantes deploys in the novel is that he never wrote it in the first place. He found a Moorish manuscript in the bazaar. It was written in Arabic, and all he did was to hire a translator. Thus at the very beginning of the work, Cervantes is stressing the special features that helped to shape Spanish identity:

> One day when I was in the Alcaná market in Toledo, a boy came by to sell some notebooks and old papers to a silk merchant; as I am very fond of reading, even torn papers in the streets, I was moved by my natural inclination to pick up one of the volumes the boy was selling, and I saw that it was written in characters I knew to be Arabic. And since I recognised but could not read them, I looked around to see if some Morisco who knew Castilian, and could read them for me, was in the vicinity, and it was not very difficult to find this kind of interpreter, for even if I had sought a speaker of a better and older language, I would have found him.

The older language is, of course, Hebrew and the sentence does offer a clue to Cervantes's origins. The title of the manuscript was *History of Don Quixote de la Mancha, written by Cide Hamete Benengeli, Arab historian.* The Muslim theme is strong in the book. How could it not be, given the Morisco 'problem' at home and the final solution being mooted in Church and Palace? In ironic mode Cervantes mocks the prevalent orthodoxy, by suggesting that the Hispanic Muslim author of the novel has underplayed the virtues of Quixote, since Muslims are 'very prone to telling falsehoods'.

So, if there are any complaints, the 'fault lies with the dog who was its author'. And historians, he continues in the same passage, 'must and ought to be exact, truthful and absolutely free of passions, for neither interest, fear, rancor, nor affection should make them deviate from the path of the truth, whose mother is history, the rival of time, repository of great deeds, witness to the past, example and adviser to the present, and forewarning to the future'.

Cervantes's venom. Could he not be saying that the Old Testament will be spared, but all else burnt? That he loathed injustice is evident in the freeing of the slaves, and from the episode of Sancho's imagined governorship of an inland *ínsula* – a practical joke played on the loyal squire by bored aristocrats. It certainly makes them laugh in the novel, though not the reader. Cervantes is suggesting that the joke is on the perpetrators.

That he intensely disliked dogma is made clear on many occasions, as when Don Quixote, lance raised, charges at a bunch of penitents and priests perceived as the enemy, or in numerous ironic asides and dialogic exchanges with Sancho Panza. At one point in the novel Sancho announces that if his only virtue lay in his loyalty to the Roman Catholic Church and his hatred for the Jews, that alone would be sufficient to save him a place in history. Or take the following, from the opening of Chapter 27 of the Second Part, where Cervantes's fictitious Moorish author is back in action:

> Cide Hamete, the chronicler of this great history, begins this chapter with the words *I swear as a Catholic Christian ...* to which his translator says that Cide Hamete swearing as a Catholic Christian when he was a Moor, which he undoubtedly was, meant only that just as the Catholic Christian, when he swears, swears or should swear the truth, and tell the truth in everything he says, so too he was telling the truth, as if he were swearing as a Catholic Christian, when he wrote about Don Quixote.

Could it be that it is Catholicism, as practised in a new, purified Spain, that is the absent centre of the novel around which everything else is constructed? The traditionalists will not like this interpretation, but it is there waiting to be gleaned from virtually every chapter.

After the knight's death, the author writes the first sentence of the last paragraph: 'For me alone was Don Quixote born, and I for him; he knew how to act and I to write ...'

We know the acts well. Phrases describing certain aspects of them have entered everyday usage, 'tilting at windmills', for example. By identifying his writing with such actions, I think Cervantes is trying to tell us something.

Don't think, he is saying, that when I charged in the direction of my literary windmills at the very beginning of the novel, I was unaware of what I was doing. It had to be done like that, because of the times in which he lived. That is what makes him so courageous and so contemporary. He wrote in his time, but for all time. What he wrote was intended to forewarn the generations to come.

And so back to our modern version of the story, written in the first decade of the 'war on terror'. Why had I introduced Don Quixote and Sancho Panza as well as their animals into the twenty-first century? Economic crises, wars and religion have dominated this century. The play itself is a homage to the giants of the last century: Meyerhold, Brecht, Weiss. This can be unsettling in today's world, where a monochrome, monotone culture is dominant, where much of what is written is written not to question but to please.

Cervantes portrayed Don Quixote as deluded in order to protect himself against the Inquisition, and he mocked the knight in order to make doubly sure. But all the targets attacked were deadly serious. Interestingly, in his farewell letter to his children, Che Guevara compared himself to Quixote, writing that he hoped his Rocinante would survive the travels.

Don Quixote has deservedly been called a universal novel, even the first modern novel produced in Europe, but it was, and could only have been, written in the Spain of Philip II, a century after the triumph of the Reconquest and when the country was beset with crises of every sort. The triumphalism generated in 1492 had long worn off.

The modern Reconquest was the defeat of communism as well as many of the utopian ideas associated with it. The absence of an enemy, however, has also torn the mask off capitalism. We see its real face all over the world.

48

English Questions

The new system for Labour leadership elections that Edward Miliband introduced in 2014 was meant as a conciliatory gesture. He had been accused of winning the leadership only thanks to the support of the hated trade unions, so he instituted a one member, one vote system, with one vote for each party member as well as for supporters who, though not party members, were prepared to part with £3. The French Socialists had used a similar method to elect Hollande. It was a step forward for democratisation, but the new rules also had the overwhelming support of the Parliamentary Labour Party. Most Labour MPs assumed that if outsiders had any effect at all it would be to help seal the status quo.

And so it might have been, had New Labour managed to come up with a halfway credible candidate. In order to preserve the fiction that the PLP remained a broad church that favoured diversity and loved a good debate, a few Blairites helped to nominate a candidate from the minuscule parliamentary left. This strategy had worked before: last time round David Miliband had nominated Diane Abbott as a candidate. In 2015 they hoped a left candidate would draw support away from Andy Burnham, who passed for left-ish, thus leaving the door open for Liz Kendall or Yvette Cooper.

Enter Jeremy Corbyn, stage left.

Jeremy may not be a charismatic figure, but he could never be mistaken for a PR confection. I have shared numerous platforms with him over the past forty years and on key issues he has remained steadfast. During the leadership debates he came across as uninterested in point-scoring and oblivious to media hostility.

The *Guardian* came out for Yvette Cooper, the *Mirror* for Andy Burnham. Absolutely nobody, including Corbyn himself, thought that he could win. His campaign was intended just to show that there was an alternative to the neoliberal leadership that had ruled the country for the last three decades. What appealed to the young and to the many who had left the party in disgust during the Blair/Brown years – what appealed to the people who turned the campaign into a genuine social movement – was precisely what alienated the political and media cliques. Corbyn's campaign generated a mass movement that renewed the base of the Labour Party – nearly 200,000 new members and counting – and led to his triumph.

He won almost as many votes as all his opponents put together. Blair's misjudged appeals ('Hate me as much as you want, but don't vote Corbyn') and Brown's out-of-touch attacks accusing Corbyn of being friendly with dictatorships (he was referring to Venezuela, rather than Saudi Arabia or Kazakhstan, states favoured by the New Labour elite) only won Corbyn more support. The Blairite cohort that dominates the *Guardian*'s opinion pages – Jonathan Freedland, Polly Toynbee et al. – had zero impact on the result, desperate though they were to trash Corbyn. They were desperate enough even to give space – twice – to Blair himself, in the hope of rehabilitating him. Naturally, the paper lost many readers, including me.

Corbyn's victory was not based on ultra-leftism. His views reflected what many in the country felt, and this is what anti-Corbyn Labour found difficult to grasp. He spelled it out himself in one of the TV debates:

> We also as a party have to face up to something which is an unpleasant truth, that we fought the 2015 election on very good policies included in the manifesto but fundamentally we were going to be making continuing cuts in central government expenditure, we were going to continue underfunding local government, there were still going to be job losses, there were still going to be people

suffering because of the cuts we were going to impose by accepting an arbitrary date to move into budget surplus, accepting the language of austerity. My suggestion is that the party has to challenge the politics of austerity, the politics of increasing the gap between the richest and the poorest in society, and be prepared to invest in a growing economy rather than accepting what is being foisted on us by the banking crisis of 2008 to 2009. We don't have to set this arbitrary date, which in effect means the poorest and most vulnerable in our society pay for the banking crisis rather than those that caused it.

How could any Labour MP disagree with that? What they really hated was Corbyn's questioning of the private sector. John Prescott had been allowed to pledge the renationalisation of the railways at the 1996 Labour Party conference, but after Blair's victory the following year the subject was never raised again. Until now.

When I asked him at what point he first realised he might actually win, Corbyn's response was characteristic of the activist that he remains: 'It was in Nottingham during the last weeks of campaigning … you know Nottingham. Normally we think that fifty or sixty people at a meeting is a good turnout. I got four hundred and there were people outside who couldn't get in. I thought then: we might win this one.' The crowds grew and grew, making it clear that Corbyn was capable of mobilising and inspiring large numbers of people, and clear too how flimsy the support was, outside the media, for the other candidates.

His election as Labour leader in September 2015 animated English politics. His horrified enemies in the PLP immediately started to plot his removal. Lord Mandelson informed us that they wouldn't destroy their new leader immediately: 'It would be wrong', he wrote, 'to try and force this issue from within before the public have moved to a clear verdict.' Blair, angered by the outburst of democracy in a party that he had moulded in his own image, declared that the Labour Party would be unelectable unless Corbyn was removed. Brown kept relatively quiet, perhaps because he was busy negotiating his very own private finance initiative with the investment firm Pimco (Ben Bernanke and the former ECB president Jean-Claude Trichet were also joining its 'global advisory board'). Simultaneously, his ennobled former chancellor, Lord Darling, was on his way to work for Morgan Stanley in Wall Street.

Blair, an adviser to J.P. Morgan since 2008, must have chuckled. At last, a New Labour reunion in the land of the free. All that 'light-touch' regulation was bearing rich fruit. Virtually every senior member of the Blair and Brown Cabinets went to work for a corporation that had benefited from their policies. It was not just the Iraq War that was responsible for the public disenchantment with New Labour.

The establishment decided to wheel out the Chief of Defence Staff, Sir Nicholas Houghton. Interviewed on 8 November, he confided to a purring Andrew Marr that the army was deeply vexed by Corbyn's unilateralism, which damaged 'the credibility of deterrence'. On the same show, Maria Eagle, a PLP sniper with a seat on the front bench as shadow defence secretary, essentially told Marr that she agreed with the general. Just another day in the war against Corbyn.

The Sunday Times had previously run an anonymous interview with 'a senior serving general'. 'Feelings are running very high within the armed forces,' the general was quoted as saying, about the very idea of a Corbyn government. 'You would see ... generals directly and publicly challenging Corbyn over ... Trident, pulling out of NATO and any plans to emasculate and shrink the size of the armed forces ... There would be mass resignations at all levels ... which would effectively be a mutiny. You can't put a maverick in charge of a country's security.'

If anything expressed the debasement of Britain's political culture it was the lack of reaction to this military interference in politics. When Corbyn tried to complain, a former Tory grandee, Ken Clarke, declared that the army was not answerable to Parliament, but to the queen. Anything but Corbyn: even a banana monarchy.

In December 2015, David Cameron sought parliamentary approval for sending British planes to bomb Islamic State in

Syria. From his point of view, a happy possible side effect of the predictably successful vote was that it might make Corbyn's position as leader untenable. Having been stabbed in the back by Maria Eagle he was about to be stabbed in the front by Hilary Benn, whose disingenuous speech – mentioning Hitler, with the Spanish Civil War thrown in for good measure – was loudly cheered by Tory and hardcore Blairite MPs. (What a pity that the two-hour row between Hilary Benn and his father over the Iraq War, of which Hilary was an ardent supporter, was never taped and transcribed in Tony Benn's printed diaries – though he did talk about it to friends.)

But this, too, failed to unseat Corbyn. On the insistence of close colleagues, the Labour leader – wrongly, in my opinion – permitted a free vote (John McDonnell, the shadow chancellor, insisted it was a 'matter of conscience'.) In the end sixty-six Labour MPs voted with the Tories to bomb targets in Syria. Some of them had been given presentations by the ministry of defence designed to convince them that there would be no collateral damage. But the majority of the PLP opposed the bombings and voted with Corbyn.

Frustrated yet again, the media sought to attribute the failure of more Labour MPs to vote for the bombing to the 'bullying' of Stop the War, an organisation of which Corbyn had been the chair since the death of Tony Benn. For a week or so it was open season on the anti-war coalition. One effect was to scare the Greens and cause the party's former leader Caroline Lucas to resign from the STW committee. Was this really her own decision or was it the idea of the inept Natalie Bennett, fearful that Green supporters were being carried away by the pied piper from Islington? Corbyn himself was unmoved: he told the audience at a STW fundraising dinner that he was proud of the work the organisation had done from the time of the Afghan war onwards, and that he was proud to serve as its chair.

Later in the week of the Syria vote, the Oldham by-election, which had, again, been talked up as a possible disaster for Corbyn (George Eaton in the *New Statesman* claimed to have been told by 'an insider' that 'defeat was far from unthinkable'), was instead a resounding victory. All this left Corbyn's enemies on the defensive. A reshuffle early in the New Year removed Eagle and a few others, but Hilary Benn was left in place, a reflection of the political difficulties confronting Corbyn. Any attempt to change the political balance of the Shadow Cabinet was greeted with threats of mass resignations. But Corbyn would not be bullied or demoralised into standing down.

While the mood in Scotland shifted leftwards, the centre of politics in England had moved so far to the right since the 1980s that even though the Corbyn/McDonnell economic programme was not very radical – what it offered on the domestic front was a little bit of social democracy to strengthen the welfare state and a modest, fiscally manipulated form of income distribution – it was nevertheless a break with the consensus established by Thatcher, Blair/Brown and Cameron. But the thoughts and habits that had dominated the culture for four decades – private better than public, individual more important than society, rich more attractive than poor, a symbiosis of big money and small politics – constituted a serious obstacle.

Many who concentrated their fire on Corbyn's supposed unelectability shied away from its corollary: under the present dispensation there was no room for any progressive alternative. The dogmatic vigour with which the EU and its Troika pushed back on any attempts by the left to shift the obstacle contributed to a disturbing growth of the right in France, the Netherlands and Germany, as well as to the election of hard-right governments in Hungary, Poland, Slovakia and Croatia. This was in part a result of the refusal to tolerate even a modicum of social democracy.

The creation of Momentum, which described itself as 'a network of people and organisations to continue the energy and enthusiasm of Jeremy Corbyn's campaign', united old Bennites long asleep in the Labour Party and young activists drawn to the leadership campaign. Corbyn liked to boast that his own local constituency party had 3,300 members and 2,000 registered supporters – more than 5,000 in all, in a constituency where the Labour vote was nearly 30,000. One in six Labour voters

Stuart Hall, the first editor of *New Left Review* (1960–61).

Susan Watkins, current editor of *New Left Review* (2002–). The journal's longest continuously serving editor.

Banquet at the Verso editorial offices – the first and the last – to honour Ernest Mandel and celebrate the publication of *The Meaning of the Second World War*. From top of table right to left: Ernest Mandel, Charles Van Gelderen, Tamara Deutscher, Hilary Wainwright, Perry Anderson, Susan Watkins, Peter Gowan, Marion Miliband, Halya Gowan, Father Carlos Rossi, Margrit Fauland-Blackburn, Neil Belton, Anne Mandel, Robin Blackburn (hidden) and Tariq Ali.

Scenes from a banquet.

John Lennon and Yoko Ono at a small IMG demonstration in solidarity with the Irish struggle. The *Red Mole* cover did not create as much of a storm as its editor (T.A.) had hoped.

Tariq Ali gave the oration at the funeral of Peter Graham in Dublin, just before a revolver salute was enacted. Peter was an Irish socialist and a member of the Fourth International. He was killed in mysterious circumstances, but not by the British. His killer was never apprehended.

Seagull's Dynamic Duo: Naveen Kishore and Sunandini Banerjee. 'Naveen, an old friend who started off by founding a highbrow cultural publishing house in Kolkata in 1982. Himself a photographer and set designer for the theatre. A decade or so later he expanded Seagull in dramatic fashion. It became an internationalist publishing house par excellence with French, German and Italian lists supplemented by new series. Sunandini gave the new-look Seagull its iconic image, making the books immediately recognisable anywhere and everywhere. One day Naveen nosing around in my study found old scripts that I had forgotten. He took them away and published them. We constantly discuss book ideas of one sort or another.'

The Oxford Union, 1964, alongside Malcolm X and Scottish poet and communist Hugh MacDiarmid (otherwise known as C. M. Grieve).

The New Adventures of Don Quixote was staged 1 November 2013, at the Grillo-Theater, Essen. Sancho Panza (Jens Ochlast) with Rosinante (Ingrid Domann) and the Mule (Jan Prohl). Photos by Arko Datto.

Silvia Weiskopf as Don Quixote.

Djibril Diop Mambéty with his favourite actor, Mansour Diouf, on the set of *Hyenas*, 1992. Mambéty was planning a continental African epic with Tariq Ali when cancer struck. He died aged fifty-three (see 'Jottings').

M-K (Mary-Kay Wilmers), dowager editor of the *London Review of Books*.

With Noam Chomsky in Santa Fe, New Mexico, after a talk at the Lannan Foundation, 2005.

Receiving the best foreign-language novel prize from the judges at Santiago Compostela, Spain, for *Shadows of the Pomegranate Tree.*

It was the worst case of a child burnt by napalm that I saw in Palestine, or rather in a refugee camp in Jordan in August 1967. I had photographed Vietnamese children in North Vietnam burnt and maimed by the United States. It was this trip that embedded Palestine in my mind forever.

was a party member. This was an astonishing figure but one not matched elsewhere. Momentum helped to build support by working within existing campaigns against war and austerity, registering voters, encouraging school leavers and students to become politically active, and regularly debating opposing views (and not just on social networks).

Corbyn's radicalism lay not so much in what he was proposing on the domestic front – for that was increasingly the common sense of many economists and others, including the self-declared democratic socialist Bernie Sanders – but in his desire to change foreign policy. His criticism of the absurdly high level of military expenditure was echoed by some prominent US economists in relation to their own country. Joseph Stiglitz (a Corbyn adviser on the economy) and Linda Bilmes argued that America's spending on wars since 2003, estimated at nearly $3 trillion, was crippling the country. 'A trillion dollars', they noted, 'could have built eight million additional housing units, could have hired some 15 million additional public school teachers for one year; could have paid for 120 million children to attend a year of Head Start; or insured 530 million children for health-care for one year; or provided 43 million students with four-year scholarships at public universities. Now multiply those numbers by three.'

There are a number of US historians and analysts – those of the realist school – who aren't shy in criticising their country's foreign policy. John Mearsheimer at Chicago, Stephen Walt at Harvard, Barry Posen at MIT and Christopher Layne in Texas are joined by a former colonel, Andrew Bacevich. In *American Empire*, Bacevich argued against the previous realist view that US Cold War policy was a defensive response to Soviet ambitions and insisted that the expansion of conflict to Eurasia in the 1940s was part of a drive to establish global hegemony. Yet such opinions when voiced by Corbyn and his circle were denounced as anti-American, extremist, a threat to Britain. Corbyn was consistently hostile to both NATO and the EU as constituted, but his views on these matters were so alien to the PLP that they had to be shelved.

During the Blair/Brown period the Labour Party unlearned social democracy of the Crosland variety, let alone anything resembling the classical model of early socialism. Corbyn knew it was vital that the party relearned social democracy. It once seemed a hopeless task. Now, amazingly, they had a chance. The statistics on global inequality desperately needed someone who could explain them in terms that angered, mobilised and inspired people. If Corbyn could do that, it would mark an important shift in English politics.

Where he floundered was in not having a strategic grasp on how to lead the party and set his political stamp on the campaign trail. Viciously sabotaged by party bureaucrats and thuggish PLP types, he failed to hit back on the 'antisemitism' slurs that targeted him personally, megaphoned by the *Guardian* and the BBC. Confusions and divisions inside Labour, many of these encouraged by his opponents in the PLP, helped to ensure the defeat of 2019. Boris Johnson won that election because the Tories pledged to implement the result of the 2016 Brexit referendum without any more shilly-shallying. Democracy matters. Labour's rejection of the referendum outcome at its bubble party conference in September 2019 did them in. John McDonnell was right to take the blame for the defeat. His insistence on a second referendum was a huge strategic blunder.

Johnson's first speech as prime minister, delivered to the cameras outside Downing Street on 24 July 2019, had been lucid and effective. This was not the knockabout party-political busker, who didn't care whether what came out of his mouth was true or not. He would revert to that when things got tougher. He often sounded like a character in a comic novel. His own. Roger Barlow, in Johnson's *Seventy-Two Virgins*, is a self-portrait that reveals a surprising degree of self-awareness:

Barlow's thoughts of political extinction had taken a philosophical turn. Did it matter? Of course not. The fate of the human race was hardly affected ... In the great scheme of things his extermination was about as important as the accidental squashing of a snail. The trouble was that until the happy day when he was reincarnated as

612

a louse or a baked bean, he didn't know how he was going to explain the idiotic behaviour of his brief human avatar.

On that first day outside Downing Street it was clear that Johnson's fears of 'political extinction' had been laid to rest, at least temporarily. Watching the Leninist Boris in action, I feared that, regardless of when the next election was held, Labour would lose it.

I didn't think that December 2019 would be such a crushing defeat, but while Labour's losses should not be underplayed, it's worth remembering that the party's share of the vote was lower under Gordon Brown in 2010 and Ed Miliband in 2015. In terms of seats and numbers, the Conservatives did worse in both 1997 and 2001. The liberal commentariat that was hoping the Lib Dems would replace Labour as the main party of opposition must have been even more disappointed than Labour supporters.

There was a counter-narrative. A few blowhards still insisted that had Labour come out as a hardcore Remainer outfit, things might have been different. This was nonsense. What more could Labour have done? It had already linked arms in Parliament with the Remainer coalition of Tories who'd had the whip withdrawn, remainiacal Lib Dems and Scottish and Welsh nationalists, with McDonnell even offering a warm welcome to the DUP if they changed sides.

These parliamentary manoeuvrings failed, since Lib Dem leader Jo Swinson (her defeat by the SNP in Remainerland was the only time I smiled on election night) refused any deal with Labour under Corbyn because he wasn't prepared to press the nuclear button and was therefore a security risk. The country was spared a coalition that would have further discredited Labour. As some Labour canvassers subsequently reported, many voters felt the conference decision to ignore the results of the Brexit referendum was the last straw. Eyal Clyne, who canvassed throughout the campaign in six northern towns – Crewe, Bolton, Altrincham, Blackpool, Bury and Leigh – described some of their concerns on his blog:

Leave voters are sometimes seen as ignorant, brainwashed or racist, images that did not correspond with my impressions overall. However, for Leave voters, Brexit now symbolises the way in which their voices were being ignored, repeatedly and undemocratically, by the losing Remainers, who are also associated with other classes and more privileged groups ... As far as they are concerned, Labour (and others) did not fully respect the will of the working class, and a democratic result. They feel betrayed.

A striking example of the political re-composition taking place was the East Midlands town of Mansfield, which had bucked the Corbyn surge in 2017, electing a Tory by a thousand-odd votes. This time the Conservative majority was 16,000.

Could this all have been avoided? Corbyn was in a very difficult position. His own close allies had moved away from him on Brexit. His statement that he would remain neutral in a new referendum was ineffective. Was there any other way? Perhaps if Labour had stated clearly that the referendum and the chaos that followed it were the result of a Tory split, and that Labour would let them get on with it, Theresa May's deal with the EU would have gone through and the scheduled April 2022 election would have centred on the NHS, education, public transport, etc. Instead the Labour Party opted for suicide.

The personal vilification of Corbyn as an 'enemy within', carried out by the mass media and Blairite remnants inside and outside the party from the moment of his election as leader, reached a crescendo during the 2019 campaign. There was not much that could be done about this since Labour does not have its own press, but the claim of antisemitism in the party wasn't effectively dealt with. Corbyn's office hoped the problem would go away but it never did.

Social networks were filled with rubbish from provocateurs. Headlines suggested that British Jews were planning to leave the country if Corbyn became prime minister. Internal Labour investigations revealed that, in a party with more than half a million members, 0.06 per cent of them had been implicated in antisemitic behaviour. We have no idea how this compares to the Conservative Party (even before the arrival in the party of a claimed 5,000 members of the far-right group Britain First) or the Lib Dems. We don't know because that was not the purpose of this campaign.

Corbyn was the most radical leader Labour has ever elected in the domain of foreign policy. His very presence questioned the special relationship with the US. His four years as Labour leader transformed the party. The leadership candidates following his resignation were all aware of this fact. Even the Blairite Jess Phillips talked about renationalising the railways being a good idea, and, to be frank, there was not much difference between Keir Starmer and Rebecca Long-Bailey. Starmer said that Labour would accept Brexit, and that was that. Social democratic normality was slowly being restored.

Starmer was duly elected Labour leader in April 2020 by 56 per cent of a demoralised membership, on a promise to 'unify the party'. Though he prefers to proceed by stealth, his strategy is transparent.

Born in 1962 to a working-class family in South London, Starmer made his name as a barrister at the liberal Doughty Street Chambers and supposedly brought a human-rights background to his appointment under Brown as Director of Public Prosecutions. But the rights protected were mainly those of police and spies. Starmer ruled not to prosecute the police killers of Jean Charles de Menezes or Ian Tomlinson, or the MI5 and MI6 officers accused of torture in Bagram and elsewhere. He showed up during the all-night trials of those arrested in the 2011 London riots to praise the judges for their harsh sentencing, and his office notoriously fast-tracked efforts to extradite Julian Assange, warning Swedish prosecutor Marianne Ny, 'Don't you dare get cold feet!'

When he stepped down as DPP in 2013, Starmer was awarded a KCB for his efforts and offered the safe Labour seat of Holborn and St Pancras by Ed Miliband. He was part of the first failed attempt to oust Corbyn in July 2016, then stepped smoothly back into the Shadow Cabinet three months later to run the block-Brexit campaign that helped seal Labour's fate. Once he'd won the leadership, he told members it was time to accept the Brexit result.

Starmer has not bothered to position himself with the voters. In a two-party system, he calculates that, sooner or later, exhaustion with the Tories means it will be his turn. Instead, he is trying to win the establishment's favour – to prove he'll be a safe pair of hands. He has been described in such terms: 'under new management', 'serious', 'professional', 'capable', 'competent', 'responsible', 'sober'. All qualities on display in October 2020, when he ran over a Deliveroo cyclist while reversing his SUV at a busy junction, en route to his tailor, and made off before the police arrived. (The *Guardian* tactfully downplayed the story. The right-wing press and local papers went big.)

Many voted for Starmer as Labour leader in the half-hope that he would 'avoid excesses' but keep the bulk of the social-democratic programme established under Corbyn and McDonnell. But he soon ditched the 'Ten Pledges' of his leadership campaign. Being 'serious' means that only 110 per cent conformism to neo-imperial principles will do.

After Russia's invasion of Ukraine, members of the left-labour Socialist Campaign Group were warned by Labour whips that if they shared anti-NATO platforms they would be punished with suspensions. Several of them hurriedly withdrew their names from a Stop the War public statement that criticised Putin strongly but also attacked NATO for having provoked the crisis. We now know that the Ukrainian government was seriously tempted by an offer from Putin for a neutral Ukraine and a restoration of friendly relations. Boris Johnson, the Ukrainian Deputy PM has revealed, flew in to scupper the deal, insisting there could be no Western negotiations with Putin.

At a Stop the War public meeting at Conway Hall in Central London, I was one of the platform speakers. Corbyn was meant to speak after me, but whispered that he had to rush to another meeting and apologised for not staying till the end. An NEU figure did the same. If these jokers, I remember thinking, are scared off by Starmer, who will they be able to fight?

49

The End of Cricket?

The cricket matches I grew up with in the Indian subcontinent during the 1940s and '50s lasted five days. The players were dressed in immaculate white or off-white flannels, the ball was dark red and the spectators were well dressed and sedate. It was no different in the West Indies: English cricket was everywhere the model. Our heroes were the great English batsmen and bowlers of the time. There were great Australians, too, but, we joked, they were only Englishmen twice removed – once from prison and once from England.

I always envied the apparently carefree life of the street children who played cricket the whole day long during the idyllic winter months from November till March. One year, when my parents were abroad, I bunked off school for a week to play with the street teams. It was bliss, even though I wasn't very good and knew the only reason I had been allowed to play was that I had a new cricket ball – then, as now, a rare luxury for them.

When the street kids weren't playing cricket, they played a game known as gulli-danda, using branches hacked off roadside trees or stray pieces of wood discarded by the shopkeepers. The gulli is a small wooden stake with pointed ends. When you lay it flat, the pointed ends rise slightly above the ground. The danda is a medium-sized stick with which you hit one end of the stake so that it jumps up in the air. As it comes down to about shoulder level, you strike it really hard with the stick to make it go as far as possible. This isn't as easy as it sounds: timing and hand–eye coordination are critical and you need a lot of practice to become an expert player. As they approached their teens, the more gifted gulli-danda players graduated effortlessly to cricket.

They shone in the matches between rival street teams, usually played on dusty patches of land and to a fixed over limit, though the teams were always bowled out before the overs were up. A number of these street cricketers could have gone far, but in the newly independent subcontinent the colonial mode persisted as much in cricket as in the officers' mess and the gymkhana clubs, where civil servants gathered every evening for scotch and political gossip, just as the British had done.

In the first decades after Independence, cricket became more popular, but without any change in its character. Old habits were not easily displaced and at the top level the game remained polite, dominated by the middle and upper classes who still deferred to English ways. Ordinary people were confined to playing in the streets and shouting bawdy comments from the stands during a Test match. In the lunch interval of the first Tests in Pakistan, there was a display by military bands. The sight of young, hairy-legged Punjabis and Pathans dressed in kilts and playing bagpipes greatly amused English journalists, though we took them for granted. Even now the sound of bagpipes reminds me of the first cricket matches I watched from the Victorian pavilion in the lush green field of the Lawrence Gardens (now the Jinnah Gardens), where Majid Khan's father (and Imran Khan's uncle), the stern-faced Dr Jehangir Khan, used to open the innings. Here too, in a crucial Test match between India and Pakistan in the fifties, our most exciting batsman, Maqsood, was dismissed one run short of his century. I also remember the nostalgia when the Indian team arrived in Lahore. For my parents' generation, it was a small, temporary, reversal of the ethnic cleansing that had accompanied Partition. In those days the Indian team was greeted warmly by the crowd.

Until fairly recently, Test umpires belonged to the country hosting the match and their role in deciding the outcome of a game was often critical. On one occasion in Peshawar in the fifties, when a partisan Pakistani umpire, Idris Beg, raised his finger every time the captain, A.H. Kardar, appealed for lbw, the visiting English team, who'd been drinking after the match, decided on a public-school-style punishment: Idris Beg was captured, debagged and dunked in a swimming pool. British umpires used to be accused of bias tinged with racism by visiting teams from the West Indies and the subcontinent.

I once tried to explain the rules of cricket to a young Chinese communist, a former Red Guard who had become disillusioned and fled to Hong Kong, where, to his amazement, he discovered that some of the local Chinese, including a supporter of the fledgling Democracy Movement, played the game. He listened intently, asked questions, and then fell silent. I assumed he was bored but I was wrong. 'Could you explain something to me?' he asked with a frown. 'Who selects the umpires?' He had grasped at once that a partial umpire could turn the game. It was thanks to Imran Khan, and despite fierce objections from the English, that the principle of neutral third-country umpires in Test matches was eventually accepted by the authorities.

The history of cricket is the history of the former colonies overtaking their imperial masters. Cricket, C.L.R. James said, is a metaphor for the empire: one way of undermining the colonists was to beat them at their favourite game. It was this that fuelled the rise of Australian, West Indian and subcontinental cricket, and, later, mass participation in the game. In the 1930s, English sensibilities were offended by the Australians, Don Bradman especially. By the 1960s, it was the turn of the West Indies' fast bowlers. They were too fast, too hostile and bowled too many bouncers. Could it be, the fogeys whispered to each other in the Long Room at Lord's, that the blacks had a special gene which enabled them to bowl so fast? Something had to be done and the white knights of cricket imposed a rule which made it illegal to bowl more than two bouncers an over. They would never get away with that now.

World cricket has changed. The rising power is the subcontinent. Cricket is an obsession in India, Pakistan and Sri Lanka. Under Indira Gandhi there was a growth of self-confidence on the part of the underclass in the big towns, and the change of mood had its effect on cricket, which discarded its colonial wardrobe, became more democratic and began to wear the colours of nationalism. In Sri Lanka in the eighties, cricket was a release for both the Tamils and the Sinhalese engaged in a debilitating civil war, and it wasn't long before the country's incredible batsmen exploded onto the world scene.

The social composition of the Pakistan cricket team began to change after the military dictatorship was toppled in 1969. This process was accelerated when Imran Khan took charge and used his prestige to cut through bureaucracy and cronyism. He encouraged talented young players who had no connections with wealth or with the functionaries in control of the game, and the emergence of players such as Wasim Akram, Waqar Younis and Inzamam-ul-Haq was a direct result. Today, a young boy in a dusty street can see boys slightly older than himself transformed into superstars.

The gulli-danda days are over. The kids now play cricket with a tape-ball – an old tennis ball encircled with red insulating tape. The bounce of the tape-ball is unpredictable. Its tendency to deviate as it hits the ground helps to develop batting reflexes and encourages unorthodox styles. The tape-ball forces bowlers to work harder on their wrist technique since a tennis ball has no seam to make it swing naturally. Ijaz Ahmed, Shahid Afridi, Wasim Akram, Saleem Malik and Yousuf Yohanna all grew up playing tape-ball cricket.

These former street players led Pakistan to victory in the 1992 World Cup. Modelled on its football equivalent, this tournament has become the most important event in cricket, easily eclipsing the annual ritual slaughter of the English by the Australians. It also marks the dominance of one-day cricket over the five-day game. The beauty of five-day cricket is that an accomplished team can be beaten by mediocre opponents lucky enough to have a captain with the strategic skills of a chess player. Victory is rarely certain and a drawn match used to be taken as a satisfactory and honourable outcome.

When they began, one-day cricket matches with limited overs were regarded as a frivolous side-show, a disruption that had to be tolerated because they drew bigger crowds and more sponsorship money. This was not my mother's view. Monumental impatience had always prevented her from enjoying a five-day match. One-day cricket consumes less time and generates more excitement. Purists were inclined to disagree, but they, too, have been won over by the sheer energy of the fifty-overs game.

Robert Winder's *Hell for Leather* is an account of a trip to India, Pakistan and Sri Lanka in 1996, when these countries were staging the World Cup. Winder found a subcontinent in love with cricket. The contrast with England could not have been more pronounced. His prose, mellifluous when describing South Asian cricket, turns caustic when he writes about his own team. The English manager, Ray Illingworth, is typically graceless and petty, always finding an excuse for the team's churlish behaviour on or off the field. He is slow to appreciate the brilliance of the Sri Lankans. Why, the despairing Winder asked, does England produce so many 'bad-tempered cheese-and-pickle types who played too much, ate too much, drank too much, travelled too much and complained too much. Goodness knows, we had plenty of money, plenty of grounds, plenty of players, plenty of every-thing. But all these other countries just seemed to have more zip. It didn't seem fair. Boo-hoo.'

I watched the 1999 World Cup hoping for a repeat of Pakistan's 1992 triumph. The star of the tournament was a Pakistani boy from the streets, Shoaib Akhtar, who bowled at 96 mph. He was discovered by a group of casual onlookers, who alerted Ramiz Raja, a batsman who had played in the national team (and a member, like Imran Khan, of the old Aitchison College cricket elite). Raja went to face Shoaib in the nets. He was scared and impressed and recommended him to Majid Khan and the selec-tors. Shoaib was given his chance.

The Pakistan team was young, although captained by a veteran, Wasim Akram. It was inexperienced, erratic, petulant, but also very exciting to watch. At the Oval, where they played Zimbabwe, the fans were ebullient, alternately cheerful and critical. Why did Ijaz Ahmed get himself run out so stupidly? Some juicy Punjabi abuse was hurled at the departing batsman's head. Several theories sprang to life around me, each involving a conspiracy of one sort or another. When I suggested that Ijaz might simply have made a mistake, I was told by my good-humoured neighbours that I was naive and didn't know anything about Pakistani cricket. But Pakistan defeated Zimbabwe, which meant that India was out of the World Cup. 'India's going home', the fans chanted joyously.

When India had beaten Pakistan at Old Trafford a couple of days earlier, angry Pakistan fans had surrounded the team coach and waved tenners at the team to suggest that they had deliberately thrown the match. I was not convinced, though I had begun to wonder after they lost to Bangladesh. The fans had no doubts. It was all about money, filthy money from the betting syndicates in Bombay, Karachi and Dubai. Bangladesh's victory, I was told, had been bought by Bangladeshi businessmen, desperate to give their fledgling team a boost. The celebrations in Dhaka were phenomenal. History, politics and sport had merged and a large Bangladeshi banner proclaimed: 'Pakistan's second defeat: 1971 & 1999'.

It is rare for a whole team to be bought: usually, a single player is sent detailed instructions. He must bowl three no-balls in his third over, for example, or make sure he is out after scoring sixteen runs, or some other agreed variant. Buying a few players is known as 'spread-betting'. The effect is to demoralise the entire team. Some players have families who can barely afford one meal a day. What do they do if a syndicate makes them an offer of 30 lakh rupees (nearly half a million pounds) for bowling several bad overs in a given match? And if the offer has come through a senior player who might victimise them if they refuse, the choice is simple.

In the Lahore High Court in the late nineties, a one-man tribunal consisting of Justice Malik Mohammad Qayyum considered whether some members of the national team were corrupt. The tribunal was established at the request of the Pakistan Cricket Board and its chief, Majid Khan. It made extensive inquiries and took sworn evidence from players such as Rashid Latif, a former wicket-keeper in the Pakistan team. Disgusted by the scale of the corruption, Latif had secretly taped conversations between leading players. A decision was delayed, probably under government pressure. In public Justice Malik said that he did not wish to damage the team ahead of the World Cup. There were strong indications that all would be forgiven if Pakistan won the Cup.

But they did not win. The final against Australia was a sad, one-sided match. Having unwisely decided to bat, Pakistan collapsed. Its top-order batsmen could not resist the Australian attack. The middle-order crumbled. Shane Warne may have looked unplayable, but Pakistan's batsmen didn't try very hard. The demoralised bowlers, feeling the game was in any case lost, failed to retrieve the situation. Wasim Akram said that they were outplayed and there was nothing more to it. I think, on this occasion, he was telling the truth, but very few people in Pakistan agree with me. The news of the defeat brought angry crowds onto the streets of the major cities (the more recent clashes with India over Kashmir have failed to produce comparable shows of feeling). Unable to accept that this Pakistan team could lose to anyone, the crowds assumed the worst. For them the real victors were not Australia, but the betting syndicates.

The team delayed its departure from London for a few days in the hope that their security could be guaranteed. When they finally landed at Karachi airport, a thousand armed policemen were waiting to protect them from the wrath of several thousand fans chanting 'Hang Wasim!' His brother was allowed into the VIP lounge to collect him but they emerged to find that their brand-new car had been set on fire. Wasim's mother issued a statement accepting that some punishment might be necessary if her son were found guilty of any misdemeanours, but pleading for him not to be hanged. When Pakistan had been beaten by India in Bangalore in 1996, it was said that Wasim Akram had failed to play in the match, not because he was ill, but on the instructions of a betting syndicate. Fans kidnapped his father and held him hostage for a few days. Perhaps that is why this time his mother decided to launch a pre-emptive strike.

Had the team beaten Australia, they could have fornicated, gambled, drunk whisky and taken all the drugs they wanted. They would have been revered by the Pakistani people, who feel that cricket players, unlike politicians, are of their own kind. And their sins would have been washed clean by the obligatory stopover at Mecca on their way home.

The game has been bought and sold in other ways as well. The BBC's decision to stop showing live cricket in the late 1980s was brought about by a combination of the cricket establishment's greed, misplaced sporting priorities on the part of public broadcasters and, according to some, strong pressure from Margaret Thatcher, who was determined to repay Rupert Murdoch for his support by helping him build up his television empire. Within a few years there was no live cricket left on terrestrial television. Numerous addicts, myself included, were forced to admit defeat, sign the document of surrender to Sky and offer our collective shilling to Murdoch. It is now impossible to watch live cricket without subscribing to Sky.

The cricket season is now global; it has neither a beginning nor an end, which can be severely disruptive of the rest of one's life. If you want to watch matches between South Asian teams, you have to pay an additional fee to Zee TV (India) and ARY (Pakistan). The creation of the Indian Premier League (IPL) in 2006, and the extravaganza that accompanied it, forced cricket fanatics to buy a temporary subscription to Setanta Sports. Watching cricket is now more expensive than the BBC licence fee.

Yet all this is trivial compared to the big changes that have taken place since the turn of the century. For many years after the end of empire, the English MCC, together with the wild colonial boys in Australia and, for a time, white South Africa, dominated the international scene. The Brits made the key decisions and went unchallenged. The West Indies have too many fast bowlers who are difficult to bat against? Change the law: restrict the bouncers to one an over. Pakistan's seamers can reverse-swing an old ball? They must be cheating: turn the cameras on them and watch every move. So it went on, with the help of a few umpires who found it difficult to rise above ancient prejudices. Mike Marqusee was harsh but accurate when he wrote in *Anyone but England* (1994) that 'the hypocrisy of the English takes root early in cricket, and is one of the things that makes English cricket English – the way it lies about itself to itself'. In the 1980s, when one of India's great batsmen, Sunil Gavaskar, declared that it was no big deal playing at Lord's and that he wasn't interested in MCC membership, his remarks were greeted with shock. (I was delighted.)

The ICC had been set up in 1909, as the Imperial Cricket Conference, when South Africa was admitted to Test match status and challenged the Anglo-Australian duopoly. It governed by consensus: there would be a discussion, and at the end of it the English chairman got his way. In 1964, the ICC became the International Cricket Conference, but until 1989 the president of the MCC was still automatically made chairman.

By the 1990s the balance of power had shifted. Sixty per cent of the world's cricketing revenue was by then being generated in South Asia. India has a population of a billion, and cricket is its national sport. The Board of Control for Cricket in India (BCCI), riled by long years of English arrogance and conde-scension, decided it was time to rid itself of the Raj. By this time, they had learned enough tricks of the trade from the old colonial bosses and were ready to declare independence. The nervous-ness at Lords was captured in Mike Atherton's comments in the *Sunday Telegraph*:

> India are the big beast of cricket and everyone is frightened of both their bark and bite. Their rise to dominance began in 1983 with an unexpected World Cup victory over the mighty West Indies ... It was a sweeping change to the balance of power but one that took England ... a long time to appreciate ... Malcolm Speed, the chief executive of the ICC, found himself in a position much occupied by Kofi Annan and the United Nations in recent years: being bullied by a superpower for whom the notions of international law and collective responsibility have long ceased to have any meaning.

In 1996, after what an Australian cricket official referred to as 'a decidedly ugly ICC meeting', Australia and England considered mounting a counter-coup. What had upset them was that South

Africa had jumped ship and sided with India. Graham Halbish, a former CEO of the Australian Cricket Board, revealed there had been acute concern that 'India, Pakistan and Sri Lanka, with the unexpected support of South Africa and Zimbabwe, were forming a powerful alliance with the potential to take over international cricket'. In *Run Out* (2003), he described how he was 'given the extraordinary task of drawing up a plan ... so secret and highly sensitive, that it even had a codename – Project Snow'. It was an attempt to split the ICC, so that Australia, England, New Zealand and the West Indies would play each other but nobody else. Halbish was sure that this 'contingency plan would allow us to keep satisfying our television networks, sponsors and crowds'.

Better heads prevailed; the South Asians made a few cosmetic concessions (such as rotating the chairmanship) and a split was averted. The ICC's function today is straightforward: it determines the rules and structure of world cricket and makes decisions that are binding on its members. I thought of Project Snow as I watched the England and Wales Cricket Board (ECB) notables – led by its chairman, Giles Clarke, and flanked by English cricketing legends (all Sky employees) – lining up to greet Sir Allen Stanford's helicopter as it landed on the nursery ground at Lord's in 2007. The Texas-born, Caribbean-based billionaire (as he was described before we learned that much of his capital was fictitious) was greeted like a monarch. The fantasist from the Antiguan St John's was not in a mood for compromise and proceeded to describe the Test cricket played in St John's Wood as 'boring'. The future, as far as he was concerned, lay with 'Twenty20', the shortest version of the game – and, no doubt, with the rah-rah girls imported from Ukraine and elsewhere whom he thought necessary to enliven proceedings.

In Twenty20, each team plays only one innings, batting for a maximum of twenty overs; the game is completed in about two and a half hours. The Indian Premier League was already a massive popular success; the global broadcasting rights alone were expected to earn the BCCI $1 billion over the next ten years. It was felt by some in the English cricketing establishment that a rival competition was badly needed; after all, Twenty20 had started out as an English innovation. The plan was simple: to set up a Twenty20 super-series to rival the IPL, which had paraded virtually every non-English cricketing star in several Indian cities before huge and cheering crowds. It would be supervised by the ECB and funded by the Stanford millions.

England's star player, Kevin Pietersen, was signed up as a Stanford ambassador, and appeared happy enough in news photographs. (He later informed the media that he was always dubious and regarded Stanford as a 'sleazebag'.) A hurried exhibition match between England and the West Indies was organised at Stanford's private club in Antigua in November 2008. The players on the winning team were each promised $1 million. The West Indies (playing as the Stanford Superstars) duly won, but five of the players agreed to let Stanford invest the money on their behalf. They were foolish, but not as foolish as the Antiguan government, whose economy was closely linked to Stanford's enterprises, or the Venezuelan oligarchs who used the Stanford Bank in Caracas to launder money.

It was only after the US Securities and Exchange Commission accused Stanford of 'massive and ongoing' financial fraud that the ECB decided to break off all links with him. The proposed Twenty20 rival to the IPL lay in ruins. If Project Snow was a childish response to the cricket establishment's loss of hegemony, the Stanford debacle was the result of thoughtless greed. In a sense it's unfair to single out the ECB. 'Soft-touch regulation' was the order of the day under Thatcher and continued under New Labour. Why should the ECB have been any different? True, allegations of one kind or another regarding Stanford's business practices had been doing the rounds for a number of years, and in 2007 the Stanford Group Company was fined $20,000 for violating disclosure norms; but nobody really cared. None of it was unusual in the world of fictitious capital laid bare by the financial crisis.

As with the world in which it is played, much has changed in cricket. The cheating – the betting scandals and the disgraced captains Hansie Cronje, Mohammed Azharuddin, Salman Butt et al. – is the least of it. A bookie, Hanif Cadbury, was murdered in South Africa, where he had fled after testifying before Justice Qayyum's inquiry into match-fixing in Pakistan, spilling the beans on how the cricketers had collaborated with the bookmakers. Some of this, as John Major revealed in *More Than a Game*, his accomplished history of cricket's early years, is not exactly new. Extensive match-fixing took place in nineteenth-century Britain, when cricket as we now know it was being invented.

What of the on-field changes? Jean-Marie Brohm, a French sociologist, has described all sport as 'a prison of measured time'. Looked at that way, five-day Test cricket is the equivalent of a life sentence. And yet Test matches can be tenser and more stimulating than any other form of the game, even when they end in a draw – a possibility that is excluded in shorter forms, where a result is vital. It's fogeyish, of course, to say that things were better in the past, but there is a serious argument here. Fifty-overs-a-side one-day cricket can be enjoyable, but Twenty20 is cricket's answer to the penalty shoot-out: its outcome depends too much on luck. The main thrust behind globalised cricket is commercial and few bother to hide the fact. It is organised by the money-wallahs and TV schedulers: floodlit night matches, played to secure prime-time audiences, are increasingly common.

Then there are the commentators who vie with each other to see who can dumb down the most, competing with mini-skirted dancers hired to do the cancan when a boundary is scored or a six hit into the crowd. Making a fool of oneself when Twenty20 matches are being played is par for the course: some of the players on the fielding side are fitted with microphones so they can be interviewed in the course of the game. The message is clear: 'We don't take it seriously and you shouldn't either. We're only trying to inject a bit of fun into the game and get the young more interested' – though this has never been a problem in South Asia or Australia.

There is, of course, lots of money to be made. Most cricketers are underpaid, and I'm in favour of them being paid more, not least because it would reduce the influence of the betting mafias on the stars, which has come close to wrecking the game altogether. One reason the public stopped turning up for Test matches in some parts of the world was a deep suspicion that the results had already been decided.

Test cricket at its best has the qualities of an exquisitely chore-ographed ballet. To watch the great spin bowlers – Abdul Qadir, Shane Warne, Muttiah Muralitharan, Anil Kumble – bowl at the same batsman for over an hour, varying each ball till they trap their victim, is to delight in their artistry. It can also be boring and predictable; but so can its abbreviated offspring, for all its frills.

When the IPL circus first began, with Bollywood stars and Indian corporations getting franchises, I feared the worst. The hoopla, the slavish commentary by overpaid pundits and the unending shots of the IPL commissioner, Lalit Modi, preening like an Indian god minus the make-up – all this was truly awful, but the cricket was exciting and I was hooked.

Meanwhile the Chinese government has decided that its youngsters should learn how to play cricket, just in case the shorter version becomes an Olympic event. Former Test players from South Asia, especially Pakistan, have been hired to go and act as coaches. If cricket were to take off in China, the ICC would be forced to shift its headquarters to Shanghai and the biggest cricketing event of the sporting calendar in 2030 would be the annual India–China Test series. Who knows? Chinese helicop-ters might be provided with a permanent pad at Lord's.

But while the game has become increasingly international, it is still haunted by an imperial ghost and, along with it, the stain of racism. Who would have imagined that the sordid saga of ingrained racism in English cricket and its consequences would be laid bare before a select committee of the House of Commons in 2021? Very few non-white British women and men engaged in professional sport on any level would have been surprised by the goings-on in Yorkshire. Much of what Azeem Rafiq revealed – the levels of racism in the changing room as well as the board room – had been known in the cricketing world and its fringes for a long, long time. There's no point pretending otherwise. The dressing room at the Yorkshire Cricket Club may have been par-ticularly nasty, but let's avoid the 'bad apple' theories so beloved in this country and always used to justify corruption, sleaze, racist atrocities, etc. Few other county clubs have a clean record. And the rot starts at the head.

Despite all the evidence, the ECB was not prepared to take on the toads in Yorkshire. Credit for the scale of the exposure must go to Sajid Javid. The shock the health secretary felt when he read an early account of what Rafiq had suffered was palpable. 'Heads must roll,' he tweeted. His far-right Cabinet colleague at the Home Office might well have thought Rafiq's head should roll or, at the very least, his citizenship be annulled for bringing English cricket into disrepute, but once Boris Johnson declared the racism unacceptable, a cover-up was impossible. Hence the select committee and the attendant publicity. And, following that, the sorry sight of embattled cricket executives bowing their heads in shame, admitting – in the case of a former boss of Yorkshire – that the county was the site of 'institutional racism'.

County cricket welcomes white 'Rhodesians' and South Africans with open arms, while tormenting British Asians and blacks. It took Rafiq, and other players of Asian and Caribbean heritage, some time to understand the extent to which racism was embedded in the consciousness of some of their white fellow players. The old colonial mentality was alive and well in English cricket. Some had assumed that a love for cricket might transcend all prejudices. This was not the case, as they had to learn the hard way. The word must have spread. Since 2015, the number of British Asian kids learning cricket has declined by 40 per cent and Rafiq has said he would not encourage his son to play.

Watching the 2021 select committee proceedings, I wondered how John Arlott, C.L.R. James and Mike Marqusee might have responded to the spectacle. They wouldn't have been surprised. Arlott, the former cemetery assistant whose commentary on *Test Match Special* was mesmerising, was horrified by the practices of the apartheid state when he visited South Africa with the English team in 1948–49. At the airport on his way back home, he famously refused to fill in his 'race' on the departure form. David Rayvern Allen describes it in his biography of Arlott (2014):

The immigration officer looked at him impatiently. 'What race are you?' he asked. 'Human,' replied Arlott. 'What do you mean?' the man asked in an aggressive tone. 'I am a member of the human race,' came the reply ... The immigration officer glowered. At last, between gritted teeth, he said: 'Get out.'

Arlott never forgot. A decade or so later, he was instrumental in helping the Cape Coloured cricketer Basil D'Oliveira move to England. D'Oliveira played for England in the 1966 Test series against the West Indies but was not selected to tour South Africa in 1968–69. The MCC caved in to apartheid. There was a huge outcry, led by Arlott, demanding the tour be cancelled. When Tom Cartwright was injured and had to drop out, D'Oliveira made himself available, though the captain, Colin Cowdrey, was desperate to keep him out of the team. At a debate at the Cambridge Union, Arlott destroyed Ted Dexter, a former captain whose colonial mindset would accompany him to his grave. In the end D'Oliveira was selected and the tour was cancelled by South Africa, leading to its ostracism from international cricket until the collapse of the apartheid regime.

Colonial attitudes in cricket were rarely absent from the thoughts of my late friend Mike Marqusee, whose *Anyone but England* was roundly denounced by most cricket writers. How could a left-wing American Jew know anything about the game? The book remains one of the most stinging assaults on the English cricket establishment. Marqusee's call for a global boycott of English cricket irked many who were otherwise sympathetic to his views. Some underestimated the problem. Matthew Engel, a former editor of *Wisden*, reviewed a reissue of Marqusee's book in 2005. He summarised its argument as: 'in all cricketing disputes, the English view is wrong'. Engel disagreed:

This may be a necessary corrective to imperial arrogance but it creates many nonsenses of its own. His account of the England-Pakistan ill-feeling at the time, in which the Pakistanis are portrayed as heroic victims, is ludicrously one-sided. Now the game has moved on; the book has not.

631

Really? In September 2021 the ECB unilaterally cancelled an England (men's and women's) tour of Pakistan. They gave no convincing reason. Ramiz Raja, the president of the PCB, said he felt as if he had been 'used and then binned'. The ECB chairman, Ian Watmore, resigned. The CEO, Tom Harrison, flew to Pakistan to apologise as the Rafiq case was building. He lasted until May 2022. Meanwhile, the government threatened the ECB: 'If they don't get their act together,' the sports minister told the select committee, 'then we have the nuclear option of legislating in order to bring in potentially an independent regulator. That is probably the route that, if we absolutely had to, we could go down.'

Marqusee would have had a few things to say about this had he been alive, but cancer took him early in 2015. His reports from the select committee would certainly have been angry, but he would also have felt vindicated. He got it right.

50

Kings and Queens

Charles is a name that the English monarchy has avoided since the seventeenth century. A century and a half before the French Revolution, the English fought a civil war and made a bourgeois revolution, funded by merchants. They executed the king – Charles I – on 30 January 1649, abolished the House of Lords and declared a republican state. The Commonwealth that ruled over England, Scotland, Ireland and Wales may not have lasted very long, but it left an enduring mark. The restoration of 1660 – and Charles II – was a compromise, and when his successor James II tried to push the boundaries he in turn was overthrown in the so-called Glorious Revolution of 1688, and a more accommodating royal family installed. The absolutist state could not be resuscitated. The 'divine right of kings' was never allowed back. But the reconstituted monarchy proved to be remarkably resilient. From his perch at Princeton, Arno Mayer explained this development in his classic 1981 account, *The Persistence of the Old Regime*:

The [post-1688] monarchy and landed elite tamed the industrialization of England without succumbing to it ... England never became a 'bourgeois order' run by a 'conquering' bourgeoisie ... There was no movement to remove the crown, the royal court, the House of Lords, and the ascriptive public service nobility. Despite the decline of agriculture and despite insular security, which vitiated the need for a strong military caste, the landed classes managed to perpetuate the 'archaic' political order and culture.

This archaic order has been modified over the centuries. A major reform was the neutering of the House of Lords in 1911, after it had rejected David Lloyd George's 'People's Budget' of 1909, provoking a constitutional crisis that was resolved in favour of the House of Commons. The second chamber could delay, but not veto, a bill that had been approved by the Commons. Nothing else happened.

In 1991, left-wing Labour parliamentarians Tony Benn and Jeremy Corbyn proposed and tabled a Commonwealth of Britain Bill that called for the radical democratisation of the country. The bill included demands that, had they been implemented, would have completed the bourgeois revolution that began in the seventeenth century. They envisioned the abolition of the monarchy and the disestablishment of the Church of England; the head of state would be a president, elected by a joint sitting of both Houses of the new Commonwealth Parliament; all the functions of the royal prerogative would be transferred to that Parliament; the Privy Council would be abolished and replaced by a Council of State. The House of Lords would be replaced by an elected House of the People and both Houses would have equal representation of men and women. England, Scotland and Wales would have their own national parliaments with responsibility for devolved matters as agreed. County Court judges and magistrates would be elected, and British jurisdiction over Northern Ireland would end.

Dream on!, some might say, especially on the day of the Coronation of Charles III, 6 March 2023, when the country was busy grovelling in public. The three main UK parties, every newspaper and all the TV channels proved themselves staunch monarchists. So, where the hell is Britain going?

Charles I did not inherit his father's brains; it was his own arrogance and stupidity that led to his trial and execution. The leaders of the Revolution were divided on the issue. Mrs Cromwell was opposed as well. She had enjoyed tea with the queen. It was Oliver Cromwell who finally put his foot firmly on the royal neck. Charles I had broken one promise too many.

Charles III is unlikely to follow the same path. At most, he might be reduced to the status of a bicycling, low-key king like his Scandinavian equivalents. In the 1960s, when hardcore Welsh nationalists threatened to bomb his investiture as Prince of Wales and claimed that a sniper was ready and waiting to cause sensational havoc, Charles Windsor presented himself as a jokey individual, not too bothered by threats, confessing to a BBC interviewer:

> As long as I don't get covered too much in egg and tomato, I'll be all right. I don't blame people demonstrating like that. They've never seen me before. They don't know what I'm like. I've hardly been to Wales, and you can't expect people to be over-zealous about the fact of having a so-called English prince come amongst them.

Not bad. But in 2010, when his car was unexpectedly surrounded just off Trafalgar Square (a short walk from the Banqueting House in Whitehall, where his namesake was executed) by student demonstrators protesting the new Conservative government with chants of 'Tory scum', 'parasites' and 'off with their heads!', the photograph that captured the moment revealed Charles and his wife Camilla in a state of bewilderment and fear. Had his namesake's fate momentarily flashed through his head?

On 9 September 2022, Charles III became king after a long reign by his mother. He had been waiting impatiently for some time, hoping his ageing parent would follow Juliana's example in the Netherlands and retire, but it was not to be. Charles's reign can't be too long, but the current state of Britain and its monarchy invites some questions. The most important of these is whether the monarchy can survive if the United Kingdom breaks up and Scotland decides to leave the UK and join the EU. Opinion polls in Scotland suggest that 49 per cent of Scots favour independence. Another few years and this could easily become 50-plus per cent. If there were a new referendum, a majority vote to exit the Union would force a rethink in England and perhaps even compel its rulers and politicians to move in the direction of a written constitution.

Why did the country that first established the tradition of successful revolutions and executions of hereditary rulers cling for so long to the monarchy, adapting it at different times to satisfy the same basic needs: maintaining a stabilisation of the ruling class and an organic embrace of all its institutions, including the Labour Party and the trade unions? As if to acknowledge this, following the death of the queen the otherwise radical leaders of the railway workers' union and the postal workers, then in the middle of a series of effective strikes, delayed further action as a mark of respect. This was obviously a tactical move, but the fact that it was considered necessary indicates the continuing grip of the institution of monarchy on the popular imagination in England. The durability of the 1688 compromise created a uniquely successful environment for British rulers.

Scottish historian Tom Nairn argued for almost half a century that the monarchy was needed to act as a balancing wheel at home, both to keep a rising working class under control (George V's behind-the-scenes interventions in the general strike of 1926 were brutal) and to try to incorporate it organically, so that its loyalty to the political system in place was never in doubt. Grateful for Labour's moderation during the general strike, the king said, 'What a wonderful people we are.'

Abroad, the British Empire needed a monarch to strengthen its hold on colonies where kings were seen as normal. In both Asia and Africa, monarchs were used as pacifiers of the natives. Elizabeth Windsor was in Kenya in 1952, while the British were crushing the Mau Mau nationalists via torture and concentration camps ('British gulags', as American academic Caroline Elkins has described them, putting English historians to shame). It was in Kenya that the queen was informed that her father had died. George had only become king because his older brother Edward had married an American divorcée (he was reputedly ensorcelled by her proficiency at fellatio) and so was forced to abdicate. Some were nervous because of Edward's openly expressed fondness for Hitler. Had the Germans taken Britain during the Second World War, Edward Windsor would have been returned to the throne, an English Pétain.

The monarchy is willingly used to meet the needs of the British state as defined by its politicians, secret services, etc. The decision to topple the Australian prime minister Gough Whitlam as punishment for bringing his country's troops home from Vietnam was taken with the approval of Elizabeth II by her governor-general. Australia, pathetically, is still not a republic.

The closest I have been to Buckingham Palace was in 1973, when a bunch of us were arrested for opposing the presence of Portuguese dictator Marcelo Caetano at the queen's dinner table. As I predicted to the policeman arresting me, Caetano would be toppled by a popular revolution the following year. Romania's murderous Nicolae Ceaușescu was knighted by Elizabeth, and slept and breakfasted at the palace. The family has a long record of hobnobbing with dictators, and Charles has often travelled with a begging bowl to the Gulf States pleading for money for his foundations. 'The Firm' – as the royals reputedly refer to themselves – is a wretched business that should be closed down.

The only serious question raised by the death of a ninety-six-year-old, extremely wealthy titled lady in her palazzo is: how long can this farce last? The mainstream press of Europe wasting so much paper on the Windsors would do well to remember that the late queen was (in private) a staunch supporter of Brexit, as revealed by Murdoch's rag the *Sun*. The last few decades have shown the monarchy (and in some ways Britain itself) to be in a state of advanced decay. The brutal treatment of Diana is now the subject of a mediocre movie. Prince Andrew's debauchery has alienated quite a few royalists. All this has been the subject of a multi-episode soap opera on Netflix. That is where the Crown belongs – and where it should be kept.

With Scottish leaders demanding a new referendum and Welsh nationalists insisting there should be no new Prince of Wales (the title given to the successor of the monarch ever since the Welsh were crushed) and threatening to disrupt any investiture in Caernarfon, what the hell is the point of going on? Why should England be left to bear the burden of a continuing monarchy? The country doesn't need it.

The empire has long gone, but the monarchy reminds people of those 'great times' when Britain did rule large tracts of the world. As Nairn argues in *The Enchanted Glass*, the British state's victory against the French Revolution was another reason to make sure it remained a monarchy. In his words: 'The advances of its industrial revolution delivered continents into its paws, in a way that no subsequent state would ever be able to emulate. The rich life-blood of a world's wealth rushed to its head, lending a new magnificence and meaning to its mediocre dynasty.' The name of the Hanoverian dynasty had to be changed as the First World War approached. It became the House of Windsor.

A few mainstream commentators have argued that the queen remained popular because she was linked to memories of the Second World War. Much of the generation that lived through the war is now dead. Their children and grandchildren would have little truck with the sentiments expressed by General de Gaulle to the queen in a letter dispatched in 1961:

> In the palace where God has put you, be who you are Madam. Be the person in relation to whom, by virtue of your legitimacy, all things in your Kingdom are ordered; the person in whom your people perceive their own nationhood; the person by whose presence and dignity, the national unity is sustained.

The monarch is redundant today. The real king of Britain sits in the White House. The House of Windsor's only function is to help preserve the antiquarian structure of the British state, but structural reforms are needed on every level – as is a written constitution. Perhaps we will have to wait for the Scots to kick-start the process. After all, they produced in James Stuart (the father of Charles I) the only monarch of Scotland and England who was a gifted intellectual.

I noticed no signs of sadness or quiet on the streets of London in the week after the queen's death. Most young people are indifferent to the monarchy. Thatcher and some of her gang had promised modernisation, but that turned out to be regressive. She got trapped as well – and ended up falling for the whole show. In the late 1980s, I described Britain as an island where 'two Queens sat on a single throne'.

The monarchy needs deaths and weddings for its cyclical renewal. Television cameras help create the charisma. Weddings are invariably shown as joyous – and by the time the marriage collapses, memories have faded. State funerals reduce Britain to the level of North Korea, as in the mindless orchestrated adulation we witnessed on 19 September 2022. That funeral was used to stress the unity of the United Kingdom. Too late, I think. She has yet to find a real home, but I think the Scottish filly has bolted.

BOOK IV

JOTTINGS

Introduction: A Homage to Lu Xun

In April 2011 I was in South Africa, being driven to the airport closest to Rhodes University, which had just awarded me an honorary doctorate for services to the anti-imperialist cause. The university's official wording was slightly different:

> Today Rhodes University is proud to honour one of the English-speaking world's foremost public intellectuals ... historian, novelist, playwright, filmmaker, activist; an incisive, often witty, political commentator; determined champion of oppressed, marginalised peoples across the globe ... Mr Chancellor, I have the honour to request you to confer on Tariq Ali the degree of Doctor of Laws, *honoris causa*.

I was sharing the car with a cultural attaché from the Chinese embassy. I was mocking him for the Chinese decision to offer a Confucius Prize to rival the Nobel Peace Prize. He was clearly irritated. 'What name would you have chosen?'

I replied: 'Lu Xun. To stress your affinities with modernity and critical thinking.'

He became even more irritated. 'Are you a communist?'

I burst out laughing. It's true that in a tribute to Lu Xun in Yenan on the first anniversary of his death, Mao Zedong had declared: 'In my view, Lu Xun is a great Chinese saint – the saint of modern China, just as Confucius was the saint of old China ... He was a great steadfast tree, not a blade of wavering grass, against the onslaught of dark and violent forces.' True, but the Maoist attempt to instrumentalise him did not quite succeed. Lu Xun (1881–1936) was undoubtedly one of the greatest writers of twentieth-century China, sympathetic to the party but never part of its cultural apparatus. He was fiercely independent-minded and his longer and short-form essays ('jottings') were widely read in the country. He could write on every subject under the sun, though he was best known as a literary critic.

In later years, well after the success of the Chinese Revolution, Mao and comrades were discussing Lu Xun. One of them wondered aloud what, were he still alive, Lu Xun would be writing. Quick as a flash and lucid as ever, Mao replied: 'He would either have fallen silent or been in prison.'

I doubt he would have fallen silent. Three of his literary followers, who did join the party and joined Mao in Yenan – Hu Feng, Xiao Jun and Feng Xuefeng – were ruthlessly purged and Hu Feng was put in prison.

My 'Jottings' below are a simple homage to Lu Xun. Collated chronologically, they span the many places, people and events that I have witnessed. They form a constellation rather than an argument for a life spent in refusal to please all.

Parchment Does Burn (1989)

Roshan Seth (who played Nehru in Attenborough's epic *Gandhi*) had become a friend in the late eighties. We worked together on some projects and met fairly regularly. Roshan was at the time married to Pepita, an English cultural historian of South India, based in Kerala, and an expert on Indian classical dances, their origins, music and language. Susan and I both remarked to each other after one dinner that Pepita was more Indian – her accents had developed Keralan undertones – whereas Roshan was a *pukka sahib* and very English in temperament. All his friends were aware of this and teased him mercilessly.

One evening, after dinner in their London flat where Pepita had excelled herself producing a number of Keralan dishes, I asked after her family. She was an upper-class lass and I wondered how her parents had taken to her marrying an Indian actor. She left the room and returned with a letter.

'Here, judge for yourself.'

'Oh God,' Roshan muttered, 'do you have to inflict this on them?'

'He asked,' said Pepita tartly. 'It's the best answer to his question.'

Pepita was Pepita Fairfax. Her father was the lineal descendent of General Fairfax, 'whose name in arms through Europe rings ...' (Milton). A leading figure in Cromwell's New Model Army, the general (like Mrs Cromwell) had been somewhat unhappy at the decision to execute the king. Now I became seriously curious. It was a very loving negative letter. He loved his daughter and wanted to see her happy. He made the case for all castes sticking to their own and wrote that he could never agree to her marriage with any Indian. To prove that this wasn't just anti-Indian prejudice, he provided a long list of races to which he would also object. These included: Hottentots, Eskimos, Red Indians (by this he didn't mean members of the Indian communist parties, but Native Americans), no African whatsoever, or Aboriginals. Maori? Certainly not. Chinamen and Nips? No! And not even the Pitcairn islanders with their polluted mixed-race blood. There were other names too, but I read this letter a long time ago. He must have searched the *Encyclopaedia Britannica* pretty thoroughly.

'You're in good company here, Roshan,' I laughed. 'So you've never met him before or after your marriage? No trips to the Fairfax family house?'

'Well,' Pepita took over, 'my mother invited us to a Sunday lunch. I didn't want to go, but Roshan did. It was awful. Father, buried in an armchair, pointedly read the Torygraph after we arrived, grunted in response to Roshan's attempt to ingratiate himself, didn't say a word during lunch and withdrew afterwards.'

I couldn't stop laughing. Terence Rattigan could have written a good play. But Roshan wasn't done. 'Everyone in the family knows her father's mad. Tell him the other story that proves this point.'

Before she could I pointed out to Roshan that nothing in the letter I had read suggested insanity. In fact, the opposite. He was a straightforward, down-to-earth racist like so many others of his race-type and caste and he spoke the truth. Better than hypocrisy and bullshit.

But Pepita's story amazed me. She described how once, in their late teens, she and her brother had come home for Christmas from their respective schools and were in relaxed mode. One day the siblings went up to explore the old attic and its secrets. Quite accidentally, one of them brushed against the seventeenth-century wood panelling and a secret compartment opened. It contained letters written on parchment.

'We unfolded them very carefully and were simply stunned. What we had found were letters from Oliver Cromwell written to our great forebear and explaining in some detail why the king had to go. He answered all General Fairfax's objections. We rushed downstairs screaming with excitement. My father asked if we'd found something.'

He looked at the letters and nodded. Then his daughter made a fatal mistake. In her own words: 'I was excited and said this was a great discovery and we must ring the relevant ministry and the British museum to hand the letters over.' Her father responded firmly: 'It's family property. I will never hand it to any government or museum.' As Pepita and her brother objected vociferously, Mr Fairfax rose from his chair and proceeded to place the letters on the blazing fire in the living room. His wife and children were so horrified they stifled their screams.

I was forced to concede that this couldn't just be a display of excessive philistinism. There must be a streak of madness in the Fairfax side of the family. As we said our farewells, Roshan gave me a sly, triumphant smile.

Gerrard Winstanley had written that the old world was 'running up like parchment in the fire'. This felt slightly different.

My Dinner with Mambety (1995)

Full name: Djibril Diop Mambety. Profession: A natural-born *auteur*. A self-taught cameraman, director, musician, script-writer; well-read son of a poor Muslim Senegalese cleric. It was October 1995. Djibril was in town for the launch of his film *Hyenas* at the London Film Festival. It had been strongly recommended to me by friends whose judgement I trusted. Susan and I trooped along to see it, not knowing what to expect. The press file they'd sent me was largely written by Djibril. He explained:

> The hyena is an animal of Africa. Singularly wild. It practically almost never kills. First cousin to the vulture. It knows how to sniff out illness in others. And then is capable of following, for a whole season, a sick lion. From a distance. Across the Sahel. To feast one evening on its corpse. Peacefully.

Mambety had read Fredrich Dürrenmatt's 1956 play *The Visit* and, as he told me, 'I fell in love with it. A real intellectual passion.' Kenneth Tynan had reviewed the London production in the *Observer* and summarised the play as only he could:

> A flamboyant, much-married millionairess returns to the Middle-European town where she was born and offers the inhabitants a free gift of a billion marks if they will consent to murder the man who, many years ago, seduced and jilted her ... Eventually, and chillingly, her chosen victim is slaughtered, but I quarrel with those

who see the play merely as a satire on greed. It is really a satire on bourgeois democracy. The citizens … vote to decide whether the hero shall live or die, and he agrees to abide by their decision. Swayed by the dangled promise of prosperity, they pronounce him guilty. The verdict is at once monstrously unjust and entirely democratic. When the curtain falls, the question that Herr Dürrenmatt intends to leave in our minds is this: at what point does economic necessity turn democracy into a hoax?

Mambety's programme notes for *Hyenas*:

> The village of Colobane, devastated by drought and unemployment, sees sudden hope for the future with the arrival of a former citizen, Linguère Ramatou (Ami Diakhate), who left her hometown when still a young woman, but now returns with a great fortune. The grocer Dramaan Drameh (Mansour Diouf), one of Colobane's leading citizens and Ramatou's former lover, is selected to lead a welcoming committee, but after a seemingly tender reunion to the two, Ramatou reveals the true depths of her bitterness towards Dramaan Drameh, who impregnated her and denied his responsibility, resulting in her being sent into an uncaring world where she had to turn to prostitution to survive. She offers the villagers a hard deal: One hundred billion dalasis (Gambian currency) in exchange for the death of Dramaan Drameh. The citizens of Colobane refuse, but as the village is flooded with consumer goods, they are driven deeper and deeper into debt, forcing them to make a hard collective decision. Will it be the money, or Dramaan Drameh's life?

After initially resisting Ramatou's demands, the need to buy the latest consumer good from the West becomes overpowering and the villagers cave in and despatch Dramaan who they had once liked. Money transcends morality. Refrigerators, washing machines, stoves fly into the kitchen. Two young men on bikes are singing Paree, Paree, Paree and imagining they're almost in Paris. Ramatou has a uniformed Japanese woman as her bodyguard. Political surrealism dominates *Hyenas*. Throughout the movie, the lure of the West is depicted as ever present, though in different shapes and on different levels. Apart from all else, it is comedy on a very high level.

We spent nearly five hours talking over supper. Our conversation would have made a little book. We spoke of the world, the West, its culture, but kept returning to Africa. Did he like Ousmane Sembene's cinema?

'He is an inspiration and always will be. Sometimes filmmaker's praise another director for public consumption. I don't do that. Never. Without Sembene many of us might not have made films. He is a socialist but also a feminist. The women portrayed in his work are strong. They don't see themselves as victims. Have you seen all of them?'

I had, but at festivals or the rare art cinema releases. Once in New York. Djibril had no firm idea for his next movie.

'Ever thought of doing an African epic?'

'What do you mean?'

'Finding a medieval mechanism to encourage a modern revolution.'

'Should we do it together? But how.'

We ordered cognacs and I started, with both of us making notes.

'We could frame it as follows. It's a film that embraces the whole continent. How? A grandfather takes his fifteen-year-old granddaughter to show her the ruins of Greater Zimbabwe and she asks "What happened?" He takes her hand and they both stand on a flat rock and look at the landscape. We tell four basic stories from the South, West and East coasts and integrate them with traveller's tales from the North.'

Djibril continued:

'OK. Good. We could start with Lord Waka in Timbuktu, a ruler without a son but not worried since the region is matriarchal. He has two daughters but their mothers have walked out on him because he gambles, drinks, fornicates most of the day. One gambling den is run by an old master of the *worra*, an old African board game. Lord Waka tries and tries to defeat the master, but never succeeds. Waka is ill, dying of syphilis. Desperate to succeed on some level … you continue, Tariq.'

'Desperate to succeed on some level, Waka wants to defeat the *worra* master. The sound of horses hooves intermingles with the noise of pebbles on the *worra* board. Build up to a crescendo. Five horsemen enter the room and inform the master they have orders. "Whose Orders?" ... Djibril takes over.

'A soldier slaps him. Old man fearful. A soldier says that unless he agrees to lose a game to Lord Waka, the consequences will be grim. The master refuses. The soldiers laugh and set the place on fire ...'

We carried on. The next day Mambety rang the Bandung office. He was excited. He could visualise it and said, 'Let's do it.' He had another short film to finish, but would get in touch in a month's time. We worked out a budget, discussed locations. It wouldn't be an expensive film.

I waited and waited. Three months had passed by. I thought he'd changed his mind. Hardly uncommon in this world. One day I got a letter from his Swiss wife or lover, no mean documentarist herself. Djibril had been diagnosed with a rapidly spreading cancer. All work had stopped. He died aged fifty-three. A huge loss to African cinema. And to me. His anarcho-surreal vision would have made *Munhumumutupa – The King* (as he wanted to call our film) a remarkable work of art. Of this I am sure. We had, I see from my notes, agreed on a rolling Epitaph with an African drum beat and Shakespeare's words (from *Coriolanus*):

> They said they were hungry, sigh'd forth proverbs,
> That hunger broke stone walls, that dogs must eat,
> That meat was made for mouths, that the gods sent not
> Corn for the rich men only ...

Better Red than Wed (1996)

A decade ago when my son was just starting school, he came home one day and asked his mother: 'Are you and Tariq married?' 'No,' replied Susan. 'Why not?' he persisted. 'Because', she explained, 'I don't want to give up any of my rights.' He thought and then asked: 'But what about your lefts?'

I was reminded of that yesterday, listening to the pious tones of Gillian Shephard informing us that the institution of marriage must be a cornerstone of all moral teachings at school. What about our lefts? Are they going to try to outbid Tory hypocrisy on this front as well? They should recall how all the cant of back-to-basics backfired over adultery. Shephard was referring, I think, exclusively to heterosexual marriages – if the Labour front bench attaches itself too firmly to her they could soon find the tabloids investigating all the bachelors in Tony Blair's entourage. One person's morality is usually another person's sin.

The suggestion that morality requires marriage was always grotesque anyway. Marriage, according to a distinguished Victorian sociologist, was little more than 'legalised prostitution'. This was an exaggerated way of stating that traditionally it was a patriarchal handing-over of a woman by her father to her husband. The sociologist (Engels) never married himself, unlike his best friend. The novelist George Sand was surely right when she insisted that the laws of the human heart were more important than those of the Church. An official blessing is not and never was a prerequisite for a happy family.

The background of politicians who have sought to impose a moral straitjacket on their citizens is mixed. The Christian right in the US Republican Party, the Taliban fundamentalists in Kabul and the Jewish fundamentalists who want to return to the morality of their ancient patriarchs (by restoring the right to concubines) are a few modern examples. The aim is usually the same: to roll back social, economic and educational policies that have made gradual advances and helped to emancipate both men and women.

We could take an earlier example of the 'Christian' ethos from Germany in the 1930s, when Adolf Hitler proclaimed at a Nuremberg rally that, while for a man the world was the state and the community, the woman had different priorities: 'Her world is her husband, her children and her home. But where would the big world be if no one wanted to look after the small world? How could the big world continue to exist if there was no one to make the task of caring for the small world the centre of their lives! No, the big world rests upon this small world! The big world cannot survive if this small world is not secure.'

If, at the recent Tory Party conference, Peter Lilley had used these exact words while justifying a further reduction in social security payments, he would have got a standing ovation.

Incapable of promoting policies to alleviate the suffering of the two million unemployed and millions of underprivileged citizens, and thus help bring about a society more at ease with itself, our politicians have instead clambered onto the morality bandwagon. Party leaders vie with each other for the approval of the Anglican Church, forgetting that in this nation there are more practising Catholics than Anglicans and more Muslims than Methodists and that all of them have slightly different moral priorities.

The two-party consensus has created a political climate of stifling conformity, the tones and themes of which are reflected in most of the press and an increasingly abject television service, where the components compete in subservience. Life-politics are all the rage; issue-based politics are frowned upon.

Both Michael Howard and Jack Straw can give only one serious explanation for an increase in crime: the moral breakdown of society. What about the ravages of the 1980s and the fissions Margaret Thatcher deliberately brought about in order to fracture communities and proclaim there was 'no such thing as society'? What about the collapsing infrastructure in town and country? The near-collapse of the National Health Service as a provider of free healthcare for all? The removal of political support and economic aid from state schools? The undermining of public service broadcasting? The encouragement of a crass philistinism and greed (as symbolised by the chairmen of privatised utilities)?

What sort of morality is it that can justify all this and then preach piety to the poor? The only thing most people could afford to invest in was hope, but the Blair project has ended even that possibility and there is little that is positive in what the shadow 'Iron Chancellor' is plotting. So cynicism increases and an interest in politics is discouraged.

As for Gillian Shephard and her marital obsession, let me suggest a model contract which could apply to both hetero- and homosexuals: 'We, X and Y, of our own free will, marry for the duration of our mutual affection. We wish and intend to put our fortunes in a common fund, but reserve the right to separate them again for the benefit of any children we may have, either in common or separately. We recognise that our property belongs to our children by whomsoever we may have had them and that all of them have the right to the name of whichever parent acknowledges them.'

The author of these words, Olympe des Gouges, was a radical pamphleteer during the French Revolution. For denouncing the brutal excesses of Robespierre and Marat, she was guillotined in November 1793; this should make her a heroine to both the Tory Party and New Labour. Either way, her proposed contract could be hurried through the first session of the next Parliament. Although I worry that some Blairite moralist might rush to the British Library, read her pamphlets, and condemn her to the guillotine yet again.

A Man without Instincts (1997)

During Michael Grade's last year or so as the boss of Channel 4, he sent Peter Ansorge, the drama commissioning editor, and myself a message to come for a chat. He asked whether we had an idea for a TV play that would shake things up. Peter looked at me. I thought aloud: 'If we could manage to do it, a ferocious satirical, surreal assault on John Birt's BBC and management-speak would certainly have an impact.'

Grade started laughing. We talked more. He told us to get on with it. As we were leaving, he said: 'I'll leave you with a clue that you should pass on to your writer. When I was leaving the Beeb to come here, Birt came into my room to wish me well. Then he asked whether I had any advice for him. I told him "Go with your instincts." His response astonished me: "I don't have any instincts, Michael." I was seriously taken aback, but said nothing. I mean, even animals have instincts.' Grade wanted the play done quickly.

As Peter and I got back in the lift, I said: 'Many BBC employees have one strong instinct. Self-preservation. I bet you Birt has that one secured.' We were both amazed that Michael had gone for the idea immediately. No problem with instincts in his case.

We discussed possible authors and finally agreed on what turned out to be a mistake. Alan Plater had written a TV play for C4 that had been a huge success. *A Very British Coup* was based on Chris Mullin's novel in which a left-wing politician (inspired by Tony Benn) manages to win an election and a coup is immediately set in motion. Tony watched that play several times. Plater had pulled it off. Might he do the same with Birt and the BBC? Could he write a semi-realist satire very different in tone and spirit from his big hit? The two other names I had in mind were Howard Brenton and Terry Gilliam. Howard is very good with villains and Gilliam, in some ways, would have been brilliant at a robotic takeover of the BBC and gone wild with all the examples of Birt-speak we got every fortnight in *Private Eye* (these were times when the *Eye* kept up a relentless assault on the Birt BBC).

We had a session with Plater, an extremely decent and good man who we both liked. He came up with a script titled *The Domino Effect*. It was like seeing the BBC through the eyes of a team of tiddly-wink players visiting from Hull after having won the national tiddly-winks championship. As soon as he left, Peter Ansorge screamed: 'I hate English whimsy. I hate English whimsy.' We sat down calmly with Alan and explained the problem. He became very defensive and said 'I've done what you wanted. A satire on the BBC with a soft outside but a hard centre.' I said gently that it was soft everywhere, that it was too sentimental, and that while I understood the desire to be kind to a public service institution, he might rewatch *Britannia Hospital*, Lindsay Anderson's 1982 satire on the NHS and its shortcomings.

He made some changes but we weren't on the same wavelength. We had no time left. Grade had a look at the script and was very disappointed. So were we.

Blowing this project is one of my deepest regrets on the cultural front. What a missed opportunity. Gilliam would have used daleks instead of actors to play top management!

Marx on Suicide (2001)

I was arrested at Munich airport at 7 a.m. yesterday (30 September). After one day of interviews and book signings and two days spent at a Goethe Institute seminar on 'Islam and the Crisis', I checked in at the departure lounge and soon my hand luggage was wending its way through the security machine.

No metal objects were detected but they insisted on dumping the contents of my bag onto a table. Newspapers, dirty underpants, shirts, magazines and books tumbled out in full view. Since news always reaches Germany a day after it has appeared in the US press, I thought the locals might be looking for envelopes containing powder, in ignorance of the FBI and CIA briefings that Osama bin Laden and gang were considered unlikely to be involved in the anthrax scare. There were no envelopes in my bag.

The machine-minder brushed aside the copies of the *Sueddeutsche Zeitung*, the *International Herald Tribune* and *Le Monde diplomatique*. He appeared to be very interested in the *Times Literary Supplement*, and was inspecting my scribbled notes in the margins of a review by Hugh Roberts of a book on Algeria. There was also a copy of a book-essay by Marx in German that had been handed to me by a local publisher. There had been no time to flick through the volume. It was still wrapped in cellophane. The minder grasped the text eagerly and then, in a state of some excitement, rushed it over to the armed policeman.

The offending book was Marx's essay 'On Suicide'. It was the reference to suicide that had got the security men really excited. They barely registered the author, but when they did real panic set in and there were agitated exchanges. The way they began to watch me was an indication of their state of mind. They really did think they had got someone. My passport and boarding card were taken away from me. I was rudely instructed to repack my bag – minus the crucial 'evidence' (the *TLS* and the offending text by Marx) – and was escorted out of the departure area and taken to the police headquarters at the airport.

On the way there the arresting officer gave me a triumphant smile. 'After September 11, you can't travel with books like this,' he said. 'In that case,' I replied, 'perhaps you should stop publishing them in Germany, or better still, burn them in public view.'

Inside the headquarters, another officer informed me that it was unlikely I'd be boarding the scheduled BA flight and that they would have to make inquiries about later departures. At this point my patience evaporated and I demanded to use a phone. 'Who do you want to ring?' he asked. 'The Mayor of Munich,' I replied. 'His name is Christian Ude. He interviewed me about my books and the present crisis on Friday evening at Hugendubel's bookshop. I wish to inform him of what is taking place in his city.'

The police officer disappeared. A few minutes later another officer – this one sported a beard – arrived and beckoned me to follow him. He escorted me to the flight, which had just finished boarding. We did not exchange words. On the plane a German fellow passenger came and expressed his dismay at the police behaviour. He told me that the policeman who had initially detained me had returned to boast to the other passengers of how his vigilance had led to my arrest. The *Sueddeutsche Zeitung* asked me to write a piece. This was Otto Schilly – a former left-wing lawyer who had defended the Baader–Meinhof people in court – who criticised me in public for making heavy weather of the incident. The German Greens could end up anywhere.

Al Jazeera (2002)

In Cairo and Abu Dhabi, the two Arab capitals I have visited this year, street and palace are for once in harmony. A pre-emptive strike against Saddam Hussein on the grounds that he might, at some point in the future, authorise the production of nuclear weapons, would be, for the people of the region, a classic display of imperial double standards. They know that the only country which possesses both nuclear and chemical weapons is Israel. Arab public opinion has not been so united for decades. And a cable television station, Al Jazeera ('the Peninsula'), has played a crucial part in both promoting and symbolising this unity. It has raised mass consciousness in the region by providing a ruthless analysis of what is wrong with the Arab world.

Unity was the recurring theme of the nationalist period of Arab political history. First there was Nasser and his dream of a united Arab republic. Then defeat in war. Then the laments of exiled poets – Nizar Qabbani from Syria, Mahmoud Darwish from Palestine and Mutlaffar al-Nawab from Iraq. The Egyptian diva Um Kalthoum sang their poetry and was revered. Then darkness. The 1991 Gulf War demoralised and atomised the Arab world. Secular dissenters continued to meet in the cafés of Damascus, Baghdad, Beirut and Cairo, but could speak only in whispers. Elsewhere, mosques became the organising centres for a confessional resistance to the New Order and the Great Satan that underpinned it.

The state media networks continued to broadcast propaganda of the crudest kind; criticism of government was unheard of. Then, in 1996, Al Jazeera arrived. It is a TV news channel that defies taboos and prohibitions. Arab viewers abandoned the state networks overnight and Al Jazeera's newsreaders and talk-show hosts became instant celebrities.

Nothing like this had been witnessed since the early 1960s, when nationalist radio stations in Cairo, Baghdad and Damascus issued daily incitements to listeners to topple every crowned head in the region. The Jordanian king was nearly overthrown and the Saudi monarchy seriously destabilised. In both countries Western aid helped to crush the nationalist revolts. Al Jazeera has no such ambitions: the men running the channel are only too aware that a crowned head, the maverick Emir of Qatar, provides the funds and the headquarters for their operation. The Emir has also allowed the US to construct the largest military base in the region, which boasts a recently completed 13,000-foot runway to handle heavy bombers. Iraq will no doubt be attacked from this base while on Al Jazeera commentators denounce US aggression.

The idea of a semi-independent Arab TV network was first suggested by BBC World Service journalists and supported by the Foreign Office. A deal was signed with the Orbit Radio and Television Service to provide a news programme in Arabic for Orbit's Middle East channel. But Orbit was Saudi-owned, and its financiers were unwilling to allow news bulletins critical of the Saudi Kingdom. The project collapsed in April 1996 after footage of a public execution was broadcast. The BBC retired hurt and the Arab journalists who had been made redundant began to search for a new home. They were lucky. Their quest coincided with a change of rulers in the tiny state of Qatar.

In 1995, the old Emir, a traditionalist, was deposed by his son, Hamad bin Khalifa al-Thani, who promised to modernise the statelet. Starting with a dramatic gesture, he abolished the ministry of information. When informed of the collapse of the BBC venture, he offered the journalists a headquarters in Doha and $140 million to restart operations. Sheikh Hamad's father and grandfather had together owned 452 cars, including some hand-built for them. The TV station must have seemed cheap by comparison, and it has given the Sheikhdom more visibility and prestige than it has ever had. Encouraged by the response to his action, Hamad allowed women to vote and to stand as candidates in municipal elections in 1999. This was a shot across the Saudi bows and was recognised as such.

Virtually none of the journalists who came to work for the new channel was a local. The Syrian-born Faisal al-Kasim, Al Jazeera's most controversial host and now one of the most respected journalists in the Arab world, studied drama at Hull and spent a decade as the anchor of the BBC's Arabic Service. His show *The Opposite Direction* features political debates and confrontations conducted with an intensity rarely seen on Western networks. When I met him in Abu Dhabi he had just finished an interview with the local paper and was fending off other journalists and well-wishers. I asked whether the complaints about his show had started to drop away. 'They never stop,' he replied. 'People can't believe that I choose the guests and the subjects. No authority has ever tried to influence or censor me and I have much more freedom than I ever did at the BBC.'

In the early days, the Qatari government received at least one official complaint about the channel every day from fellow Arab governments – 500 in the first year alone. Gaddafi withdrew his ambassador from Qatar after the station broadcast an interview with a Libyan opposition leader; Iraq complained when the channel revealed the amount of money that had been spent on Saddam Hussein's birthday celebrations; Tunisia was angry at having been accused of human rights violations; Iranian newspapers resented 'slurs' against Ayatollah Khomeini; Algeria cut off the electricity in several cities to prevent its citizens from watching a programme that accused its army of complicity in several massacres; Arafat objected to Hamas leaders being interviewed; and Hamas was angered by the appearance of Israeli politicians and generals on *The Opposite Direction*.

The Saudi and Egyptian governments were enraged at criticisms made by dissidents on Al Jazeera. As loyal allies, both countries have had a relatively good press in the West. Before 11 September it required the death of a Westerner in Saudi Arabia to focus attention on the Kingdom, but the furore never lasted long. Over the last decade, the Saudis have spent hundreds of millions of pounds to keep Western and Arab media empires and their employees on side. Al Jazeera's broadsides were viewed as treachery. Riyadh and Cairo put massive pressure on Qatar to muzzle the station, but the Emir ignored the protests and his government denied that the channel was the instrument of Qatari foreign policy.

During its early years, Al Jazeera was warmly welcomed in Washington and Jerusalem. Thomas Friedman, the *New York Times* columnist, celebrated the birth of the station with a bucketful of praise: it marked, he said, the dawn of Arab freedom. Ehud Yaari was similarly praising two years ago in the *Jerusalem Report*: 'Out of a modest, low-rise prefab, five minutes' drive from the Emir's diwan, the tiny Sheikhdom of Qatar is now producing a commodity much in demand in the Arab world: freedom.' The channel's 'powerful video signals', he continued, 'are gradually changing the cultural and political order in the Middle East'.

What happened last September put a stop to these eulogies, especially after Al Jazeera broadcast interviews with bin Laden and his Egyptian deputy, al-Zawahiri. The bin Laden interviews were banned on Western TV on the spurious grounds that they might contain coded instructions for future terrorist hits. In fact, it was because bin Laden's soft features undermined the portrayal of him as evil incarnate. A senior TV producer in Berlin complained to me last October that his ten-year-old son, after seeing bin Laden on the news, had remarked: 'Papa, he looks like Jesus.'

Qatar now came under very heavy pressure to do something about Al Jazeera. Maureen Quinn, the US ambassador, delivered a strongly worded complaint to the foreign minister. It had little impact. In October, Colin Powell was sent to browbeat the Emir, who once again defended the freedom of the press and stressed that the state could not interfere with what he described as a 'private commercial operation'. US officials who met Al Jazeera executives were heard politely and told that the channel would be delighted to interview the American president or his nominees: Condoleezza Rice, Tony Blair and Colin Powell were allowed unlimited time to explain their point of view. The effect of these broadcasts on Arab public opinion was non-existent.

When the bombing of Afghanistan began, Al Jazeera was the only TV network sending out regular reports. And so began its dazzling ascent. Its footage was eagerly sought, bought, carefully edited and shown on CNN, BBC and every major European network. Then the building in Kabul it was using as a temporary studio was bombed, just as a BBC journalist using its facilities had begun to broadcast a live report. He hit the floor and we witnessed the 'accidental bombing' live on our TV screens. When a Belgrade TV station was targeted by NATO forces in 1999, Clinton and Blair admitted the bombing was deliberate, and justified it on the grounds that 'deliberate misinformation' was being broadcast. Qatar could hardly be categorised as an enemy and so the spin-doctors were far more careful when it came to explaining the bombing in Kabul: the building was targeted, they claimed, because of 'reports' that it housed al-Qaeda suspects, and they hadn't known that it was Al Jazeera's base.

It is on the second front of the 'war against terror', however, that Al Jazeera's coverage has made the most significant impact. After Israeli tanks entered Nablus earlier this month, the channel broadcast a story about the following incident (the description here comes from LAW, a Palestinian human rights organisation):

> Khaled Sif (41), who is married and has four children, received a call on his cellular phone. In order to get a better signal he went to the balcony. The moment he reached the balcony, Israeli forces shot him in the head and killed him. After he heard the shot, Muhammad Faroniya, who is married and has six children, went to the balcony. Israeli forces opened fire and also shot Muhammad Faroniya, wounding him in his chest and abdomen. Mahmoud Faroniya, Muhammad's brother, tried to save his brother, but Israeli forces pointed their guns at him and he was prevented from doing so. Muhammad bled to death. According to eyewitnesses, Israeli forces deliberately left Muhammad Faroniya bleeding for ninety minutes.

The daily coverage on Al Jazeera of stories such as this one stands in contrast to what is shown in Europe, let alone the

United States. CNN established its reputation during the Gulf War through the work of its correspondent, Peter Arnett, who remained in Baghdad and whose reports of civilian casualties and the bombing of non-military targets enraged the US, with the result that Western governments are now much more careful to control access to information during times of conflict. They also try hard to stop anyone else covering the stories they are trying to suppress.

Having failed to curb Al Jazeera's influence, however, the US is now going to try to mimic its success. With a war in Iraq seemingly imminent – a war about which the West is profoundly divided, and for which there is no support at all in the Arab world – there are plans to launch a satellite channel in Arabic funded by the US Information Service, to which can be added the expertise of CNN and BBC World. The Israelis have already launched their own version, with little effect. The notion that the Arabs are brainwashed and all that is needed to set them right is regular doses of Bush and Blair is to ignore every reality of the region. But the plot is far advanced.

'What will they name their channel?' I asked Faisal al-Kasim. 'The Empire?'

'No,' he said. 'They have a name for it already. Al-Haqiqat.' It translates into 'Pravda' in Russian.

In Tripoli (2006)

'We've been trying to get you to come and talk here for the last three years,' my host complained as we shook hands at the airport. 'Here' was Tripoli, capital of the Socialist People's Arab Jamahiriya, bathed in mild February sunshine; my host a functionary from the World Centre for the Studies and Researches of the Green Book (the Libyan equivalent of the Little Red Book). 'The lecture is just an excuse,' I told him. 'I'm really here to see Leptis Magna.' We both laughed. He because he thought I was joking, and me because I wasn't.

I was billeted at the state-funded Funduq al-Kebir, rebuilt in 1982 on the site of the colonial Grand Hotel. The old place looks much nicer in photographs than its soulless replacement, with its surly receptionists, appalling service and second-rate food (the worst breakfasts ever, and that includes Pyongyang circa 1972).

The hotel overlooks the waterfront and is within walking distance of the main sights, including the great old mosque-church-mosque, the Ottoman souk and the museum. Close by are the huge marble arcades of the colonial period. Some have a belle époque charm; others are more reminiscent of grandiose Italian Fascist architecture, such as the railway station in Milan. Above both varieties of arcade are beautiful apartments with baroque plaster mouldings and shuttered windows, which once housed the colonials. Walking through the decaying arcades, crowded with noisy men-only cafés, one gets a glimpse of prewar Italy, far preferable to the imitations of Dallas that are so typical of the cities of the Gulf States.

I meet up at a waterfront café with a lively Libyan intellectual, freshly returned from Canada and excited about his plans for launching a weekly magazine. We notice that most of the young women, including those arm-in-arm with a boyfriend, are hijabed. Very few are worn tight like a nun's cowl; more often they are designer versions, and usually (as is also the case in Cairo) it's what is worn below the neck that attracts attention. It is not unusual to see hijabed women wearing tight-fitting tops and jeans. In such cases a display of hair might well be thought a distraction. But my companion is shocked. 'It was very different when I left for Montreal several years ago,' he said. Only a minority covered their heads and most wore skirts. And at least half the people in this café would have been women.'

Has there been pressure from the state?'Exactly the opposite,' he said.'The government doesn't impose any norms in matters of dress. Not now and not under the monarchy.' But Gaddafi is pious, I insist. Why else would he have ordered the uprooting of the wonderful vineyards surrounding Tripoli?' Libya's neighbours, Tunisia, Morocco and Algeria, have maintained their vineyards.

'It was a mistake,' my companion declared. 'And our wines were better.' We discussed his project for a cultural magazine. He was confident that changes were on the way in Libya. The secret police were less visible and had stopped harassing citizens. There were a few hundred political prisoners, mainly in Benghazi, a centre of Salafism, crushed fifteen years ago after an insurrection. It was in Benghazi last month that several hundred Islamists stormed the Italian consulate, after a Northern League member of Berlusconi's government was seen wearing a T-shirt with one of the Danish cartoons on it. The minister was sacked the following day and Berlusconi apologised.

The next day I met a chain-smoking freelance journalist in his late fifties. In reality he was a creature of the café and did very little during the day apart from smoke and drink Turkish coffee – a character familiar to readers of Mahfouz's *Cairo Trilogy*. He, too, was slightly puzzled by the rapid growth of the hijab industry. His own wife had taken to wearing one about five years ago. Since she was present, I asked her why. She smiled and shrugged.

I explained that I was curious to know whether it was a globalised fashion trend or a reflection of the increase in religiosity.

'Both,' she replied. 'And also the proliferation of cable TV. We can now get everything. Pornography and preachers. The hijab in my case is a response to both.'

After his wife had left, the journalist said more. 'I think it is an increase in religiosity, but in men more than women. Many young women do it to please men and think it will put them on the fast track to marriage.' He told me that a few years earlier, a Moroccan woman had accosted him in a hotel restaurant. She was wearing a hijab and he was taken aback to realise that she was a prostitute. 'If we walk out and get in your car, nobody will think twice because I'm wearing a hijab,' she had told him. 'I could be your sister, a cousin or even your wife. So I wear it to make things easier for you men.'

The two internet cafés in the hotel lobby have young male workers wearing jeans, who greet customers with a friendly 'hi'. There are over a dozen messages waiting for me from various media outlets wanting comments or interviews about the Danish cartoons. Nobody in Libya has mentioned them so far. I have a look at the cartoons: most of them are unfunny and the one of Muhammad as a turbaned terrorist is a provocative and crude stereotype. I reply to the questions of the Swedish liberal daily, *Dagens Nyheter*, but ignore most of the other requests.

It took five months of concentrated lobbying in the Muslim world by a travelling imam from Denmark to manufacture this 'anger'. In occupied Afghanistan about 500 people joined a demonstration. Were their thoughts on the cartoons, or the ruin and destruction around them? Feeling powerless, they used the cartoons as an excuse to march outside a US military base. The marines opened fire and two young boys died. In Lahore the violence was orchestrated by the Jamaat-i-Islami, who tried to regain the political initiative by getting young men armed with clubs to attack a bank. Perhaps they needed some cash. One cleric who clearly doesn't is Maulana Yousaf Qureshi of Peshawar, who is offering a million dollars and a new car to anyone who kills the cartoonist. The make of car is not specified.

All this is very different from the restraint shown by the Muslim Brotherhood in the Arab world and Western Europe, whose members objected but in a newfound, moderate way. They are seriously interested in power and want the United States to believe they are pretty much the same as Christian Democrats. That this is largely the case can be seen in Turkey, where a pro-EU, pro-NATO Islamist party is in power.

The next day I'm driven to Leptis Magna, the capital of Rome's African Empire, on a road running alongside an unspoilt coastline. The satanic cartoons fade from memory. As we turn a corner the columns of Leptis suddenly appear, with the turquoise Mediterranean as their backdrop. The size and scale are astonishing. Like much else on the shores of this sea, the city was founded by Phoenician traders, around 1100 BC; later it fell to Carthage and was incorporated into the Roman Empire by Tiberius after the defeat of Carthage in the Third Punic War in 146 BC. It provided Rome with an emperor, Septimus Severus, and the arch commemorating him still stands. The Vandals took Leptis in 439, destroying its walls to prevent Roman resistance.

By the time the Arabs arrived in 650, the city had been abandoned, but its stones weren't looted and the city was hidden under the sand, until in 1912 Italian archaeologists uncovered it. I was mostly alone for the three hours I spent at Leptis, apart from a few Italian tourists and some Libyan families with picnics.

Many artefacts from Leptis and Sabratha (an ancient Greek city) are now in the museum in Tripoli, which has a stunning collection of virtually intact statues from the ancient world. But another object in the museum catches my attention. Preserved in a glass case, surrounded by antiquities, is a blue 1960s Volkswagen. This is the car which Gaddafi, then a young army captain, drove around Tripoli, encouraging his fellow officers to follow the path of Nasser and topple the pro-Western monarch, King Idris. Gaddafi has run the country since 1969 without feeling the need to create a single political party. He has declared, *pace* Ibn Khaldun, that tribalism is a curse of the Maghreb and that since political parties are only a modern version of tribes, they are dispensable. This thought and others can be found in the Green Book, a collection consisting for the most part of verbose and turgid declamations, with the odd original reflection reflecting the zaniness of its author.

It's difficult to gauge what is really happening in Tripoli. Some things we know. Libya's earnings from oil stand at $36 billion a year. Its annual budget is $10 billion. Its population is nearly six million. Naturally nobody starves. The bazaars are full of food, but the level of education and the health facilities are primitive. Thousands of Libyans cross into Tunisia to get medical treatment. The contrast with Cuba, an island always strapped for cash, is instructive. The Medical University of the Americas in Havana trains and educates hundreds of students from South and North America (mainly Afro-Americans and Hispanics). The level of culture and education is very high. Why not in Libya? The state bureaucracy produces a population in its own image. Isolated, provincial, with more than a touch of brutality, it conditions the population, who in return display fear combined with prudence and cunning.

It need not be like this, and the latest turn towards the West is an attempt to join the globalised world. Few in Libya believe that Gaddafi was responsible for the Lockerbie disaster, but in order to end sanctions and shift Libya's political position he admitted guilt and agreed to pay a fortune in compensation. The acceptance of imperial hegemony requires tributes of this sort. Does it also require a hereditary leadership? One of Gaddafi's sons, Saif al-Islam, is being groomed for the succession. Since he's a PhD student at the LSE and enamoured of the neoliberal West, there is little criticism there of the proposed handover. Gaddafi, after all, is no longer the head of a 'rogue state' but a 'great statesman' (in the words of Jack Straw), and has received Blair in his tent. This helps maintain the pretence that he's caved in to London, not Washington. It's simple: Saif wants to privatise everything and turn Libya into a Gulf statelet. But his dad has been flattered by the West into relinquishing the country's nukes. The family will end sooner rather than later.

ॐ

Ahmad Ibrahim al-Faqih, a novelist I had asked to see, was in town. His autobiographical trilogy (*I Shall Present You with Another City, These Are the Borders of My Kingdom* and *A Tunnel Lit by a Woman*) has won him renown throughout the Arab world. Like many Arab writers inspired by the nationalist wave of the 1960s, he became disaffected after the Arab defeat in the Six-Day War. This is not uncommon. Numerous Arab intellectuals, writers and poets are alienated from both their own societies and the West.

Few have embraced religion. Al-Faqih's first novel opens: 'A time has passed and another time is not coming.' The final sentence of the trilogy is: 'A time has passed and another time has not come and will not come.' He told me that he is close to finishing a ten-novel work. 'I've just been appointed ambassador to Romania. As you can imagine there is not much to do there, so I will have plenty of time to write.' Gaddafi, too, writes short stories. One of them, 'Suicide of an Astronaut', is said to be surreal, but my requests for a copy went unheeded.

The Road to Damascus (2006)

Land in Beirut for a meeting. An old Palestinian friend, Fawaz Trabulsi, picks me up at the airport. Notices that I am in a very long queue. I see him on the phone. Ten minutes later a security officer emerges, calls my name, has my passport stamped and escorts me out to where Fawaz is waiting. We embrace. I haven't seen him for a very long time. He explains: 'The security this week is the responsibility of the Druze guys, loyal to our friend Walid [Jumblatt]. Walid rang and said you were his guest. That's all.'

Supper with Syrian oppositionists of the left. The next day a car is waiting to drive me to Damascus. A lunch is being laid on by the UK ambassador to Syria, a strong opponent of the Iraq War. As I arrive at the embassy, he greets me warmly: 'Not a free lunch, I'm afraid. I've invited various representatives from different political currents to question you while we eat. There will be a senior figure from the Ba'ath as well.' I agree. The Syrian guests are slightly nervous. The ambassador starts the ball rolling: 'Tariq Ali, welcome. A short while ago you wrote in the *Guardian* that our prime minister, Tony Blair, should be charged for war crimes in Iraq. Would you care to elucidate?'

I was taken aback, as were the Syrian guests. I explained the reasons in a calm and judicious fashion. The ambassador nodded: 'I agree with you completely. Any other questions?'

There were, but on safer themes. After all the guests had departed, most of the embassy staff present burst out laughing.

'It was worth it just to see your face when he asked you the question,' one of them said. When I expressed concern for the ambassador's career, I was reassured by another staff member (probably MI6, since we later discussed Chávez as well): 'Don't worry. He's retiring at the end of the year!'

That same evening, I spoke at a well-attended public lecture organised by the British Council and appealed for some form of democratic accountability and the opening of debates in the media on the future of the Arab world, including Syria. Better to do it yourselves than wait for some form of US intervention. I ended by warning liberal and a few left intellectuals in Syria and Iran: 'Some of you, I know, would prefer regime-change organised by Washington. Look at Iraq. Listen to the bells tolling in Baghdad and Basra. They toll for you.'

I spent the next afternoon and evening with Suad and Yasser Munif, the widow and son of the late novelist Abdurahman Munif, whose work I admire greatly. He had died prematurely two years previously. First we wandered through the old parts of the city on foot, the best way. I had last visited in 1967 after the Six-Day War. This time was more relaxed. Yasser informed me that he had read *Bush in Babylon* to his father as he lay ill in bed and he had liked it, saying: 'Tariq has said everything that needed to be said about the Ba'ath.' Suad had, courageously, rejected the request of the Saudi ambassador to come and condole when he died. They had deprived him of his nationality for his *Cities of Salt* quintet, amongst the finest work produced on the Peninsula.*

Supper at the Munif household. Exquisite food. Met Ossama Nagib, now eighty, who had set up the PLO propaganda network in Washington in the 1960s. He was scathing about Yasser Arafat: 'From the very beginning he was a crook and an operator.' He's disgusted with the PLO for agreeing to split the movement and ganging up against Hamas. He is not a supporter of the latter. Just thinking of Palestine.

Syrian intellectuals, old and young, also present. Yasin, a leftist,

---

* Probably the finest essay on Munif ever written in any language is that in English by the Egyptian critic Sabry Hafez in *New Left Review* 37, January/February 2006.

in prison for fifteen years and tortured, insists the leftists were not brutalised as badly as the Islamists: 'They were tortured every day. It was purposeless torture, not designed to gain information but exact revenge and assert power.'

Suad showed me Munif's study. Very moving to see his notebooks. On the wall a painting by an Iraqi of the writer in bed, depicting his last months. The general view was that there were three factions in the regime: (1) Pro-US, cave in completely, like the Egyptians; (2) pro-EU, cave in partially; (3) carry on as before using Syrian policy as a lever to amass wealth (like South Africa and Iran). But even this faction prepared for a deal with the United States on the Golan heights. On this depressing note I depart.

Diyarbakir (2006)

It was barely light in Istanbul as I stumbled into a taxi and headed for the airport to board a flight for Diyarbakir, the largest Kurdish city in eastern Turkey, not far from the Iraqi border. The plane was full, thanks to a large party of what looked like chattering students with closely shaved heads, whose nervous excitement seemed to indicate they'd never left home before. One of them took the window seat next to my interpreter. It turned out he wasn't a student but a newly conscripted soldier, heading east for more training and his first prolonged experience of barrack-room life, perhaps even of conflict. He couldn't have been more than eighteen; this was his first time on a plane. As we took off he clutched the seat in front of him and looked fearfully out of the window. During the flight he calmed down and marvelled at the views of the mountains and lakes below, but as the plane began its descent he grabbed the seat again. Our safe landing was greeted with laughter by many of the shaven-headed platoon.

Only a few weeks previously, some young soldiers had been killed in clashes with guerrillas belonging to the Kurdistan Workers' Party (PKK). It used to be the case that when Turkish soldiers died in the conflict, their mothers were wheeled on to state television to tell the world how proud they were of the sacrifice. They had more sons at home, they would say, ready and waiting to defend the Fatherland. This time the mothers publicly blamed the government for the deaths of their sons.

Diyarbakir is the de facto capital of the Turkish part of Kurdistan, itself a notional state that extends for some 600 miles through the mountainous regions of south-eastern Turkey, northern Syria, Iraq and Iran. Turkish Kurdistan is home to more than fourteen million Kurds, who make up the vast majority of the region's population; there are another four million Kurds in northern Iraq, some five million in Iran and a million in Syria. The Turkish sector is the largest and strategically the most important: it would be central to a Kurdish state. Hence the paranoia exhibited by the Turkish government and its ill-treatment of the Kurdish population, whose living conditions are much worse than those of the Kurds in Iraq or Iran.

Kurdish language and culture were banned at the foundation of the unitary Turkish Republic in 1923. The repression intensified during the 1970s, and martial law was imposed on the region in 1978, followed by two decades of mass arrests, torture, killings, forced deportations and the destruction of Kurdish villages. The PKK, founded by the student leader Abdullah Öcalan in 1978, began a guerrilla war in 1984, claiming the Kurds' right to self-determination within (this was always stressed) the framework of a democratised and demilitarised Turkish state. By 'democratisation' Kurds mean the repeal of laws used to harass minorities or to deny them basic political rights The constitution, for example, established in 1982, requires a party to get 10 per cent of the vote nationally before it can win parliamentary representation – the highest such threshold in the world. Kurdish nationalists consistently receive a majority of the votes in parts of eastern Turkey but have no members of parliament. When, in 1994, centre-left Kurdish deputies formed a new party to get over the 10 per cent barrier, they were arrested on charges of aiding the PKK and sentenced to fifteen years in jail.

An estimated 200,000 Turkish troops have been permanently deployed in Kurdistan since the early 1990s, and in 1996 and 1998 fierce battles resulted in thousands of Kurdish casualties. By February 1999, when the fugitive Öcalan was captured in Kenya – possibly by the CIA – and handed over to Turkey, more than 30,000 Kurds had been killed and some 3,000 villages burned or destroyed, which resulted in a new exodus to Diyarbakir; the city now has a population of more than a million. At the end of 1999, after heavy American lobbying, the EU extended candidate status to Turkey, with further negotiations conditional on some amelioration, at least, of the Kurdish situation.

The pace of reforms accelerated after the election of Recep Tayyip Erdoğan's government in November 2002. In 2004, the Kurdish deputies who had been arrested ten years earlier were finally released, and a Kurdish-language programme was broadcast for the first time on state television. In line with EU cultural heritage provisions, restoration work began on the old palace in Diyarbakir – even while Kurdish prisoners were still being tortured in its cellars.

My host, Melike Coskun, the director of the Anadolu Cultural Centre, suggested a tour of the walls and the turbot-shaped old town. We picked up Seymus Diken, cultural adviser to the recently elected young pro-PKK mayor. He took us to a mosque that was once a cathedral and before that a pagan temple where sun-worshippers sacrificed virgins on large stone slabs in the courtyard. It was a Friday during Ramadan and the mosque was filling up. The majority belonging to the dominant Sunni Hanafi school occupied the main room while the Shafii prayed in a smaller one.

We then visited three empty Christian churches. The first was Chaldean, built in 300 AD, its brick dome exquisitely held in place by intertwined wooden arches. The second, which was Assyrian, was square, and even older, with Aramaic carvings on the wood and stones. The caretaker lives in rooms attached to the church and grows vegetables in what was once the garden of the bishop's palace. Hens roam about, occasionally laying eggs beneath the altar. The Armenian church was more recent – sixteenth century – but without a roof. It was a more familiar shape, like a Roman Catholic church, and the priest confirmed that the Armenians who had once worshipped here were Catholics. Seymus began to whisper something to him. I became curious. 'It's nothing,' Seymus said. 'Since my triple bypass the only drink I'm allowed is red wine and there's a tiny vineyard attached to a monastery in the countryside. I pick up a few bottles from this church. It's good wine.' This was strangely reassuring.

We walked over to the old city walls, first built with black stone more than 2,000 years ago, with layers added by each new conqueror. The crenelated parapets and arched galleries are crumbling; many stones have been looted to repair local houses. From an outpost on the wall, the Tigris is visible as it makes its way south. Seymus told me that he had been imprisoned in the palace cells by the Turkish authorities. 'The next time you come,' he promised, 'this building will be totally restored and we will sip our drinks and watch the Tigris flow.' In a large enclosed space below the wall there was an exhibition of photographs of Diyarbakir in 1911. The images, of a virtually intact medieval city, seemed to show little interest in the people who lived there but concentrated on the buildings. The photographer was Gertrude Bell, who later boasted that she had created modern Iraq on behalf of the British Empire by 'drawing lines in the sand'. These lines, of course, also divided the territory of the Kurdish tribes, which claim an unbroken history in this area, stretching back well before the Christian era.

The first written records come after the Arab Muslim conquest. In the tenth century, the Arab historian Masudi listed the Kurdish mountain tribes in his nine-volume history, *Meadows of Gold*. Like most of the inhabitants of the region they converted to Islam in the seventh and eighth centuries, and were recruited to the Muslim armies. They were rebellious, however, and took part in uprisings such as that of the Kharijites in the ninth century. (The Kharijites denounced the hereditary tradition as alien to Islam and demanded an elected caliph. They were crushed.) The Kurds settled around Mosul and took part in the epic slave revolt of the Zanj in southern Mesopotamia in 875. This, too, was defeated. Subsequently Kurdish bands wandered the region as mercenaries. Saladin's family belonged to one such group, whose military skills soon propelled its leaders to power. During the sixteenth-century conflicts between the Ottoman Empire and the Safavids who ruled Iran, Kurdish tribes fought on both sides. Inter-tribal conflicts made Kurdish unity almost impossible.

When Gertrude Bell visited Diyarbakir in 1911, Muslims (mostly Kurds) constituted 40 per cent of the population.

Armenians, Chaldeans and Assyrians, groups that had settled in what is now eastern Turkey well over a thousand years before the Christian era, remained the dominant presence. Istanbul was becoming increasingly unhappy with the idea of such a mixed population, and even before the Young Turks seized power from the sultan in 1909, a defensive nationalist wave had led to clashes between Turks and Armenian groups and small-scale massacres in the east. The Armenians began to be seen as the agents of foreign countries whose aim was to dismember the Ottoman Empire.

It's true that various wealthy Armenian (and Greek) factions were only too happy to cosy up to the West during the dying days of the Ottoman Empire, but much of the Armenian population continued to live peacefully with their Muslim neighbours in eastern Anatolia. They spoke Turkish as well as their own language, just as the Kurds did. But Armenian nationalist revolutionaries were beginning to talk of an Armenian state and the communities increasingly divided along political lines. A Kurdish militia was set up by the sultan to cow the Armenians, and then Mehmed Talat, the minister for the interior (who would be assassinated by an Armenian nationalist), decided to get rid of them altogether. The Kurdish irregulars carried out the forced expulsions and massacres of 1915 in which up to a million Armenians died.

Melike told me that her grandmother was Armenian, and that Kurdish families had saved many lives and given refuge to Armenian women and children who had converted to Islam in order to survive. Two years ago, Fethiye Çetin, a lawyer and a historian, published a book about her grandmother, who in old age had confessed to Çetin that she wasn't a Muslim, but an Armenian Christian. The book was launched at the cultural centre Melike runs. 'The hall was packed with women who had never been near our centre before,' Melike said. 'After Fethiye had finished so many women wanted to speak and discuss their Armenian roots. It was amazing.' Çetin writes that her grandmother was a 'sword leftover' child, which is how people whose lives had been spared were described: 'I felt my blood freeze. I had heard of this expression before. It hurt to find it being used to describe people like my grandmother. My optimism, which was formed with memories of tea breads, turned to pessimism.'

The political logic of ultra-nationalism proved deadly for both victim and perpetrator. The aim of the Young Turks had been to expel the non-Muslim minorities with a view to laying the foundations of a new and solid unitary state. The exchange of populations with Greece was part of this plan. In 1922 Atatürk came to power and made the plan a reality under the slogan 'one state, one citizen and one language'. The language was Latinised, with many words of Arab and Persian origin cast aside very much like the unwanted citizens. Given that virtually the entire population was now Muslim, the secular foundations of the new state were extremely weak, with the military as the only enforcer of the new order. The first blowback came with the 1925 Kurdish uprising. Then, as now, religion could not dissolve other differences. The rebellion lasted several months, and when it was finally put down all hopes for Kurdish autonomy disappeared. The Kurds' culture and language were suppressed. Many migrated to Istanbul and Izmir and other towns, but the Kurdish question would never go away.

I had been invited to give a lecture in Diyarbakir on the Kurdish question and the war in Iraq. Four years ago, while the war was still being plotted in Washington, Noam Chomsky and I were invited to address a public sector trade-union congress in Istanbul. Many of those present were of Kurdish origin. I said then that there would be a war and that the Iraqi Kurds would wholeheartedly collaborate with the US, as they had been doing since the Gulf War, and expressed the hope that Turkish Kurds would resist the temptation to do the same. Afterwards I was confronted by some angry Kurds. How dare I mention them in the same breath as their Iraqi cousins? Was I not aware that the PKK had referred to the tribal chiefs in Iraqi Kurdistan as 'primitive nationalists'? In fact, one of them shouted, Barzani and Talabani (currently the president of Iraq) were little better than 'mercenaries and prostitutes'. They had sold themselves successively to the Shah of Iran, Israel, Saddam Hussein, Khomeini and now the Americans. How could I even compare them to the PKK? In 2002 I was only too happy to apologise. I now wish I hadn't.

The PKK didn't share the anti-war sentiment that had engulfed the country in 2003 and pushed the newly elected parliament into forbidding the US from entering Iraq from Turkey. But while Kurdish support for the war was sheepish and shamefaced in Istanbul, no such inhibitions were on display in Diyarbakir. Virtually every question after my talk took Kurdish nationalism as its starting point. That was the only way they could see the war. Developments in northern Iraq, or southern Kurdistan, as they call it in Diyarbakir, have created a half-hope, half-belief, that the Americans might undo what Gertrude Bell and the British did and give the Kurds their own state. I pointed out that America's principal ally in Turkey was the army, not the PKK. 'What some of my people don't understand is that you can be an independent state and still not free, especially now,' one veteran muttered in agreement. But most of the people there were happy with the idea of Iraqi Kurdistan becoming an American–Israeli protectorate. 'Give me a reason, other than imperial conspiracy, why Kurds should defend the borders which have been their prisons,' someone said. The reason seemed clear to me: whatever happened they had to go on living there. If they started killing their neighbours, the neighbours would want revenge. By collaborating with the US, the Iraqi Kurdish leaders in the north are putting the lives of fellow Kurds in Baghdad at risk. It's the same in Turkey. There are nearly two million Kurds in Istanbul, including many rich businessmen integrated in the economy. They can't be ignored. A conspiratorial Kurd came and whispered a message from the imprisoned PKK leader in my ear: 'Commander Öcalan is advising all members to read your book *Clash of Fundamentalisms*. He likes it very much.'

As I was flying back to Istanbul the PKK announced a unilateral ceasefire. Turkey's moderate Islamist government must be secretly relieved. The PKK decision offers the possibility of genuine reforms and autonomy, but this will happen only if the Turkish Army agrees to retire to its barracks. Economic conditions in the Kurdish areas are now desperate: the flow of refugees has not stopped and increasing class polarisation is reflected in the growth of political Islam. A Kurdish Hezbollah was formed some years ago (with, so it's said, the help of Turkish military intelligence, which hoped it might weaken the PKK), and the conditions are ripe for its growth. Its first big outing in Diyarbakir was a 10,000-strong demonstration against the Danish cartoons. If things don't change, the movement is bound to grow.

Return to Cochabamba (2007)

In 2005 Bolivia witnessed another Bolivarian victory. Evo Morales, a popular trade union leader and the founder of the Movement for Socialism (MAS), had defeated the traditional elites. I had met him briefly in Caracas in 2003 and was impressed by his confidence. He was sure that unless there was a military coup, his side would win. In a country where almost 70 per cent of the population was indigenous, Evo M was the first ever to be elected president. The excitement in the country was palpable when I was at another conference – this time 'defending humanity', something I often do – in Cochabamba in Bolivia. I had last been there forty years ago as part of a four-man team (the others were Perry Anderson, Robin Blackburn and Ralph Schoenman) sent by Bertrand Russell to attend the trial of Régis Debray in Camiri, not far from where a besieged Che Guevara was fighting to escape the Bolivian Army.

Debray had been captured while attempting to leave the guerrilla encampment and head home. I had also been asked by the Cubans to photograph every Bolivian army officer in the region. This got me into trouble a few times. On one occasion a colonel, pistol drawn, walked up to me and asked for the film. I gave him a blank roll. 'If you take any more photographs of me,' he said, 'I'll shoot you.' I didn't. These photographs and others (including one of Robin Blackburn having a long shower) were dispatched to Havana, where they must still be held in some ageing archive. A detailed narrative can be found in *Street Fighting Years*.

Cochabamba was where the US Military Advisory Group, which was supervising the operation to capture and kill Guevara, established its HQ. And it was to Cochabamba that I fled from Camiri in 1967 after being briefly arrested, accused of being a Cuban guerrilla called Pombo, Che's bodyguard and one of those who escaped the encampment and returned safely to Cuba. I holed up there till I could get a flight to La Paz and a connection to Europe via Brazil. Hearing me reminisce with Richard Gott, who was also at the conference defending humanity, and who had been the *Guardian*'s chief Latin America correspondent in 1967, a young Telesur journalist from Madrid said: 'God. It's just like listening to Spanish Civil War veterans returning to Spain.'

Bolivia has a large Indian population: 62 per cent describe themselves as indigenous; 35 per cent live on less than a dollar a day. It has a turbulent history: wars, coups, revolutions, the odd guerrilla *foco* and numerous uprisings. There were 157 coups between 1825 and 1982, and seventy presidents, half of whom held office for less than a year. Neoliberal slumber lasted throughout the 1990s, before anti-government protests culminated in the 'water wars'. The government sold the water in Cochabamba to Bechtel, who told people it was illegal to collect rainwater. There were clashes with the army, a young demonstrator was killed and the protesters won. The municipality regained control of the water. Such unrest created the basis for the triumph of Morales and the Movement for Socialism in the elections of 2005. Not only was Morales on the left, he was an Aymara Indian, and his victory ended a century and a half of Creole rule. The rich were furious.

Within a few months, a campaign of destabilisation had begun, centred in the Creole stronghold of Santa Cruz. 'They predicted economic chaos,' Rafael Puente, a former government minister and Jesuit priest, told us. 'They said Bolivia would become another Zimbabwe. They accused Evo of starting a civil war. They exchanged doctored photographs on their cell phones depicting their elected president bleeding from a gunshot wound in the head with the words "Viva Santa Cruz" painted above him in blood.' The government went ahead and carried out its election promises, nationalising energy resources and taking direct control of operations. The increase in state revenues was to be used to help poor families keep their children at school. The aim was to reduce poverty by 10 per cent, a modest enough goal, but the Santa Cruz businessmen screamed 'Communism!' When economic conditions improved, the opposition moved on to Morales's relationship with Chávez. The walls of Santa Cruz were plastered with posters reading 'Evo, Chola de Chávez' (*chola* meaning 'Indian whore'). When one looks at the newspapers here it is hard to work out which man they hate more.

Richard Gott and I wandered around Cochabamba. The Paris Café on the Plaza de 14 Septembre was still there, looking much less dilapidated. The Roxy cinema where I watched Lee Marvin and Jane Fonda in *Cat Ballou* in 1967 has also survived, although it is now an evangelical church. Gott insisted that we visit La Cancha. This is the indigenous market opposite the old railway station, reminiscent of an Arab bazaar with its narrow lanes and commodities transported by wheelbarrow; among other things it has to offer is the most ravishing assortment of multicoloured potatoes anywhere in the world. Little has changed since 1967, though the quality seems to have declined a bit. I bought two cheap tin plates painted with flowers, which turned out to have been made in China.

Back at the hotel I was ambushed by a Spanish journalist from *El Mundo*: 'You've described Venezuela, Bolivia, Cuba and Ecuador as an axis of hope. What is your axis of evil in this continent?' I told her that I avoid the terms good and evil because they are religious concepts, but that my axis of despair consists at the moment of Brazil, Chile and Mexico. 'Could you please add the Dominican Republic?' asked Scheherazade Vicioso, a feminist poet. 'We're always being ignored.' I did so. Then I asked the reason for her name. Her father, a composer, adored *The Thousand and One Nights*. 'I got off lightly,' she added. 'My brother is called Rainer Maria Rilke.'

Murder in the Family (2008)

If cheating in bed was always settled by the bullet, many of us would be dead. Gerald Martin's new biography of Gabriel García Márquez reveals that *Chronicle of a Death Foretold* was based on the murder of the novelist's friend Cayetano Gentile in Sucre in 1951. He had seduced, deflowered and abandoned Margarita Chica Salas. On her wedding day Margarita's husband was told that she was no longer a virgin. The bride was sent back to her family home. Her brothers then found Gentile and chopped his body into pieces. Márquez blamed the socio-moral dictatorship of the Catholic Church.

But of course it is usually women who are killed for breaking codes of sexual conduct. There have been several recent cases in Britain. Banaz Mahmod, a twenty-year-old of Kurdish origin, was murdered in Surrey at the behest of her father because she'd left an arranged marriage and he didn't approve of her new boyfriend. Iraq has lately seen a spate of such murders. Last month acid was thrown at three women in Basra who were talking to a male friend. Yet Iraq once had the highest proportion of women integrated into every level of society of any Arab country.

And then there is Pakistan. In 2005 General Pervez Musharraf pushed through legislation making honour killing a capital offence, yet official statistics admit to 1,261 such killings in 2006 and half that number again the following year. The actual figures are probably much higher, since many deaths go unreported. 'Women are considered the property of the males in their family irrespective of their class, ethnic or religious group, and the owner of the property has the right to decide its fate,' Tahira Shahid Khan of Shirkat Gah, a group that campaigns for equal rights for women, reported in 1999. Domestic violence too, according to the Human Rights Commission of Pakistan, is 'considered normal … A sample survey showed 82 per cent of women in rural Punjab feared violence resulting from their husbands' displeasure over minor matters; in the most developed urban areas 52 per cent admitted being beaten by their husbands.'

Consider the following. A man dreams his wife has betrayed him. He wakes up and sees her lying next to him. In a fury he kills her. This really happened in Pakistan and the killer escaped punishment. If dreams are to be treated as justification for an honour killing, what woman is safe? Since the police and the judicial system regard murder in the family as a private affair, most cases don't get to court even if they're reported. Society, it's said, needs to protect its foundations. So mostly we rely on the information collected by the Human Rights Commission and on courageous lawyers like Hina Jilani and Asma Jehangir, two sisters both of whom have received numerous death threats.

In 1999, Hina Jilani was in her office with Samia Sarwar, a mother of two from Peshawar seeking a divorce from her husband, when Sarwar's mother burst into the room with two armed men in tow and had her daughter shot dead. In 1989 Samia Sarwar had married a first cousin. For six years he beat her and kicked her. But after he threw her downstairs when she was pregnant with their second child, she went back to her parents' house. The minute she told them she wanted a divorce they threatened to kill her. Yet they were educated and wealthy people.

One widely reported murder this year was that of Tasleem Solangi, the seventeen-year-old daughter of a livestock trader in the Khairpur District of Sindh. She wanted to go to university and become a doctor like her uncle, but instead agreed to marry a cousin in order to settle a protracted family dispute over property. Her mother, Zakara Bibi, tried to stop her, but Tasleem was determined. Her father-in-law, Zamir Solangi, came to collect her and swore on the Quran that no harm would befall her. A month after the marriage, Zakara had a message from her daughter: 'Please forgive me, mother. I was wrong and you were right. I fear they will kill me.' On 7 March, they did. She was eight months pregnant. The Koran-swearer accused her of infidelity and said the baby was not his son's. She went into labour, her child was born and instantly thrown to the dogs. She pleaded for mercy, but the dogs were set on her as well and the terrified girl was then shot dead. On this occasion at least there was an inquiry. Her husband was charged with Tasleem's murder and is currently awaiting trial.

Another case much discussed is that of five women in Baluchistan who were buried alive in Baba Kot village, about 250 miles east of Quetta, the Baluch capital. Three of the women were young and wanted to marry men they'd chosen for themselves; two older women were helping them. Three male relatives have been arrested. According to the local police chief, the brother of two of the girls has admitted that he shot three of the women and helped bury them, though they weren't even dead. The trial date is awaited.

Traditionalists have always considered love to be something that brings shame on families: patriarchs should be the ones to decide who is to be married to whom, often for reasons to do with property. *If you fall in love*, the eighteenth-century Urdu poet Mir Hassan explained (more than once), *you will be burned by its fire and perish*. That is what happened in the Punjabi city of Wah in late October. Nowadays Wah has half a million inhabitants and Pakistan's largest ordnance factories, but it was once an idyllic village almost floating on water.

Other ghosts lurk there now. A mile and a half from the old village, my youngest maternal uncle, Sardar Ghairat Hyat Khan, built himself a house and moved out of the decaying manor house we'd all shared. My Kashmiri great-grandmother, Ayesha, moved with him. In the last week of October, my uncle's granddaughter, Zainab, barely eighteen years old, was shot dead by her brothers, Inam and Hamza Ahmed. Zainab apparently had a lover and despite repeated warnings refused to stop seeing him. She was on the phone to him in her grandfather's house when her brothers pumped seven bullets into her body.

I don't know whether her mother, Ghairat's oldest daughter Roohi, whom I last saw when she was about ten, was part of the plot. Whether or not she was involved, I find it deeply shocking that my uncle allowed the young woman's body to be buried that same day without at least insisting that a First Information Report be lodged at the local police station, let alone demanding an autopsy. Zainab deserved at least that. I am told that Ghairat is old and frail, that he was angry and wanted to ring the police, but was talked out of it by his daughter and other members of his immediate family, who collectively recoiled at having to accept the consequences of what they had witnessed. Perhaps his faith in a just and merciful Allah was not as strong as he used to claim. Whatever the reason, it's unacceptable. The body should be exhumed, the murderers arrested and put on trial, as the law requires. None of that happened.

The Nobel War Prize (2010)

Last year's recipient of the Nobel Peace Prize escalated the war in Afghanistan a few weeks after receiving the prize. The award surprised even Obama. This year the Chinese government were foolish enough to make a martyr of the president of Chinese PEN and neocon, Liu Xiaobo. He should never have been arrested, but the Norwegian politicians who comprise the committee, led by Thorbjørn Jagland, a former Labour prime minister, wanted to teach China a lesson. And so they ignored their hero's views. Or perhaps they didn't, given that their own views are not dissimilar. The committee thought about giving Bush and Blair a joint peace prize for invading Iraq but a public outcry forced a retreat.

For the record, Liu Xiaobo has stated publicly that in his view:

(a) China's tragedy is that it wasn't colonised for at least 300 years by a Western power or Japan. This would apparently have civilised it for ever.

(b) The Korean and Vietnam wars fought by the US were wars against totalitarianism and enhanced Washington's 'moral credibility'.

(c) Bush was right to go to war in Iraq and Senator Kerry's criticisms were 'slander-mongering'.

(d) Afghanistan? No surprises here: Full support for NATO's war.

He has a right to these opinions, but should they get a peace prize? The Norwegian jurist Fredrik Heffermehl argues that the committee is in breach of the will and testament left behind by the inventor of dynamite whose bequest funds the prizes: 'The Nobel committee has not received prize money for free use, but was entrusted with money to give to the pivotal element in creating peace, breaking the vicious circle of arms races and military power games. From this point of view the 2010 Nobel is again an illegitimate prize awarded by an illegitimate committee.'

Against the Extreme Centre (2011)

After the hopeful Wisconsin flutter in April, when thousands of public employees came out on strike and occupied the state building, I wondered whether this might be the harbinger of an Egyptian summer in New York. Spring has absconded from the heart of political America for far too long. The frozen winters of the Reagan and Bush years didn't melt with Clinton or Obama – hollow men who rule over a hollow system where money overpowers all and the much-maligned state is used mainly to preserve the financial status quo and fund the wars of the twenty-first century. Discussion, serious debate and openness have virtually disappeared from mainstream political life in the United States and from its more extreme versions in Europe, with Britain as the cock on the dung heap. The extreme right is small. The extreme left barely exists. It is the extreme centre that dominates political and financial life.

The Occupy Wall Street protesters are consciously or subconsciously demonstrating against a system of despotic finance capital, a greed-infected vampire that must suck the blood of the non-rich in order to survive. The protesters are showing their contempt for bankers, for financial speculators and for their media hirelings who continue to insist that there is no alternative. Since the Wall Street system dominates Europe, local versions of that model exist here too. The young people being pepper-sprayed by the NYPD may not have worked out what they want, but they sure to hell know what they're against and that's an important start.

Over the last two years I've been in the US dozens of times. During the Occupy movement, I attempted at Yale, Berkeley, Chicago and other places to force the audience to engage in some programmatic reflections. Three pithy demands on a free health service, education and minority rights would be enough. The next wave of struggles could take these up and add to them. In Berkeley I was heckled by a member in the audience: 'Are you a commie? Where are you from? You know you can't say these things in our country.' He was booed away, including by the anarcho-libertarians. In Wisconsin at a large university gathering a Hitchens fan stood up and asked: 'Why did Verso publish a book by Osama bin Laden?' I explained that knowledge of the enemy is vital to improve one's own understanding and that the scholarly apparatus and introduction by Professor Bruce Lawrence were useful for everyone. I added: 'There is another reason. Unlike Hitchens, our Arab author is not able to pester us for royalties and he's been selling well.' Much merriment.

Later I was told that Hitchens had delivered a talk at the same location a month earlier, and when asked 'Should we support the bombing of Iran' had replied: 'Yes. Destroy everything in that country.' Half the audience had applauded enthusiastically.

Brazil (2011)

Very comfortable flight to Sao Paulo. Slept for eight hours undisturbed. As we approach the city, a large Brazilian moon frames the window. The airport has become familiar. Enough time to get a shave plus neck and head massage before getting a local two-and-a-half-hour flight to Recife for the Literature Festival. Never been to Pernambuco before. Recife on the northern jutting-out tip of Brazil on the Atlantic. Alas, the sea is out of bounds for swimming because of a shark infestation. Several surfers have died this year alone. Spend a lot of time chatting to Derek Walcott. I find him soft and unassuming. His Nobel is not mentioned except by Sigrid who enjoys the fame of the prize a bit too much. At one point Derek takes me aside:

'Any idea why the *LRB* is so hostile to me?'

'No, I can't believe that. Why should it be?'

'I was told they were backing a woman called Ruth Badelle ...'

'Padel.'

'Whatever. And two of her sponsors went around slandering me and attempted to "me-too" me as well. The names mentioned were O'Hagan and Toibean.'

'Derek, surely you are referring to the Oxford Poetry Professorship.'

'Yes, of course. Badelle went round feeding rumours to the tabloids and disgraced herself in the process. She won but had to resign within a week when her stupid intrigues were revealed.'

'I remember that business now, but I know for a fact that it was some individuals who sabotaged your bid, with Padel in the lead. Not the *LRB*. Or its editor.'

'Good to know. Pathetic and petty, that Badelle. Terrible poet, too. Mediocre and mean-spirited.'

'The Nobel Committee vindicated you.'

He smiled. I changed the subject to Brazilian culture and politics. We decamp to Francesco's in Olinda. Family restaurant, Italian. Excellent fish, vegetable starters. Given that many Italian fascist families fled to South America after Mussolini was hanged from a lamppost, I wanted to make sure Francesco's wasn't run by one of them. Francesco replied to my provocation by giving us a rendering of 'Bella Ciao'. Derek W. and Sigrid insisted on coming to my event. I spoke of PT (Partido dos Trabalhadores, the Workers' Party) weaknesses on health, land reform and education, criticised the uniformity of 'global' (US) culture and the decline of European and South American cinema. After the talk as I'm signing books, a striking Brazilian woman joins the queue. Her arrival trebles its size, and the paparazzi are clicking away, etc. I have no idea who she is and smile and sign her copy at which point she links arms with me and poses for pics. Her English is very warming: 'I need to speak. Quick drink afterwards?' It turns out she's Maria Paula Gonçalves da Silva, the top soap-opera actress, has recently divorced a very well-known PT politician and strongly approved of my critical remarks. Also hated mimicry in the cultural realm. Sharp, political and critical. I suggested she should write a TV series on corporate exploitation of body surgery. Given that her ex-husband's first wife (also a senior PT politician) had been outed by radical students (they found and published her huge beauty surgery bill), she should investigate the whys and wherefores of this practice. A crime-comedy?

She suggests dinner in Rio to further discuss this project. I apologise but explain that I've got a conference in Porto Allegre, after which I'm already booked into the Chávez suite at the Venezuelan Embassy in Brasilia, where my thirty-something friend, Maximilien Arvelaiz, is ambassador, and I must see Brasilia, if only once. We agree to keep in touch. And we do. She emails to say she's working on the script we discussed in Recife. Nothing more is heard.

A terrible eight-hour TAM flight from Recife to Porto Allegre. Its only 8 p.m. but the city appears dead. I manage to find the Italian where some of us used to eat during World Social Forum gatherings. I've been invited by PSOL, a leftist split from the PT that has together with PT leftists a strong presence in the local government. At the Book Fair I am 'honoured for all your books'. The next day I meet the PSOL leaders, starting with Luciana Genro, whose father Tarso is currently the PT governor of the province: Rio Grande de Sul. Luciana was a young PT MP but split soon after Lula came to power, as did some of the leading left PT intellectuals. She's sharp, very critical of the PT government. She collects me in a car driven by her security guard, a Bond 'girl', both pretty, but armed and tough and very political. At lunch we are joined by another PSOL activist, Fernanda: early twenties, tough-minded and quite bitter that the Mandelista leaders have 'betrayed' PSOL by insisting on remaining in the PT. Lucinda's twenty-three-year-old son joins us ('I had him when I was seventeen'). He is torn between his grandfather and his parents but is veering towards the latter. He asks my opinion. I point out that it's a purely tactical choice. No big issue of principle is involved. Now I understand why Luciana Villas-Boas, my editor at *Record*, was so keen to translate and publish Redencao (Redemption). Without warning they all turn on me and ask why NLR still takes PT intellectual Emir Sader seriously. They're scathing: 'Bad writer, bad thinker', 'permanently enveloped by the stench of opportunism', 'licks the arse of power', 'tried very hard to get a government job but snubbed by Dilma'. Poor Emir. I've known him a long time. Could this be true? Others informed me, in more temperate language, that Emir 'had played his cards badly'. Evening talk in the chamber of the local parliament. Several hundred people. Saw Raul Pont in the balcony. We exchanged waves but he disappeared very rapidly after the event. A real pity. Evidently he had been expelled by the Fourth International. Why? 'For opportunism.' Difficult not to laugh.

Flew to São Paulo the next day for a session with João Pedro Stedile, the charismatic leader of the MST (landless peasants movement) at their headquarters. Max joined us as well. João Pedro had few illusions. The agribusinesses backed by the PT government are winning the battle against poor peasants. The Left is very isolated. Economic upturn has strengthened the PT electorally. Corruption, scandals, exposures of other wrongdoings seem to have no effect. PSOL well meaning, but a premature birth.

Later that afternoon, Max and I flew to Brasilia. I for a few days' rest and to see the architecture, and Max to carry on with his diplomatic duties. The city itself is a bit spooky. Very few people on the streets. Workers and others live far away from the centre. The shape of the new capital completed in 1960 was determined by Oscar Niemeyer. He has no equivalent anywhere else in the world. While he built Brasilia, his works are dotted all over Brazil. His Marxism did him few favours with the economic–military elites, but they could neither ignore nor harm him. His work typified the modernism that was overtaking classicism in key Brazilian cities. I spent the best part of a day admiring his architecture in Brasilia. The cathedral, parliament, National Art Gallery are undoubted masterpieces, but why here?

Niemeyer was still alive, but a meeting was now impossible. He was one hundred and four years old.

Max had encountered him last year and recounted a meeting. After discussing Chávez and Lula, it was time to get down to the nitty-gritty:

Oscar Niemeyer: Do you know what the secret of long life is?
Maximilien: I was hoping to learn from you.
O. N.: Red wine every day. Watching a beautiful woman you can admire from a distance. Faith in Marxism. (Then, looking closely at Max.) How old are you?
M: Thirty-six.
O.N.: Then what the hell are you doing here wasting your afternoon talking to an old man? You should be in an apartment or hotel fucking someone. Get out of here.

Brazil (2011)

During a farewell dinner for me, an urgent call. Max whispers: 'Some good news. The Commandante's (Chávez's) cancer seems to be under control.' Back to São Paulo the next day to catch a flight to London. Hope the Chávez news is true.

Blitz Spirit: Alex Cockburn (2011)

The general impression of the Blitz, fostered by war movies and many books, is of a period when intense national solidarity reigned supreme and class was transcended as everybody sang defiant songs and went about their work. Not so. Alexander Cockburn in *Counterpunch* draws attention to a piece in *The First Post* by Gavin Mortimer (author of *The Blitz**), on looting during 'our finest hour':

> It didn't take long for a hardcore of opportunists to realise there were rich pickings available in the immediate aftermath of a raid – and the looting wasn't limited to civilians. In October 1940 Winston Churchill ordered the arrest and conviction of six London firemen caught looting from a burned-out shop to be hushed up: 'In April 1941 Lambeth juvenile court dealt with 42 children in one day, from teenage girls caught stripping clothes from dead bodies to a seven-year-old boy who had stolen five shillings from the gas meter of a damaged house. In total, juvenile crime accounted for 48 per cent of all arrests in the nine months between September 1940 and May 1941 and there were 4,584 cases of looting.'
>
> Perhaps the most shameful episode of the whole Blitz occurred on the evening of March 8 1941 when the Café de Paris in Piccadilly was hit by a German bomb: 'Some of the looters in the Café de

---

* A very good book which, alas, I forgot to include in my own book on Churchill, which I deeply regret.

Paris cut off the people's fingers to get the rings,' recalled Ballard Berkeley, a policeman during the Blitz who later found fame as the 'Major' in Fawlty Towers. Even the wounded in the Café de Paris were robbed of their jewellery amid the confusion and carnage.

This piece was written a year before Alex was felled by cancer. Still missed by some of us. He often talked about his father, Claud, who I knew before I met Alexander, Andrew and Patrick Cockburn. 'Not a day goes by that I don't think of him.' We discussed a Fathers and Sons trilogy with essays by him, Perry and myself, but it never got off the ground, though Perry's piece on his father – a gem – in the *LRB* revealed what was possible. He had never written like that before, nor has he since. Of course, Claud and my father were staunch communists, whereas Perry's father was a tough-minded realist civil servant based in China, with intellectual gifts that left a genetic trail. I remember when Perry returned from a trip to China with his father's correspondence files, he showed me a document that had predicted an event that did happen, a Chinese People's Liberation Army capture of a town. His boss had scribbled on it: 'Another brilliant Anderson prediction.' Anderson *père* had little doubt that the Chinese Communists would ultimately win.

Pissing on Insurgents
(2012)

It's now official. Urinating on dead insurgents, the US Marine Corps informs the world, is 'not consistent with its core values'. I think we need a list of non-core values as soon as possible. Pissing on the dead is considered loathsome in most cultures, but clearly can be a morale-booster for demoralised troops in an occupied country where the war is going badly for Western civilisation. What better way to assert civilisational values against the barbarians and win local hearts and minds? And why stop here? The next stage surely is to excrete on them and use their beards as toilet paper. That would enhance the value of the videos and might even win the innovators the Santorum Prize for Moral Superiority.

Urinating on the dead is bad enough, but what of those who do it on the living? One of the earlier complaints in this regard came from Gitmo prisoners who alleged that their guards pissed on them from above and that some of the drops fell not just on them, but on the Korans they were reading. At the time nobody thought fit to say that such acts 'were not consistent with core values'. Limited progress has been made. Why the employees of imperial powers feel obliged to act in such a way requires psychiatric investigation. During the British occupation of India it was common practice for British police officers to order their men (who included Muslims, Sikhs and 'low-caste' Hindus) to unbutton themselves and let fly at non-violent Gandhian protesters occupying railway tracks to enforce a strike and non-cooperation call by the Congress Party. Nobody talked about core values at that time. Most Indians knew what they were.

Lincoln in His Lover's Nightgown (2012)

Steven Spielberg's *Lincoln* is consciously restrictive, concentrating as it does on how the vote was manipulated and the 13th Amendment passed, but Mrs Lincoln is not exactly missing from the movie. So why didn't the scriptwriter Tony Kushner, a staunch gay rights activist who 'personally believe[s] that there is some reason to speculate that Lincoln might have been bisexual or gay', include any of that speculation in the film? There is a great deal of circumstantial evidence to suggest that Lincoln slept with a number of men. In an interview with *Gold Derby*, Kushner said:

> I wanted to write about a very specific moment and I chose this moment and I don't feel that there's any evidence at this particular moment that Lincoln was having sex with anybody … He seems to have not slept and taken no time off and during this period I think he was beginning to feel ground to a pulp by the war and by the pressures of his job. I find it difficult to believe that Lincoln was banging anybody.

Not very convincing. Especially when you consider that one of the men who shared Lincoln's bed was his military aide and bodyguard, Captain David Derickson (in 1862–63, before the film begins). Kushner may find it difficult to believe that at the height of a political crisis 'banging' is possible. But history and present times contradict such a narrow view.

The teenage Abe was much more relaxed than his current

sycophants. He wrote a pre-homage to gay marriage (quoted in William Herndon's 1889 *Life*), which at the moment appears to be the only issue that divides centre-left from centre-right in Euro-American political life:

> I will tell you a joke about Joel and Mary,
> It is neither a joke nor a story.
> For Reuben and Charles have married two girls,
> But Billy has married a boy.

A few years ago, not long after reading C. A. Tripp's pioneering *The Intimate World of Abraham Lincoln*, I had lunch with Gore Vidal in LA, and taped our conversation for later use. The following exchange is revealing:

T.A. Given the recent book and materials on Lincoln's homosexuality how do you feel having portrayed him as a raving heterosexual in your novel?

G.V. You're a bastard. What a bastard question. It hurts. It hurts. How could I have missed that?

T.A. You didn't look?

G.V. I had no idea, but since Tripp's book I've gone back and devoured everything on the subject. There is no doubt in my mind. Once he was in bed with the Captain and the latter's son walked in. On another occasion they were disturbed and Lincoln opened the door wearing his lover's nightgown. Oh what a fool I was …

Kushner missed an opportunity to give the issue an airing and in so doing caved in to what the marketing people think is a homophobic audience. Daniel Day-Lewis would surely have risen to the occasion under Derek Jarman's direction.

'Indian Army Rape Us' (2013)

The rape in Delhi has shocked India. Has it really? Or was it the sight of thousands of young students, male and female, demonstrating on the streets and being assaulted by the police for daring to protest that made some Indian citizens think seriously about the problem? As for the Congress government that has, like most of the opposition parties, tolerated this for decades, it was the bad publicity abroad that finally did the trick, but only as far as this case is concerned.

Rape takes place in police stations, in military barracks, in the streets and occasionally in some provincial parliaments. The feminist communist parliamentarian Brinda Karat, who has long campaigned on the issue, pointed to the assault of a member of the Trinamool assembly by a male oppositionist on 11 December last year. 'Women were not safe even inside the assembly,' she said.

Legal activists in Kashmir and Manipur, both areas occupied by the Indian Army, have produced report after report highlighting cases of women raped by soldiers. Response from the top brass: nil. In a country where the culture of rape is so embedded, only a determined effort on every level can change things. This will not happen if this case and others are forgotten. Indian courts, following government orders, have now ruled that soldiers cannot be charged with rape.

In 2004, a group of middle-aged mothers were so enraged by the military raping their daughters and sisters that they

The most amazing anti-rape demo ever. Indian women from age eight to eighty demonstrate naked outside the Indian Army HQ in Manipur.

organised a protest unique in the annals of the women's movement. They, from the ages of eight to eighty, gathered outside the Indian Army barracks, stripped, and held up a banner that read 'Indian Army Rape Us'. That image, too, shocked India, but nothing changed. Only a few weeks later another rape scandal erupted in Manipur. If the Indian state is incapable of defending its women, perhaps the world's largest democracy should seriously consider a change of name. Rapeistan comes to mind.

Ships in the Night (2013)

I'm rung from Enniskillen (Beckett's birth town) by classical musician Sean Doran, who is organising the Beckett Festival this year. He asks whether I might agree to give a lecture on the playwright. I'm a bit flummoxed by the request. I'm certainly a fan but by no means an authority on the writer. Also, I wondered whether I could say anything that had not been said before. As Sean and I were speaking an idea occurred.

'Would it be possible to find two male actors?'

'Not a problem.'

'I could have a go and see if I could conjure a conversation between Beckett and Brecht that we could stage.'

I did think about it quite seriously. Had the two ever met? Did they know each other's work? I searched all of Beckett and books on him. I went through every index. Not a single reference. It was obvious that the Irish writer had ignored the German poet's output. That annoyed me. Brecht was six years older but their generation was confronting the same horrors and hopes of the same world, writing plays and poetry and stories. The idea grew. The cart and the skeletal tree were amongst the best-known stage props of the twentieth century. Mother Courage pushing a cart over-filled with refugees. The skeletal tree designed to hang resistance fighters is vacated while Vladimir and Estragon are waiting for Godot. To hang him? No. That would be more Brecht than Beckett. Goethe's dictum that 'If the poet you'd understand/ You must go into the poet's land.' A café. A table for two. Brecht is waiting. Another table in the same space. Beckett is waiting. Neither has seen the other. Two monologues with silences? Then

I found Brecht's brief notes on how the East Berliner Ensemble could stage *Waiting for Godot*. Very simple: 'While the two men are talking, screen at back is playing silent archive of the Algerian and Vietnamese fighters, resisting the French ...' A great idea.

Brecht: You were ten during the Easter uprising. Your father took you and your brother to a hill from where you could see the fires burning in the city centre. Did you ever forget that image?

(*Long pause. Beckett doesn't reply. Just smokes.*)

Three years later Rosa Luxemburg was murdered by the Freikorps predecessors of the SS in Berlin, her dead body thrown in the canal. I didn't see it, but I remembered that event. It reappears in my poems and plays. I know you don't want to hear one of these poems so you can walk out while I recite.

(*Beckett remains seated. Doesn't look at Brecht's face while he reads:*)

> As she drowned, she swam downwards and was borne,
> From the smaller streams to the large rivers,
> In wonder the opal of the heavens shone,
> As if wishing to placate the body that was hers.
> Catching hold of her were the seaweed, the algae,
> Slowly she became heavy as downward she went,
> Cool fish swam around her legs, freely,
> Animals and plants weight to her body lent.
> Dark light smoke in the evenings the heavens grew,
> But early in the morning the stars dangled, there was light,
> So that for her, there remained too,
> Morning and evening, day and night,
> Her cold body rotted in the water there,
> Slowly step by step, god too forgot,
> First her face, then her hands, and finally her hair
> She became carrion of which the rivers have a lot.

Ships in the Night (2013)

(*Silence. Brecht walks away. When he is off stage, Beckett looks in his direction and smiles.*)

I had an idea for the ending as well. In *Endgame* Hamm speaks: 'I love the old questions. (*With fervour*) Ah, the old questions, the old answers, there's nothing like them!' Brecht replies: 'Don't start from the good old things, but the bad new ones.'

In the end I abandoned the two-hander. Just gave a talk on 'Ships in the Night'.

A Tear Gas Canister, Made in Brazil, Used in Turkey (2013)

How it changes. When I was in Istanbul in April the mood was sombre. Even the most ebullient of friends were downcast. The latent hostility to the regime was always present, but the AKP's hegemony, I was told many times, went deep. Erdoğan was a reptile, cynical but clever, and not averse to quoting the odd verse from Nâzım Hikmet, the much-loved communist poet imprisoned by Atatürk. The poet had escaped in a boat and been rescued by a Soviet tanker. 'Can you prove you're Hikmet,' the captain asked him. He laughed and pointed to a poster in the captain's cabin which had his photograph on it. He died in Moscow in 1963. His remains are still in exile.

Talk now was of food (the exquisite wafer-thin pizzas from the Syrian border) or the delights of children produced in middle age. Complaints were varied. An old cinema on İstiklal was about to be dynamited. It would be replaced by yet more characterless shops that have already disfigured this historic street with its arcades and belle époque apartments (where, once upon a time, many wealthy Armenian merchant families lived). There had been a few mild demonstrations against the execution of the movie house, but symbolic in character. The newspapers were talking of the regime's latest PR triumph: sixty 'wise men' who would be consulted from time to time. There were photographs of their first assembly in the Dolmabahçe Palace, a suitably kitsch setting for a kitsch gathering. An old acquaintance, Murat Belge, was among their number.

Encouraged by the indifference, Erdoğan proceeded with other plans: a shopping mall in Gezi Park, a new bridge over the Bosphorus and a new grand mosque to steal the landscape from Sinân's delicate creations. The citizens of Istanbul were never asked for their views. It was this lack of any consultation that angered them and triggered the occupation of the tiny green space in the heart of the city. As we all now know, the spirit of conciliation is not the Turkish prime minister's strong point. Nor is generosity of heart or mind. He loathes secular intellectuals, refers to the founders of the republic as drunkards or alcoholics (as if those were their defining characteristics rather than out-witting Lord Curzon and the British Empire to create a republic) and talks constantly of the danger from left-wing 'terrorists'. When angry, which is often, Erdoğan takes on the character of a village bully, sometimes embarrassing his colleagues.

Socially conservative, politically unscrupulous, economically beholden to the building industry, and militarily/politically NATO's favourite Islamists, the party in power ignored the voices on the street. They were meant to be the model for other Muslim countries. Erdoğan's arrogance in using violence – baton charges, water cannon and tear gas, against mainly young people – has wrecked the model. Hence the note of exasperation from the White House, and the familiar request that 'both sides should show restraint'.

The police assault on unarmed and peaceful occupiers back-fired badly. Within forty-eight hours every city, bar four, had experienced solidarity demonstrations and occupations of public places. The tiny protest had grown into a national uprising against the sultan of the building trades, large and small. When I arrived in Ankara on the evening of 15 June, the tell-tale signs were visible. Water tanks and Scorpions (police command cars) were stationed on the main streets, ready to go into action.

It's the first time I've experienced protests that begin at night. People come home from work, change, eat, discard their ties and get ready. Water bottles and handkerchief, soaked to protect against tear gas. At 10 or 11 p.m. they come out, usually in small groups, crossing streets like shadows till they reach Kuğulu Park and smile as thousands are already there, chanting slogans, singing songs, taunting Erdoğan. The police attack. Barricades hurriedly go up using advertising boards, the odd car and anything to hand. Water cannons are used to try to disperse them. They fail. Then the tear gas (imported from Brazil). It keeps coming. The demonstrators disperse, assemble again, and so it goes on till 3 a.m. or later. Action will be resumed the following night.

While this is happening on the streets, in apartment windows the mothers and grandmothers of the demonstrators bang pots and pans in solidarity – and as a warning to Erdoğan, for this is a very old Turkish style of protest pioneered by Janissary corps to warn the Ottoman sultan that enough was enough. In Istanbul, when Erdoğan asked parents to take their kids home, thousands of mothers joined the occupation, bringing pots, spoons and pans with them.

Erdoğan denounced the protestors as *çapulcu*: 'looters'. As in Paris in May 1968, the young Turks chanted: 'We are all çapulcu.' When I visited Kuğulu Park there was a slogan on the wall: 'Welcome to the çapulcu fest.' Passionate arguments were taking place, free libraries in every corner, free food brought by parents, and hope written on young faces. Steve Bell's cartoon of Erdoğan as a water tank dousing the people is on all their phones. I asked a young woman about the word. She laughed: 'Yes. Our response was immediate. The semiotics of this uprising are certainly very interesting. But more importantly, what next? Our demobilisation would be a big tragedy.' A young man interrupted: 'We can't hold on to the squares for ever. We need something more.'

How the new opposition regroups is difficult to say, but if a new democratically structured political movement is formed (like, for instance, Syriza in Greece) it could give a permanent voice to the people from below. A monthly public assembly in Istanbul, Ankara, Izmir, Bodrum, Antakya and other cities to discuss the situation at home and abroad and report on the building of a new movement would create something permanent and make the clearing and re-clearing of the squares a bit meaningless. This is my hope. Some agreed, but a young student piped up: 'I'm a neoliberal capitalist and I'm here.' Others laughed. I asked him why he was there.

'Because of the police violence.'

'But the police violence is being used to defend neoliberal values.'

'No. Neoliberalism promotes liberal values.'

'Where?'

'In the United States.'

I said what had to be said.

A woman doctor told me she had to leave for a doctor's assembly. The government is demanding that doctors hand over the names of the thousands of wounded demonstrators they have been treating. The assembly is unanimous. No.

Turkey has suddenly changed. The new generation is on the parapets. To demonstrate that he still has mass support, Erdoğan has had to bus his supporters in from all over the country. Few were impressed. The battle lines for the next elections have been laid. The builder's friend can't be the prime minister again. He was hoping to amend the constitution and make it presidential or, failing that, to become president à la Putin. It will be more difficult now. He should read Aziz Nesin's popular short story, 'The New Prime Minister', in which the sultan, tiring of a politician who is getting all his ideas from a mule, appoints the animal in his stead.

Gaza: A Disgrace to the World (2014)

The United Nations secretary-general, Ban Ki-moon, denounced the bombing of the UN school in Gaza as 'outrageous' and 'unjustifiable'. His officials have described the massacres as 'a disgrace to the world'. Who stands disgraced? The UN General Assembly has regularly voted in favour of an independent Palestine. It is the Security Council that has vetoed the very thought, and the Security Council, as everyone knows, is dominated by the United States; on this issue, Russia and China have remained on message.

What of the broader 'international community', in other words the United States, the EU and NATO? They have backed Israel. As for the ideologues of the human rights industry, Samantha Power, the queen of 'humanitarian interventions', is the US rep on the Security Council and staunchly pro-Israel. Both the House and the Senate have unanimously written Israel a blank cheque; the French Socialist government banned demonstrations against the Gaza horrors in Paris on the grounds that they would encourage antisemitism (not well received by the French Jewish organisations who co-sponsored the march); the British Foreign Office is compliant as usual; the Germans are too busy imposing sanctions against Russia, while turning a blind eye to Gaza and refusing to accept that the Palestinians are the indirect victims of the Judeocide unleashed by the Third Reich and for which successive democratic governments in Germany have been paying ever since. The US satellite states in Eastern Europe have followed suit. Scandinavia, too, with this exception: Carl Bildt, the Swedish foreign minister and veteran NATO hack, supports US policies, but the Swedish king and queen donned Palestinian scarves and joined a public demonstration against Israeli atrocities.

In the Arab world there is great anger from below, but the Wahhabi monarch in Riyadh, the Israeli-protected king in Jordan and General Sisi in Egypt have effectively backed Israel's assault on Gaza. They loathe Hamas and make no secret of the fact that they would rejoice if the Israelis exterminated the organisation. And what about those who vote for it? Dissolve the people and elect another? In Turkey, Erdoğan makes a lot of noise, mostly ineffective and over-the-top, but refuses to break diplomatic relations with Israel. Turkey is after all a long-standing member of NATO, and if Iraqi Kurdistan becomes 'independent' as a US-Israeli protectorate, Erdoğan will need their help to prevent a spillover in eastern Turkey.

While Asia is effectively silent – China thinks trade, India is close to Israel, Japan is still not allowed its own foreign policy – in South Africa there is growing support led by Desmond Tutu and others for the Boycott, Divestment and Sanctions (BDS) campaign. The apartheid analogies are not taken lightly and the ANC in the South African parliament voted unanimously to expel the Israeli ambassador, a demand ignored by President Zuma.

The strongest political reaction has come from a continent where Muslim populations are either non-existent or tiny. Venezuela and Bolivia broke relations with Israel after the attack on Gaza in 2009. The Israeli ambassadors in Ecuador, Peru, Chile, Salvador and Brazil have now been asked to pack their bags.

In the occupied territories themselves there is strong unity from below, and Mahmoud Abbas, who initially remained silent and refused to visit Gaza, is now talking of 'Israeli war crimes', even though his security apparatus and the PLO leadership have been collaborating with the IDF ever since the Oslo Accords. Hamas might have been drawn to this position with the help of the Muslim Brotherhood in Egypt, whose elected leaders were willing to capitulate to Washington like the PLO. Sisi's coup put paid to all of that and Hamas was, as a result, able to reassert its independence.

There is no military solution in the region. Israel is a nuclear state and has the sixth largest army in the world (so any talk of parity with Hamas – moral, political or military – is grotesque). It is threatened by itself, not by an outside force. The only solution left is the creation of a single state with equal rights for all, and till this is achieved the only way to help the Palestinians in the medium term is via the BDS campaign. It is not enough, I know, but it is the very least we can do.

And what of the media's role in all of this? In July, I received four calls from the BBC's *Good Morning Wales*. First morning call: was I available to be interviewed about Gaza tomorrow morning? I said yes. First afternoon call: could I tell them what I would say? I told them: (a) Israel is a rogue state, pampered and cosseted by the US and its vassals; (b) targeting and killing Palestinian children (especially boys) and blaming the victims is an old Israeli custom; and (c) the BBC coverage of Palestine was appalling and, if they didn't cut me off, I would explain how and why. Second afternoon call: was I prepared to debate a pro-Israeli? I said yes. Afternoon message left on my phone: Terribly sorry. There's been a motorway crash in Wales, so we've decided to drop your item.

Benedict Anderson: An Irishman Abroad (2015)

When it was time to decide nationalities, Ben chose Irish after his father. Perry opted for Anglo-Irish dual nationality and made it a triple by getting a US passport too, and Melanie opted for English after their mother. The death of a friend, a comrade, a family member, sometimes even a casual acquaintance, usually comes as a shock if not a surprise. Born in Kunming in China, Ben exited in Batu, Java, Indonesia. He had suffered a heart attack some years ago. 'What did the doctor say, Ben?' I asked the next time we met. 'Too much whisky, too many chocs. But too difficult to give up completely. I will try.' He did for a while. The most remarkable thing about him was not simply that his intellect, life, work, knowledge was dominated by the culture and politics of South-East Asia, but that he was treated and regarded by the locals as one of their own.

This became very clear to me when I was in Indonesia in October 2011, first at the Literature Festival in Ubud, Bali, and subsequently to deliver a public lecture in Djakarta. What was striking about both events was the number of people who asked whether I knew Ben Anderson or what I thought of his work, or simply: 'Is Benni fine. His health good?' Or complaints, as in this case from a lady in Jakarta: 'When you see him next, please tell him I'm still waiting for a response to my last three emails.' Remarking on this phenomenon to the novelist Eka Kurniawan, who Ben had translated and introduced to Verso, I got the following response: 'Ever since I was at school we had knowledge of Ben, but not because of the curriculum. It was through word of mouth. Some teachers would mention him as the great storyteller of our country. At university his works were known. He belongs to us, not to the West.'

I suddenly felt very proud that I knew Ben. A white man who never spoke with a forked tongue. Fluent in Bahasa and Thai he could communicate easily with members of every social class. He describes his own formation from childhood onwards in his memoir *A Life Beyond Boundaries*, written initially for his Japanese audiences at the request of Endo Chiho, an experienced and persuasive editor at the NTT Publishing company in Japan. *Imagined Communities* and other books had been translated into Japanese and she wanted to know who this erudite scholar was, how he had developed his interest in South-East Asia and learnt some of its languages.

Thus began the struggle to let Verso publish it in the US and UK. Ben didn't think it was good enough. Perry it was who convinced him, though Ben writes that in addition to pressure it was the realisation that he was nearly eighty and might never produce a 'proper memoir'. The book is both very readable and informative and sheds some light on the family history. Perry's own essay on his father, first published in the *LRB* and later included in one of his essay collections, is a remarkable piece of writing. In fact, both the brothers could easily have become novelists. In his memoir Ben writes:

> Although the Thai and Indonesian languages have no linkages and belong to quite different linguistic ancestries, both have long had a fatalistic image of a frog who lives all its life under half a coconut shell – commonly used as a bowl in these countries. Sitting quietly under the shell, before long the frog begins to feel that the coconut bowl encloses the entire universe. The moral judgement in the image is that the frog is narrow-minded, provincial, stay-at-home and self-satisfied for no good reason. For my part, I stayed nowhere long enough to settle down in one place, unlike the proverbial frog.

Most of his life was spent at Cornell and in Java and Thailand. I met him in London and at Cornell, but never in Asia. It would have been nice to hang out with him in Java. We talked a great deal about world politics and matters culinary and cultural. Fuad Makki, one of his closest friends at Cornell, once questioned me why I was such close friends with Perry but not with Ben. He said that Ben had posed the question. I was surprised, since the answer was so obvious: *NLR* was in London, and at the height of the radical wave that swept Europe from 1967 to 1975, Perry was in London. Generationally, too, we were closer. Before the internet, maintaining contact was more cumbersome, though also rewarding.

In his memoir, Ben has a quite amusing sentence regarding his younger brother's competitiveness. The subject came up the last time we had supper together, at Fuad's pad in Cornell in 2011. I had spoken at a conference organised by the Department of Comparative Modernities on the origins of modern Europe and, later, shared a panel with Ben and Martin Bernal on a related theme. At supper, Ben made us laugh by recounting how he had found an old letter written by his mother to her sister (Ben adored his aunt) while they were still in China. At the age of two, when their Vietnamese amah was having a noisy bad dream, Perry's character formation was proceeding apace. He sat up in his cot and said in a stern voice: 'No noise!' A bit later, when Ben was riding a bike that Perry couldn't ride because his legs weren't long enough: Ben: 'Look Rory, I'm riding the bike.' Perry (staring at his brother): 'I can't see!' As we laughed, Ben muttered affectionately: 'It was ever thus.'

The Quintet (1992–2016)

From 1994 till 2016 my Islam Quintet novels, which were being translated into different languages, were responsible for my non-stop travels and dominated my life. Though not exclusively. First the Yugoslav civil war and then the *attentats* of 9/11 trebled the amount of travel. It took Covid to stem the flow.

My decision to write *Shadows of the Pomegranate Tree*, the first book in the series, was prompted by hearing an LSE professor of international relations, a staunch supporter of the 1991 Gulf War, proclaim on a BBC News bulletin that the Arabs were without 'a political culture'. I was shocked and angry, because I knew he knew better. It was part of his recantation. For me this period began a process of self-education in a subject I had grown up with but never studied seriously: the history of Islam.

I went off to Spain to explore that country and its past – a bastion of Islamic thought and culture for well over half a millennium. I spoke with Juan Goytisolo, incredibly knowledgeable on this subject, and with Antonio Muñoz Molina, Rodrigo Zayas and various others. After many weeks of travel, I produced a film for Channel 4, *Islam in Spain: The Final Solution*, that marked the anniversary of 1492 by reminding viewers that the year being celebrated also marked the expulsion of the Jews and a wave of ethnic cleansings in Iberia. The Reconquest. The Muslim expulsions followed later. I thought I would write a lengthy essay, but everywhere I visited, especially Granada, Cordoba and Sevilla, I began to think that to reconstruct the last years of this civilisation it might be easier to write a novel.

After it was published a note from Edward Thompson on 21

April 1992 cheered me considerably. He was in hospital again and had found time to read the novel: 'A stirring book ... its an imaginative achievement ... an unexpectedly straight historical novel – a departure for you. And it arouses the readers' imagination, certainly mine. The last chapter must have been agony to write.' He knew. The novel starts with a book-burning and ends with a massacre. It's a short chapter but was very painful to write and even at the time a critic wrote that the fictional tragedy reminded him of a Palestinian family under siege in Lebanon.

The first person who read the draft of the Spanish translation was Juan Goytisolo. He was dissatisfied, took charge and corrected it at various points, for which I was ever grateful – the publishers even more than me. The other person whose support I valued was Edward Said. He rang, said he liked the book very much and 'Don't stop now. You've got to tell the whole bloody story.' He meant the story of the clashes between Western Christendom and Islamic civilisation. I thought long and hard, not at all sure whether I could ever complete such a project. Since *Shadows* had been a commercial success, my publishers added to the pressure, especially the Germans.

It took over twenty years to complete. For two of the books I vanished to writers' retreats. I like working in isolation. I made a note of my productivity rates and they were similar in both cases: starting with 800–1,000 words a day, moving upwards to 2,000-plus by the end of the week, and settling down in the final spurt to 4,000–5,000 after suppressing the entry of any new characters. *The Book of Saladin* entailed travelling to Damascus, Aleppo and Cairo, wandering through streets where twelfth-century buildings from Saladin's time were still intact. I wanted to go to Jerusalem as well, but Edward advised against it. 'It will not inspire, just depress you and distract you from the novel.' Written as a biography of Saladin compiled by a Jewish scribe (well over 50 per cent of Saladin's advisers in court were Jews), it was the only book of mine ever to be published in Hebrew. After defeating and expelling the Crusaders, Sultan Saladin had provided state funding to rebuild the synagogues and mosques burnt by the Christians.

What was intended as a trilogy grew. After *The Stone Woman*, a story of a family declining in tandem with the Ottoman Empire, I thought I'd stop. One amusing byproduct of this was that when the book was announced, the sexologist Shere Hite rang up the Verso publicists in New York and said she was pleased I was writing on these subjects. Would I go on her show? Hite's publicist rang me excitedly: 'Tariq, is *The Stone Woman* about frigidity?' Anything but, I explained.

After this many Italian friends, acquaintances and readers began to send me letters or ring. 'Are you going to completely ignore southern Italy and Sicily?' After a long holiday in Sicily I holed up in a hotel in Sardinia and started writing *A Sultan in Palermo*. The book was finally finished in Lahore in a race against power cuts, making sure I saved the files every half an hour. An abiding memory is that of a young couple queuing in a Palermo bookshop. He was over six-foot, blond hair, blue eyes. She was a few inches shorter, dark skinned, brown eyes, black hair. Finally it was their turn. I looked at him, but before I could say anything he pointed at himself, laughed and said: 'Norman and I learnt a lot about them in your book.' I looked at her and she said: 'My family were originally from Damascus.' Originally, in this case, meant the twelfth century. That's how it should be everywhere.

Three areas remained uncovered. South Asia, China and West Africa. *Night of the Golden Butterfly* mixed Lahore and Yunnan. Some readers felt that the story of a barely known Chinese uprising led by Chinese Muslim leaders in the nineteenth century should have been a separate book. I disagreed. I think the mix worked. I started making notes for a novel provisionally titled *The Lost Manuscript of Timbuktu*. Looking back at them I see that the plan was to write largely about women in pre- and post-Islamic West Africa, with the self-regarding Arab travel writer, Ibn Battuta, depicted as an ultra-conservative blowhard, shocked by the matrilinear characteristics of the region. Since all the earlier novels had required both research and travel, a trip to West Africa was essential. I needed the scents, the smells, the cuisine, the architecture of Timbuktu. The project was stymied by the NATO assault on Libya, with Obama and the dreaded Hillary

Clinton approving the lynching of Gaddafi (Clinton boasting in public: 'We came, we saw, he died'). Libya descended into murderous chaos and Gaddafi was no longer there to protect the large numbers of black Africans he had given refuge to. NATO's new Libyan friends (mostly fundamentalists, including shoots of al-Qaeda) began to drive the Africans out of the country on mainly racist grounds. As a consequence, Timbuktu was occupied by fleeing African refugees, who formed themselves into vigilantes of one sort or another and took the city.

One other factor, slightly childish, came into play. Had the Timbuktu novel been written, the entire series would have had to be renamed *The Islam Sextet*. Which might have created a few misunderstandings.

Mr Ford's Hacienda (2018)

V.S. Naipaul never saw himself as just another face in the mural of twentieth-century literature. The mural was, in any case, not his favourite art form. He loved Persian and Indian miniatures and possessed a very fine collection. But this wasn't a frame in which he saw himself either. Long before the knighthood and the Nobel Prize, it was the mirror that excited him. Destiny stared him in the face every morning. He believed in himself. The Trinidadian was to become a very fine writer of English prose.

Naipaul and C.L.R. James were educated at the same colonial school. The high quality of the teaching in classics and English literature left its mark on both men. Both came to England. There the similarity ends. James embraced Marxism and became a great historian in that tradition. Naipaul put politics on the back burner, joined the lesser ranks of vassalage (the BBC) and cultivated a cultural conservatism that later became his hallmark both politically and socially. The classical heritage of the European bourgeoisie had completely bewitched him. He saw it as the dominant pillar of Western civilisation and this led him to underplay, ignore and sometimes to justify its barbaric sides both at home and abroad.

In later years, James (in private conversation) would refer to Naipaul as someone who, in an imperialist country trying to create a postcolonial culture, is often needed to say things about native peoples that are no longer acceptable in polite society. Naipaul was never, by any stretch of the imagination, a card-carrying Tory. He lived his life through a circle of friends he had carefully selected. Most, if not all, were figures on the right.

Whatever his politics, the novels were very good, especially the earlier ones. The autobiographical A *House for Mr Biswas* remains a comic masterpiece. And it would have made an excellent TV series, or so I thought. Would he ever agree? It wasn't a secret that Naipaul had long opposed his work being transferred to small or big screen. Twenty-odd years ago I rang him up and was invited to lunch. He confirmed that he had always hated the idea of his work being polluted by cinema or television and told me how his excited US agent had once forced him to fly out to 'Mr Ford's hacienda' to discuss filming A *Bend in the River.* 'Mr Ford' was his name for Francis Ford Coppola.

Against his own instincts, Naipaul arrived on the West Coast. At the hacienda, Coppola informed him that the only other guest apart from family would be George Lucas. Naipaul was amazed. 'Georg Lukács, the Hungarian philosopher? I thought he was dead?' It got worse. During supper Coppola handed Naipaul a script that he had commissioned. He wanted Naipaul to have a quick read of the adaptation and see what he thought. While handing over the script, 'Mr Ford was also trying to swallow some spaghetti which he managed to spill on his shirt. It was a very vulgar occasion. I decided to leave.' Which he did. Since then, he had turned down every proposal.

His second wife, Nadira, who he married in 1996, persuaded him to calm down and let Ismail Merchant commission Caryl Phillips to write a script of *The Mystic Masseur*. Naipaul was filled with foreboding that it might turn out to be awful. 'It did.' This was not a promising start. He asked why I liked A *House for Mr Biswas*. 'It's pure,' I replied, 'and very funny.' He agreed we should have a go. Farrukh Dhondy knew the book well and Channel 4 commissioned the script. Peter Ansorge was a stern invigilator and made sure that most of the dialogue from the novel was retained. When we discussed the script and possible directors over dinner at my place several months later, Naipaul and Nadira and Gillon Aitken (his agent) were pleased with the final product.

Channel 4 had appointed a new boss who had brought in a new drama editor, Gub Neal, who also liked the script. But the marketing folk at the channel were surprised to discover that no white star could be cast in a main role, since there was none in the novel. No black characters either except in minor roles. It was Trinidadian Asians all the way through, a 'problem' that would never have bothered Satyajit Ray or Ken Loach. And so the project was cancelled. Naipaul was shocked but not surprised. The script still works and if Ian Katz seriously wants to lift Channel 4 a tiny bit from the ratings sewer where it has been immersed for many years, he might have a read.

'I'm Glad Edward Said Is Dead' (2022)

Looking at a diary jotting of 11 April 2002: 'Spoke today at Columbia University to launch CoF [*Clash of Fundamentalisms*]. Chaired by Edward [Said]. He looks frail and exhausted. On the platform, he asked me to feel his arm: only bones. He's lost a lot of weight but exhorts me in public to maintain *my* intransigent spirit on Palestine. He gives the book and me an ultra-generous introduction ...'

Yet he always managed to muster enough strength to travel and lecture around the world. This was how he deceived us. It was his indomitable fighting nature that kept him alive for so long. When the cursed cancer finally took his life the shock was terrible.

I was at the Gothenburg book fair in Sweden when the news reached me. I had already spoken twice, ironically mostly about Palestine. I'd been thinking about Edward, and a Swedish admirer of his had asked me about his health. Later, after the news had come through, we paid homage to the man and his work at a meeting organised by the Swedish publisher Ordfront.

I spoke: 'With the death of Edward Said, the Palestinian people have lost their richest and most articulate voice in the Global North, a world that fundamentally ignores the endless suffering of the Palestinians. It was precisely in this world – in the heart of American academia, to be precise – that Edward lived and worked. It was here that his controversial theses on culture and politics and on the use of Western academic knowledge as an

instrument of domination earned him the admiration of some
and the envious rancour of many ...'

From Gothenburg I flew to Rome and changed flights for
Naples. I was scribbling notes on Edward for *La Repubblica* and
Il Manifesto. I finished these lines in Naples at a gathering of
writers for the 'Napoli Prize'. By pure coincidence I met, together
with others, the Israeli novelist Avraham (A.B.) Yehoshua. He
insisted on snatching/borrowing the Italian edition of *Clash* to
read the section on Palestine and then disappeared. He returned
and handed the book back. 'Nothing new there,' he said grump-
ily. I laughed. He continued: 'Your position is the same as that of
Matzpen and other anti-Zionist Jews.' I agreed. The organisers
had laid on a huge boat to show us the Bay of Naples in all its
glory. Yehoshua to me aggressively: 'Well, aren't you coming? I
could bark some more at you.'

I explained that I had to finish an article in memory of a
friend. When I mentioned Edward's name, Yehoshua exploded:
'I'm glad he's dead.' I moved forward to slap his face but the
Italians separated us, muttering 'an Arab–Israeli war is about
to break out'. Yehoshua continued unabashed: 'Edward Said
was in New York and criticised us from there ... what did he
know about the conditions of the Palestinian camps ... he and
Mahmoud Darwish only created problems ... misleading the
Palestinians who lived at home.' I responded harshly, pointing
out that his remarks mirrored European colonial talk. If there
weren't outside troublemakers, the oppressed would be happy.
Somehow the exchange was reassuring. Edward Said has many
lives ahead of him.

We met again the next day and had to pose together for a photograph. He had won the fiction prize for that year and *Clash of
Fundamentalisms* the non-fiction. Neither of us even pretended
to smile. Later, I was told that he and Amos Oz were childhood
friends; that Yehoshua was of Sephardic origins and his family
had lived in Jerusalem for centuries; that he was not an anti-Arab
racist like most Israeli Jews today, who continuously elect semi-
fascist governments; that he was equally critical of diaspora Jews;
that he opposed the 1982 war in Lebanon and was a member of

'Peace Now'. Fine, but you still must be blind to blame Yasser Arafat for 'throwing away the chance of peace at Oslo'.

I thought of all this in July 2022, when I read his obituary. I certainly wasn't glad he had died. He needed to see what Likud had become and how there was an astronomical leap in the number of school kids chanting 'Death to the Arabs'. They were, perhaps, unaware of who they were mimicking. A.B. Yehoshua would have known.

Adieu, Boris, Adieu (2022)

In 1985, all Britain's living ex-prime ministers were invited to 10 Downing Street to mark the 250th anniversary of the building. Macmillan, Douglas-Home, Wilson, Heath, Callaghan and the then incumbent, Margaret Thatcher, were all there. To break the ice, Callaghan supposedly asked the others what they thought they had in common. 'A lack of principle,' Macmillan immediately replied.

The rot at the top has deepened measurably since then. Thatcher helped her son to millions in kickbacks for smoothing Saudi arms sales. Major's government was embroiled in unending cash-for-questions and kiss-and-tell scandals, the PM himself conducting torrid affairs in Number 10, while his chief secretary to the Treasury, Jonathan Aitken, was eventually jailed for perjury after denying Riyadh had settled his Ritz Hotel bills in Paris.

Blair and Brown, both accused of lying about legal exemptions for Formula One racing after a million-pound donation from Bernie Ecclestone, turned to tarring each other over the cash-for-peerages scandal, which saw Scotland Yard knocking on numerous ministerial front doors; not to mention the still unexplained death of whistleblower David Kelly and Blair's misleading of Parliament over the invasion of Iraq. Cameron was deeply embroiled in the celebrity phone-hacking scandal involving the Murdoch press and his close chum Rebekah Brooks. Theresa May, always coy about her tax returns, was revealed to be linked via her husband to Panama Papers tax-avoidance schemes.

And Johnson? Office parties during lockdown, or sparing the rod to spoil your Pincher, fade in comparison. Claiming not to know about the notorious Mr Pincher (his Deputy Chief Whip) fondling young men's posteriors at his club was a stupid decision, but a sacking offence? The hallowed domain of the Carlton has surely witnessed worse. The frothing indignation of the liberal pundits – 'toxic', 'poison', tarnishing 'good people' according to the *Economist*'s Bagehot column – makes one wonder what these people know of their own history.

Comparisons between Johnson and Trump were always far-fetched. Trump is a disruptive novelty who has succeeded in creating something like a political movement on the right of US politics: numerically quite small, perhaps, but capable of exploiting the radicalising dynamic that the predominance of gerrymandered one-party constituencies has built into America's two-party system. Johnson – a social liberal by inclination, who presided over the most diverse cabinet in British history (a litany of opportunists and useful idiots, many of whom are now vying for the top job) – is very different. More of a louche old-school politician with a popular touch, the closest US equivalent would be an upper class Chris Christie. Johnson has no extra-parliamentary movement. He rode the Brexit wave; he didn't create it.

It's miscategorising Johnson to see him as some right-wing populist excrescence on the fair face of liberal democracy. While the *Daily Mail* has risen in Johnson's defence – 'What the Hell Have They Done?', 'Day Tories Lost Their Marbles', 'Red Wall Backlash Against Tory Traitors' – the *Daily Telegraph* has been attacking him from the right for turning the Conservative Party into a 'semi-socialist party' with big-state handouts and tax rises. Whatever else his ouster is, it's definitely not a revolt from below. If Johnson had seized the initiative and called a snap election, the voters would likely have returned him with a much-diminished majority. It is rumoured that the queen baulked at agreeing to dissolve Parliament and call a fresh election. Then BJ baulked at going head-to-head with his monarch. This is England, after all. Amid soaring inflation and rising interest rates there is plenty of discontent in the country, as the widespread support for the striking railway workers and their plain-speaking leader Mick Lynch has shown. But Starmer is desperate to avoid any association with it, banning Labour MPs from joining RMT picket lines, while adopting all the Tory policies he can. Johnson, of course, has presided over a hawkish foreign policy and sadism towards refugees, but this is continuity politics in Britain.

What we are witnessing is an internal Tory Party revolt, set in motion by some of Johnson's long-term personal enemies: ex-Foreign Office mandarin Simon McDonald, the energetic Dominic Cummings. The real puzzle is why Tory MPs have lost their heads in this fashion and defenestrated one of their very few leaders capable of galvanising popular support. True, Conservatives have always been ruthless in dumping prime ministers viewed as an electoral liability (in polar contrast, Labour is only ruthless in removing any leader who poses a threat to the values of the extreme centre: before Corbyn there was George Lansbury, considered too radical and replaced by Attlee). But the Tories were not doing so badly in the polls and have done worse since Johnson's overthrow. Their deep divisions over tax-cutting Thatcherism or 'One-Englandist' pork will still prevent them from presenting a coherent programme to the electorate.

Why then are the Tories behaving so irrationally? It appears to be a galloping case of the post-imperial entropy diagnosed by Tom Nairn many decades ago, through which 'the English conservative Establishment has begun to destroy itself'. Enoch Powell was an early sign of this; as Nairn put it: 'symptomatic of the growing paralysis and deterioration of the consensus itself'. Posing as the answer to British malaise, Thatcher succeeded in rebooting returns on capital and crushed the organised working class as a political force for two generations. But the radicalism she injected into Conservative politics – combined with the decimation of the Tories' provincial base of local gentry, bank managers and businessmen through the waves of transatlantic acquisitions and privatisations she unleashed – has left the Tory Party permanently damaged. Cameron's attempts to remodel it on New Labour opened up a vacuum to its right, instantly filled by UKIP and the tyros of the European Research Group.

Worstward Ho (2022)

Whatever else, the last forty-five days in British politics have been hugely diverting. The *Daily Star*, a newspaper I had thought was long dead, has spent the last week publishing pictures of Prime Minister Liz Truss alongside those of a cabbage, encouraging readers to bet on which would go off first. And was I dreaming when I read the Survation poll which put Truss's support at minus 70, making her almost as unpopular with the British public as Vladimir Putin? Last Monday, Penny Mordaunt, standing in for Truss at the dispatch box, felt the need to reassure MPs that the leader was not 'hiding under a desk'. Backbenchers seated behind her tried hard not to giggle. Meanwhile a German newscaster took great delight in quoting a Tory MP who remarked, 'I'm fucking furious and I don't fucking care anymore.' The French are mocking Truss by suggesting she will only be remembered for seeing off the queen.

Having got rid of Johnson because they thought he would lose them the next election, the Tories accepted his choice of successor to avoid rewarding Sunak for wielding the knife. Had he no idea that she was incompetent, incapable of making basic decisions and frankly not very bright? Regardless, it didn't take the country long to realise. Remember Heseltine bringing down Thatcher and Major reaping the reward?

The free-market ghouls Truss appointed as chancellor and home secretary sat and watched as the pound collapsed and the market they worship booted them out, backed by a nervous claque of businessmen, an assortment of Tory MPs and a panicky *FT*. Evidently, the market would have preferred a chunk of the

Labour 2019 programme to the gibberish of the Kwarteng mini-budget and a Tory Party entirely out of touch with reality.

Rung yesterday by the Jamaican national broadcaster to comment on the shenanigans in Westminster, I was prepared:

'On. Say on. Be said on. Somehow on. Till nohow on. Said nohow on. Say for be said. Missaid. From now say for be missaid. Say a body. Where none. No mind. Where none. That at least. A place. Where none. For the body. To be in. Move in. Back into. No. No out. No back. Only in. Stay in. On in. Still. All of old. Nothing else ever. Ever tried. Ever failed. No matter. Try again. Fail again. Fail better.'

There was a silence: 'Mr. Ali is that you? I'll try again in case I got the wrong number.'

The words were obviously not mine. They were drawn from one of Beckett's final texts, *Worstward Ho*. What for him was an expression of existential suffering has for us become the best description of a sociopolitical pathology which won't go away with Truss or her successor. The outgoing PM is herself a symptom of this social crisis, shaped by Britain's exhausted financialised economy, bankrupt post-imperial foreign policy, exclusionary parliamentary system and creaking multinational state. What the British ruling class needs is a real conservative government – with or without the capital C – to protect and stabilise this political order. In this sense Starmer would be more sellable than Sunak, since he can be framed as something new rather than something borrowed and something blue. Yet mimicking Thatcher has so far proven useless, and imitating Blair will be no better. Starmer is the worst opposition leader that Labour has ever had.

What can we look forward to over the next six months or so? Why the coronation, of course, for which Starmer has pledged to clear the decks and delay May Day. Surely the time has come for republican democracy. Let's launch it with a huge street party in Whitehall and food banks galore outside the Banqueting Hall. And let's look to the French, who are holding large assemblies in all the major cities to protest living conditions and threatening a general strike. How long until Britons follow their lead?

Celebrations (2023)

At last. He's finally gone. The *Rolling Stone* headline says it all: 'Henry Kissinger, War Criminal Beloved by America's Ruling Class, Finally Dies.' He was a world-class criminal and – as in better times the late Verso author Christopher Hitchens argued, in his excellent polemical book *The Trial of Henry Kissinger* – many offences huge and small had to be laid at his door. I debated him in 1965 and wrote an account of it in *Street Fighting Years*. Kissinger's latest biographer, Niall Ferguson, has tracked down and listened to an audio recording of the debate.

Kissinger's principal crimes were in Indo-China and Chile. He endlessly delayed the peace talks; suggested, organised and defended extending the war to Kampuchea; and supported the crazed Pol Pot regime that emerged in its wake. Over a million died in Kampuchea alone. Prior to that, the 'great statesman' had applauded the genocidal massacres in Indonesia, where US point man General Suharto wiped out over a million members and supporters of the Indonesian Communist Party (PKI).

For his role in Indo-China, he was awarded the Nobel Peace Prize by the Cold War scumbags who ran the organisation. In an attempt to cover their posteriors they awarded it jointly to Le Duc Tho, the prime negotiator for Vietnam. Tho refused to accept the award with a very dignified statement.

In Chile, as is now well known, Kissinger was centrally involved in helping plot the Pinochet coup d'état of 11 September 1973 that toppled the popular socialist government of President Salvador Allende. It was not yet the custom for the United Sates (aka 'the international community') to describe such events as 'regime changes' to defend 'humanitarian values'. The tension ratcheted up by Kissinger, Pinochet and the generals was leading to a confrontation. What was to be done? A huge debate erupted on the Chilean left. From Havana, Fidel Castro sent a private message to Allende:

> I can imagine that tensions must be high, and that you want to gain time to improve the balance of power in case fighting breaks out and, if possible, find a way to continue the revolutionary process without civil strife, avoiding any historical responsibility for what may happen. These are praiseworthy objectives. But if the other side, whose objectives we are not able to judge from here, continues to carry out a perfidious and irresponsible policy, demanding a price which is impossible for Socialist Unity to pay, which is quite likely, don't forget the extraordinary strength of the Chilean working class and the firm support it has always given you in difficult moments ... it can block those who are organising a coup, maintain the support of the fence-sitters, impose its conditions and decide the fate of Chile ...

Kissinger got there first. The more liberal chief of the army, Carlos Prats, was forced out (and later assassinated); Allende died under a hail of gunfire inside the Moneda Palace; Pinochet acceded to power and the *golpistas* triumphed. We lost. Neoliberal economics under a brutal dictatorship was a perfect model for that period. The total casualties among socialists, communists, trade unionists and left intellectuals ran into thousands. Thousands of Chilean refugees sought asylum in Europe.

Elsewhere in the world, the US with Kissinger in the lead backed apartheid South Africa and the despatch of South African troops to crush the liberation forces in Angola. Cuba sent in troops to help the Angolans and the white regime in Pretoria suffered its first major defeat. Some suggest it was Kissinger who proposed that Israel send the apartheid state the know-how to make nukes, which it did. It would certainly be in character for him to have done so, but I have yet to see evidence of his direct involvement in what was dubbed 'Operation Samson'.

In South Asia, with India possessing nukes already, the Bhutto government was determined that Pakistan should get its own. Libya agreed to fund the whole show. The US got worried, not so much for India as for Israel. The latter saw this development as an 'Arab bomb'. In his death-cell memoir *If I Am Assassinated*, Zulfikar Ali Bhutto wrote that Kissinger, during one of his visits to Pakistan in 1976, had threatened him mafia-style. Unless Bhutto desisted on the bomb, 'We'll make a horrible example out of you.' A senior Pakistani Foreign Office person present at the meeting confirmed this years later – in January 2008 to be precise – to an interviewer from *Business Recorder*:

> Kissinger waited for a while, and said in a cultured tone, 'Basically I have come not to advise, but to warn you. The USA has numerous reservations about Pakistan's atomic programme; therefore you have no way out except agreeing to what I have to say.' Bhutto smiled and asked, 'Suppose I refuse, then what?' Kissinger became dead serious. He locked his eyes on Bhutto's and spewed out deliberately, 'Then we will make a horrible example out of you.' Bhutto's face flushed ...

On the night of 4–5 July 1977, a US-greenlighted coup toppled the Pakistan government. The previous September, the large crowds greeting Bhutto throughout the country had scared the military. Bhutto was arrested and charged with murder. At 2 a.m. on 4 April 1979, after two lengthy and controversial trials (a 4–3 Supreme Court verdict is usually enough to avoid execution), Bhutto was hanged. Yet another successful Kissinger operation. He was now worshipped in Foggy Bottom and regularly invited to the White House. His verbal advice was sought re both Mrs Gandhi and Sheikh Mujibur Rahman. Did he suggest that they both be bumped off? No evidence, but not unlikely. She was very hostile to the Zia dictatorship and Mujib had moved too close to the Soviet Union. So why not? A triple murder would be quite an achievement for a once-modest Harvard professor.

A year before the Soviet Union collapsed, Kissinger advised the White House that even if the result was a 'Pinochet-style dictator', a new system could still work. Among the BRICS, China alone mourned Kissinger's death. He had been very helpful in organising Nixon's visit to Beijing and the political-economic rapprochement that soon followed, and in recent months he had been critical of the Cold War tone being adopted towards China.

A decade ago, he was invited to the *Nation*'s annual party in New York. He was reluctant to attend, but couldn't resist mingling with the enemy. A friend of mine overheard him saying to Katrina vanden Heuvel: 'Strange being at a party where I know that most of the other people here think I'm a war criminal.' Probably the truest sentence he ever spoke.

The day he died New York was the scene for a spirited pro-Palestine demonstration. As the news was announced everyone briefly stopped chanting 'Biden, Biden, You Can't Hide, We Charge You With Genocide' and burst into applause, laughter, and there was dancing in the streets. Literally.

A Missed Churchill Footnote (2023)

It was the late Mike Davis – West Coast historian, gifted writer, old friend, *NLR* colleague and radical Marxist – who had repeatedly insisted that I write a critical biography of Winston Churchill. It was published just before he died in 2022 of protracted cancer. I sent him an email saying the book was out and that Verso had despatched an express delivery from Brooklyn. He wrote back immediately: 'I'm going right now to lay siege to the local post office.'

I wanted so much for him to read it and approve the content or point out what I'd missed or ask why I'd left out all reference to Churchill's fling with sexy Labour MP, Raymond Blackburn, who happened to be Robin's father. They were both regular bisexuals at a time when any form of homosexuality was a criminal offence as far as the state was concerned, but not for most enlightened citizens. 'His Crimes' in the title of my book certainly does not refer to that 'crime'.

The reason I didn't include this as a footnote was because the *unexpurgated* 'Chips' Channon diaries had not then been published. I did mention Churchill's warm political relations with my own grandfather. Mike would have been tickled by the coincidence that two members of the *NLR* board had family links with Churchill, one more intimate than the other. He would, no doubt, have come up with a suitable description and analysis.

A Fatal Flashback:
The Dying Palestinian

October 1974. The old Palestinian revolutionary lay dying in the geriatric ward of Hammersmith Hospital in West London. His son had rung. His father was insistent that I go and see him immediately. I obeyed. He was Jabra Nicola, born in Haifa in 1912, a Palestinian of Christian origin, a leading Marxist intellectual and an organiser of the Palestinian Communist Party, responsible for its publication *al Ittihad* (Unity). He had joined the party in 1931, before he reached twenty. I saw him lying there surrounded by English geriatrics, glued to their TV sets. They had no idea who he was and just as well. The presence of a Palestinian Arab and revolutionary might have hastened their own departures. That year alone, fifty years ago now, the tabloids and their older cousins were filled with news of Palestinian terror attacks, etc. A security guard who had killed a hijacker on a 747 was the hero of that week. Then, as now, few asked why. Refugee camps? A nomadic existence? A people deprived of their homes? It's their own fault. The BBC was less biased then, but not all that different from now. The global political context was different. Jabra Nicola was not a great admirer of George Habash or Yasir Arafat or the PLO. He understood their motives but disagreed strongly with their politics. He had left the PCP on the urging of a close friend, Ygael Gluckstein (pen name: Tony Cliff), and both went Trotskyist. One created another Trotskyist faction. The other (Jabra) joined an existing one. Simple choices.

'You think I'm too rigid,' he once told me.'But no. You are wrong for being too soft on the nationalists. My hardness is the result of a deep conviction. Their politics are impractical. They will never defeat Zionism unless they have a strategy to defeat Arab reaction. An alliance with Saudi Arabia is not very reassuring to the Jewish masses. It will drive them closer to Zionism. And they should never forget that Zionism is capable of reaching a bargain with the national bourgeoisie of Egypt, Syria and Jordan.'

He said all this ten years prior to Anwar Saadat's fatal Jerusalem handshake with Begin. Both were given the Nobel War Prize and, for once, Golda Meir spoke the truth: 'They both deserve an Oscar.'

I sat on his bed. The nurse told me he had not eaten for the last two days and had been force-fed that very morning. I felt awful. I had not seen him for nearly a year, even though we lived in the same city, held similar views and belonged to the same political organisation. He had changed completely. His face a few bits of flesh on a skeleton. He explained in a low voice why he'd sent for me.

'I'm dying.'

'No, you're not. You can't go yet. You haven't finished your book. You must fight back.'

His eyes smiled.

'I'm useless now. There's not much more I can do. Someone else will finish the book. The movement has grown.'

'What rubbish. You can't give up now. Believe me, your book will educate people for many decades. It will become a classic on the Arab world and the national question.'

Suddenly he clutched my hand. For someone so frail the strength of his grip surprised me. He side-glanced at the TV viewers in the ward.

'I hate television.' The old passion appeared to have returned. 'They have it on all the bloody time. It's worse than the drugs they inject in me.'

Was that why he had grasped my hand? Solidarity against philistinism? What he did say was that his death was timely. He had failed. This made me sad and angry. He started to weep and indulge in self-recriminations.

'Listen to me, old friend,' I said. 'You know what you're saying is false. Why is it that tens of thousands in Europe alone have joined the movement since 1968? You know why. It's because people like you refused to go along with the lies and perversions that disfigured Marxism, the Moscow Trials, the camps and all that stuff. It was because there were men and women like you that we are here today. So no more self-reproaches please. And no tears. Your book is unfinished. You must complete it. Books are legacies as our movement knows only too well.'

Born in Haifa, under blue skies and the scent of orange blossoms, he was dying in Hammersmith. What a fate. I withdrew my hand from his and promised to return the following week. He died on 25 December 1974. We cremated him without undue fuss. A fortnight later Matzpen, the Israeli socialist organisation he had helped create with a cluster of anti-Zionist Jews, organised a memorial in the smaller Conway Hall in Red Lion Square in central London. They don't allow anti-war or pro-Palestinian meetings today. At the memorial we relived seventy years of his existence. Another Matzpen founder, Moshe Machover, made the oration. 'Arguing with him was no joke,' he said to applause and laughter. 'You felt the kitchen floor cracking as a new divide appeared.'

Epilogue: The Ashes of Gaza

I am a Palestinian. Hath not a Palestinian eyes? Hath not a Pal-
estinian hands, organs, dimensions, senses, affections, passions?
Fed with the same food, hurt with the same weapons, subject to the
same diseases, healed by the same means, warmed and cooled by
the same winter and summer, as a Jew is? If you prick us, do we not
bleed? If you tickle us, do we not laugh? If you poison us do we not
die? And if you wrong us, shall we not revenge? If we are like you in
the rest, we will resemble you in that   the villainy you teach me,
I will execute; and it shall go hard but I will better the instruction.

With apologies to W. Shakespeare

Eric Hobsbawm argued that the twentieth century was short,
starting in 1917 and ending with the collapse of Soviet Russia in
1991. However, it is turning out to be a much longer century for
those who remain oppressed by capital and empire. The United
States may have been challenged economically, and sometimes
politically, but militarily it still calls the shots. What could be a
better example than the US-backed Israeli war on Gaza and the
West Bank? US, UK and EU politicians watch and defend the
genocidal war being waged by the most far-right Zionist gang
in Israel without lifting a finger.

A large percentage of Israel's Jewish citizens proudly support
the genocide, while others feel that the government elected by
them could go much further. How much further can they go?
This is the barbarian world we live in. The bulk of the world's

citizens are indifferent to this daily slaughter that pollutes their TV screens, but there is an active opposition on the streets.

The demonstrations got larger with every week. They reveal an angry generation that is horrified by what is happening. When asked why Britain has been in the lead on mass mobilisations, I point out that we set up the Stop the War Coalition in 2002 to oppose the occupation of Afghanistan. Here, as with our protests against the invasion of Iraq, history has vindicated our actions and the political analyses on which they were based. The movement maintained a base throughout these years, as can also be found with the Palestine Solidarity Campaign. No such organisations were formed in any other European country or the United States.

In July 2023, I had a silent black-and-white dream. It was night-time. The locale was the West Bank. The bomber jets were flying low. Suddenly they swooped a bit lower and bombed the settlements. That's all. It was such a vivid dream that, slightly shaken, I woke up. The next morning, I shared the dream with Susan. Her response: 'Dream on.' And then I recalled how often I'd been thinking of Palestine and its future that year. How depressing it was to see the gangster regimes in Israel punish Gaza, Jerusalem and the West Bank. Was the resistance completely dead?

A few months later Hamas launched a surprise guerrilla attack and killed nearly 400 IDF soldiers and sixty police. The 700 civilian casualties were high and included twenty-nine children under eighteen years of age. I read the report of the Hamas attack and its scale before these details were released. My first reaction was: 'At last ...' And I immediately wrote a piece for *Sidecar*, the *NLR* blog, which was published on 7 October. Civilian deaths are always upsetting, but the civilian casualties suffered by Palestinians since the first Nakba (catastrophe) began in 1947–48 have been largely ignored by the world. The occupation of Palestine, like other variants elsewhere, as the Israeli Zionist historian Benny Morris tells us, was 'founded on brute force, repression and fear, collaboration and treachery, beatings and torture chambers and daily intimidation, humiliation, and manipulation ... and was always a brutal and mortifying experience for the occupied'.

Ever since the Six-Day War in 1967 and the occupation that followed, I have been a staunch supporter of the Palestinian political and armed resistance. I was sympathetic to the PFLP and the DPFLP, in particular the latter, since it fought for a single state together with the Jewish citizens of Israel and worked closely with the Israeli socialist organisation, Matzpen.

Once you back a side in an armed conflict – as I did with the NLF in Vietnam, the FLN in Algeria, the ANC in South Africa and the anti-colonial resistance in the African colonies of Portugal – you are faced with certain facts. Your side may carry out actions of which you disapprove. How this disapproval is expressed is up to you. The NLF bombed many cafés in Ho Chi Minh city (then Saigon) during the Vietnam War. They were denounced as terrorists, etc. They replied that the cafés were used by first the French and later the American soldiers. 'We will stop when they leave our country.' An Algerian FLN leader said words to the same effect when he told French journalists that if France provided them with an air force then they would select their targets more judiciously.

I don't agree politically with Hamas as I did with the organisations mentioned above. But I do not and will not criticise them in public for defending Gaza. Neither do their Palestinian opponents (including die-hard collaborationists) nor the millions who are marching in the streets – a fact that speaks for itself. The continuous lies fed by Israel via Western propaganda networks are not having the impact they once had. The genocidal assault on Gaza has opened many eyes, as has the shameful and shameless support for Israel provided by the US (let's automatically include the UK as a de facto US statelet), the EU and India.

I once had a long talk with the revolutionary, poet and novelist Ghassan Kanafani at a Palestinian conference in Kuwait, I think in 1967. He was, apart from anything else, a wonderful human being. I asked him if the PFLP was opposed to any negotiations with Israel on principle. He asked whether I was aware of the true history of Palestine.

'No,' I said. 'I need to catch up.'

'Because of the Jewish tragedy in Europe, it's difficult, but we Palestinians know that once you stop seeing the conflict between Israel and Palestine as one between colonial settlers and a national liberation movement you're politically finished. They will crush you. How can a neck ever negotiate with a sword on equal terms? You tell me.'

I couldn't. If Ghassan were still alive, I would tell him that I caught up with the history. I'm not alone. Many young Jewish people from the present generation in the United States and Britain have done so as well. Ghassan Kanafani and Mahmoud Darwish were the two greatest literary figures produced by the Palestinian resistance. One can only speculate on how Kanafani might have developed. But the Israelis did not doubt his strategic intelligence for a moment, and paid their own unique tribute: he was only thirty-six when, in 1972, he was assassinated by a Mossad car bomb. Targeted killings have long been a speciality of this state.

As I write, Gaza is still being bombed, its citizens massacred by a state that has dehumanised itself as well as its powerful supporters. The Indian prime minister Narendra Modi is among the more recent apologists, and New Delhi is the only significant global city where there have been no demonstrations against Israeli war crimes. There is no moral, political or military equivalence as far as the two sides are concerned. Israel is a nuclear power, armed to the teeth by the US. Its existence is not under threat. It is the Palestinians, their lands and their lives that are under permanent attack. This must be resisted by all means necessary. Or is Western 'civilisation' going to stand by while the indirect victims of the Judeocide are also gradually exterminated or expelled from their homes? A new Nakba has been in motion for some years. That is what this dispute is now about.

The far-right regime in Israel, with some serious fascists in key posts, is making exterminist threats and carrying some of them out. They are, as usual, blaming the victims for the war crimes that are taking place. The *New York Times*, which once published pieces telling lies about Iraq (weapons of mass destruction, etc.), is carrying on in the same way by backing absurd and discredited stories about Palestinian groups bombing a hospital in Gaza. But very few are falling for the propaganda this time. Every untruth has been challenged and answered by the huge demonstrations taking place.

The Israelis want as many Gazan Palestinians killed as possible, with northern Gaza occupied by Israeli troops and southern Gaza decimated by weekly targeting to drive people into Egypt. They will move on to the West Bank soon. As Israeli prime minister Netanyahu boasted at the UN, there will only be one Israel, in the shape of an authoritarian apartheid state. That is, in fact, what most Israeli leaders have wanted from the very beginning. Labour and Likud have adopted different styles, but the aim is the same. Eretz Israel.

In December 1987, after a traffic accident on the Gaza–Israeli border saw four Palestinians killed, a new intifada erupted in Palestine, shaking Israel as well as the Arab elites. It started spontaneously and spread rapidly. Benny Morris, despite his own Zionist views, described it accurately: 'It was not an armed rebellion, but a massive, persistent campaign of civil resistance, with strikes and commercial shut-downs, accompanied by violent (but unarmed) demonstrations against the occupying forces. The stone and, occasionally, the Molotov cocktail and knife were its symbols.' How did the Israel Defense Forces respond? Back to Morris: 'Almost everything was tried: shooting to kill, shooting to injure, beatings, mass arrests, torture, trials, administrative detention, and economic sanctions ... a great many [of the Palestinian dead] were children.'

The uprising took both the Palestine Liberation Organization leadership in Tunis and the Israeli regime by surprise. Yasser Arafat sent feelers to Yitzhak Rabin via Norwegian intermediaries, and after much secret negotiation the Oslo conference took place. This was a direct result of the intifada, but the actual leadership of the uprising was sidelined. The Israelis preferred to deal with the PLO.

A few weeks later, the grand old Syrian poet Nizar Qabbani wrote a long poem, 'The Trilogy of the Children of Stones', in which he denounced the older generation of Palestinian leaders (today represented by the corrupt, collaborationist

Palestinian Authority). It was sung and recited in many an Arab and Palestinian café:

> The children of the stones
> have scattered our papers
> spilled ink on our clothes
> mocked the banality of old texts ...
> O Children of Gaza
> Don't mind our broadcasts
> Don't listen to us
> We are the people of cold calculation
> Of addition, of subtraction
> Wage your wars and leave us alone
> We are dead and tombless
> Orphans with no eyes.
> Children of Gaza
> Don't refer to our writings
> Don't be like us.
> We are your idols
> Don't worship us.
> O mad people of Gaza,
> A thousand greetings to the mad
> The age of political reason has long
> departed
> So teach us madness ...

The Palestinian people and their organisations have tried every method to achieve some form of meaningful self-determination. Every Israeli political party has sabotaged this hope. 'Renounce violence,' they were told. They did, despite the odd response to an Israeli atrocity. There was massive support among Palestinians at home and in the diaspora for the Boycott, Divestment and Sanctions (BDS) movement to put pressure on Israel. Here was a peaceful movement par excellence and it has been partially successful. Precisely for this reason, the US and its NATO family have been trying to criminalise it in Europe and America. To support BDS and defend the Palestinians apparently encourages 'antisemitism', as defined by weightless organisations such as the International Holocaust Remembrance Alliance (IHRA). The genocide has revived BDS and encamped US and UK students are demanding divestments and winning in a number of instances.

The Labour Party in the UK banned meetings during its last conference that used the word 'apartheid' in their advertising. The Labour left is too scared of being expelled and has largely fallen silent on the issue. South Africa, Bolivia, Venezuela, Chile and Mexico support BDS and the Palestinian cause. But neither Turkey nor Egypt nor most of the Arab states speak up for the Palestinians. And the keeper of the holiest of holy Muslim cities, Saudi Arabia, is currently negotiating with the White House on recognising the Israeli government. The latest events will at most delay the process.

Backing the fascism of the settlers are the 'democracies' of the Western world, with a few notable exceptions (Spain and Ireland). For decades, the IDF has attacked and killed Palestinians at will. A handful of retired IDF generals and their Mossad equivalents have admitted that what is being done to the Palestinians is shameful, but what is the point of saying this after they have retired? The IDF and Mossad have stood by as settlers in the occupied territories burned houses, destroyed olive plantations, poured cement in wells, drove Palestinians out, chanted 'Death to the Arabs' and targeted and killed young men – all with hardly a murmur from Western leaders.

Then one day the elected Palestinian leadership in Gaza decides to fight back. The headlines on this event bring Palestinians back into the news. Shock, horror. They are resisting again! Why should they not? They know better than most that the far-right government in Israel will retaliate viciously, backed as usual by the US and the mealy-mouthed EU. What did they think? That there would be no blowback at all? That Netanyahu and the criminals in his Cabinet might slowly expel or kill most of the Palestinians? Let there be no doubt – some of the fascist elements in the Israeli government have quite openly backed mass killings of Palestinians. A far-right politician described them as 'human animals'. The Nazis referred to Jews, Slavs, the Roma, the disabled and gays in similar terms as *Untermensch*, subhuman.

Jewish liberals in Israel and the diaspora are upset that Bibi Netanyahu is trying to neuter the highest court in the land to protect himself against very serious charges of corruption. But the sustained and mammoth demonstrations in Tel Aviv by Israelis defending their Supreme Court against the government's threats cut little ice as far as Palestinians are concerned. They know full well that most of the marchers who defend Jewish civil rights do not care a whit for the rights of Palestinians. They know that this same Supreme Court is part of the apartheid state's systematic oppression of the occupied and besieged Palestinians in the West Bank and Gaza. Many Israelis who despise Netanyahu are nonetheless staunch supporters of the IDF and its genocidal actions.

Do the oppressed Palestinians have a right to resist the nonstop aggression to which they are subjected? There can be only one answer: Yes. Subjugated people have long asserted their right to resist. This is a right they give themselves, a right that goes far back to Spartacus and Toussaint L'Ouverture, leaders, respectively, of white and black slaves against the Roman Empire and black slaves against the French Empire. This is what anti-colonial resistance fighters did throughout the twentieth century, in China, Vietnam, Korea, Algeria, Angola, Mozambique, and so on.

To exclude Palestinians from this list because the forebears of those who currently occupy, torture, kill and destroy are the descendants of those who were burnt in the Judeocide no longer serves as penitence for an event that the Allies watched and did nothing to prevent. The Jewish Agency asked Churchill to bomb the Treblinka and Auschwitz concentration camps, to raze them to the ground. They were told that the RAF was too busy. This historical guilt felt by Europe is a partial explanation of its refusal to understand that Palestinians, too, are indirect victims of the Judeocide.

The Israelis obtained a green light from the US and its European satraps to march into Gaza and destroy more buildings and kill more people. They have not yet obtained permission from the White House to take on Hezbollah in Lebanon. The US, worried by the closeness of Iran with China, is engaged in negotiations with Tehran and does not want further disruption at this moment. While the Israelis wait, they torture Gaza every day. They take hostages from both Gaza and the West Bank. They froth and fume because they know that the Palestinian offensive masterminded by Hamas has ignited mass global support for Palestine. The fact that the King of Jordan – a country that is little more than an American–Israeli protectorate – refused to meet with US president Joe Biden and made a sharp speech at the recent regional summit in which he defended self-determination and support for the Palestinians is a clear sign that the question of Palestine is no longer on the back burner. It is everywhere.

Those who had imagined that the Palestinians were in the grip of an unshakeable apathy and despair have suffered a rude shock. Many who oppose Hamas in the region have refused to attack them. This is the real triumph of the Hamas initiative and of the millions who have marched all over the world, including thousands of non-Zionist young Jewish people in the States and Britain. But nobody in the US or EU is demanding elections in Palestine. They are scared by democracy. They fear that Mahmoud Abbas and his minions will be swept aside and replaced by Hamas and possibly others. The Palestinian Authority and the collaborationist Abbas have largely been discredited, just like Abdel Fattah el-Sisi in Egypt and the King in Morocco.

The strength of the demonstrations in the Arab world has created an impressive unity from below. Half a million people on the streets of Morocco (which recognises Israel); two huge street assemblies of over a quarter of a million each on successive days in Amman; Tahrir Square occupied in Cairo once again, flanked by hundreds of thousands on the streets in other parts of the city. And the Algerian government is offering full support to the Palestinian cause on many levels.

It has been reported that during a recent meeting between US secretary of state Antony Blinken and the Saudi Crown Prince Mohammed bin Salman Al Saud (MBS), the latter was sharp-tongued and asked the American to order a ceasefire and end the siege of Gaza. This, of course, would be the simplest and most effective method to bring this phase to an end and create a space to discuss a possible resolution to the crisis. Biden vetoed any such possibility and MBS fell silent. From their own experience in Afghanistan and Iraq, the Americans know that bombings and occupations rarely work, as Biden admitted when he half-heartedly cautioned Israel this time. They should explain this better to their client state in Jerusalem.

Neither Ariel Sharon nor Benjamin Netanyahu and his fascist sidekicks have succeeded in crushing Gaza yet. Now, the world is watching again. This is the triumph that ordinary Palestinians of every hue are celebrating despite the ongoing pain and atrocities. From October to December 2023, the IDF, backed by the US, destroyed more than half of Gaza, its hospitals and universities, its bakeries and water tanks, its mosques and churches, and above all its people. It has targeted and killed doctors, journalists, professors and teachers. The US State Department has declared that 'it sees no evidence' that Israel targets civilians. As of February 2024, the total number of dead was over 28,000, including, 12,000 children and 8,000 women. Over 67,000 Gazans have been injured, seeking help from hospitals all of which have been rendered barely functional by the constant bombardments.

The two books I have read on Palestine this year, and that have educated me further, were written by, respectively, a Palestinian and an anti-Zionist Jew. Rashid Khalidi's *The Hundred Years' War on Palestine* (2020) is a biography of the Khalidi family and its remarkable cluster of intellectuals. It was in Walid Khalidi's beautiful Beirut garden, immediately after the Six-Day War, that I got a proper account of the 1947 Nakba and the massacre of Palestinians. Tarif Khalidi helped me decipher important aspects of early Islamic history when I was working on *The Clash of Fundamentalisms* early in this century.

Rashid, the Edward Said Professor of Arab Studies at Columbia, is an old friend, as is his wife Mona, whose Facebook interventions make it impossible to forget the Palestinian past. I was very pleased to read his sharp criticisms of Arafat in this book.

Norman Finkelstein's *Gaza: An Inquest Into Its Martyrdom* was first published by the University of California Press in 2018. Those who want to understand Gaza and the carnage inflicted on it by Israel over a long period will not find a better book.

I was very tempted to quote extensively from both books, but since they exist I recommend that they be read whole. The genocide has been going on, backed by Western colonial barbarism, for nine months as I finally part company with this manuscript.

Acknowledgements

At Verso (London) my editor Leo Hollis had to deal with structural and length problems that were overcome amicably as always; Sebastian Budgen found me documents I thought were long lost; and Michal Schatz (an intern when the project started, now an assistant editor) dug out articles and references that I could never have found, displaying admirable forensic skills. To them heartfelt thanks. Mark Martin and Bob Bhamra, the production supremos in New York and London, made sure nothing went out of control. Tim Clark, who has copy-edited many of my books, has always been and remains a pillar of strength. For the chapters on our family, my sister in Lahore, Tauseef Hyat, and my brother in Sydney, Mahir Ali, were very helpful. Mahir, in fact, went beyond the call of fraternal duty in going through the first three books thoroughly, fixing multiple typos, removing infelicities and correcting factual inaccuracies, for which I am very grateful. My nephew Taimur Hyat designed a new typeface, Fermata, in 2023, and this is the first book to be set in it.

I must also thank my editors at various publications for their support and encouragement over the years: Richard Ingrams at *Private Eye*, Alastair Hetherington and Peter Preston at the *Guardian*, and after them Alan Rusbridger, the best editor the paper has ever had in terms of offering space to diverse and critical opinions (including my own). In addition, W. L. Webb, Richard Gott and Seumas Milne helped make sure that I wrote for the paper fairly regularly over fifty years. Mary-Kay Wilmers always offered useful and sometimes irritating advice on pieces I wrote for papers and mags other than the *London Review of Books*.

Acknowledgements

My three editors (and longtime colleagues) at the *New Left Review* – Robin Blackburn, Perry Anderson and Susan Watkins – have already been thanked in this book. Susan did a heroic job in removing repetitions, correcting factual errors and making important structural suggestions. Thanks also to Alexander Zevin for suggesting a much improved chapter title. Oliver Eagleton at the remarkable *NLR* blog *Sidecar* kept me mentally and politically alert by getting me to write on current events, which helped keep the book up to date as well. The *LRB* blog-meister Thomas Jones will be familiar with some of the final book's 'Jottings'. To all the newspapers and magazines that published me, a very profound thanks; without them it would not have been possible to complete this book. A special thanks is due to Annalena McAfee, literary editor at the *Financial Times*, who commissioned me regularly to the surprise of the many authors I reviewed for her.

Over the last two years I have also had many memory-reviving conversations with friends and comrades on every continent. They were generous with their time and the only reason some of them are not mentioned in the volume was lack of space. Other are, alas, dead and gone both politically and otherwise.

Finally, I must also thank myself for not being forced to rely on anyone else to cook while I wrote this book. That has been a huge relief.

Tariq Ali
March 2024

Chronology: 1943–2024

1943   Born in Lahore, then called British India, later Pakistan. Brought up for first few years in Wah, later in Lahore.

1947   Partition of India. Aged three, is handed Pakistani flag by family retainer and taught to shout, 'Pakistan zindabad' ('Long live Pakistan'). Does not recall doing so again except at cricket matches. A sister, Tauseef, is born in April.

1949   Accompanies parents to May Day meeting. Speeches and slogans cheer on the victories of the Chinese liberation armies. Mao Zedong enters Beijing in October and proclaims a People's Republic.

1950   Admitted to St Anthony's High School, run by Catholic Irish Brothers addicted to corporal punishment and buggery. Some can teach as well.

1954   A party at home to celebrate French defeat at Dien Bien Phu. An apolitical distant uncle (also a film director) informs the media that he has named his son (born on the day) Ho Chi Minh.

1956   Joins first public demonstration against Suez War, the unleashed Anglo-French-Israeli invasion of Egypt, after university students march and close down schools. Meets Chinese revolutionary leaders on a state visit to Pakistan at a lunch in their honour held by radical writers, poets and journalists.

1957   Organises first direct encounter with US democracy after reading that an all-white jury in Montgomery,

Alabama, has sentenced young black man Jimmy Wilson to death for stealing $1.95 from an eighty-year-old white woman. Only fifteen others join protest march to US Consulate. Figures enhanced by street urchins bribed with soft drinks to swell the 'crowd'. Hard-faced US consul-general accepts letter of protest, but defends court decision and threatens to have students expelled from the school.

1958 Martial law declared to pre-empt Pakistan's first general election. Backed by US and UK, General Ayub Khan becomes the country's first dictator. Revolution in Iraq topples UK-installed monarchy. King Feisal and uncle are hanged from the lamp-posts in Baghdad.

Confined to bed for some months by rheumatic fever, reads the *Communist Manifesto*, the William novels by Richmal Crompton, and starts on Alexander Dumas series beginning with *The Three Musketeers*.

1959 Military regime takes over country's largest newspaper chain, Progressive Papers Limited. TA's father, Mazhar Ali Khan, resigns as editor of the *Pakistan Times*. Younger brother, Mahir, is born.

Reads the Russian classics – Gogol, Chekhov, Dostoevsky, Tolstoy – and moves on to Jane Austen, the

Jimmy Wilson after death sentence

Brontës, Charles Dickens, Harriet Beecher Stowe, Upton Sinclair and then, not exclusively for literary reasons, to Pierre-Félix Louÿs, Boccaccio's *Decameron*, Fanny Hill and Henry Miller. Magazines regularly arriving at home from abroad are the *New Statesman, Nation, Labour Monthly, Masses and Mainstream* and a plethora of journals from the Soviet Union, China, Vietnam and India.

1960–61   Joins Government College Lahore, elected vice-president of Students Union, secretary of the Drama Club and becomes active member of Film Society. Attends first Marxist cell meeting with four others. First chapter of *Capital* abandoned in frustration, replaced by the *Communist Manifesto*. On hearing (February 1961) that Congolese leader Patrice Lumumba has been assassinated, summons an emergency student meeting. Alleges US ordered the killing, calls on students to break the law by defying dictatorship restrictions and march to US consulate. Five hundred join the Lumumba march, the first such in the world. On returning to college, students demand democracy and chant anti-dictatorship slogans. Government orders he be expelled from the university and externed from Lahore. Ban lifted on condition he does not speak at any political event in college. TA respects decision by organising a culinary debate: 'We Prefer Lassi to Coca-Cola.' The motion is won by a huge majority.

1962   Organises strike of underpaid Christian cleaners (who also clean the pre-flush thunder-boxes) at the exclusive summer hill resort of Nathiagali. As a stench envelops the place, elite families panic and, within twenty-four hours, order local bureaucrats to pay equal wages to the Christian workers. Total victory. Celebrated in workers' café in local one-street bazaar.

Parents begin to insist he studies abroad. Is

virtually forced to sign application form to Exeter College, Oxford. Unhappy with decision.

1963 Battle of Ap Bac in Vietnam, the NLF trounce American 'advisers' and puppet soldiers. Visits Wah to bid emotional farewell to maternal great-grandmother. Protracted farewells in Lahore. Dr Nazir Ahmed, head of college, sends messages for Victor Kiernan and others. Father's old wet-nurse extracts pledge never to marry a white woman and weighs his arms down with amulets. Arrives at Oxford and joins Socialist Society, the Humanist Group and the Oxford Union. Repelled by the sectarianism of the Socialist Labour League, saddened by ineffectual reformism of the Communist Party and depressed that the food in the country is little more than edible garbage, apart from breakfast. JFK assassinated. Oxford Left indifferent. Goes to Putney Heath in London to hear Harold Wilson, leader of the opposition (the best Labour has ever had) denounce the Tory government and remind very large crowd of the political debates that took place here during the English Revolution. Reads Christopher Hill's *The Century of Revolution*, meets the author and works his way through all his books.

1964 As Vietnam War escalates, sets up Oxford Vietnam Committee together with Richard Kirkwood, Rip Bulkeley, Heather Spooner, Trevor Pateman, Stephen Marks and other Socialist Society stalwarts. The first demo outside US Embassy in Grosvenor Square is organised by this committee.

1965 Arrested on another Oxford Vietnam Committee outing outside US Embassy and arrested for 'breach of the peace'. Defended in court by veteran civil liberties communist lawyer Jack Gaster and acquitted. In a politically polarised election, he defeats Douglas Hogg and becomes president of the Oxford Union. The debates become left-wing and the motion that

'American Political Friendship Is the Kiss of Death' is defended by Chinese novelist Han Suyin and undergraduate Fred Halliday, who becomes a friend. Parents visit Oxford, the first meeting in three years. On insistence of Faiz Ahmed Faiz, TA joins him as a Pakistani delegate to the Helsinki Peace Conference, doubling the size of delegation. It turns out to be the last gathering of the unified communist movement. The Chinese walk out, accusing the Soviet Union of open manipulation. As the Algerian delegate is introduced a few, including him, heckle from the floor since Ben Bella has been toppled. TA falls out with Faiz, who complains of juvenile ultraleftism to parents, who agree with the poet. Puritanical social restrictions at conference prevent TA and Heather Spooner from sharing a room, leave alone a bed.

1966   Writes a letter to the *Observer* denouncing the Vietnam War. It results in a note from Bertrand Russell expressing appreciation and an invitation to tea at his Chelsea house. Russell is sympathetic to the Chinese and desperate for the Vietnamese to win. Establishes contact with the Bertrand Russell Peace Foundation (funded by book royalties) and meets Ralph Schoenman, Ken Coates, Pat Jordan and Geoff Coggan. Has no idea they're all Trotskyists.

BBC person rings to suggest participation in inaugural satellite debate on Vietnam – Oxford versus Harvard – two undergrads and one senior figure from each side. TA suggests fellow socialist Stephen Marks and alumni Michael Foot from Oxford. CBS in States has sent unknown names. BBC DG, Sir Hugh Carleton-Green, whispers in TA's ear before the debate begins: 'Sock it to them. Awful bloody war.' Oxford do as asked. The senior figure from Harvard is Henry Kissinger. They lose. TA destroys Kissinger. Debate shown coast-to-coast in US but not in Britain. TA receives hundreds of letters from the States, supporting Oxford's stance.

A phone call from Michael Heseltine offers him a job on *Town* magazine. TA becomes its theatre critic and later takes charge of the entire review section. In this capacity and after a critical review of Peter Brook's *US* meets literary and theatre agent Clive Goodwin and his circle: Christoper Logue, Trevor Griffiths, Ken Tynan, David Mercer, Lynn Horsford, Roger Smith, Dennis Potter, Ken Loach, et al.

Ralph Schoenman informs him that Sartre and De Beauvoir are on board for a BRPF initiative to create an independent International War Crimes Tribunal on Vietnam. TA will form part of project and is sent on investigation team to North Vietnam. From December 1966 to January 1967 is in war-torn country. Details of trip recorded in *Street Fighting Years: An Autobiography of the Sixties.*

Attends Kuwait conference on Palestine. Meets among others, Ghassan Kanafani, who educates him on Palestinian history and the futility of negotiations with the Zionists ('Like a sword negotiating with a neck').

1967	Visits Camiri in Bolivia with Perry Anderson and Robin Blackburn to attend the trial of Regis Debray. Arrested and accused of being Cuban guerrilla Pombo (Che's bodyguard). *NYT* correspondent sounds the alarm, and he is released. Leaves the country. Visits Middle East – Amman, Damascus, Cairo – after Six-Day War on behalf of the BRPF, gathering evidence and talking to shaken and shattered Palestinian refugees. In Damascus he has a lengthy conversation with Prime Minister Yusuf Zuayyin representing the Ba'ath left wing. He will be toppled the following year. Helps set up the Vietnam Solidarity Campaign.
1968	At Berlin Vietnam Congress in February shares a

platform with Rudi Dutschke and Ernest Mandel and during lunch break is recruited by latter to the Fourth International.

Helps launch the *Black Dwarf* and becomes its editor, the first of three magazines he will edit. A Labour Cabinet minister (Robert Mellish) asks his colleague, the home secretary (James Callaghan) why 'Tariq Ali can't simply be deported'. Callaghan sympathises but explains that the law does not permit it, since he has been resident now for five years and only arrest and conviction could justify such a course. Bertrand Russell and others denounce the pair for encouraging the police to frame him. He receives an informal message from Irish politicians that he would be welcome to shift to the Republic.

Student movement erupts in Pakistan demanding an end to the military dictatorship. A message from Raja Anwar, a student leader in Rawalpindi insists TA return to the country immediately.

1969   Invited by Ibrahim Abu-Lughod to give keynote at conference on Palestine in Chicago, he is denied a visa and informed he is not permitted to enter the country without a State Department waiver. Expelled from France after speaking at a big rally in Toulouse with Alain Krivine, presidential candidate for the far-left LCR. Informed he is not allowed entry into Turkey.

Addresses students at Queen's University in Belfast. Audience includes Bernadette Devlin and Michael Farrell.

Receives several invitations from student action committees all over Pakistan asking him to return and join the movement. He arrives in Karachi the day the dictator is toppled and travels throughout the country. Greeted by large crowds in Rawalpindi, Multan, Lyallpur (Sahiwal) and Dhaka. At rally under the amtala tree in Dhaka university predicts that unless country's rulers (Army) come to their senses, the country will split. Meets and interviews every political leader. Prepares to write book explaining his position in detail.

1970–71 *Pakistan: Military Rule or People's Power?* is published by Jonathan Cape. Elections in Pakistan result in overall majority for the East Pakistan-based nationalist Awami League. Army and Bhutto's People's Party refuse to accept result and disallow new Parliament from convening. Pakistan Army invades East Pakistan. Civil war ensues, ended by Indian military intervention in December 1971. Bangladesh is born. Together with a handful of others in the diaspora from West Pakistan – Aijaz Ahmed, Eqbal Ahmad, Feroz Ahmad – he drafts and signs statement defending right of Bengalis to self-determination. Military dictator, General Yahya Khan, signs order banning him from entering Pakistan. He obtains UK passport, automatic at the time for all Commonwealth citizens after completion of five years' residency. Tour of Australia.

1972–73 Natasha, his daughter with radical actor Jane Shallice, is born in January '73.

Two long trips to India: series of lectures at Jawaharlal Nehru University; meetings in Hyderabad with Naxalite dissidents; Calcutta, where police chief in charge of hunting Maoists informs him at a dinner that he has named his Labrador Rosa Luxemburg, 'who I admire and would have opposed terrorism'. Points out coldly: 'She would never have supported a chief of police who hunts down and kills militants whatever their political complexion.'

Trips to Pakistan in a hopeful period, to China and North Korea as well as a lengthy tour of Japan. In the latter joins encampment opposing the construction of Narita airport, though daily 6 a.m. exercises find him seriously wanting. His hotel in Bangkok is surrounded by military personnel. Arrested and immediately expelled from Thailand for demanding abolition of monarchy in newspaper interview.

After brutal US-backed military coup in Chile that toppled an elected socialist government, he helps to set up and is active in the Chile Solidarity Campaign.

1974 Stands as IMG candidate at Attercliffe (Sheffield) in February 1974 general election. Numbers attending his meetings are larger than the vote obtained. IMG van tours empty streets. He cheers up the comrades by calling for the 'transformation of Attercliffe into the English Sierra Maestra'. At a miners' meeting above a pub outside Sheffield, the brothers are in a state of advanced inebriety but friendly. After his brief talk on the railway strike in India, a miner asks, 'Is it true that the Indian government chops off your goolies to stop you having babies?' TA explains the forced sterilisation programme against the poor. Another miner: 'Seems like a good idea to me. We should try it here.' Laughter.

Supports and speaks at Imperial Typewriters' strike initiated by Asian workers for equal pay with whites. Racist members of Transport Workers Union pressure the management to refuse. Within IMG, together with Peter Gowan and Robin Blackburn, opposes decision to take on the cops at Red Lion Square who are defending a fascist rally at Conway Hall. In clashes with police, Kevin Gately is killed – the first fatality on a British demo for fifty-five years. Scarman Inquiry reveals incoherence of political line and police spies expose leadership follies.

Arrested in March outside Buckingham Palace for opposing welcome dinner for Portuguese dictator Marcelo Caetano. Portugal itself approaches a pre-revolutionary upheaval. In April. The masses topple Caetano.

762

1975   Visits India to lecture at JNU, St Stephen's College, etc. Meets George Fernandes and other opposition leaders. Interviews K. Damodaran, veteran leader of the CPI, on the birth and evolution of Indian Communism, published in the *New Left Review*.

Portugal gripped by pre-revolutionary crisis in which soldiers and younger officers participate freely and play a crucial rule. In November the revolutionaries are politically defeated by Mario Soares and financially crushed by the Ebert Foundation. On a speaking tour of Canada, TA breaches FI discipline by arguing at public meetings that the revolution in Europe is over. Bob Dylan's latest LP, *Shelter from the Storm*, is playing in too many comrades' homes for political and other reasons. In Vancouver, after-event social cannot start till a leading comrade arrives. Her evening job is as a strip artist under the name of Rosa Luxemburg. She was delayed by an earthquake.

1976   The SWP sets up the Anti Nazi League, with a cultural adjunct Rock against Racism, organised mainly by Red Saunders and David Widgery. A huge success. He is on the national committee of the ANL and speaks at meetings throughout the country. Launches and edits a third paper, *Socialist Challenge*. It is an IMG paper but designed to encourage debates and discussions on the left as a whole. Writers include Angela Carter, John Fowles, Tom Nairn, Sheila Rowbotham and Hilary Wainwright. Other organisations are allowed their own supplements except for PIE (the Paedophile Information Exchange).

1977   Denounces General Zia-ul-Haq's military coup in Pakistan. Zia, a US-trained officer, had previously led the military assault on the Palestinians in Jordan in September 1970. Penguin commissions new book on Pakistan. Starts to make notes for *Can Pakistan*

Survive? Socialist Challenge Christmas issue intro-
duces humour to the left, appreciated by itinerant
songwriter Ian Birchall.

1978   *Inside the Revolution*, a balance sheet of the first
decade after 1968, is published by Anthony Blond.
Political lectures in Sweden, India, Sri Lanka,
Mexico City and Germany.

1979   Stands as Socialist Unity candidate in Southall.
Is beaten senseless by rioting police and arrested.
Margaret Thatcher wins the election defeating
right-wing Labour.

1980   Interviews C.L.R. James, Ken Livingstone and Tony
Benn. Fails to understand that the political consensus being put in place by Mrs Thatcher represents
something new. Interviews with Livingstone published as a Verso book: *Who's Afraid of Margaret
Thatcher?* with Steve Bell cover.

Meets and establishes relationship with Susan
Watkins, a fellow IMGer and socialist feminist
activist; also at the time manager of IMG printshop,
FI Litho, highly regarded for its punctuality.

1981   Announces resignation from IMG in a *Guardian*
article and decision to link arms with the Bennite
upsurge in Labour. The secretary of his local party
(Hornsey), Jeremy Corbyn, issues him with membership card and defies Labour NEC injunction to
withdraw card. A year-long battle follows which
NEC wins. TA is formally expelled. Neil Kinnock
informs *Guardian* readers that socialism will only
come in Britain after repeated Labour electoral victories. Laughter in the valleys. A firm riposte by
Raymond Williams in a Socialist Society pamphlet
settles the issue. Banned from entering Pakistan.

1982   Invited to lunch by Tony Elliot who offers him a
regular column in *Time Out* that he writes for two
years on wide-ranging themes. Travels to Mexico
with Susan for holiday (train from Mexico City to

Oaxaca takes a day and a half) and to speak at conference together with Robert Brenner and others.
Entertaining lunch with avocado heiress in her
sixties who describes how she met Ernest Mandel
last week and asked him what he thought of US
historian, widower and activist George Novack
(who belonged to a different Trot faction). Ernest
rubbishes him. The heiress replied: 'Good to know,
because I've decided to marry him.'

Speaks at Trafalgar Square with Tony Benn, Tam
Dalyell and others against the Falklands War, which
is eagerly and orgasmically supported by Labour
leader Michael Foot in parliament.

1983   Susan gives birth to their son, Chengiz, named after
the great Soviet novelist Chingiz Aitmatov. Right-
wing gossip columns mock *NLR* editors for naming
their children after 'Atilla and Chengiz Khan'.

After the Thatcher–Pinochet victory in the Falklands, participates in a BBC Radio 1 debate with
Douglas Hogg MP on whether one should always
fight for 'Queen and country'. Listeners were asked
to phone in and register their votes throughout
the programme, and at the end, 10,000 people had
phoned in, 6,000 of whom were on his side. Thatcher
wins the election.

Asked by Oxford University magazine *Isis*
whether Oxford needs reforming, TA replies, 'It's
an anachronism like the House of Lords and the
Monarchy. Oxford is part of that complete failure of
the English bourgeoise to institute a thoroughgoing
bourgeoisification of the previous system. Now it has
become an ideological pillar of an antiquated ruling
class and when it gets threatened, they get upset.'

Commissioned by Carmen Callil and Sonny
Mehta to write a book (for Chatto and Picador)
on the culture and politics of India, leaves for the
subcontinent. Interviews among others Bhupen

Khakhar over a week in Baroda, the dancer Chandralekha for two days at her beach house and studio in Chennai, Shabana Azmi as well as her parents in Mumbai, Jyoti Basu and Aparna Sen in Kolkata and Indira Gandhi at the Prime Minister's Office in New Delhi.

1984   Indira Gandhi assassinated by her Sikh bodyguards. Mayhem in India. Anti-Sikh pogroms in Delhi. Sonny rings and insists that the India book be changed to a biographical history of the Nehru-Gandhi family. Spends early part of year writing *The Nehrus and the Gandhis*. It is translated into many languages. Updated and reprinted four times in English. Carmen Callil insists he acquire a literary agent. Sonny suggests Andrew Nurnberg.

Farrukh Dhondy, the new commissioning editor at Channel 4, asks him and Darcus Howe to produce a new-style programme that caters for Asians, West Indians, Africans, etc. *The Bandung File* is born.

1985–99   TA and Susan's daughter, Aisha, born on 19 September 1986. Hectic decade and a half spent producing documentaries and drama and writing the first novels of the Islam Quintet. *The Bandung File* ended in 1989. He and Darcus part company amicably. He starts a new show, *Rear Window*, that combines culture, politics and ideas. Finds time, however, to attend and speak at political conferences in North and South America. Denounces the Gulf War and organises a TV debate on the subject. When, in 1999, Channel 4 bosses decide to turn down dramatised series of V.S. Naipaul's *A House for Mr Biswas* on the grounds that there are no Trinidadian Asian stars, he denounces them in the *New Statesman*. Naipaul awarded the Nobel some months later. Fearing that Channel 4 is mimicking the rest of television and will soon be in breach of its parliamentary writ and not worth sending ideas to, he closes Bandung. A documentary idea on the Belgian genocide (10–12 million Africans died] in the Congo is rejected by both Channel 4 and BBC TV's *Timewatch*.

Disappears to a writers' and artists' retreat near Almeria to complete *The Stone Woman*. Already in the Verso catalogue, it is attracting attention. A mainstream sex programme on US TV rings up Verso in NY to get him on the show when the book comes out. They assume the novel centres on 'frigidity'.

2000 *The Stone Woman*, third in the Quintet, is published. Edits a collection on the break-up of Yugoslavia: *Masters of the Universe? Nato's Balkan Crusade*. It includes a striking contribution from Harold Pinter. Criticises strongly the US/ISI decision to hand over Afghanistan to the Taliban. Publishes 'Throttling Iraq' in the *New Left Review* on the punishments being inflicted on the Iraqi people via sanctions and bombing raids by the US and its allies.

2001 Pre-9/11: makes two trips to Brazil, one for a book launch, the other to attend the worst post-modernist conference – Identity and Difference in the Global Era – he has ever attended, where chief guest Luc Ferry arrives by helicopter and on meeting him whispers that Pierre Bourdieu is a 'bad intellectual'. Pass the sickbag time again.'

Izmir Book Fair to launch Turkish edition of *Fear of Mirrors*. New York for Socialist Scholars' Conference, followed by SOAS rally for Palestine in London and Sheffield. Turin for the bookfair and roundtable on Europe and its future. In August to Weimar for moonlit open-air talk on German edition of *The Stone Woman*.

9/11 and after. On Mary-Kay Wilmers' advice decides to change gear on a book he has just begun to write on Islam (*Mullahs and Heretics*) and instead to write a history of the conflict between the United States and the House of Islam. Starts making notes for *The Clash of Fundamentalisms*. Public talks in Athens and Darmstadt as well as Frankfurt Book Fair. Then trip to Lahore to soak in the post-9/11 atmosphere. Book launch of *The Stone Woman* in Munich with Christian Ude, the mayor of the city. Temporarily detained by security at the airport for carrying German edition of *Marx on Suicide* and marked copy of the *TLS*. Year ends with trips to Toronto and NYU conference in New York, where temperature is a bit heated following the al-Qaeda attacks.

Opposes US invasion of Afghanistan. Speaks at anti-war assembly in Trafalgar Square and helps found the Stop the War Coalition.

2002   *The Clash of Fundamentalisms* is published in the UK, Germany, Brazil, Spain, Portugal, Italy, Pakistan, Egypt, Qatar, etc. Global sales reach 250,000. Book launches and lectures in UK, US, Brazil Germany, Switzerland (with Oscar Lafontaine in Zurich), New York (with Edward Said at Columbia), Sydney Literature Festival, Melbourne, Adelaide. Lectures in Cairo and Beirut, Sweden, Italy, Spain. With Iraq War in sight speaks on criminality of such a plan at numerous cities in Europe and North America. Defends Hugo Chávez against pro-US generals who launch a coup that fails.

2003–04   Speaks at anti-Iraq War meetings on four continents, culminating in huge million-plus demo in London, the largest ever in British history. Calls for regime change in Britain. Starts writing *Bush in Babylon: The Recolonisation of Iraq* while travelling. Speaks at Menil Museum in Houston, Texas, to an audience largely consisting of oilmen and their wives. Over a small dinner is gently reprimanded by hostess for being 'too rough' on Bush. As others laugh, the host explains that his wife is a bit sensitive because she once 'stepped out' with Bush. She explains: 'He was great fun as a young man. Baseball, rock and roll and not the least bit political.' General agreement around table that he should have remained such.

2005–09 Receives an average of thirty invitations a month. Above pattern continues. Most trips to Germany, Turkey, US, Canada, Mexico, Brazil, Venezuela. The wars interrupt work of finishing the Islam Quintet. Holes up in Sardinia to start and finish *Night of the Golden Butterfly.* Quintet completed. Gives Edward Said Memorial Lecture at Adelaide University followed by feast organised by Palestinian family. Their forebear had fled here after the Nakba, set up a roadside petrol station and prospered. Tiny Jerusalem recreated on hillside outside city. Animated discussion on the future of Palestine. The same at the International Literary Festival of Paraty, Brazil, where Toni Morrison ignores advice to the contrary and signs a writers' statement that he drafted (together with Mourid Barghouti, Radwa Ashour and Susan Watkins) denouncing the Israeli assault on Gaza. Barack Obama is elected US president.

2010 In the closing sequences of *Night of the Golden Butterfly* as described in the *Guardian* 'characters congregate for a viewing of Plato's last great painting. It is a triptych, at centre of which is Barack Obama, "the first dark-skinned leader of the Great Society", with the stars and stripes "in a state of cancerous decay" tattooed on his back. "The newest imperial chieftain was wearing a button: 'Yes we can ... still destroy countries'." Elsewhere in Plato's painting, tumours sprout and bearded jihadis are shown "developing a life of their own".'

As US liberals and liberal campuses close ranks behind Obama, he fires a non-fiction missile: *The Obama Syndrome: Surrender at Home, War Abroad.* This produces a magical effect. A sharp decline in invitations to speak in the US, but an increase in South America and Asia.

Visits Granada to receive the 2010 Granadillo Prize for the Islam Quintet. In his acceptance speech, he is sharply critical of the growing Islamophobic currents in Europe.

2011 The Arab Spring demonstrations lead to another long bout of travel to Cairo, Beirut, Sanaa, Qatar as well as Germany and Switzerland. A *Guardian* piece ('An Arab 1848') pleases Eric Hobsbawm and he rings to say so, but another historian is critical: of the three demands of the French revolution, 'Liberty' is visible in the uprisings. 'Fraternity' and 'Equality' are missing. Soon 'Liberty' will disappear as well.

At the Perth Literary Festival, his critique of Obama's presidency is broadcast live by the Australian Broadcasting Corporation's *Big Ideas*.

Delivers the Sir Douglas Robb Lectures (three in total) in Auckland, New Zealand, on Islam, China and the American Empire. When asked by a member of the audience what people in Europe think about New Zealand, he replies, 'New Zealand is not a country one thinks of when one isn't here.' Suggests they disband their standing army and foreign office, simply utilising US and Australian facilities to save money.

2012 Public lecture in Zagreb on 'The Rotten Heart of Europe' and a second lecture for the Subversive Festival in the same city on *The Obama Syndrome*. Notes that the new post–civil war generation in the former Yugoslavia is one of the more promising developments in Europe.

In Houston, he speaks on 'The Uses and Abuses of History' at the Rothko Chapel. A cousin he hasn't seen for decades asks, 'Where is the Rothko painting?'

2013 Visits Bangladesh for the first time since the breakup of Pakistan in 1971 to speak at the Hay Festival in Dhaka. During the opening ceremony denounces the organisers for pandering to the NGOish Hay Festival and hopes they will change name to Dhaka Festival of Literature. Meets many old friends and in press interviews recalls the processes that led to the break-up: 'Both countries appear to be addicted to uniforms.'

Hugo Chávez dies of mysterious cancer. Speaks at several memorial meetings.

2014   Invited again, this time to the Dhaka Literary Festival, TA regrets inability to attend. Interviewed by E-International Relations on the Israel–Palestine conflict, TA is blunt:

There has been much discussion in the media of the so-called moral high ground in the current crisis involving Israel–Palestine. Taking into consideration how events have played out, do you see either side having a serious claim to this?

'Moral high ground' is not a phrase I ever use. One person's moral high ground can be another person's dungeon. In the overall conflict the Palestinians are in the right. Much wrong has been done to them by Israel and its principal backer, the United States. The Israelis treat them as untermensch, have tried to destroy their past, their historical memory, and are now attempting to destroy them as a political entity.

What do you feel are the Israeli government's current political aims in Gaza?

The destruction of Hamas, the intimidation of those who vote for it, and the institution of a puppet regime that is a twin of the Palestinian equivalent of the Judenrat that exists on the West Bank. This aim is supported by Washington, Riyadh, and Cairo, as well.

Visits Athens for a public meeting (sharing platform with Alexis Tsipras) and warns them not to trust the EU. They are determined to punish Greece.

Three lectures in Scotland to speak for the Radical Independence Campaign.

2015 Addresses the Festival of Dangerous Ideas at the Sydney Opera House on 'The Twilight of Democracy' ('The most amazing indoor location I've ever spoken at') based on a book – *The Extreme Centre* – also published this year. Delivers the *London Review of Books* Winter Lecture on 'The New World Disorder.'

In Athens to attend a conference, he and others learn that the Tsipras government, despite a referendum that wanted rejection, has accepted the EU's punishing terms. He stands up at a largely pro-government conference and denounces the betrayal of the Greek people as an event that will lead, sooner or later, to a huge triumph for the Greek Right.

2016–22 In Brazil to speak at a conference for trade-union activists, he could not vote in the Brexit Referendum, but made no secret of his view that one could vote Leave on left-wing socialist grounds, while sharply criticising right-wing support for Brexit based on opposition to European migration. He rejected the view of the EU as a gold standard, pointing out its undemocratic character and to the strength of anti-democratic currents in France and Italy that were even more opposed to immigration than their British counterparts.

Has a lengthy dialogue with Norman Finkelstein at the Left Forum in New York on Israel–Palestine. They disagreed on a single-state solution, but agreed on the centrality of Gaza.

With the centenary of the Russian Revolution approaching, he started work on a book challenging conventional views of Lenin that appeared in 2017.

The Dilemmas of Lenin: Terrorism, War, Empire, Love, Revolution was also published in a number of European countries as well as in Arabic and Turkish.

The Covid lockdown ended travel and, under pressure from Mike Davis, the West Coast historian and a friend, he starts work on a book about Churchill. It was briefly interrupted by the political necessity of producing *The Forty-Year War*, his collection of essays on Afghanistan. *Winston Churchill: His Times, His Crimes* was published in 2022 and challenged the glorification of the wartime leader. All his former German publishers refused to publish the book.

2023–24 Began work on a new volume of memoirs while still speaking at meetings on various subjects and after the Israeli genocide that began in October 2023, largely on Palestine, Israel and the United States.

April 2024 Memoirs completed.

Index